good word guide

seventh edition

good *word* guide

seventh edition

The fast way to correct English –
spelling, punctuation, grammar and usage

edited by Martin H. Manser

Foreword by Martin Cutts,
Plain Language Commission

Consultant editors: Jonathon Green and Betty Kirkpatrick

Compilers: Rosalind Fergusson, David Pickering and
Jenny Roberts

Bloomsbury Publishing Plc

1 3 5 7 9 10 8 6 4 2

Bloomsbury Publishing Plc
36 Soho Square
London W1D 3QY
www.bloomsbury.com.

Copyright © 1988, 1990, 1994, 1997, 2000, 2003, 2007, 2011
Bloomsbury Publishing Plc

First published in 1988
Second edition published 1990
Third edition published as Bloomsbury Guide to Better English
Fourth edition published 1997
Fifth edition published 2003
Sixth edition published 2007
Seventh edition published 2011

A CIP catalogue record for this book is available from the British Library

ISBN: 978 1 408 12294 5

Typeset by Margaret Brain, Wisbech, Cambs
Printed and bound in Great Britain by CPI Cox & Wyman

contents

foreword

Miscommunication is the spice of history. James Hutton, the great eighteenth-century geologist, discovered that the Earth must be many millions of years old instead of originating in 4004BC as biblical scholars insisted; but his writings were so obscure most readers didn't get the point. In the nineteenth century the disastrous Charge of the Light Brigade in the Crimean War occurred because vague and confusing written orders became ever more garbled as they rose up the chain of command. And in the twentieth century the politician and linguist Enoch Powell confessed that he'd not wed his sweetheart fifty years before, because she'd misunderstood his high-flown marriage proposal; so the pair drifted apart and met other people instead.

There's a battle between those who think that the essence of clear communication – which is putting the right words in the right places and punctuating sentences properly – is important, and those who couldn't care less. The *Good Word Guide* is right to be in the first camp. Being loose and creative with meaning and punctuation is fine for some purposes – in songwriting, for example – but when it comes to most professional tasks, standard English is still what most readers prefer. Even academics who take the 'anything goes' line tend to use standard English in their own writing.

Too few professionals in business and government bother to check their writing before sending it to their readers. Here, for example, is part of a sales email sent to thousands of companies by a British firm:

'Rather than spending £35,000 twittering, perhaps Lincolnshire should focused on sorting out the complaince, quality and finctionality of thier own site...'

English is full of words that sound similar but have different meanings. The following email confuses 'ensured' with 'assured' and 'weather' with 'whether', as well as spelling several words wrongly. There's also the strange use of 'yourself' to mean 'you':

'I have spoken to the branch and they have ensured me they will get the paint to yourself this week. I have made a note to clall them on wedensday to check weather this has been done yet or not. I hope this is okay but if you have any prolbems come back to me.'

One error that's rare in newspapers and books is common on the web, perhaps because it's often left uncorrected in schools and universities. This is to mark a sentence boundary with a comma instead of a full stop or semicolon. In this example, my bullet points mark the places where extra full stops or semicolons should be:

'Thanks for all of this, * I am happy with all the points you have made * they make perfect sense. You need a purchase order from 1 May * at the moment you can just submit an invoice for payment.'

Even the secretarial staff at 10 Downing Street have caught this bug. They responded to an artist's letter in the 1990s about Humphrey (the resident cat) by getting most of the punctuation wrong – all the commas should have been full stops or semi-colons:

'Thank you for your recent letter addressed to the Prime Minister, I have been asked to reply. Your portfolio of pen portraits was very impressive, however we already have a portrait of Humphrey hanging on the walls of the Cabinet Office. An artist sent it in two years ago, she copied his likeness from press photographs.'

Of course, an interest in words too often declines into obsessive pedantry in which old rules and conventions are observed and prescribed long after any reason for them has gone. One of the strengths of English is its willingness to embrace change – new words emerge, new usages thrive, new norms are established. So linguistic chafing is inevitable as the old gives way to the new. But if we lose the distinction between full stops and commas, people will often misread the text and meaning will become unsure.

The *Good Word Guide* is a rare stock of riches for writers and speakers, and will help sticklers to decide at what precise point to pin their flag. It could help people like the soccer manager who said he was 'under no disillusions' about his team's plight near the relegation zone; the cricket commentator who always says 'risqué' when he means 'risky'; and the politician who informed a Paris press conference that the French president had been 'prevaricating' – accurately translated into French as 'lying' – when merely 'procrastinating' was meant. The book could even help all those radio and TV reporters who misuse 'refute' to mean 'deny' – which matters, because they are helping to extinguish the word's special meaning, 'to disprove'.

Whatever you write, the book will help you do it correctly and precisely. It may also help you be clear for your intended audience, which is the goal of 'plain language' writing and editing. Plain language can be described as:

'The writing and setting out of essential information in a way that gives a co-operative, motivated person a good chance of understanding the intended meaning at first reading.'

This reference to 'essential information' means that businesses like ours, Plain Language Commission, are far less concerned about novels, poetry and journalism – whose appeal will live or die by market forces – than the clarity of government, legal, medical and business English in web and print documents meant for the public. For those, we recommend mainly familiar words (but with technical terms such as 'endometriosis' and 'vasovagal syncope' explained where necessary) and an average sentence length of 15–20 words. If the reading-age level can be kept to 12–14 years (US grade 7–9), that will often help.

Lack of clarity can endanger lives. At the inquest into the July 2005 terrorist attacks in London, the assistant deputy coroner Lady Justice Hallett complained of the emergency services' 'ludicrous use of English' that had caused delay and confusion. She said job titles were so obscure that 'when it comes to managing incidents, people don't understand what the other person is'. She criticised the kind of management jargon that called a portable incident room a 'conference demountable unit from a management centre'.

There's still too much inflated writing around, and regrettably schools and universities often encourage it as a mark of education. Only graduates write things like this:

* 'The fish exhibited a 100 percent mortality response.' (In other words, 'All the fish died.')
* 'The physical condition of a property is the fundamental determinant of its quality.' (In other words, 'A property's quality depends mainly on its condition.')
* 'Ironically, the expansion of virtual networks have [sic] appeared to render some aspects of social life increasingly anachronistic, so much so that people find ways to reconnect in real-time and real-pace [sic].' (In other words, 'Facebook is too faceless: it's good to have a coffee and a chat for a change.')

And it takes many years of learning to produce swampy officialese like this, from a public body in Northern Ireland:

'To the contrary the Commission envisages that in documenting the case for filling any particular posts employers will be required to demonstrate that their actions in avoiding redundancies are justifiable having considered the relevant data and statistical analysis of options under consideration to demonstrate that the decisions they are adopting are a proportionate means of achieving the aim of filling a vacancy and avoiding a redundancy.'

Job descriptions often belie an organisation's public statements about the value of clear communications. An advert for a 'reputation manager' at the Foreign and Commonwealth Office said the role required:

'Maintenance and development of the UK narrative around FCO and its value proposition, using insights from research and evaluation as well as knowledge of the evolving FCO strategy to inform resonant messaging.'

And the job summary for a £75,000-a-year 'head of culture and performance' at the Care Quality Commission implied a working life fraught with jargon and waffle:

'To achieve in this area the successful candidate will work closely with the directors to ensure that a significant shift in culture is sustained and directly impacts on the originations [sic] performance. They will embrace initiatives to shape the organisations [sic] success by means of focused leadership, empowerment and values and ensure that key messages are communicated to promote reputation and culture. Other responsibilities will include talent management, performance management, development of a dashboard of human capital metrics and a detailed strategy for employee branding.'

Puncturing inflated writing by using plain words and short sentences is not, as some may think, dumbing down, but clearing up; and it's good and worthwhile work that will be helped by this book. As Lord Denning, famed for his lucid legal judgements, once put it: 'It is better to be clear and brief than to go drivelling on.'

Martin Cutts
Research director
Plain Language Commission
Whaley Bridge, Derbyshire
www.clearest.co.uk

note on the seventh edition

In this edition, the text has been revised to take into account the latest changes to the language: new entries and new panels have been added. Quizzes have been added at the end of the book, so that readers can check their proficiency in different aspects of English usage.

I wish to acknowledge my gratitude to David Pickering for his compilation of new material, Betty Kirkpatrick for her comments on the text, and Martin Cutts for his Foreword.

Martin H. Manser
www.martinmanser.com

how to use this book

Entries, listed in a single alphabetical ordering, cover five main areas of the English language: spelling, pronunciation, grammar and punctuation, usage, and writing tips.

• Spelling

accommodation The word *accommodation* is often misspelt. Note the *-cc-* and *-mm-*.

Pronunciation

See also **Guide to pronunciation** on page xvii.

controversy In the traditional pronunciation of this word, the stress falls on the first syllable [*kon*trŏvĕrsi]. The variant pronunciation, with stress on the second syllable [kŏn*trov*ĕrsi], is widely heard, but is disliked by many users. *See also* **stress**.

Grammar and punctuation

participles All verbs have *present participles*, which are formed with *-ing*: • *see-ing* • *walking*, and *past participles*, formed with *-d* or *-ed* for regular verbs and in other ways for irregular verbs: • *loved* • *finished* • *given* • *gone* • *thought*. *Participles* are often used as adjectives: • *broken promises* • *a leaking tap*. They are also used, with an inversion of the usual sentence construction, to introduce a sentence such as: • *Sitting in the corner was an old man.* • *Attached to his wrist was a luggage label.* Care should be taken with such introductory participles, as they are sometimes used to link items that are quite unrelated: *see* **dangling participles**.

The pronunciation most frequently used is [*part*isipl]; [*part*isipl] is an older variant. *See also* **-ed** *or* **-t?**; **-ing forms**; **stress**. For irregular parts of verbs *see* table at **verbs**.

full stop The principal use of the full stop as a punctuation mark is to end a sentence that is neither a direct question nor an exclamation. In creative writing, reference books, etc., the full stop may also mark the end of a group of words that does not conform to the conventional description of a sentence: • *He had drunk six pints of beer and two whiskies. Two very large whiskies.* A full stop is often used in decimal fractions, times, and dates: • *3.6 metres of silk* • *at 9.15 tomorrow morning* • *your letter of 26.6.07.*

Full stops are also used in some abbreviations, although the main problems with abbreviations concern punctuation. The modern tendency is to omit full stops whenever possible: • *BBC* • *AD* • *D H Lawrence* • *Prof.* Full stops are increasingly being omitted from capital abbreviations: • *USA* • *EU*, and they are always omitted from acronyms: • *NATO* • *UNESCO*. When an abbreviation is a contraction (i.e., the final letter of the abbreviation corresponds with the final letter of the word) there is usually no full stop: • *Mr* • *Dr* • *Rd*. There is more likely to be a full stop when the abbreviation is just the first part of the word: • *Rev.* • *Feb.*, although here too the modern trend is to omit it. Abbreviated names can take a full stop or not: • *C.S. Lewis* • *A S Byatt*. There should be no full stop if a capital letter does not stand for a whole word: one should not write *T.V.* (television) or *D.N.A.* (deoxyribonucleic acid) as *tele-* and *deoxyribo-* are not complete words. There are usually no full stops in the abbreviations of weights and measures: • *km* • *oz* and never in chemical symbols: • *Fe* • *Cu*.

A full stop is sometimes called a *stop*, a *point*, or (in American English) a *period*. In email addresses it is pronounced as *dot*.

See also **brackets; exclamation mark; question mark; quotation marks; semicolons; sentences.**

Usage

affect or **effect**? The noun *effect* means 'result'; the verb *affect* means 'influence' or 'have an effect on', hence its frequent confusion with the verb *effect*, which means 'bring about' or 'accomplish': • *The new legislation may have an effect on small businesses.* • *The new legislation may affect small businesses.* • *We have effected a number of improvements. Affect* and *effect* are often misused, one in place of the other: • *Officials said yesterday the downturn could effect the future of the scheme* (*The Guardian*). • *'It will have very little affect,' says ... the chief economist at the merchant bank Morgan Grenfell* (*The Times*). The verb *effect* is largely restricted to formal contexts. The verb *affect* is also used in the sense of 'assume', 'pretend', or 'feign': • *I affected an air of indifference.* • *She affected to despise them.* • *He affected ignorance.*

that or **which**? Whether to use *that* or *which* depends on whether it appears in a restrictive clause (a clause that limits the meaning of another part of a sentence) or a non-restrictive clause (a clause that conveys parenthetical or incidental information). *That* and *which* are both used in restrictive (or defining) clauses: • *the school that/ which they go to.* Furthermore, a restrictive clause is not followed by a comma: • *The school that I go to burnt down.* In non-restrictive (or non-defining) clauses, only *which* can be used: • *The programme, which was broadcast by the BBC, caused much controversy.* Non-restrictive clauses are always preceded by a comma and, unless at the end of a sentence, followed by one. Some people dislike the use of *which* in restrictive clauses, maintaining that only *that* can be used. However, the usage described above is widespread and generally accepted. *Which* is also useful to relieve a sentence that already has several thats: • *His Ford Capri. He remembered that*

that was the car which [not *that*] *had run out of petrol on the M1.* On the use of *that* or *who/whom, see* **who**. *See also* **comma**; **restrictive clause**.

Writing tips

PLAIN ENGLISH The most effective writing is both clear and concise. By observing some basic rules about writing and speech, anyone may be confident of conveying their meaning both neatly and efficiently. See tips in the following panel.

WRITING TIPS	
1 Thinking	It is always good policy to devote time to thinking about the task in hand and about the aims to be fulfilled before putting pen to paper or touching the computer keyboard. This is arguably the most important stage in the whole process, as the success of the finished piece of writing will depend largely upon the quality of the thinking and researching done at the outset. Experienced writers know the value of good preparation and recognise that time spent at this initial stage is never wasted. In the case of an email or a letter, this would include thinking about who the message is being sent to, the content of the message, and the response that is desired from the recipient.
2 Organising	It is essential to give some thought to planning how best to organise and present your writing, making decisions about the proposed structure, layout, etc. There may be more than one way to present an argument or other material, and choosing between these alternatives at this early stage may save a lot of time later. Being properly organised will reduce the overall time needed to complete the task and will help ensure that all the intended aims are met at the desired standard. If there is a deadline to be met, it is vital to decide how much time to dedicate to the task, making sure there will still be an opportunity at the end to go back over what has been written and make any necessary corrections and improvements.

Examples of the use of words are preceded by *. Many of the examples are drawn from actual quotations of contemporary usage:

hi-tech The adjective *hi-tech* specifically refers to high technology, or sophisticated electronics; many careful users object to its indiscriminate application to basic electrical appliances or to anything remotely connected with computing: * *a beautiful hi-tech modern home* * *high-tech benefits* [a reference to the computerisation of the social security benefits system] * *This transition of the cycle from leisure 'toy' to hi-tech pedal machine* (*Daily Telegraph*). The word *hi-tech* has a number of variant spellings: *high-tech, high tech, hi-tec, high-tec*, etc. It is also used as a noun: * *Reflecting the world of high tech* [spelt *hi-tech* in the headline], *the first museum devoted to the chemical industry opens today* (*The Guardian*).

Indications of incorrect usages are sometimes shown to contrast with the correct forms:

your or **you're**? These two words may be confused. *Your* means 'belonging to you': • *your house* • *your rights*. *You're* is a contraction of *you are*: • *Hurry up, you're going to be late!* Note also the spelling of *yours*: • *That's mine not yours*; the spelling with an apostrophe, *your's*, is wrong.

A distinction is made between the use of many words in informal and formal contexts:

incredible or **incredulous**? *Incredible* means 'unbelievable'; *incredulous* means 'disbelieving': • *He told her an incredible story.* • *She looked at him with an incredulous expression.* The use of the adjective *incredible* in the sense of 'wonderful' or 'amazing' should be restricted to informal contexts: • *We had an incredible holiday. See also* **credible, creditable** or **credulous**?

Differences between British English and American English spelling, usage, etc., are highlighted:

fulfil Note the spelling of this word: in British English neither *l* is doubled. The spelling of the derived noun in British English is *fulfilment*. The spellings *fulfill* and *fulfillment* are almost exclusively restricted to American English. However, the final *l* of the verb is doubled in British English before a suffix beginning with a vowel, as in *fulfilled* and *fulfilling* (*see also* **spelling**).

Cross-references are used to show where an entry may be found or where there is additional information:

uninterested *see* **disinterested** or **uninterested**?

government In the sense of 'the group of people who govern a country, state, etc.', *government* may be a singular or a plural noun: • *The government is blamed for the rise in unemployment.* • *The government have rejected the proposal. See also* **collective nouns; singular** or **plural**?

guide to pronunciation

a as in bad
ă as in arrest
ah as in father
air as in dare
ar as in carpet
ăr as in burglar
aw as in saw
ay as in may
b as in bed
ch as in cheese
d as in dig
dh as in these
e as in get
ĕ as in open
ee as in see
eer as in here
er as in bird
ĕr as in butcher
ew as in few
ewr as in pure
f as in fit
g as in go
h as in hat
i as in it
ĭ as in pencil
ī as in try
j as in jam
k as in keep
kh as in loch
ks as in mix
kw as in quiz
l as in lie
m as in mad

n as in nod
ng as in sing
n(g) as in restaurant
o as in hot
ŏ as in cannon
ō as in no
oi as in boy
oo as in zoo
oor as in cure
or as in tore
ŏr as in doctor
ow as in now
p as in pat
r as in rim
rr as in marry
s as in sat
sh as in ship
t as in take
th as in thin
u as in up
ŭ as in crocus
uu as in push
v as in van
w as in water
y as in yes
yoo as in unite
yoor as in urine
yr as in tire
z as in zoo
zh as in treasure

stressed syllables are shown in italics:
[sistĕr]

A

@ *see* **at**.

a or **an**? *A* is the form of the indefinite article used before words or abbreviations that are pronounced with an initial consonant sound, regardless of their spelling; *an* is used before words that begin with a vowel sound: * *a light* * *an LCD screen* * *a unit* * *an uncle* * *a horse* * *an heir* * *a one-armed bandit* * *an ostrich* * *a seat* * *an SOS* * *a ewe* * *an egg* * *a UFO* * *an IOU*. The use of *an* before words that begin with an *h* sound and an unstressed first syllable, such as *hotel, historic, hereditary, habitual*, etc., is optional. Nowadays, the preference is increasingly to use *a* followed by *hotel*, etc., with the *h* sounded, rather than *an* followed by *hotel*, etc., with the *h* not pronounced.

A and *an* are usually unstressed. The pronunciations [ay] and [an] are used only for emphasis: *He told you to take a biscuit, not the whole plateful!* In this example *a* would be pronounced [ay].

abbreviations Abbreviations are useful space-saving devices. They are used heavily both in informal writing and in technical or specialised writing, but less in formal writing. Some abbreviations stand for more than one thing, and it is better to spell these out unless the context makes the meaning clear. * *He was a CO in the war* is confusing, as the abbreviation means both 'commanding officer' and 'conscientious objector'. The main problems with abbreviations concern punctuation. The modern tendency is to omit full stops whenever possible: * *BBC* * *AD* * *D H Lawrence* * *Prof*, and so on. Full stops are increasingly being omitted from capital abbreviations: * *USA* * *EU*, and they are always omitted from acronyms: * *NATO* * *UNESCO*. When an abbreviation is a contraction (i.e. the final letter of the abbreviation corresponds with the final letter of the word), there is usually no full stop: * *Mr* * *Dr* * *Rd*. There is more likely to be a full stop when the abbreviation is just the first part of the word: * *Rev.* * *Feb.*, although here too the modern trend is to omit it. Abbreviated names can take a full stop or not: * *C.S. Lewis* * *A S Byatt*. There should be no full stop if a capital letter does not stand for a whole word: it is wrong to write *T.V.* (television) or *D.N.A.* (deoxyribonucleic acid), as *tele-* and *deoxyribo-* are not complete words. There are usually no full stops in the abbreviations of weights and measures: * *km* * *oz*, and never in chemical symbols: * *Fe* * *Cu*.

Apostrophes tend no longer to be used for shortened forms that are in general use: * *bus* * *flu* * *phone* * *photo* * *vet*.

Most abbreviations form their plurals with an *s*: * *JPs* * *PhDs*. A few abbreviations form their plurals by doubling: * *pp* (pages) * *ll* (lines).

Most abbreviations (except for

acronyms) are pronounced by spelling out the letters. When preceded by the indefinite article, those abbreviations that begin with a vowel sound take *an*: * *an EC directive* * *an LSE graduate*; those beginning with a consonant sound (even if they actually start with a letter that is a vowel) take *a*: * *a DBE* * *a UN spokesman*. *See also* **acronyms**.

aberration This word, meaning 'deviation from the norm': * *a temporary mental aberration*, is sometimes misspelt. Note the spelling: a single *b* and *-rr-*, as in *error*.

ability *see* **capability**, **capacity** or **ability?**

-able or **-ible?** Both forms of this suffix are added to words to form adjectives, *-able* being the suffix that is productive and the more frequently used: * *washable* * *comfortable* * *collapsible*. The form *-able* is always used for words composed of other English words: * *drinkable*; *-ible* being used for some words of Latin origin: * *credible* * *defensible*.

On whether to retain the silent final *-e* in words such as *lik(e)able*, *see* **spelling** and individual entries.

The suffix *-able* may be active or (more frequently) passive in usage. In such words as *washable, eatable, dispensable*, etc. it has the passive meaning of 'able to be washed, eaten, dispensed (with), etc.'. In the adjectives *changeable, perishable*, etc. it has the active meaning of 'able (or likely) to change, perish, etc.'. The suffix is frequently used to produce new words, such as *microwav(e)able*, meaning 'able to be cooked in a microwave oven', and *photocopiable*. Some people dislike the overuse of words coined in

this way, preferring *can it be found?* to *is it findable?*, for example.

abled The term *abled* is sometimes used as a synonym for 'able-bodied'; it is also used in alternatives for 'disabled' or 'handicapped': * *differently abled* * *Marshall rejects the term 'disabled' for these children... She calls them 'uniquely differently abled'* (*Daily Telegraph*). Users feel that such phrases project a more positive image of people with disabilities, but these alternatives are widely disliked as much by the supposed beneficiaries as by the public at large. *See also* **ableism; challenged; disabled; political correctness**.

ableism The term *ableism* refers to discrimination against people with disabilities, especially in employment and in the provision of facilities in public places. *See also* **political correctness**.

Aboriginal or **Aborigine?** Either noun may be used in referring to a member of the indigenous people of Australia who settled there prior to the arrival of European settlers, but *Aboriginal* is now generally preferred to *Aborigine* by the people themselves. In recent years the alternative *indigenous Australian* has gained ground within Australia.

abound The verb *abound* is followed by the preposition *with* or *in*: * *The river abounds with* [or *in*] *salmon*.

about Care should be taken in using *about* in describing the essential characteristics of something or as an intensifier after a negative, as many people consider such usages acceptable only in informal contexts: * *Being a teenager today is all about* appearances. * She was not about to give in to his demands at this late stage. See also **around** or **about**?

above or **over**? The preposition *above* means 'at a higher level than'; *over* means 'vertically or directly above', 'on top of' or 'across': * He raised his hand above his head. * She held the umbrella over her head. * There's a mark on the wall above the radiator. * I've put my towel over the radiator. * The aeroplane flew above the clouds. * The aeroplane flew over Southampton. In many contexts the two words are interchangeable: * Hang the picture above/over the mantelpiece. * Our bedroom is above/over the kitchen.

In reference to numbers, *over* is generally preferred to *above*: * over 40 people volunteered * meeting the needs of the over-eighties. Note, though, that many people dislike such usages and would themselves use *more than* instead: * More than 100 people were drowned.

The use of *above* as a noun or adjective, with reference to something previously mentioned, is disliked by some users but acceptable to most: * You will need several items in addition to the above. * Please quote the above reference number on all correspondence.

abridgment or **abridgement**? Both spellings of this word, meaning 'a shortened version of a work such as a book', are fully acceptable.

abscess This word, meaning 'a collection of pus surrounded by inflamed tissue', is often misspelt. Note the *sc* at the beginning of the second syllable.

absence This word is sometimes misspelt. The most frequent error is the substitution of -*sc*- for the -*s*-, as in *abscess*; note also the -*ence* ending.

absolutely Some users dislike the frequent use of *absolutely* in place of *yes*. Others feel that the adverb is overused as an intensifier, in the sense of 'completely': * it's absolutely disgraceful! The pronunciation of *absolutely* varies according to its meaning. In normal adverbial use it is stressed on the first syllable [*absŏ*lootli]; in the sense of 'yes' it is stressed on the third syllable [absŏ*loot*li].

absolve The verb *absolve* is followed by the preposition *of* or *from*: * They absolved us of [or *from*] blame.

absorption Note the spelling of this word. The final -*b* of the verb *absorb* changes to -*p*- in the derived noun. It should not be confused with *adsorption*, which refers to a chemical process in which a gas or other substance accumulates on the surface of a solid.

abstention or **abstinence**? Both these nouns are derived from the verb *abstain*, meaning 'to refrain' or 'to refrain from voting'. The noun *abstention* is chiefly used in the second of these senses: * 24 votes for the motion, 16 against, and 5 abstentions. *Abstinence* refers to the act or practice of *abstaining*, often from something that is enjoyable but possibly harmful: * abstinence from alcohol * total abstinence from sexual intercourse.

abstractedly or **abstractly**? *Abstractedly* is derived from the adjective *abstracted*, meaning 'lost in thought': * He stared abstractedly out of the window. The adverb *abstractly*, meaning 'in the abstract', is less frequent in usage.

abuse or **misuse**? The noun *abuse* denotes wrong, improper, or bad use or treatment; the noun *misuse*, denoting incorrect or unorthodox use, is more neutral: * *the abuse of power* * *child abuse* * *the misuse of words* * *misuse of the club's funds.* The same distinction applies to the verbs *abuse* and *misuse*: * *to abuse a privilege* * *to misuse money.*

In some contexts the two words are interchangeable: * *The misuse of drugs among teenagers is but one aspect of drug abuse currently being examined by government bodies.* * *He predicted that it would not lead to an upsurge in alcohol misuse… But Action on Alcohol Abuse attacked the move at a time of increased medical concern about excessive drinking* (*Daily Telegraph*).

The word *abuse* also refers to insulting language: * *The president was abused by the crowd.* * *The pickets shouted abuse at the strikebreakers.*

As in the word *use*, the final [s] sound of the nouns *abuse* [ăbews] and *misuse* [misews] changes to [z] in the verbs. *See also* **substance abuse** or **substance misuse**?

abysmal This adjective, meaning 'very bad; dreadful': * *abysmal weather*, is sometimes misspelt. The word comes from *abyss*, hence the *y* in the spelling. The adverb *abysmally* is also sometimes misspelt.

academic The adjective *academic* is widely used in the sense of 'theoretical': * *an academic question* * *of academic interest only*, but some people object to its frequent use in place of *irrelevant*: * *Whether he wins this race or not is academic, because he is already several points ahead of his nearest rival.*

accede or **exceed**? *Accede*, used in formal contexts, means 'agree'; *exceed* means 'go beyond' or 'be greater than': * *They will accede to our demands.* * *Do not exceed the speed limit.* The two verbs are similar in pronunciation but quite different in spelling: *accede* [akseed] ends in -*ede*; *exceed* [ikseed] ends in -*eed*.

The verb *accede* is usually followed by *to*; it can also be used in the expression *to accede to the throne*, meaning 'to become king (or queen)'. Compare *to succeed to the throne*, meaning 'to be the next person to become king or queen, especially as an inheritance'.

accelerate The word *accelerate*, meaning 'speed up', is sometimes misspelt. Note the -*cc*- and single -*l*-.

accent or **accentuate**? Both verbs can be used in the sense of 'to emphasise'. *Accent* usually refers to the act of stressing a sound in speech or music, whereas *accentuate* is used in a wider range of visual and abstract contexts: * *He accented the word 'life'.* * *to accent the first beat in the bar* * *to accentuate an outline/a problem.* The word *accent* is stressed on the second syllable [ak*sent*] when it is used as a verb and on the first syllable [*ak*sĕnt] when it is used as a noun.

accents Accents are sometimes used on words that are now accepted into English, though the tendency is increasingly to omit them. Accents are generally used when they show the pronunciation of the word: the cedilla in *façade* shows that the *c* is soft; the acute accent on *cliché* shows that the word is pronounced [*klee*-shay] not [kleesh]. A circumflex accent on the *o* of *role* is unnecessary and is usually omitted.

accentuate *see* **accent** or **accentuate**?

accept or **except**? These two verbs should not be confused, being virtually opposite in meaning. *Accept* means 'receive' or 'admit'; *except*, used in formal contexts, means 'exclude' or 'leave out': • *She was accepted for the job.* • *He was excepted from the team.* *Accept* only exists as a verb, whereas *except* may also be used as a preposition, meaning 'excluding', and as a conjunction, meaning 'if it were not for the fact that' or 'otherwise than': • *Everyone had to attend except heads of department.* • *She did not pause except to pick up her hat.* The two words are similar but not identical in pronunciation: *accept* is pronounced [ăk*sept*] and *except* is pronounced [ik*sept*].

access The use of the word *access* as a verb was formerly mostly restricted to the field of computing, where it means 'gain access to (stored information or a computer memory)': • *Customers will shortly be able to access this information with minimum delay through personal computer or mobile phone.* Some users dislike the more recent, extended use of the verb in general contexts: • *We often receive requests to 'access' our membership lists and these are almost always refused* (*Club Lotus News*).

access or **accession**? The noun *access* refers to the act, right, or means of approaching, reaching, entering, or using: • *Access to the laboratory is restricted.* The noun *accession* is derived from the verb *accede* (*see* **accede** or **exceed**?) and is most frequently used in the sense of 'becoming king (or queen)': • *Elizabeth II's accession (to the throne) in 1952.*

access or **excess**? The noun *access* means 'entry' or 'opportunity to make use of something': • *He obtained access to the building.* • *We hope to promote access to further education.* It should not be confused with *excess*, which variously means 'surplus' or 'unrestrained behaviour': • *The department has an excess of materials.* • *He abandoned himself to a life of excess.* Note that in *access* the stress falls on the first syllable, while in *excess* the noun it falls on the second syllable.

accessible The adjective *accessible*, meaning 'easy to use, enter, or approach', is sometimes understood to have particular relevance to access for people whose mobility is impaired, specifically for people in wheelchairs: • *The site is fully equipped with accessible toilets.* • *The brochure includes information about accessible holidays.*

accessory or **accessary**? In British English, the spelling of this word in the sense of 'supplementary attachment' is *accessory*: • *a car accessory.* In the legal sense of 'a person who incites another to commit a crime', the spelling is usually *accessory, accessary* being an older variant: • *an accessory before the fact.*

In American English, *accessory* is the spelling in all senses.

accommodation The word *accommodation* is often misspelt. Note the *-cc-* and *-mm-*.

accompany The passive verb *to be accompanied* may be followed by the preposition *by* or *with*, depending on the sense in which it is used: • *She was accompanied by her friend.* • *His words were accompanied with/by a* *gesture of impatience.* In the first example the verb *accompany* means 'go somewhere with someone as a companion; escort'; in the second it means 'supplement'. *With* is also used with the active verb, *accompany*: * *He accompanied his words with a gesture of impatience.*

accountable The adjective *accountable*, meaning 'answerable', should be applied only to people: * *Union leaders are accountable to the rank-and-file members.* * *We were accountable for their welfare.* In other contexts the adjective is often better replaced by its synonym, *responsible*: * *An unexpected fall in demand was responsible* [not *accountable*] *for the company's financial problems.*

The noun *accountability* is best avoided where *responsibility* would be adequate or more appropriate: * *the individual responsibilities* [not *accountabilities*] *of the directors.*

accumulative or **cumulative**? The adjective *cumulative* refers to something that gradually increases with successive additions: * *the cumulative total* * *a cumulative effect.* It should not be confused with *accumulative*, an adjective that is derived from the verb **accumulate** but is rarely used.

acetic *see* **aesthetic, ascetic** or **acetic**?

achieve This word is often misspelt. Note the *-ie-* spelling, which conforms to the rule 'i before e except after c'. *See also* **spelling**.

acknowledgment or **acknowledgement**? This word may be spelt with or without the *e* after the *g*; both spellings are fully acceptable.

acoustics The word *acoustics* is often misspelt, the most frequent error being the doubling of the first *c*. For the use of *acoustics* as a singular or plural noun, *see* **-ics**.

acquaint The verb *acquaint* is best avoided where *tell* would be adequate or more appropriate: * *He acquainted me with his plans,* for example, may be more simply expressed as *he told me his plans.* The passive form *be acquainted with* can often be replaced by *know*: * *I am not acquainted with* [I do not know] *the rules.*

Note the spelling of *acquaint* and its derivatives, particularly the presence and position of the letter *c*.

acquiesce The word *acquiesce*, meaning 'agree or consent to something (especially reluctantly)', is sometimes misspelt. Note the *-uie-* in the middle of the word and the *-sce* ending. The word is pronounced [akwee*es*].

acquirement or **acquisition**? In the sense of 'something acquired', *acquirement* is largely restricted to abilities or skills and *acquisition*, the more frequent word, to material things or people: * *Fluency in spoken and written Japanese is one of her many acquirements.* * *He showed me his latest acquisition.* Both nouns may be used to denote the act of acquiring: * *the acquirement/acquisition of specialist knowledge* * *the acquisition/acquirement of wealth.*

Note the spelling of *acquirement* and *acquisition*, particularly the *-c-* before the *-qu-*.

acquit The verb *acquit* is followed by the preposition *of* or *on* in the sense of 'acquit a person of (a charge)': * *She was acquitted of* [or *on*] *all charges,* and of in the sense of 'acquit a person of (a crime)': * *She was acquitted of manslaughter.*

acronyms An *acronym* is a word formed from the initial letters or syllables of other words: * *OPEC* (Organisation of Petroleum Exporting Countries) * *radar* (radio detecting and ranging). The punctuation of acronyms varies. The usual style is capitals without full stops: *WHO* * *NICAM*, although some of the better-known acronyms are sometimes seen with only an initial capital: * *NATO/Nato* * *AIDS/ Aids*. Acronyms which refer to some piece of technical equipment, rather than an organisation: * *sonar* (sound navigation and ranging) * *radar* * *laser* (light amplification by stimulated emission of radiation) * *scuba* (self-contained underwater breathing apparatus), become so accepted that they are written in lower-case letters like ordinary words and many people do not even realise that they are acronyms. Other acronyms have become so well known that it is rare to hear their full names: * *Naafi* [Navy, Army and Air Force Institutes] * *Tomcat* (theatre of operations missile continuous-wave anti-tank weapon).

Recently there has been a tendency to make acronyms correspond with actual English words: * *SEAL* (sea-air-land (US Navy)) * *PACE* (Police and Criminal Evidence Act). The more appropriate the word to the organisation or concept, the better: * *ASH* (Action on Smoking and Health) * *MAD* (mutual assured destruction). It sometimes seems almost as though organisations and systems are made to fit the acronyms, rather than vice versa: * *In 1984, Holmes, the Home Office Large Major Enquiry System,*

was set up. In spite of its name, Holmes is not an electronic version of the master detective, but a means of investigating crimes through computers (The Times).

The development of electronic communications in recent years has greatly increased the number of acronyms in daily use (*see* **email**; **netspeak**; **text messaging**). *See also* **nimby**; **yuppie**.

acrylic This word is sometimes misspelt. Note particularly the *yl*, not *il*, in the middle.

act or **action**? Both these nouns mean 'something done', but *action* tends to emphasise the process of doing, whereas *act* denotes the deed itself: * *Terrorist action has increased.* * *It was an act of terrorism.* The use of the word *action* as a verb, meaning 'take action on' or 'put into action', is disliked by many people, including Fritz Spiegl (*Daily Telegraph*), who criticised '…*the many new verbs spawned by the Caring Industry. They no longer do things. They "action" them.*'

activate or **actuate**? Both words, meaning 'make active or operative', are acceptable, but careful users reserve *actuate* for more formal or technical contexts: * *The young scientist activated the machine.* * *The government decided to activate the dormant security unit.* * *The system is actuated by a series of switches.* *Actuate* is preferred to *activate* when referring to personal motivation: * *The old man's interest in the girl's welfare was actuated by greed.*

active An active verb is one in which someone or something (*see* **subject**) performs the action of the verb (compare **passive**). The sentence * *The* *mechanic mended my car* contains the active verb *mended*. Most clauses and sentences containing an active transitive verb can be converted into the passive: • *My car was mended by the mechanic*, but the result is sometimes clumsy or needlessly complicated.

actor or **actress**? *see* **non-sexist terms**.

actual Many people object to the frequent, redundant use of the adjective *actual* simply for emphasis: • *This is the actual place where the crash happened*. • *That is an actual Picasso*. The word *actual* may, however, be used perfectly legitimately in, for instance, comparing real and projected totals: • *The actual figure is probably much lower*.

actualise The verb *actualise*, meaning 'make actual', is disliked by some users as an example of the increasing tendency to coin new verbs by adding the suffix *-ise* to nouns and adjectives: • *They have actualised their plans*. See also **-ize** or **-ise**?

actually Many people object to the frequent use of the adverb *actually* where it adds nothing to the meaning of the sentence: • *Actually, I prefer coffee to tea*. • *We weren't actually very impressed by his performance*. • *She doesn't live here, actually*. In some contexts, however, *actually* may serve the useful purpose of contrasting that which is actual or real with that which is theoretical or apparent: • *I know how to make a soufflé but I've never actually made one*. • *It sounds difficult but it's actually quite easy*. See also **in fact**.

actuate *see* **activate** or **actuate**?

acute *see* **chronic**.

AD and **BC** The abbreviation *AD*, which stands for *Anno Domini*, is traditionally placed before the year number; *BC*, which stands for *before Christ*, always follows the year number: • *The custom dates back to AD 1462*. • *The city was destroyed in 48 BC*. In modern usage *AD* sometimes follows the year number: • *The battle took place in 1127 AD*.

It is strictly tautological to precede *AD* with *in*, since *Anno Domini* literally means 'in the year of the Lord'; however, the omission of *in* is generally considered to be unidiomatic: • *He died in AD 1042*.

BC and *AD* are also applied to centuries, although the use of *AD* for this purpose is disliked by some people and is often unnecessary: • *since the fourth century BC* • *until the ninth century AD*.

The abbreviations are always written in capital letters (small capitals are sometimes used in printed texts), with or without full stops (*see also* **abbreviations**).

Some contemporary writers prefer to use *BCE* (Before the Common Era) and *CE* (Common Era), or *PE* (Present Era), to avoid the Christian connotations of *BC* and *AD*.

address Note the spelling of this word, particularly the *-dd-* and the *-ss* ending. See also **letter writing**.

adequate The adjective *adequate* is followed by the preposition *to* or *for*: • *Their income was no longer adequate to* [or *for*] *their needs*.

adherence or **adhesion**? Both these nouns are derived from the verb *adhere*, meaning 'stick'. *Adhesion* is largely confined to the literal sense of the word, whereas *adherence* is used for the figurative senses of 'loyalty' or 'obedience': * *the adhesion of the tape to the fabric* * *their adherence to the cause* * *strict adherence to the rules.* In medical contexts *adhesion* is the abnormal union of usually separated body tissues, for example as a result of inflammation.

ad hoc The Latin phrase *ad hoc* denotes something that is made or done for a particular purpose, rather than as a general rule. It is most frequently used as an adjective: * *an ad hoc decision* * *on an ad hoc basis.* The phrase is also used as an adverb: * *The committee will meet ad hoc, as needs arise.* It is not usually written or printed in italics.

ad infinitum The Latin phrase *ad infinitum* means 'endlessly': * *This series of events repeats itself ad infinitum.*

adjectives An *adjective* is a word which provides information about a noun: * *fat* * *blue* * *happy* * *intelligent* * *dirty.* The main division of adjectives corresponds to the position that they take. Attributive adjectives come before a noun: * *a stupid boy.* Predicative adjectives follow a verb: * *the sky is grey.* Postpositive adjectives follow a noun: * *the chairman elect.* Of course, some adjectives can be used in all three positions: * *a long walk* * *the sides are long* * *two yards long.* Most can be used both attributively and predicatively: * *sweet tea* * *The tea is sweet.* Some adjectives can only be attributive: * *the principal reason,* not *The reason is principal.* Some can only be predicative: * *The baby is awake,* not *the awake baby.* Some are used only in the postpositive position: * *There were drinks galore.*

Nouns can sometimes be used as attributive adjectives: * *a glass bowl* * *a Meissen plate* * *cotton shirts.* Adjectives can be used as nouns: * *the poor* * *the accused* * *the quick and the dead*; they are also used in the place of adverbs: * *They sell their goods dear.* * *It tastes delicious.* Such words as: * *fast* * *late* * *early* function both as adjectives and as adverbs.

Absolute adjectives are such words as: * *entire* * *extreme* * *total* * *unique,* which cannot be used in the comparative or superlative, and cannot be modified by words like very, utterly, or totally. They can, however, be modified by almost or nearly: * *an almost total disaster* * *a nearly perfect round.* Other absolute adjectives cannot be modified in any way: * *a postgraduate student* * *a deciduous tree,* but it is occasionally possible to modify an apparently absolute adjective for effect: * *He looked very dead.*

The overuse of adjectives should be avoided, particularly when they are tautologous: * *true facts (see **tautology**).* Care should be taken with choice of adjectives, and the less informative ones should be avoided. *He's a nice man* says very little about a man; he might be good-natured, sympathetic, witty, attractive, respectable, or none of these. Long strings of adjectives should also be avoided in ordinary speech or writing, unless they are needed for a precise description: * *a small brown one-eyed mongrel.* In poetry, several adjectives can be used to good effect: * *A poor, weak, palsy-stricken, churchyard thing* (Keats). *See also **comparative** and **superlative**; **nouns**.*

adjourn This word, which means 'stop for a short time' and 'go', is sometimes misspelt. Note the *d* in front of the *j*, and the *our*, as in *journey*.

administer or **administrate**? Either verb may be used in the sense of 'manage', 'supervise', 'control', or 'direct', with reference to the work of an administrator: • *She has administered/administrated the company since the death of her father. Administer* also means 'give', 'apply', or 'dispense': • *to administer first aid* • *to administer justice. Administrate* is not used in such contexts.

admissible This word, meaning 'acceptable' or 'having the right to be admitted', is sometimes misspelt. Note the *-ible* ending.

admission or **admittance**? Both these nouns mean 'permission or right to enter'. *Admission* is the more frequent, *admittance* being largely restricted to formal or official contexts: • *Admission is by ticket only.* • *No admittance.* • *He presents the picture of a boy for whom an early admission could well be advantageous... Education officials say they blocked his admittance because class sizes at the school were too large* (Sunday Times). Of the two words, only *admission* may be used to denote the price charged or a fee paid for entrance.

The noun *admission* also means 'confession' or 'acknowledgment': • *an admission of guilt* • *by her own admission.*

admit In the sense of 'confess' or 'acknowledge', *admit* is generally used as a transitive verb: • *He admitted his mistake.* • *I admitted that I had lied.* • *Do you admit writing this letter?* Many users dislike the insertion of the preposition *to* in such contexts: • *He*

admitted to his mistake. • *Do you admit to writing this letter?*

Admit is followed by *to* in the sense of 'allow to enter' or 'give access': • *We were not admitted to the club.* • *This gate admits to the garden.* In the formal sense of 'be open to' or 'leave room for', *admit* is followed by *of*: *The phrase does not admit of a different interpretation.*

admittance *see* **admission** or **admittance**?

ad nauseam The Latin phrase *ad nauseam* is used to refer to something that happens, is said, etc., again and again so that it is boring or irritating: • *to discuss politics ad nauseam.* Literally, the phrase means 'to a sickening degree'.

adolescence This word is sometimes misspelt. Note particularly the *-sc-* and the *-nc-*.

adopted or **adoptive**? The adjective *adopted* is applied to children who have been adopted; *adoptive* relates to adults who adopt another person's child: • *their adopted daughter* • *her adoptive parents.* Careful users maintain the distinction between the two words.

adrenalin or **adrenaline**? Both spellings of this word, denoting a hormone secreted by the adrenal glands, are acceptable. In British English *adrenaline* is preferred; in American English, *adrenalin* (also a tradename). Another US alternative is *epinephrine*.

adult The noun *adult* may be stressed on either syllable, but the pronunciation [adŭlt] is heard more frequently than [ădult] in British English. The adjective *adult*, which principally means 'mature' or 'of or for adults': * *an adult approach* * *adult education*, is often used as a euphemism for 'pornographic': * *adult videos* * *an adult film*.

advance or **advancement**? The noun *advance* means 'forward motion' or 'progress': * *the advance of the enemy.* The noun *advancement* is chiefly used in formal contexts to refer to 'promotion' or 'increased status': * *opportunities for personal advancement.* The two nouns are sometimes confused in the context of progress in development: * *advances in medical science* * *the advancement of medical science.* Here, *advancement* refers to the act of assisting progress or development.

advantage or **vantage**? *Advantage* means 'superiority' or 'benefit': * *to have the advantage over a rival* * *the advantages of co-education.* *Vantage* is chiefly found in the phrase *vantage point*, meaning 'a place that affords a good overall view'. In tennis, the words *vantage* and *van* are sometimes used as shortened forms of the scoring term *advantage*: * *(ad)vantage Smith.*

advantageous This word is sometimes misspelt, the most frequent error being the omission of the *-e-*. Note also the pronunciation of this word, stressed on the third syllable [advăn*tay*jŭs].

adverbs *Adverbs* modify other parts of speech and answer questions such as how? (adverbs of manner): * *quietly* * *greedily;* when? (adverbs of time): * *then* * *tomorrow;* where? (adverbs of place): * *there* * *outside.* They can modify verbs: * *She wrote neatly;*

adjectives: * *extremely hot;* other adverbs: * *fairly well;* whole clauses or sentences: * *Anyway, it doesn't matter now* – or can be used to link clauses or sentences: * *I dislike him; nevertheless, I feel responsible for him.* Adverbs are frequently formed by adding *-ly* to an adjective: * *darkly* * *wisely,* but this does not apply to all adverbs: * *to work late* * *to jump high.*

It is usually acceptable to place an adverb between parts of a verb: * *I have often spoken about the matter,* but adverbs should not come between a verb and its direct object. Whether the adverb is positioned after the object or before the verb depends on the length of the object clause: * *They tortured the prisoners cruelly.* * *They cruelly tortured the political prisoners who had been arrested for demonstrating against the regime.* Careful positioning of the adverb is sometimes necessary in order to avoid ambiguity in a sentence: * *She disliked intensely sentimental films.* If *intensely* relates to *disliked,* it should be placed before the verb. *See also* **adjectives; sentence adverb; split infinitive.**

adversary The pronunciation of this word with stress on the second syllable [ăd*ver*sări] is disliked by many users, who prefer the traditional pronunciation with stress on the first syllable [*ad*vĕrsări]. *See also* **stress.**

adverse or **averse**? *Adverse,* meaning 'unfavourable', 'antagonistic', or 'hostile', usually precedes an abstract noun; *averse,* meaning 'disinclined', 'unwilling', or 'having a strong dislike', usually relates to people and is never placed before the noun it qualifies: * *adverse criticism* * *an adverse effect* * *These working conditions are* *adverse to efficiency.* * *The committee was not averse to the proposal.* * *Her father is not averse to using violence.* * *They are averse to all publicity.* The two adjectives are sometimes confused in the sense of 'opposed'.

Averse is often preceded by *not* and may be followed by *to* or *from* – *to* being preferred in modern usage.

Adverse may be stressed on either syllable, but the pronunciation [*ad*vers] is more frequent than [ă*d*vers]. *Averse* is always stressed on the second syllable [ă*vers*].

advertise This word, meaning 'promote or publicise': * *a brochure advertising holidays*, is sometimes misspelt. It is one of the words ending in -*ise* that cannot be spelt -*ize*; *see also* -**ize** or -**ise**?

advise The use of the verb *advise* as a synonym for 'tell', 'inform', 'notify', etc., is widely regarded as commercialese and is best avoided in general usage: * *Please advise us of your new address.* * *I told* [not *advised*] *him that the meeting had been cancelled.* The -*s*- of advise should not be replaced by -*z*- in British or American English. *See also* **counsel** or **advise**?; -**ize** or -**ise**?

adviser or **advisor**? This word, meaning 'person who gives advice', may be spelt either *adviser* or *advisor*. *Adviser* is preferred in British English but *advisor* is more frequent in American English.

advisory This word, meaning 'for the purpose of giving advice', is sometimes misspelt: note the -*ory* ending. In American English *advisory* may also be used as a noun to denote advance warning of something, especially of severe weather: * *hurricane advisory.*

-ae- and **-oe-** In such words as *archaeology* and *amoeba*, the vowel combinations -*ae*- and -*oe*- were once represented by the characters æ and œ. They are now usually written or printed as separate letters and there is an increasing tendency for the -*a*- and -*o*- to be omitted. In American English such words as *haemorrhage*, *oestrogen*, and *anaesthetic* are spelt *hemorrhage*, *estrogen*, and *anesthetic*, although, conversely, *esthetic* is not usually preferred to *aesthetic*. In British English the -*o*- has already been dropped from *ecumenical* (formerly *oecumenical*) and the -*a*- and -*o*- are gradually disappearing from *medi(a)eval*, *encyclop(a)edia*, *f(o)etus*, etc. This process of simplification, which is particularly associated with scientific and technical contexts, is disliked and resisted by some users.

The -*ae* ending of such plural nouns as *vertebrae* and *formulae* (*see* **plurals**) should not be reduced to -*e*. *See also* **archaeology**; **encyclopedia** or **encyclopaedia**?; **foetus** or **fetus**?, etc.

aegis This word, meaning 'authority' or 'protection', is sometimes misspelt. Note the *ae*- at the beginning of the word. * *The committee operates under the aegis of the state legislature. Aegis* is pronounced [*eejis*].

aerial This word, meaning 'of the air; from an aircraft' and 'device that receives or sends out broadcast signals', is sometimes misspelt. Note particularly the *ae*- at the beginning of the word.

aero or **air**? Both these words may be used adjectivally or as prefixes in the sense of 'relating to aeroplanes or aircraft': * *aerobatics* * *airliner* * *aerodrome* * *airport* * *an aero engine* * *the airforce* * aerospace * airspace. In some American words the prefix *aero-* is replaced by *air-*: the nouns *aeroplane* and *aerofoil*, for example, are rendered as *airplane* and *airfoil* in American English.

aeroplane *see* **aero** or **air**?; **plane**.

aerosol Note the spelling of this word, particularly the *ae-* at the beginning and the *-ol* at the end. An *aerosol* is a fine spray dispensed from a pressurised container; the noun may refer to the container or the contents.

aesthetic, **ascetic** or **acetic**? These three words should not be confused. The adjective *aesthetic* means 'relating to beauty or good taste': * *aesthetic value*. An *ascetic* is a person who practises self-denial; *acetic acid* is the main component of vinegar. Note the spelling of *aesthetic*, particularly the *ae-*; the variant spelling esthetic is restricted to American English.

Ascetic and *acetic* are not identical in pronunciation. The middle syllable of *ascetic* is pronounced with the short [e] sound of *set*, whereas the middle syllable of *acetic* is usually pronounced like the word *seat*.

affect or **effect**? The noun *effect* means 'result'; the verb *affect* means 'influence' or 'have an effect on', hence its frequent confusion with the verb *effect*, which means 'bring about' or 'accomplish': * *The new legislation may have an effect on small businesses.* * *The new legislation may affect small businesses.* * *We have effected a number of improvements.* *Affect* and *effect* are often misused, one in place of the other: * *Officials said yesterday the downturn could effect the future of the scheme* (The Guardian). * *'It will have very little*

affect,' says... the chief economist at the merchant bank Morgan Grenfell (The Times). The verb *effect* is largely restricted to formal contexts. The verb *affect* is also used in the sense of 'assume', 'pretend', or 'feign': * *I affected an air of indifference.* * *She affected to despise them.* * *He affected ignorance.*

affectation or **affection**? *Affectation* is false behaviour that is intended to impress; *affection* means 'fondness' or 'tenderness'. The two nouns are related to different meanings of the verb *affect* and should not be confused.

affinity The use of the preposition *for* with the noun *affinity*, in the sense of 'liking' or 'attraction', is disliked by some users but acceptable to most: * *He has a natural affinity for lost causes.* Those who object to this usage restrict the noun to the meaning 'reciprocal relationship or similarity', in which sense it is followed by *between* or *with*: * *the affinity between the two friends* * *her affinity with her brother.*

afflict or **inflict**? To *afflict* is to distress or trouble; to *inflict* is to impose: * *He afflicted the prisoners with cruel torture.* * *He inflicted cruel torture on the prisoners.* * *Egypt was afflicted with a plague of locusts.* * *A plague of locusts was inflicted on Egypt.* The direct object of *afflict* is the sufferer; the direct object of *inflict* is the suffering. The two verbs should not be confused.

affront or **effrontery**? *Affront* may be used as a noun or as a verb, meaning 'insult': * *an affront to his pride* * *I felt affronted.* The noun *effrontery* means 'impudence': * *She had the effrontery to suggest that we were mistaken.*

Afghan or **Afghani**? *Afghan* is an adjective relating to the country Afghanistan: * *the Afghan people* * *Afghan culture*. *Afghani* is the name of the standard monetary unit of Afghanistan.

aficionado This noun, meaning 'an expert on or devotee of something', is sometimes misspelt. Note the single *-f-* and the *-c-* in the middle of the word. The word can be pronounced [ăfishyă*nah*dō] or [ăfisyă*nah*dō]. The original Spanish pronunciation [ăfithyă*nah*dō] is best avoided.

African American *African American* is the term now generally applied to Americans of African descent. It has been preferred to *Afro-American* since the late 1980s, when the latter term was judged to have derogatory overtones, and is often used in place of **black**. **Black American** is also widely used today. Equivalent coinages recorded in other countries, such as *African Canadian*, are known but are not yet widely familiar.

African Caribbean *African Caribbean* is the term generally applied to people of African descent who live in or come from the Caribbean. The alternative *Afro-Caribbean* is equally acceptable to most people.

Afro-American *see* **African American**.

Afro-Caribbean *see* **African Caribbean**.

afters *see* **dessert, sweet, pudding** or **afters**?

afterward or **afterwards**? In British English, *afterwards* is the usual form of the adverb meaning 'subsequently', the variant *afterward* being more frequently used in American English: *I'll do the washing-up afterwards.* * *His foot was sore for days afterwards.* See also **-ward** or **-wards**?

again This word is pronounced either [ăgen] or [ăgayn]. The first of these is probably the more frequently used.

aged This word is pronounced [ayjid] in the sense 'very old': * *his aged uncle* * *looking after the aged*. When the word is used with a specific age: *She was aged twenty*, it is pronounced [ayjd].

ageing or **aging**? This word, meaning '(the process of) becoming old', may be spelt *ageing* or *aging*.

ageism *Ageism* is discrimination against people on the grounds of age, especially in employment, or the offensive use of stereotypical images of old people. In the first sense the noun is not restricted to old age: any job advertisement that puts an upper (or lower) limit on the age of applicants may be described as *ageist*. In the second sense, the noun refers to the assumption that all people over retirement age are dependent, unproductive, intolerant, conservative, infirm, senile, unhappy, poor, etc. Such stereotypes are best avoided wherever possible in both speech and writing. *See also* **political correctness**.

agenda The word *agenda* is used as a singular noun, with the plural form *agendas*: * *The agenda for tomorrow's meeting has been changed.* * *This item has appeared on a number of previous agendas.* Originally the plural form of the singular noun *agendum*, *agenda* literally means 'things to be done'.

The singular form *agendum* remains in occasional very formal use, in the sense of 'item on the agenda'.

aggravate The use of the verb *aggravate* and its derivatives in the sense of 'annoy', 'irritate', or 'exasperate' dates back to the early 17th century but is still disliked by some people. It is therefore best restricted to informal contexts, with the offending word replaced by one of its synonyms: * *I was aggravated by the noise.* * *She has a number of aggravating habits.* * *His lackadaisical attitude is a constant source of aggravation.* The principal meaning of *aggravate* is 'make worse': * *Your resignation will aggravate our problem.* * *The child's suffering was aggravated by the intense heat.*

Note the spelling of *aggravate*, particularly the -*gg*- and the single -*v*-.

aggressive The use of the adjective *aggressive* in the sense of 'assertive' or 'forceful' is best avoided where there is a risk of confusion with its principal meaning of 'belligerent' or 'hostile': * *an aggressive salesman* * *an aggressive approach.* The derived noun *aggressiveness* may be used for both senses of the adjective, but *aggression*, with its connotations of hostility, should be restricted to the principal meaning: * *the aggressiveness of the salesman's approach* * *an act of aggression.*

Note the spelling of aggressive and aggression, particularly the -*gg*- and -*ss*-.

aging *see* **ageing** or **aging**?

agnostic or **atheist**? Strictly speaking, an *agnostic* is a person who holds that knowledge of a Supreme Being, a first cause of everything, etc., is impos-sible. In general usage, however, the word *agnostic* is often used in the broader sense of 'a person who doubts the existence of God', in contrast to an *atheist*, 'a person who denies the existence of God'. The word *agnostic* was coined in 1869 by the English biologist Thomas Henry Huxley (1825–95).

ago or **since**? It is wrong to place *ago* and *since* side by side: * *It was a fort-night ago that* [not *since*] *I posted the letter.* * *It is a fortnight* [not a *fortnight ago*] *since I posted the letter.* Note that *ago* is preceded by the past tense, and *since* by the present tense, in sentences of this type; also that the first example could be more simply expressed as: * *I posted the letter a fortnight ago.* The adverbial use of *since* for this purpose: * *I posted the letter a fortnight since*, is regarded as very old-fashioned.

The word *since* is also used as a prep-osition: * *We have lived here since 2001.* If a period of time rather than a spe-cific time is mentioned, the preposi-tion *for* should be substituted for *since*: * *We have lived here for three years.*

agoraphobia This word, describing a fear of open spaces or public places, is sometimes misspelt. Note the -*o*- after the *ag*-. The word originates from the Greek word *agora*, 'marketplace'. *Agoraphobia* should not be confused with *acrophobia*, which means 'fear of heights'.

agreement and **person** Modern English lacks any formalised system under which the form of a verb changes in order to agree with the subject. Verb endings rarely indicate whether the subject is the person speaking (the first person), the person being addressed (the second person), or someone or something else being spoken about (the third person). This simplified approach makes matching verb endings with their subject relatively straightforward, with the only changes relating to the third person present singular, which requires the addition of a final -s to the verb, and such exceptions as *to be*, which retains such forms as *am* (first person singular) and *are* (second person singular, and first, second, and third person plural): *It remains a question to be resolved.* *We are going to town.* The lack of distinctive verb endings in English can lead to confusion in the case of multiple subjects, especially where one of them is in the third person. Thus, both *Neither she nor I know where it will lead* and *Neither she nor I knows where it will lead* may be used, although some users will match the verb with the subject closest to it (*see also* **neither**).

People may also disagree over the choice of matching pronoun in the case of nouns that may refer to either gender: *How to keep your child and his phone safe (The Times).* *Always let your baby adjust to her new surroundings in her own time.* *Let your toddler have its own way now and then.* See also **he** or **she**?

ahead of The phrase *ahead of* should be avoided when it is intended in the sense of 'before' or 'in advance of'.

-aholic The suffix *-aholic* (or *-oholic*), derived from the noun *alcoholic*, is being attached to an increasing number of words to denote a person who is obsessed by or addicted to something: *golfaholic* *shopaholic* *spendaholic* *chocoholic.* The noun *workaholic*, coined in the late 1960s,

is now firmly established in the English language, but more recent examples are best avoided in formal contexts.

aid The noun *aid* is specifically used to denote a tangible source of help, assistance, or support, such as a device: *hearing aid* *teaching aids* *audiovisual aids* or money, supplies, equipment, etc., given to those in need: *overseas aid.* In the second sense the word was used in a series of fundraising campaigns inspired by the rock musicians of Band Aid (1984) and the immensely successful rock concert *Live Aid* (1985): *Live Aid raised millions for the starving in Africa.*

The noun *aid* also occurs in certain fixed expressions, such as *legal aid, first aid*, and *in aid of*, but its use as a general synonym for 'help', 'assistance', or 'support' is disliked and avoided by many users.

The spelling of *aid* should not be confused with that of *aide*, a noun meaning 'assistant': *one of the president's aides.*

Aids This acronym, for *Acquired Immune Deficiency Syndrome*, was originally written with capital letters when first identified in the early 1980s as a serious disease of the immune system. It is now generally rendered in the form *Aids*, although both versions are acceptable. Care should be taken not to confuse *Aids* with *HIV*, the abbreviation for *Human Immunodeficiency Virus*, the infective retrovirus from which the full-blown disease *Aids* may or may not subsequently develop. *Her son was diagnosed HIV-positive five years ago but has not yet displayed any of the symptoms of full-blown Aids.*

ain't As a contraction of *are not, is not, have not,* or *has not, ain't* is wrong. It is however generally widely used in speech and in such jocular expressions as: * *Things ain't what they used to be.* * *You ain't heard nothing yet.* As a contraction of *am not, ain't* is regarded by some users as slightly more acceptable, especially in informal American English in the interrogative form *ain't I,* which is replaced in British English by the grammatically irregular *aren't I* and in formal contexts by the full form *am I not.*

air *see* **aero** or **air?**

airman or **airwoman?** *see* **non-sexist terms.**

air miss or **near miss?** An *air miss* is the near collision of two aircraft in the sky. Such a situation is traditionally called a *near miss,* and both terms are in current use: * *The Civil Aviation Authority has launched an investigation into a near miss 33,000 feet over Exmoor* (*Daily Telegraph*). * *The Civil Aviation Authority is investigating an air miss over Sussex this morning* (*BBC South Today*). The expression *near miss* is also used figuratively to describe something that almost succeeds: * *It was a near miss, failing by just 1%; better luck next time.*

aisle This word is sometimes misspelt, the most frequent mistake being the omission of the silent *-s-.* Note also the initial *a-.*

à la carte On a menu in a restaurant, *à la carte* refers to a range of individually priced dishes, in contrast to a complete meal charged at a fixed price: * *We only have an à la carte menu.* The expression comes from French, and means literally 'according to the card'. *See also* **table d'hôte.**

alibi The use of the noun *alibi* as a synonym for 'excuse' or 'pretext' is disliked by many people and is best restricted to informal contexts: * *He used the power cut as an alibi for not finishing his essay.* * *Her illness provided her with an alibi to leave early.* The word *alibi,* which literally means 'elsewhere', is principally used in law to denote a defendant's plea (or evidence) that he or she was somewhere other than at the scene of a crime: * *I have an alibi for the afternoon of the robbery – I was at a conference in Birmingham.* The plural form of the noun is *alibis.*

align This word, meaning 'bring or come into line; support', is sometimes misspelt. Note the single *-l-* and also the silent *-g-.*

all The use of the preposition *of* between *all* and *the, this, that, these, those,* or a possessive adjective is optional, *all* being preferred in British English and *all of* in American English: * *All (of) the birds have flown away.* * *I can't carry all (of) that.* * *Do all (of) these books belong to you?* * *All (of) her children are right-handed.* * *They spent all (of) their leave in France. All* is used alone before nouns that are not preceded by the, these, my, their, etc.: * *All birds have wings.* * *All leave has been cancelled. All of* is always used before personal pronouns: * *all of us* * *all of it. See also* **all right** or **alright?**; **all together** or **altogether?**; **not.**

allege The verb *allege,* meaning 'state without proof', is sometimes misspelt, the most frequent error being the substitution of -*edge* for the -*ege* ending.

alliteration *Alliteration*, the use of successive words that begin with the same or a similar sound, can be employed to striking effect in poetry or newspaper headlines, for instance, but should never be overused: * *Round the rugged rock the ragged rascal ran.* * *Full fathom five thy father lies* (*Shakespeare, The Taming of the Shrew*). * *Down in the deep dark dell* (*from an elegy by Sextus Propertius*).

allowed or **aloud**? These words are occasionally confused, as they are pronounced in the same way. *Allowed* is the past participle of the verb, *allow*: * *Such behaviour should not be allowed.* It should not be confused with *aloud*, meaning 'audible': * *She did not dare to voice her concerns aloud.*

all ready *see* **already** or **all ready**?

all right or **alright**? The spelling *all right* is correct; the spelling *alright* is wrong. Some users defend the spelling *alright*, arguing that *altogether* and *already* are analogous spellings. Such users want to distinguish *alright*, 'satisfactory or acceptable': * *The play was alright for children* from *all right*: * *The answers were all right*, i.e. all the answers were right.

all together *see* **altogether** or **all together**?

allude The verb *allude* means 'refer indirectly'; it should not be used in place of the verb *refer* itself: * *He was alluding to the death of his father when he spoke of the loss of a lifelong friend.* * *She referred* [not *alluded*] *to*

'the spectre of redundancy' in her speech on unemployment. Allude should not be confused with *elude* (*see* **avoid**, **evade** or **elude**?). *See also* **allusion**, **illusion** or **delusion**?; **allusive**, **elusive** or **illusive**?

allure or **lure**? Both these words may be used as a noun or as a verb. The verbs *allure* and *lure* are virtually synonymous in the sense of 'entice', 'tempt', or 'attract', but *lure* is by far the more frequent: * *They tried to lure her away.* The verb *allure* is most frequently found in the form of the present participle, used as an adjective: * *an alluring proposition.* The nouns *allure* and *lure* share the meaning 'attraction', but they are used in different contexts. *Lure* refers to the act of *attracting*, whereas *allure* refers to the *attractiveness* of the person or thing concerned: * *the lure of the gambling table* * *the allure of show business.*

allusion, illusion or **delusion**? An *allusion* is an indirect reference (*see* **allude**); an *illusion* is a false or misleading impression or perception; a *delusion* is a false or mistaken idea or belief: * *an allusion to his schooldays at Eton* * *an optical illusion* * *to destroy a person's illusions* * *delusions of grandeur* * *to labour under a delusion.* The nouns *allusion* and *illusion* are confused because of their similarity in pronunciation; *illusion* and *delusion*, because of their similarity in meaning.

Illusion and *delusion* are virtually interchangeable in some contexts, but careful users maintain the distinction between them where necessary. An *illusion* is often pleasant and harmless; a *delusion* may be a sign of mental disorder: * *the illusions of childhood* * *the* delusion that she is Queen Elizabeth I. An *illusion* temporarily deceives the senses and is sometimes known to be false; a *delusion* is a strongly held opinion that is not easily eradicated. *See also* **allusive, elusive** or **illusive?**; **disillusion**.

allusive, elusive or **illusive?** The adjectives *allusive* and *illusive* relate to the nouns *allusion* and *illusion* respectively (*see* **allusion, illusion** or **delusion?**); *elusive* means 'difficult to catch, find, achieve, describe, define, remember, etc.': * *an allusive style* * *an illusive hope* * *an elusive quality*. *Elusive* and *illusive* are identical in pronunciation [i*loo*siv]; *allusive* differs only in the pronunciation of the first syllable [ă*loo*siv].

Of the three adjectives, *elusive* is the most frequent. *Allusive* is rarely used and *illusive* is usually replaced by its synonym *illusory*.

alma mater The Latin phrase *alma mater* is a formal expression used to refer to a person's school, college, or university. The phrase, which is sometimes written with capital initials, *Alma Mater*, literally means 'bounteous mother'. It is pronounced [almă *mah*tĕr] or [almă *may*tĕr].

almond This word is sometimes mispronounced. The *-l-* is silent, as in *calm*; the correct pronunciation is [*ah*mŏnd].

alone or **lone?** *Alone* and *lone* are both used in the sense of 'solitary' or 'by yourself', but *alone* is always placed after the verb and *lone* before the noun: * *She was alone.* * *a lone cyclist* * *The house stood alone.* * *a lone tree.* *Lone* tends to be used more in literary or poetic contexts. There is also some difference in meaning: *alone* is more likely to suggest loneliness or a desire for solitude, whereas *lone* usually describes a person or thing that simply happens to be on his/her/its own. When *alone* is placed directly after a noun or pronoun it means 'only': * *He alone can help us.* Care should be taken to avoid ambiguity when *alone* is used in this sense: * *She drinks whisky alone* probably means that she drinks no other alcoholic liquor, but it could imply that she drinks in solitude.

along with In the phrase *along with*, the word *along* is often superfluous: * *The package was delivered along with the rest of the mail* could be changed to: * *The package was delivered with the rest of the mail* without affecting the meaning.

aloud *see* **allowed** or **aloud?**

already or **all ready?** The adverb *already* should not be confused with the phrase *all ready*, as both have distinct meanings. *Already* variously means 'at a time earlier than expected' or 'by or before a particular time', whereas *all ready* means 'in a state of complete readiness': * *Have you finished your homework already?* * *They are already in the building.* * *Is everything all ready?* The use in American English of *already* as an intensifier following an exclamation, command, or other statement is best restricted to informal use: * *Enough already!* * *Get over here already!*

alright *see* **all right** or **alright?**

also The use of the adverb *also* in place of the conjunction *and* is disliked and avoided by many users, especially in formal writing: * *Please send me a copy of your new catalogue and a list of local stockists* [not... *a copy of your new catalogue, also a list...*]. The combination *and also*, however, is generally acceptable: * *Please send me a copy of your new catalogue and also a list of local stockists.*

In some sentences, *also* must be carefully positioned in order to convey the intended meaning: * *She also [as well as someone else] was carrying an umbrella.* * *She was carrying an umbrella also [as well as something else].* * *She was wearing a raincoat and she was also carrying an umbrella.* See *also* **not only... but also**.

altar or **alter**? These words are sometimes confused. An *altar* is a place where sacrifices are offered to a god, and also the table on which the bread and wine are blessed in Communion services: * *The priest approached the altar. Alter* with an *e* means 'change': * *a scheme for radically altering the whole tax system.* The different words both have the same pronunciation [*awl*tĕr].

alternate or **alternative**? The adjective *alternate* means 'every other' or 'occurring by turns'; the adjective *alternative* means 'offering a choice' or 'being an alternative': * *on alternate Saturdays* * *alternate layers* * *alternative routes* * *an alternative suggestion.* The use of *alternate* in place of *alternative* is acknowledged by most dictionaries but disliked by many users. *Alternative* should not be used in place of *alternate*.

Note the difference in pronunciation between the adjective *alternate* [awl*tern*ăt] and the verb *alternate* [*awl*tĕrnayt].

The adjective *alternative* is used with increasing frequency in the specific sense of 'not conventional' or 'not traditional': * *alternative medicine* * *alternative comedy* * *alternative technology* * *alternative energy.* This usage is best avoided where there is a risk of ambiguity: * *I decided to buy an alternative newspaper.*

The noun *alternative* traditionally denotes either of two possibilities, or the opportunity of choosing between them, but is widely used with reference to three or more options or choices: * *Are the current alternatives to the dole effective?* (*Daily Telegraph*). * *If the campaign against terrorism is not successful within a few months, the only alternatives will be surrender, negotiation, or a long drawn-out war of attrition.* Most authorities dismiss as pedantry, criticism of this usage on etymological grounds (*alternative* is derived from the Latin word *alter*, meaning 'other [of two]').

alternative medicine *see* **complementary medicine** or **alternative medicine**?

although or **however**? The conjunction *although* should not be treated as interchangeable with the adverb *however*, which is used to introduce contrasting information: * *The team should do well, although they have been hit by injuries; their opponents, however, are unlikely to make much impression.* Note that *however* is usually followed by a comma, but *although* is not.

although or **though**? As conjunctions, meaning 'despite the fact that', *although* and *though* are interchangeable in most contexts: * *We bought the table, although/though it was damaged.*

Though is slightly less formal but more versatile than *although*: it may be used in combination with *even* for extra emphasis; in the phrase *as though* (*see* **as if** or **as though**?); after an adjective; and as an informal substitute for the adverb *however*. • *We bought the table, even though it was damaged.* • *We bought the table, damaged though it was.* • *Ground coffee tastes better than instant coffee; it's more expensive, though. Although* is not used in any of these contexts.

Though and (less frequently) *although* are also used in the sense of 'but' or 'and yet': • *They applauded, though not enthusiastically.* • *It's possible, though unlikely.*

The shortened forms *altho'*, *altho*, *tho'*, and *tho* are best avoided in formal writing. *See also* **if**.

altogether or **all together**? The adverb *altogether* means 'in all' or 'completely'; *all together* means 'at the same time' or 'in the same place': • *She has nine pets altogether.* • *Your system is altogether different from ours.* • *They disappeared altogether.* • *They arrived all together.* • *We keep our reference books all together on a separate shelf.*

aluminium Note the spelling of this word, which refers to the silvery-white metallic element: *-inium* in British English. In American English, the spelling is *aluminum*. In British English, the stress falls on the third syllable; in American English on the second syllable.

Aluminum was the name given to the element in 1812 by its discoverer, the English chemist Sir Humphry Davy (1778–1829), although he had originally proposed *alumium*. By analogy with the names of such other

elements as potassium and sodium, the name *aluminium* was also suggested and this is now the standard form in British English.

alumnus The word *alumnus*, meaning 'former pupil or student', is reserved for males; note however that the plural form *alumni* may refer to former students of both sexes. The equivalent for a female student is *alumna* [plural *alumnae*].

a.m. and **p.m.** Full stops are often retained in the abbreviations *a.m.* (for *ante meridiem*, meaning 'before noon') and *p.m.* (for *post meridiem*, meaning 'after noon') to distinguish *a.m.* from the verb *am*. The use of capital letters is acceptable but rare. The abbreviation *a.m.* refers to the hours from midnight to midday; *p.m.* refers to the hours from midday to midnight: • *12.05 a.m. is five minutes after midnight* • *12.05 p.m. is five minutes after midday.* Such phrases as *8.15 a.m. in the morning* and *11.45 p.m. at night* are tautological; either *a.m.* or *in the morning* and either *p.m.* or *at night* should be omitted. *See also* **abbreviations**.

amanuensis This word, meaning 'person employed to take dictation or copy manuscripts', is sometimes misspelt. Note the single *-n-* and the *-ue-* in the middle of the word. *Amanuensis*, pronounced [ămanyooensis], is best restricted to formal contexts. The plural form is *amanuenses*, pronounced [ămanyooenseez].

amateur This word, meaning 'person who follows an activity as a pastime rather than as a profession': • *an amateur golfer*, has several pronunciations, the most frequent being [*amătĕ*]. The pronunciations [*amāchĕ*], [*amă-tewr*], and [*amāter*] are also heard.

ambience Some people object to the frequent use of the noun *ambience* as a pretentious synonym for 'atmosphere': * *the ambience of the restaurant*. The French spelling *ambiance* and an anglicised form of the French pronunciation are sometimes used in English. The English pronunciation of *ambience* is [*ambiĕns*].

ambiguous or **ambivalent**? *Ambiguous* means 'having two or more possible interpretations or meanings' or 'obscure'; *ambivalent* means 'having conflicting emotions or attitudes' or 'indecisive': * *The phrase 'a French horn player' is ambiguous.* * *Many people are ambivalent about the issue of disarmament: they recognise the importance of the nuclear deterrent but feel that the money spent on nuclear weapons could be put to better use.* Careful users maintain the distinction between the two adjectives, avoiding the temptation to use *ambivalent* in place of *ambiguous*. In some contexts, including the above example, *be ambivalent* may be better replaced by *have mixed feelings* or *be in two minds*.

ameba *see* **amoeba** or **ameba**?

amen The word *amen*, meaning 'so be it', may be pronounced [*ay*men] or [*ah*men]. Both pronunciations are correct.

amend or **emend**? Of these two verbs, *amend*, meaning 'correct', 'improve', or 'alter', is the more general, *emend* being restricted to the correction of errors in a printed or written text: *

The ambiguous wording of the opening paragraph has been amended. * *They have amended the rules.* * *The manuscript was emended by an eminent scholar.* The pronunciation of amend [*ămend*] is very similar to that of *emend* [*imend*]; their derived nouns, however, are quite different: * *an amendment* * *an emendation*.

amenity The noun *amenity* is ultimately derived from the Latin word for 'pleasant'. A few users prefer to restrict the term, which is generally used in the plural form *amenities*, to that which is conducive to comfort or pleasure, objecting to its extended application to that which is merely useful or convenient: * *The amenities of the hotel include a sauna, swimming pool, licensed restaurant, and 24-hour room service.* * *The town lacks some of the basic amenities, such as public toilets and a rubbish dump. Amenity* is usually pronounced [*ameeniti*], with a long *e*, but the pronunciation [*ameniti*], with a short *e*, is an accepted variant and is usual in American English.

America The word *America* is most frequently used with reference to the United States of America, although it strictly denotes the whole landmass comprising Canada, the USA, Central America, and South America. The United States of America may be shortened to the United States, the USA, the US, or (in informal contexts) the States: * *I often go to the States on business.* USA and US are sometimes written or printed with full stops (*see also* **abbreviations**).

Like *America*, the adjective *American* is largely restricted in general usage to the meaning 'of the USA'.

The abbreviation *US* may be used adjectivally to avoid ambiguity: * *a US actor.* There is no single noun that specifically denotes a native or citizen of the USA, but American is generally used for this purpose: * *The book was written by an American.*

American Indian *see* **Native American.**

AMERICANISMS For many years American English has had a significant influence on British English. Although many British purists dislike American English, in some respects its differences arise from greater conservatism than British English. Such words as: * *gotten* * *fall* (autumn), as well as many American spellings, were originally the British forms and have changed in Britain but not in the United States. American English is also a fertile ground for new words and idioms, and there is no reason why British English should not borrow the more striking ones. Such American words as: * *truck* * *commuter* * *teenager* have become part of British vocabulary. Other words of American origin that have been widely transmitted elsewhere reflect the country's particular cultural influences, such as that exerted by Native American culture: * *moccasin* * *squaw* * *prairie.*

The most noticeable differences between American and British English are those of vocabulary. Most British people are familiar with the better-known American equivalents: * *sidewalk* (pavement) * *elevator* (lift) * *cookie* (biscuit) * *vacation* (holiday) * *chips* (crisps) * *fries* (chips) * *hood* (bonnet). It is when the same word or phrase is used with different meanings that confusion arises. If an American says: * *I put on my vest and pants and washed up*, an English person might think of him washing the dishes in his underwear, while in fact he had put on his waistcoat and trousers and washed his hands.

There are various differences between British and American spellings: * *tyre – tire* * *mould – mold* * *connection – connexion.* Many words ending in -re in British English have the ending -er in American English: * *centre – center* * *theatre – theater* * *fibre – fiber*; many words ending in -our in British English have the ending -or in American English: * *colour – color* * *humour – humor.* British English has in most cases resisted American spellings, such as *traveler* (for *traveller*) and *analyze* (for *analyse*), although the American tendency to drop the *o* or *a* in words like *foetus* or *encyclopaedia* is growing increasingly familiar in British spelling (*see also* -**ae**- and -**oe**-; **spelling**).

The significant differences in grammar include a few past tenses like the American *dove* (dived) or *gotten*, and the American tendency to say: * *Do you have...?* where the British would say: * *Have you...?* or: * *Have you got...?* Speakers of British English generally tend to use less direct forms of approach than do Americans, preferring such forms as: * *Would you mind if...?* or * *I'm afraid that...* and may find more direct American approaches lacking in politeness. Americans in turn may consider such Briticisms forced and overly formal (*see also* **quotation marks**; **shall** or **will**?; **subjunctive**; **tense**).

Differences in pronunciation between British and American English can lead to confusion even over identical words, as for instance in the cases of *missile* (pronounced [*misīl*] in British

AMERICANISMS			
American word	**British equivalent**	**American word**	**British equivalent**
airplane	aeroplane	first floor	ground floor
aluminum	aluminium	flashlight	torch
analyze	analyse	flat	puncture
ash can	dustbin	freeway	motorway
baby carriage	pram	fries	chips
baggage	luggage	garbage	rubbish
bathroom	lavatory	gas	petrol
beltway	ringroad	grade crossing	level crossing
billfold	wallet	hood	bonnet
bobby pin	hair grip	humor	humour
bookstore	bookshop	kerosene	paraffin
can	tin	labor union	trade union
candy	sweets	mail	post
casket	coffin	mailbox	pillar box
center	centre	math	maths
check	bill	molasses	treacle
checkers	draughts	mold	mould
chips	crisps	pacifier	baby dummy
color	colour	pants	trousers
comforter	eiderdown	pantyhose	tights
cookie	biscuit	sidewalk	pavement
cot	camp bed	sneakers	trainers
cotton candy	candy floss	snuck	sneaked
diaper	nappy	squash	marrow
dove	dived	stroller	pushchair
drapes	curtains	subway	underground
druggist	pharmacist	theater	theatre
elevator	lift	tire	tyre
encyclopedia	encyclopaedia	traveler	traveller
expressway	motorway	truck	lorry
fall	autumn	undershirt	vest
faucet	tap	vacation	holiday
fender	bumper	vest	waistcoat
fetus	foetus	wrench	spanner
fiber	fibre		

English but [*mi*sil] in American English) and *laboratory* (pronounced [la*bor*ătree] in British English but [*la*brătree] in American English).

Much as many British people deplore the adoption of such American words and phrases as • *laid-back* • *no way* • *cookbook* (instead of *cookery book*), and • *truck* (instead of *lorry*), it can be assumed that such words will continue to cross the Atlantic and that they will continue to be absorbed into British English. *See* the panel, on page 24.

amiable or **amicable**? *Amiable* means 'friendly', 'pleasant', 'agreeable', or 'congenial'; *amicable* means 'characterised by friendliness or goodwill': • *an amiable man* • *an amicable agreement* • *She smiled at me in an amiable manner.* • *The dispute was settled in an amicable manner.* The two adjectives should not be confused.

amid, amidst, mid or **midst**? *Amid* and *amidst* are synonymous, and both are used in formal or poetic contexts, although *amidst* is used more rarely. Both mean 'in the middle of', or 'among': • *amid the crowd* • *amidst the waving reeds*. The word *mid* also means 'in the middle of'; in modern usage it is chiefly found in combination with nouns: • *mid-September* • *mid-air*. *Midst* is most frequently used as a noun, in the phrases *in the midst of*, meaning 'in the middle of', and *in our/their/etc. midst*, meaning 'among us/them/etc.': • *in the midst of the election campaign* • *There is a traitor in our midst*.

amoeba or **ameba**? There are two possible spellings for this word, which refers to a very small single-cell organ-

ism. The first is more frequent in British English, but both forms are used in American English. *See also* **-ae-** and **-oe-**.

amok or **amuck**? The word *amok*, pronounced [ă*muk*] or [ă*mok*] and used especially in the phrase *run amok* ('behave in a violent manner; go berserk'), has the rarer variant spelling *amuck*, pronounced [ă*muk*]. The word derives from Malay *amoq*, 'frenzied attack'.

among or **amongst**? The words *among* and *amongst* are interchangeable in all contexts, *among* being the more frequent in modern usage: • *They hid among/amongst the bushes*. Some users prefer *among* before a consonant sound and *amongst* before a vowel sound: • *among strangers* • *amongst ourselves*. *See also* **between** or **among**?

amoral or **immoral**? *Amoral* means 'not concerned with morality' or 'having no moral standards'; *immoral* means 'not conforming to morality' or 'infringing accepted moral standards': • *an amoral matter* • *an amoral politician* • *immoral behaviour* • *an immoral young man* • *Some people consider vivisection to be immoral; others have an amoral attitude to the issue.* Careful users maintain the distinction between the two adjectives, both of which can be used in a derogatory manner.

The first syllable of *amoral* may be pronounced as a long *a* [ay*mor*răl] or a short *a* [a*mor*răl]; *immoral* is pronounced [i*mor*răl]. Note the spellings of the two words, particularly the single -*m*- of *amoral* and the -*mm*- of *immoral*.

amount or **number**? The words *amount* and *number* are not synonymous. *Number* refers to a countable quantity and is preferred to *amount* in reference to plural nouns, while *amount* refers to something uncountable: ∗ *a large number of volunteers*: ∗ *any amount of rubbish*. Note that while it is correct to talk about a large or small *number* or *amount*, some people consider it less correct to talk about a big or little *number* or *amount*.

amuck *see* **amok** or **amuck**?

an *see* **a** or **an**?

anaemia or **anemia**? There are two possible spellings for this word, which refers to a medical condition resulting from a deficiency in red blood cells in the blood. *Anaemia* is the accepted spelling in British English, while *anemia* is the usual form in American English.

anaesthetic This word, meaning 'a substance that produces a loss of feeling', is sometimes misspelt. Note the *-ae-* in the middle of the word. In the American English spelling, the second *a* is dropped: ∗ *anesthetic*. *See also* **-ae-** and **-oe-**.

analogous The adjective *analogous* should be employed only where the relationship between two things goes beyond mere similarity: ∗ *The shriek of an emergency siren is analogous to the warning cry of a bird*. It is best avoided where *similar, equivalent, comparable, corresponding, like*, etc., would be adequate or more appropriate: ∗ *The new system is analogous to that used in the electronics industry*. The usual pronunciation of *analogous* is

[ănal̆ŏgoŭs], with the hard *g* of *goat* and *analogue*, not the soft *g* of *gem* and *analogy*.

analyse The *s* of *analyse* should not be replaced with *z* in British English, *analyze* being the American spelling of the word (*see also* **-ize** or **-ise**?). Some people object to the use of the verb *analyse* in place of discuss, examine, etc.: ∗ *Your proposal will be analysed at the next committee meeting*. The frequent use of the noun *analysis* in general contexts is also disliked, especially the phrases *in the last analysis, in the final analysis*, and *in the ultimate analysis*, which can usually be replaced by *in the end, at last, finally, ultimately*, etc.

analysis *see* **analyse**.

ancillary This word, meaning 'supplementary or subsidiary': ∗ *ancillary services*, is sometimes misspelt. Note particularly the *-c-*, the *-ll-*, and the ending *-ary*, not *-iary*.

and The use of *and* at the beginning of a sentence is disliked by some users but acceptable to most. And it can sometimes be an effective way of drawing attention to what follows. Two or more subjects joined with *and* are used with a plural verb unless they represent a single concept (*see also* **singular** or **plural**?).

For the use of a comma before and in a series of three or more items, *see* **comma**. *And* may also be preceded by a comma in other contexts, especially in complex sentences or where there is a risk of ambiguity: ∗ *Jenny owns the red car, and the black car belongs to her brother*. ∗ *He unlocked the door with the key that he had found inside the* stolen purse, and went in. • *She has been to Spain, Portugal, and Italy, and hopes to visit Greece next year.* The omission of the first *and* in the last example and similar sentences is a frequent error.

The use of *and* in place of *to* is best avoided in formal contexts: • *We'd better try and find it.* • *I'll come and see you tomorrow.* See also **and/or**; **I** or **me**?

and/or The phrase *and/or* should only be used where three possibilities are envisaged: • *cash and/or postage stamps*, for example, means 'cash, postage stamps, or both'. The phrase should not be used where *and* or *or* would be adequate: • *This food is suitable for hamsters and* [not *and/or*] *gerbils.* • *The bank is not open on Saturdays or* [not *and/or*] *Sundays.*

And/or is best restricted to official, legal, or commercial contexts and replaced elsewhere by a slightly longer phrase: • *The casserole may be served with potatoes or carrots or both* [not *potatoes and/or carrots*].

anemia *see* **anaemia** or **anemia**?

anesthetic *see* **anaesthetic**.

angle Some people object to the frequent use of the noun *angle* in place of *point of view, standpoint,* etc.: • *The report has been written from a unilateralist angle.* The verb *angle* implies a lack of objectivity: • *The play was angled to make the audience sympathise with the criminal.*

angry The adjective *angry* is followed by the preposition *about* or *at* in the sense of 'angry about something': • *She was angry about* [or *at*] *the way they had treated him,* and *with* in the

sense of 'angry with a person': • *Are you angry with me?*

annex or **annexe**? In British English, *annex* is a verb meaning 'add' or 'appropriate'; *annexe* is a noun that denotes a building built or used as an extension: • *to annex a state* • *a room in the annexe.* The variant spelling of the noun without the final -*e* is largely restricted to American English. It is wrong to spell the verb with a final -*e*: • *He had no ambitions to annexe the Department of Transport* (*The Guardian*).

annual, **biennial** or **perennial**? An *annual* plant, e.g. the marigold, completes its life cycle in only one growing season. A *biennial* plant, e.g. the strawberry, germinates and accumulates food reserves in the first year and flowers, fruits, and dies during the second year. A *perennial* plant, e.g. a woody tree, and a herbaceous plant such as the foxglove, grows for more than two years, sometimes lasting for several years and usually having a new growth of flowers each year. Note the -*nn*- spelling in these words.

anonymous This word, meaning 'of unknown origin or identity': • *an anonymous donor,* is sometimes misspelt, the most frequent error being to replace the *y* with an *i*.

anorexic or **anorectic**? The words *anorexic* and *anorectic* have the same meaning. Either may be used as a noun or as an adjective to describe a person suffering from the disorder *anorexia nervosa,* although *anorexic* is used more frequently and *anorectic* is usually restricted to more technical contexts.

-ant or **-ent**? The suffixes *-ant* or *-ent*, identical in pronunciation, cause frequent spelling problems. Either suffix may be used to form nouns and adjectives: * *the defendant* * *a superintendent* * *a defiant child* * *an irreverent remark*. However, in many cases where both *-ant* and *-ent* forms exist, *-ant* is the usual form for the noun and *-ent* for the adjective (*see* **confidant** or **confident**?; **dependant** or **dependent**?; **pendant** or **pendent**?). It may be useful to remember that nouns and adjectives formed from verbs ending in *-ate* take the suffix *-ant* rather than *-ent*: * *predominant* * *stimulant* * *tolerant* * *mutant*.

ante- or **anti-**? These two prefixes are sometimes confused. *Ante-*, from Latin, means 'before': * *antenatal* * *anteroom* * *antecedent*. *Anti-*, from Greek, means 'against; opposite to': * *anti-apartheid* * *anti-aircraft* * *anti-American* * *anticlockwise*. In British English, both prefixes are pronounced [*ant*i]; in American English *anti-* is pronounced [*ant*ī] or [*ant*i], *ante-* [*ant*i].

In informal spoken English, *anti* is sometimes used as a preposition, meaning 'opposed to': * *He's very anti politics*, or as an adjective: * *He's very anti*.

antecedent An *antecedent* is a word, phrase, or clause to which a subsequent word refers: * *She passed the book to him and he took it* (in which *the book* is the antecedent). Care should be taken to avoid confusion over the *antecedent* being referred to: * *She passed the book through the window and he opened it* (where the antecedent could be either *the book* or *the window*).

antennae or **antennas**? The noun *antenna* has two plural forms, *antennae* and *antennas*. The plural form *antennae*, pronounced to rhyme with *my* or *tree*, is used to denote an insect's or crustacean's feelers; when *antenna* is used to mean 'aerial' (this sense being of American origin) the plural form *antennas* is preferred.

anti- *see* **ante-** or **anti-**?

anticipate The verb *anticipate* is widely used as a synonym for 'expect': * *We do not anticipate that there will be any problems.* * *Oil prices showed their expected leap yesterday.... But the rally was not as strong as some traders anticipated* (*Daily Telegraph*). This usage is disliked by many people, who restrict the verb to its accepted more formal senses of 'forestall', 'act in advance of', etc.: * *Preventative medicine anticipates disease.* * *They anticipated the attack by boarding up their doors and windows.* * *You must learn to anticipate his needs.* The verb is best avoided altogether where there is a risk of ambiguity, for example in such sentences as *I anticipated her resignation* and *The driver anticipated the accident*.

antidote The noun *antidote* is followed by the preposition *to* or *for*: * *Alcohol should not be used as an antidote to* [or *for*] *depression*.

antihistamine The word *antihistamine*, which denotes a medicinal substance that is used to treat allergies, is sometimes misspelt. Note the third syllable, *-hist-* (not *-hyst-*), and the *-ine* ending.

antique or **antiquated**? The adjective *antique* is used to describe a piece of furniture or a work of art that is old and valuable: * *a beautiful antique vase.* The adjective *antiquated*, meaning 'old-fashioned' or 'obsolete', is usually derogatory: * *an antiquated washing machine* * antiquated procedures.*

antisocial, **asocial**, **unsocial** or **unsociable**? These four adjectives are sometimes confused. Both *antisocial* and *unsociable* can mean 'unfriendly', describing somebody who avoids the company of others: * *Our new neighbours seem rather antisocial/unsociable.* *Antisocial* is the stronger of the two and may also describe behaviour that causes harm or inconvenience to others: * *an antisocial act/habit. Asocial,* a much rarer word, implies a deeper hostility to or withdrawal from society; *unsocial* is chiefly used in the phrase *unsocial hours*, referring to the time when most people are not at work: * *You must be prepared to work unsocial hours. See also* **sociable** or **social**?

antonym An *antonym* is a word that has the opposite meaning to another word: * *right* (the antonym of *wrong*) * *quick* (the antonym of *slow*). It yields the adjective *antonymous*, but this is less familiar in daily use than *synonymous*, which signifies two words with the same meaning and is best avoided in informal contexts.

any The use of a singular or plural verb with the pronoun *any* depends on the sense and context in which it is used: * *Is any of the furniture damaged?* * *Ask him if any of his children watch/watches the programme.* In the first example, *any*, like furniture, must be used with a singular verb. In examples of the second type, a singular verb is preferred if *any* is used in the sense of 'any one'

and a plural verb if *any* implies 'some' (*see also* **singular** or **plural**?).

The use of *any* in place of **at all** is used in American English but should be avoided in British English: * *Her manners haven't improved any. See also* **anybody** or **anyone**?

anybody or **anyone**? The pronoun *anybody* and its synonym *anyone* are interchangeable in all contexts. Both are used with a singular verb but are sometimes followed by a plural personal pronoun or possessive adjective (*see* **they**): * *Has anybody/anyone finished their work?*

Note the difference between the one-word compound *anyone* and the more specific two-word form *any one*, both of which may be applied to people: * *Anyone could have started the fire.* * *Any one of the tenants could have started the fire.* Only the two-word compound is used of things: * *These tables are not reserved, so you can sit at any one you like.*

anymore or **any more**? This word, variously meaning 'any longer' or 'nowadays', is generally rendered *any more* in British English and careful users avoid *anymore*, the accepted form in American English: * *She does not live there any more.*

anyplace or **any place**? This word is usually rendered *any place* in British English and careful users avoid *anyplace*, the accepted form in American English: * *Have you seen my jacket any place?* British English in any case tends to prefer *anywhere*.

anytime or **any time**? This word is usually rendered *any time* in British English and careful users avoid *any-*

time, the accepted form in American English: • *Come round any time.*

apartheid The name of the former South African political system *apartheid* may be pronounced in several different ways. Some users prefer the pronunciation [ăpartḥayt], following the Afrikaans original. Other frequently used pronunciations are [ăparthīt] and pronunciations in which the *h* is not sounded: [ăpartīt] and [ăpartīd].

apophthegm This word, meaning 'aphorism', is sometimes misspelt. Note the *-ph-* in the middle of the word and the *-egm* ending. It is sometimes rendered *apothegm* in American English: • *This truth is expressed in a pungent apophthegm.* The word is pronounced [apăthem].

apostasy This word, meaning 'renunciation of a religious or political belief, cause, or allegiance', is sometimes misspelt. Note the *-asy* ending.

APOSTROPHE The *apostrophe* is used mainly to denote possession and other relationships: • *Angela's house* • *the Church of England's doctrines* • *the rabbits' warren*, and to indicate omitted letters in contractions: • *can't* • *you're* • *there's. See* panel on page 31; *see also* **contractions; dates; -ing forms; its** or **it's?; possessives**.

appal Note the spelling of this verb, especially the *-pp-* and (in British English) the single *l*. The usual American English spelling of the word is *appall*. In British English the final *-l* is doubled before a suffix beginning with a vowel, as in *appalled* and *appalling* (*see also* **spelling**).

apparatus This word is usually pronounced [apăraytŭs] or [apăraytus], though the pronunciation [apărahtŭs] is also sometimes heard.

appendixes or **appendices**? The noun *appendix* has two accepted plural forms, *appendixes* and *appendices*. The use of the plural form *appendixes* is largely restricted to the anatomical sense of the word: • *During his early years as a surgeon he removed countless tonsils, adenoids, and appendixes.* In the sense of 'supplement (to a book, document, etc.)', most users prefer the plural form *appendices*, pronounced [ăpendiseez]: • *One of the appendices lists foreign words and phrases in general usage.*

applicable In the more traditional pronunciation of this word, the first syllable is stressed [aplikăbl]. The pronunciation with the second syllable stressed [ăplikăbl] is probably more frequently heard, however. *See also* **stress**.

apposition A noun or phrase that is in *apposition* supplies further information about another noun or phrase. Both nouns or phrases refer to the same person or thing; they are equivalent in meaning. In the sentence • *Mary Jones, an accountant, was elected*, the phrases *Mary Jones* and *an accountant* are in apposition. In the phrase • *the accusation that he had stolen the car*, the *accusation* and *that he had stolen the car* are in apposition. Like relative clauses (*see* **clause**), appositive nouns or phrases may be defining or non-defining. The phrase • *that he had stolen the car* is non-defining in • *The accusation, that he had stolen the car, was untrue* and defining

APOSTROPHES

1 Apostrophes and pronouns	Possessive personal pronouns do not take apostrophes: ● *his book* ● *its name* ● *it is ours*, but indefinite pronouns do: ● *anybody's guess* ● *no one's fault*. Purists have maintained that as *else* is not a noun or pronoun it cannot take an apostrophe, and have used the form: ● *someone's else*, but *someone else's* is now generally acceptable.
2 Problems with apostrophes	Difficulties with the possessive use of the apostrophe centre on its presence or absence and its position before or after the *s* (for the basic rules *see* **'s** or **s'**?). Advertisers are particularly guilty of leaving apostrophes out when they should be included: ● *mens clothes* ● *last years prices* ● *special childrens menu*, while market stalls are especially prone to forming plurals with apostrophes when they should not be included: ● *potato's* ● *apricot's*. Other errors recorded in recent years have included: ● *cres's* ● *gateaux's* ● *Beware of the dog's*. Units of measurement often have their apostrophes omitted; it should be: ● *50 years' service* ● *a six months' stay in America*. With well-known commercial organisations and products, the tendency is now to drop the apostrophe: ● *Barclays Bank* ● *Macmillans* ● *Pears soap*.
3 Apostrophes and plurals	There are a few exceptions to the rule that apostrophes cannot be used for plurals. They can be used to indicate the plurals of individual letters, words, and numbers in expressions like: ● *It takes two l's in the past tense.* ● *mind your p's and q's* ● *She often begins sentences with and's and but's.* ● *He writes his 7's in the continental way.* The apostrophe is also sometimes used for the plural of abbreviations: ● *MP's*, but this usage is becoming less frequent.
4 Apostrophes and contractions	Apart from the use of the apostrophe to indicate contractions such as *shouldn't, I'm, 'n'* (for and: ● *salt 'n' vinegar flavour crisps*), it is used to indicate missing letters in poetic forms such as *e'er, o'er*, in terms such as *o'clock, will-o'-the-wisp*, and in names like *O'Connor*. It might also be used when writing dialogue to indicate Cockney or dialect speech: ● *'E was goin' to 'Ackney.* ● *... 'tis said 'a was a poor parish 'prentice* (Hardy, *The Mayor of Casterbridge*). Apostrophes are also sometimes used to indicate missing numbers: ● *the generation who were young in the '60s.* Apostrophes are no longer generally used for shortened forms that are in general use: ● *flu* ● *phone* ● *photo* ● *plane*.

in * *The accusation that he had stolen the car was the most upsetting.*

Many names and titles are made up of two nouns in *apposition*; for example, *Lake* and *Geneva* in * *Lake Geneva* or *Prince* and *Charles* in * *Prince Charles*. Longer titles are better placed after the proper noun with which they are in apposition: * *Mr Green, managing director of the company* (the insertion of *the* before *managing director* is optional). *See also* **comma**.

appraise, **apprise** or **apprize**? To *appraise* is to assess the quality or worth of something; *apprise* means 'inform': * *She appraised their work.* * *He apprised me of the details. Apprize* is listed in some dictionaries as a less frequent variant spelling of *apprise*; it is also an archaic verb meaning 'appraise'. The verb *apprise* is largely restricted to formal contexts.

appreciate The frequent use of the verb *appreciate* in place of *realise* or *understand* is disliked by a few users: * *I appreciate that the child's parents were unaware of the risk.* * *Do you appreciate our problem?* The principal senses of *appreciate* are 'be grateful for', 'recognise the worth of', and 'increase in value': * *He would appreciate some assistance.* * *She does not appreciate good wine.* * *Their house has appreciated considerably during the past six months.*

apprehend or **comprehend**? These two verbs are sometimes confused when they have the meaning 'understand'. *Comprehend* implies a complete understanding, sometimes emphasising the mental activity needed to come to such knowledge: * *They did not fully comprehend the motives that lay behind her decision. Apprehend*, which is used

fairly rarely in this sense, implies a perception – not always complete – of the essential quality or significance of something: * *to apprehend the nature of beauty.* Both verbs have other meanings. *Apprehend* means 'arrest' and is used in formal contexts: * *to apprehend a criminal.* In formal contexts *comprehend* means 'include', in which sense it is more frequently found in the form of the adjective *comprehensive* (*see* **comprehensible** or **comprehensive**?): * *a comprehensive survey.* The noun *comprehension* means 'understanding'; *apprehension* is rarely used in this sense.

apprise, **apprize** *see* **appraise**, **apprise** or **apprize**?

appropriate The adjective *appropriate* is followed by the preposition *to* or *for*: * *language that is appropriate to* [or *for*] *the situation in which it is used.* Care should be taken not to overuse the jargonistic phrase, *appropriate person*: * *The child was placed in the care of an appropriate person.*

approval The noun *approval* is followed by the preposition *of* or *for*: * *They expressed their approval of* [or *for*] *our plan.*

a priori The Latin phrase *a priori*, which literally means 'from the previous', is applied adjectivally to deductive or presumptive reasoning, arguments, statements, etc. The phrase is usually pronounced [ay prīorī], the pronunciation [ah preeoree] being an accepted variant.

apropos As a preposition meaning 'with regard to', *apropos* may be followed by *of*: * *apropos (of) your* enquiry * apropos (of) the new development. In formal contexts *apropos* is also used as an adjective, meaning 'appropriate', and as an adverb, meaning 'incidentally': * *Your remark was not quite apropos.* * *Apropos the contract, is it concluded?*

Apropos is always written as one word in English, unlike the French phrase *à propos*, from which it is derived. Note that the initial *a* is followed by a single *p*.

The pronunciation of this word is [apro*po*]: the *s* is not sounded.

apt *see* **liable** or **likely**?

aqueduct The noun *aqueduct*, describing a structure that carries water, is often misspelt. Note that the word begins *aque-*, not *aqua-* (as in *aqualung*, *aquaplane*, etc.).

Arab, Arabian or **Arabic**? The adjective *Arab* relates to the people of Arabia and their descendants; *Arabian* to Arabia itself; and *Arabic* to the language of Arabia and other Arab countries: * *an Arab sheikh* * *the Arab nations* * *the Arabian peninsula* * *the Arabian Sea* * *an Arabic numeral* * *Arabic literature*. All three words are used as nouns, *Arabian* being a rare variant of *Arab*: * *His sister married an Arab.* * *Arabic is the official language of Egypt.*

The word *Arab* is also applied to a breed of horse that is used for riding; the *Arabian Nights* is a collection of oriental tales; and *gum arabic* (note the lower-case *a*) is a gum obtained from certain acacia trees.

arbiter or **arbitrator**? An *arbiter* is a person who has the power to judge or who has absolute control; an *arbitrator* is a person who is appointed to settle a dispute: * *an arbiter of fashion* * *an arbiter of human destiny* * *The arbitrator's decision proved acceptable to both parties.* The general term *arbiter* may be used in place of the more specific *arbitrator*, but the two nouns are not fully interchangeable.

arbitrarily The adverb *arbitrarily* should be stressed on the first syllable [*ar*bitrǎrĕli]. The pronunciation [arbi-*trerr*ĕli], in which the primary stress shifts to the third syllable, although unacceptable to many people, is the most frequently used.

arbitrator *see* **arbiter** or **arbitrator**?

arch- and **archi-** The prefixes *arch-* and *archi-* are both derived from a Greek word meaning 'to rule'. In words beginning with the prefix *arch-* the -*ch*- sound is soft, as in *choose*; in words beginning with the prefix *archi-* the -*ch*- sound is hard, as in *chord*: * *archbishop* [arch*bish*ŏp] * *architect* [*ark*itekt]. The word *archangel* [*ark*aynjĕl] is an exception to this rule. In the suffixes -*arch* and -*archy* the -*ch*- sound is always hard: * *patriarch* [*pay*triark] * *anarchy* [*an*ǎrki].

archaeology This word, describing the study of the material remains of ancient cultures, is spelt with the vowels -*aeo*- in the middle of the word in both British and American English. The alternative spelling *archeology* is occasionally encountered in American English. *See also* -**ae**- and -**oe**-.

archetypal The adjective *archetypal* is best avoided where *typical*, *characteristic*, *classic*, *original*, etc., would be adequate or more appropriate: * *an archetypal Yorkshire village*.

archi- *see* **arch-** and **archi-**.

aren't The use of this informal contracted form of *are not* is widely avoided in formal contexts. Note that in questions, *aren't* may also be used in informal contexts as a contraction of *am not*: * *I'm next, aren't I?* * *Aren't I clever?*

Argentine or **Argentinian**? Either word may be used as an adjective, meaning 'of Argentina', or as a noun, denoting a native or inhabitant of Argentina. Though purists prefer *Argentine*, *Argentinian* is more frequent in both senses: * *the Argentinian/Argentine flag* * *an Argentinian/Argentine ship* * *Her stepfather is an Argentinian/ Argentine.* The word *Argentine* may be pronounced [arjĕntīn] or [arjĕnteen], rhyming with *mine* or *mean*.

The republic of Argentina is sometimes called the *Argentine*: * *They lived in the Argentine for several years.*

argument Note the spelling of this word. The final *-e* of the verb *argue* is dropped when the suffix *-ment* is added to form the noun.

arise or **rise**? *Arise* means 'come into being', 'originate', or 'result'; *rise* means 'get up', 'move upwards', or 'increase': * *A problem has arisen.* * *The quarrel arose from a misunderstanding.* * *He rose to greet her.* * *The water level is rising.* *Arise* may be substituted for *rise* in some senses of the latter, but this usage is largely restricted to formal or poetic context and is generally regarded as old-fashioned.

The verb *arise* is followed by the preposition *from* or *out of*: * *issues arising from* [or *out of*] *the discussion.* See also **raise** or **rise**?

around or **about**? In British English, *about* is preferred to *around* in the sense of 'approximately': * *We have about/around 200 employees.* * *He left at about/around eleven o'clock.* Many people regard the use of *around* in this sense as an Americanism.

In the sense of 'here and there', *around* and *about* are interchangeable in most contexts: * *to run around/ about* * *sitting around/about all day* * *toys scattered around/about the room.* In the sense of 'surrounding', *about* is less frequent than *around* (in American English) and *round* (in British English). In the sense 'concerning', both British and American English use *around*: * *He has issues around his childhood.* * *A lot of people have expressed worries about the threat of biological terrorism.* See also **around** or **round**?

around or **round**? *Around* and *round* are synonymous in most of their adverbial and prepositional senses, *around* being preferred in American English and *round* in British English: * *I turned round/around.* * *The wheels went round/around.* * *They sat round/ around the table.* * *She wore a gold chain round/around her ankle.* See also **around** or **about**?

arouse or **rouse**? *Arouse* means 'stimulate' or 'excite'; *rouse* means 'wake' or 'stir': * *Their curiosity was aroused.* * *The ban on smoking has aroused widespread opposition.* * *The noise of the aeroplanes roused the child.* * *I was roused to anger by his accusations.* The direct object of *arouse* is usually an abstract noun; the direct object of *rouse* is usually a person or animal. The substitution of *arouse* for *rouse* in the sense of 'wake' is acceptable but rare.

arpeggio This word, meaning 'the notes of a chord played in succession', is sometimes misspelt. Note the *-gg-* in the middle of the word. *Arpeggio* is pronounced [ah*pejee*ō].

artefact or **artifact**? Both spellings of this noun, referring to an object made by a person, e.g. a tool with special historical interest, are correct. *Artefact* is probably more frequent in British English and *artifact* in American English.

articles *see* **a** or **an**?; **the**.

artifact *see* **artefact** or **artifact**?

artist or **artiste**? An *artist* is a person who is skilled in one or more of the fine arts, such as painting or sculpture; an *artiste* is a professional entertainer, such as a singer or dancer: * *the Dutch artist Vincent Van Gogh* * *the music-hall artiste Marie Lloyd*. In its extended sense of 'skilled person' the noun *artist* may be substituted for *artiste*, which is becoming less frequent. Both nouns can be applied to people of either sex.

as The *as... as* construction may be followed by a subject pronoun or an object pronoun: * *She loves the child as much as he* [as much as he does]. * *She loves the child as much as him* [as much as she loves him]. In informal contexts the subject pronoun is sometimes replaced by the object pronoun, especially in simple comparisons: * *as tall as me* * *as old as them*. This usage, which is unacceptable to many people, should be avoided in formal contexts.

The *as... as* construction is sometimes ambiguous: * *She loves the child as much as her husband*, for example, may mean 'she loves the child as much as her husband does' or 'she loves the child as much as she loves her husband'. In such cases the missing verb may be inserted for clarity.

The substitution of *so... as* for *as... as* in negative constructions is optional: * *He is not so/as clever as his sister*. When the construction is followed by an infinitive with *to*, however, *so... as* is preferred: * *I would not be so careless as to leave my car unlocked*.

When the *as... as* construction is followed by a comparative adjective or adverb, the second *as* is sometimes omitted in informal contexts but is retained by careful users in formal contexts: * *Her car is as old (as) or older than mine.* * *He dances as badly (as) or worse than you.*

The use of the *as... as* construction when *as* alone is required, in the sense of 'though', is widely disliked in British English: * *Tired as he was* [not *As tired as he was*], *he finished the race.*

The dialectal use of *as* in place of *that* or *who* should be avoided in formal contexts: * *I don't know that* [not *as*] *I agree.* * *the man who* [not *as*] *cleans our windows. See also* **as far as**; **as from**; **as if** or **as though**?; **as per**; **as to**; **as well as**; **as yet**; **because, as, for** or **since**?; **comparative and superlative**; **like**; **such as** or **like**?

ascent *see* **assent** or **ascent**?

ascetic *see* **aesthetic, ascetic** or **acetic**?

as far as The phrase *as far as... is concerned* can often be replaced by a simple preposition: * *The course is a waste of time for the more experienced students* [not as *far as the more experienced students are concerned*].

as follows The phrase *as follows* should be used when introducing a list or other enumeration. Note that *follows* retains the -*s* ending regardless of whether it succeeds a singular or plural noun: • *The conditions demanded by the hijackers are as follows.* • *The result is as follows.*

as for *see* **as to.**

as from The phrase *as from* is best avoided where *from*, *on*, *at*, etc., would be adequate or more appropriate: • *I shall be available for work from* [not *as from*] *next Monday.* • *Sunday deliveries will cease on* [not *as from*] *1 November.* • *The increase will come into effect at* [not *as from*] *midnight. As from* may serve a useful purpose in the context of retrospective payments, agreements, etc.: • *The reduced interest will be payable as from last July.*

Asian or **Asiatic**? Either word may be used as an adjective, meaning 'of Asia', or as a noun, denoting a native or inhabitant of Asia. *Asian* is preferred in both senses, the use of *Asiatic* with reference to people being considered racially offensive: • *an Asian/Asiatic country* • *an Asian* [not *Asiatic*] *doctor* • *an Asian* [not *Asiatic*] *living in Europe.* The word *Asian* may be pronounced [*ay*shăn] or [*ayz*hăn], although [*ay*shăn] is more common among younger people. *See also* **Indian.**

as if or **as though**? *As if* and *as though* are interchangeable in most contexts: • *The car looked as if/though it had been resprayed.* • *She trembled, as if/though aware of our presence.* • *He opened his mouth as if/though to speak. As if* is preferred in emphatic exclamations: • *As if it mattered!* • *As if I*

needed their advice! See also **subjunctive; were** or **was**?

asocial *see* **antisocial, asocial, unsocial** or **unsociable**?

as of *see* **as from.**

as per The use of the phrase *as per* in place of *according to* is widely regarded as commercialese: • *as per instructions* • *as per the specifications.* The use of the expression *as per usual* in place of *as usual* is best restricted to informal contexts: • *The train was ten minutes late, as (per) usual.*

asphalt This word, used to describe a material used in road-surfacing, is often misspelt. Note particularly the -*sph*-. The preferred pronunciation is [*as*falt], although [*ash*falt] is also heard.

asphyxiate This word, meaning 'suffocate', is sometimes misspelt. Note particularly the -*phy*-, as in *physics.*

assassinate This word, meaning 'murder an important person': • *The president was assassinated*, is often misspelt. Remember the -*ss*-, which occurs twice. The nouns *assassin* and *assassination* follow the same spelling pattern.

assent or **ascent**? These two words are sometimes confused, being identical in pronunciation. The noun *assent* means 'agreement' (*see* **assent** or **consent**?); the noun *ascent* means 'the act of ascending', 'a climb', or 'upward slope': • *She gave her assent.* • *the ascent of Everest.*

assent or **consent**? Either word may be used as a verb, meaning 'agree', or as a noun, meaning 'agreement'. The verb *consent* sometimes implies greater reluctance than *assent*: * *They readily assented to our plan.* * *After hours of persuasion they consented to end the strike.* The noun *assent* has connotations of acceptance or acquiescence, whereas the noun *consent* denotes approval or permission: * *with the assent of my colleagues* * *without her parents' consent.*

assertion or **assertiveness**? An *assertion* is a positive statement or declaration; *assertiveness* is the state of being dogmatic or aggressive: * *to make an assertion* * *assertiveness training.* Careful users maintain the distinction between the two nouns. The use of *assertion* in place of *assertiveness* is probably due to confusion with the noun *self-assertion*, which means 'putting yourself forward in a forceful or aggressive manner'.

assignation or **assignment**? Both these nouns may be used to denote the act of assigning: * *the assignation/assignment of household chores. Assignation* has the additional meaning of 'secret meeting'; *assignment* also means 'task': * *an assignation with her lover* * *having completed his first assignment.* The two words are not interchangeable in either of these senses.

assimilate This word, meaning 'absorb or integrate', is often misspelt. The only double letters are the *-ss-*. The verb *assimilate* should not be confused with *simulate* (*see* **dissemble**, **dissimulate** or **simulate**?; **simulate** or **stimulate**?).

assist The verb *assist* is followed by the preposition *in* or *with*: * *He assisted her in* [or *with*] *her research.*

assonance *Assonance*, meaning 'the repetition of similar sounds in successive words', can be employed to striking effect in headlines or poetry, etc., but overuse is best avoided: * *History's greatest mystery.* * *light-stifling night.*

as such The phrase *as such* means 'as already explained or understood': * *a government as such will soon fall*; or 'in itself or themselves': * *Knowledge as such is no guarantee of happiness.* Note, however, that it is used increasingly to mean 'therefore': * *The project is just a first step and as such should not be expected to change the situation very much.* Careful speakers and writers avoid overusing this expression in that sense.

assume or **presume**? In the sense of 'suppose' or 'take for granted', the verbs *assume* and *presume* are virtually interchangeable: * *I assume/presume you will accept their offer.* In some contexts, *assume* may suggest a hypothesis postulated without proof, and *presume* a conclusion based on evidence: * *He assumed that she was an experienced player and did not offer her any advice.* * *From her performance in the opening game he presumed that she was an experienced player.*

Both verbs have a number of additional senses. *Assume* means 'undertake', 'feign', or 'adopt': * *to assume responsibility* * *to assume an air of astonishment* * *to assume a new name. Presume* means 'dare' or 'take advantage of': * *I did not presume to contradict him.* * *They presumed on our hospitality.*

assurance or **insurance**? Both *assurance* and *insurance* are used to denote financial protection against a certainty, such as the death of the policyholder: * *life assurance* * *life insurance*. Of the two nouns, only *insurance* is used with reference to financial protection against a possibility, such as fire, accidental damage, theft, or medical expenses: * *motor insurance* * *household insurance* * *travel insurance* * *health insurance*.

The noun *assurance* has a number of other meanings derived from the verb *assure*, such as 'guarantee' and 'confidence': * *an assurance of help* * *an air of assurance*. See also **assure, ensure** or **insure**?

assure, ensure or **insure**? To *assure* is to state with conviction or to convince; to *ensure* is to make certain; to *insure* is to protect financially: * *He assured me that the carpet would not be damaged*. * *Please ensure that you do not damage the carpet*. * *I insured the carpet against accidental damage*. In American English the word *insure* is sometimes used in place of *ensure*. See also **assurance** or **insurance**?

asterisk The *asterisk* (*) has several different uses. It may be employed to indicate that some letters in a word have been omitted, for instance, when rendering swearwords: * *Some bas***d cut me up on the way to work this morning!*, to create a break between passages of text (sometimes with a row of several asterisks side by side), to separate items in a list or to refer readers to a footnote. Care should be taken, however, not to use asterisks too frequently.

Note the spelling and pronunciation of *asterisk*, particularly the *-sk* ending.

asthma This word, which describes the disorder that makes breathing diffi-

cult, is sometimes misspelt – the most frequent error being in the combination of the consonants *sthm*. It is not easy to pronounce the word in its entirety, and [*asmă*] is probably more frequently heard than the full pronunciation [*asthmă*].

as though *see* **as if** or **as though**?

as to Many people object to the unnecessary use of *as to* before *whether, what, why*, etc.: * *There is some doubt (as to) whether she is suitably qualified*. * *He offered no explanation (as to) why he was late*. *As to* is also best avoided where *of, about, on*, etc., would be adequate or more appropriate: * *Please give me your opinion as to the efficiency of the system*. * *They received no warning as to the risks involved*.

The phrase *as to* (or *as for*) may serve a useful purpose at the beginning of a sentence, in the sense of 'with regard to' or 'concerning': * *As to/for the results of the survey, they will be published in next month's magazine*. * *As for his sister, she survived the accident*.

astrology or **astronomy**? These two nouns are sometimes confused. *Astrology* is the study of the movements of the planets and their effect on human affairs; *astronomy* is the scientific study of the universe.

astronomical The use of the adjective *astronomical* in the sense of 'very large' is best restricted to informal contexts: * *an astronomical increase in crime* * *astronomical prices*. This usage probably originated in the very high figures required for the expression of measurements in *astronomy*.

astronomy *see* **astrology** or **astronomy**?

as well as When two or more verbs are linked by the phrase *as well as*, in the sense of 'in addition to', the verb that follows *as well as* is usually an *-ing* form: * *The burglar broke a valuable ornament, as well as stealing all my jewellery.* * *As well as weeding the borders, the gardener pruned the roses* and *mowed the lawn.* For the use of a singular or plural verb after nouns linked by *as well as*, *see* **singular** or **plural**?

    As well as is best avoided where there is a risk of confusion with the literal sense of the phrase: * *Mark plays golf as well as Peter,* for example, may mean 'both Mark and Peter play golf' or 'Mark and Peter are equally good at golf'.

as yet The phrase *as yet*, meaning 'up to now' or 'so far', is best avoided where *yet* would be adequate: * *Have you sold any tickets yet* [not *as yet*]? * *I haven't sold any tickets (as) yet.* * *No tickets have been sold (as) yet.* * *Only a few tickets have been sold as yet.*

asylum seeker The phrase *asylum seeker* should be used with caution. It is often employed pejoratively as a blanket term to describe migrants from other countries, typically people hoping to gain access to a country's internal welfare system to which they are deemed to have no right. Asylum is a legal process, however, and those seeking it may well be in genuine need of refugee status or humanitarian protection. Consequently, although it is correct to refer to an *illegal immigrant* when discussing a person who has outstayed the right to remain, *illegal immigrant* is not synonymous with

asylum seeker, and furthermore there is no such thing as an 'illegal asylum seeker'.

at The word *at* features in many email addresses and is conventionally represented by the symbol @, usually placed between a person's name and their organisation or Internet service provider: * *Please send your reply to fsmith@infocenter.com.* The symbol @, again representing (and pronounced) *at*, may also be used in other technical contexts: * *200 packets @ £4 each* * *2,000 miles @ 23 miles per gallon,* and increasingly in non-technical contexts: * *Come to a party @ our house.*

at or **in**? *At* is traditionally used before the name of a village or small town; *in* before the name of a large town, city, country, etc.: * *He lives at Great Snoring.* * *They stayed at Keswick.* * *She works in Southampton.* * *We have a house in Scotland.* *At* may be replaced by *in* when the speaker or writer is referring to his or her own place of residence, work, etc.: * *I live in Southbourne.*

    In other contexts, *at* generally indicates a more exact or specific position than *in*: * *He lives in North Street.* * *He lives at 27 North Street.* * *She works in a bank.* * *She works at Barclays Bank.*

ate This word, which is the past tense of the verb *eat*, is pronounced [et] or [ayt] in British English. In American English the usual pronunciation is [ayt], the pronunciation [et] being considered non-standard.

-ate A number of words ending in *-ate* may be used as adjectives (and/or nouns) and verbs. In these adjectives and nouns, the ending *-ate* is pro-

nounced [-ăt]; in verbs it is pronounced [-ayt]. For example, the adjective
animate is pronounced [*ani*măt],
whereas the verb is pronounced
[*ani*mayt]; the noun *delegate* is pronounced [*deli*găt], whereas the verb is
pronounced [*deli*gayt].

atheist *see* **agnostic** or **atheist**?

attach This word, meaning 'join or fasten', is sometimes misspelt. Note the
-*tt*- and the -*ch*. There is no *t* before
the -*ch*.

attempt The noun *attempt* is followed
by the preposition *at* in the sense of
'trying to do something': * *Her first
attempt at setting up a business ended
in failure*, and *on* in the sense of
'trying to kill someone': * *He had survived two earlier attempts on his life.*

at the sharp end To be *at the sharp end*
of an activity is to be involved in the
area in which there is the greatest difficulty or danger: * *football referees at
the sharp end of violence on the field
and also criticism from the media* *
'*Nurses*'... *a repeat of the* [television]
*series on life at the sharp end of
the National Health Service* (*The
Guardian*). Care should be taken to
avoid overusing this expression,
which is best restricted to informal
contexts. The expression is a figurative extension of the term *sharp end*,
which is nautical slang for the bows of
a ship.

at this moment in time Many people
object to the frequent use of the
cliché *at this moment in time* in place
of *now*: * *I am not in a position to
comment on the situation at this
moment in time.*

attribute The verb *attribute*, meaning
'ascribe', is generally used with the
preposition *to*: * *They attributed the
accident to careless driving.* * *To what
do you attribute your success?* * *The idea
was attributed to his colleague.* The use
of *attribute* with the preposition *with*,
in the sense of 'credit', is wrong: * *His
colleague was credited* [not *attributed*]
with the idea.

Note the difference in pronunciation between the verb *attribute*
[ă*tri*bewt] and the noun *attribute*
[*a*tribewt]. *See also* **stress**.

attributive *see* **adjectives**.

au fait *Au fait* means 'familiar', 'informed',
or 'competent': * *Are you au fait with the
procedure?* The phrase *au fait* is of
French origin and is sometimes written
or printed in italics in English texts. It is
pronounced [ō *fay*].

aural or **oral**? These two words are
sometimes confused, partly because
they both often have the same pronunciation [*aw*răl]. *Aural* means 'of
the ear or the sense of hearing', while
oral means 'of the mouth; expressed in
speech'. An *aural comprehension* tests a
person's ability to understand a spoken
language; an *oral examination* is one in
which the questions and answers are
spoken, not written. In order to distinguish *aural* and *oral*, the variant
pronunciations [*ow*răl] for *aural* and
[*o*ral] for *oral* are sometimes used.

Australianisms There are fewer differences between Australian and British
English than between American and
British English, probably because
until comparatively recently nearly all
settlers in Australia were British or
Irish. The words that were adopted by

the early settlers from the Aboriginal languages: * *koala* * *boomerang*, are now in general use, and most British people are familiar with those Australian words which were coined in the context of the early days of European settlement: * *outback* * *bushranger* * *swagman* * *digger* * *walkabout*. Although the speech of many Australians is not markedly different from British forms, for most British people Australian English is associated with the pronunciation known as Broad Australian or Strine. In the amusing book *Let Stalk Strine*, published in 1965, examples are given of this characteristic pronunciation: * *egg nishner* (air conditioner) * *garbler mince* (couple of minutes) * *chee semmitch* (cheese sandwich).

Australian English seems particularly adapted to informal use (the very formal British *good day* becomes the informal Australian greeting *g'day*) and it abounds in colourful slang. Although * *cobber* (mate) * *dinkum* (perfect) and * *chunder* (vomit) are now dated, other Australianisms, such as * *pom* (a British person) * *sheila* (woman) and * *rubbish* (as a verb, *see* **nouns**) remain widely familiar in Britain. Slang words are often formed by adding *-ie* or *-o* to an abbreviated word: * *barbie* (barbecue) * *garbo* (refuse collector) * *sickie* (day taken off work for real or invented illness) * *tinnie* (can of beer).

Australian spelling has traditionally been identical to British. In recent years, however, it has been influenced by American English – as has Australian pronunciation and vocabulary.

Australoid This word, describing a member of the indigenous aboriginal population of Australia and the southern Pacific, is avoided by careful users because of its potentially offensive racial connotations. *Aboriginal* is one of the preferred alternatives.

author The use of the word *author* as a verb, in place of *write*, is disliked and avoided by careful users in all contexts: * *She has written* [not *authored*] *a number of books on the subject*. On the use of *authoress*, see **-ess**; **nonsexist terms**.

authoritarian or **authoritative**? The adjective *authoritarian* means 'favouring obedience to authority as opposed to individual freedom'; *authoritative* means 'having authority' or 'official': * *an authoritarian father* * *an authoritarian regime* * *an authoritarian policy* * *an authoritative voice* * *an authoritative article* * *an authoritative source*. The word *authoritarian*, which is also used as a noun, usually has derogatory connotations, whereas *authoritative* is generally used in a complimentary manner.

Authoritative is often misspelt, the most frequent error being the omission of the third or fourth syllable.

avenge *see* **revenge** or **avenge**?

averse *see* **adverse** or **averse**?

avoid, **evade** or **elude**? *Avoid* means 'keep away from'; *evade* and *elude* mean 'avoid by cunning or deception': * *He avoided the police by turning down a side street*. * *He evaded the police by hiding in the cellar*. * *He eluded the police by using a series of false names*. All three verbs have other senses and uses: * *She managed to avoid damaging the car*. * *He is trying to evade his responsibilities*. * *Your name eludes me.*

The difference between the terms *tax avoidance* and *tax evasion*, both of which relate to methods of reducing or minimising tax liability, is that *tax avoidance* is legal and *tax evasion* is not.

avoidance *see* **avoid**, **evade** or **elude**?

await or **wait**? *Await* is principally used as a transitive verb, meaning 'wait for' or 'be in store for'; *wait* is chiefly used intransitively, often followed by *for*, in the sense of 'remain in readiness or expectation': ◦ *They awaited the verdict of the jury with trepidation.* ◦ *I wonder what adventures await you in your new career.* ◦ *She asked us to wait outside.* ◦ *He waited for the rain to stop.* In the sense of 'wait for', *await* is largely restricted to formal contexts, where its direct object is usually an abstract noun. In other contexts *wait for* is preferred: ◦ *We're waiting for* [not *awaiting*] *a taxi.*

In the phrase *wait your turn* and similar expressions, *wait* is used as a transitive verb. The phrasal verb, *wait on* means 'serve'; its use in place of *wait for* or *await* is disliked by many people: ◦ *They're waiting on the results.*

awake, **awaken**, **wake** or **waken**? All these verbs may be used transitively or intransitively in the literal senses of 'rouse or emerge from sleep' and the figurative senses of 'make or become aware': ◦ *Please waken me at six o'clock.* ◦ *He wakes earlier in the summer.* ◦ *Her sister's plight awakened her to the problems faced by single parents.* ◦ *They awoke to the dangers of drug abuse.* *Wake* and *waken* are preferred in literal contexts, and *awake* and *awaken* in figurative contexts. The verb *wake*, which is more frequently used than *waken*, is often followed by *up*: ◦

Don't wake the baby up. ◦ *I woke up in the middle of the night.* *Woke* and *woken* respectively are the usual forms of the past tense and past participle of *wake*, although *waked* is also used from time to time. *Waken* is a regular verb.

Awaken and (less frequently) *awake* are also used in the sense of 'arouse': ◦ *His absence from work may awaken/ awake her suspicions.* The usual forms of the past tense and past participle of the verb *awake* are *awoke* and *awoken* respectively, *awaked* being an accepted variant. Like *waken*, *awaken* is a regular verb.

The word *awake* is also used as an adjective, meaning 'not asleep' or 'alert': ◦ *Did the children manage to stay awake?* ◦ *The police are awake to the situation.*

award-winning The adjective a*ward-winning*, which is frequently used in advertising, is meaningless unless the nature of the award is specified: ◦ *an award-winning design* ◦ *an award-winning writer.* It is therefore best avoided or replaced with a more precise synonym, such as *excellent* or *remarkable.*

aware The use of the adjective *aware* before the noun it qualifies, in the sense of 'knowledgeable' or 'alert', is disliked by many users: ◦ *one of our more aware students* ◦ *financially aware individuals.* *Aware* is usually placed after a noun or pronoun and is often followed by *of*: ◦ *I am aware of the need for secrecy.*

awesome The adjective *awesome* is used as a slang term of approval, especially by young people: ◦ *'What was the party like?' 'Awesome!'* In formal contexts it should be restricted to the sense of 'inspiring admiration or dread': * *an awesome responsibility.*

awful *see* **awfully.**

awfully The use of the adverb *awfully* as an intensifier is best restricted to informal contexts: * *I'm awfully sorry.* * *It's awfully difficult to decide which to buy.* The substitution of *awful* for *awfully* in this sense is wrong.

Ultimately derived from the noun *awe*, *awful* and *awfully* are rarely used in their literal senses ('being inspired or filled with awe') today. Their principal meanings in modern usage are 'bad' or 'badly': * *The weather is awful.* * *They played awfully in yesterday's match.*

awhile or **a while**? *Awhile* and *a while*, both referring to a brief period of time, are used in different grammatical contexts. *Awhile* is an adverb: * *Come inside awhile*, but *a while* is a noun phrase, usually preceded by 'for': * *Sit still for a while. Awhile* is often preferred in poetical contexts.

axe In journalese, the verb *axe* is frequently used in the sense of 'dismiss', 'terminate', 'remove', etc.: * *Britain's biggest teaching union, the National Union of Teachers, is to axe a third of its head office staff* (*Sunday Times*). * *Coloroll, the wallpaper and furnishing company, is to axe 120 jobs* (*Daily Telegraph*). * *Saturday Review, the BBC's current arts magazine programme... will be axed after a final series starting in October* (*Sunday Times*). This usage is best avoided in general contexts.

axes *Axes* is the plural of *axe* or *axis*: * *axes for chopping wood* * *the horizontal and vertical axes.* The plural of *axe* is pronounced [*aks*iz] and the plural of *axis* is pronounced [*aks*eez].

B

-babble Many people dislike the increasing use of the suffix *-babble* to coin new words for particularly incomprehensible types of jargon: * *technobabble* * *psychobabble* * *Eurobabble* * *ecobabble*. See also **-speak**.

babe *Babe* is a slang term frequently applied approvingly to a sexually attractive young woman or (increasingly) man. Because it focuses on a person's superficial attributes, without reference to character or intelligence, the word may cause offence: * *He walked in with a long-legged babe on each arm.* * *Her brother is a real babe.*

bachelor This word, meaning 'unmarried man': * *a confirmed bachelor*, is sometimes misspelt. The most frequent error is to insert a *t* before the *-ch-*. Note that use of the word is becoming old-fashioned.

back This word can be a cause of confusion when used in relation to time. When referring to the past, *back* refers to a change to an earlier time: * *The date of the temple has been pushed back 1000 years* [i.e. 1000 years earlier than previously thought]. When referring to the future, *back* refers to a change to a later time: * *Because of this difficulty, hopes of a successful Mars landing have been pushed back another 20 years* [i.e. 20 years later than previously expected].

back burner The phrase *on the* [or *a*] *back burner* is often used, especially in informal contexts, in the figurative sense of 'deferred' or 'postponed': * *'Priorities will be made, and some things will be put on a back burner.'* (*The Guardian*). Care should be taken not to overuse this expression.

back formation *Back formation* is a way of creating new words, usually verbs, by removing an affix from an existing word: * *donate* (from *donation*) * *extradite* (from *extradition*). Many such words have been used for so long that they are no longer recognised as back formations: * *edit* (from *editor*) * *laze* (from *lazy*) * *burgle* (from *burglar*) * *enthuse* (from *enthusiasm*). *Back formations* often arise as a result of false assumptions about the composition of a word. Hearing the word *scavenger*, people might assume, incorrectly, that the noun comes from a verb, *scavenge*, and so come to use this verb. Often, however, the removed affix is not a genuine affix at all: the 19th-century writer on obesity and slimming, William Banting, invented a system of diet which became known as *the banting system*, which in turn gave rise to the verb *bant*.

New verbs are regularly being formed in this way: * *televise* * *automate* * *explete* * *euthanase*. Many, like *liaise* (from *liaison*), are disliked when newly coined, but when such verbs are created from a genuine need for them in the language, they tend to be retained.

background Some people object to the use of the word *background* to mean 'the circumstances that relate to, lead up to, or explain an event or experience', preferring to use such words as *circumstances*, *conditions*, *context*, or *setting* instead. Recently, *background* has also been used for a person's work or professional experience and training: • *The successful applicant will probably have a building background* (*Executive Post*).

backlash *Backlash* is used metaphorically to describe a strong adverse reaction to a recent event or political/social development or tendency: • *the backlash against the Government's radical new changes in education policy*. The metaphor suggests a sudden reaction, but in fact the word is often used in describing a gradual reaction, perhaps over years: • *The philosophy of the New Right can be seen as a backlash against the pacifism and permissiveness of the 1960s*.

back of The phrases *back of* and *in back of*, meaning 'behind', are largely restricted to American English and are avoided elsewhere, although the opposite phrase, *in front of*, is universally accepted: • *The car was parked in back of the hotel*. • *A bomb had been placed back of the building*.

backward or **backwards**? In British English, *backward* is principally used as an adjective, *backwards* being the usual form of the adverb meaning 'towards the back' or 'in reverse': • *a backward step* • *a backward child* • *walking backwards* • *written backwards*. The adverb *backward* is more frequently used in American English. *See also* **-ward** or **-wards**?

bacteria The term *bacteria* refers to all micro-organisms exhibiting certain characteristics. They are thought of as disease-bearing, but in fact many are harmless and some essential to human life, although others do cause disease. *Bacteria* is a plural noun, so expressions such as: • *I think it's caused by a bacteria* are incorrect; the singular term is *bacterium*.

bad The adjective *bad* is used as a slang term of approval, especially by young people. The potential ambiguity of this usage is obvious. This sense derives originally from American black English. *See also* **wicked**.

bade *Bade* is a form of the past tense of the verb *bid*: • *He bade them farewell*. Its traditional pronunciation is [bad], but [bayd] is also acceptable.

baguette The noun *baguette*, describing a long narrow French loaf, is sometimes misspelt. Note the *-guette* ending.

bail or **bale**? The primary senses of these words are as follows (their spellings are often confused): *bail* is the security deposited as a guarantee of the appearance of an arrested person; *a bale* is a large, bound quantity of hay, old newspapers, etc. The associated verbs also follow these spellings: • *Davies was released on £10,000 bail*. • *His friends bailed him out for £10,000*. • *bales of old papers* • *to bale hay*. In the senses of scooping water out of a boat, helping someone out of a difficult situation, and escaping from an aircraft in an emergency by using a parachute, either *bail out* or *bale out* can be used.

The *bails* are the two crosspieces over the stumps in cricket.

baited or **bated**? These two words are occasionally confused. *Baited* means 'provoked or teased', or 'hooked or trapped with food to attract a fish or animal'. *Bated* is used only in the expression with *bated breath*, meaning 'tense with anxiety or excitement': * *They waited for news of the missing child with bated breath.*

balance Some people dislike the frequent use of the noun *balance* in the sense of 'remainder', especially in non-financial contexts: * *The balance of the work will be completed by the end of the month.*

bale *see* **bail** or **bale**?

balk or **baulk**? Either spelling may be used for this word: * *He balked* [or *baulked*] *at paying such a high price.* * *The horse balked* [or *baulked*] *at the fence.* * *As usual she was balked* [or *baulked*] *in her ambitions by a man.*

ball game or **ballpark**? Both these terms have informal idiomatic uses, of American origin. In the phrase *a whole new ball game*, *ball game* means 'state of affairs'; in the phrases *in the right ballpark* and *not in the same ballpark*, *ballpark* means 'range' or 'area': * *a ballpark figure* is an estimate or approximate figure. The two terms are sometimes confused, producing such expressions as: * *It was a completely new ballpark.*

balmy or **barmy**? These words are sometimes confused. *Balmy* means 'mild and pleasant': * *a balmy evening*. *Barmy*, an informal word in British English, means 'foolish': * *I've never heard of such a barmy idea!* *Balmy* derives from *balm*, a plant with fra-

grant leaves that is used for flavouring foods and for scenting perfumes. The word itself derives from the Latin *balsamum* – 'balsam'. *Barmy* comes from the Old English *beorma*, 'the yeasty froth of fermenting beer'.

In American English and sometimes in British English, *balmy* is the main spelling for both senses.

banister A *banister*, a handrail supported by posts fixed alongside a staircase, has the less usual variant spelling of *bannister*.

baptismal name *see* **first name, christian name, forename, given name** or **baptismal name**?

barbarian, barbaric or **barbarous**? *Barbaric* means 'crude, primitive, uncivilised': * *They discovered a barbaric tribe living in the bush*; or sometimes merely 'uncultured, unsophisticated': * *Most teenagers have barbaric tastes in music. Barbarian* as a noun means 'someone living barbarically'; as an adjective it is synonymous with *barbaric*. *Barbarous* means 'cruel, harsh, or inhuman': * *Torture is condemned as a barbarous practice. Barbaric* is often used with the same condemnatory meaning as *barbarous*, although it can be used approvingly: * *The dance had a barbaric vitality.*

barbecue The word *barbecue* is often misspelt. The most frequent error is the substitution of -*que* for the -*cue* ending, perhaps influenced by advertisements that use the non-standard phonetic spelling *bar-b-q*.

bare or **bear**? Care should be taken not to confuse the spelling of the adjective *bare*, meaning 'naked' or 'simple', with that of the noun *bear*, referring to the animal, and the verb *bear*, meaning 'support', 'withstand', 'give birth to', etc. All three words are pronounced the same: [bair].

barely *see* **hardly**.

barman or **barmaid**? *see* **non-sexist terms**.

barmy *see* **balmy** or **barmy**?

base or **basis**? Both *base* and *basis* mean 'a foundation, substructure, or support'. *Base* is usually used to refer to the bottom support of a tangible object: • *the base of a pillar*, while *basis* is used for abstract or theoretical foundations: • *on the basis of all the evidence received* • *The new pay scale provides a sound basis for the new contract* • *on a daily basis*. Careful writers avoid the overuse of *basis*. *Base* is also used to mean 'a principal ingredient': • *The cocktail has a whisky base*, and 'a centre', as in: • *We used the flat as our London base*. *Base* can be used as a verb: • *The company is based in Sheffield*, and as an adjective: • *base unit*.

The plural of both *base* and *basis* is *bases*, but the plural of *base* is pronounced [*bay*siz] and the plural of basis [*bay*seez].

base or **bass**? The noun *base* means 'a foundation, substructure, or support'; the noun *bass* means 'a voice, instrument, or sound of the lowest range': • *The company has been established on a sound base*. • *He sings bass in the local choir*. The two words are pronounced the same: [bays]. The fish *bass* is pronounced [bas].

basically The literal sense of *basically* is 'concerning a base or basis, fundamentally': • *His argument has a superficial persuasiveness but it is basically flawed*. • *I believe that she is basically a good person*. It is often used to mean no more than 'importantly': • *It is basically the case that fats can cause heart disease*; and it has recently become fashionable to put the word at the beginning of a sentence, where its presence is often wholly superfluous: • *Basically, I don't think he should have been offered the job*.

basis *see* **base** or **basis**?

bass *see* **base** or **bass**?

bastard The word *bastard*, meaning 'person born to unmarried parents', should be used with caution, as many people find it offensive when used in this original sense. In its alternative use as a slang term for a despicable or unlikable person, *bastard* is, however, increasingly considered a relatively mild term of abuse, especially when referring to something inanimate: • *That machine can be a real bastard to control*. It is equally likely to be encountered as a term of jocular affection or sympathy: • *You lucky bastard!* • *He lost all his money on the horses, poor bastard*.

bated *see* **baited** or **bated**?

bath or **bathe**? In British English, the verb *bath* means 'have a bath (in a bathroom)', or 'wash someone else in a bath': • *bath the baby*, while the noun means 'the vessel in which a person baths, or the act of washing in a bath'. *Bathe* means 'immerse in liquid, apply water or soothing liquid to (a wound)', or 'swim, usually in the sea, for pleasure': • *Who's coming for a bathe?* In American English *bathe* is used to mean 'have a bath' and does not have the transitive use of *bath*. *Bath* is pronounced [bahth] and *bathe* [baydh]. The past tense of both verbs is *bathed* and the present participle *bathing*, but the pronunciation differs: *bath*: [bahtht], [*bah*thing]; *bathe*: [baydhd], [*bay*dhing].

bathos or **pathos**? *Bathos* means 'anti-climax' and is used in literary criticism to describe a sudden change from something serious or grand to something absurd or commonplace. The word *pathos* is used more frequently and in less specialised contexts to refer to a quality that evokes pity or compassion: • *The play highlights the pathos of pain and mortality.* Both words are Greek in origin: *bathos* means 'depth'; *pathos* means 'suffering, experience, emotion'. The derived adjectives are *bathetic* and *pathetic*.

bathroom *see* **toilet, lavatory, loo** or **bathroom**?

battalion The word *battalion*, denoting a military unit, is sometimes misspelt. Note the consonants -*tt*- and -*l*-, which are the same as those in the word *battle*.

baulk *see* **balk** or **baulk**?

BC *see* **AD** and **BC**.

BCE *see* **AD** and **BC**.

be The infinitive *be* is used in some British dialects in place of other parts of the verb: • *It be a fine day.* In standard speech it is used mainly in impera-

tives: • *Be quiet!*, after *to*: • *You ought to be careful*; and after an auxiliary verb: • *He should be home soon.* Two common uses after an auxiliary verb concern age and money: • *She'll be 40 tomorrow.* • *That'll be £10 exactly.* *Be* is often used to mean 'become': • *What do you want to be when you grow up?*

beach or **beech**? These two words are occasionally confused, as they are pronounced in the same way [beech]. The noun *beach* means 'strip of sand or pebbles on a shoreline'; the noun *beech* refers to a species of tree with greyish bark and shiny leaves: • *There were hundreds of tourists on the beach.* • *The old beech fell during the storm.*

bear *see* **bare** or **bear**?

beat or **beaten**? *Beat* is the past tense and *beaten* the past participle of the verb *beat*: • *He beat the eggs.* • *She has beaten the champion.* The use of *beat* as a variant form of the past participle is largely restricted to the informal phrase • *dead beat*, meaning 'exhausted'.

beat or **beet**? These two words are occasionally confused, as they are pronounced in the same way [beet]. The verb and noun *beat* should not be confused with the noun *beet*, which refers in British English to *sugar beet* and in American English to *beetroot*: • *He beat the iron into a rough circle.* • *The following year the field was planted with beet.*

beautiful This word, meaning 'delightful to the senses': • *a beautiful woman* • *a beautiful sunset*, is sometimes misspelt. Note particularly the first letters, *beau*-. The word derives from the

Old French word *biau* and comes ultimately from the Latin *bellus*, meaning 'pretty'.

because The conjunction *because* means 'for the reason that': • *You're cold because you need warmer clothes.* It is often used incorrectly in such constructions as: • *The reason her accent is so good is because her mother is French,* which should be: *Her accent is so good because her mother is French,* or: *The reason for her accent being so good is that her mother is French.* Another mistaken use of *because* is to mean 'the fact that': • *Because he's deaf doesn't mean he's daft. See also* **not**; **reason**.

because, as, for or **since**? All these words are used to introduce clauses that give the reason for whatever has been said in the main clause. *As* and *since* are similar in use, although *since* is rather more formal. They are used more often at the beginning of a sentence than *because,* and tend to be used when the reason is already well known, or when the reason is considered to be less important than the main statement: • *As you're only staying a little while, we'd better have tea now.* • *He refrained from smoking between courses, since he knew that was generally thought to be impolite.* • *As/Since we went there in the summer, the weather was gloriously hot. Because* tends to put the emphasis on the cause: • *He married her because she was rich. Because* is also sometimes used to introduce a reason for stating a fact: • *You must have forgotten to invite him, because he didn't turn up. For* would be better here, although it would have a more formal sound. *For* always comes between the elements it joins and places equal emphasis on

the main statement and the reason: • *She never saw him again, for he returned to Greece soon afterwards.*

Ambiguity in the use of *as* should be avoided, since it can mean both 'while' and 'because': • *As Hugh went out to do the shopping, Sandra looked after the baby.*

because of *see* **due to, owing to** or **because of**?

beech *see* **beach** or **beech**?

beer or **bier**? These two words are occasionally confused, as they are pronounced in the same way [beer]. The noun *beer* refers to the alcoholic drink made from hops; the noun *bier* describes the platform or stand upon which a coffin or corpse may be placed before burial or cremation: • *The waiter brought them two pints of beer.* • *The princess's lifeless body was placed upon a bier in the chapel.*

beet *see* **beat** or **beet**?

befriend Some people dislike the increasing use of the verb *befriend* in the sense of 'make friends with': • *She soon befriended her new neighbours.* The traditional meaning of the verb is 'act as a friend to (by giving assistance or showing kindness)': • *They befriended me when I first came to work at the hospital.*

beggar This word, describing a person who begs, is sometimes misspelt. Note the ending: *-ar,* not *-er.* This spelling is different from other 'doer' words such as *hunter, miner,* and *writer.*

beggar belief The phrase *beggar belief* means 'be unbelievable or beyond all reason' and is usually used to convey criticism of the act or opinion, etc., in question: * *That they should even contemplate doing such a thing beggars belief.* Care should be taken not to overuse this already widely quoted phrase.

begin The verb *begin* is followed by the preposition *with* in the sense of 'have something at the beginning': * *The word 'knee' begins with the letter 'k'.* When referring to doing or saying something as the first part of an activity, *begin* is followed by the preposition *by*: * *Begin by mixing the dry ingredients.* * *He began by thanking the visiting speaker.*

beg the question To *beg the question* is sometimes used as if it meant 'evade the question skilfully' or 'raise the question'. Its principal meaning – and the only one accepted by some people – is 'base an argument on an assumption whose truth is the very thing that is being disputed'. For example, to argue that God must exist because of the evidence of his creation in the natural beauties that surround us is *begging the question*, for the premise that these natural beauties are evidence of God's creation is unproved, and dependent on the truth of God's existence, which is supposed to be the conclusion of the argument.

behalf To speak or act *on behalf of* someone else is to act as the representative of that person or those people: * *I am speaking on behalf of my union.* In American English, *in behalf of* is also used; a distinction is sometimes drawn between *on behalf* (acting for) and *in behalf* (in the interest of). A frequent mistake is to use *on behalf* instead of

on the part: * *That was a serious error on behalf of the Government.*

beige This word, describing a very pale brown colour, is sometimes misspelt. Note the *ei* and the soft *g*. *See also* **spelling**.

bells and whistles The phrase *bells and whistles* is used in informal English to refer to the non-essential facilities and special features that are used to promote sales of a particular computer, software package, or similar product: * *This system's got fewer bells and whistles, but it's half the price.* The phrase should not be overused.

beloved This word, meaning 'dearly loved', may be pronounced [bi*luv*id] or [bi*luvd*]. Either is acceptable.

below, beneath, under or **underneath**? These words all mean 'lower than', and the distinctions between them are subtle. *Below* and *under* are often synonymous; *below* is contrasted with *above*, and *under* with *over*. *Below* alone is used to refer to written material following: * *see chapter 5 below*, and is more often used in comparison of levels: * *She lives in the flat below.* * *He was below me in rank.* *Under* is used in reference to being subject to authority: * *He served under Montgomery.* *Underneath* is used mainly for physical situations, and often suggests proximity: * *She kept her savings underneath her mattress.* *Beneath* can be synonymous with *underneath* but sounds either old-fashioned or poetic; it is now used mainly to mean 'unworthy of': * *beneath contempt*.

beneficent, beneficial *see* **benevolent, benign, beneficent** or **beneficial**?

benefit Note the single *t* in the spelling of the past tense: * *benefited* and of the present participle: * *benefiting*. The *t* is not doubled, because the syllable containing this consonant is not stressed. The verb *benefit* is followed by *from* or *by*: * *Most old age pensioners will benefit from* [or *by*] *these changes in taxation. See also* **spelling**.

benevolent, **benign**, **beneficent** or **beneficial**? These are all adjectives suggestive of doing or intending good. *Benevolent* means 'disposed to do good; charitable': * *a donation from a benevolent well-wisher. Benign* means 'kind, mild, and well-disposed' and can be used of things as well as people: * *a benign climate*; it is also used as a medical term meaning 'non-cancerous': * *a benign tumour. Beneficent* means 'doing good; promoting good' and is used of people, while *beneficial* means 'promoting good or well-being' and is often used of things: * *The waters are said to be beneficial to the health.*

bereft *Bereft* was formerly synonymous with *bereaved* but is now used mainly to suggest loss or deprivation of any non-material thing: * *He was now bereft of all hope.* When used of death, *bereft* suggests the desolation of loss more forcefully than does *bereaved*: * *A year after his death she still wandered through the silent house, bereft.* It should not be used merely as a synonym for 'without', with no sense of loss, as in: * *I was unable to help, being bereft of any mechanical skill.*

beside or **besides**? *Beside* means literally 'by the side of': * *Come and sit beside me*, and is also used in the expression *beside oneself*, meaning

'extremely agitated': * *He was beside himself with grief. Besides* can mean 'moreover': * *I won't be able to go; besides, I don't want to.* It can also mean 'as well as': * *Besides the usual curries, the restaurant offers some unusual tandoori specialities*, and 'except for; other than': * *He's interested in nothing besides cricket.* This last use is always inclusive, not exclusive – as with *except*: * *Besides Ben, my colleagues are all Jewish* implies that Ben is Jewish; *Except for Ben...* implies that he is not.

best or **better**? Careful writers prefer *better* when comparing two persons or things, reserving *best* for comparisons between a larger number of persons or things, or in idiomatic contexts: * *On the night they proved the better of the two teams.* * *This painting is the best in the exhibition.* * *She had decided to keep the best till last. See also* **comparative** or **superlative**.

best-before date *see* **sell-by date**.

bet or **betted**? *Bet* is the usual form of the past tense and past participle: * *They bet me £10 I wouldn't do it. Betted* is a much rarer word, preferred in more general intransitive contexts: * *He has never betted in his life*; even here, a phrase such as *place a bet* is more usual: * *He has never placed a bet in his life.*

bête noire A *bête noire* is something that a person fears or hates: * *Rock music is her bête noire.* The phrase is of French origin and is sometimes written or printed in italics in English texts. Note the spelling, particularly the accent on the first *-e-* of *bête* and the *-e* ending of *noire.* The plural is formed by adding *s* to both words: * *What are your bêtes noires?*

betted *see* **bet** or **betted**?

better The phrase *had better* means 'ought to' or 'should': * *You had better close the window.* * *She'd better stay here.* Careful users do not drop the word *had* (or its contraction *'d*), even in informal contexts: * *I'd better apologise*, not *I better apologise*. This last form, without *had* or *'d*, is commonplace in informal speech, but should be avoided when writing. The negative form of the phrase is *had better not*: * *He had/He'd better not be late*, but *better hadn't* is also heard in informal speech: * *He better hadn't be late*. See also **best** or **better**?

between The preposition *between* is used either before a plural noun: * *the interval between the acts* or in conjunction with *and*; it should not be used with *or*: * *You must choose between your family life and* [not *or*] *your work*. *Between* should not be used with *each* or *every* followed by a singular noun: * *There is a gap of one foot between the skittles* [not *between each skittle*]. See also **I** or **me**?

between or **among**? *Between* is traditionally used when speaking of the relationship of two things, and *among* of three or more: * *There was a clear hostility between George and Henry.* * *There was dissent among the committee members.* However, in current usage *between* is acceptable as a substitute for *among*: * *agreement between the NATO countries*, although *among* is still only used for several elements. *Between* is also used when discussing the joint activities of a group: * *The*

carol-singers collected £50 between them, and in the expression *between ourselves*, meaning 'in confidence': * *Between ourselves, I think he's heading for a nervous breakdown*. See also **among** or **amongst**?

bi- The prefix *bi-* always means 'two', but sometimes in the sense of doubling: * *bicycle* * *bifocal*, and sometimes of halving: * *bisection*. This is particularly confusing with words like *biweekly*, which can mean 'every two weeks' or 'twice a week'. It is probably best to avoid *biweekly* and *bimonthly* and to express in a fuller form what is intended. *Biannual* means 'twice a year', while *biennial* means 'every two years'.

A *bicentenary* (or *bicentennial*) is a 200th anniversary. *Bicentennial* is used more frequently in American English and can also be used as an adjective: * *bicentennial celebrations*. It should be noted that *bi* has a particular significance in certain sexual contexts, in which it may be understood as a shortened form of the word *bisexual*.

bias The doubling of the final *s* of the word *bias* before a suffix beginning with a vowel is optional. Most dictionaries give *biased*, with *biassed* as an acceptable alternative. See also **spelling**.

Bible or **bible**? The noun *Bible* is spelt with a capital *B* when it refers to the sacred writings of the Christian religion: * *the first book of the Bible* * *a Bible reading*. When referring to a copy of the book containing these writings, it may be spelt with a lowercase *b*: * *I bought her a bible for Christmas*. The noun is also spelt with a lower-case *b* when it refers to an authoritative book on a particular subject: * *the gardener's bible*. The adjective *biblical* is usually spelt with a lower-case *b*: * *in biblical times.*

bid The noun *bid*, normally meaning 'an offer', takes on a new meaning in popular journalism, where it is used – particularly in headlines – to mean 'an attempt or effort': * *Athlete's bid for title* * *Rescue bid fails* * *Vicar's bid to cut family breakdowns.*

biennial *see* **annual, biennial** or **perennial?**

bier *see* **beer** or **bier?**

big bang The cosmological theory of the *big bang* suggests that the universe originated in an explosion of a mass of material. The term *Big Bang* was also used to describe the radical re-organisation of the London Stock Exchange, which took place in 1986.

The term is increasingly used in general contexts to denote any sudden radical change or reform: * *the big-bang approach to solving the problems of the National Health Service.*

big brother The phrase *big brother* refers to a person or organisation that observes and controls the lives of others. It was coined by George Orwell in his book *Nineteen Eighty-Four* (1949), describing a totalitarian state, and has been subsequently applied to any action by a government or similar body that is considered to be an invasion of privacy, such as the installation of CCTV cameras or the monitoring of personal Internet use and email communica-

tions. The phrase was substantially revived in the late 1990s through the television show *Big Brother*, seen in many countries around the globe.

billion In Britain, *billion* has traditionally meant 'one million million'; however, in the United States it means 'one thousand million' and this usage has been increasingly adopted in Britain and internationally. When used with specific figures, the word *of* is not used: * *Five billion dollars* (not *five billion of dollars*). When used informally to mean 'a great number', *billions of* is sometimes used: * *Billions of people are living in poverty.*

Trillion has replaced *billion* as the word for 'one million million' – or 10 to the power of 12. The word *trillions* may be treated as synonymous with *billions* when referring to an otherwise unspecified large number: * *There were trillions of wasps in the nest.* See also **large numbers**.

bio- The prefix *bio-* comes from the Greek word *bios*, meaning 'life', and words beginning with it have a connection with life or living organisms: * *biology* * *biography* * *biopsy*. There are several recently coined words having the *bio-* prefix: * *bionic* 'the application of knowledge about living systems to the development of artificial systems' * *biodegradable* 'able to decompose organically without harming the environment' * *biorhythms* 'supposed regular cycles in human physiological processes that affect emotions and behaviour' * *bioethics* 'study of moral problems connected with issues like euthanasia, surrogate motherhood, genetic engineering, etc.' * *biometrics* 'statistical analysis of biological data' * *bioweapon* 'a missile or other weapon containing harmful bacteria' * *bio-terrorism* 'the employment of biological warfare by terrorists'.

bivouac The verb *bivouac* adds a *k* before the suffixes *-ed* and *-ing*: * *We bivouacked halfway up the mountain.* See also **spelling**.

bizarre Note the spelling of this word, meaning 'eccentric or odd', particularly the single *-z-* and the *-rr-*. Do not confuse *bizarre* with *bazaar*, 'a type of market'.

black *Black* is the word now usually applied in British English to dark-skinned people of Afro-Caribbean origins, sometimes extended to include other non-white races. It is broadly acceptable to most black people, although **African American** has replaced it to a substantial degree in American English among people of African descent. Note that (in line with *white*) it is usually written with a lower-case *b*: * *black power* * *black consciousness*. *Coloured* is considered offensive, as it groups together all non-white people; under the former policy of apartheid in South Africa it was a technical term used to refer to South Africans of mixed descent. The phrase *people of colour* is, however, considered by some an acceptable alternative to African American and other terms. The terms *Negro* and *Negress* are also considered offensive. *Black* is used in many words and phrases, usually having negative connotations: * *black magic* * *blackleg* * *black market*. Some black people resent the association of the colour black with evil and unpleasantness and, while it is difficult to find synonyms for established words like

blackmail, it is desirable to avoid such possibly offensive (and overused) terms as: * *a black look* * *blacken someone's name*.

black hole The term *black hole*, originally used in astronomy, is increasingly found in figurative contexts, where it is used with a variety of meanings: * *If a region of the UK gets into trouble through high wages, underinvestment or because it is regarded by business as an economic black hole, Whitehall can bail it out with grants* (*The Guardian*). In astronomy, *a black hole* is a hypothetical region of space with such a high gravitational field that nothing can escape from it.

blame *Blame*, as a verb, means 'hold responsible; place responsibility on': * *He was blamed for the accident.* Some careful users dislike the expression *blame (it) on*: * *They all blame it on me* and would substitute: * *They blame me for it* or: *They put the blame on me*. However, the usage is well established and is acceptable in all but very formal contexts.

blanch or **blench**? Both these verbs mean 'make or become white' or 'make or become pale'. *Blanch* may be applied to people or things and is more frequently used as a transitive verb: * *The sun had blanched the rug.* * *Her face was blanched with fear.* *Blench* is chiefly applied to people and is more frequently used as an intransitive verb: * *He blenched with shock.* In this sense the verb *blench* is a variant of *blanch*, which is derived from the Old French *blanc*, 'white'. There is an unrelated verb *blench*, meaning 'recoil (in fear)', which is derived from the Old English *blencan*, 'to deceive'.

In cookery, the verb *blanch* refers to the process of immersing vegetables, nuts, etc., in boiling water: * *blanched almonds*.

blatant or **flagrant**? *Blatant* and *flagrant* are both concerned with overtly offensive behaviour, but their usage is not identical. *Blatant* means 'crassly and conspicuously obvious': * *The article was blatant propaganda.* *Flagrant* means 'conspicuously shocking or outrageous': * *The European parliament sees the tougher measures as a 'flagrant violation of human rights and justice'* (*Sunday Times*). Blatant can be used of a person: * *a blatant liar*, but *flagrant* is used only of abstract things and carries a stronger suggestion of moral disapproval.

blench *see* **blanch** or **blench**?

blends A *blend*, also known as a *portmanteau word*, is a new word that is formed by joining parts of two other words – usually the beginning of one and the end of the other. Examples include: * *brunch* (*br*eakfast + l*unch*) * *motel* (*mo*tor + ho*tel*). Many of these words fill a genuine gap in the English language; others are best restricted to informal contexts. Some people dislike the increasing number of neologisms coined in this way: * *camcorder* ([video] *camera* + *recorder*) * *docudrama* (*documentary* + *drama*) * *infotainment* (*information* + *entertainment*) * *Japanimation* (*Japanese* + *animation*) * *affluenza* (*affluence* + *influenza*).

blessed This word sometimes causes problems with pronunciation. The word *blessed*, the past tense of the verb *bless*: * *He blessed the child*, is pronounced [blest]. The noun or adjective *blessed*: * *the Blessed Sacrament*, is usually pronounced [*bles*id] but is occasionally pronounced [blest].

blind Because of its negative associations, and because there are many different degrees of visual impairment, the word *blind* is increasingly avoided by careful writers in general reference to people who have difficulties with their eyesight. It is especially important to avoid the impersonal plural form *the blind*. Preferred terms, depending upon the loss of vision involved, include *visually impaired, visually challenged, unsighted*, and *partially sighted*: * *The hotel has been redesigned throughout to accommodate the needs of visually impaired guests.*

blip *Blip*, a term used in radar, has developed the figurative sense of 'sudden change or interruption; temporary minor problem'. It became a vogue word in the late 1980s when the Chancellor of the Exchequer, Nigel Lawson, dismissed a sudden rise in the Retail Price Index as a 'temporary blip'. The word should not be overused in this figurative sense. A *blip* on a radar screen is the sharp peak or flash of light that indicates the position of something.

bloc or **block**? The noun *bloc* denotes a group of people or nations that have political aims or interests in common: * *the Communist bloc*. It should not be confused with *block*, which has a wide range of meanings and uses: * *a block of wood* * *a mental block* * *a block of flats*.

blond or **blonde**? These two spellings of the word meaning 'light in colour' are sometimes a cause of confusion. As a noun, *blonde* is generally reserved for a girl or woman with fair hair, while *blond* may refer to fair-haired people of either sex. As an adjective, the distinction between *blond* and *blonde* is frequently ignored and both may be employed for either sex, although *blonde* is more common in British English: * *She is a blonde.* * *A blond man entered the room.* * *Both brother and sister have blonde hair.*

blue-chip *Blue-chip* is originally a Stock Market term referring to a share issue which is considered to be both reliable and profitable: * *a blue-chip investment*. It is extended to companies and any extremely worthwhile asset or property: * *one of the world's most successful manufacturers... with a blue-chip reputation* (*Sunday Times*). The meaning has now become further extended, to 'fashionable and exclusive' or 'of the highest standard': * *polo, the blue-chip sport* (*Daily Telegraph*) * *Parents in Britain believe they are entitled to blue-chip facilities when they go out and about with their children* (*Daily Telegraph*). Many people dislike the use of the word in this way.

blue-sky This is a vogue term describing wild, ambitious, or purely theoretical research, thinking, etc.: * *One day, childcare could be up there along with health, education and transport as one of the government's big spending departments. But that's blue-sky thinking for now* (*The Guardian*). It should not be overused in formal contexts.

blueprint A *blueprint* is literally a print used for mechanical drawing, engineering, and architectural designs.

The word is used metaphorically to mean any plan, scheme, or prototype: * *a blueprint for a successful life* * *the London launch of a policy document, 'A Blueprint for Urban Areas'* (*The Times*). Although a literal *blueprint* is a finished plan, the metaphorical use, very popular as a jargon and journalistic term, is just as often applied to preliminary schemes. Care should be taken, however, not to overuse this word.

blush or **flush**? Both these verbs mean 'go red in the face'. To *blush* may be a sign of modesty, embarrassment, shame, or guilt; to *flush* may indicate any of these emotions as well as stronger feelings, such as anger, or the effects of alcohol or physical causes. The verb *flush* is also used transitively, often in the passive or in the form of the past participial adjective: * *He was flushed with rage*. To be *flushed* may also indicate excitement, or result from exertion or illness: * *You look flushed – have you got a temperature?* *Blush* cannot be used in this way.

board or **bored**? The noun *board* variously denotes a flat piece of wood or other material, a group of people chosen to head an organisation, daily rations of food, etc.: * *a sheet of board over the window* * *suggestions put before the board* * *to set out in search of board and lodging*. It should not be confused with *bored*, past participle of the verb *bore*: * *She quickly grew bored with* [or *by*] *the work*. *See also* **bored of** or **bored with**?

boat or **ship**? The use of *boat* or *ship* is mainly a matter of size. *Boat* is usually applied to smaller vessels, especially those that stay in shallow or sheltered waters: * *a rowing boat* * *a lifeboat*, and *ship* to larger vessels that travel the open seas: * *steamship* * *warship*. The rule is by no means invariable: cross-Channel ferries are informally described as *boats*, and most sailing expressions refer to *ships* even when applied to *boats*: * *amidships* * *aboard ship* * *The fishing boat was shipwrecked*.

bona fide *Bona fide* is an adjective meaning 'of good faith; genuine or sincere': * *I will accept any bona fide offer*. *Bona fides* is a singular noun, meaning 'good faith, sincerity, honest intention': * *He had no documentary proof but we did not doubt his bona fides*. *Bona fide* is also sometimes used to mean 'authentic', as in: * *It's not a reproduction; it's a bona fide Matisse*.

Bona fide is pronounced [bōnă fīdi] in British English, but sometimes [bōnă fīd] in American English. *Bona fides* is pronounced [bōnă fīdeez].

bored of or **bored with?** Careful users avoid the construction *bored of* except in very informal contexts, preferring *bored with* or *bored by*: * *He was soon bored with tidying up*. * *Modern audiences are bored by old-fashioned farces*. See also **board** or **bored?**

born or **borne?** These two spellings are sometimes confused. *Borne* is the past participle of the verb *bear*: * *They had borne enough pain*. * *The following points should be borne in mind*. * *His account is simply not borne out by the facts*. * *airborne supplies*. In the sense of 'giving birth', *borne* is used in phrases where the mother is the subject: * *She has borne six children*, and also in the passive with *by*: * *borne by her*. *Born* is used for all other passive constructions

without *by*: * *He was born in Italy*. * *Twins were born to her*. * *a born leader* * *his Burmese-born wife*.

born again The term *born again* was originally confined to the context of evangelical Christianity, to mean 'converted': * *a born-again believer*. It is now often used generally to refer to a conversion to any cause or belief, particularly when accompanied by extreme enthusiasm or fervour: * *a born-again conservationist* * *Having declared himself born again as a Republican, he set about nurturing old contacts within the party*. Occasionally, *born again* is also used to mean 'renewed; fresh, new, or resurgent': * *a born-again car* * *born-again post offices with refurbished premises* * *the mini-skirt appears to have been born again*.

The origin of the term *born again* is John 3:3 in the Bible.

borne *see* **born** or **borne?**

borrow Besides its literal meaning of 'take something for a limited period with the intention of returning it': * *I borrowed this book from the library*, borrow can also be used metaphorically to refer to words, ideas, etc., taken from other sources: * *Wagner borrowed this theme from Norse mythology*. * *Some American slang is borrowed from Yiddish*. A person *borrows from*, not *off*, someone: * *I borrowed it off my friend* is generally considered wrong. See also **lend** or **loan?**

both *Both* is used as an adjective, a pronoun, a conjunction, and an adverb: * *Both legs were amputated*. * *I like both*. * *He is both an artist and a writer*. * *The room has both hot and cold water*.

It should not be used where more than two elements are involved, as in: * *She's both selfish, mean, and malicious*. The constructions: * *Both his parents are teachers* and * *Both of his parents are teachers* are equally acceptable. However, in possessive constructions with *us*, *them*, etc., it is usually necessary to use *of*: * *the opinion of both of them*, not *both of their opinions*.

When two things are being considered separately, it is often better to use *each* to avoid ambiguity. * *We were both given a box of chocolates* might involve two boxes or one shared box. In general, care should be taken in placing the word *both*, in order to avoid ambiguity: * *He has insulted both his aunts and his grandmother* might suggest that he has two aunts.

Both as a conjunction goes with *and*; as with all such pairs of conjunctions, it must link grammatically similar things. So it is possible to say: * *She is both charming and intelligent*, but not: * *She is both charming and an intellectual*.

Both is often used redundantly, when some other phrase in the sentence conveys the same sense: * *They are both identical*. * *Both of them are equally to blame*.

bottleneck A *bottleneck* is a term originally applied only to narrow stretches of road which cause traffic hold-ups. It is now extended to anything that holds up free movement or progress: * *A bottleneck at the Traffic Area Office is resulting in long waits for driving tests*. As a vogue word it is sometimes overworked and its literal meaning forgotten. The original metaphor refers to the narrowness of the neck of a bottle, which makes absurd such phrases as:

* *an enormous bottleneck* * *an increasing bottleneck* * *reducing the bottleneck*.

bottom line *Bottom line* is a vogue expression, taken from financial reports where the final line registers the net profit or loss. It can mean 'the most important or primary point or consideration': * *The bottom line is that we have no more resources for the project*. It can also mean 'the final result': * *The bottom line was their divorce*. Care should be taken not to overuse this phrase, which may sometimes be used as an adjective to mean 'having a pragmatic concern for cost and profit': * *He has a bottom-line approach to running the company*.

bottom out *Bottom out* was formerly used to describe a levelling-out of something that has reached its lowest point: * *Industrial output is now bottoming out*. It is now often used to suggest that the low point is prior to an upsurge: * *The market has bottomed out and is expected to improve by the spring*.

bough or **bow**? The noun *bough* denotes a large branch of a tree: * *a bough fell on the lawn during the storm*. It should not be confused with *bow*, which describes the front of a boat or ship, or refers to bending as a sign of respect: * *She greeted the duke with a bow*. Both words are pronounced [bow]. *See also* **bow**.

bought or **brought**? As the past tense and past participle of the verb *buy*, *bought* is correct: * *I bought* [not *brought*] *the dress in the January sales*. *Brought* is the past tense and past participle of the verb *bring*: * *She brought an umbrella with her*.

bouquet This word is usually pronounced [boo*kay*] or [bō*kay*], but some users prefer to stress the first syllable.

bourgeois This word, meaning 'middle class': * *a bourgeois mentality*, is sometimes misspelt. Note the first syllable *bour-* and the *e*, which softens the *g* in the second syllable. The word comes from the Old French word *borjois*, meaning 'burgher or merchant'.

bow The word *bow* has two pronunciations. The noun and verb *bow*, referring to the bending of (part of) the body as a sign of respect, etc., are pronounced to rhyme with *how*. The same pronunciation is used for the noun meaning 'front of a boat or ship'. The noun *bow*, meaning 'looped knot', the *bow* that is used as a weapon, the *bow* that is used to play a violin, etc., and the verb *bow*, meaning 'curve', are pronounced to rhyme with *toe*. In the adjective *bow-legged* and the noun *bow window*, the word *bow* is pronounced to rhyme with *toe*. *See also* **bough** or **bow**?

boy A *boy* is a male child or adolescent. The use of the noun as a synonym for 'man' is largely restricted to informal contexts: * *one of the boys* * *a local boy* * *the new boy* * *a night out with the boys.*

boycott This word, meaning 'refuse to deal with': * *boycott the Olympic games*, is sometimes misspelt: note the *-tt* at the end of the word. The term originates from the name of Charles Cunningham Boycott (1832–97), an Irish land agent who was ostracised for refusing to grant reductions in rent.

bracket Some people object to the frequent use of the noun **bracket** in place of group, level, range, etc.: * *the 25–35 age bracket* * *a lower income bracket.*

BRACKETS The most frequently used kind of brackets are round brackets, also known as parentheses. They are used to enclose supplementary or explanatory material that interrupts a complete sentence: * *William James (1842–1910) was the brother of the novelist Henry James.* * *He asked his scout (as college servants are called in Oxford) to wake him at nine.* The material in parentheses could be removed without changing the meaning or grammatical completeness of the sentence. Round brackets are used, in preference to commas or dashes, when the interruption to the sentence is quite a marked one. *See* the following panel, on page 60.

brake or **break**? These words are sometimes confused. A *brake* is a device to slow something down: * *the handbrake on a car. Break* has many meanings, including '(cause to) fall into pieces', 'stop', and 'transgress': * *break a vase* * *break for lunch* * *break the law.*

bravado, bravery or **bravura**? These three nouns are sometimes confused. *Bravery* means 'courage'; *bravado* is a false or outward display of courage or daring; *bravura* is an ostentatious or brilliant display of daring, skill, etc.

breach or **breech**? The word *breach* means 'the breaking or violating of a rule or arrangement': * *a breach of the peace. Breach* should not be confused with *breech*, 'the rear part of the body' and 'the part of a gun behind the

BRACKETS

1 Round brackets (also called parentheses)	*Round brackets* are used to enclose subsidiary information within sentences and are also used for letters or numbers in a series: • *The Chartists demanded (1) annual elections, (2) universal manhood suffrage, (3) equal electoral districts ...* They are also used to indicate alternatives or brief explanations: • *boy(s)* (meaning 'boy' or 'boys') • *it cost 15 euros (roughly £10)* • *the payment of VAT (value added tax)*.
2 Square brackets	*Square brackets* are used for brackets within brackets: • *Browning's wife (the poet Elizabeth Barrett Browning [1806–61]) was an invalid.* They are also used to indicate editorial comment or explanation in quoted matter: • *The Young Visiters [sic]* • *'who would fardels [burdens] bear'.* To use ordinary round brackets implies that the words inside them are part of the original quotation.
3 Punctuation within brackets	Punctuation within brackets is that appropriate to the parenthetic material; however, even if it is a complete sentence, capital letters and full stops are usually not used. Punctuation of the sentence containing the brackets is unaffected, except that any punctuation which would have followed the word before the first bracket is placed after the second bracket: • *Worst of all, their confidence is undermined by a lurking fear of the meaninglessness of those basic questions in themselves (is this good? is this right?), which yet they find themselves unable to cease from asking* (Richard Hoggart, *The Uses of Literacy*). If the material within the brackets comes at the end of a sentence, the full stop falls outside the second bracket. The only time when a full stop appears inside brackets is when the parenthetic material in brackets comes between two sentences, rather than within a sentence: • *He came from a humble background. (His mother was a charwoman.) Yet he mixed with people of all classes.*

barrel': * *a breech birth*. The nouns *breach* and *breech* are pronounced [breech], but the plural noun *breeches*, meaning 'knee-length trousers', may be pronounced [*bree*chiz] or [*brich*iz].

bread or **bred**? The word *bread* refers to the foodstuff: * *a loaf of bread*. *Bread* should not be confused with *bred*, the past participle of the verb *breed*: * *This species has been bred for speed*. Both words are pronounced [bred].

break *see* **brake** or **break**?

breakthrough *Breakthrough* as a metaphor meaning 'a sudden advance in (particularly scientific or technological) knowledge' has become something of a journalistic cliché. Phrases like: * *a major breakthrough in cancer research* are used so frequently that they have lost all impact. *Breakthrough* is also sometimes used to mean 'success': * *Olympic breakthrough for British athletes*, or 'new idea': * *The Great Borrowing Breakthrough* (advertisement for a loan company).

bred *see* **bread** or **bred**?

breech, breeches *see* **breach** or **breech**?

bridal or **bridle**? The word *bridal* means 'of or relating to brides or weddings': * *a bridal veil*. *Bridal* should not be confused with *bridle*, used as a noun meaning 'harness for a horse's head' and as a verb meaning 'restrain' or 'show resentment': * *The soldier slipped the bridle over the horse's head.* * *She needs to bridle her tongue.* Both words are pronounced [*brī*dăl].

bring or **take**? The verbs *bring* and *take* differ in meaning. *Bring* generally denotes the fetching of something and carrying of it to the speaker: * *Please bring me that book*; *take* generally denotes the removal of something to a more distant location: * *Take this rubbish with you*. Note that *brought* is the correct past tense and past participle of *bring*, and that *brung* is incorrect: * *He brought the money with him.*

Brit The noun *Brit*, meaning 'British person', is often used derogatorily. It should be restricted to informal contexts. A British person may be called a *Briton*, but this term is most frequently found in newspaper reports about the British abroad: * *A coach carrying 58 Britons... was preparing last night to spend a third night trapped in a motorway service area south of Paris* (*Daily Telegraph*). The informal term *Britisher* is chiefly used by people of other English-speaking nations, not by the British themselves.

Britain The expression *Britain* is often used vaguely, sometimes as a substitute for *Great Britain*, sometimes for the *United Kingdom* or the *British Isles*. As an abbreviation of *Great Britain* it means England, Scotland, and Wales. The *United Kingdom* includes Northern Ireland as well as England, Scotland, and Wales. The *British Isles* includes all the United Kingdom, together with the Republic of Ireland, the Isle of Man, and the Channel Islands.

Briticisms British English is the basis on which the English of America, Australia, New Zealand, South Africa, the West Indies, and the rest of the English-speaking world is built. To greater or lesser degrees the English of these countries has gone its own way, producing distinct varieties, while the English spoken in Britain has its own characteristics, sometimes known as *Briticisms*. Specifically British – usually in contrast to American – usage of grammar, spelling, and so forth, is discussed under various headings in this book. It is vocabulary and idiom that mark the speaker or writer of British English. A sentence like: * *I rang you from a call box but the line was engaged* marks the speaker as British; in other English-speaking countries it would be: * *I called you from a phone booth but the line was busy.* Such familiar words or phrases as: * *bank holiday* * *fortnight* * *white coffee* * *spring onion* * *Father Christmas* * *roundabout* (in the senses of both merry-go-round and traffic junction) are peculiarly British uses.

Of course there is no one standard form of English spoken throughout Britain; marked differences in pronunciation, vocabulary, grammar, and usage are found in the different countries and regions. *See also* **dialect**; **Americanisms**.

Britisher, **Briton** *see* **Brit**.

Brittany *Brittany*, the English name of a region of northwest France, is often misspelt. Note the *-tt-* and single *-n-*, unlike in *Britannia*.

broach or **brooch**? A *brooch* is a piece of jewellery that is pinned to a garment: * *a diamond brooch*. *Broach*, a rare variant spelling of this noun, is most frequently used as a verb, meaning 'introduce' or 'mention': * *to broach a subject.* Both words are pronounced [brōch]. To *broach* a barrel or a bottle is to open it in order to use the con-

tents: * *We broached a second bottle of champagne.*

In nautical contexts, *broach* means 'to swerve dangerously in a following sea, so as to lie broadside to the waves'.

brochure This word is usually pronounced [brōshĕr], although the French-sounding [brōshoor] is also possible. Note also the *-ch-*, not *-sh-*, in the spelling.

brooch *see* **broach** or **brooch**?

brought *see* **bought** or **brought**?

brownie points *Brownie points* are notional marks of approval for an action or achievement, especially something that is deliberately or ostentatiously done to win favour: *You should get some brownie points for that.* * *There are political brownie points in opening hospitals* (*The Guardian*). The phrase may be spelt with a capital *B* or with a lower-case *b*; it is best restricted to informal contexts. The expression derives from the erroneous belief that Brownie Guides receive points for doing something good.

buffet In the senses 'a counter where food is served' and 'food set out on tables': * *a buffet car* * *a buffet lunch*, *buffet* is pronounced [buufay]. In the sense 'strike sharply': * *buffeted by the wind*, the pronunciation is [bufit].

bulk *Bulk* means 'thickness, volume, or size; a heavy mass': * *the vast bulk of the castle walls.* It is also used in the expression *in bulk*, to mean 'in large quantities': * *We buy rice in bulk.* The noun is frequently used to mean 'the greater part, the majority': * *The bulk of the population support the new legislation.* Some people object to the application of *bulk* to anything other than mass or volume, but this usage is well established and generally acceptable.

bulletin This word, meaning 'statement of news': * *No further bulletin will be issued this evening,* is sometimes misspelt. Note the *-ll-* and single *t,* as in *bullet.*

bullet points *Bullet points* can be used for various purposes, typically to introduce examples (as in this book) or items in a list, generally with each item being introduced on a new line. They are commonly rendered in the form of a black dot (•) but may also appear as a small black square (▪) or other shape, such as a lozenge, arrow or stylised hand. Useful to differentiate between main points, they are probably best confined to technical contexts, official documents, spreadsheet presentations, etc.

There are few set rules concerning punctuation of phrases or sentences introduced by *bullet points.* If followed by a single word or phrase, not a full sentence, the usual convention is to begin with a lower-case (not capital) letter and to end with no punctuation (although some writers choose to end each point with a semicolon instead) and to have a final full stop at the end of the final item. In the case of a full sentence, a closing full stop may or may not be included at the end of each line.

When using bullet points, it is important to make sure that the opening 'platform text' runs on grammatically with each point.

bulwark This noun, meaning 'fortification' or (figuratively) 'defence against something', is sometimes mispronounced. The second syllable is unstressed; the *-ark* ending has the same pronunciation as the *-ock* ending of *hillock.*

buoy The noun and verb *buoy,* meaning 'type of float' and 'keep afloat' respectively, and the derived adjective *buoyant,* are sometimes misspelt. The most frequent mistake is to place the *-u-* and the *-o-* in the wrong order. *Buoy* should not be confused with the noun *boy,* which is identical in pronunciation in British English. In American English, *buoy* is pronounced [*booi*].

bureaucracy Note the spelling of this word: the first *u,* the vowels *eau,* and the suffix *-cracy* (not *-crasy*).

burgle, rob or **steal?** To *steal* is to take other people's possessions without permission: * *He stole her jewellery. Burgle* is a **back-formation** from *burglar* and means 'break into a building in order to steal': * *Their house was burgled when they were on holiday. Burglary* always involves unlawful entry. To *rob* is to steal money or property from a person or place, often with violence: * *rob a bank* * *rob an old lady. Rob* is sometimes incorrectly used in place of *steal:* * *to rob a car* is to take things from a car, not to take the car itself. The verb *burglarise* is chiefly confined to American English.

burned or **burnt?** Either word may be used as the past tense and past participle of the verb *burn.* In transitive contexts *burned* is preferred in American

English and *burnt* in British English; in intransitive contexts *burned* is the preferred form in both: * *We burnt/ burned the letters.* * *He has burnt/ burned his hand.* * *She burned with anger.* * *The fire had burned all night.*

Burnt is also used as an adjective in British and American English: * *burnt toast* * *a burnt offering.*

Burned may be pronounced [bernd] or [bernt]; *burnt* is always pronounced [bernt]. *See also* –**ed** *or* –**t**?

bus Although the noun *bus* was originally short for *omnibus*, it is now never spelt with an apostrophe. The word was rarely used as a verb until the 1960s, when controversy in the United States over the practice of sending schoolchildren by bus to different districts in order to achieve a racial balance in the schools gave rise to the need for such a verb. The problem of how to spell the various forms of the verb has not been wholly resolved. Traditional British spelling rules dictate *bussed* and *bussing*, but the American preference was for *bused* and *busing* and these spellings have now been widely accepted in Britain.

business This noun, meaning 'occupation', 'commercial activity', or 'matter', is sometimes misspelt. The most frequent mistake is the omission of the letter *i*, which is silent in speech. *Business* is a two-syllable word, pronounced [*biz*nis]. It should not be confused with the noun *busyness*, meaning 'the state of being busy', which has three syllables and is pronounced [*biz*inis].

businessman or **businesswoman**? *see* **non-sexist terms**.

but There are various problems with the usage of the word *but*. As a conjunction it is used to link two opposing ideas: * *He lives in Surrey but works in London.* It should not be used to link two harmonious ideas: * *She is not British-born but originates from Kenya*; nor should it be used in a sentence with *however*, which conveys the same meaning: * *But their suggestions for improvement, however, were ill-received.* Careful users avoid inserting a comma after *but*: * *I agree but I have reservations.* * *That's a good point but not an original one.* The problem with *but* used to mean 'except' is this: is it functioning as a conjunction or as a preposition, and should it be followed by an object or subject pronoun? Is it *all but he* (conjunctional) or *all but him* (prepositional)? There is no absolute rule here, but a rough guide to natural usage is to use the object when it falls at the end of a clause and the subject when it comes in the middle: * *They had all escaped but her.* * *All but she had escaped.*

Some users dislike the use of *but* at the beginning of a sentence. But it is acceptable to most and can be used to good effect.

The expressions *can but* and *cannot but* are slightly formal and old-fashioned but still used: * *setting a standard others can but hope to follow* (advertisement, *Sunday Times*). The oddity is that the expressions mean much the same thing, for the *not* of *cannot* combines with the *but* to form a double negative. When used with *help* in *cannot* (or *can't*) *help but*, a triple negative is formed; in fact, the expression is used positively: * *I can't help but regard your attitude as hostile.* The phrase is awkward and should be avoided; the expressions *can but* and *cannot but* can also be rephrased: * *I can only regard your attitude as hostile.* * *I can't help regarding your attitude as hostile.* See also **conjunctions**; **help**; **nothing but**; **not only... but also**.

buzz word A *buzz word* is a vogue word or expression, especially one that is first used in technical jargon and subsequently enters everyday language, usually in a figurative sense. Examples of *buzz words* that are dealt with in this dictionary are: *bottom line*, *matrix*, *traumatic*.

by and large or **by in large**? The correct rendering of this phrase, meaning 'in the main' or 'on the whole', is *by and large*: * *We were content with the decision, by and large.*

by or **bye**? These spellings are sometimes confused. Note the spelling of the following compounds and expressions: * *by-election* (occasionally, *bye-election*) * *by-law* (sometimes, *bye-law*) * *bypass* * *by-product* * *by and by* ('later') * *by and large* ('generally') * *by the bye* (occasionally, by the by, 'incidentally') * *a bye in sports*, and * *bye-bye* (informal for goodbye). Further problems may arise from confusion with *buy* and *bi-*, which are pronounced the same [bī].

by the same token *By the same token* is an expression meaning 'for the same reason; in a similar way': * *Middle-aged men should avoid overworking because of the effects of stress on the heart; and by the same token they should avoid fatty foods.* Care should be taken to avoid overusing this phrase.

C

cache or **cash**? *Cache* means 'secret store' or 'place where valuables are concealed': ▪ *For years he had suspected her of keeping a secret cache of money.* It should not be confused with *cash*, which means 'ready money' or 'money in the form of coins and banknotes': ▪ *He paid for the car in cash.* Both words are pronounced [kash].

Caesarean This word, meaning 'of or relating to any of the Caesars', is used particularly in the expression *Caesarean section*, 'the surgical operation for the delivery of a baby by cutting through the wall of the mother's abdomen and into the womb'. The variant spellings *Caesarian*, and, in American English, *Cesarean* or *Cesarian*, are also used. Note, too, that any of these spellings may be written with a lower-case *c*: ▪ *She had a caesarean.* The word derives from Julius Caesar; it is traditionally thought that he was born by this method.

café or **cafeteria**? The noun *café* refers to any small restaurant or coffee-bar serving non-alcoholic drinks, snacks, light meals, etc.: ▪ *a seaside café.* The noun *cafeteria* is more specific, meaning 'self-service restaurant': ▪ *There is a cafeteria on the third floor.* Note the spelling of *café*, particularly the acute accent, which should never be omitted. The noun may be pronounced [*ka*fay] or [*ka*fi].

Cafeteria should not be confused with the noun *cafetière*, denoting a type of coffee-pot with a plunger, in which coffee can be brewed and served. The grave accent on the second *e* of *cafetière* is optional in English.

caffeine *Caffeine*, pronounced [*ka*feen], is a stimulant substance found in tea and coffee. Note the spelling of the word, especially the *-ff-* and the vowel sequence *-ei-*. It is an exception to the 'i before e' rule (*see* **spelling**). *Caffein* is a rare variant spelling of the word.

calendar, **calender** or **colander**? These words are often confused. A *calendar* tells the date; a *calender* is a machine used to smooth paper or cloth; and a *colander* is a perforated bowl used for draining food. The first two words are pronounced in the same way [*kal*indĕ]. *Colander* is pronounced [*kol*ăndĕ] or [*kul*ĕndĕ]. This second pronunciation of *colander* is reflected in the variant spelling *cullender*.

callous or **callus**? *Callus* is a noun, denoting a hardened or thickened area of skin, especially on the hand or foot. The adjective *callous* is related to this noun, but is most frequently used in the figurative sense of 'unfeeling' or 'insensitive': ▪ *a callous attitude to the poor.*

calorie Note the spelling of this word, which is a unit for measuring the energy value of food and also a measurement of heat.

Calvary *see* **cavalry** or **Calvary**?

66

cameraman or **camerawoman**? *see* **non-sexist terms**.

camouflage This word, meaning 'disguise': *The trees provided excellent camouflage*, is sometimes misspelt: note the *-ou-*. Note also the soft *g*.

can or **may**? The verb *can* means 'be permitted' or 'be able'; the verb *may* means 'be permitted' or 'be likely'. In the sense of 'be permitted', *may* is preferred in formal contexts and *can* is best restricted to informal contexts: *Can I come to your party? May I borrow your pen, please?* Many people dislike the negative contraction *mayn't*, which is usually replaced with *can't*: *Can't* [not *Mayn't*] *she stay?*

    Both verbs can be ambiguous: *He can go* may mean 'he is permitted to go' or 'he is able to go'; *He may go* may mean 'he is permitted to go' or 'he is likely to go'. *Could* and *might*, the past tenses of *can* and *may* respectively, are equally ambiguous: *She said he could go. She said he might go.*

    Could and *might* are also used in polite requests: *Could/Might I have another cup of tea, please? See also* **but**; **cannot** and **can't**; **help**; **may** or **might**?

candelabra The word *candelabra*, meaning 'a branched candlestick or lamp', was originally a plural noun, from the singular *candelabrum*. Purists therefore consider it incorrect to speak of: *a valuable candelabra*, or to say: *There were candelabras in every room*, although such usage is widespread. *Candelabra* are often confused with *chandeliers*, which hang from the ceiling, while *candelabra* stand on surfaces.

cannon or **canon**? These two words are sometimes confused. A *cannon* is a large gun and a shot in billiards; a *canon*, with a single *n*, is a ruling laid down by the church, or a title given to a clergyman. Both words are pronounced [*ka*năn].

cannot and **can't** In American English, *can not* is sometimes written as two words; in British English *cannot* is standard. It may be necessary to write *can not* when the *not* is stressed: *No, I can not lend you any more money*, or in sentences like: *It can not only blend vegetables but also grind coffee beans*, where the *not* goes with *only*, rather than *can*. Care should be taken when using *cannot* in constructions like: *Her work cannot be too highly praised. You cannot put too much pepper in*, where ambiguity can arise. Was her work excellent or poor? Should a large or small amount of pepper be put in?

    The contraction *can't* is normally used in speech and often in writing. The standard British English pronunciation is [kahnt]. *See also* **but**; **can** or **may**?; **help**.

canon *see* **cannon** or **canon**?

can't *see* **cannot** and **can't**.

canvas or **canvass**? *Canvas* is a certain type of woven cloth: *a canvas bag* • *a painting on canvas. Canvass*, with *-ss* at the end, means 'solicit votes': *He canvassed for the Labour Party.*

capability, **capacity** or **ability**? These words all refer to the power to do something. *Capability* suggests having the qualities needed to do something: *She has the capability to handle the* work. *Capacity* suggests being able to absorb or receive: * *Children are born with the capacity to acquire language.* *Ability* can sometimes suggest above-average skills: * *He has considerable mathematical ability.* *Capacity* has several other meanings: 'volume': * *The pot has a capacity of two litres,* '(maximum) output': * *The factory is working at (full) capacity,* 'a particular role': * *I am speaking in my capacity as treasurer.* It is also used as an adjective in the journalistic phrase: * *a capacity crowd at the ground.*

capital or **capitol**? *Capital* denotes the seat of government of a country or state: * *Tokyo is the capital of Japan.* *Capitol* refers to the building housing a state legislature, often specifically to the headquarters of the US Congress: * *The party's control of the Capitol is no longer in question.*

capital letters *Capital letters* are used to draw attention to a particular word. There are some generally accepted rules for their use, and some areas where it is a matter of choice.

Capitals are used to mark the first word of a sentence, a direct quotation, or a direct question within a sentence (*see also* **question marks; quotation marks; sentences**). They are sometimes used after a colon (*see* **colon**). Traditionally they are used for the first word of each line of poetry: * *Forewarned of madness/In three days time at dusk/The fit masters him* (Robert Graves), and for the major words of titles of literary, musical, or artistic works: * *The Mill on the Floss* * *Peter and the Wolf.*

Capitals are used for proper nouns and most adjectives derived from them: * *John Brown* * *New York* *

Sainsbury's * *Oxford Street* * *French* * *Jewish* * *Freudian.* If an adjective is not closely connected with its original proper noun it does not usually take a capital: * *brussels sprouts* * *french windows,* and capitals are not used for verbs derived from proper nouns: * *anglicise* * *boycott* (*see also* **eponyms; trade names**). Note that academic subjects should only take a capital if they are proper nouns (a rule that is often ignored in practice): * *He is studying French and history.* Titles of people or places are capitalised when part of a proper name, but not when used alone: * *my aunt* * *Aunt Jane* * *redbrick universities* * *Cambridge University* * *a professor of history* * *Professor Thomson.* For institutions, the rule is that capitals are used in specific references but not in general ones: * *many world governments* * *the Government has agreed* * *he goes to a Baptist church* * *St Mark's Church, a church in the centre of town* * *the Church of England.* The same rule applies more widely in relation to formal titles and names: * *The Regional Code of Practice is an excellent document. The code sets out...* The pronoun *I* always takes a capital, but no other pronouns apart from those referring to *God,* where some people choose to capitalise *He, Him, His.*

Capitals are used for days of the week, months, holidays, and religious holidays: * *Monday* * *February* * *Easter* * *Yom Kippur,* but not for seasons. They are used for historical, cultural, and geological periods: * *the Restoration* * *the Enlightenment* * *the Spanish Civil War* * *the Stone Age.*

Capitals should never be used for emphasis; italics should be used for this purpose: * *an* enormous [not *ENORMOUS*] bear!

In recent years the conventions relating to capitals have been considerably relaxed in the context of electronic communications, simply because it is quicker and easier to type lower-case characters than upper-case ones. It is usually not necessary to distinguish between capital and lower-case letters in email addresses and Internet searches, and computer users have accordingly fallen into the habit of using lower-case letters to open sentences, write names, etc.: * *joe did u get my message about the new york trip?* The same tendency has been observed in other contexts, such as company names, in conscious imitation of the abbreviated, simplified writing styles associated with modern electronic communications. *See also* **abbreviations; colon; east, East** or **eastern?; email; hyphen; north, north** or **northern?; south, south** or **southern?; west, west** or **western?**

carat or **caret?** These words are sometimes confused. A *carat* is a unit for measuring the weight of precious stones and a unit for measuring the purity of gold; in this second sense, the spelling *karat* is usually used in American English. A *caret*, spelt with an *e*, is a character used in written or printed matter to indicate that an insertion should be made.

carburettor Note the spelling of this word, particularly the *-u-*, the *-tt-*, and the *-or* ending. The spelling in American English is *carburetor*.

care The verb *care* is followed by the preposition *for* or *about* in the sense of 'feel affection': * *Most people care for* [or *about*] *their family*, and *for* in the sense of 'like': * *I don't care for foreign food*. In the sense of 'look after' it is followed by *for*: * *He cared for the wounded fox*, and in the sense of 'be concerned' it is followed by *about*: * *She doesn't care about the cost*. Some people avoid using the phrase *in care* to describe a person whose welfare is the responsibility of the social services, believing that this carries a stigma: * *Both children have been in care since the arrest of their parents*. The alternative *looked-after* is now widely used within the social services and has appeared with increasing frequency elsewhere in recent years: * *You will chair child protection case conferences and reviews of Looked After Children...* (*The Guardian*, job advertisement). Note also the phrase *personal care* in reference to nursing-care of the old or infirm.

caret *see* **carat** or **caret?**

Caribbean This word, referring to the region extending from the southeastern tip of Florida to the northern coast of South America, is often misspelt. Note the single *-r-* and the *-bb-* in the middle of the word. Caribbean is pronounced [kari*bee*ǎn] in British English and [kǎr*i*beeǎn] in American English.

caring *Caring* has been used in recent years in such phrases as: * *the caring professions* * *the caring services*, to describe people professionally involved in various kinds of social work – sometimes also including healthcare and education. It combines the idea of 'taking care of' and the idea of 'concerned': * *The welfare state itself, and all the caring professions, seemed to be plunging into... uncertainty, self-questioning, economic crisis* (Margaret Drabble, *The Middle Ground*).

The noun *carer* is used to denote a person who looks after a sick or old relative: * *The new benefit is payable to carers and their dependants.*

carte blanche The French phrase *carte blanche* means 'complete freedom or authority to do whatever you think is right'. * *He was given carte blanche to do what he wanted.* The literal French meaning of *carte blanche* is 'blank document'.

case *Case* is very often loosely used to mean 'state of affairs, the truth' in sentences where it is either redundant or could be replaced by simpler or more specific wording: * *Is it the case that you are his aunt?* could be changed to: *Are you his aunt?* * *Teenage pregnancies are now less common than was the case ten years ago* could be changed to: *... than they were ten years ago.* The expression is acceptable in sentences like: * *This rule applies in your case.* *In case* is used as a conjunction: * *in case it rains.* The use of *just in case*, with no clause: * *Take your mac, just in case,* is acceptable only in informal contexts.

cash *see* **cache** or **cash**?

caster or **castor**? For the senses 'a swivelling wheel on furniture' and 'a container from which sugar may be shaken', the spelling may be either *castor* or *caster*. Finely granulated white sugar is usually *caster sugar*, although the spelling *castor sugar* is also found. The medicinal or lubricating oil, *castor oil*, is, however, always spelt with an *o*.

catalyst *Catalyst* is a scientific term that applies to a substance that speeds up a chemical reaction while itself remaining chemically unchanged. The word is also used as a metaphor to apply to someone who, or something which, by a particular action provokes significant change: * *The shooting of Archduke Ferdinand acted as the catalyst for the outbreak of World War I.* Some people dislike the overuse of this word.

catarrh This word, which describes an inflammation of the throat and nasal passages, is sometimes misspelt. Note particularly the single *t* and the *-rrh* ending.

catastrophic The adjective *catastrophic* comes from *catastrophe*, which was originally used in Greek drama to describe the denouement of a tragedy. The word should only be applied to extremely severe disasters and tragic events: * *the catastrophic earthquake in Mexico City*, although it is often used informally for quite minor disasters: * *Do you remember that catastrophic dinner party when I burnt the casserole?*

cater The verb *cater* is followed by the preposition *to* or *for*: * *The leisure centre caters to* [or *for*] *the needs of the local people.*

Catholic or **catholic**? The word *catholic*, with a lower-case *c*, is an adjective meaning 'general, wide-ranging, or comprehensive': * *It is a catholic anthology which includes poems by Shelley, Auden, and Allen Ginsberg. Catholic*, with a capital, as a noun or adjective, usually refers to the *Roman Catholic Church*: * *He's a good Catholic.* * *They go to a Catholic school.* As some 'high' Anglicans prefer to refer to themselves as *Catholics*, it is advisable to use the term *Roman Catholic* when speaking in a specifically theological context.

cavalry or **Calvary**? These words are sometimes confused. *Cavalry* is used to refer to soldiers trained to fight on horseback and the branch of the army that uses armoured vehicles. *Calvary* is the hill near Jerusalem where Christ was crucified.

caviar or **caviare**? Both of these spellings are acceptable for the word that describes the salted roe of the sturgeon.

CE *see* **AD** and **BC**.

cede or **seed**? These two verbs, which are pronounced the same, should not be confused. *Cede* means 'surrender' or 'give way to': • *The defending champion ceded the match.* • *The President ceded the point. Seed* means 'scatter seed in', 'initiate', or 'rank a sportsperson as a seed': • *The farmer seeded the field.* • *This money will help to seed economic recovery.* • *seeded tennis players.*

ceiling *Ceiling* is frequently used, particularly in economic jargon, to mean 'an upper limit': • *The organisation is urging the Government to put a ceiling on rent rises.* As the word *ceiling*, in its literal meaning, is in constant use, it can sound odd to speak of *increasing* or *reducing a ceiling, an unworkable ceiling,* and so on: • *Sir Gordon Borrie... said, 'If money and manpower ceilings were to become too tight in relation to the demands put upon my office, then the taxpayer... would be likely to pay the price in other ways'* (*The Guardian*).

celeb This abbreviated form of *celebrity* has been heard with increasing frequency since the 1990s, but remains essentially a slang term and should be avoided in formal contexts, especially if referring to people who are not really famous: • *The usual posse of celebs turned up for his birthday bash.* • *She's a bit of a celeb around here.*

celibate *Celibacy* means 'the state of being unmarried, often because of a religious vow'. *Celibate* is used as a noun to describe a person living in a state of celibacy and, by implication, chastity: • *As celibates, priests find it difficult to give advice on marital problems*; it is also used as an adjective: • *She never married but chose a celibate life.* The word is sometimes used to mean 'abstaining from sexual intercourse': • *After twenty years of marriage, they decided to live a celibate life together.* This usage was formerly considered incorrect but is now widely accepted.

Celsius, **centigrade** or **Fahrenheit**? All these terms denote scales of temperature. The Celsius and centigrade scales are the same; the degree Celsius is now the principal unit of temperature in both scientific and non-scientific contexts. The Fahrenheit scale, on which water freezes at 32 and boils at 212, remains in informal use, particularly with reference to the weather: • *The temperature reached the eighties today.* The centigrade scale, on which water freezes at 0 and boils at 100, is now known as the Celsius scale, to avoid confusion with other units of measurement.

Celsius and *Fahrenheit* should always begin with a capital letter, being the surnames of the scientists who devised the scales.

Celtic The word *Celtic*, referring to a language or to people of Scotland, Wales, Ireland, or Brittany, is usually pronounced [*kel*tik], with a hard initial *C*. The variant pronunciation [*sel*tik], with a soft initial *C*, is most frequently associated with the Scottish football team of that name.

censure, censor or **censer**? The verbs *censure* and *censor* are often confused. *Censure* means 'blame, criticise strongly, or condemn': * *The judge censured them for the brutality of the attack. Censor* means 'examine letters, publications, films, etc., and remove any material which is considered obscene, libellous, or contrary to government or official policy': * *All prisoners' mail is censored.* The person who examines letters, etc., in this way is also known as a *censor.* The adjective from *censor* is *censorial*, and from *censure, censorious.*

Censor should not be confused with the noun *censer*, meaning 'a vessel used for burning incense'.

centenary or **centennial**? Both *centenary* and *centennial* are used to mean a hundred-year anniversary: * *1982 was the centenary of Joyce's birth. Centennial* is used more frequently in American English and can also be used as an adjective: * *a centennial celebration.* The recommended pronunciation of *centenary* is [sen*teen*ărĭ], although some people pronounce it [sen*ten*ărĭ]. *Centennial* is pronounced [sen*ten*ĭăl].

centigrade *see* **Celsius, centigrade** or **Fahrenheit?**

centre or **middle**? *Centre* and *middle* are sometimes used virtually synony-mously: * *Put it in the centre/middle of the table. Centre* is used as a precise geometrical term: * *the centre of the circle*, whereas *middle* is more often used generally in situations where the geometric centre is not obvious or measurable: * *the middle of the sea. Centre* is also used to mean a place where activity is concentrated: * *shopping centre. Middle* is used to mean the point equally distant from extremes, either literally: * *middle name*, or figuratively: * *middle-of-the-road politics.*

centre on or **centre around**? The verb *centre* can be used with *on* or *upon*, or (of a place) *at*: * *His argument centres on Marxist theory.* * *The European Parliament is centred at Brussels.* The expressions *centre round* and *centre around* are frequently used: * *The film centres around the Vietnam War.* * *Her hobbies centred around the arts*; however, they are disliked by many careful users as being illogical, because, it is argued, a centre cannot be around anything. Since this usage is so widely objected to, it is best avoided. One alternative is to use the more acceptable *revolve around* instead: * *Everything revolves around the children in this house.*

centuries People often become confused about when centuries start and end and how they should be referred to. As there was no year AD 0, we calculate in hundred-year periods from the year AD 1. This means that the twentieth century ended on 31 December 2000 and the twenty-first century began on 1 January 2001. Despite the reckoning above, 31 December 1999 was popularly accepted as marking the end of the twentieth century, and 1 January

2000 the beginning of the twenty-first century. *See also* **millennium**.

cereal or **serial**? These two words are sometimes confused. A *cereal* is a plant that produces grain for food: * *breakfast cereals*. A *serial* is a novel or play produced in several parts and at regular intervals: * *a television serial.*

ceremonial or **ceremonious**? The adjectives *ceremonial* and *ceremonious* are sometimes confused. *Ceremonial* means 'marked by ceremony or ritual': * *The Queen wears her crown only on ceremonial occasions like the opening of Parliament. Ceremonious* means 'devoted to formality and ceremony' and usually carries a slightly pejorative suggestion of over-punctiliousness or pomposity: * *She presided over the dinner table with a ceremonious air.*

certainty or **certitude**? Both these nouns mean 'the state of being certain'. *Certainty* is by far the more frequent, and is used in a wider range of contexts: * *a feeling of certainty* * *the certainty of death. Certitude* is a formal or literary word, largely restricted to the state of mind of somebody who is certain: * *Nothing could disturb his certitude. Certainty* may also be used as a countable noun: * *She may win, but it's not a certainty. Certitude* is not used in this sense.

cervical There are two pronunciations for this word, both of which are perfectly acceptable: [*ser*vikăl] and [sĕr*vī*kăl]. Note that the word, denoting the neck or cervix, may be used in reference to various parts of the body.

cession or **cessation**? These two nouns should not be confused. *Cession* is

derived from the verb *cede*, meaning 'yield'; *cessation* is derived from the verb *cease*, meaning 'stop': * *the cession of territory* * *the cessation of warfare*. Both words are largely restricted to formal contexts. *See also* **cession** or **session**?

cession or **session**? *Cession* is the act of yielding (*see* **cession** or **cessation**?); a *session* is a meeting or a period of time devoted to a specific activity: * *the cession of rights/property* * *a parliamentary session* * *a recording session* * *The court is in session.* The two nouns are identical in pronunciation and should not be misspelt; *session* is the more frequent in usage.

cf. or **ff.**? The abbreviation *cf.* (from Latin *confer*) means 'compare': * *cf. table on page 47.* The abbreviation *ff.* stands for 'folios following' and means 'see subsequent pages or lines': * *For more details, see page 172 ff.*

chafe or **chaff**? The verb *chafe* means 'rub'; the old-fashioned verb *chaff* means 'tease': * *These boots chafe my ankles.* * *She was chaffed by her colleagues.* The two verbs should not be confused. *Chaff* is also a noun, meaning 'husks (of wheat, etc.)', and is used figuratively in the phrase *to separate the wheat from the chaff*, meaning 'separate the good from the bad'.

chain reaction *Chain reaction* is an expression from scientific terminology that refers to a chemical or nuclear reaction which creates energy, or to products that cause further reaction. It is now more often used to mean any series of events where each one sets off the next one, although some dislike this usage: * *The shooting*

started a chain reaction which culminated in the street riots.

chair The noun *chair* is sometimes used
to denote a person presiding over a
meeting, committee, etc., to avoid the
potentially sexist terms *chairman* and
chairwoman and the controversial
neologism *chairperson*: * *The new
chair will be elected next week*. Some
people dislike this usage. The verb
chair, meaning 'preside over', is
acceptable to most users: * *The leader
of the Union chaired the conference. See
also* **non-sexist terms; person.**

challenge Some people object to the
frequent use of the word *challenge* in
the sense of 'stimulate' or, as a noun,
'something that is stimulating or
demanding': * *Gifted children need
challenging work.* * *The job presents a
challenge.* In recent years the word has
also emerged as a jargonistic euphemism for bad or unruly behaviour,
usually with reference to children: *
*Her son John is one of several in the class
who present challenging behaviour.* The
verb *challenge* sometimes means little
more than 'interest; excite': * *The film
challenged us visually and musically.*

challenged *Challenged* is a vogue word
used to form euphemisms for disability or disadvantage: * *physically challenged.* The use of this term is widely
satirised by opponents of political
correctness, who have coined such
phrases as *follicularly challenged*
('balding'). It is often used facetiously
or ironically: * *Robert Lindsay... is
about to play the nasally challenged
Cyrano de Bergerac in the West End
(Daily Telegraph).* * *The Borrowers are
a vertically challenged family – 6in tall,
to be exact (Sunday Times).* *

*Financially challenged souls cannot
afford to cast aside the clothes that have
been key fashion investments over the
past three years (Daily Telegraph).* *
*The usual assumption made about those
still watching the TV of their youth –
that they're sad, socially challenged crea-
tures (Sunday Times). See also* **abled;
political correctness.**

chamois This word may cause problems
with pronunciation and spelling. The
antelope *chamois* is pronounced
[*sham*wah]. The leather *chamois* made
from the skin of this animal or a
sheep is usually pronounced [*sham*i].

changeable This word, meaning 'liable
to change': * *changeable weather*, is
sometimes misspelt. Note the *e* of
change, which is retained before the
suffix *-able. See also* **spelling.**

chaperon or **chaperone**? An older
woman who accompanies a young
unmarried woman on social occasions
is known as a *chaperon* or a *chaperone*.
The noun, and its derived verb, may
be spelt with or without the final *e*.
The usual pronunciation for both
spellings is [*shap*ĕrŏn].

character The word *character* can be
used of the distinguishing qualities
that make up individual people or
things, of people with unusual traits,
of people portrayed in works of fiction, and of moral firmness and
integrity: * *Such behaviour did not
seem consistent with what I knew of her
character.* * *It is a lively town with a
great deal of character.* * *Everyone
knows him – he's a real character.* * *Mrs
Gamp is a minor character in Martin
Chuzzlewit.* * *Anyone who takes this
job on will need character and deter-*

mination. Character is often used vaguely in such phrases as: * *the strange character of this declaration * programmes of an intellectual character * the intimate character of our conversation.* Where it is used to mean no more than 'type' or 'quality', *character* would be better replaced with an alternative.

charisma The word *charisma* was originally used only in theological contexts to refer to supernatural spiritual gifts of healing, speaking in tongues, etc. A *charismatic church* is one where emphasis is placed on the exercise of these gifts. *Charisma* and *charismatic* are now often used to describe a person with unusual qualities of leadership, personal appeal, and magnetism, though care should be taken to avoid overusing these words: * *Lange is planning to run a presidential-style election campaign, based on his own charisma* (*Sunday Times*). The word *charismatic* is sometimes used more loosely to mean 'charming or showing a confident efficiency': * *Our client... is looking for two charismatic sales managers* (advertisement, *Daily Telegraph*).

charted or **chartered**? A *chartered accountant/surveyor/engineer/*etc. is a person who has the required professional qualifications and experience. A *chartered yacht* is a hired yacht. *Chartered* should not be confused with *charted* (derived from the word *chart*): * *charted territory.* Similarly, the adjective *uncharted*, describing something that has not been mapped or surveyed: * *uncharted waters*, should not be misspelt as *unchartered*.

chat The verb *chat* is followed by *to* or *with*: * *chatting to* [or *with*] *his friend*

on the telephone. The advent of *chat rooms* on the Internet, enabling people to communicate directly with others via a computer network, has brought a whole new linguistic dimension to *chat*, with participants adopting a radically abbreviated style of writing that makes much use of coded phrases and symbols: * *got to go ttyl :-)* (meaning 'got to go, talk to you later', followed by a symbol indicating happiness). *See also* **email**; **smiley**; **text messaging**.

chauvinism The word *chauvinism* means 'excessive or fanatical patriotism' and comes from Nicolas Chauvin, a soldier of Napoleon's army who was noted for his overzealous patriotism. It is used more loosely to describe any prejudiced belief in the superiority of a group or cause, particularly in the term *male chauvinism*: * *The media... fanned the flames of male chauvinism, stereotyping all women who took a serious interest in the issues as bra-burners* (Elaine Storkey, *What's Right with Feminism*). Some people, encountering the word for the first time in the context of male chauvinism, wrongly assume *chauvinist* to be synonymous with sexist: * *Her husband's an awful chauvinist.* The word should not be used in this sense unless preceded by male.

cheat The verb *cheat* is followed by the preposition *of* or *out of*: * *She had been cheated of* [or *out of*] *her inheritance.* To *cheat on* your husband or wife is to be unfaithful to them.

cheque or **check**? A *cheque* is an order to a bank to pay money from a person's account. *Check* is the spelling preferred in American English, but is never preferred to *cheque* in British English. Both spellings are pronounced [chek].

chequered Note the spelling of this adjective, meaning 'varied; marked by many changes in fortune', most frequently used in such phrases as a *chequered career* and *chequered past*. In British English the adjective is spelt *chequered*; *checkered* is the American English spelling.

chick or **chicken**? A *chick* is a young bird: * *The chicks have hatched.* * *eagle chicks.* A *chicken* is a type of domestic fowl and *chicken* is the meat of this fowl: * *He keeps geese and chickens.* * *roast chicken.* Either noun may be applied to the young of a domestic fowl: * *a hen and her chicks* [or *chickens*]. *Chick* is also used offensively as a slang term for a young woman. This is now dated, although the derivatives *chick flick* and *chick lit*, respectively denoting a film and book aimed at a female audience, are relatively recent coinages: * *It's a romantic chick flick that won't appeal to many men.* Some women consider these phrases to be derogatory.

chihuahua Note the unusual spelling of this word, which denotes a breed of tiny dog. The dogs are named after the state of *Chihuahua* in Mexico; the noun is sometimes written with a capital *C*. *Chihuahua* is usually pronounced [chi*wah*wah] or [chi*wah*wǎ].

chilblain A sore that is caused by exposure to the cold is known as a *chilblain*. The word is sometimes misspelt, the most common error being to retain the second *l* of *chill*, which has been lost in the formation of this compound noun.

childish or **childlike**? *Childish* is almost always used in a pejorative sense to indicate immaturity and the less endearing characteristics of childhood: * *She refused to tolerate his selfish behaviour and childish outbreaks of temper.* * *The drawings looked like childish scribbles.* *Childlike* is usually applied to the attractive qualities of childhood, such as enthusiasm and innocence: * *At 85, she retains a childlike curiosity about her environment.*

chill This word, meaning 'relax' or 'take time out', is a vogue term of 1990s origin, probably coined in imitation of *cool*: * *I plan to stay at home tonight, just chilling.* It is best restricted to informal contexts and is often encountered in the form *chill out*, in which case it may also mean 'calm down': * *Everyone needs to chill out occasionally.* * *Stop yelling at me and chill out.* A *chillout room* is a quiet, restful place in a club where dancers may relax.

Chinese *Chinese* as an adjective means 'of or from China': * *Chinese writing.* It is also used as a singular or plural noun for a person or people of Chinese nationality: * *I took a party of Chinese around London.* * *There is a Chinese studying at my college.* The singular expression *a Chinese* sounds odd to some people, who prefer to say *a Chinese man/woman*. The term *Chinaman* is out-of-date, derogatory, and offensive.

chiropodist This word, describing a person who treats and looks after people's feet, may be pronounced [ki*rop*ŏdist] or [shi*rop*ŏdist], although the first of these is preferred by many users.

cholesterol This word is sometimes misspelt. The most frequent error is the omission of the second *e*, often silent in speech. Remember also that the first syllable is *chol-*, not *chlo-* as in *chlorine*.

chord or **cord**? These spellings are sometimes confused. In the musical or mathematical senses, the spelling is *chord*. *Chord* is also used when describing an emotional reaction: * *He struck the right chord.* In the anatomical sense: * *umbilical cord* * *spinal cord*, either spelling is acceptable, although in *vocal cords* the word is nearly always spelt without the *h*. The word that describes any type of string is spelt *cord*: * *nylon cord*.

Christian name *see* **first name, Christian name, forename, given name** or **baptismal name**?

chronic *Chronic* means 'long-standing; permanently present': * *She has suffered from chronic asthma all her life.* * *Malnutrition is a chronic problem in the Third World.* It is often confused, in its medical context, with *acute*, which means 'intense and of sudden onset': * *I suddenly got an acute* [not *chronic*] *pain in my shoulder.* Because *chronic* is so often used of pains and illnesses that are very bad, the word is also sometimes used in informal British English to mean 'bad' or 'dreadful': * '*Drank! My word! Something chronic*' (Shaw, *Pygmalion*).

chute or **shoot**? *Chute* means 'slide' or 'slope' and is also an abbreviated form of 'parachute': * *Three sacks of grain came down the chute.* * *He opened the chute as soon as he left the plane.* *Shoot* means 'to fire a weapon', 'to travel quickly', etc.: * *He shot several times at his enemy* * *The dog shot out of the pipe.* Both words are pronounced [shoot].

circumstances *In the circumstances* and *under the circumstances* are used in slightly different ways. *In the circumstances* is more general, and merely acknowledges the existence of a situation: * *In the circumstances, you had better do nothing.* *Under the circumstances* suggests more of a connection between the circumstances and the action: * *He was starving and under the circumstances cannot be blamed for stealing food.* *Under* is more often used than *in* in a negative context: * *Under no circumstances will I allow it.*

cirrhosis This word, denoting a disease of the liver, is sometimes misspelt. Note particularly the *-rrh-* combination.

cite, **site**, or **sight**? These words may occasionally be confused, since they are all pronounced in the same way [sīt]. *Cite* means 'to give something as an example', 'to order', or 'to praise': * *The prisoner cited several cases in his defence.* * *The two men were cited for their bravery.* *Site* means 'to locate something': * *The memorial will be sited in that corner.* *Sight* means 'to see someone or something': * *They sighted a ship on the far horizon.*

city or **town**? In general a *city* is a place that is larger and more important than a *town*: * *She had only lived in small towns before and was apprehensive about moving to the city.* The British 'rule' that the possession of a cathedral confers city status on a town is misleading; it is the monarch who grants a town the right to call itself a city, and though cities very often do have cathedrals, this is not always the case. Cambridge, for example, was granted city status and has no cathedral.

civic, civil or **civilian**? These words all refer to citizenship but have different meanings. *Civic* means 'of a city': * *civic centre*, or is used of the attitudes of citizens to their city: * a *sense of civic pride*. *Civil* relates to citizens of a state, rather than a city: * *civil rights*, or is used as distinct from criminal, religious, or military: * *civil law* * *civil marriage* * *civil defence*. *Civilian* refers to a person who is not a member of the armed forces, police, or other official uniformed state organisation: * *The major had been a bank manager in civilian life*. *Civil* is also used to mean 'polite or courteous': * *The proprietor was very civil to us*.

clad or **clothed**? *Clad* means the same as *clothed* but, except in expressions like *thinly clad* or *ill-clad*, is considered archaic or poetic. It can be used of things other than clothes: * *rose-clad trellises*, or of clothes where the note of archaism is appropriate: * *clad in armour*, but for ordinary dress, *clothed* is used: * *She was clothed completely in black*. *Clothed*, not *clad*, may be used as the opposite of naked: * *With that paunch, he looks sexier clothed these days*.

claim The verb *claim* means 'demand something as a right': * *The dismissed workers are claiming redundancy pay*; 'take something you rightfully own or that is your due': * *He claimed his father's estate*. * *She claimed the prize*; and 'assert forcefully, especially when faced with possible contradiction': *

He claims that there have been no composers of genius since Beethoven. This last use was at one time disliked, having no connection with the recognition of rights, but it is now widely used and accepted. It should, however, be avoided when the assertion is not particularly forceful or controversial; in such instances *maintain*, *allege*, *contend*, or sometimes just *say*, is often better.

clandestine This word, meaning 'secret', is generally stressed on the second syllable [klan*de*stin], although it is acceptable to stress the word on the first syllable [*klan*dĕstin].

clarity *see* **plain English**.

classic or **classical**? There is some overlap in the meanings of *classic* and *classical*, but they have distinct separate meanings. *Classic* means 'typical of or unusually fine in its class': * *classic symptoms of diabetes* * a *classic example of 1960s pop art*. *Classical* essentially means 'of the classics, i.e. the literature, history, and philosophy of ancient Greece and Rome': * a *classical education*.

Classic is also used to mean 'elegant and unlikely to date': * a *classic dress* * *classic design*, and 'definitive, absolute': * *Your behaviour was a dirty trick of classic dimensions... (The Guardian)*. While the *classics* are the works of ancient Greece and Rome, a *classic* is any work of high standard and enduring quality, whatever its date: * *the jazz classic 'St Louis Blues'*.

Classical, too, can suggest elegance, but there is a definite link with the standards and forms of ancient Greece and Rome. *Classical music*, in its narrowest sense, is the music of about 1750–1830, which is characterised by its formal beauty. The term is, however, widely applied to all serious music, as distinct from jazz, folk, and popular music.

clause A *clause* is a group of words, including a finite verb, within a compound or complex sentence. A *main clause* can stand alone as a sentence in its own right; it is expanded by a *subordinate clause*. A *relative clause* modifies the subject or object of a sentence. In the sentence * *She stayed at home because it was raining, She stayed at home* is the main clause and *because it was raining* is the subordinate clause. The sentence * *She stayed at home but her sister went out* contains two main clauses.

Relative clauses may be defining (identifying) or non-defining (non-identifying). They are usually introduced by *that, which, who,* etc. A defining clause provides essential information; a non-defining clause provides parenthetical information. The clause *who lives in India* is non-defining in the sentence * *My sister, who lives in India, is coming home for Christmas,* and defining in * *My sister who lives in India is coming home for Christmas.* The first sentence implies that she is the only sister the speaker has; the second sentence implies that the speaker's other sisters are not coming home for Christmas. *See also* **comma; that** or **which?**

claustrophobia The fear of being in confined spaces is known as *claustrophobia.* Note the *claustro-* in the spelling.

clean or **cleanse?** While *clean* functions as adjective, noun, adverb, and verb,

cleanse is used only as a verb. The two words are almost synonymous but *cleanse* has more of a suggestion of very thorough cleaning which also purifies: * *I'll just clean the flat quickly.* * *The wound must be cleansed before a dressing is applied. Cleanse* has a more formal sound than *clean* and is sometimes used figuratively to mean 'purify', as it is in the older translations of the Bible: * *Wash me throughly from mine iniquity, and cleanse me from my sin (Psalm* 51:2).

cleft lip *Cleft lip,* referring to a congenital split in the upper lip, is preferred to the former term *harelip,* which is now considered offensive and should be avoided.

clench or **clinch?** These two words are sometimes confused. The verb *clench* means 'close tightly' or 'grasp firmly': * *he clenched his teeth* * *She clenched the key in her hand.* The verb *clinch* is most frequently used in the figurative sense of 'settle definitely': * *to clinch a deal.* The literal meaning of the verb *clinch* is 'secure by bending over the protruding point of a driven nail'. *Clinch* is also used as a noun and verb to refer to two people holding each other tightly with the arms in boxing or wrestling, or in an amorous embrace.

clergyman or **clergywoman?** *see* **nonsexist terms.**

clever The adjective *clever* is followed by the preposition *at* in the sense 'clever at a subject, an activity, etc.': * *He's not very clever at maths,* and by *with* in the sense 'clever with a tool, your hands, etc.': * *She's clever with a needle.*

clichés The word *cliché*, referring to a phrase or idiom that has become stale through overuse, is almost always used pejoratively. Examples of clichés are: • *from time immemorial* • *as old as the hills* • *last but not least.* Not all fixed phrases are necessarily bad; some were quite apt when first used but have become hackneyed over the years. It is virtually impossible to avoid using the occasional cliché, but those that are inefficient in conveying their meaning or are inappropriate to the occasion should be avoided.

There are various categories of cliché. There are overworked metaphors and similes: • *leave no stone unturned* • *as good as gold,* overused idioms: • *add insult to injury* • *a blessing in disguise*, the clichés of public speakers: • *someone who needs no introduction* • *in no uncertain terms* • *without fear or favour*, and the quotation (or usually misquotation) from the Bible or Shakespeare: • *pride goes before a fall* • *a poor thing, but mine own.* Journalists are perhaps the worst offenders; to them, all countries at war are *strife-torn*, all battles are *pitched*, and all denials *categorical.*

Many clichés have become such through years of use – but it can take a very short time for a newly coined phrase to become a cliché. Some modern examples are: • *sixty-four thousand dollar question* • *at the end of the day* • *at this moment in time* • *keep a low profile* • *a level playing field* • *a game of two halves.*

client or **customer**? A *client* is someone who receives the services of a professional person or organisation, while a *customer* is someone who buys goods from a shop or other trading organisation: • *The solicitor had several showbusiness clients.* • *She was a regular customer at the fish market.* A collective noun for regular clients is *clientele*, and this word is also sometimes used for customers, particularly if there is a suggestion of superiority in the shop or its customers: • *The customers at the Co-op have less exacting tastes than the clientele of Harrods.* The rather formal word *patron* is also sometimes used in place of *customer*, when they are regarded as bestowing the favour of their custom on an establishment.

clientele The preferred pronunciation of this word, which means 'clients' (*see* **client** or **customer**?): • *an exclusive clientele*, is [kleeon*tel*]. Note also the spelling, particularly the *-ele* (not *-elle*) ending.

climactic or **climatic**? These two words have completely different meanings. *Climactic* is the adjective from *climax*: • *This aria marks the climactic point of the opera*. *Climatic* is the adjective from *climate*: • *The climatic conditions are unsuitable for outdoor activities.* Both words should be distinguished from the noun *climacteric*, which means 'a crucial stage in life; the menopause or corresponding male equivalent'.

climate The word *climate* has been extended in meaning to embrace not just the atmosphere as regards the weather, but atmosphere in general: • *a climate of hope.* It is used rather more specifically of the prevailing state of affairs or the attitudes and opinions of people at a particular time: • *the economic climate* • *the change in the moral climate of America* (Franklin D. Roosevelt).

climatic *see* **climactic** or **climatic**?

clinch *see* **clench** or **clinch**?

clique The noun *clique*, often used pejoratively to denote a small exclusive group of people, may be pronounced to rhyme with *teak* or *tick*. The first of these pronunciations, [kleek], is closer to the French original and is preferred by many users.

clone *Clone* is a word taken from genetic science, where it means 'the asexually, and often artificially, produced offspring of a parent, which is genetically identical to the parent, or a group of such offspring, which are genetically identical to each other'. The word is now used popularly to suggest anything very similar to something else: * Marketing the Arts *is a new magazine, tabloid size, a clone of* Campaign (*Daily Telegraph*). It is also used synonymously with *lookalike*: * *a dozen Elvis Presley clones*.

close or **closed**? Confusion between these two words sometimes arises when they are used in compounds, especially *close/closed season* (the period of time when the killing of certain animals, birds, or fish is forbidden). In British English *close season* is preferred; in American English, *closed season*. In most other compounds *close* and *closed* are not interchangeable: * *a close shave* * *a closed-shop agreement* * *at close quarters* * *closed-circuit television*.
  In all of these compounds, *close* is pronounced [klōs] and *closed* is pronounced [klōzd].

close proximity *Proximity* means 'being close or near in space or time': * *Its* proximity to the station made the house particularly convenient. As 'close' is part of the meaning of the word, it is never necessary to add *close* before *proximity*: * *His close proximity made me feel uneasy. See also* **tautology**.

clothed *see* **clad** or **clothed**?

clout Some people object to the overuse of the noun *clout* to mean 'influence; political power': * *financial clout* * *The union doesn't carry much clout with the government.* This usage is best restricted to informal contexts.

co- The prefix *co-* is increasingly attached without a hyphen in modern usage. Some users prefer to retain the hyphen when the prefix is attached to a word beginning with *o*: * *co-ordinate* * *co-operate* (*see also* **hyphen**). Some dictionaries retain the hyphen in words referring to a person who does something jointly with another: * *co-author* * *co-star*, but the spellings *coauthor*, *costar*, etc., are acceptable.

coarse or **course**? These words are sometimes confused. *Coarse* means 'rough or crude': * *coarse behaviour* * *coarse cloth*. The noun *course* means 'progression of events': * *in the course of time*, or 'route': * *The ship steered a difficult course*. The verb *course* means 'hunt or pursue'; *coursing* is the sport in which hares are hunted with dogs. *Coarse* [not *course*] fishing is the activity of catching freshwater fish other than salmon or trout.

cocoon This word, which means 'protective covering': * *The butterfly emerged from its cocoon*, is sometimes misspelt. Note the second *c* and the *-oo-*.

coherent or **cohesive**? *Coherent* and cohesive have the same roots in the verb to *cohere*, but they are used differently. *Coherent* means 'logically consistent; comprehensible': * *a coherent argument* * *coherent speech. Cohesive* means 'clinging or sticking together': * *the cohesive properties of the mortar,* but is more frequently used figuratively of anything that holds together or has unity: * *Union members should think of themselves as a cohesive group.*

cohort This word, meaning 'united group of people', is encountered with increasing frequency in the singular, referring to an individual supporter or accomplice: * *He has emerged as a loyal cohort of the President.* This usage is more frequent in American English than in British English, and is avoided by careful users. A *cohort* is also a group of people sharing a particular statistical characteristic: * *to compare the exam results of children within the various cohorts.*

coiffure This word, meaning 'hairstyle', is usually pronounced [kwah*fewr*]. This should be clearly distinguished from the pronunciation of *coiffeur*, meaning 'hairstylist' [kwah*fer*]. Note the different endings of these nouns and also the -*ff*- in the spelling.

colander *see* **calendar, calender** or **colander**?

collaborate or **cooperate**? Both *collaborate* and *cooperate* mean 'work together for a common purpose': * *The two scientists have collaborated/ cooperated for years on various projects. Collaborate* has the extra sense of working with or assisting an enemy, particularly an enemy occupier of a country: * *The French politicians who had collaborated with the Nazis were discredited after the war. Collaborate* is more likely to be used of a cooperative enterprise of an intellectual or artistic nature: people might *collaborate* in writing a book, but *cooperate* in organising a party.

The verb *collaborate* is followed by the preposition *in* or *on*: * *They have collaborated in* [or *on*] *a number of musicals.*

collective nouns This term applies to such nouns as: * *flock* * *gang* * *troop,* which are usually followed by *of* and another noun: * *a flock of sheep,* to other nouns which apply to groups, such as: * *audience* * *orchestra* * *crowd,* and to 'class' collectives, which include various things of a certain kind: * *furniture* * *underwear* * *greengrocery* * *cutlery.* Some collective nouns have very restricted uses: a *pride* can only be of lions; a *school* only of fish and other aquatic animals. Others, such as *herd,* have a more general use.

The main problem with collective nouns is whether to treat them as singular or plural. With some nouns there is no choice. Class collectives always take a singular verb: * *My luggage is missing.* Words for people in general or a particular class of person: * *folk* * *the police,* take a plural verb: * *The clergy are up in arms about it.* It is with group nouns such as: * *audience* * *jury* * *committee* that problems arise. American English treats them as singular: * *The Government is undecided,* but British English treats them as either singular or plural: * *The Government is/are undecided.* For the use of singular and plural verbs, see individual entries and **singular** or **plural**?

COLON A *colon* introduces a clause or word which amplifies, interprets, explains, or reveals what has gone before it: ● *He was beginning to be anxious: they had been gone for five hours.* ● *Only one party cares: Labour.* Its other main uses are to introduce lists: ● *The Thames Valley Police Authority covers three counties: Berkshire, Buckinghamshire, and Oxfordshire*, and to introduce lengthier quotations, often when quotation marks are not used and the quoted material is indented. *See* panel below.

colonnade Note the spelling of this noun, meaning 'row of columns' –

particularly the *-l-* (as in *column*) and the *-nn-*.

coloration Note that the *u* of *colour* is omitted in this derived form of the word, which refers to a pattern or arrangement of colours: ● *the distinctive coloration of the feathers.* The same principle applies to the noun *discoloration*, derived from the verb *discolour*.

coloured *see* **black**.

colourise The verb *colourise* refers to the process of adding colour to black-and-white films: ● *the controversial*

COLONS

1 Colon clauses	The clause preceding a colon should usually be able to stand on its own grammatically: ● *The firing died down as night fell: officers on both sides gathered to discuss their options.*
2 Capitals	Capitals should be used after colons only if the word following is a proper noun; if the first word of a quotation is capitalised; if the colon follows a formal salutation or brief instruction: ● *To whom it may concern*: ● *Note*: ● *Warning*: or sometimes if the material following the colon is a whole sentence or sentences expressing a complete thought.
3 Uses	As well as introducing additional or explanatory material, or introducing lists or quotations, colons are also used to introduce speech in plays: ● *Cecily: Are you called Algernon? Algernon: I cannot deny it.* They are used between titles and subtitles: ● *Men Who Play God: The Story of the Hydrogen Bomb*; in biblical references between chapter and verse: ● *James 2:14–17*; in business correspondence: ● *To:* ● *Reference:* and to show the relationship of one number to another: ● *The ratio was 2:1.* Colons are also used in books such as this, to introduce examples.
4 Dashes	The use of the dash following a colon is restricted to lists, usually where each item starts on a new line and is indented. Even then the practice is old-fashioned and not recommended. *See also* **dash**.

practice of colourising classic films.
Note that the verb is spelt *-our-* in
British English, and with an *s* (the
American spelling is *colorize*), unlike
the verb *decolorise*, meaning 'remove
the colour from', which is spelt *-or-* in
British and American English.

columnist The *n* of this word is sometimes not sounded in speech. The
pronunciation [*kol*ŭmnist] is strictly
correct, but [*kol*ŭmist] is becoming
increasingly common; [*kol*ŭmist]
reflects the pronunciation of *column*,
with its silent *n*.

come The tendency to follow the verb
come with *and* is avoided by some users
and is best restricted to informal contexts: * *Come and tell me all about it.*

comedian or **comedienne**? *see* **non-
sexist terms**.

comic or **comical**? *Comic* and *comical*
are not quite synonymous. *Comic*
means 'of comedy, intended to cause
laughter or amusement': * *a comic
actor* * *a comic poem*. *Comical* means
'having the effect of causing laughter
or amusement': * *a comical sight*.
Something can be *comic*, in that it is
intended to be funny, even if it fails
actually to arouse mirth: * *His comic
songs did not raise a smile*. *Comical* is
often used in cases where the humour
is unintentional: * *It was comical to see
their attempts to appear sophisticated.*

COMMAS Of all the punctuation marks,
the *comma* is the most likely to cause
confusion or ambiguity through its
misuse, overuse, or omission. Some of
the conventions that formerly governed its use are now regarded as
optional; it is important, however, to

be consistent within a single piece of
writing. Excessively long sentences
containing many clauses separated by
commas are best divided into shorter
units; short sentences that require
many commas for clarity should be
reworded if possible. The principal
uses of the comma are listed in the
panel on pages 85–6. *See also* **dates**;
letter writing; **numbers**; **quotation
marks**.

commandant, **commander** or **commandeer**? *Commandant* and *commander* are nouns; *commandeer* is a
verb. The noun *commandant* refers to
an officer in command of a particular
group or establishment, such as a
military academy or prisoner-of-war
camp; the noun *commander* refers to
an officer in command of a military
operation, ship, etc. *Commander* is
also the name of a rank in the Navy
and is used in non-military contexts
to denote anybody who is in command: * *the commander of the expedition*. The verb to *commandeer* means
'seize, especially for military or public
use': * *They commandeered our car.*

commemorate This word, meaning
'remember with a ceremony': * *They
commemorated the 50th anniversary of
the revolution*, is sometimes misspelt.
Note particularly the *-mm-* followed
by a single *m*.

commence *Commence* means the same
as *begin* or *start* but should be used
only in formal contexts, where its
opposite is *conclude*, rather than *end*:
* *The meeting will commence at 9.30
a.m. and conclude at noon*. It sounds
affected or pompous to use *commence*
in contexts where *begin* or *start* is
appropriate: * *I shall commence my*

COMMAS

1 Commas in lists	The individual items of a series of three or more are separated by commas; the final comma preceding *and* or *or* is optional: • *We have invited Paul, Michael, Peter, and Mark.* • *She plays tennis, hockey and netball.* • *He doesn't like cabbage, carrots, or beans.* The same conventions apply to series of longer units: • *I closed the window, drew the curtains, and went to bed.* Omission of the final comma may cause confusion if the last or penultimate item contains *and*: • *They only serve pies, fish and chips, and beefburgers.*
2 Commas between adjectives	The use of a comma between adjectives that precede the noun they qualify is optional in most cases: • *a large, red, juicy tomato* • *a small round black button.* When the final adjective has a closer relationship with the noun, it should not be preceded by a comma: • *a picturesque French village* • *an impertinent little boy* • *an eccentric old woman.* In the following examples, omission of the comma could cause ambiguity or confusion: • *bright, blue curtains* • *a freshly ironed, neatly folded shirt.*
3 Commas and non-restrictive clauses.	Commas separate non-restrictive (or non-defining) clauses or parenthetical clauses and phrases (material that could otherwise be placed within brackets) from the rest of the sentence: • *The mayor, who is very fond of gardening, presented the prizes at the flower show.* • *My diamond necklace, a valuable family heirloom, has been stolen.* It is important to ensure that both commas are present (unless the clause or phrase falls at the end of the sentence) and that they enclose the appropriate information: it should be possible to remove the words between the commas without affecting the basic message of the sentence. As a general rule, the subject of a sentence should not be separated from its verb by a single comma, although this rule is being flouted with increasing frequency when the subject is a long phrase: • *A man killed by an inter-city express train at Haddenham station two weeks ago, was one of the county's leading bridge players* (*Bucks Herald*). Commas are not used around restrictive (or defining) or essential clauses or phrases: • *The classical guitarist Andrés Segovia has died.* • *The skirt that I bought last week has a broken zip.* In some cases, the removal or insertion of parenthetical commas can alter the meaning of a sentence: • *My daughter Elizabeth is a doctor* implies that the speaker has two or more daughters, one of whom is called Elizabeth; • *My daughter, Elizabeth, is a doctor* implies that the speaker has only one daughter. *See also* **apposition**; **brackets**; **clause**; **dash**; **restrictive clause**; **that** or **which**?

4 Separating commas	The use of the comma or commas to separate such words and phrases as *however, therefore, nevertheless, of course, for example,* and *on the other hand* from the rest of the sentence is optional: • *I wondered, however, whether he was right.* • *The holiday will include visits to some of the local attractions, for example the caves and the pottery.* • *We could go by train or of course we could use the car.*
5 Commas and terms of address, interjections, etc.	Commas are always used to separate terms of address, interjections, and closing question tags from the rest of the sentence: • *I'm sorry to have troubled you, madame.* • *Please sit down, Mr Smith, and tell me what happened.* • *Oh, what a beautiful garden!* • *It's cold today, isn't it?*
6 Commas and clauses	The main clause of the sentence may be separated from a preceding subordinate clause or participial phrase by a comma: • *When fiscal times are hard, waste is a favourite target for politicians* … (*The Economist*). • *After loading all their luggage into the car and locking up the house and garage, they set off on their holidays.* The comma is often omitted after a short clause or phrase: • *When it stops raining we will go out. See also* **dangling participles**.
7 Commas and conjunctions	Two or more main clauses linked by a coordinating conjunction (*and, or, but,* etc.) may be separated with a comma if necessary. The comma is usually omitted if the clauses have the same subject or object: • *Tom washed the dishes and Sarah dried them.* • *He shut the door but forgot to turn out the light.* If the clauses are fairly short, the comma is optional: • *The lorry overturned but the driver was uninjured.* • *The hotel is very comfortable, and the food is excellent.* Between longer or more complex main clauses, a comma is often necessary to avoid ambiguity or confusion. (Where such clauses are not linked by a coordinating conjunction, they should be separated by a semicolon rather than a comma.)
8 Commas and repeated verbs	A comma may be used in place of a repeated verb in the second of two related clauses: • *She speaks French and German; her husband, Spanish and Italian.*

new job tomorrow. • *The car commenced making a rattling noise.*

Commencement is the noun from *commence* and should be used in similar contexts: • *the commencement of the financial year.* It has a special meaning in the United States, where *Commencement* is the ceremony at which students receive degrees.

commensurate *Commensurate* means 'equal in measure or extent; proportionate': • *The rent charged is commensurate with the flat's current value.* The word is frequently used in connection with job salaries: • *Remuneration will be commensurate with the importance of this key role* (*Executive Post*).

commercialese *Commercialese* is a usually pejorative term applied to the jargon used in the business and commercial world. Typically such jargon is found in business letters and includes such abbreviations as: * *inst.* (this month) * *ult.* (last month) * *prox.* (next month), as well as such phrases as: * *Please find enclosed* * *Further to your letter* * *I beg to remain* * *your esteemed favour* * *your communication to hand.* Unlike other forms of jargon, commercialese is becoming distinctly old-fashioned and most modern companies prefer to conduct their correspondence in plain English. *See also* **management-speak**.

commissionaire This word, meaning 'attendant in uniform': * *the commissionaire at the theatre*, is sometimes misspelt. Note the *-mm-*, *-ss-*, single *n*, and the *-aire* ending. Do not confuse this word with *commissioner*, meaning 'an important official of a government, etc.': * *a high commissioner* * *the police commissioner.*

commitment The *sense of commitment* which means 'loyalty to a cause or ideology' is an increasingly popular one: * *a genuine Christian commitment* * *his commitment to the animal rights movement* * *As my commitment to the struggle for a racial justice intensified, I wanted to go further in my relationship with the black community* (Jim Wallis, *The New Radical*). Many people dislike this word's overuse, especially in reference to personal relationships: * *She doubted his commitment.* Note the *-mm-* and single *t* of *commit.* The *-t-* is not doubled in *commitment*, unlike in *committed, committing*, etc.

committee The noun *committee* may be singular or plural: * *The committee meets on Thursdays.* * *The committee were unable to reach a unanimous decision.* Note the spelling of *committee*, particularly the *-mm-*, *-tt-*, and *-ee.* *See also* **collective nouns; singular** or **plural?**

common *see* **mutual, common** or **reciprocal?**

communal This word, meaning 'of a community': * *communal living*, has two different pronunciations. Both [*kom*yuunăl] and [kŏ*mew*năl] are widely used. Careful speakers, however, prefer the first of these pronunciations.

communicate The verb *communicate* is followed by the preposition *with* or (something) *to*: * *They communicated with each other through an interpreter.* * *She communicated the news to her staff.*

community *Community* has become a vogue word in two different ways. The application of the word to a recognisable group within a larger society: * *the Jewish community* * *the black community*, has given the word an association with minority racial groups, and now a *Council for Community Relations,* a *community relations officer*, and so on, are those that deal with the problems of black and Asian minorities in Britain. *The community* is also used in a much more vague sense to mean 'society in general'. When psychiatric patients are discharged from hospital and it is recommended that they be *cared for in the community*, it usually means no more than that they are to live in society.

comparable The traditional pronunciation of this word is [*komp*ărăbl]. Careful speakers avoid the variant [kŏm*parr*ăbl]. *See also* **stress**.

comparative and **superlative** The *comparative* form of an adjective or adverb is used when two things or people are compared: * *Anne is smaller than her sister*, while the *superlative* is used as the highest degree of comparison between three or more things: * *Anne is the smallest girl in her class.*

The two main ways of forming comparatives and superlatives are by adding the suffixes -*er* and -*est*, or preceding the word with *more* or *most*: * *sad–sadder–saddest* * *eager–more eager –most eager.* One-syllable words always take -*er* and -*est*, as do two-syllable words ending in -*y*: * *big–bigger* * *pretty–prettiest.* Two-syllable words ending in -*le*, -*ow*, -*er* sometimes also take -*er* and -*est*: * *little–littlest* * *shallow–shallower* * *clever–cleverer.* Other two-syllable words and all words of three or more syllables take *more* and *most*: * *more abject* * *most horrific* * *most interesting.* Most compound adjectives can use either form: * *fairer minded* * *more fair-minded.* There are two well-known words with irregularly formed comparatives and superlatives: * *good/well–better–best* * *bad/badly–worse–worst.*

More is used instead of -*er*, even with one-syllable words, in certain contexts: when two adjectives are being compared with each other: * *He's really more shy than aloof*; and when the aptness of an adjective is being challenged: * *She's no more fat than a stick insect!*

Absolute adjectives (*see* **adjectives**) cannot be used in comparative or superlative forms. It is impossible to

say *more total* or *finaller.* It is, however, possible to use comparative forms when suggesting a closer approximation to perfection: * *A fuller description will be given tomorrow.*

Mistakes concerning comparatives and superlatives include the use of the comparative in phrases like: * *three times wider* * *ten times more expensive*, instead of: * *three times as wide* * *ten times as expensive* – although when an actual measure is specified, it is appropriate to say: * *three feet wider* * *ten pounds more expensive.* Another mistake is the use of *more* or -*er* in phrases like: * *one of the more promising of the new novelists*, when it is clear that more than two things or people are being compared, and the use of *most* or -*est* when only two things or people are being compared: * *We have two sons; Tom is the youngest.* A (possibly deliberate) mistake much used by advertisers is the use of the comparative when it is unclear what is being compared: * *X washes whiter and cleaner!* * *Y gives you a better, closer shave!*, and the unbridled use of superlatives: * *The most luxurious holiday ever!*

Finally, a frequent mistake is the misspelling of *comparative* as *comparitive*, probably based on *comparison*.

comparatively *Comparatively* means 'relatively, as compared with a standard': * *It was comparatively inexpensive for vintage champagne.* It is often used as a synonym for 'rather, fairly, or somewhat', with no question of comparison: * *It is a comparatively small resort*, but many people dislike this usage.

compare to or **compare with**? *Compare to* and *compare with* are not interchangeable. *Compare to* is used when things are being likened to each other: * *He compared her skin to ivory.* *Compare with* is used when things are being considered from the point of view of both similarities and differences: * *Tourists find London hotels expensive compared with those of other European capitals.* When *compare* is used intransitively, *with* should always be used: * *His direction compares with early Hitchcock.* In American English, *compared to* and *comparable to* are frequently used where *with* is appropriate: * *Compared to my brother, I'm poor.* * *It's not comparable to the home-made version*, and these uses are coming into British English.

compel or **impel**? Both these verbs mean 'force', but they differ in usage. *Compel* is used with human and non-human subjects and implies strong obligation: * *They compelled us to take part.* * *Financial necessity compelled him to accept the job.* *Impel* is chiefly used with non-human subjects and implies an urge rather than an obligation: * *She felt impelled to protest.* * *Fear impelled him to turn back.*

compete The verb *compete* is followed by the preposition *with* or *against*: * *We found ourselves competing with* [or *against*] *three other companies for the contract.*

competent The adjective *competent* is followed by the preposition *at* or *in*: * *Applicants must be competent at* [or *in*] *word processing.*

competition or **contest**? *Competition* and *contest* both involve rivalry with an opponent or opponents and can be synonymous: * *At 18 she won a*

contest/competition for young musicians. However, *contest* is restricted to the sense of organised competitive events or exertions to achieve victory over opponents: * *the contest for nomination as candidate.* *Competition* is used more generally of rivalry: * *There will be keen competition for tickets*, and is also used of the people or organisation against which others are competing: * *We must assess the strengths and weaknesses of the competition.*

complacent or **complaisant**? A *complacent* person is smug or self-satisfied; a *complaisant* person is obliging or willing to comply. Both adjectives may be applied to the same noun: * *'We can't lose,' she said with a complacent smile.* * *He opened the door with a complaisant smile.*

The two words should not be confused: they are similar in pronunciation but quite different in spelling: *complacent* [kŏm*plays*ĕnt] ends in *-cent*; *complaisant* [kŏm*playz*ănt] ends in *-sant*.

Complacent is the more frequent word, *complaisant* being rather old-fashioned.

complement The *complement* of a clause or sentence provides essential additional information about the **subject** or **object**. A complement may be a noun, adjective, pronoun, or phrase.

A subject complement usually follows such verbs as *be, become, turn, look, appear, seem, feel*, and *sound*. In the sentence: * *He became a teacher, a teacher* is the complement. In: * *They felt disappointed, disappointed* is the complement. The clause: * *where we live* is the complement of the sentence *This is where we live.*

An object complement usually follows the direct object of such verbs as *make, find, declare, elect,* and *call.* In the sentence: * *You made me very proud, very proud* is the complement. In: * *The judges declared him the winner, the winner* is the complement. *See also* **complement** or **compliment**?; **complement** or **supplement**?

complement or **compliment**? These two words are often confused. Both as a noun and a verb, *complement* suggests the addition of something necessary to make something whole or complete: * *a ship's complement* * *The flowers complemented the room's decor perfectly. Compliment* is used as a noun and verb to refer to an expression of praise, respect, or admiration: * *She complimented her host on the excellent meal.* * *with the compliments of the management.* To avoid mistakes, remember that the *e* of *complement* is also in *complete.* The derived adjectives *complementary* and *complimentary* are also confused, particularly when *complimentary* is used in the sense of 'given free': * *a complimentary* [not *complementary*] copy of his latest book * *two complimentary* [not *complementary*] *tickets to the exhibition.*

complement or **supplement**? *Complement* and *supplement* have a distinct difference in meaning. Both as a noun and a verb, *complement* suggests the addition of something necessary to make something whole or complete: * *The closures were forced by the hospital's inability to recruit 92 nurses out of its full complement of nearly 800* (*Daily Telegraph*). * *The music complemented the mime aptly. Supplement* suggests an addition to something

that is already complete: * *Her fees for private tuition supplemented her teacher's salary.* * *Most Sunday newspapers publish a colour supplement.*

complementary medicine or **alternative medicine**? *Complementary medicine* is the treatment of illnesses by such techniques and systems as osteopathy, acupuncture, and homoeopathy. The term *complementary medicine* suggests that the treatments and therapies complement – fit in with and work alongside – orthodox scientific medicine; the term *alternative medicine*, used for treatments such as herbalism and naturopathy, emphasises that such treatments are completely different from those of 'conventional' medicine. Note, however, that the distinction between the two phrases is increasingly ignored and that alternative therapies are often called complementary.

complete When used to mean 'total', *complete* is an absolute adjective (*see* **adjectives**) and many people dislike any modification of it: * *We were in almost complete darkness.* However, complete also has the meaning of 'thorough': * *a complete overhaul,* and in that sense can be modified with more or most: * *This is the most complete study of the period yet published.*

complex The noun *complex* is taken from psychoanalysis, where it means 'a set of subconscious repressed ideas and emotions which can cause an abnormal mental condition': * *an Oedipus complex* * *an inferiority complex.* The term has been taken up and used popularly to mean any behavioural problem or obsession, even if it is completely conscious; some people dislike this usage: * *She's got a complex about spiders.* * *'You're crazy,' Clevinger shouted... 'You've got a Jehovah complex'* (Joseph Heller, *Catch 22*). *Complex* is also used to mean 'something made up of interrelated parts' and this is now often applied to a group of buildings, as in: * *shopping complex* * *housing complex.*

complex or **complicated**? *Complex* and *complicated* are very similar in meaning, and the differences in usage are subtle ones. Both mean 'consisting of many parts which are intimately combined': * *This is a complex/complicated problem. Complicated* emphasises the fact that the multifaceted nature of a thing makes it difficult to solve or understand, and there is sometimes a negative connotation to it – a suggestion that it could possibly be simpler: * *Compared with Scottish procedure, house buying in England is unnecessarily complicated. Complex* is more neutral and emphasises the intricacy of the combination of parts rather than the resulting difficulties: * *The blood-clotting system is a complex mechanism.*

compliant The word *compliant*, meaning 'acquiescent' or 'complying', may be used in combination with other nouns to indicate that something conforms to a particular system, set of rules, etc.: * *This program is fully web-compliant.* * *We have checked that the machine is industry-compliant.*

compliment, complimentary *see* **compliment** or **compliment**?

compose, comprise or **constitute**? All these verbs are concerned with parts making up a whole. *Compose* and *constitute* are both used to mean 'come

together to make (a whole)' but *compose* is usually used in the passive and *constitute* in the active: * *The team is composed of several experts.* * *the commodities that constitute the average household diet. Comprise* can only be used to mean 'consist of': * *The house comprises three bedrooms, a living room, kitchen, and bathroom.* Its use in place of *constitute*: * *Eleven players comprise a team* is not generally considered acceptable; its use in place of *compose*: * *The team is comprised of eleven players* is wrong. *See also* **consist of** or **consist in?**; **include** or **comprise?**

compound A *compound* is a word that consists of two or more other words joined together, with or without a space or hyphen: * *breakdown* * *forget-me-not* * *dining room.* There are no absolute rules governing the use of spaces and hyphens in many compounds (*see* **hyphen**).

The plural of a compound noun is usually formed by making the noun element plural: * *passers-by* * *sons-in-law* (*see also* **plurals**).

The coining of new compound verbs, such as *drug-test* or *rubber-stamp*, is disliked by some people (*see also* **verbs**).

As a noun or adjective, the word *compound* is stressed on the first syllable [*kom*pownd]; as a verb it is stressed on the second syllable [kŏmp*ownd*].

comprehend *see* **apprehend** or **comprehend**?

comprehensible or **comprehensive**? These two adjectives are derived from different senses of the verb *comprehend* (*see* **apprehend** or **comprehend?**). *Comprehensible* means 'understandable'; *comprehensive* means 'including all or most things': * *The explanation must be comprehensible to the average reader.* * *fully comprehensive car insurance.*

comprise *see* **compose, comprise** or **constitute?; include** or **comprise?**

compulsive or **compulsory?** Both these adjectives are derived from the verb *compel,* meaning 'force'. *Compulsive* refers to something that a person is forced to do by an internal or psychological urge; *compulsory* refers to something that a person is forced to do by an external rule or law: * *a compulsive gambler* * *a compulsory payment.*

concede This verb, meaning 'admit' or 'yield', is sometimes misspelt. Note the *-cede* ending, as in the verb *cede,* which is similar in meaning.

concept The precise meaning of *concept* is 'an idea of a category or thing which is formed by generalisation from particular instances'. The meaning has widened to embrace ideas in general, and is often now used to mean 'an accepted idea of a particular thing': * *the concept of alternative medicine.* It is frequently used very loosely to mean little more than 'an idea or notion', particularly in advertising; many people dislike this usage: * *a new concept in slimming.* *Conceptualise* means 'form a concept' or 'interpret conceptually': * *The Greeks conceptualised all their experiences in terms of the gods.* It should not be used to mean 'think', 'imagine', or 'visualise'.

concerned The adjective *concerned* may be followed by *about* or *for* when it

means 'anxious', and by *with* when it means 'on the subject of': * *We are very concerned about pollution.* * *The article is concerned with pollution.* * *They are concerned for his health.* * *The organisation is concerned with public health.* For discussion of the phrase *as far as... is concerned, see* **as far as.**

concerning *Concerning* means 'relating to, on the subject of, or about': * *The head teacher is available to talk to people concerning their career choices.* It is normally used between two clauses rather than at the beginning of a sentence and is rather more formal than *about.*

condemn or **condone?** These words are opposite in meaning. To *condemn* means 'declare something to be unacceptably bad or evil' or 'give a punishment to someone': * *to condemn the atrocities/terrorist activities* * *The prisoners were condemned to death.* To *condone* behaviour that is wrong means to accept it, or turn a blind eye to it, considering it harmless or unimportant. *Condone* is sometimes used with a negative, hence the possible confusion with *condemn:* * *The association does not condone reckless driving.*

condition or **precondition?** A *condition* is a requirement or stipulation on which an agreement or contract depends: * *I will let you go on condition that you are back before midnight.* While a condition can be fulfilled either before or after the agreement is made, a *precondition* is a requirement that must be satisfied in advance of an agreement being made: * *Assent to the manifesto was a precondition of membership.* *Condition* can be used, not just of agreements, but also of situations and states of being: * *the condition of the world* * *in good/poor condition*. The words *condition* and *precondition* are used synonymously to mean anything that has to be true or must occur before something else can happen: * *The establishment of a just society is an essential condition/precondition for peace.*

condone *see* **condemn** or **condone**?

conducive The adjective *conducive* is followed by the preposition *to*: * *an environment conducive to mental concentration.*

confidant or **confident**? A *confidant*, feminine *confidante*, is someone in whom a person can confide. Both words are pronounced either [*kon*fidant] or [konfi*dant*]. These nouns should not be confused with the adjective *confident*, which means 'assured or certain': * *a confident young man.*

confide The verb *confide* is followed by the preposition *in* or *to*: * *He confided in his sister.* * *He confided his problems to his sister.*

conform The verb *conform* is followed by the preposition *with* or *to*: * *The results did not conform with* [or *to*] *our expectations.*

confrontation A *confrontation* is a face-to-face meeting, especially in the context of opposition, challenge, or defiance: * *St George's confrontation with the dragon.* Popular journalism has weakened the meaning so that any disagreement or conflict of ideas is now inevitably referred to as a confrontation. Similarly, anyone with a

tendency to argumentativeness is described as confrontational: * *Mr Underhill said Mr Senchak's style 'was that of the old-fashioned confrontational "us and them" union official'* (*The Times*).

congenial, **genial**, **congenital** or **genetic**? Both *congenial* and *genial* mean 'pleasant'; *congenial* is usually applied to abstract nouns and *genial* to people: * *a congenial atmosphere* * *He finds the work congenial.* * *a genial host.* *Congenial company* refers to people who share a person's interests or attitudes; *genial company* refers to people who are friendly and cheerful.

Congenital means 'existing from birth'; *genetic* means 'relating to genes': * *congenital brain damage* * *genetic engineering.* A *congenital defect* is not hereditary or inherited; a *genetic defect* is.

The adjectives *congenital* and *congenial* are sometimes confused, being similar in spelling; note that the *e* of *congenital* is short, as in *men*, whereas the *e* of *congenial* is long, as in *mean*.

congressman or **congresswoman**? *see* **non-sexist terms.**

congruent or **congruous**? Both *congruent* and *congruous* are formal words. If one thing is *congruent* with another, there is a similarity or connection between them: * *ritualistic and mystical elements congruent with the expectations of converted pagans.* *Congruous* refers to something that is in harmony with something else: * *decorations congruous with their surroundings.* *Congruous* is more often found in its negative form *incongruous*, which is less formal than *congruous* and is used to refer to a person or thing that seems strange and out of place: * *behaviour that was incongruous with his beliefs*. In mathematics, two shapes are *congruent* if they are equal in size and shape: * *congruent triangles*.

conjoined *Conjoined* twins is the preferred term for babies that are born joined together, replacing the previous *Siamese twins*: * *The doctors have succeeded in separating conjoined twins delivered at the hospital last Sunday.*

conjunctions *Conjunctions* are words which link two or more words, clauses, or sentences: * *and* * *but* * *or* * *because* * *when*.

And, but, yet, and *or* are known as coordinating conjunctions. They connect words and clauses of the same grammatical type: * *Martha and Mary* * *I love Mozart but I detest Mahler.* They often connect clauses that share a common verb, and this does not need to be repeated: * *She is young yet surprisingly wise. But* and *yet* can be used only to link two sentence elements, but *and* and *or* can link more than two: * *I'm tired and cold and hungry and miserable.*

Conjunctions such as *because,* when, *if, though, unless* are known as subordinating conjunctions, as they connect a subordinate clause to its main clause: * *He's fat because he eats too much.* * *It won't work unless everyone cooperates.*

Correlative conjunctions are the pairs *either... or* and *neither... nor* which are always used together: * *Neither Williams nor Jenkins is now an MP.* * *He's either wicked or mad.*

Few people still have objections to sentences starting with the conjunctions *and, but,* and *or,* which can be effective if used sparingly. *See also*

individual entries for **conjunctions** and **singular** or **plural**?

conjurer or **conjuror**? Either spelling is perfectly acceptable.

connect The verb *connect* is followed by the preposition *to* or *with* in the sense 'join': * *A narrow lane connects the farm to* [or *with*] *the village.* In the sense of 'associate' it is followed by the preposition *with*: * *The broken window may not be connected with the robbery.*

connection or **connexion**? This word, meaning 'a relationship between two things; joint': * *His death must have had some connection with the stormy weather.* * *faulty electrical connections,* is usually spelt *connection. Connexion* is a rare variant spelling, especially in British English.

connoisseur A person who is an expert within a certain field is called a *connoisseur.* Note the *-nn-, -oi-,* and *-ss-* in the spelling.

connote or **denote**? These two verbs are sometimes confused. *Denote,* the more frequent of the two, refers to the literal or primary meaning of something: * *The word 'bachelor' denotes an unmarried man.* * *Tears do not always denote sadness. Connote,* a more formal word, means 'imply' or 'suggest', referring to secondary meaning or association: * *For some people, the word 'bachelor' connotes freedom.*

conscience Note the spelling of this word, particularly the *-sci-* in the middle and the *-ce* ending. The second syllable is identical in spelling (but not in pronunciation) with the noun *science.*

conscientious or **conscious**? *Conscientious* means 'diligent and careful': * *She was a conscientious worker.* *Conscious* means 'aware' or 'awake': * *He was so tired he was barely conscious.* The words are sometimes misspelt: note in particular the *-sc-* in the middle of both, and the *t* in *conscientious*.

consensus *Consensus* means 'opinion shared unanimously; a view generally held or accepted': * *He had broken the pro-nuclear consensus shared by all postwar leaders* (*Sunday Times*). As the meaning contains the idea of a generally held opinion, careful users avoid the expressions *general consensus* and *consensus of opinion*, since they are tautologies.

   Consensus is frequently misspelt as *concensus*, perhaps from a mistaken belief that it is connected with the word *census*. In fact, it derives from the same root as *consent*.

consent *see* **assent** or **consent**?

consequent or **consequential**? *Consequent* means 'following as a direct result': * *She was knocked down by a lorry and her consequent injuries left her a permanent invalid.* *Consequential*, a more rare word than *consequent*, is also used to mean 'following as a direct result': * *the improvement in the local economy and the consequential loss of the area's special status.* *Consequential* also means 'important': * *Their decisions were becoming increasingly consequential in determining the direction of the company.* It is also used in legal expressions such as *consequential loss* to mean 'an indirect result', and has the additional meaning of 'self-important; pompous': * *His manner was pretentious and consequential.*

consequent or **subsequent**? *Consequent* and *subsequent* are sometimes confused. While *consequent* means 'following as a direct result', *subsequent* simply means 'occurring after': * *her bereavement and consequent grief* * *her bereavement and subsequent remarriage.* *Consequent* takes the preposition *on*, while *subsequent* takes *to*: * *increase in salaries consequent on the pay review* * *his behaviour subsequent to his arrival.*

consequential *see* **consequent** or **consequential**?

conservative or **Conservative**? The word *conservative* with a lower-case *c* means 'tending to support tradition and established institutions; opposed to change; moderate, cautious, conventional': * *The college has a reputation for being conservative and still refuses to admit women students.* * *He has conservative tastes and dresses in sombre colours.* * A *Conservative*, with a capital *C*, is someone who supports or is a member of the Conservative Party in Britain or elsewhere; it is also used as an adjective: * *a Conservative MP.* A *conservative estimate* is one that is cautious and moderate, but the term is often used to mean 'a low estimate': * *It's worth a million pounds at the most conservative estimate.*

consider *Consider* means 'regard as being': * *I consider him a nonentity,* 'think about carefully': * *I have considered all aspects of the problem,* and 'regard sympathetically': * *We will not fail to consider your feelings on the matter.* In the first sense given above, *consider* is more or less synonymous with *regard as*, and this leads some people to add *as* to *consider*: * *He considered* *their work as vitally important.* This construction is wrong; it is however correct to use *as* when *consider* is used in the sense of 'think about, give consideration to': * *The songs are tuneful, but considered as an opera, the work lacks solidity.*

considerable *Considerable* means 'worth consideration; significant': * *She has made a considerable contribution to biochemical research.* It has been extended to mean 'large in amount': * *They have saved a considerable amount of money,* although some people dislike the imprecise nature of this use. *Considerable* is usually attached to abstract nouns: * *a considerable quantity* * *considerable numbers of,* but in American English it can be used with concrete nouns: * *They have mined considerable gold.* This use is not yet acceptable in British English, although when the meaning is 'significant' it is possible to attach *considerable* to a concrete noun: * *a considerable pianist.*

consist of or **consist in**? *Consist of* means 'comprise, be made up of': * *Breakfast consists of bread, croissants, jam, and coffee. Consist in* means 'have its essence in': * *The appeal of the writing consists in its use of language rather than its content. Consist of* usually precedes a list of concrete nouns, while *consist in* is usually applied to abstract nouns.

consonant A *consonant* is the sound represented by any of the letters *b, c, d, f, g, h, j, k, l, m, n, p, q, r, s, t, v, w, x, y,* and *z* in the English language (compare **vowel**). The presence of a consonant at the beginning of a word may affect the form or pronunciation of

the preceding word (*see* **a** or **an**?; **the**).
Note that in such words as *party* and *rhyme,* the letter *y* functions as a vowel.

consortium or **consortia**? *Consortia* is a plural form of the noun *consortium,* which means 'association of companies': * *a consortium of insurance brokers.* The plural form *-ia* is sometimes wrongly used in place of the singular noun: * *Now only Phonepoint, a consortia led by British Telecom, and Byps, owned by Hutchison Telecom UK, are keen to offer the mobile phone service* (*The Guardian*). The plural form *consortiums* is also acceptable.

constable A police officer of the lowest rank is known as a *constable.* The word has two pronunciations: [*kun*stăbl] or [*kon*stăbl], both of which are acceptable.

constitute *see* **compose, comprise** or **constitute**?

constrain or **restrain**? Both these verbs mean 'hold back' or 'limit', but there are differences of usage and application between them. *Constrain* is more formal and implies an abstract or undesirable restriction; *restrain* may involve physical force: * *Such strict guidelines constrain creativity.* * *He struggled to restrain the dog. Constrain* has the additional and more usual meaning of 'compel': * *I felt constrained to resign.*

contact The meanings of *contact* as a noun include 'the state of touching': * *He avoided all physical contact with dogs,* 'link or relationship': * *The two towns have commercial contacts,* and 'communication': • *I am in regular contact with her*. A modern use is 'a person you knows who may be useful to you': • *I have a good contact at the Home Office*. The use of the verb *contact* to mean 'communicate with': • *I will contact you next week* is still disliked as an Americanism by some people. It is, however, particularly useful in cases where a person wishes to avoid specifying whether communication will be made by letter, telephone, message, or personal visit.

contagious or **infectious**? *Contagious* and *infectious* are both used of diseases that can be passed on to others. *Contagious* diseases are those passed on by physical contact, like venereal diseases or impetigo; *infectious* diseases are those passed on by airborne or waterborne microorganisms, like measles or influenza. In figurative use, the words are synonymous: • *His optimistic mood was infectious/contagious*.

containerise *Containerise* is a verb formed from the noun *container* in its sense of a large packing case in which goods are transported by road and sea, being handled mechanically throughout. To *containerise* means both 'pack into containers for transport, and transport in this method': • *The beans must be containerised before the end of the week*; and 'change over to the use of containers': • *We are containerising our shipping procedures*.

contemporary The primary meaning of *contemporary* is 'happening or living at the same time as': • *Joyce was contemporary with the Bloomsbury group, though not a member of it*. It has more recently been used to mean 'happening at the present time; current': •

Contemporary values are materialistic and selfish. A development of this meaning has been the use of *contemporary* to mean 'modern, up-to-date', sometimes qualified with *very*, *extremely*, etc.: • *They sell the most contemporary fashions in town*. This use is disliked by many people and is best avoided. Care should be taken to distinguish between the first and second meanings of *contemporary* where the meaning may be ambiguous: • *a contemporary biography of Shelley* may mean one written when Shelley was alive, or one written recently.

contemptible or **contemptuous**? Both *contemptible* and *contemptuous* are concerned with *contempt*, but they have distinctly different meanings. *Contemptible* means 'despicable; deserving scorn or contempt': • *His meanness was contemptible*. *Contemptuous* means 'scornful, feeling or showing contempt': • *She observed his feeble efforts with a contemptuous smile*.

contest *see* **competition** or **contest**?

contingency A *contingency* is 'something that happens by chance; something unforeseen that might possibly occur in the future': • *We must prepare ourselves for every contingency*. In modern use, the word almost always appears in the phrase *contingency plans* and is usually applied, not to unforeseen future events, but to those that are predictable (although not inevitable): • *The council has made contingency plans in case of a severe winter*.

continual or **continuous**? *Continual* means 'frequently repeated'; *continuous* means 'without break or interruption': • *Our neighbour's continual*

complaints forced us to move house. *
The continuous noise from the genera-
tor kept him awake all night. The fundamental difference in sense, which
also applies to the adverbs *continually*
and *continuously*, is that something
continual stops from time to time,
whereas something *continuous* does
not stop until it reaches its natural
end. It is acceptable in certain contexts to interchange the two words,
but this may lead to ambiguity and is
therefore best avoided if possible.
Continual is not used of physical
objects, such as a *continuous roll of
paper*, nor should *continuous* be substituted for *continual* in such phrases
as: * *continual interruptions.*

continuance, continuation or **continuity**? All three nouns are derived
from the verb *continue*. *Continuance*
is the act of continuing, usually without a break, whereas *continuation* may
be the act of continuing after a break:
* *the continuance of the strike* * *a continuation of yesterday's discussion.* In
some contexts, such as the first example above, *continuance* and *continuation* are interchangeable. *Continuity*
is the state of being continuous (*see*
continual or **continuous**?): * *the continuity of the action.*

continuous *see* **continual** or **continuous**?

continuous tense *see* **progressive
tense**.

contractions The most common *contractions* in English are those of the
verbs *am, are, is, have, has, had, will,
shall, would*, and the word *not* combined with an auxiliary verb: * *I'm* *
you're * *she's* * *we've* * *he'll* * *they'd* *

can't * *shouldn't*. An apostrophe indicates the missing letter(s), although in
the contraction *shan't*, where there are
actually two sets of missing letters,
only the missing *o* is indicated. The
contracted form *'d* can stand for
either *had* or *would*, and *'s* can be
either *is* or *has* – or *us* when used in
the word *let's*; it should always be clear
from the context which word is
intended. Two irregular contractions
are *won't* (will not) and *aren't* (are
not), which can also mean *am not*, as
in: * *Aren't I right?* * *Aren't I clever!*

Contractions are almost always
used in speech. They should always be
used in written passages of dialogue,
and are generally acceptable in all but
the most formal writing. Some contractions are more likely to be written
than others. * *He's late* and: * *Jill's late*
are more acceptable in writing than: *
Dinner's late * *The train's late*, and the
'll contraction (except when used with
personal pronouns: * *I'll*: * *Tim'll be
there.* * *The bus'll be on time* is not
usually used in writing.

Care should be taken with the placing of the apostrophe. A frequent
mistake is placing it where the syllables break, rather than where the letter is missing: * *wouldn't* [not
would'nt]. *See also* **ain't**; **'s** or **s'**?

contrary This word, meaning 'opposed
in position': * *On the contrary, I
would like to go for a walk*, is stressed
on the first syllable [*kon*trări]. Only in
the sense 'perverse or stubborn': *
such a contrary girl, is it stressed on the
second syllable [kŏn*trairi*].

contribute In the traditional pronunciation of this word, the stress is on the
second syllable [kŏn*trib*yoot]: some
users dislike the pronunciation with

the word stressed on the first syllable [*kon*tribyoot].

controversy In the traditional pronunciation of this word, the stress falls on the first syllable [*kon*trŏversi]. The variant pronunciation, with stress on the second syllable [kŏn*trov*ĕrsi], is widely heard, but is disliked by many users. *See also* **stress**.

convalescence This word, meaning 'recovery after an illness', is sometimes misspelt. Note the combinations *-sc-* and *-nc-*.

convenient The adjective *convenient* is followed by the preposition *to* or *for*: * *Come whenever it is convenient to* [or *for*] *you.*

converse, inverse, obverse or **reverse**? These four words share the sense of 'opposite'; in some contexts they are interchangeable. The noun *converse* specifically denotes something that is opposite in meaning: * *the converse of this statement. Inverse* is more frequently used as an adjective in such phrases as * *in inverse proportion*; *obverse*, a formal word and the least common of the four, refers to a counterpart: * *The obverse of the company's success is the failure of its rivals. Reverse*, the most frequent and general of the four words, may be used as a verb, noun, or adjective: * *to reverse a decision* * *to do the reverse* * *in reverse order. Obverse* and *reverse* may also refer to the two sides of a coin, *obverse* being 'heads' and *reverse* 'tails'.

The *converse* of a statement or proposition is one that reverses the elements of the proposition: * *You say that your mother dislikes you but in fact the converse is true – you dislike your mother.* The word is now usually used much more loosely to mean 'opposite': * *The previous speaker claimed that nuclear weapons help to preserve peace, but I maintain the converse.* The adverb *conversely*, similarly, is now used to mean just 'on the other hand': * *In such an emergency the driver can stop the car or, conversely, can accelerate out of danger.*

The noun or adjective *converse* is stressed on the first syllable [*kon*vers]. The verb *converse*, meaning 'have a conversation', is stressed on the second syllable [kŏn*vers*].

convertible This word, meaning 'capable of being changed': * *convertible car*, is sometimes misspelt. The ending is *-ible*, not *-able*.

cool *Cool* is widely employed as a slang term variously meaning 'fashionable' or 'excellent': * *He looks really cool in that jacket.* * *We had a cool time at the party.* As the dominant slang term of approval among young people since the late 1980s, it is used both in longer sentences and on its own as an exclamation. Its overuse should be avoided: * *'We could go to a restaurant later.' 'Cool.' See also* **chill**.

cooperate *see* **collaborate** or **cooperate**?

cord *see* **chord** or **cord**?

co-respondent *see* **correspondent** or **co-respondent**?

corporal or **corporeal**? *Corporal* means 'relating to the body': * *corporal punishment.* It should not be confused with *corporeal*, which means 'physical' or 'material': * *Her imaginary friend* has no corporeal reality. *Corporal* is pronounced [*kor*prăl]. *Corporeal* is pronounced [kor*poree*ăl].

corps or **corpse**? The noun *corps*, meaning 'body of people', should not be confused with the noun *corpse*, meaning 'dead body': * *the diplomatic corps* * *The corpse lay undiscovered for several weeks.* Both are ultimately derived from the Latin *corpus* – 'body' – via the French noun *corps*. The English word *corps* retains the French pronunciation [kor], whereas *corpse*, which entered English from Old French some 400 years earlier, is pronounced [korps].

correspond There are two main meanings of *correspond*. One is 'communicate with someone by exchange of letters': * *He met his Italian penfriend after they had corresponded for years.* The other meaning is 'match or be equivalent or comparable in some respect': * *Your account corresponds exactly with the description of the other witnesses.* * *The French baccalauréat roughly corresponds to the British A-level exam.* In this second meaning *correspond to* is considered correct by many careful users, although *correspond with* is often used.

correspondent or **co-respondent**? A *correspondent* is someone who communicates by letter: * *She has correspondents in three continents,* or someone who contributes news reports to a newspaper or to radio or television programmes: * *And now a report from our Middle East correspondent.* A *co-respondent* is the person cited in divorce proceedings as the lover of the husband or wife who has been accused of adultery: * *Divorced couples*

hobnobbed with each other and with each other's co-respondents (Noël Coward, *Present Indicative*).

cosmetic Some people dislike the use of *cosmetic* as an adjective to apply to anything that improves the outward appearance of something: * *One supplier of decaffeinated coffee... plans to switch from the chemical process... although a spokesman insisted this was necessary for 'cosmetic' reasons only* (*Sunday Times*). It is extended further to anything which makes a superficial improvement but does not make any fundamental change: * *Opposition claims that the Government's inner-city plans would have only a cosmetic effect were hotly denied by the Department of the Environment.*

cost or **price**? As nouns, *cost* and *price* are often used synonymously to mean 'the amount paid or charged for something': * *We were afraid that the cost/price would be more than we could afford.* *Cost* is more likely to refer to an amount paid and *price* to an amount charged: * *An increase in manufacturing costs will result in higher prices.* *Price* is more often used when preceded by an adjective: * *an exorbitant price* * *bargain prices,* and when speaking of the amount needed in order to bribe someone: * *'All those men have their price'* (Sir Robert Walpole). *Cost* is used in the plural for the expenses of a lawsuit: * *The court awarded him costs,* and either *cost* or *price* is used to describe the expenditure in terms of effort and sacrifice made in order to achieve an end: * *'To give and not to count the cost'* (St Ignatius Loyola). * *This was indeed a high price to pay for success.*

couch potato The slang term *couch potato* originated in American English in the mid-1970s and entered British English in the late 1980s. It is applied to people who spend most of their leisure time watching television: * *We are inexorably mutating into a coast-to-coast allotment of couch potatoes* (*The Guardian*). The term is best avoided in formal contexts.

could *see* **can** or **may**?

could have or **could of**? *see* **of**.

council or **counsel**? The noun *council* means 'a body of people meeting for discussion and consultation': * *the county council*. The noun *counsel* means 'advice': * *She always gave wise counsel*, and the corresponding verb *counsel* means 'give advice to someone': * *She was counselled about her future career*. * *He was counselled against acting rashly*. * *psychiatric counselling*.

A *councillor* (in American English, sometimes *councilor*) is a person who belongs to a *council*, just as a *counsellor* (in American English, sometimes *counselor*) is a person who *counsels*: * *Relate counsellors*.

A *counsel* is a lawyer or group of lawyers: * *Queen's Counsel* * *the counsel for the defence*.

counsel or **advise**? In many instances *counsel* and *advise* are synonymous, although *counsel* is rather more formal: * *I would advise/counsel you not to drink any more if you're driving home*. *Advise* is more likely to be used in informal contexts and when the advice is not of great importance: * *He advised me to go on the ring road*. *Counsel* is more appropriate when the advice is serious and when given by trained or profes-sional counsellors: * *He has been counselled by social workers, doctors, and clergy but he still can't sort out his problems*. *See also* **council** or **counsel**?

country or **countryside**? Both these words may be used to denote a rural area: * *We went for a walk in the country/countryside*. *Countryside* is commonly preceded by *the*; usually only *country* occurs before a noun: * *the English countryside* * *a country cottage/lane*. In the sense of 'nation' or 'state', the noun *country* cannot be replaced by countryside: * *A flu epidemic is sweeping the country* [not *countryside*].

country or **nation**? These words are often used interchangeably: * *the poorer countries/nations of the world*. Strictly speaking, *country* should be used when the context is one of geographical characteristics: * *Wales is a mountainous country*, and *nation* when speaking of the people or of social and political characteristics: * *Wales is a nation of musicians and orators*. *Nation* carries a suggestion of a people with a common culture, language, and traditions, and is often better replaced with the more general *people* when describing a multi-cultural society like modern Britain.

countryman or **countrywoman**? *see* **non-sexist terms**.

countryside *see* **country** or **countryside**?

coup de grâce The French expression *coup de grâce* is a formal phrase used to refer to an event that finally destroys something: * *The latest bombings have effectively dealt a coup de grâce to the whole peace process*. The literal meaning

COUNTRIES AND PEOPLES

The right-hand column lists the words used as adjectives and nouns referring to the countries – and their people – given in the left-hand column. A single item in the right-hand column, such as 'Albanian', indicates that the same word is used as adjective and noun. 'Argentinian *or* Argentine' indicates that either of these words may be used as an adjective or a noun.

Where the adjective and noun are not identical, they are separated by a semicolon, with the adjective first: 'Danish; a Dane' indicates that *Danish* is the adjective and *Dane* the noun.

Most of the nouns can be converted to plural or collective form by adding -*s*: ● *the Albanians* ● *a party of Danes.* However, the plural and collective form of nouns ending in -*ese* and -*ois* is identical to the singular form: ● *the Chinese* ● *the Seychellois.* Other irregular plurals and collective forms are separated from the singular noun by a second semicolon, as at 'Lesothan; a Mosotho ...; the Basotho ...' and 'Irish; an Irishman (*or* -woman); the Irish'.

Note that the following list includes some overseas territories (such as Bermuda and the Cayman Islands), unincorporated territories (such as Puerto Rico) and aspirant states (such as East Timor and Taiwan) that are not universally recognised as fully independent countries in their own right. Cross-references, e.g. *see* **Chinese**, to main entries in the *Good Word Guide* are also included.

Afghanistan	**Afghan**	Bolivia	**Bolivian**
Albania	**Albanian**	Bosnia-	
Algeria	**Algerian**	Herzegovina	**Bosnian**
Andorra	**Andorran**	Botswana	**Botswanan**
Angola	**Angolan**	Brazil	**Brazilian**
Antigua and	**Antiguan**	Brunei	**Bruneian**
Barbuda		Bulgaria	**Bulgarian**
Argentina	**Argentinian** *or*	Burkina Faso	**Burkinabé**
	Argentine	Burma	*see* **Myanmar**
(*see* **Argentine** *or* **Argentinian**?)		Burundi	**Burundian**
Armenia	**Armenian**	Byelorussia	*see* **Belarus**
Australia	**Australian**	Cambodia	**Cambodian**
Austria	**Austrian**	Cameroon	**Cameroonian**
Azerbaijan	**Azeri** *or* **Azerbaijani**	Canada	**Canadian**
Bahamas, the	**Bahamian**	Cape Verde	**Cape Verdian** *or*
Bahrain	**Bahraini**		**Cape Verdean**
Bangladesh	**Bangladeshi**	Cayman Islands, the	**Caymanian;**
Barbados	**Barbadian**		**a Cayman Islander**
Belarus	**Belarusian**	Central African	
Belau	*see* **Palau**	Republic, the	**Central African**
Belgium	**Belgian**	Chad	**Chadian**
Belize	**Belizean**	Chile	**Chilean**
Benin	**Beninese** *or* **Beninois**	China	**Chinese** (*see* **Chinese**)
Bermuda	**Bermudan** *or*	Colombia	**Colombian**
	Bermudian	Comoros, the	**Comoran**
Bhutan	**Bhutanese**	Congo	**Congolese**

Costa Rica	**Costa Rican**	Grenada	**Grenadian**
Côte d'Ivoire	**Ivorian**	Guatemala	**Guatemalan**
Croatia	**Croatian; a Croat** *or*	Guinea	**Guinean**
	a Croatian	Guinea-Bissau	**Guinea-Bissauan**
Cuba	**Cuban**	Guyana	**Guyanese**
Cyprus	**Cypriot**		*or* **Guyanan**
Czech Republic	**Czech**	Haiti	**Haitian**
Denmark	**Danish; a Dane**	Holland	*see* **Netherlands, the**
Djibouti	**Djibouti**	Honduras	**Honduran**
Dominica	**Dominican**	Hungary	**Hungarian**
Dominican		Iceland	**Icelandic; an Icelander**
Republic, the	**Dominican**	India	**Indian**
East Timor	**East Timorese**	Indonesia	**Indonesian**
Ecuador	**Ecuadorean** *or*	Iran	**Iranian**
	Ecuadorian *or*	Iraq	**Iraqi**
	Ecuadoran	Ireland, Republic	**Irish; an Irishman**
Egypt	**Egyptian**	of (Eire)	(*or* **-woman**); **the**
El Salvador	**Salvadorean** *or*		**Irish**
	Salvadorian *or*	(*see also* **Northern Ireland** *in table*)
	Salvadoran	Israel	**Israeli**
England	**English; an**	Italy	**Italian**
	Englishman (*or*	Ivory Coast	*see* **Côte d'Ivoire**
	-woman);	Jamaica	**Jamaican**
	the English	Japan	**Japanese**
Equatorial Guinea	**Equatorial Guinean**	Jordan	**Jordanian**
Eritrea	**Eritrean**	Kazakhstan	**Kazakh**
Estonia	**Estonian**	Kenya	**Kenyan**
Ethiopia	**Ethiopian**	Kiribati	**Kiribati**
Falkland Islands,	**Falklands; a Falkland**	Korea	**Korean**
	Islander	(*see also* **North Korea, South Korea** *in*
Fiji	**Fijian**	*table*)
Finland	**Finnish; a Finn**	Kosovo	**Kosovan**
France	**French; a Frenchman**	Kuwait	**Kuwaiti**
	(*or* **-woman**);	Kyrgyzstan	**Kyrgyz; a Kyrgyzstani**
	the French	Laos	**Laotian** *or* **Lao**
Gabon	**Gabonese**	Latvia	**Latvian** *or* **Lettish;**
Gambia *or*			**a Latvian** *or* **a Lett**
the Gambia	**Gambian**	Lebanon	**Lebanese**
Georgia	**Georgian**	Lesotho	**Lesothan; a Mosotho**
Germany	**German**		*or* **a Lesothan; the**
Ghana	**Ghanaian**		**Basotho** *or* **the**
Gibraltar	**Gibraltarian**		**Lesothans**
Great Britain	**British; a Briton; the**	Liberia	**Liberian**
	British	Libya	**Libyan**
(*see* **Britain; Brit**)		Liechtenstein	**Liechtenstein;**
Greece	**Greek**		**a Liechtensteiner**
(*see* **Greek** *or* **Grecian**?)		Lithuania	**Lithuanian**

Luxembourg	**Luxembourg** *or* **Luxembourgian** *or* **Luxembourger;** a **Luxembourger**	Norway	**Norwegian**
		Oman	**Omani**
		Pakistan	**Pakistani**
		Palau	**Palauan**
Macedonia	**Macedonian**	Panama	**Panamanian**
Madagascar	**Madagascan** *or* **Malagasy;** a **Madagascan** *or* a **Malagasy**	Papua New Guinea	**Papua New Guinean**
		Paraguay	**Paraguayan**
		Peru	**Peruvian**
Malawi	**Malawian**	Philippines, the	**Philippine;** a **Filipino**
Malaysia	**Malaysian**	Poland	**Polish;** a **Pole**
Maldives, the	**Maldivian**	Portugal	**Portuguese**
Mali	**Malian**	Puerto Rico	**Puerto Rican**
Malta	**Maltese**	Qatar	**Qatari**
Marshall Islands	**Marshallese**	Romania	**Romanian**
Mauritania	**Mauritanian**	Russia	**Russian**
Mauritius	**Mauritian**	Rwanda	**Rwandan**
Mexico	**Mexican**	St Kitts and Nevis	**Kittitian**
Micronesia, Federated States of	**Micronesian**	St Lucia	**St Lucian**
Moldova	**Moldovan**	St Vincent and the Grenadines	**St Vincentian**
Monaco	**Monacan** *or* **Monegasque**	Samoa	**Samoan**
		San Marino	**San Marinese** *or* **Sanmarinese**
Mongolia	**Mongolian** *or* **Mongol**	Sâo Tomé and Príncipe	**Sâo Toméan**
Montenegro	**Montenegrin**		
Montserrat	**Montserratian**	Saudi Arabia	**Saudi Arabian** *or* **Saudi**
Morocco	**Moroccan**		
Mozambique	**Mozambican**	Scotland	**Scottish;** a **Scot** *or* a **Scotsman** (*or* -woman); the **Scots** *or* the **Scottish**
Myanmar (Burma)	**Myanmar** *or* **Burmese**		
Namibia	**Namibian**		
Nauru	**Nauruan**		
Nepal	**Nepalese**	(*see* **Scotch, Scots** *or* **Scottish**?)	
Netherlands, the	**Dutch;** a **Netherlander** *or* a **Dutchman** (*or* -woman); the **Dutch**	Senegal	**Senegalese**
		Serbia	**Serbian** *or* **Serb**
		Seychelles, the	**Seychellois**
		Sierra Leone	**Sierra Leonean**
New Zealand	**New Zealand;** a **New Zealander**	Singapore	**Singaporean**
		Slovakia	**Slovakian**
Nicaragua	**Nicaraguan**	Slovenia	**Slovenian**
Niger	**Nigerien**	Solomon Islands, the	**Solomon Islands;** a **Solomon Islander**
Nigeria	**Nigerian**		
Northern Ireland	**Northern Irish;** a **Northern Irishman** (*or* -woman); the **Northern Irish**	Somalia	**Somalian** *or* **Somali**
		South Africa	**South African**
		South Korea	**South Korean**
North Korea	**North Korean**	Spain	**Spanish;** a **Spaniard;** the **Spanish**

Sri Lanka	**Sri Lankan**	United Arab Emirates, the	**Emirati**
Sudan	**Sudanese**	United Kingdom, the, or the UK	**British; a Briton; the British**
Suriname	**Surinamese**		
Swaziland	**Swazi**		
Sweden	**Swedish; a Swede**	(see also **Great Britain**, **Northern Ireland** in table)	
Switzerland	**Swiss; a Swiss; the Swiss**		
Syria	**Syrian**	United States of America, the or the USA or the US	**American**
Taiwan	**Taiwanese**		
Tajikistan	**Tajik** or **Tadjik**		
Tanzania	**Tanzanian**	Uruguay	**Uruguayan**
Thailand	**Thai**	Uzbekistan	**Uzbek**
Togo	**Togolese**	Vanuatu	**Vanuatuan**
Tonga	**Tongan**	Vatican City	**Vatican**
Trinidad and Tobago	**Trinidadian** or **Tobagoan**	Venezuela	**Venezuelan**
		Vietnam	**Vietnamese**
Tunisia	**Tunisian**	Wales	**Welsh; a Welshman (or -woman); the Welsh**
Turkey	**Turkish; a Turk**		
Turkmenistan	**Turkmen**		
Tuvalu	**Tuvaluan**	Yemen	**Yemeni**
Uganda	**Ugandan**	Zambia	**Zambian**
Ukraine	**Ukrainian**	Zimbabwe	**Zimbabwean**

of the expression is 'stroke of mercy'. It is sometimes written or printed in italics and its anglicised pronunciation is [koo de *grahs*]. The accent on the *a* in *grace* is sometimes omitted.

coup d'état The French expression *coup d'état* is used to refer to a sudden, violent seizure of power in a country. The phrase is often shortened to simply *coup*. The literal meaning of the expression is 'stroke of state'. Note that it is sometimes written or printed in italics. The plural of *coup d'état* is *coups d'état*. Both the singular and plural have the same pronunciation: [koo day*tah*].

course see **coarse** or **course**?; **of course**.

cover The verb *cover* is followed by the preposition *in* or *with*: ● *The floor was covered in* [or *with*] *sawdust.*

crafted This word, meaning 'skilfully made', is sometimes used simply as a synonym for 'made' or 'produced' in exaggerated sales descriptions: ● *fitted cupboards crafted from the finest wood.* Many people dislike this usage.

craftsman or **craftswoman**? *see* **non-sexist terms**.

crash The adjectival use of *crash* in the sense of 'intensive' is best restricted to the few phrases in which it is most familiar: ● *a crash diet* ● *a crash course.* The word should not be used in contexts that may be associated with its sense of 'collision': ● *an intensive* [*crash*] *course in air-traffic control.*

creak or **creek**? *Creak* means 'make a scraping sound': ● *The door creaked on* *its hinges.* It should not be confused with *creek*, which variously means 'inlet or bay on a shoreline' or, in American English, 'stream flowing into a river': * *The smugglers hoped to lure the ship into the creek.* * *They followed the creek to the main river.* Both words are pronounced [kreek].

creative The adjective *creative* traditionally refers to originality and imagination used for artistic purposes: * *a creative mind* * *She is very creative.* It is increasingly used in a less favourable sense, describing something that stretches the limits of convention, legality, or truth: * *creative accounting/bookkeeping.*

credence or **credibility**? *Credence* is the state of believing something; *credibility* is the state of being believable: * *He gave credence to her explanation.* * *Her explanation lacked credibility.* The two nouns should not be confused.

    Credence, a formal word, is also used in the phrase *letters of credence*, meaning 'credentials'.

    Credibility is increasingly used as a vogue word meaning 'power to convince or impress': * *Appointing such a senior figure to the post would give instant credibility to any administration.*

    Credence and *credibility* should not be confused with *creed*, 'a set of beliefs'. *See also* **credible, creditable** or **credulous**?

credible, creditable or **credulous**? The three adjectives *credible, creditable*, and *credulous*, and their corresponding nouns *credibility, credit*, and *credulity*, are sometimes confused. *Credible* means 'believable': * *My story may sound barely credible but I assure you that it's true. Creditable* means

'deserving praise': * *Her readiness to forgive her attacker is creditable. Credulous* means 'gullible; too ready to believe': * *Only the most credulous person could believe such nonsense.* There is a further, fashionable use of *credible* to mean 'authentic; convincing': * *They serve a credible paella. See also* **credence** or **credibility**?

creed *see* **credence** or **credibility**?

credit crunch The term *credit crunch* became current during the worldwide financial collapse of 2008–9, referring specifically to the sudden reduction in the availability of bank loans or other credit: * *Construction businesses have been badly hit by the credit crunch.* It largely superseded such existing terms as *credit squeeze* and *credit crisis* but it remains to be seen whether it will enter general usage with reference to any credit shortage. Because of its slang characteristic, some users avoid the term in formal contexts. *See also* **toxic**.

creek *see* **creak** or **creek**?

creep *Creep* has recently acquired a new meaning beside that of 'move slowly' or 'approach' and may as a noun now denote an expansion of something beyond its intended or officially sanctioned scope: * *The American forces in Afghanistan could be leaving themselves open to charges of mission creep.* * *This a clear example of jargon creep.* In this usage, *creep* remains a vogue term and is best avoided in formal contexts.

crème de la crème The French expression *crème de la crème* is used to refer to the best people or things of their kind: * *The fee-paying schools take the* *crème de la crème of local children*. The literal meaning of the example is 'cream of the cream'. It is pronounced [krem dĕ lah *krem*].

crescendo *Crescendo* is a musical term that is frequently misused in both its technical and figurative senses. In music it describes a gradual increase in volume: • *The brass sections take up the theme as the crescendo builds up.* It can be used of other sounds or to describe any build-up of intensity: • *The baby's whimpering increased in a crescendo to a howl.* • *Public interest in the matter has risen in a crescendo.* Because people sometimes mistakenly refer to *building up/rising to a crescendo*, the word is often interpreted to mean the loud climax which is actually the culmination of a crescendo, and it is used to mean both 'a loud noise' and, in figurative contexts, 'peak, climax, or milestone': • *The drum solo ended in a deafening crescendo.* • *She reached the crescendo of her career before she was 30.*

cripple The term *cripple* is considered offensive by many people when referring to a person with a physical impairment. Careful users avoid *cripple* or *crippled* and prefer other terms: *see* **disabled**.

crisis *Crisis* literally means 'turning point' and it should be used for situations that have reached a turning point for better or worse, for decisive moments in dramas, and for crucial states of affairs where significant changes are likely: • *The illness had passed its crisis and it was clear that she would live.* • *the worsening economic crisis* • *It is feared that the crisis which resulted in the military coup may lead to civil war.* To the dislike of some

people, *crisis* is now often applied to situations which are worrying or serious but without any definite implication of imminent change: • *Independent television is facing a crisis through declining audiences* (*Daily Telegraph*), or for quite trivial problems: • *I've got a crisis here – my zip's broken.*

Note the spelling of the plural of *crisis*, which is *crises*, pronounced [*krīseez*].

criterion or **criteria**? The word *criterion*, meaning 'a standard by which to judge or evaluate something', is a singular noun: • *Exam results were the only criterion for deciding whether candidates should be interviewed.* The plural of *criterion* is *criteria*: • *on the condition that the basic criteria of the code are accepted and met* (*The Bookseller*). Many people take *criteria* to be a singular noun with the plural *criterias*. This is wrong. It is, however, acceptable to use the phrase *set of criteria* as an alternative to *criterion* when a singular expression is required: • *Pay awards may be given according to the following set of criteria.*

The noun *criterion* is followed by the preposition *of* or *for*: • *the only criterion of* [or *for*] *success.*

critic or **critique**? A *critic* is someone who criticises. The word is sometimes used in the sense of someone who finds fault or expresses disapproval: • *Acupuncture has many critics in the medical profession.* It is also used of someone who is employed to evaluate works of art, music, or literature: • *The public loved the play but the critics did not have a good word to say for it.* A *critique* is a work of criticism, usually applied to an academic work which analyses and discusses ideas in depth: * *This is a thoughtful critique of logical positivism.*

critical *Critical* means 'inclined to judge severely': * *My mother is so critical of the way I bring up the children*; 'involving careful or scholarly evaluation': * *a critical account of Jung's work*; or 'involving a turning point; crucial': * *We are at a critical point in our negotiations.* This last use is often applied to serious or dangerous illnesses or injuries: * *in a critical condition* and has in its turn led to such uses as: * *A woman was later described as 'critical' in hospital, with one wrist almost severed* (*Daily Telegraph*).

critique *see* **critic** *or* **critique**?

crochet *or* **crotchet**? The noun *crochet* refers to a type of needlework; the noun *crotchet* is the name of a note in music. *Crochet* is a word of French origin that retains the French pronunciation [krōshay] in English. The past tense of the verb *crochet* is *crocheted*, spelt with a single *t* and pronounced [krōshayd].

The noun *crotchet*, pronounced [krochit], has the derived adjective *crotchety*, which means 'irritable' in informal English.

cross-section A *cross-section* is a piece of something which has been cut off at right angles, or a drawing of the dimensions revealed by such a cutting: * *The diagram shows an artery in cross-section.* The expression is more often used popularly to mean 'a typical or representative sample': * *Over five thousand people were interviewed as a cross-section of the general public.*

crotch *or* **crutch**? Either noun may be used to denote the angle between a person's legs (hence, the genital area) or the corresponding part of a garment (such as a pair of trousers). The term *crotch* is more frequently used in these senses, but *crutch* is not incorrect. The principal meaning of the noun *crutch* is 'support used by people with injured legs or feet': * *She was on crutches for three months after the accident.*

crotchet *see* **crochet** *or* **crotchet**?

crucial The use of *crucial* as a synonym for *important* is best avoided in formal speech and writing, where it should be restricted to the sense of 'decisive' or 'critical': * *constituencies where the self-employed vote could be crucial to the outcome of the election* (*Daily Telegraph*). *Crucial* is widely used in informal contexts, and increasingly by journalists, broadcasters, advertisers, and others, to emphasise the importance of events or issues that are by no means decisive or critical. The word has the same derivation as *crux*, meaning 'a decisive point', which is most frequently encountered in the expression *the crux of the matter.*

crutch *see* **crotch** *or* **crutch**?

cue *or* **queue**? *Cue* means 'signal': * *The actor heard his cue.* It also means 'rod, as in the games of billiards, snooker, etc.': * *teach someone how to hold their cue properly.* It should not be confused with *queue*, which means 'line' or 'sequence': * *a queue of traffic.*

cuisine The word *cuisine* is used to describe a style of cooking food, particularly one which is typical of a particular country or region: * *Peppers and tomatoes are characteristic of Basque cuisine*; for the food itself: * *Their cuisine is excellent*; and in various phrases which convey a particular style of cooking: * *nouvelle cuisine* * *cuisine minceur*. *Cuisine* carries a suggestion of good food skilfully cooked, so its use in such a sentence as: * *It was typical service-station cuisine – chips with everything* is either inappropriate or jocular. The word is pronounced [kwiz*ee*n].

cullender *see* **calendar**, **calender** or **colander**?

culminate *Culminate* means 'form a summit; reach the highest or most crucial point': * *The church culminates in a steeple.* * *Her rise in society culminated in her marriage to an earl.* The word is very often used as though it were merely a synonym for result or conclude: * *The growing unrest culminated in industrial action.* This use is so widespread as to be generally accepted, although some careful users object to it.

The verb *culminate* is followed by the preposition *in*: * *The rebellion culminated in civil war.*

cult Some people dislike the adjectival use of the word *cult* to refer to a particular person, idea, activity, etc., that arouses great popular interest, especially for a short period of time: * *a cult movie* * *a cult book* * *a cult figure.* Care should be taken to avoid overusing the word in this way.

cultured or **cultivated**? *Cultured* and *cultivated* are almost synonymous in that they are both used to mean 'edu-

cated, refined'. *Cultured* is particularly applied to education in terms of an understanding and appreciation of the arts: * *They were cultured people who attended concerts and art galleries*, while *cultivated* is applied to behaviour and speech: * *He gradually dropped his Cockney twang and spoke in a soft, cultivated accent.* Both *cultured* and *cultivated* also have connections with things that are produced artificially: * *cultured pearls* * *cultivated plants.*

cumulative *see* **accumulative** or **cumulative**?

curb or kerb? These two spellings may sometimes be confused. *Curb* means 'check or control': * *He curbed his anger.* A *kerb* is the edge of a pavement; in American English this word is spelt *curb*.

currant or **current**? A *currant* is a small seedless dried grape used in cookery: * *She always put lots of currants in her cakes*, or any of several different soft fruits: * *redcurrant jam* * *blackcurrant juice.* A *current* is a steady flow: * *They did not swim because the current was very strong.* * *250 volts, alternating current.*

current The adjective *current* means 'occurring in or belonging to the present time; presently existing or in progress': * *Current techniques for treating the disease are acknowledged to be inadequate*; a further meaning is 'accepted or prevalent at this time': * *The current opinions of American Catholics are in conflict with the Vatican.* *Current* and *currently* are often used superfluously where there is no need to emphasise that the present is being discussed, rather than the past or future: * *The company currently employs over a thousand people.*

curriculum This word, meaning 'programme of courses available or subjects studied in a school or college': * *a wide-ranging sixth-form curriculum* * *the National Curriculum,* is sometimes misspelt. Not that the only double letters are *-rr-*, as in *current.* A *curriculum vitae*, often abbreviated to *CV*, is a summary of a person's career and qualifications, often required when applying for a job. *Vitae* may be pronounced [veetī] or [vītee].

curtsy or **curtsey**? The noun and verb *curtsy* refer to a formal greeting made by a girl or woman in which the head and shoulders are lowered, the knees are bent and the skirt is held outwards with both hands: * *She curtsied to the Queen.* The alternative spelling *curtsey* is also acceptable.

customer *see* **client** or **customer**?

cutting edge Some people dislike the frequent use of the phrase *cutting edge* in the figurative sense of 'forefront': * *at the cutting edge of information technology.* See also **leading-edge**.

cyber- This prefix is commonly used in the context of high-technology communication and information systems and virtual reality: * *cybercafe* * *cybercrime* * *cyberoptics* * *cyberspace*. The word may also be used independently: * *the cyber age*. Caution should be exercised in adopting some of the very informal coinages: * *cybersex* * *cybersquatting*.

cymbal or **symbol**? Note the spelling of these words, which have the same pronunciation [simbăl]. A *cymbal* is a circular brass percussion instrument; a *symbol* is a sign or design that represents something else: * *the clash of cymbals* * *The dove is a symbol of peace.*

cynical or **sceptical**? A *cynical* person is a person who has a distrust of human nature and sincerity, believing others to be motivated by self-interest: * *He had a cynical belief that nobody took up law or medicine for any reason but the money. Sceptical* (American English, *skeptical*) means 'doubtful, unwilling to believe without rational proof': * *While accepting Jesus' moral teachings she remained sceptical about the miracles and the resurrection.*

czar *see* **tsar** or **czar**?

D

dangling participles Participles that are used to introduce a phrase which is attached to a later-mentioned subject: * *Startled by the noise she dropped her book.* * *Being by now very tired, we stopped at a pub.* There is a tendency, though, for such introductory participles to become apparently attached to the wrong noun: * *Startled by the noise, her book fell to the floor.* * *Being by now very tired, a pub was a welcome sight.* It was not the book that was startled or the pub that was tired. Then there is the sentence where the participle appears to have no subject at all, which is the thought behind the term *dangling participle* (also known as *unattached*, or *unrelated participle*): * *Lying in the sun, it felt as though it had always been summer.* Who, or what, was lying in the sun? Some participles are habitually used in a manner where they might be thought to dangle, but they are usually being used as prepositions or conjunctions, and such use is acceptable: * *Speaking of fruit, does anyone want an apple?* * *Considering the odds against them, they did well.* * *Regarding your enquiry, I have pleasure in enclosing our catalogue.* On the borderline is the increasingly popular use of *having said that*: * *Having said that, the West Indies still look certain to win*, which is considered unacceptable by many people.

dare The verb *dare* can be used in two different ways. It can be used as a full verb, followed by an infinitive with *to*: * *I dare you to jump.* * *We'll see if she* *dares to contradict him*; or it can be an auxiliary or modal verb, followed by an infinitive without *to*: * *He dared not go there at night.* * *How dare you say that?* As an auxiliary the verb is only used in the forms *dare* and *dared*, and only in negative and interrogative constructions.

The expression *dare say* means 'suppose, expect, or think likely': * *I dare say we'll go to Bognor again.* It is only used in the present tense and in the first person, and is sometimes written as one word: * *I daresay.*

DASH Dashes can be used both singly and in pairs. Though the dash is useful, most of its functions can be performed by other punctuation marks, and excessive use of the dash is sometimes considered to be a mark of a careless writer. A sentence should never contain more than one dash or pair of dashes. *See* panel, on page 112.

data *Data* means 'facts, information that can be used as a basis for analysis, etc.': * *We have data on road accidents for the past thirty years. Data* is actually a plural, with the singular *datum*, but the singular is rarely used and *data* has come to be regarded as a collective noun, which is appropriate to its use for a body or aggregate of information. There is still considerable controversy as to whether it should take a singular or plural verb. In American English the singular verb is now usual: * *This is essential data*, and such use is becoming increasingly

111

DASH	
1 Double dash	The double dash is used to mark a break in a sentence, very much in the same way as round brackets: * *My mother – a Yorkshire-woman by birth – had little time for Londoners.* As with parentheses, the material enclosed by dashes should be able to be removed leaving the sentence grammatically complete. Commas should not be used with double dashes.
2 Single dash	A single dash is used to introduce a statement summarising what has gone before: * *Beer, chips, and cigarettes – these are the main threats to the nation's health.* It is also used to introduce an after-thought or a sharp change in subject or continuity: * *I'm surprised to see Nigel here – he's usually late.* * *You take two eggs – but perhaps you don't even like omelettes?* * *I don't believe it – caviare!*
3 Other uses	Dashes are used to indicate an unfinished sentence or hesitant speech: * *I think he's – ? I – um – er – I don't er – know.* They are often used to precede the attribution of a quotation: * *'No man is an island'* – *Donne.* They are, occasionally, used to indicate an omission of part of a name, and to replace all or part of an obscenity: * *I travelled to the small mountain town of L–.* * *It's none of your –ing business.* They are also used between points in space or time, where they are equivalent to *to*: * *London–Paris* * *1914–18.*
4 Use as a colon	A dash may be thought of as a less formal punctuation mark than a colon: * *This word means 'like a goat' – Lloyd George was known as 'the Goat'.* For dashes with colons, *see* **colon**.

frequent in British English. However, some careful users (especially those working within scientific and medical circles) still insist on using the noun as a plural: * *These are essential data.*

The pronunciation [*day*tă] is pre-ferred, although [*dah*tă] is acceptable and is usual in American English.

dates It is usual to write dates in figures, rather than words, except in some very formal contexts, such as legal documents. There are various ways of expressing dates: * *5 October 2012* is becoming the standard form in Britain in preference to *5th October, 2012* and *October 5th, 2012.* The

standard form in the United States is *October 5 2012.* The abbreviated form *5.10.12* or *5/10/12* is acceptable in informal use but should be used with caution, as this abbreviation would mean the tenth of May in the United States, where the fifth of October would be abbreviated to *10.5.12.* In at least one exceptional circumstance, however, the US version has become widely familiar else-where in the world and is not reordered: * *9/11* (or *9-11, nine-eleven, nine-one-one*), referring to the terrorist attacks on the United States that took place on 11 September 2001.

Centuries may be written as numbers or written out in full: * *the 19th century* or * *the nineteenth century*, and the abbreviation AD usually precedes the date, while BC follows it: * *AD 527* * *1000 BC* (*see also* **AD** and **BC**).

The apostrophe in a series of years is nowadays generally omitted: * *in the 1990s* * *the 1800s*.

Specific years are usually rendered in numerical form. Sometimes a year date may be rendered in abbreviated form where the fuller form is felt to be unnecessary: * *He died in the 14–18 war.* * *If only we had known that back in '39.* * *Let's have another bottle of '47 Lafitte.* * *Do you remember the summer of '69?* Another abbreviated form appears to be limited to the year 2000, marking the turn of the millennium: * *Y2K* (for 'the year 2000'). *See also* **centuries**; **numbers**; **millennium**.

de- The prefix *de-* is used to signify 'the opposite or reverse': * *declassify*, 'removal': * *descale*, or 'reduction': * *degrade*. As a productive prefix, *de-* is constantly being used to create new words: * *desegregate* (to reverse a practice or law involving racial segregation), * *de-escalate* (to decrease in scope or extent), * *deinstitutionalise* (to release patients from an institution), * *delist* (to remove from a list of approved items), * *demerger* (the separation of previously merged companies). Some users object to the coining of such forms.

deadly or **deathly**? *Deadly* means 'likely to cause death'; *deathly* refers to a characteristic of death: * *a deadly weapon* * *a deathly silence*. *Deadly* is sometimes used in place of *deathly* in figurative contexts: * *'Goodbye,' she said, with a deadly finality*. Both words may be used adverbially: * *deadly quiet* * *deathly pale*. In informal contexts the adjective *deadly* can also mean 'extremely boring': * *The party was deadly*.

deaf Because of its negative associations, and because there are many different degrees of hearing-impairment, the word *deaf* is sometimes avoided by careful writers in general reference to people who have difficulties with their hearing. Preferred terms include *hearing-impaired*: * *This loop system is a great help to the hearing-impaired*. Similarly, those with perfect hearing may be termed *hearing-people*. *See also* **profoundly deaf**.

deaf-mute This term, describing a person who cannot hear or speak, is no longer considered acceptable by many people, who prefer the less offensive alternative **profoundly deaf**. The alternative *deaf-and-dumb* is similarly considered old-fashioned and offensive as it may suggest that the person concerned is incapable of communication of any kind.

deal The verb *deal*, in the sense of 'buy and sell', is followed by the preposition *in*: * *They deal in antique furniture*. In the sense of 'see to, tackle, look after' it is followed by *with*: * *The police were called in to deal with the riot*.

dear or **deer**? *Dear* variously means 'beloved', 'expensive', or 'appealing': * *This is my dear wife*. * *The prices in that shop are very dear*. * *What a dear little picture*. It should not be confused with *deer*, which denotes the animal. Both words are pronounced [deer].

debris This word, meaning 'rubble or remains': *They removed the debris from the building site*, is stressed on the first syllable [*deb*ri]. The variant pronunciation [*day*bri] is widely used, and this pronunciation should be used when the word is written with an acute accent: * *débris*.

debut *Debut*, meaning 'first appearance': * *He made his debut in a James Bond film*, may be pronounced [*day*bew] or [*de*bew]. If the word is spelt with an acute accent: * *début*, the first pronunciation should be used. Many users dislike the use of *debut* as a verb: * *She debuted last month*.

deca- or **deci-**? The prefix *deca-* means 'ten times'; the prefix *deci-* means 'one tenth': * *decagon* * *decibel*. A *decametre* is ten metres; a *decimetre* is one tenth of a metre. Note the difference in pronunciation, particularly the hard *c* [k] of *deca-* and the soft *c* [s] of *deci-*.

decade The word *decade*, denoting a period of ten years, is variously pronounced [*de*kayd] or [di*kayd*]. Either pronunciation may be used, although some people disapprove of the latter, more recent, version.

deceitful or **deceptive**? Both *deceitful* and *deceptive* imply misleading appearances or cheating. However, *deceitful* suggests an intention to deceive or mislead, even if not successful, and therefore carries negative moral overtones: * *It was deceitful of you to pretend to be an orphan*. *Deceptive* applies to a misleading effect or result rather than dishonest motivation, and something might be unintentionally deceptive: * *The ring's dull appearance was deceptive, for on closer inspection it turned out to be gold*.

deceive This word is often misspelt. Note the *-ei-* spelling, which conforms to the rule '*i* before *e* except after *c*'. *See also* **spelling**.

decent or **decorous**? Both these adjectives can mean 'socially acceptable': * *decent/decorous behaviour*. *Decorous*, a formal word, is largely restricted to this sense, whereas *decent* has the additional meanings of 'not obscene', 'adequate', 'morally correct', 'obliging; pleasant', etc.: * *decent language* * *a decent meal* * *to do the decent thing* * *He's a decent enough fellow*. In the sense of 'not obscene', *decent* is not as frequent as its opposite *indecent* ('obscene').

deceptive *see* **deceitful** or **deceptive**?

deceptively The adverb *deceptively* suggests misleading appearances and is used to indicate that something is not as suggested by the following adjective: * *a semi-detached house offering deceptively spacious accommodation* (advertisement, *Chichester Observer*).

deci- *see* **deca-** or **deci-**?

decidedly or **decisively**? *Decidedly* usually means 'definitely; unquestionably': * *It was a decidedly welcome suggestion*. It is also sometimes used to mean 'firmly; resolutely', and *decisively* is used in the same way: * *'I'm going ahead with it,' she said decidedly/decisively*. *Decisively* is also used to imply decision-making that is marked by firmness, confidence, and lack of wavering: * *He studied the options* *briefly before decisively choosing the second one. Decisive* can be applied to anything which makes a particular outcome inevitable: * *a decisive goal* is the one that decides the result of the match; *decisively* is also used in this sense: * *Her conduct at the interview influenced the board decisively.*

decimate *Decimate* literally means 'destroy one in ten', from the Roman practice of killing every tenth soldier as a punishment for mutiny. The word is now used popularly to mean 'inflict considerable damage; destroy a large part of': * *The weather decimated today's sports programme* (BBC TV). This use probably arises from the mistaken belief that the word means 'destroy all but a tenth' and, although the usage is very widespread, many careful users still dislike it. *Decimate* should not be used to mean 'annihilate totally', or in such constructions as: * *badly decimated* * *utterly decimated* * *Some 75 per cent of the cattle were decimated by the disease.*

decisively *see* **decidedly** *or* **decisively**?

decolorise *see* **colourise**.

décor The noun *décor*, meaning 'interior decoration' or 'stage decoration', may be spelt with or without the acute accent in English. The pronunciation is [*day*kor] or [*de*kor]. Some users prefer the spelling *décor* and the pronunciation [*day*kor], being closer to the original French.

decorous *see* **decent** *or* **decorous**?

decriminalise *or* **legalise**? These two verbs are virtually interchangeable in the sense of 'make no longer illegal': *

to legalise [or *decriminalise*] *the smoking of cannabis. Legalise* is the more frequent, and is used in a wider range of contexts in the sense of 'make legal': * *to legalise independent radio stations.* The verb *decriminalise* emphasises the (former) criminality of the practice to which it refers, and may be more emotive than *legalise*: * *He was an ardent supporter of the campaign to decriminalise homosexuality.*

decry *or* **descry**? To *decry* an idea or plan is to criticise or denounce it strongly: * *The report decried television news for concentrating on disaster and conflict. Descry* is a formal word and is much more rare than *decry*; it means 'to notice something, especially at a distance': * *descry the coast on a clear day.* Etymologically both *decry* and *descry* derive from Old French *descrier*, to proclaim or decry.

deduce *or* **deduct**? To *deduce* is to come to a logical conclusion; to *deduct* is to subtract: * *I deduced that she was lying.* * *He deducted £10 from the bill.* The two verbs have the derived noun *deduction* in common: * *the deduction that she was lying* * *a deduction of £10.*

deer *see* **dear** *or* **deer**?

de facto The Latin phrase *de facto* refers to something that exists in actual fact, whether or not that is justified or was intended: * *de facto recognition of the state's independence.* The literal meaning of the phrase is 'in actual fact'. Note that it is sometimes written or printed in italics. *See also* **de jure**.

defective *or* **deficient**? *Defective* means 'having a fault; not working properly':

* *The washing machine I bought yesterday turned out to be defective.* *Deficient* means 'having a lack': * *She sings well but her voice is deficient in power.* While *deficient* can be applied to concrete as well as abstract nouns: * *Your diet is deficient in calcium,* it is not usually applied to manufactured objects. *Defective* is usually applied to concrete nouns, including manufactured objects, but can be applied to some abstract nouns, particularly those denoting some physical quality: * *His colour vision is defective.*

defence The noun *defence*: * *the importance of the country's defence,* is spelt with a *c* in British English, while the adjective *defensive* is spelt with an *s*: * *The players adopted a defensive strategy.* In American English the noun is spelt with an *s*.

defensible or **defensive**? An opinion, idea, etc., that is *defensible* is one that is capable of being defended: * *the most morally defensible method of calculating payment.* *Defensive* is used more frequently and refers to things or actions that protect someone or something: * *the strong defensive walls of the city.* *Defensive* is also used to describe the behaviour of a person reacting to criticism and, in sports contexts, actions that prevent an opponent from scoring in a competition: * *take up a defensive position.* To be *on the defensive* is to be prepared to fend off an expected attack or criticism.

defer The verb *defer* is followed by the preposition *to*: * *She deferred to our wishes.*

deficient *see* **defective** or **deficient**?

defining clause *see* **restrictive clause.**

definite or **definitive**? These two words are sometimes confused, although their meanings are different. *Definite* means 'precise, exact, or unambiguous': * *The rules draw a definite distinction between professionals and amateurs.* *Definitive* means 'final; conclusive': * *This is the definitive game in the tournament,* and is frequently used in criticism in the sense of 'authoritative' to describe a work or performance that is unlikely to be improved on: * *Painter has written the definitive biography of Proust.* Careful users avoid the vague use of *definite* for emphasis: * *He has a definite resemblance to Winston Churchill.*

definite article *see* **the.**

definitely This word, meaning 'certainly': * *He was definitely going to win,* is sometimes misspelt, the most frequent error being the replacement of the second *i* with an *a*.

definitive *see* **definite** or **definitive**?

defuse or **diffuse**? To *defuse* is to remove the device that causes a bomb to explode; to *diffuse* is to spread: * *The bomb was defused.* * *The light was diffused.* The two verbs are sometimes confused, being similar in pronunciation: *defuse* is pronounced [dee*fewz*] and *diffuse* is pronounced [di*fewz*]. The adjective *diffuse*, meaning 'widely spread', has a final *s* sound [di*fews*].

The verb *defuse* is also used in figurative contexts, meaning 'make less tense': * *The President hopes to defuse the current highly charged atmosphere.*

degree The phrase *to a degree* has two meanings, 'somewhat' and 'extremely':
* *The match was exciting to a degree.*
This may give rise to ambiguity, as in the above example: how exciting was the match? The use of the phrase in the sense of 'extremely' should be restricted to informal contexts.

The phrases *to a surprising/considerable/lesser/etc., degree* are often better replaced by a simple adverb, such as *surprisingly/considerably/less/etc. To what degree...?* may be replaced by *How much...?* or *To what extent...?*

deity The pronunciation of *deity* is either [*day*iti] or [*dee*eiti]. Although the former is widely used, the latter is the more traditional pronunciation.

déjà vu The French phrase *déjà vu* is used to refer to the feeling a person may get that they have already experienced a present situation: * *As we came into the village we had a strange sense of déjà vu.* In modern usage it may also describe something that is so often repeated it has become hackneyed and stale: * *That style is so déjà vu.* The literal meaning of *déjà vu* is 'already seen'. Its anglicised pronunciation is [dayzhah *voo*].

de jure The Latin phrase *de jure* refers to something that exists or is so by legal right: * *the de jure leaders.* The literal meaning of the phrase is 'by right'. Note that it is sometimes written or printed in italics. It is pronounced [day *jooray*] or [day *yooray*]. *See also* **de facto**.

delirious Note the spelling of this adjective, particularly the first two vowels - *e*- and -*i*-. The correct pronunciation is [di*lirr*iŭs], with the short [i] of

squirrel, not [di*leer*iŭs]. *Delirious* is the adjective that derives from *delirium*, 'a confused mental state resulting from a feverish illness' or 'a state of great excitement or happiness'.

deliver Some people dislike the intransitive use of the verb *deliver* in the sense of 'fulfil a promise or commitment': * *The government has failed to deliver on tax cuts.* * *We don't just want people with good ideas; we want people who will deliver.* This usage is derived from the very informal expression *deliver the goods*, which originated in American slang in about 1850 and has the same meaning.

deliverance or **delivery**? Both these nouns are derived from the verb *deliver*. *Deliverance* specifically refers to the act of delivering from danger, captivity, evil, etc., and is used in formal or literary contexts; *delivery* is used in the many other senses of the verb: * *to pray for deliverance* * *the delivery of a baby* * *postal deliveries* * *the delivery of a speech*.

delusion *see* **allusion**, **illusion** or **delusion**?

demi-, **hemi-** or **semi-**? All three prefixes mean 'half': * *demigod* * *hemisphere* * *semicircle*. *Semi-* is the most frequent, and may be used to form new words: * *semiprofessional* * *semi-independent*. *Hemi-* is found in a number of scientific terms: * *hemihydrate* (a term used in chemistry) * *hemiplegia* (paralysis of one side of the body). *Demi-* is chiefly found in words of French origin: * *demitasse* (a small cup) * *demilune* (a crescent-shaped formation). The noun *hemidemisemiquaver* – the name of a note in music that is one eighth of the length of a quaver – is the only word in English that makes use of all three prefixes.

demise The original meaning of *demise* was 'the transfer of an estate or of sovereignty'; because such a transfer was frequently the result of death, the word came to mean 'death': * *We were sad to hear of the demise of your husband.* This usage is formal and somewhat outdated. *Demise* can be used figuratively to mean 'the ending of existence or activity': *The demise of the steel industry in Consett caused massive unemployment in the area.* Its use to mean merely 'failure' or 'decline': *the demise of the cinema* should be avoided.

denote *see* **connote** or **denote**?

denouement This word, meaning 'final outcome': * *the stunning denouement of the novel,* may be spelt *denouement* or *dénouement.* Note the *-oue-* vowels in the middle of the word. The usual pronunciation is [day*noo*moon(g)], although in American English the word may be stressed on the first or third syllables.

deny *see* **refute** or **deny**?

depend *Depend* means 'be contingent': * *It depends on the weather,* or 'be reliant': * *They depend on Social Security.* It is normally used with *on* or *upon,* except in certain constructions where it is the subject: * *It depends whether I'm well enough.* * *It depends what you mean by socialism.* This usage is widespread but disliked by some careful users who insist on the word *on* or *upon* following *depend* in all cases. The expression: * *It all*

depends, as a complete utterance, is acceptable only in informal speech.

dependant or **dependent**? The adjective, meaning 'reliant', is spelt *dependent*: * *industries that are dependent on North Sea gas* * *He is completely dependent on other people's help.* The noun, meaning 'someone who relies on another person for financial support', is spelt *dependant*: * *Apart from your children, do you have any dependants?* The two are often confused, as in a leaflet for Exmoor Area Tourist Attractions: * *But this freedom will remain largely dependant upon visitors respecting the life of the countryside.* Note that in American English the noun *dependant* is often spelt *dependent.*

dependence or **dependency**? Either noun may be used to mean 'the state of being dependent', but *dependence* is the more frequent in this sense: * *his dependence/dependency on his parents* * *her dependence/dependency on alcohol.* *Dependency* can also mean 'territory that is controlled by another nation': * *one of Britain's dependencies.* It cannot be replaced by *dependence* in this sense. Note the spellings of the two words: the endings *-ance* and *-ancy* are American variants. *See also* **dependant** or **dependent**?

dependent *see* **dependant** or **dependent**?

deploy *Deploy* is a military term meaning 'organise troops or equipment so that they are in the most effective position': * *the decision to deploy the Marines in the Middle East.* Careful users object to the frequent use of the word with reference to any utilisation or organisation of resources: * *It will be up to you to set ambitious revenue targets and then train, develop, and deploy your team-members to ensure that those targets are met and surpassed* (*Daily Telegraph*).

deprecate or **depreciate**? *Deprecate* means 'express disapproval of': * *She deprecated the Government's record on equal opportunities*. *Depreciate* means 'reduce in value', where it is usually used intransitively: * *It depreciates by about £100 every year*, and 'belittle or disparage': * *He depreciated their attempts to talk English*. *Deprecate* is often used instead of *depreciate* in the sense of 'disparage' and is also extended to mean 'play down; show modesty'. This usage of *deprecate* is disliked by some people, although it is acceptable in the well-established use of *self-deprecating*: * *Jewish humour tends to be ironical and self-deprecating*.

depression or **recession**? The terms *depression* and *recession* are sometimes confused. Definitions of both terms are hotly debated by economists, and different authorities stipulate different conditions that must be met before a *recession* (a relatively subdued economic slowdown) can properly be said to have become a *depression* (a full-blown collapse in economic activity). These typically relate to the rate of growth in an economy, to rates of investment and to rising unemployment figures. One definition of *depression* that is often accepted in the press, if not by economists, is a decline in the gross domestic product over two or more consecutive quarters.

deprived *Deprived* means 'having something taken away or withheld': *

Brain damage can occur if a baby is deprived of oxygen during labour. It should properly be applied to things that were once possessed or would be possessed in normal circumstances, but the modern tendency is to connect it with basic necessities and rights. As an adjective it has become a vogue word often meaning little more than 'poor': * *It is always the most deprived women, usually with housing problems or of low intelligence, who are involved* (*The Times*).

de rigueur The French expression *de rigueur* means 'required by social custom': * *Evening dress is de rigueur at the dinner*. The literal meaning of *de rigueur* is 'of strictness'. It is pronounced [dĕ rĭ*ger*].

derisive or **derisory**? *Derisive* means 'expressing derision; mocking or scornful': * *His speech was received with derisive mirth*. *Derisory* means 'deserving derision': * *It was a derisory performance*. *Derisory* is used particularly in the sense of 'ridiculously inadequate; contemptibly small': * *He was retired with a derisory pension* (BBC Radio).

derived words *Derived words* are formed by adding fixed groups of letters at the beginning or end of another word. The noun *sadness* is derived from the adjective *sad*; the adjective *readable* is derived from the verb *read*; the adverb *boldly* is derived from the adjective *bold*; the noun *membership* is derived from the noun *member*. Sometimes the base form of the word changes in the derived form: the *-y* of *happy*, for example, changes to *-i-* in the derived forms *happily* and *happiness*.

New words are also formed by adding prefixes or inflectional endings, such as *-s*, *-ed*, *-ing*, *-er*, and *-est*: * *unhappy* * *members* * *reading* * *bolder*. Some derived words are more complex: * *unknowingly*, for example, consists of the base form *know* plus *un-*, *-ing*, and *-ly*. *See also* **prefixes**; **suffixes**.

descendant or **descendent** *Descendant* is a noun meaning 'someone descended from a particular ancestor': * *She was a descendant of the fourth duke.* It should not be confused with the adjective *descendent*, which describes something moving downwards: * *The aeroplane continued in a descendent arc towards the hills.* Both words are pronounced [disendănt].

descry *see* **decry** or **descry**?

desert or **dessert**? These words are sometimes confused. *Dessert* is the last course of a meal (*see* **dessert**, **sweet**, **pudding** or **afters**?): * *a deliciously sweet dessert* * *a dessert spoon.* *Desert* is used in all other contexts: * *the Sahara desert* * *She got her just deserts.* * *a deserted city.* The verb *desert* is often followed by the preposition *from*: * *He deserted from his regiment.*

As a noun, *desert* is usually pronounced [dezăt]; as a verb (or in the noun phrase *just deserts*) it is pronounced [dizert]. *Dessert* is pronounced [dizert].

desiccated This word, meaning 'dried': * *desiccated coconut*, is sometimes misspelt. Note the single *s* and the *-cc-*. It is worth remembering the Latin words *de* and *siccare*, meaning 'to dry', from which the word originates.

design *see* **invent**, **design** or **discover**?

desirable or **desirous**? *Desirable* means 'worth desiring or having': * *a desirable residence* * *Confrontation with the union is not desirable at this stage.* *Desirous*, which means 'desiring; wanting', is a more formal adjective, usually placed after the verb and followed by *of*: * *to be desirous of peace* * *The president is desirous of your opinion.* The two adjectives should not be confused.

despair or **desperation**? The noun *despair* means 'loss of hope': * *a feeling of utter despair* * *She gave up in despair.* The noun *desperation* is often applied to a reckless act that results from despair: * *In desperation he jumped out of the window.* Note the spelling of *desperation*, particularly the second *-e-*, which is sometimes wrongly replaced with the *-a-* of *despair*.

despatch or **dispatch**? Both of these spellings are acceptable for the verb meaning 'send quickly' or the noun meaning 'message or report': * *The letter was immediately despatched/dispatched.* * *The despatch/dispatch arrived that afternoon.*

desperate This word, meaning 'having no hope': * *a desperate man* * *a desperate situation*, is sometimes misspelt. The middle part of the word is spelt *-per-*, not *-par-* as in *separate*.

desperation *see* **despair** or **desperation**?

despite or **in spite of**? *Despite* and in spite of are completely interchangeable: * *Despite/In spite of his injury, his playing was superb.* *In spite of* is used rather more frequently, although *despite* has the advantage of brevity. *Despite* needs no preposition; *despite of* is incorrect, and it is never necessary to precede either *despite* or *in spite of* with *but*.

dessert, **sweet**, **pudding** or **afters**? The question of how the sweet (usually) last course of a meal is referred to in Britain is not fixed. Usage not only varies slightly from one individual, family, etc., to another, but also is currently changing. Generally, *dessert* is found in both spoken and written contexts: * *For dessert we were offered ice cream and fruit.* *Sweet* is more informal, is found in spoken English, and is considered by some middle- and upper-class people to be unacceptable. Such users prefer the word *pudding* to refer generally to the last course of a meal, but this may be becoming slightly old-fashioned. *Afters* is used in very informal spoken English: * *What's for afters, Mum? Pudding* has a number of other culinary senses. It may refer to a cooked sweet or savoury dish containing flour, eggs, etc.: * *treacle pudding* * *Yorkshire pudding*, or to a sausage-like savoury preparation * *black pudding*. These connotations may make it seem an inappropriate term for a light dessert, such as ice cream or fruit. *Dessert* traditionally denotes a course of fruit, dates, nuts, etc., served at the end of a meal. *See also* **desert** or **dessert**?

destined *Destined* means 'being determined or intended in advance; directed towards, or having a particular purpose or end': * *She believed her son was destined to be the messiah.* * *The convict ship was destined for Australia.* Some people object to the use of *des-*

tined as a synonym for *intended*, with no suggestion of *destiny*. The use of *was destined to be* to mean 'later became': * *He was destined to be prime minister* is also disliked. However, these uses are well established and generally acceptable.

detach The verb *detach*, meaning 'separate', is often misspelt, the most frequent error being the substitution of *-tch* for the *-ch* ending.

detract or **distract**? *Detract* means 'take away from; diminish' and is usually used figuratively to describe the diminishing of some desirable quality: * *The new hotels can only detract from the resort's charm. Distract* means 'take someone's mind off something; divert attention elsewhere': * *I tried to concentrate but I was distracted by the noise outside.*

detrimental The adjective *detrimental* is followed by the preposition *to*: * *Smoking is detrimental to health.*

development Since Third World countries have been referred to as *under-developed countries*, and then *less-developed countries*, *least-developed countries*, or *developing countries*, the word *development* has come to have a specialised meaning in terms of the economic growth and improvements in living conditions of these countries: * *the World Development Movement* * *The rich world need provide only $5 billion a year in development assistance* (Ronald Sider, *Rich Christians in an Age of Hunger*). Note the spelling: there is no *e* after the *p*.

While more developed countries are frequently referred to as belonging to the First World, and less-developed or least-developed countries (*LDCs*) are commonly said to belong to the Third World, the phrase Second World, describing the former countries of the Communist bloc, is rarely used today and is not likely to be understood without explanation.

device or **devise**? These words are sometimes confused. *Device* is a noun meaning 'contrivance or gadget': * *a device for opening bottles*, or 'scheme or ploy': * *It was a cunning device to get his own way*. *Devise* is a verb meaning 'plan': * *They devised a new method of classifying the books*. Note that *devise* is one of the few verbs that cannot be spelt *-ize*: *see also* **-ize** or **-ise**?

devoid The adjective *devoid* is followed by the preposition *of*: * *The landscape is devoid of interesting features*.

devolve on or **devolve to**? The verb *devolve*, meaning 'pass to' or 'transfer', may be followed by either *on* or *to* and little distinction is made between the two in general modern usage. Careful users, however, reserve *devolve on* for the transfer of powers or authority, etc., and use *devolve to* when referring to the passing of a right or benefit to someone: * *The power to impose tax will devolve on local government bodies*. * *The property will devolve to her surviving relatives*.

devotee The noun *devotee*, meaning 'enthusiast', 'supporter', or 'follower', is sometimes mispronounced. The correct pronunciation is [devŏtee], with the stress on the last syllable. The first two syllables rhyme with *clever*: they do not have the same vowel sounds as the verb *devote*.

dexterous or **dextrous**? This word, meaning 'skilful or nimble': * *a dexterous artisan*, may be spelt *dexterous* or *dextrous*, although the former is the more frequently used spelling. Note that *ambidextrous* is always spelt without the extra *e*.

diagnosis or **prognosis**? Both *diagnosis* and *prognosis* are most often used in medical contexts. A *diagnosis* is the identification of a disease, from studying the symptoms: * *The doctor's diagnosis, based on her spots, was chickenpox*. A *prognosis* is a forecast of the likely course of an illness and the prospect of recovery: * *The doctor's prognosis is that he will never fully regain his eyesight*. Both *diagnosis* and *prognosis* can be used of problems in general, with the meanings, respectively, of 'an analysis of the cause of the problem' and 'a forecast of the course and outcome of a problem': * *They diagnosed a major fault in the wiring*. * *His prognosis indicated that the company was heading for bankruptcy*.

The plural of both nouns is formed by changing the *-sis* ending to *-ses*: * *diagnoses* * *prognoses*.

dialect *Dialect* usually refers to an established variety of a language, confined either to a region or to a social group or class. The dialect used by educated middle- or upper-class people is often regarded as the standard form of a language and other dialects as non-standard (*see* **pronunciation**). At one time non-standard regional dialects were considered a handicap to acceptance in 'civilised' English society; regional accents have now gained wide acceptance, for example among BBC announcers, although non-standard grammar or vocabulary is still considered unacceptable.

Dialect is seen not only in pronunciation: vocabulary, grammar, and sentence construction vary too. Compare the Northern English: * *He'll not be coming* with the Southern: * *He won't be coming,* or the North-East English: * *You suit that dress* with the standard: * *That dress suits you.* An example from William Trevor shows the Irish use of *the* for *a*: * '*Well, Bridie, isn't that the grand outfit you have on*' (*The Ballroom of Romance*). Social dialects are often associated with the working-class dropping of *h*'s, use of double negatives, and so on, but upper-class cultures have their own dialect forms too.

There is a wealth of dialect words. Often the same word has different meanings in different regions. *Canny* means 'thrifty or shrewd' in Scotland, but 'pleasant or agreeable' in North-East England.

dialectal or **dialectic**? *Dialectal* is an adjective, meaning 'relating to dialect': * *a dialectal term. Dialectic* is a noun, meaning 'disputation'; it has a number of specialised uses in logic and philosophy. *Dialectic* is also a variant of the adjective *dialectical,* meaning 'relating to dialectic'.

dialogue *Dialogue* is now rarely used for an ordinary conversation between two or more people, but is increasingly applied to exchanges of opinion and high-level negotiation between organisations and individuals who are usually ideologically opposed or have a conflict of interest: * *We must bring about meaningful dialogue between management and unions.* * *It is hoped that military conflict can be avoided through international dialogue. Dia-*

logue is used as a verb in American English: * *We must dialogue with each other,* but this use is not generally acceptable in British English.

diaphragm A *diaphragm* is a separating membrane and especially refers to the partition that separates the chest from the abdomen. The word also refers to a contraceptive device. In spelling, note the *-ph-* and the silent *g*.

diarrhoea This word is often misspelt. Note particularly the *-rrh-* and also the *-oea* ending. In American English the *o* is usually omitted. *See also* **-ae-** and **-oe-**.

dice *Dice* was originally the plural form of a singular noun *die,* but this singular form is now almost never used in British English except in the expression: * *The die is cast. Dice* is used now both as a singular and as a plural: * *He made a dice out of a sugar cube.* * *You need two dice for that game.* The word is also used for a gambling game played with dice: * *I cannot believe that God plays dice with the cosmos* (Albert Einstein).

The word *dice* may also be applied generally to cube-shaped pieces of something: * *Next place the parsnip dice in a saucepan of boiling water.*

die The verb *die* is followed by the preposition *of* or *from*: * *Thousands died of* [or *from*] *starvation during the drought.* * *He died from his wounds.*

dietician or **dietitian**? A person who studies the principles of nutrition is known as a *dietician* or *dietitian.* Both spellings of the word are perfectly acceptable. Note that the science itself is called *dietetics.*

difference or **differentiation**? These two words differ slightly in meaning and cannot be used as synonyms for each other. *Difference* means 'dissimilarity', while *differentiation* denotes the process of becoming dissimilar: * *There are several marked differences between the two machines.* * *Scientists have followed the differentiation of the two species over several decades.*

different from, **different to** or **different than**? It is possible to follow *different* with *from*, *to*, or *than*. *Different from* is the most frequently used form and the most acceptable: * *Your life is different from mine. Different to* is often used in informal British English: * *That suit is different to this one*; it is, however, disliked by some people and is not used in American English. *Different than* is in frequent use in American English but is disliked by many users of British English and generally should be avoided; it is considered most acceptable when followed by a clause: * *My values now are different than they were when I was a teenager*, as it removes the need for clumsy phrases such as * *from those that I had.*

differential *Differential*, as both adjective and noun, is a term in mathematics and has the non-technical meanings of 'based on a difference; a difference between comparable things'. It is now most frequently used in reference to differences in pay rates for various jobs in the same industry, based on differences in skills, work conditions, etc.: * *Pay differentials between nursing and administrative staff have widened.* The use of *differential* in place of *difference*: * *a differential of £20 a week* is inappro-

priate, as a *differential* is a discrepancy based on related differences, not the difference itself.

differentiation *see* **difference** or **differentiation**?

differently abled *see* **abled**.

different than, **different to** *see* **different from**, **different to** or **different than**?

diffuse *see* **defuse** or **diffuse**?

digital The adjective *digital*, meaning 'storing information as numbers or electronic signals', has specific technical uses in computing, sound recording, and broadcasting: * *digital superhighway* * *digital recording* * *digital television. Digital* also refers to the presentation of information in the form of digits rather than pointers on a dial or scale: * *digital watch* * *digital display* * *digital thermometer.*

dilapidated This word, meaning 'falling into ruin': * *a dilapidated cottage*, is sometimes misspelt, the most frequent mistake being to begin the word with *de-*, rather than the correct *di-*.

dilemma A *dilemma* is a situation in which a person is faced with two equally unsatisfactory alternatives: * *It was a hopeless dilemma – she could stay with her husband and be miserable, or she could leave him and lose the children.* It is usually considered acceptable to use *dilemma* when more than two choices are involved, provided they are equally unattractive, but *dilemma* should not be used for desirable things: * *His mouth watered as he pondered the dilemma of whether* *to choose the chocolate soufflé or the pistachio ice-cream.* The word is often used to mean just 'a problem', where there is open choice or no element of choice at all: * *the dilemma of what to wear* * *the dilemma of how to attract new members.* Careful users dislike this imprecise use of the word.

The *i* of dilemma may be short [di*lemă*] or long [dī*lemă*]. Some users prefer the first of these pronunciations.

dimension The literal uses of *dimension* are concerned with measurement, *dimensions* being also used figuratively to mean 'scope or extent': * *They were now in a position to assess the dimensions of the tragedy.* The word is also fashionably used as a synonym for aspect or factor: * *The fact that one of the applicants was black and one a woman added a new dimension to their decision.* Some people dislike the overuse of the non-literal senses of this word.

diminution This word means 'decrease in size, intensity, etc.': * *the possible diminution in readers.* Note the spelling and the pronunciation [dimi*new*shŏn].

dinghy or **dingy**? These words are sometimes confused. A *dinghy* is a small boat; *dingy* is an adjective meaning 'gloomy or shabby': * *a dingy basement flat.* *Dinghy* is pronounced with a hard *g* [*ding*gi] or [*ding*i]. The pronunciation of *dingy* is [*din*ji].

dining room *see* **lounge**.

dinner, **lunch**, **tea** or **supper**? The question of how meals and mealtimes are referred to in Britain is fraught with class and regional considera-

tions. In general, middle- and upper-class people have their main meal in the evening and call it *dinner* or *supper*; *lunch* is taken around midday and is usually a light meal or snack, although Sunday lunch may be the main meal of the day. *Tea* (or *afternoon tea*), if it is taken, is eaten late in the afternoon and consists of small sandwiches and cakes. *High tea* is a meal eaten in the late afternoon rather than *dinner* or *supper* later in the evening. Some people, especially those living in Northern England and Scotland, have *dinner* at midday, while *tea* is a substantial meal eaten at about six o'clock. *Supper* is always the last meal of the day and is sometimes a light bedtime snack for those who have had a large tea, or it can be the main evening meal for those who choose not to call the main evening meal *dinner* or *tea*. *See also* **lunch** or **luncheon**?

diphtheria This word causes problems with spelling and pronunciation. Note the *-phth-* in the spelling. The *ph* sound is pronounced *f* [dif*thee*riă] or *p* [dip*thee*riă].

diphthong Note the *-phth-* in the spelling. The *ph* sound is pronounced *f* [*dif*thong] or *p* [*dip*thong].

direct speech *Direct speech* is a record of the actual words used by a speaker. These words are usually enclosed in quotation marks and followed or preceded by a verb such as *said, whispered, shouted,* etc.: * *'Get out!' he cried.* * *She replied, 'I don't know.'* In passages of conversation, the words of different speakers are often placed in separate paragraphs. The verbs that follow or precede the direct speech are sometimes omitted once the identity of the speakers has been made clear. *See also* **reported speech**.

dis- or **dys-**? Confusion between these two prefixes can cause spelling mistakes. *Dis-* is the more frequent, indicating lack, reversal, negation, removal, etc.: * *disagreement* * *discontinue* * *dissimilar*. *Dys-* means 'abnormal', 'faulty', 'difficult', or 'bad' and is chiefly found in technical words relating to physical or mental problems: * *dyspepsia* * *dyslexia* * *dysfunction*.

disabled *Disabled* is the preferred word in both British and American English for people with physical or mental disabilities, replacing *handicapped, crippled, defective*, etc.: * *He was disabled as the result of an accident at work.* * *I believe from personal experience of having a disabled mother that it is not disabled-friendly and we will look at it.* (*Bucks Herald*). As preferred terms in sensitive areas such as disability tend to change, some users now consider even *disabled* unacceptable and prefer such terms as *person with disabilities, differently abled,* or *physically challenged. See also* **accessible; people with disabilities**.

disadvantaged Like **underprivileged** and **deprived**, *disadvantaged* has become a fashionable euphemism for 'poor', with particular emphasis on the lack of a reasonable standard of housing, living conditions, and opportunities for gaining basic rights: * *Up to 100 teachers from each country are to spend one or two months studying such matters as how to motivate disadvantaged children* (*The Times*).

disappear Note the spelling of this

word, particularly the single *s* and the *-pp-*.

disappoint The verb *disappoint* and its derivatives are often misspelt, the most frequent error being the doubling of the *s*. Note also the *-pp-*.

disassemble *see* **dissemble** or **disassemble**?

disassociate *see* **dissociate** or **disassociate**?

disassociation or **dissociation**? *Disassociation* and *dissociation* are close in meaning, denoting the separation of two things, persons, or concepts: * *She has completed the process of disassociation from all her old friends.* * *The party's disassociation from the affair has not been entirely successful.* The two words are, however, not always exact synonyms of each other; in psychology and psychiatry, *dissociation* specifically denotes the separation of emotions as a defence mechanism: * *As an adult he protected himself through dissociation from this childhood trauma.*

disastrous This word is sometimes misspelt. Note that the *e* of disaster is dropped before the suffix *-ous* is added. In pronunciation, careful users avoid sounding the *e* of *disaster*: [di*zah*strĕs] rather than [di*zah*stĕrĕs]. Many people dislike the overuse of this word to describe something very bad in its performance or results.

disc or **disk**? These spellings are sometimes confused. A *disc* is a flat round or circular shape: * *a slipped disc* * *compact disc*. In American English this word is usually spelt *disk*. In

British English *disk* is reserved for use in computer science, to describe a thin plate on which data is stored: * *a floppy disk*. This is occasionally spelt *disc*.

discipline Note the *c* following the *s* in the spelling of this word.

discoloration *see* **coloration**.

discomfit or **discomfort**? There is some overlap between these words, and often confusion as to the distinction between them. *Discomfit* means 'defeat or thwart': * *He discomfited his opponent*, and 'disconcert, confuse, or embarrass': * *They were discomfited by his strange manner*. *Discomfort* means 'make uncomfortable or uneasy'; this might be physical distress: * *The hard seats discomforted her*, or mental uneasiness, in which case the distinction between *discomfort* and *discomfit* often becomes blurred: * *His ominous tone discomforted them*. *Discomfort* is both a verb and a noun, but the noun from *discomfit* is *discomfiture*.

discover *see* **invent, design** or **discover**?

discreet or **discrete**? These two words are sometimes confused. *Discreet* means 'judicious or prudent': * *You can confide in him; he is very discreet*; *discrete* means 'separate or distinct': * *discrete elements in the composition*.

discrepancy or **disparity**? Both these nouns mean 'difference'. A *discrepancy* is a difference between things that should be the same; a *disparity* is a greater difference that suggests imbalance or inequality: * *a discrepancy between the accounts of the two witnesses* * *a disparity between the wages of factory and office workers*.

discriminating or **discriminatory**? Both these adjectives are derived from *discrimination* and are connected with 'distinguishing, making distinctions'; they are however used in very different ways. *Discriminating* is applied to someone who is discerning in matters of taste, and able to tell the difference between good and poor quality: * *We'd better serve the Bordeaux because Paul is discriminating when it comes to wine*. *Discriminatory* is now almost always applied to discrimination that is unjust and based on prejudice: * *Feminists are organising a boycott of the bank because of its discriminatory practices*.

disillusion *Disillusion* is a verb meaning 'to make someone realise that something they thought was good is not really as good as they thought it was'. It is most often found in the form *disillusioned*: * *disillusioned voters* * *He quickly became disillusioned with his new job*. *Disillusion* is also occasionally used as a noun meaning 'disillusionment; the state of being disillusioned': * *There is a deep public disillusion with the government's decision*. Careful users avoid confusing *disillusion* with *delusion* or *illusion*: * *We are under no illusions* [not *disillusions*] *about how challenging the task is*. See also **allusion, illusion** or **delusion**?

disingenuous or **ingenuous**? *Disingenuous* means 'devious and dishonest' and implies that something is being concealed: * *The statement put out by the police is disingenuous*. It should be distinguished from *ingenuous*, which means 'innocent', 'naïve', or 'frank'. *See also* **ingenious** or **ingenuous**?

disinterested or **uninterested**? *Disinterested* means 'impartial; having no self-interest': * *As a disinterested party he felt free to intervene in the dispute.* *Uninterested* means 'having no interest; indifferent; bored': * *I was quite uninterested in their holiday photos.* Perhaps because uninterested is not in frequent use, *disinterested* is now often used in its place to mean 'lacking interest' – which was, in fact, the original meaning of *disinterested*: * *Charles, in turn, appeared cold and disinterested in his wife* (*Sunday Times*). However, many people object to its use in this sense.

disk *see* **disc** or **disk**?

disorganised or **unorganised**? Either adjective may be used in the sense of 'not organised'. As the past participle of the verb *disorganise*, *disorganised* specifically refers to something organised that has been thrown into confusion, but it is also used in a general informal sense: * *I'm a bit disorganised this morning*. *Unorganised* is more neutral and less frequent: * *an unorganised method of working.*

disorient or **disorientate**? *Disorient* and *disorientate* are interchangeable and mean 'cause to lose bearings or sense of identity; confuse': * *They had organised a one-way traffic system since his last visit and he was completely disoriented/disorientated.* * *After years of being institutionalised she was disoriented/disorientated after her discharge.* *Disorient* is preferred by some users as the shorter and simpler

alternative; it is also the standard form in American English, while *disorientate* is more frequently used in British English. *See also* **orient** or **orientate**?

disparity *see* **discrepancy** or **disparity**?

dispassionate, **impassioned** or **impassive**? The adjectives *dispassionate* and *impassive* are sometimes confused because of their similarity in meaning; *impassioned* and *impassive*, because of their similarity in form. *Dispassionate* means 'not influenced by emotion; objective', whereas *impassive* means 'showing no emotion': * *a dispassionate assessment of the problem* * *She remained impassive, ignoring his cries.* *Impassioned* means 'full of passion': * *an impassioned attack on the government.*

dispatch *see* **despatch** or **dispatch**?

dispel or **disperse**? *Dispel* means 'scatter; drive away' and is often used for abstract things: * *He allowed them to see the original document so as to dispel their doubts about its authenticity.* *Disperse* means 'break up': * *The family were dispersed over Europe*, 'spread over a wide area': * *The gas dispersed over half the town*, and 'dissipate, evaporate, or vanish': * *The mist had now dispersed and visibility was normal.*

dispute The noun dispute may be pronounced with the stress on the first syllable [*di*spewt] or the second [dis*pewt*]. The first of these pronunciations is becoming increasingly frequently heard, although many users dislike it. The verb *dispute* is always stressed on the second syllable.

dissect This word, meaning 'separate or cut up for analysis', is spelt with -ss-, unlike *bisect*. Although *dissect* is often pronounced to rhyme with bisect [dīsekt], careful users prefer [disekt].

dissemble or **disassemble**? *Dissemble*, a literary word, means 'pretend' or 'conceal'; *disassemble* means 'take apart': * *He dissembled his excitement.* * *She disassembled the machine.* The two verbs should not be confused. Note the spellings of the words, particularly the -s- and -ss-.

dissemble, **dissimulate** or **simulate**? The verbs *dissemble* and *dissimulate*, both of which are formal, mean 'pretend not to have; conceal'; *simulate* means 'pretend to have; feign': * *to dissemble* [or *dissimulate*] *your anger* * *to simulate enthusiasm.* See also **simulate** or **stimulate**?

dissension or **dissent**? The noun *dissension* refers to a state of disagreement, discord, or conflict: * *The proposal caused much dissension.* The noun *dissent*, the opposite of *assent*, means 'difference of opinion'; it refers to the act of disagreeing or an expression of disagreement: * *a voice of dissent.* Confusion between the two nouns may lead to the misspelling of *dissension*, with -t- in place of the third -s-.

dissimilar The adjective *dissimilar* is followed by the preposition *from* or *to*: * *The flavour is not dissimilar from* [or *to*] *that of chicken.*

dissimulate *see* **dissemble**, **dissimulate** or **simulate**?

dissociate or **disassociate**? *Dissociate* and *disassociate* are interchangeable opposites of associate: * *One of the committee members told me after the meeting that she wished to dissociate/disassociate herself from what the chair had said.* Most careful users prefer the form *dissociate*.

dissociation *see* **disassociation** or **dissociation**?

distil In British English the verb *distil* ends in a single *l*, which is doubled before a suffix beginning with a vowel: * *distillery*. The American English spelling of the verb is *distill*. See also **spelling**.

distinct or **distinctive**? These two adjectives are frequently confused although they are not interchangeable. *Distinct* means 'definite; clearly perceivable or distinguishable': * *There's a distinct taste of garlic in this stew.* *Distinctive* means 'characteristic, peculiar to, distinguishing': * *He had the distinctive rolling gait of a sailor.*

distract *see* **detract** or **distract**?

distribute The traditional pronunciation in British English of this word, meaning 'share out' or 'spread', is [distribyoot], with the stress on the second syllable. The alternative pronunciation [distribyoot], with the stress on the first syllable, has, however, become equally acceptable in both British and American English.

distrust or **mistrust**? *Distrust* and *mistrust* are often used interchangeably: * *Somehow I distrust/mistrust the whole business.* *Distrust* is more frequently used and has a far more emphatic suggestion of suspicion and lack of trust: * *I have known him to be deceitful in* *the past and I have come to distrust everything he says.* Mistrust is rather more tentative and is used for a less positive lack of trust or when the doubt is directed against the subject him- or herself: * *There was something about her manner that made me uneasy and I found myself beginning to mistrust her.* * *I tend to mistrust my critical judgment when it comes to my own writing.*

disturb or **perturb**? Disturb can mean 'interrupt; inconvenience': * *His reverie was disturbed by a ring at the doorbell.* * *I hope I'm not disturbing you by phoning so late,* 'throw into disorder': * *The cleaner had disturbed all her papers,* and 'upset; destroy the mental composure of': * *I was deeply disturbed by this revelation.* In this last use, *disturb* is virtually synonymous with the less frequently used word *perturb*, which means 'cause disquiet to; cause mental disturbance': * *His violent language and abrupt departure had perturbed her.*

dived or **dove**? In British English the past tense of *dive* is almost always *dived*: * *They all dived for cover.* However, the past tense *dove* exists in some British dialects and is the standard form in several regions of the United States and Canada: * *She dove beautifully, and a moment later she was swimming back to the side of the pool* (Philip Roth, *Goodbye Columbus*). The use of *dove* (pronounced [dōv]) is now generally considered acceptable in all but the most formal writing in American English. It is still considered non-standard in British English.

divorcee A divorced person of either sex is known as a *divorcee* [divaw*see*]. A

divorced man is also called a *divorcé* [divaw*say*] or [divaw*see*], and a divorced woman is also called a *divorcée* [divaw*see*].

do Do is used as an informal replacement for various different verbs, for example 'prepare': * *Shall I do you a sandwich?,* 'clean': * *I'm just going to do my teeth,* 'visit': * *We're doing the British Museum tomorrow,* 'perform': * *The local rep are doing The Cherry Orchard,* 'study': * *She's doing maths at Cambridge,* 'provide': * *Do they do breakfasts?* There are also the slang meanings of 'cheat': * *You've been done!,* 'arrest': * *He was done for burglary,* 'rob': * *They did the bank last night,* 'attack': * *I'll do you,* and 'have sexual intercourse with': * *Glober did me on the table* (Anthony Powell, *Temporary Kings*). Do is used informally as a noun to mean 'a party or social event': * *I'm going to the firm's Christmas do.*

The addition of *do* in constructions when a previously mentioned verb is omitted: * *They behaved just as I wanted them to do* is best reserved for informal use.

Do is also used as an auxiliary verb in questions: * *Do you like it?,* in negative sentences: * *They don't want to go,* and for emphasis: * *I do wish he'd phone!*

The construction *do have* in British English (probably under the influence of American English) is often used in questions and negative statements as an alternative to have got: * *Do you have the new edition of this?* * *Do we have his reply yet?* * *We don't have time to wait.* In such contexts, some users find *do have* more acceptable than *have got*, although both are equally correct grammatically.

Domesday or **doomsday**? The
Domesday Book is the survey of
England carried out during the reign
of William I. The noun *doomsday*,
sometimes spelt with a capital *D-*,
means 'Judgement Day; Last Judgement' in the Christian religion, and
'day of reckoning' or 'end of the
world' in general usage. The phrase
till doomsday means 'for ever': * *You
can wait till doomsday, but I won't
change my mind*. Both words are pronounced [*doomz*day].

dominate or **domineer**? To *dominate*
means 'rule, exert power or control
over': * *Her charm and energy were
such that she came to dominate the
whole company*. It can also mean
'occupy a preeminent position': * *Our
products dominate the pet-food market*,
and 'overlook from a superior height':
* *The church is built on a hill and
dominates the town*. *Dominate* is often
used in a negative way that would be
better reserved for *domineer*, which
means 'tyrannise, exert power in an
arbitrary or overbearing manner'. It is
most frequently used as a present participle that functions as an adjective: *
his cruel domineering manner.

done or **finished**? Both *done* and *finished* signify completing something: *
Everything's been done. * *The race has
finished*. Some users prefer *finished* to
done in formal contexts, preferring *I
have finished with the computer* to *I'm
done with the computer*.

doomsday *see* **Domesday** or **doomsday**?

do's and **don'ts** In the phrase *do's and
don'ts*, note that the apostrophe in
don'ts comes after the *n* and not after

the *t*. The apostrophe in *do's* is sometimes omitted.

dot.com The phrase *dot.com* refers to a
commercial computer website or
company operating through the Internet, the origin of the phrase being the
.com ending of many website addresses.
Though widely understood, *dot.com*
should be avoided in formal contexts.
It is increasingly spelt as one word: *
*He works for one of the new dotcom out-
fits*. The phrase *dot.com* has inspired a
host of subsidiary phrases relating to
computer-based business, often with a
hyphen in the place of the full stop: *
dot-com millionaire * *dot-commer* *
dot-comback. During the so-called
dot.com bubble of the 1990s, many
conventional retailers restyled themselves as *dot.com* organisations by
establishing websites to promote their
goods and services.

double entendre The French expression *double entendre* refers to an
ambiguous word or phrase, one of
whose meanings has indecent connotations. The literal meaning of *double
entendre* is 'double meaning'. It is pronounced [dooběl on*tond*rě].

double negative The *double negative*, as
in: * *I didn't do nothing*. * *He hasn't
had no tea*, is always avoided by careful users. The objection to such constructions is that the negatives cancel
each other out and reverse the meaning of the sentence. When two negatives are intended to cancel each
other: * *She is not without talent*. * *It
is not impossible*, they are, however,
acceptable. Another generally acceptable, if colloquial, use is in such sentences as: * *I shouldn't be surprised if it
doesn't snow*.

The cruder *double negative* is not difficult to avoid. It is more likely to occur with the semi-negative adverbs *hardly, scarcely, barely*: * *They were left for hours without hardly any food*, or in complex sentences where the various negative words and phrases might get muddled: * *Despite his injury, he denied that it was unlikely that he would not play again this season.*

The word *neither* should not be used in sentences that are already negative: * *I'm not hungry and I'm not thirsty neither.* * *I didn't neither.*

doubling of consonants On the general rule of doubling consonants in such words as: * *drop–dropped* * *refer–referred*, see individual entries and **spelling**.

doubt The main problem with *doubt* is what preposition or conjunction to use with it. When *doubt* is used as a noun it is most often followed by *about*: * *I have my doubts about it*, but it can be followed by *that* in a negative construction: * *There is no doubt in my mind that he is telling the truth.* When *doubt* is used as a verb it can only be followed by *that* in negative constructions: * *I don't doubt that you are right*, and in most other constructions it is followed by *whether*: * *They doubted whether she would be welcome.* *If* is a possible alternative to *whether* but is suitable for more informal use: * *I doubt if I can make it.*

doubtful or **dubious**? Both *doubtful* and *dubious* mean 'giving rise to doubt, uncertain, questionable' and they are more or less interchangeable: * *They were doubtful/dubious whether the car was safe. Doubtful* is more neutral and is more likely to be used

when expressing uncertainty: * *The eventual result remains doubtful. Dubious* carries more negative overtones and is often used to suggest a suspicion that a person or practice is underhand or dishonest in some way: * *He was involved with some dubious export company. Doubtful* is always preferable in constructions starting with 'it is': * *It is doubtful whether he has ever actually visited Germany.*

doubtless *see* **undoubtedly**.

douse or **dowse**? Either spelling of this verb may be used in the sense of 'soak' or 'extinguish'; the pronunciation is [dows]. *Douse* is the more frequent: * *doused with petrol* * *to douse a candle.* The verb dowse, in the additional meaning of 'search for water using a divining rod', should never be spelt *douse*. It is pronounced [dowz].

dove *see* **dived** or **dove**?

download and **upload** *Download* and *upload* are both computer terms that have been absorbed to some extent into the English language to denote the copying or transfer of information, data, etc. *Download* refers to the transfer of data from a larger computer or other information system, such as the Internet, while *upload* denotes the opposite: * *He downloaded the file onto his PC.* * *The program will take about twenty minutes to upload from the disk.*

downside The vogue word *downside* means 'unfavourable aspect'; it is best avoided where *disadvantage* would be more appropriate: * *the downside of the new system* * *Every scientific breakthrough has its downside.*

downsizing *Downsizing* is the act of reducing in size. In America in the late 1970s it referred to the production of smaller cars: * *With the whole industry downsizing, big-car addicts will find fewer alternatives* (*Time*). In Britain in the late 1980s it referred to redundancy: * *downsizing the workforce* * *In the case of the latest cuts – 55 jobs to go at US investment bank L.F. Rothschild – downsizing is something of an understatement* (*The Guardian*). The term is also used in computing: * *'Downsizing' simply means that firms are tending to buy smaller computers to do jobs which used to require big ones* (*The Guardian*).

Down's syndrome This is the preferred modern term for the congenital disorder formerly known as *mongolism*, a term that is now widely considered unacceptable. Named after the English physician J.H.L. Down (1828–96), the disorder is known as *Down syndrome* in American English.

downward or **downwards**? In British English, *downward* is principally used as an adjective – *downwards* being the usual form of the adverb meaning 'to a lower level': * *a downward slope* * *to look downwards.* The adverb *downward* is more frequently used in American English. *See also* -**ward** or -**wards**?

dowse *see* **douse** or **dowse**?

draft *see* **draught** or **draft**?

dramatist or **playwright**? *Dramatist* and *playwright* are synonymous words, both dating from the late seventeenth century and meaning 'a person who writes plays': * *He is a poet as well as a dramatist/playwright.* There may be a slight tendency to apply *dramatist* to those who write more serious plays or plays which conform to the traditional categories of drama: * *Racine was a dramatist writing in the classical tradition*, and *playwright* to modern writers and those whose work is less serious: * *playwrights like Neil Simon who are popular on both sides of the Atlantic.*

Note the spelling of the final syllable of *playwright*: -*wright*, not -*write*.

draught or **draft**? These words are sometimes confused. A *draft* is a preliminary outline: * *a rough draft of the essay*; it is also a money order and a group of soldiers. *Draught* is the spelling for: * *draught beer* * *draught animals* * *a draught from an open door.* The American English spelling of *draught* is *draft*. A person who draws up a rough version of a document is a *draftsman*; an artist or someone who prepares detailed drawings of buildings, machinery, etc., is a *draughtsman* (feminine, *draughtswoman*; American English *draftsman*).

The board game called *draughts* in British English is known as *checkers* in American English.

draughtsman or **draughtswoman**? *see* **non-sexist terms.**

drawing room *see* **lounge.**

dreamed or **dreamt**? Either word may be used as the past tense and past participle of the verb *dream*: * *I dreamed/dreamt I was in Australia.* *Dreamed* may be pronounced [dreemd] or [dremt]; *dreamt* is always pronounced [dremt]. *See also* -**ed** or -**t**?

drier or **dryer**? *Drier* is the usual spelling of the comparative form of the adjective *dry*; both are used for the noun derived from the verb *dry*: * *These socks are drier than those.* * *a hair-dryer/drier* * *a spin-dryer/drier.*

drugs slang The drugs subculture has contributed a large number of slang coinages to British and American English. Some of these terms are useful as they provide succinct names for otherwise unwieldy chemical titles, but care should be taken over their use; they tend to come into and go out of fashion very rapidly. Examples of slang terms that have remained current through the years are: * *E* or *Ecstasy* (for the drug MDMA) * *speed* (amphetamines) * *crystal* (methamphetamine) * *weed* (cannabis) * *smack* (heroin) * *acid* (LSD). Terms that are less common today include: * *pot* (cannabis) * *horse* (heroin).

drunk or **drunken**? Both *drunk* and *drunken* are adjectives applied to alcoholic intoxication, but *drunk* is normally used after a verb: * *She got drunk on cheap white wine*, while *drunken* is normally used before a noun: * *We were just sipping sherry – it was hardly a drunken orgy.* * *the campaign against drunken driving.* However, *drunk* implies temporary intoxication, while *drunken* suggests a habitual state of being drunk. When this distinction is being emphasized, it is possible to reverse the usual rule and use *drunk* before a noun: * *drunk driving* and, though less frequently, *drunken* after a verb: * *He was drunken, foul-mouthed, and inconsiderate.*

dryer *see* **drier** or **dryer**?

dual or **duel**? These two words are sometimes confused, being identical in pronunciation. *Dual* is an adjective, meaning 'double'; *duel* is a noun or verb referring to a rather formal fight between two people: * *dual-purpose* * *a dual carriageway* * *the duel of the champions* * *to settle a quarrel by duelling.* Note that in British English the final *l* of *duel* is doubled before *-ed, -ing, -er*, etc.

dubious *see* **doubtful** or **dubious**?

duel *see* **dual** or **duel**?

due to, **owing to** or **because of**? Although these phrases have roughly the same meanings, they are not used in the same way. *Due to* should strictly speaking be used only adjectivally: * *His shakiness is due to Parkinson's disease*; whereas *owing to* and *because of* are used as prepositions: * *We were delayed owing to an electrical fault on the line.* * *Because of poor health he took early retirement.* Although the use of *due to* as a preposition is objected to by careful users, this usage is becoming increasingly widespread: * *Due to the sheer size of the operation, we now need additional people to join our... Membership Recruitment and Corporate Marketing Departments* (*Sunday Times*).

du jour This French phrase, meaning 'of the day', has become a standard term used in menus to indicate a dish available on a particular day: * *le plat du jour.* It has recently been adopted in a wider context to denote something that is currently popular or fashionable but not likely to remain so for long: * *The health scare du jour is the claim that such products can raise* *cholesterol levels.* It is best restricted to informal use.

dumb or **mute**? A person who is *dumb* cannot speak. As *dumb* also means 'stupid' in very informal contexts; many users of English prefer to use the word *mute* when referring to people who are unable to speak. However, *mute* can also cause offence (*see* **deaf-mute**). A more acceptable alternative of fairly recent coinage is *speech-impaired*.

duplication or **duplicity**? The noun *duplication* is derived from the verb *duplicate*, meaning 'copy' or 'repeat'; the more formal noun *duplicity* means 'deception' or 'double-dealing': * *There may be some duplication in the text.* * *They were unaware of his duplicity.* The two nouns should not be confused.

duration or **length**?

dustman or **dustwoman**? *see* **non-sexist terms.**

dwarf *Dwarf* is no longer considered an acceptable term for an abnormally small person. None of the alternatives so far coined, such as *person of restricted growth*, has achieved wide acceptance. The term *midget* may also cause offence and should be avoided.

Note that *dwarfs* is the more frequent plural of *dwarf*, although *dwarves* is also acceptable.

dwelled or **dwelt**? Either may be used as the past tense and past participle of the verb *dwell*. *Dwelled* is more frequent in American English than in British English, but *dwelt* is the preferred form in both: * *He dwelt on her infidelity. See also* **-ed** or **-t**?

dying or **dyeing**? These spellings are sometimes confused. *Dying* is the present participle of the verb *die*, meaning 'cease to live': * *Her son is dying.* * *his dying words. Dyeing* is the present participle of the verb *dye*, meaning 'change the colour of': * *She was dyeing her hair blonde.*

dynasty The preferred British English pronunciation of *dynasty*, which means 'series of hereditary rulers', is [*din*ǎsti]. The American English pronunciation [*dīn*ǎsti] is sometimes also used in British English.

dys- *see* **dis-** or **dys-**?

dyslexic or **dyslectic**? The words *dyslexic* and *dyslectic* are interchangeable; either may be used as a noun or adjective to describe a person suffering from *dyslexia*, though *dyslexic* is used much more frequently.

E

e- The prefix *e-*, meaning 'electronic', has been used to form numerous new words since the advent of the Internet and web-based business: * *e-mail* * *e-business* * *e-commerce* * *e-trade* * *e-book* * *e-shopping* * *e-bill* * *e-learning* * *e-ticket*. Note the growing tendency to drop the hyphen: * *email* * *ezine* * *emarketing*.

each When *each* is used as a determiner or as a pronoun which is the subject of a sentence, the rule is that subsequent verbs and pronouns should be singular: * *Each man has his price.* * *Each of the operas was sung in English.* The rule is frequently broken, partly because those who are sensitive to sexism in language prefer: * *Each student had a paper handed to them* [rather than *to him*]. Of course, it is possible to avoid both sexism and grammatical error by rephrasing such sentences: * *All the students had a paper handed to them.* When *each* follows a plural noun or pronoun which is the subject of the sentence, the subsequent verb is plural: * *The cakes each have cherries on top.*

each or **both**? *see* **both**.

each or **every**? *Each* and *every* are interchangeable in some contexts: * *He picked up each book in turn* * *He picked up every book in turn.* There is, however, a subtle but important difference between the two, in that *each* emphasises the individuality of each person or item under consideration, while *every* treats them collectively, within a group: * *each car in the garage* * *every ship in the fleet.* Note, however, that *each*, not *every*, should be used after a plural noun: * *The guests each have their own room*, and also that *each* refers to two or more in number, while *every* refers to at least three in number: * *She put a shoe on each foot.* * *She had frostbite in every finger.*

each and every *Each and every* is used for emphasis in such phrases as: * *Each and every person has a vital part to play.* * *I am deeply grateful to each and every one of you.* Most careful users dislike it as a cliché, and as an unnecessarily wordy construction for which *each*, *everyone*, or *all* can often be substituted.

each other or **one another**? The traditional rule is that *each other* is used when two elements are involved, and *one another* when more than two are involved: * *Helen and Charles love each other deeply.* * *All the people at the party already knew one another.* However, there is no particular reason for this rule and most people feel free to ignore it. There is a slight difference between the two phrases, in that *each other* tends to emphasise each individual element whereas *one another* sounds more general. So it would be preferable to say: * *They were throwing one another into the swimming pool* rather than *throwing each other*; the former gives a general impression of horseplay and allows for the odd person who was neither thrown nor throwing, while the latter suggests something much more systematic.

earthly or **earthy**? *Earthly* relates to the earth as opposed to heaven; *earthy* refers to earth in the sense of 'soil': * *our earthly life* * *an earthly paradise* * *an earthy taste/texture*. The two adjectives are not interchangeable. Both words have other meanings: *earthly* is used informally in the sense of 'possible', usually in negative contexts or in questions: * *What earthly reason could she have for saying that?* * *They haven't an earthly chance of success*, while *earthy* means 'coarse' or 'crude': * *an earthy remark*.

east, **East** or **eastern**? As an adjective, *east* is always written with a capital *E* when it forms part of a place-name: * *East Anglia* * *the East End*. The noun *east* is usually written with a capital *E* when it denotes a specific region, such as the countries of Asia: * *She has travelled extensively in the East*. * *East–West relations*. In other contexts, and as an adverb, *east* is usually written with a lower-case *e*: * *They sailed east in search of land*. * *The east wind chilled him to the marrow*. * *The sun rises in the east*.

The adjective *eastern* is more frequent and usually less specific than the adjective *east*: * *the eastern shore* * *in eastern Australia*.

Like *east*, *eastern* is written with a capital *E* when it forms part of a proper name, such as: * *the Eastern Orthodox Church*. With or without a capital *E*, it also means 'of the East': * *eastern/Eastern philosophy*.

eastward or **eastwards**? *Eastward* is the correct choice when an adjective is needed: * *an eastward direction*. Either *eastward* or *eastwards* may be used when an adverb is required: * *They travelled eastward from the city*. * *The skies were full of birds flying eastwards*. See also **-ward** or **-wards**?

eatable or **edible**? *Eatable* means 'palatable', but with the suggestion of 'not actually tasting unpleasant' rather than 'delicious': * *He had managed to get together a reasonably eatable meal*. *Edible* means 'suitable for eating as food': * *Common sorrel is edible but wood sorrel is poisonous*. If something is not *edible* it would be either impossible or dangerous to eat, but a substance can be *edible* without being *eatable* – for example, raw potatoes. Despite these differences the two words are often used interchangeably in informal contexts: * *The cabbage was overcooked but just about eatable/edible*.

The distinction between *eatable* and *edible* is also applicable to their antonyms, *uneatable* and *inedible*: * *The meal was uneatable*. * *Toadstools are inedible*.

eco- The growing popularity of the science of *ecology*, the study of living things in their relation to the environment, has given rise to several words with the prefix *eco-*, some legitimate terms in ecology: * *ecospecies* * *ecotype* * *ecosystem*, and some more modern coinages: * *ecocatastrophe* * *eco-freak* * *ecotourism* * *ecotoxicology*. New *eco*-words are being spawned all the time: * *a new magazine... described as the journal of eco-politics* (*The Guardian*) * *the eco-warriors of Greenpeace* (*Sunday Times*).

economic or **economical**? *Economic* is the adjective from *economics* or *the economy* and is concerned with the production, distribution, and structure of wealth: * *Friedman's economic theories* * *the Government's economic policies*. *Economical* is the adjective from *economy* and is concerned with thrift and the avoidance of waste: * *an economical car* * *a large economical pack*. An *economic price* is one that benefits the seller, but an *economical price* benefits the buyer. Although careful users keep the distinction between the two words, each is frequently used with the meaning belonging to the other: * *Labour gave fewer details of their economical brief* (BBC Radio). * *Buying a whole chicken makes economic sense* (advertisement, *Bejam* magazine).

The initial *e-* of both words may be short [ekŏnomik(l)] or long [eekŏnomik(l)].

economics *see* **-ics**.

ecstasy This word, meaning 'intense emotion', especially of happiness, is sometimes misspelt. Note particularly the *-cs-* and the *-asy* ending, as in *fantasy*. *Ecstasy*, usually spelt capitalised or referred to as 'E', is the slang name for the drug methylenedioxymethamphetamine, or MDMA.

-ed or **-t**? The past tense and past participle of the verbs *burn*, *dream*, *dwell*, *kneel*, *lean*, *leap*, *learn*, *smell*, *spell*, *spill*, and *spoil* may end in *-ed* or *-t*. In most cases the *-ed* form is preferred in American English and the *-t* form is slightly more frequent in British English. For further discussion and specific information on pronunciation and adjectival use, *see* the entries at the individual words.

edible *see* **eatable** or **edible**?

-ee or **-er**? In general, the suffix *-ee* can be applied to the recipient of an action denoted by the verb to which the suffix is attached, and the suffix *-er* is applied to the thing or person who performs the action: * *employer-employee* * *trainer-trainee*. However, this rule does not apply in all cases. The suffix *-ee* can sometimes indicate someone who behaves in a particular way: * *absentee* * *arrestee* * *escapee*, and the suffix *-er* can be applied to something that is a suitable object for an action: * *prisoner* * *cooker* (type of apple). The suffix *-ee* is also found as a substitute for *-ie* or *-y*, suggesting smallness, in the word *bootee*, and is sometimes applied to people or things associated with a particular noun: * *townee* * *goatee*, although *-er* is more often used in this way: * *docker* * *villager*.

effect *see* **affect** or **effect**?

effective, **effectual**, **efficacious** or **efficient**? The distinction between these words is subtle. *Effective* means 'having or producing the desired effect': * *The talks were effective in settling the dispute*. *Effectual*, a formal word, means 'capable of achieving the desired effect': * *All plans to reduce the trade deficit have not so far proved effectual*, and in religious contexts: * *effectual prayer* * *God's effectual calling of his people*. *Efficacious*, also a formal word, means 'having the power to achieve the desired effect' and is usually applied to medical treatment: * *an efficacious remedy*. *Efficient* is applied to people or things producing results through a good and economical use of resources: * *an efficient* *machine* ⁕ *an efficient secretary*. Similar distinctions apply to *ineffective*, *ineffectual*, and *inefficient*: ⁕ *an ineffective remedy* ⁕ *an ineffectual policy/leader* ⁕ *an inefficient system/clerk*.

Effective is used in various other ways. It can mean 'impressive': ⁕ *an effective performance*, 'operative; in force': ⁕ *The law is effective as from today*, and 'actual; in practice if not theory': ⁕ *He had become the effective leader*.

effeminate or **effete**? To describe a man or boy as *effeminate* suggests that he shows, in an excessive manner, qualities which are usually thought of as being feminine: ⁕ *he spoke in a high-pitched, effeminate voice*. *Effete* is used more rarely, particularly in formal contexts, and means 'weak or powerless': ⁕ *charming but effete aristocrats*. *Effete* is derived originally from Latin *ex* and *fetus* 'fruitful', meaning 'worn out by producing offspring'. It became applied to systems that were no longer effective and in the 20th century has also been applied to effeminate boys and men.

effrontery *see* **affront** or **effrontery**?

e.g. and **i.e.** The abbreviation *e.g.* stands for *exempli gratia* and means 'for example'. It is used before examples of what has previously been mentioned: ⁕ *We could show you some of the sights, e.g. Buckingham Palace and the Tower of London*. The abbreviation *i.e.*, often used in error for *e.g.*, stands for *id est* and means 'that is'. It is used before amplifications or explanations of what has previously been mentioned: ⁕ *They were vegans, i.e. vegetarians who also avoid eggs and dairy products*. The abbreviations *e.g.* and *i.e.* are best confined to official writing or very informal writing; in other contexts and in speech, *for example* and *that is* should be used.

It is usual in American English to render *e.g.* and *i.e.* with both full stops, but there is an increasing tendency to omit them in British English.

Note that it is incorrect to end a list that begins with *e.g.* with *etc.*

egoism or **egotism**? The words *egoism* and *egotism* are frequently used interchangeably but there are differences between them. *Egoism* is applied to the ethical theory that all actions and motivation are based on self-interest. An *egoist* is a believer in this theory or, much more often, a person who is selfish and self-seeking: ⁕ *His conduct was characterised by ruthless egoism*. *Egotism* means 'being self-obsessed; self-centred'. The typical *egotist* is vain, boastful, and uses the word *I* constantly: ⁕ *Her egotism makes her oblivious to other people's concerns*. The conspicuous self-obsession of *egotists* often makes them absurd, pathetic figures, whereas *egoists* may pursue their own interests in a covert, though calculating, manner.

eighth Note that in the spelling of this word, the letter *h* occurs twice: *eight* plus *h*.

either As an adjective or pronoun, *either* is used with a singular verb: ⁕ *Is either child left-handed?* ⁕ *Is either of your children left-handed?* In the *either... or* construction, a singular verb is used if both subjects are singular, and a plural verb is used if both subjects are plural: ⁕ *Either David or Peter is responsible.* ⁕ *Either their parents or their teachers are responsible*. The use of a plural verb with the pronoun *either* or with singular subjects in an *either... or* construction is avoided by careful users, especially in formal contexts.

When a combination of singular and plural subjects occurs in an *either... or* construction, the verb traditionally agrees with the subject that is nearest to it: * *Either David or his parents are responsible.* * *Either his friends or his brother is responsible.* The same principle is applied to singular subjects that are used with different forms of the verb: * *Either you or I am* [not *are*] *responsible.* If the resulting sentence sounds awkward or unidiomatic it may be reordered or rephrased.

The alternatives presented in an *either... or* construction should be grammatically balanced: * *Dilute the soup either with milk or water* may be changed to: *Dilute the soup either with milk or with water* or: *Dilute the soup with either milk or water.*

As a pronoun *either* should be used only of two alternatives: * *I haven't seen either of my parents since June.* * *Any* [not *Either*] *of the four knives may be used to cut vegetables.* However, the use of the *either... or* construction with three or more subjects is acceptable to some: * *Either Sarah, Jane, or Pauline will be there.*

The first syllable of *either* may be pronounced to rhyme with *try* or *tree*. The pronunciation [*ī*dhĕr] is more frequent in British English. *See also* **neither**.

eke out The original meaning of *eke out* is 'make something more adequate by adding to it': * *She eked out the meal with extra rice.* It is frequently used in two other senses: 'make something last longer by using it economically': * *They eked out the supplies over two weeks*, and 'make (a living) with laborious effort': * *The children eked out a living by selling wild flowers to tourists.* Some careful users dislike both these uses, particularly the latter, but they are well established and generally acceptable.

elder, eldest, older or **oldest?** *Elder* and *eldest* are applied only to people, and usually within the context of family relationships: * *my eldest brother* * *She is the elder of my two daughters.* It is incorrect to say: * *Rachel is elder than Sarah* or: * *He is elder/eldest* without adding *the*. *Older* and *oldest* can be used of things as well as people and in a far wider range of constructions: * *I am older than David.* * *He is older.* * *It is the oldest church in Yorkshire.* *Elder* is also used in such expressions as: * *I am his elder by eighteen months* although: * *I am older than him by eighteen months* sounds less formal. It is also used for people noted for age and experience: * *an elder statesman* * *village elders* * *his elders and betters*, and for an officer in various nonconformist churches. *See also* **comparative** and **superlative**.

electric or **electrical?** *Electric* and *electrical* can both mean 'worked by electricity', although *electric* tends to be applied more to specific, and *electrical* to general, things: * *electrical lighting* * *an electric motor* * *electrical appliances* * *electrical equipment.* *Electric* is also applied to things that produce or carry electricity: * *an electric socket* * *electric current* * *an electric shock*, and is used figuratively to describe something stimulating or thrilling: * *The atmosphere was electric.* *Electrical* is also used to mean 'concerned with electricity': * *electrical engineering.*

elemental or **elementary**? *Elemental* means 'of or like the elements or forces of nature': • *This evoked a flood of elemental passion*. It is also sometimes used to mean 'fundamental or essential': • *an elemental truth of Christianity*. It should not be confused with *elementary* which means 'very simple; introductory': • *I know nothing about computers so I need an elementary manual*. A further possible mistake is the confusion of *elementary* with *alimentary*, which means 'to do with the provision of nourishment': • *the alimentary canal*.

elicit *see* **illicit** or **elicit**?

eligible *see* **illegible** or **eligible**?

ellipse or **ellipsis**? An *ellipse* is an oval; *ellipsis* is a term used in grammar and linguistics (*see* **ellipsis**). The two nouns share the derived adjective *elliptical*: • *an elliptical shape* • *an elliptical phrase*. *Elliptical* also means 'ambiguous' or 'obscure' in formal contexts: • *an elliptical reference*.

ellipsis There are two meanings of the term *ellipsis* in grammar: one is for the punctuation marks…, usually indicating omission; the other is for the omission of words in a sentence, as an abbreviation or in order to avoid repetition: • *See you Friday*. • *I ought to write some letters and make some phone calls*.

The ellipsis… is used mainly to indicate an omission from a quoted passage: • *'There's rosemary, that's for remembrance… and there is pansies, that's for thoughts.'* If the quotation does not start at the beginning of a sentence, the ellipsis precedes it: • *'… a good fellow of infinite jest'*, and when

the end of a sentence is omitted, the three dots of the ellipsis are sometimes followed by a fourth, to indicate a full stop: • *'Cudgel thy brains no more….'*; if a whole sentence is left out, the sentence before the omitted one has a full stop and the ellipsis follows. An ellipsis is always three dots, or four if a full stop is included, except when a whole line of poetry is omitted, when a row of dots can be used to fill the length of the line.

The ellipsis is also used in the same manner as the dash, to indicate halting speech, an unfinished sentence, or an omitted obscenity (*see* **dash**). When used for an unfinished sentence, a dash suggests a more abrupt break, while an ellipsis gives an impression of speech tailing off: • *'I suppose I had hoped that you might…'* An ellipsis should not be used at the end of a passage to suggest that the rest of an episode can be left to the reader's imagination.

When using ellipsis in sentences to avoid repetition, the danger is that the omitted word(s) might not correspond with the word(s) repeated, as in the following two examples. In: • *I know him as well or even better than you do*, which in full would be *I know him as well as or even better than you know him*, the second *as* is omitted after *as well* but does not appear later in the sentence. In: • *No one has ever or will ever solve the mystery*, the omitted word is *solved*, not *solve*. The only case in which such a false ellipsis is acceptable is when the omitted word is part of the verb *to be*: • *I'm going to London and Sarah to Edinburgh*.

elliptical *see* **ellipse** or **ellipsis**?

else *Else* is often followed by either *than* or *but*: * *Nothing else than revolution is possible.* * *Anybody else but him would be preferable.* Some careful users object to following *else* with *but*; difficulties can be avoided by substituting such phrases as *nothing but* or *anyone other than*. Many people also dislike the use of *else* as a conjunction: * *Stop, else you'll have an accident.* Unless it is used in very informal speech, *or else* should be substituted.

For possessive forms, *see* **apostrophe.**

elude *see* **avoid**, **evade** or **elude**?

elusive *see* **allusive**, **elusive** or **illusive**?

EMAIL There are a number of broadly accepted conventions relating to the style and layout of emails (or e-mails), as described in the following panel, on pages 143–4. *See also* **letter writing; netspeak; smiley; text messaging; underscore.**

emanate or **exude**? *Emanate* and *exude* are sometimes confused. *Emanate*, meaning 'issue or proceed from', is generally employed as an intransitive verb and is usually followed by *from*: * *a foul smell emanated from the wound* whereas *exude*, meaning 'release or be released from' or 'make apparent by behaviour', is used as a transitive verb: * *The wound exuded a foul smell* * *The infant exuded happiness.*

embarrass This word, meaning 'cause to feel shy, ashamed, or self-conscious': * *She was embarrassed by her brother's behaviour*, is often misspelt. Note the -*rr*-, the -*ss*-, and the last vowel, which is an *a*, not an *e*.

emend *see* **amend** or **emend**?

emigrant or **immigrant**? An *emigrant* is someone who is migrating from his or her country: * *Thousands of emigrants left Britain for Australia under the assisted passage scheme.* An *immigrant* is someone who is migrating into another country: * *Some of the immigrants had only been in the country for a week.* The word *immigrant* should not be applied to non-white British residents unless it is known for certain that they were actually born abroad.

The word *émigré* is applied to someone who has been forced to leave a country, usually because of a repressive political regime or intellectual atmosphere. The reasons for leaving are generally less pressing than for those described as *refugees*, and *émigré* carries a suggestion of refined class and intellect that *refugee* lacks * *Nabokov is the most famous of Russian émigré writers.*

eminent, **imminent** or **immanent**? *Eminent* means 'outstanding, notable, or distinguished' and is particularly applied to people who have achieved some distinction or fame in their profession, or in the arts or sciences: * *an eminent barrister* * *an eminent poet.* *Imminent* means 'impending; about to happen; threatening': * *It now seemed that war was imminent.* *Imminent* should not be confused with the far less frequently used word *immanent*, which means 'inherent, indwelling', and has the respective philosophical and theological meanings of 'inherent' and 'pervading all things throughout the universe'.

emoticon *see* **smiley.**

142

EMAIL	
1 Headers	The layout of the headers (giving the identity of the sender, the person or people to whom the message has been sent, etc.) is inserted automatically by the software and is thus rarely subject to stylistic variation. Note that it is considered good practice always to complete the one optional element of the header – the subject box in which the sender briefly summarises the content of the message. Care should be taken over the wording of this summary, as some computer software will filter out messages that appear from this summary to be junk mail or to contain obscene or offensive material. Choose a concise title that also indicates the level of importance of the message attached. Copy the message only to people who really need to see it.
2 Opening phrase	The style for greetings is less rigid for emails than for letters, though some recipients may consider the lack of any opening greeting at all to be unfriendly. Some users prefer the formal greetings associated with letter writing (*Dear Mr Smith*, etc.) and dislike the informality of *Hi Sam!* or *Hello Joe!* Others may simply state the addressee's name: * *Mr Smith* * *Bill*, or alternatively launch straight into the message itself, particularly if replying to another's message: * *That's fine with me; let's meet on Friday.*
3 Presentation	Ideally, the email itself should immediately be visible in its entirety on the screen, avoiding the need for the reader to scroll down to get to the end. If a longer message is unavoidable, it is a good idea to summarise in an opening paragraph that which follows, so that the reader can choose whether to scroll down further or not. Longer blocks of text should be broken down into paragraphs. The use of empty lines between paragraphs and the insertion of bullet points or numbered sections makes for greater clarity. When replying to a previous message and making use of the 'reply to' facility, it is best to add a reply either above or below the received message and to avoid interspersing the existing text with responses. When sending a long message is unavoidable, one alternative is to send the bulk of the information as an attachment (a separate file sent with the email), making sure that the recipient's attention is drawn to the accompanying material.
4 Style	In terms of content, writers should observe the usual conventions of letter writing, taking care over spelling, grammar, and punctuation. Some users, however, deliberately flout the usual conventions in the interests of making their writing feel spontaneous and informal: * *hiyaaaa! wot u reckon to this then i think its cool*. The use of capital letters is similar to shouting and should be avoided. Asterisks can be used to highlight particular words *like this*. As in any other

4 Style (cont.)	kind of writing, it is good practice at the end to go back and check issues of style and presentation – if necessary printing the text out and checking it on hard copy.
5 Closing phrase	Many people close their emails with the fixed phrases traditionally used in letter-writing (*Kind regards, Best wishes, Love from, With thanks,* etc.). Note, however, that the more formal *Yours faithfully* and *Yours sincerely* are relatively rare. Some people type their name as a signature or have it appended automatically, while others omit any closing phrase altogether. If a response is expected, this should be clearly indicated. If not added automatically, it is sometimes sensible to conclude with details of telephone number, mobile telephone number, fax number and postal address.

emotive or **emotional**? *Emotive* means 'causing or arousing emotion, especially as opposed to reason': * *Taxation is always an emotive subject* (*Mind Your Own Business*). *Emotional* means 'expressing emotion, showing excessive emotion': * *an emotional woman* * *an emotional meeting*. *Emotive* is often used when *emotional* is intended, especially since the word has become more fashionable: * *She is very emotive and gets emotionally involved herself* (*The Times*). *Emotional* is also sometimes used when *emotive* would be better, although it is acceptable to use *emotional* in this sense: * *It features television spots of almost wrenching pathos, and is being supported by equally emotional posters* (*Sunday Times*).

empathy *Empathy* means 'an imaginative identification with another's feelings or ideas': * *He read all he could about the king, and meditated on his character, so by the time he came to play the part he felt a real empathy with Henry*. It has recently become a fashionable word and its frequent use as a mere synonym for *sympathy* is disliked by some: * *Essential attributes are... an empathy for the ideals within a voluntary organisation* (*Daily Telegraph*).

emulate *Emulate* means 'attempt to equal or do better than, especially by close imitation': * *Since the company's success, all our competitors are trying to emulate our products*. The word is often used in the sense of 'imitate closely' without the idea of rivalry: * *As a teenager he had admired John Lennon devotedly and had tried to emulate him in his dress and speech.*

enable The word *enabled* is in increasing use as a suffix, meaning 'made capable of working with a particular system': * *a WAP-enabled phone*. As a suffix, it should not be overused, as some people may find it jargonistic. Note also the use of *enabling* to describe the conferring of additional legal powers: * *enabling legislation.*

en bloc The French expression *en bloc* means 'all together, all at the same time': * *The whole committee decided to resign en bloc.*

encyclopedia or **encyclopaedia**? Both spellings of this word are acceptable, *encyclopaedia* being the more traditional in British English. In American English *encyclopedia* is the more frequent spelling and is now becoming standard in British English. *See also* -ae- *and* -oe-.

end The verb *end* is followed by the preposition *in* or *with*: * *words ending in* [or *with*] *'-er'*, and by *in* in the sense 'have as a result': * *Their marriage ended in divorce.* In the sense of 'finish' it is followed by *with*: * *He ended his speech with a vote of thanks.*

endemic or **epidemic**? *Endemic*, a formal word, is most frequently used as an adjective, meaning 'occurring in a particular area': * *an endemic disease* * *The plant is endemic in* [or *to*] *Africa.* An *epidemic* is the widespread occurrence or rapid spread of a disease: * *a flu epidemic* * *an epidemic of measles.* *Endemic* may also be used as a noun and *epidemic* as an adjective. Both words have figurative uses: * *Vandalism is endemic in the inner cities.* * *There was an epidemic of resignations after the takeover.*

end product and **end result** *End product* usually means 'the final product of a process, or series of processes': * *We use the best materials so that the end product is a quality item.* * *These young men are the end products of expensive public schools and the most exclusive colleges.* Both phrases may simply mean 'the eventual outcome', as in the phrase *end result*: * *The agreement is the end product/end result of many years of negotiation.* Many careful users dislike both these phrases, as *end* is clearly redundant.

enervate *Enervate* means 'weaken, to

lessen vitality or strength': * *It was an enervating climate and they felt listless most of the time.* It is sometimes used as though it meant quite the opposite, as a synonym for *invigorate* or *energise*, and is also sometimes used as though it meant 'irritate' or 'get on someone's nerves'. *Enervate* is most often used in the forms *enervated* or *enervating*.

England *see* **Britain**.

engrossed The adjective *engrossed* is followed by the preposition *in*: * *She was engrossed in her work and didn't hear the doorbell.*

enhance *Enhance* means 'improve, increase the value or attractiveness of': * *The new windows have considerably enhanced the value of the house.* * *The images had been digitally enhanced.* It has become a fashionable word, particularly used by employers in connection with extra benefits offered to employees: * *Excellent salaries are enhanced by a wide range of benefits including relocation assistance* (*Daily Telegraph*).

en masse The French expression *en masse* means 'all together; in a crowd or group': * *The people stormed the president's palace en masse.*

enormity or **enormousness**? *Enormity* means 'the quality of being outrageous or wicked, a very wicked act': * *Those experiences alerted him to the enormity of what was being done to the Jews* (*The Guardian*). *Enormousness* means 'the quality of being extremely large': * *They were daunted by the enormousness of the task.* *Enormity* is frequently used as though it meant *enormousness* but, although this usage is now acceptable in American English, most careful users of British English still dislike it.

enquiry or **inquiry**? For many users of British English the spellings of the nouns *enquiry* and *inquiry* (and of the verbs *enquire* and *inquire*) are completely interchangeable. Some users, however, maintain that *enquire* and *enquiry* should be used for simple requests for information: * *He enquired after her health.* * *an enquiry office* * *directory enquiries*, and *inquire* and *inquiry* for investigations, especially official ones: * *Police are now inquiring into the events that led up to his disappearance.* * *MPs are calling for a public inquiry into the causes of the disaster.* In American English, the general preference is to use *inquiry*.

enrol In British English the verb *enrol* ends in a single *l*, unlike the word *roll*. The *l* is doubled before suffixes beginning with a vowel: * *enrolled* * *enrolling*. Note that the derived noun *enrolment* has only one *l* in British English. The American spellings are *enroll* and *enrollment*.

en suite *En suite*, denoting an adjoining bathroom and bedroom, has long been in use as an adjective: * *an en suite bathroom*. The adoption of *en suite* as a noun is disliked by some and is best restricted to informal contexts: * *Does the bedroom have an en suite? En suite* is pronounced [on *sweet*].

ensure *see* **assure, ensure** or **insure**?

-ent *see* **-ant** or **-ent**?

enterprise Some people dislike the overuse of the noun *enterprise* in the context of self-employment and the setting up of new small businesses: * *the enterprise culture* * *the government's Enterprise Allowance Scheme* * *a network of Local Enterprise Agencies* * *Britain's enterprise economy* * *the enterprise initiative*. An *enterprise* is also simply a business or company: * *several large industrial enterprises*. *Private enterprise* is industry and business owned by independent individuals or groups, i.e. not receiving financial help from the government.

Note the spelling of *enterprise*, which always ends in *-ise*, unlike the word *prize*.

enthral In British English the verb *enthral* ends in a single *l*, which is doubled before suffixes beginning with a vowel: * *enthralled* * *enthralling*. Note that the derived noun *enthralment* has only one *l* in British English. The American spellings are *enthrall* and *enthrallment*.

enthuse The verb *enthuse* is a back-formation from *enthusiasm* and means 'show enthusiasm': * *The critics enthused over her new play*, or 'make enthusiastic': * *The minister enthused his congregation with his vision of a new church*. Although it has been in use, especially in American English, for over a century, it is still disliked by many people and is perhaps best avoided in formal use.

entomology or **etymology**? *Entomology* is the study of insects; *etymology* is the study of the origin and development of words. The two nouns should not be confused. An *etymologist* may think that all centipedes have a hundred legs, as the word is derived from Latin *centum* 'hundred' and *pes* 'foot', but an *entomologist* knows that they do not.

entourage Of French origin, the noun *entourage*, meaning 'attendants; retinue', is pronounced [ontuu*rahzh*] in English.

entrepreneur Like **enterprise**, the noun *entrepreneur* is losing its traditional connotations of risk and initiative and is indiscriminately applied to any person who becomes self-employed or sets up a new small business: * *Skills appear to be the main requirement for successful entrepreneurship... in contrast with the simple traditional view of the entrepreneur as someone who is risk loving (The Guardian).* * *She regularly scoured the Businesses for Sale columns of the papers for the inspiration that would turn her into an entrepreneur (Daily Telegraph).* Of French origin, the noun *entrepreneur* is frequently misspelt: note that it begins with *entre-*, not *enter-*, and ends in *-eur*, not *-er*.

envelop or **envelope**? The verb *envelop* means 'enclose, surround, or enfold' and is used both literally and figuratively: * *He was enveloped in a blanket and barely visible.* * *She spent a happy childhood, enveloped in love and security.* The noun *envelope* means 'something that envelops, a wrapper (particularly for a letter)': * *It arrived in a plain brown envelope. Envelop* is pronounced [in*vel*ŏp]. The preferred pronunciation of *envelope* is [*en*vălōp], although [*on*vălōp] is also heard.

enviable or **envious**? Both these adjectives are derived from the word *envy* (*see* **envy** or **jealousy**?). *Enviable* means 'causing envy'; *envious* means

'feeling envy': * *the enviable task of showing the film star around the building* * *He was envious of his sister's success.* The two words are not interchangeable.

environment *Environment* can be applied to the surrounding conditions of people and other organisms and can include physical and social influences, though many people are careful not to overuse this word. *Environment* and its derived nouns *environmentalism* and *environmentalist* are now much used in relation to ecology and the protection of the world's physical environment from pollution: * *The present wave of environmentalism is now being viewed as a long-term influence on the market. See also* -**friendly**; **green**.

envisage or **envision**? Both *envisage* and *envision* mean 'have a mental image of, especially of something hoped for in the future': * *They envisaged/envisioned a world where war and poverty no longer existed. Envisage* is more often used in British English and *envision* in American English. The words should not be used as mere synonyms for 'expect': * *A further downward trend in share prices is envisaged.* Careful users avoid using these words with *that*: * *We envisage an improvement in the situation* [not *envisage that the situation will improve*].

envy or **jealousy**? *Envy* involves the awareness of an advantage possessed by someone else, together with a desire to have that advantage yourself: * *She gazed at his car with envy.* * *I envy your ability to relax. Jealousy* involves a person's concern to avoid the loss of something they consider their own, and includes the tendency to be suspicious of rivalry and infidelity in relation to another person they are close to: * *Her husband's jealousy forced her to conceal even the most innocent encounters with other men.*

ephemeral This word, meaning 'lasting only a short time': * *the ephemeral pleasures of life,* is sometimes misspelt. Note particularly the *ph*, pronounced [f], and the sequence of vowels.

epic *Epic* originally applied to long narrative poems on a grand, heroic scale, like Homer's *Iliad* and *Odyssey* or the Finnish *Kalevala*. It was extended to other works with some of these qualities, or to series of events or episodes that might be fit subjects for an epic: * *a marvellous epic novel* (*Newsweek*, review of Salman Rushdie's *Midnight's Children*) * *the epic battle between Greenpeace and the whaling ships.* It is also sometimes used of anything more than usually large and impressive: * *an epic gathering,* but it is preferable not to use the word so that it entirely loses its connection with its heroic origins.

epicentre This overused word, which strictly speaking refers to the point above the centre of an earthquake or underground explosion, is often misinterpreted as meaning 'at the very centre of'. In this looser and inaccurate sense, its use has been much extended in recent years to refer to all manner of more or less 'cataclysmic' events: * *The prime minister stands at the epicentre of a looming international row.* * *The club is the epicentre of this developing new sport.* Careful users may prefer to replace the word in such contexts simply with 'centre'.

epidemic *see* **endemic** or **epidemic?**

epigram, epigraph, epitaph or **epithet?** These four nouns should not be confused. An *epigram* is a short witty saying; an *epigraph*, the least frequent of the four words, is a quotation or motto printed at the beginning of a book or engraved on a monument. An *epitaph* is a commemorative statement about a dead person, often inscribed on a gravestone; an *epithet* is a short descriptive word or phrase applied to a person, such as *Lionheart* in *Richard the Lionheart.* Some people dislike the extended euphemistic use of the word *epithet* in the sense of 'term of abuse': * *shouting epithets at each other.*

epitome This word, meaning 'typical example': * *He is the very epitome of the absent-minded professor,* is sometimes mispronounced. Note that there are four syllables [ipitŏmĭ].

eponym An *eponym* is a person from whose name a word is derived: * *sandwich* * *quisling* * *cardigan* * *ampere.* There are eponymous nouns: * *martinet* * *salmonella* * *listeria* * *watt*, adjectives: * *quixotic* * *herculean,* and verbs: * *bowdlerise* * *guillotine.* The only problem with the use of eponymous words is whether or not they are written with a capital letter. The rough rule is that the closer the connection between the word and the name, the more likely it is that a capital should be used. When a young man given to amorous adventures is called a *Romeo,* a definite allusion is being made to the Shakespearean character and a capital should be used. A capital would also be used when referring to *Platonic forms,* but not when referring to *platonic love*, a concept further removed from Plato. There are no firm rules with things named after the person who invented or popularised them. Generally such words are more likely to be capitalised when used adjectivally than when used as nouns: * *Wellington boots* * *wellingtons*, but this is very much a matter of custom. *Pullman cars* and *Bunsen burners* are nearly always capitalised, while *diesel engine* hardly ever is. Eponymous verbs such as: * *boycott* * *pasteurise* never have capital letters.

equable or **equitable**? *Equable* means 'regular, moderate, not given to extremes' and is frequently applied both to climates which are consistently mild and not subject to sudden changes, and to people who are placid and even-tempered. *Equitable* means 'fair, reasonable, impartial': * *It was an equitable agreement which both parties found satisfactory.*

equal Careful users avoid modifying the word *equal*, believing it to be incorrect to say that one thing can be more or less equal than another: * *All animals are equal but some animals are more equal than others* (George Orwell, *Animal Farm*).

equally The word *equally* should not be followed by *as* in such sentences as: * *She is a brilliant pianist, and her brother is equally talented* [not *equally as talented*]. The word *equally* may, however, be replaced by *as* in the above example, in which case it is stressed.

In the sentence: * *This dress is as expensive as that one*, the first *as* should not be preceded or replaced by *equally*. The sentence can, however, be rephrased as: * *The two dresses are equally expensive.*

equal to or **equal with**? When briefly indicating identity, equivalence, or similarity, *equal* is used as a verb with no preposition: * *x equals 5* or as an adjective followed by *to*: * *x is equal to 5*. In longer constructions, using *equal* as an adjective, it is preferable to use *equal with*, rather than *equal to*: * *The Bradford team have gained five points and are now equal with the team from Liverpool. Equal to* has the specific meaning of 'capable of meeting the requirements of': * *He seemed too young and inexperienced to be equal to the task.*

equitable *see* **equable** or **equitable**?

-er *see* **-ee** or **-er**?

-er or **-or**? The suffix *-er* is used to form nouns to indicate an occupation: * *lawyer* * *bricklayer*, or an action performed by a person: * *steeplechaser* * *messenger* * *enquirer*. The suffix *-or* is used in the same way with other words, normally those formed from Latin roots. Often these are words where there is no English verb base: * *sponsor* * *doctor* * *author* * *mentor*, but this is not always the case: * *actor* * *investigator* * *sailor*. It is not always possible to guess which ending should be used and sometimes both are acceptable: * *adviser/advisor* * *vendor/vender*. The *-er* ending is more frequent and more likely with recently coined nouns and those that do not have Latin roots. *See also* **-ee** or **-er**?

erogenous *Erogenous* zones are the parts of the body that are sensitive to sexual stimulation. Note the spelling of the word *erogenous*: a single *r* and *-gen-*, not *-gyn-* as in *misogynist*.

escalate *Escalate* is a back formation from *escalator*, and as a vogue word meaning 'expand, rise, intensify' tends to be overused. It is best confined to the description of an upward movement that increases step by step: * *Rents have escalated over the last five years.* * *Officials killed by mine as Tamil attacks escalate* (*The Times*).

Eskimo *see* **Inuit**.

esophagus *see* **oesophagus** or **esophagus**?

especially or **specially**? These adverbs are often used interchangeably, but there is a difference in their meanings. *Especially* means 'more than usual, in particular, above all': * *He was especially hungry.* * *I hate dogs, especially big ones.* *Specially* means 'specifically, purposely, in this particular way': * *The car is specially designed for handicapped people.* * *I made it specially for you.* *Specially* is often used where *especially* is intended, and sometimes, as in the last example, this might lead to confusion; *specially for you* might mean 'for you above all' or 'specifically for you'.

-ess The use of the feminine suffix *-ess* is sometimes regarded as patronising or sexist and is often unnecessary. Such nouns as *author*, *poet*, *sculptor*, *editor*, *manager*, etc., can be applied to people of either sex, making *authoress*, *poetess*, *sculptress*, *editress*, and *manageress* redundant. *Actress* and *hostess* are retained in some

contexts, although *actor* and *host* are generally considered to be of neutral gender. Certain occupational titles, such as *waiter* and *steward*, tend to be used as masculine nouns, *waitress* and *stewardess* being their feminine equivalents. The suffix *-ess* is obligatory in such words as *princess*, *duchess*, *countess* and *marchioness*. It is also used without risk of controversy in relation to certain female animals: * *lioness*. *See also* **non-sexist terms**; **sexism**.

essential The adjective *essential* is followed by the preposition *to* or *for*: * *Money is not essential to* [or *for*] *happiness*.

essentially *Essentially* should be used primarily to mean 'basically, inherently, or most importantly': * *The play is essentially a tragedy although there is some comic relief.* It tends sometimes also to be used with a weaker meaning of 'in general terms': * *It was essentially a good match*, or 'importantly': * *Your view isn't essentially different from mine.* Some people dislike this usage.

establishment *The Establishment* refers to the powerful figures in government (especially the civil service), the legal system, the established church, the armed forces, and the City of London, who are thought to control the country: * *The Prime Minister, the Archbishop of Canterbury, and the Lord Chief Justice were among the Establishment figures present.* *The Establishment* (sometimes with a lower-case *e*) is thought to have a conservative outlook, generally opposing changes to the existing order, and as such is often used as a derogatory term. A further meaning of *establishment* is 'a controlling or influential group': * *the pedigree-dog establishment*.

esthetic *see* **aesthetic**, **ascetic** or **acetic**?

estimation, **estimate** or **esteem**? *Estimation* is the act of estimating. An *estimate* is a figure, idea, cost, etc., arrived at by the process of estimation: * *an estimate of the time it will take.* * *a tradesman's estimate.* *Esteem*, a more formal word, means 'great respect': * *He held her in high esteem.* The noun *estimation* also means 'opinion' or 'regard': * *What, in your estimation, is the cause of the problem?* * *She went down in their estimation when the truth came out.*

Misunderestimate is an invalid elaboration of *estimate* and should be avoided. It attracted attention when used in a speech by US President George W. Bush.

et al. *Et al.* is an abbreviation of *et alii* and means 'and other people'. It is used particularly in writings of a formal technical nature to indicate the omission of other names: * *Similar findings have been recorded by Jones, Bernstein, et al.* Alternatively, it is sometimes used informally in ironic or humorous contexts: * *Here comes Bill, et al.* It should not be used in ordinary writing or in speech, and should be used only when a list is specific and does not start with *for example* or *such as*.

etc. The abbreviation *etc.* stands for *et cetera*, which means 'and other things; and so forth': * *The college offers several non-academic subjects – home econom-*

ics, physical education, craft and design, etc. It is used in technical or informal writing; in formal writing, however, *and so on* or *and so forth* are preferred. It is incorrect to write *and etc.*, or, in a list, to precede *etc.* by *for example* or *such as*. There is never any point in writing *etc. etc.*, although this is sometimes used in informal speech.

The correct pronunciation of etc. is [etsetĕră] or [etsetră], not [ekset(ĕ)ră].

ethics *see* **-ics**.

ethnic The original meaning of *ethnic* is 'classified according to distinctive social characteristics, e.g. race, culture, or language': * *There are many different ethnic groups in the USA*. The word is now used to mean 'belonging to a particular social group, especially a minority one': * *Shooting continued last night in Sukhumi, ... more than 24 hours after the start of ethnic clashes in which 11 people have been killed* (*Daily Telegraph*). Because ethnic groups tend to be defined in relation to the majority population, it has also come to mean 'belonging to a non-Western culture', 'foreign': * *But a great deal of ethnic food is not hot, but spiced, with pronounced flavours* (*Sunday Times*), and 'non-white': * *Labour now has three other ethnic MPs* (*Sunday Times*).

ethnic cleansing The phrase *ethnic cleansing* is a euphemism originally applied to the deportation and murder in 1991 of thousands of Muslims and Croats living in Bosnia. It has since been adopted to refer to similar programmes of extermination elsewhere in the world, such as in Rwanda and Kurdish Iraq, and is occasionally applied to earlier atrocities of this kind, including the extermination of Jews by the Nazis in the 1930s. Stephen Burgen (*The Guardian*) warns against the adoption of euphemisms coined by the perpetrators of atrocities: 'Already some newspapers have started taking ethnic cleansing out of quotation marks, thus moving the phrase one more step along the road to respectability.'

etymology *see* **entomology** or **etymology**?

euphemisms A *euphemism* is an inoffensive term used as a substitute for one that might give offence. Euphemisms tend to be used particularly when referring to sexual and bodily functions: * *private parts* (genitals) * *smallest room* (toilet) * *pass water* (urinate), and to death: * *She passed away.* * *I lost my wife two years ago.* Some euphemisms have arisen out of genuine feelings of sensitivity, but many are an attempt to cover up something reprehensible: * *the Nazi Final Solution* (mass extermination of the Jews) * *being economical with the truth* (lying).

The invention of new euphemisms in the business and professional worlds is becoming almost an art form: * *At one international computer company the accepted wording for falling behind is 'achieving schedule overrun'* (*Sunday Times*). * [An American] *hospital recently announced the relapse of an important patient by saying he 'did not fully achieve his wellness potential'. He later experienced a 'terminal episode'... previously known as death* (*The Times*).

Eurasian The meaning of *Eurasian* has changed over recent decades. Formerly it was used to describe a person of mixed British and Indian parentage; today it is used more widely to refer to a person of mixed white and Asian parentage: * *Politicians are becoming increasingly aware of the needs of the country's Eurasian population.*

Euro- Although the United Kingdom is part of Europe, British people have traditionally spoken of *Europe* to mean the whole continent apart from the United Kingdom. When United Kingdom membership of the European Community was mooted, it was often referred to as *going into Europe*, and *Europe* is now quite often used as a synonym for the European Union. The prefix *Euro-* is sometimes used in words which are connected with Europe in general: * *Eurocommunism* * *Eurobond* * *Eurovision* * *Eurobank*, but more often with those having connections with the European Union * *Euro-sceptic* * *Europhile* * *Eurocrat* * *Demand for the 'rare breed' of Euro-manager will far outstrip the supply in the single market* (*Daily Telegraph*).

Euro is the name of the single currency of the European Union.

evade, **evasion** *see* **avoid**, **evade** or **elude**?

evangelical or **evangelistic**? Evangelism is the activity of declaring the Christian gospel in order to bring about conversion to Christianity. *Evangelistic* is the adjective used to describe such activities: * *an evangelistic mission to the city. Evangelical* describes people and beliefs that emphasise salvation by faith in the death of Jesus Christ, personal conversion, and the authority of the Bible: * *evangelical Christians* * *an evangelical church.*

Evangelical is also used in the extended sense of 'very enthusiastic': * *speak with evangelical fervour.*

even The position of the word *even* in a sentence can influence its meaning. Compare the following sentences and their implications: * *Even I like opera on television* (so other people would like it still more). * *I like even opera on television* (presumably I would prefer things other than opera). * *I like opera even on television* (though it is inferior on television). In formal writing it is best to put *even* before the word it modifies, in order to make the meaning unambiguous – although in speech it is often more natural to put *even* before the verb: * *He doesn't even stop working on holiday.*

eventuate *Eventuate* is used, usually in formal contexts, to mean 'result': * *If the proposed merger takes place, this might eventuate in the new company having a monopoly of the market.* Many people think it pompous and affected, and believe it conveys nothing that is not conveyed by simpler and more usual words.

ever Some people dislike the use of *ever* with superlatives in such constructions as: * *the largest pie ever* * *his fastest speed ever*, as they feel that *ever* includes the future, as well as the past. The usage is well established, but the criticism can be met by changing the constructions slightly: * *the largest pie ever baked* * *his fastest speed to date/the fastest he has ever run.* The expressions *ever so* and *ever such* as intensives: * *He's ever so clever.* * *It's ever such a nice*

house should be confined to informal contexts, and *ever so* without an adjective or adverb following: * *Thanks ever so* is better avoided.

On whether to write *whatever* or *what ever*, *wherever* or *where ever*, etc., in such sentences as: * *What ever did he say next?* * *Wherever you travel you'll find businesses that accept our credit card*, see **whatever** or **what ever**?

every *Every* is used with singular nouns; all related words should be in the singular form: * *Every machine is equipped with a safety device.* The temptation to use plurals arises when a person wishes to avoid such gender-specific constructions as: * *I hope every committee member has remembered to bring his agenda.* Rather than use the controversial *their agendas* or the rather clumsy *his or her agenda*, it is better to rephrase the sentence: * *I hope all committee members have remembered to bring a copy of the agenda with them.* See also **each** or **every**?

everybody or **everyone**? The pronoun *everybody* and its synonym *everyone* are interchangeable in all contexts. Both are used with a singular verb but are sometimes followed by a plural personal pronoun or possessive adjective (see **they**): * *Everybody/Everyone has paid their fare.*

Note the difference between the one-word compound, *everyone* and the more specific two-word form, *every one* – both of which may be applied to people: * *Everyone knew the answer.* * *Every one of the contestants knew the answer.* Only the two-word compound is used of things: * *I bought six glasses and every one was cracked.*

everyday or **every day**? *Everyday* means 'completely ordinary' and is used as an adjective or (more occasionally) a noun: * *her everyday clothes* * *not part of the everyday*. *Every day* can be used as an adverb, meaning 'daily', and as a noun, meaning 'each day': * *Brush your teeth every day*. * *He starts every day with a half-hour exercise routine.*

evince *Evince* is a formal verb meaning 'show clearly; make apparent': * *Her writing evinces keen perception and skills of observation*. Some careful users believe that it should be applied only to qualities, not to attitudes or emotions, although it is generally acceptable in such applications.

ex As a prefix, *ex-* means 'former' or 'outside': * *the ex-chairman* * *an ex-directory telephone number*. It is usually attached with a hyphen. The noun *ex*, meaning 'former spouse' or 'former partner', should be restricted to informal contexts: * *She had a letter from her ex this morning*. The preposition *ex* is used in financial contexts in the sense of 'without' or 'excluding': * *ex interest* * *£150 ex VAT*. In commercial contexts it means 'from': * *ex stock* * *ex warehouse* * *ex works*. The phrase *ex stock* is sometimes misinterpreted as 'no longer in stock', through confusion with the prefix *ex-* in the sense of 'former'.

exaggerate This word, meaning 'represent as greater than is true', is sometimes misspelt. Note the *-gg-* and single *r*, as in *stagger*. See also **over-exaggerate**.

exalt or **exult**? *Exalt* means 'elevate' or 'praise'; *exult* means 'rejoice' or 'triumph': * *She was exalted to the position* of sales director. * *to exalt a hero* * *He exulted at his success.* * *to exult in victory*. Both words are formal and more frequently found in their derived forms, such as the adjectives *exalted* and *exultant* and the nouns *exaltation* and *exultation*.

exceed see **accede** or **exceed**?

excel The verb *excel* is followed by the preposition *at* or *in*: * *She excels at* [or *in*] *creative writing.*

except It is usually better to use *except* rather than *except for*: * *We all went for a walk except Flora*. The exceptions are at the beginning of a sentence: * *Except for Stuart, we are all under 40*, and when a whole statement is being qualified and *except for* means 'if it were not for': * *The room was silent except for the occasional squeak of a pen*. *Except for* is also used with the meaning 'without; but for': * *I wouldn't have got this far except for your support*, but this is an informal use and some careful users dislike it.

Excepting (meaning 'except, excluding') is considered acceptable only when used after 'always', 'not', 'only', or 'without': * *It was the happiest day of her life, not excepting her wedding day.*

Except as a preposition should be followed by the object form: * *except me* [not *I*] * *except him* [not *he*]. See also **accept** or **except**?

exceptional or **exceptionable**? *Exceptional* means 'out of the ordinary; uncommon': * *Apart from the exceptional quiet day, we've been kept busy all month*, and 'unusually good': * *This is an exceptional wine*. In British English, *exceptional* is often used of people to mean 'above average; superior; gifted': * *an exceptional student* * *an exceptional musician*. In American English, however, *exceptional* is applied to children of both below and above average ability, and is now applied particularly to physically challenged children, or those with learning difficulties. *Exceptional* should not be confused with *exceptionable*, which means 'objectionable; something to which exception might be taken': * *His words were not offensive in themselves but there was something in his manner that we found exceptionable.*

excess see **access** or **excess**?

exclamation mark Exclamation marks are used to indicate strong feeling or urgency: * *Hurray!* * *Go away!* * *Help!* They may come at the end of a sentence, as a substitute for a full stop, or at the end of a quotation, within quotation marks: * *'Ouch!' he cried.* Occasionally, they may occur in the middle of a sentence. Exclamation marks are used after interjections, oaths, and words representing loud noises: * *Oh!* * *Ow!* * *Crash!* * *Damn!* * *Gracious!*; after alarms and commands: * *Look out!* * *Quiet!* * *Fire!*; and after insults and curses: * *You bastard!* * *Rot in hell!* They are used after various exclamations expressing surprise, indignation, pleasure, or displeasure – often starting with *how* or *what* – and after some which have the form of questions: * *How beautiful!* * *What fun!* * *What a mess!* * *How we laughed!* * *Aren't you silly!* They are also used after longer sentences when strong emotion is being expressed: * *I'm absolutely sick to death of the lot of you!*

There are no words or utterances that always need an exclamation mark. The presence or absence of one indicates the intonation required when reading a word or sentence. * *You can't be serious!* would be read with a different intonation from: * *You can't be serious?* or: * *You can't be serious.*

Exclamation marks should be used sparingly, and never doubled or trebled. The excessive use of exclamation marks in writing, particularly when used in an attempt to create an atmosphere of excitement, fun, or humour, generally has a negative effect on the reader.

exclamations *Exclamations* are words, phrases, or sentences that express a strong feeling, such as surprise, anger, shock, excitement, etc.: * *Gosh!* * *Get out!* * *Oh dear!* They are always followed by an **exclamation mark**. In writing, exclamations are best restricted to direct speech. They may also be used in informal letters, but become less effective if overused.

exclude or **preclude**? *Exclude* means 'leave out' or 'prevent from entering'; *preclude* is used in formal contexts and means 'make impossible' or 'prevent from happening': * *A number of items were excluded from the list.* * *Lack of resources precluded further research.* The two verbs should not be confused.

executive An *executive* is a senior businessman or businesswoman. Many people object to the increasing use of the word in the sense of 'fashionable', 'luxurious', or 'expensive', describing items that are designed to appeal to those who aspire to the social level of an executive or to an executive's (supposed) high income: *

an exclusive development of executive homes * an executive bathroom. The adjectival use of the noun to describe items intended for or used by the executives of a company is more acceptable: * the executive restaurant * an executive jet.

exercise or **exorcise**? These two words should not be confused. *Exercise* is a noun and verb with various meanings, including 'a set of energetic movements', 'a short piece of school work', and, in formal contexts, 'make use of': * *You should take more exercise.* * *He exercised his right to remain silent.* The verb *exorcise* means 'expel evil spirits from': * *The house had been exorcised.* Both words are sometimes misspelt with -xc- in place of the -x-. Note also the -ise endings: *exercise* is one of the few words in which -ise cannot be replaced by -ize (see **-ize** or **-ise?**). *Exorcise* has the variant spelling *exorcize*, but the -ise ending is sometimes preferred by those who use the -ize form for other verbs.

The two words are not identical in pronunciation. The unstressed -or- in the middle of *exorcise* is pronounced [-or-], whereas the unstressed -er- in the middle of *exercise* has the weak sound of the final -er of *baker, tumbler*, etc.

ex gratia An *ex gratia* payment is one that is given as a favour, rather than because it is legally necessary. The literal meaning of the phrase *ex gratia* is 'by favour' and it is pronounced [eks *gray*shă].

exhausting or **exhaustive**? *Exhausting* means 'extremely tiring': * *I find Christmas shopping exhausting.* It should not be confused with *exhaus-*

tive, which means 'thorough; comprehensive; considering all possibilities': * *They made exhaustive enquiries but to no avail.* * *This is an exhaustive study, covering every aspect of the subject.*

exhilarate This word, meaning 'thrill or excite': * *an exhilarating experience*, is sometimes misspelt. Frequent errors include the omission of the *h* and the substitution of -ler- for -lar-.

existential *Existential* usually means 'relating to existence, particularly human existence': * *an existential statement*, or 'grounded in human existence; empirical': * *an existential argument for the existence of God*. It is also sometimes used to mean 'existentialist, based on existentialist philosophy': * *existential angst* * *Sartre's existential theories*. It may be used as a vogue word to mean 'referring to a subjective intellectual viewpoint', but this is generally considered pretentious.

ex officio The Latin phrase *ex officio* is used in formal contexts to describe a right or rank to which someone is entitled because of his or her occupation or position: * *The chairman is an ex officio member of all the subcommittees.* The phrase literally means 'by virtue of office'.

exorbitant This word, meaning 'excessive': * *an exorbitant price to pay*, is sometimes misspelt. There is no *h* in the spelling, unlike in *exhilarate*.

exorcise *see* **exercise** or **exorcise?**

exotic The original meaning of *exotic* is 'from another country, not native to the place it is found': * *exotic flowers*. By this definition the potato would be an exotic vegetable in Britain, but it is never spoken of as such, because *exotic* is now almost always used with the meaning of 'unusual, excitingly different, interestingly foreign': * *exotic food* * *exotic dances* * *travel to distant exotic lands*.

expatriate The word *expatriate*, meaning 'a person who is living in a country that is not his or her native country', is sometimes misspelt. Note the ending of this word: *-ate*, not *-ot* as in *patriot*.

expeditious or **expedient**? *Expeditious* and *expedient* come from the same root, but have quite different meanings. *Expeditious* means 'speedy; efficient': * *Our courier service is the most expeditious method of sending parcels*. *Expedient* means 'convenient for a particular situation or aim': * *It would not be expedient to change the law at the present time. Expedient* is associated with practical action and often also a concern for self-interest rather than moral considerations: * *You can't learn too soon that the most useful thing about a principle is that it can always be sacrificed to expediency* (W. Somerset Maugham, *The Circle*).

explicable In the traditional pronunciation of this word, which means 'able to be explained': * *no explicable reason for their behaviour*, the stress was on the first syllable [*ek*splikăbl]. It is now more usual and perfectly acceptable to stress the second syllable [ik*spli*-kăbl]. *See also* **stress**.

explicate *Explicate* means 'explain in detail; analyse and explore the impli-

cations of': * *This series of lectures aims to explicate Kant's critical philosophy and explore its influence on German idealism*. It is a formal word, usually confined to intellectual contexts, and it is pretentious to use it merely as a synonym for *explain*.

explicit or **implicit**? *Explicit* means 'clear; unambiguous, stated or shown in a direct manner': * *He gave them explicit instructions so there was no question of their making a mistake. Implicit* means 'implied; understood although not directly expressed': * *He detected an implicit criticism in her words*, and 'without reservation; unquestioning': * *I have implicit faith in your organisational abilities*. Because *explicit* is often used in phrases like: * *explicit scenes of sex and violence*, some people now use the word to mean 'frankly portraying (usually) sexual material': * *It is very explicit and is not suitable for family viewing*. It would be preferable to say *explicitly sexual* or *sexually explicit*, if that is what is meant.

exquisite *Exquisite*, meaning 'very delicate and beautiful': * *exquisite carvings*, may be pronounced in two ways. Some users prefer the stress to fall on the first syllable [*ek*skwizit]. Other users find this pronunciation slightly affected and prefer to stress the second syllable [ik*skwi*zit]. Many people dislike overuse of this word.

extant or **extinct**? *Extant*, a formal word, means 'surviving' or 'still in existence': * *Seven of Sophocles' plays are extant.* * *an extant law. Extinct* is usually applied to a species of animal or plant that has died out or to a volcano that is no longer active: * *The*

African elephant is in danger of becoming extinct. The two adjectives are virtually opposite in meaning.

extempore or **impromptu**? These two words have similar meanings but are not quite interchangeable. Both are applied to speeches and performances that are not rehearsed in advance; however, *extempore* suggests that nothing has been memorised or written down beforehand, even though the speaker or performer may have thought about the content in advance: * *He never wrote his sermons down but preached extempore. Impromptu* suggests something improvised on the spur of the moment, with no prior notice: * *She was surprised to be asked to address them but managed a splendid impromptu speech.*

extemporise or **temporise**? To *extemporise* is to act, make a speech, play music, etc., without preparation; to *temporise* (a rarer word) is to gain time by delaying, stalling, or being evasive: * *He extemporised an accompaniment on the piano.* * *She temporised, being unable to think of a reasonable excuse.* The two verbs should not be confused. Note the spellings, especially the *-or-* in the middle, unlike the *-er* ending of *temper.*

extensive or **extended**? *Extensive* means 'large' or 'widespread'; *extended* means 'lengthened in time or space': * *an extensive search* * *an extended contract.* Both adjectives may be applied to the same noun: * *an extensive discussion* covers a wide range of subjects; * *an extended discussion* goes on for longer than usual or longer than planned.

exterior, **external** or **extraneous**? *Exterior* means 'on the outside; relating to the outside': * *The house needs some minor exterior repairs.* * *Beneath his charming exterior he has a cold and selfish nature. External* means 'outwardly visible; suitable for the outside; coming from the outside; not essential': * *He has a few external injuries.* * *This ointment is for external use only.* * *The paper will be marked by the external examiners.* * *Do not be misled by these external details. Extraneous* means 'from the outside; not essential or relevant to the issue': * *We try to impart our values to our children but they are influenced by extraneous pressures.* * *Let's concentrate on the main issue and ignore those extraneous points.*

extinct *see* **extant** or **extinct**?

extract or **extricate**? Both these verbs have the sense of 'remove' or 'withdraw', but *extricate* is more formal and specifically refers to disentanglement or setting free from a difficult situation: * *to extract a tooth* * *to extract information* * *to extricate yourself from a complex relationship* * *to extricate a ball from a thorn bush.*

extraordinary This word, meaning 'unusual or exceptional': * *an extraordinary memory for details*, is sometimes misspelt, the most frequent mistake being the omission of the first *a*. Remember the two elements of the word: *extra* plus *ordinary*.

extrapolate Apart from specialised mathematical uses, *extrapolate* is usually applied to the estimation or prediction of unknown factors by the examination, analysis, and extension

of known data and past experience: *
We can extrapolate from the existing figures and our knowledge of the previous trends in mobility and birth control to produce an estimate of the populations of major cities in twenty years' time. Careful users, however, are aware that this word is in danger of overuse.

extricate *see* **extract** or **extricate**?

extrinsic *see* **intrinsic** or **extrinsic**?

extrovert or **introvert**? *Extrovert* and *introvert* are terms coined by the psychologist Jung that are now in general use. *Extroverts* are people who are more concerned with their surroundings than with their own inner selves; they are generally sociable, outgoing, and confident: * *He is an extrovert and enjoys nothing better than a noisy, crowded party. Introverts* are primarily concerned with their own mental and emotional lives. They are withdrawn and quiet, and prefer reflection to activity: * *She tends to be an introvert and is happiest in her own company.* The original spelling was *extravert*, and this is still more frequently used than *extrovert* in American English. The spelling *extrovert* was formed by analogy with *introvert* and is now standard in British English.

exuberant This adjective is sometimes misspelt, a frequent error being the insertion of *h* after the *x*. Note also the *-ant* ending.

exude *see* **emanate** or **exude**?

exult *see* **exalt** or **exult**?

F

façade This word, which means 'front', as in: * *the palace's ornate façade*, is usually spelt with a cedilla under the *c* in British English. The spelling is sometimes anglicised by dropping the cedilla, but the French pronunciation [fă*sahd*] is retained.

face or **face up to**? Some users object to *face up to* as an unnecessary extension of the verb *face*, meaning 'confront' or 'accept', but there is a slight difference in sense and usage between the two: *to face up to one's punishment* suggests a greater degree of effort and courage than *to face one's punishment*. The verb *face* often requires qualification: * *He faced death with equanimity.* * *They face the future with hope/fear. Face up to*, on the other hand, conveys the subject's feelings of resignation, determination, etc., by implication: * *I will just have to face up to the prospect of redundancy.*

facia *see* **fascia**.

facile In the sense of 'easily achieved' or 'superficial', the adjective *facile* is often used in a derogatory manner: *facile prose* is produced with little effort and lacks substance; a *facile argument* is glib and lacks sound reasoning. The usual pronunciation of *facile* is [*fas*il], rhyming with *mile*; the alternative pronunciation [*fas*il], rhyming with *mill*, is an accepted but rarer variant.

facilitate The verb *facilitate* means 'make easier' and is largely restricted to formal contexts. It should not be used as a synonym for 'help' or 'assist': * *His cooperation facilitated our task.* * *We were helped* [not *facilitated*] *in our task by the information he gave us.*

facility or **faculty**? These two words are sometimes confused in the sense of 'ability'. *Facility* is ease or skill that is often gained from familiarity; *faculty* is more likely to denote a natural power or aptitude: * *a facility for public speaking* * *a faculty for understanding complex scientific concepts.*

Both words have additional meanings. A *faculty* is a division of a college or university: * *the faculty of arts.* A *facility* provides the means for doing something; with this sense, referring to buildings or equipment, the word is usually found in the plural: * *conference facilities* * *sports facilities* * *facilities for the visually impaired.* Careful users avoid the extended use of *facility* or *facilities* as synonyms for 'premises', 'factory', or 'shop' (or, euphemistically, for 'toilet' – as in: * '*May I use your facilities?*').

factitious or **fictitious**? Both these adjectives mean 'not genuine', but they differ in usage and application and should not be confused. *Factitious*, which is largely confined to formal contexts, means 'artificially created' or 'unnatural': * *factitious enthusiasm. Fictitious* means 'false' or 'invented': * *a fictitious address*. *See also* **fictional** or **fictitious**?

factor A *factor* is a contributory element, condition, or cause; many people object to its frequent use as a synonym for 'point', 'thing', 'fact', 'event', 'constituent', etc.: * *A rise in the cost of raw materials and a fall in demand were important factors in the company's collapse.* * *We must discuss all the relevant points* [not *factors*].

faculty *see* **facility** or **faculty**?

Fahrenheit Note the spelling of this word, which should always begin with a capital letter. *See also* **Celsius**, **centigrade** or **Fahrenheit**?

fail Some people dislike the frequent use of the verb *fail* as a simple negative: * *Those who fail to pay the tax will be imprisoned.* The principal meaning of *fail* is 'try unsuccessfully (to do something)': the verb should not be used with reference to something that is deliberately not done. This misuse of *fail* can lead to ambiguity: * *The driver of the car failed to stop* may mean that the driver applied the brakes ineffectively, or that he or she made no attempt to stop.

faint or **feint**? *Faint* means 'not clear' or 'not strong'; it is also a noun or verb referring to a brief loss of consciousness. *Feint*, derived from the verb *feign*, refers to an action or movement intended to distract or mislead: * *On hearing the news she fell to the floor in a faint.* * *The boxer made a feint with his left fist then struck with his right.* The confusion between these two words may be due to the use of *feint* by printers and stationers to denote

the fine lines on ruled paper. In this sense either spelling is acceptable, *feint* being by far the more frequent.

fair or **fare**? These words, which are pronounced the same, are occasionally confused. The noun *fair* variously refers to an event with amusements, sideshows, stalls, etc., or a commercial exhibition: * *That was the week the fair came to town.* It should not be confused with *fare*, which means 'a fee for travel', 'passenger in a taxi', or 'choice of food or entertainment': * *He paid the fare and climbed on the coach.* * *The driver carried just two fares that evening.* * *This restaurant offers the usual fare.*

fait accompli A *fait accompli* is something that has already been done and cannot therefore be changed: * *She was afraid he might not agree to her selling the car, so she decided to present him with a fait accompli* [i.e. she did not tell him until she had sold the car]. Of French origin, the phrase is sometimes written or printed in italics in English texts. The plural is formed by adding *s* to both words: * *faits accomplis.* The anglicised pronunciation is [fayt ă*kom*plee].

false friends *False friends* are words in different languages that appear similar but in fact have different meanings. Examples of potentially confusable pairs include the English *gusto* ('enthusiasm') and the Italian *gusto* ('taste') and the English *assist* ('to help') and the French *assister* ('to attend').

falsehood, falseness or **falsity**? All three nouns are formal and are derived from the adjective *false*, meaning 'untrue', 'not genuine', or 'disloyal'. *Falsehood* and *falsity* are largely restricted to the first sense: * *the difference between truth and falsehood/falsity*. A *falsehood* is a lie; a *falsity* is an act of deception. *Falseness* may be used in all three senses, occurring most frequently in the sense of 'disloyalty': * *the falseness of his statement/name/behaviour*.

fantastic The use of *fantastic* as a synonym for 'excellent' or 'very great' is best restricted to informal contexts: * *a fantastic holiday* * *fantastic wealth*. *Fantastic*, related to the noun *fantasy*, originally meant 'fanciful' or 'unreal': * *a fantastic tale*. The word should be used with care, however, even in these senses, to avoid misinterpretation through association with its informal usage.

FAQ *see* **netspeak**.

Far East The countries of East Asia and South-East Asia were formerly known as the *Far East*, but this term is now considered outdated; *East Asia* and *South-East Asia* are the preferred terms.

fare *see* **fair** or **fare**?

farther, farthest, further or **furthest**? In the sense of 'more (or most) distant or advanced', and as the **comparative** and **superlative** of *far*, *farther* is interchangeable with *further* and *farthest* with *furthest*: * *London is farther/further from Manchester than it is from Bristol*. * *Which of the three can run the farthest/furthest?* Some users restrict *farther* and *farthest* to physical distance, using *further* and *furthest* in more figurative senses: * *the farthest country* * *further from the truth*. In the

sense of 'additional', *further* is more acceptable than *farther*. * *further supplies* * *further questions*. *Further* is also preferred in certain set phrases, such as: * *further education* * *until further notice* * *Further to your letter of...* *Farther* is not interchangeable with *further* when the latter is a verb, meaning 'advance' or 'promote': * *to further one's career*.

fascia The noun *fascia* may be spelt *facia*, without the *s*, but many careful users prefer *fascia*, the spelling of the Latin noun from which the word is derived. The word is pronounced [*fay*shă].

fascinate This word, meaning 'attract and capture the interest of', as in *fascinating tales about her experiences in China*, is sometimes misspelt. The most frequent error is the confusion of the *-sc-*. The term originates from the Latin *fascinare*, 'to bewitch'.

fatal or **fateful**? *Fatal* means 'causing death or ruin'; *fateful* means 'decisively important': * *a fatal illness* * *a fatal mistake* * *their fateful meeting that fateful night*. Both words are related to *fate*: *fatal* originally meant 'decreed by fate'; *fateful* means 'controlled by fate'. In its extended sense of 'having momentous and disastrous effects', *fatal* is sometimes interchangeable with *fateful*: * *a fatal/fateful decision*. *Fatal* should not be used in this sense if there is a possibility of misinterpretation: * *a fateful journey* may change one's life; *a fatal journey* may end in death. It is also worth remembering that the consequences of something *fateful* can be good, although the word is very rarely used in this sense.

fate or **fête**? *Fate* means 'destiny' or 'death': ＊ *She met her fate without flinching*. It should not be confused with *fête*, which denotes a celebration or fund-raising festivity: ＊ *There were hundreds of people at the fête. See also* **fête**. Note that both words are pronounced [fayt].

faun or **fawn**? The spelling of these two words, which have the same pronunciation [fawn], is sometimes confused. A *faun* is a wood spirit of classical mythology: ＊ *The goddess was surrounded by fauns*, and should not be confused with *fawn*, denoting a young deer: ＊ *The hunter killed a fawn with his first arrow.*

faux The French word *faux*, meaning 'artificial' or 'imitation', has appeared with increasing frequency over recent years in discussions of contemporary fashion: ＊ *faux marble* ＊ *faux pearls*. It is pronounced [fō].

faux pas A *faux pas* is a social blunder: ＊ *Inviting her ex-husband to the party was a faux pas*. Of French origin, the phrase literally means 'false step'; it is occasionally written or printed in italics in English texts. The plural form is the same as the singular: ＊ *faux pas*. The anglicised pronunciation is [fō pah].

fawn *see* **faun** or **fawn**?

fax The word *fax*, short for *facsimile* (a system for transmitting documents telegraphically), is now well established as a noun (referring to the system of transmission, the machine used for transmission, or the document transmitted) and as a verb: ＊ *by fax* ＊ *a combined fax, photocopier, and answering machine* ＊ *fax number* ＊ *a fax from head office* ＊ *I faxed the confirmation to the solicitors*. This abbreviation is acceptable in most contexts.

Fax is also used as a respelling of the plural noun *facts*, as in the trade names *Ceefax* and *Filofax*. This usage is less acceptable and may be confused with the sense of 'facsimile'; it is best restricted to informal contexts.

faze or **phase**? *Faze* is a verb, meaning 'worry' or 'daunt': ＊ *She was not fazed by the accusation*. *Phase* is a noun, meaning 'stage': ＊ *the next phase of the development* ＊ *He went through a rebellious phase in his early teens*, or a verb, often found in the phrasal forms *phase in/out*, meaning 'introduce/withdraw gradually': ＊ *The benefit will be phased out over a period of five years*. *Faze* is regarded by some people as an Americanism and is best restricted to informal contexts.

fearful or **fearsome**? Both adjectives can mean 'frightened' or 'frightening', but *fearful* is the more common: ＊ *fearful of what might happen* ＊ *a fearsome sight*. Either adjective may also be used in informal contexts as an intensifier, meaning 'extremely bad': ＊ *I had a fearful cold*. ＊ *fearsome weather.*

feasible The use of *feasible* to mean 'probable', 'likely', or 'plausible' is avoided by some careful users, especially in formal contexts, where the word is restricted to its original sense of 'practicable' or 'capable of being done': ＊ *The committee decided that the project was feasible*. Note the spelling of the word: *feasible* ends in -*ible*, not -*able*.

In informal usage, *feasible* now shares the double meaning of *possible*, describing something that can be done or something that might happen, and is therefore equally ambiguous: * *Raising prices is a feasible solution to the problem.*

feature The verb *feature* is best avoided where *have, include, display, appear,* etc., may be more appropriate: * *a new leisure centre, featuring squash and badminton courts and an indoor swimming pool with flumes.* It is principally used in the entertainment world: * *The concert will feature such singers as Britney Spears and Whitney Houston.* Both as a noun and as a verb, *feature* should be reserved for that which is prominent, distinctive, characteristic, or important: * *The spiral staircase is a feature of the house, which also has* [not *features*] *central heating, double glazing, and fitted carpets.*

February This word causes problems of spelling and pronunciation, the most frequent being the omission of the first *r*. The full pronunciation of the word is [*feb*rooări]. In informal speech, however, the simplified pronunciation [*feb*rări] and [*febe*wri] are often heard. The first of these is more acceptable than the second.

feedback The common use of *feedback* as a synonym for 'response' or 'reaction' is disliked by some people, who prefer to restrict the term to its original scientific or technical usage. In science and technology, *feedback* is the return of part of the output of a system, device, or process to its input, the most familiar example being the high-pitched whistle heard when the output from a loudspeaker returns to the microphone. Both in scientific contexts and in general usage, *feed-back* often leads to modification: * *We must try to get as much feedback as possible from the public to see if our ideas are being successfully put over. Feedback from customers helped us choose the most practical design.*

feel Some people dislike the use of the noun *feel* in the sense of 'impression' or 'quality', as in the phrases *a nice feel about it, a different feel about it,* etc.: * *The car has a strange feel about it.* Such expressions may be more succinctly worded by using the verb *feel*: * *The car feels strange.*

feet *see* **foot** or **feet**?

feint *see* **faint** or **feint**?

fellow- The word *fellow* may be combined with other nouns to denote a person in the same category: * *fellow passengers* are the people with whom one is travelling; * *fellow workers* are people who work in the same place. The two words are sometimes hyphenated in British English: * *fellow-students* * *fellow-sufferers*. A *fellow-traveller* is someone who sympathises with the aims of a political party (especially the Communist Party), but is not actually a member of it. *See also* **hyphen**.

female or **feminine**? The adjective *female* refers to the sex of a person, animal, or plant; it is the opposite of **male**: * *a female giraffe* * *female reproductive cells*. *Feminine* is applied only to people (or their attributes) or to words (*see* **gender**); it is the opposite of **masculine**: * *feminine charms*.

With reference to people, *female* is used only of the childbearing sex; it is used to distinguish women or girls from men or boys but has no further connotations: ＊ *There are more female students than male students at the college.* Care should be taken, however, in using the term *female* in certain contexts, as it may be considered denigrating or condescending. In such cases it may be better to use *woman* instead: ＊ *a woman doctor.*

Feminine, on the other hand, may be used of both sexes; it refers to characteristics, qualities, etc., that are considered typical of women or are traditionally associated with women: ＊ *a feminine hairstyle* ＊ *a feminine voice.* Note that some inanimate objects are conventionally considered feminine, among them ships and cars (although an official decision was taken in 2002 to the effect that ships were henceforth to be treated as genderless): ＊ *She's/It's a beautiful vessel.* ＊ *She corners very smoothly.*

Feminine is occasionally confused with *feminist,* which refers to the movement or belief (*feminism*) that women should have the same rights, opportunities, etc., as men, particularly in economic, political, and social fields. A *feminist* is a person who supports feminism, especially someone who is actively trying to bring about change: ＊ *She regards herself as a staunch feminist.*

For female, male, and neutral (gender-inclusive) terms for people, *see* table at **non-sexist terms**. *See also* **woman**.

ferment or **foment**? These two verbs are virtually interchangeable in the sense of 'stir up': ＊ *to foment/ferment trouble.* The principal meaning of *ferment* is 'undergo fermentation', referring to the chemical reaction involved in the formation of alcohol.

Its figurative usage is an extension of this sense. *Foment* is most frequently used figuratively; in medical contexts it retains its original meaning of 'bathe or apply warmth to'.

Confusion may be caused by the identical pronunciation of the two words [fĕ*ment*]; they may be more clearly distinguished, if necessary, by using the variant pronunciation of *foment* [fō*ment*].

-fest The suffix *-fest* has appeared with increasing frequency over recent years and is considered by many readers to have become a cliché and thus a coinage to be avoided. Based on the German *Fest,* meaning 'festival' or 'celebration', it has led to such unlovely creations as *songfest, fashionfest* and *foodfest.*

fête In British English this word, used as a noun or verb, is usually spelt with a circumflex accent over the first *e.* The word may be pronounced to rhyme with *gate* or *get,* the first of these being the more frequent. *See also* **fate** or **fête**?

fetid or **foetid**? Both spellings of this adjective, which describes something that has a very unpleasant smell, are acceptable. The spelling *fetid* is preferred in British English and is standard in American English. The first syllable of *fetid* may be pronounced with a short *e* [*fet*id] or with a long *e* [*feet*id]; *foetid* is usually pronounced [*feet*id]. See also **-ae-** and **-oe-**.

fetus *see* **foetus** or **fetus**?

few The difference between *few* and *a few* is one of expectation or attitude rather than number; both expressions mean 'some, but not many': * *They brought few books.* * *They brought a few books.* The first of these sentences suggests that more books were expected; the second, that no books were expected. The actual number of books may be the same in both cases. *Few* has negative force, contrasting with *many*; *a few* has positive force, contrasting with *none*: * *I have many acquaintances but few friends.* * *There are no pears left, but there are a few apples.* The same principles may be applied to *little* and *a little*: * *I added little salt to the soup.* * *I added a little salt to the soup.* For the distinction between (*a*) *few* and (*a*) *little*, see **fewer** or **less**?

fewer or **less**? *Fewer*, the comparative of *few*, means 'a smaller number of'; *less*, the comparative of *little*, means 'a smaller amount or quantity of': * *fewer cars* * *less unemployment*. The general rule is that *fewer* (or *few*) is used with plural nouns and *less* (or *little*) with singular nouns, whether the nouns are concrete or abstract: * *fewer pleasures* * *few chairs* * *less wood* * *little hope* * *fewer noises* * *less noise*.

The use of *less* in place of *fewer* occurs widely in informal speech and also, occasionally, in more formal contexts: * *Please remember, on Tuesdays and Thursdays there are less queues in the afternoon* (Post Office advertisement, *The Guardian*). Many people find this usage unacceptable in formal speech and writing.

The same principles apply to the phrases *fewer than* and *less than*: * *fewer than four people* * *less than a pint of milk*. However, plural units of measurement, time, money, etc., are regarded as singular in such cases: * *It took less than ten seconds.* * *He earned less than £100 last week.*

ff. see **cf.** or **ff.**?

fiancé or **fiancée**? An engaged woman's future husband is her *fiancé*; an engaged man's future wife is his *fiancée*. The feminine form is sometimes misspelt, the second *e* being dropped in error. Unlike some other words of French origin, *fiancé* and *fiancée* are always written with an acute accent over the (first) *e*. The pronunciation of both words is identical [fionsay].

fictional or **fictitious**? *Fictional* means 'of fiction' or 'not factual'; *fictitious* means 'false' or 'not genuine': * *a fictional detective* * *his fictional works* * *a fictitious address* * *her fictitious companion*. The two words are largely interchangeable in the sense of 'imaginary', 'invented', or 'not real': * [of Tom Sharpe's *Porterhouse Blue*] *he reassured dons that the college was fictitious and that no individual tutors had been singled out* (*Sunday Times*). However, *fictional* is more frequently used with direct reference to stories, novels, plays, etc.; *fictitious* is preferred for deliberate justification that is intended to deceive: * *Fagin, Scrooge and other fictional characters* * *this fictitious character you claim to have met in the park*. See also **factitious** or **fictitious**?

fifth The second *f* in this word is sometimes not sounded in speech. The pronunciations [fifth] and [fith] are both acceptable, but some people object to the latter.

figurative *Figurative* describes language that is used imaginatively to evoke a picture in the mind rather than used in a literal way: * *That lad's a real* *devil.* • *She's a tiger when she gets going.* Figurative language can be highly effective in creative writing and as a tool in colloquial speech, but it should be used only sparingly and with care in formal contexts. *See also* **metaphors**.

fill in or **fill out**? In British English, application forms and other official documents are usually *filled in* rather than *filled out*: • *Fill in this form and give it to the receptionist. Fill out* is the more frequent verb in American English and is disliked by some British users for this reason alone. It is also considered less appropriate – the blank spaces are to be *filled in*, like holes, to make the form complete. *Fill out* suggests enlargement or extension. The verb *fill up* is also occasionally used for this purpose.

finalise The verb *finalise* is best avoided where *complete, finish, conclude, settle*, etc., would be adequate or more appropriate: • *The preparatory work must be finished* [not *finalised*] *as soon as possible*. The word does, however, serve a useful purpose in some official contexts, combining the senses of 'reach agreement on' and 'put into final form': • *The committee met to finalise arrangements for the prime minister's visit.*

finished *see* **done** or **finished**?

finite verb A *finite verb* is a verb in any of the forms that change according to the person or number of the subject, or according to the tense in which the verb is used. • *She helps.* • *The train stopped.* • *I am cold.* • *They were leaving.* • *He has lost his key.* The follow-ing verbs are not finite: • *going* to school [present participle] • *covered* with dew [past participle] • I want *to leave* [infinitive].

fiord or **fjord**? Either spelling of this word is acceptable. Derived from the Old Norse *fjôrthr*, the word is usually applied to the narrow inlets of the sea along the Scandinavian coastline. Some users prefer *fjord*, the Norwegian spelling.

fireman or **firewoman**? *see* **non-sexist terms**.

first or **firstly**? *Firstly* may be used in place of the adverb *first* when enumerating a list: • *There are three good reasons for not buying the house: firstly, it is outside our price range; secondly, it is too close to the railway; thirdly, the garden is too small*. The use of *first... secondly... thirdly*, in accor-dance with a former convention that rejected the word *firstly*, remains acceptable and is still favoured by some users. Others, however, find this usage inconsistent, preferring *first... second... third* or *firstly... secondly... thirdly*, according to the context.
  Firstly should not be substituted for *first* in any of its other adverbial uses: • *When he first* [not *firstly*] *came to this country, he could hardly speak any English.* • *Janet came in first* [not *firstly*], *followed by the others.*

first name, Christian name, forename, given name or **baptismal name**? All these expressions are used to denote the name or names a person may have, additional to their surname; in British English *first name* is replacing *Christian name* as the most frequent choice: • *a dictionary of first names.*

The principal objection to *Christian name* is that it is inapplicable, and possibly offensive, to non-Christians. For this reason the expression is generally avoided on official forms, although it remains in regular use in informal contexts: • *We never address our teachers by their Christian names.*

The term *first name* may lead to confusion among people who bear more than one such name: • *My first name is Leonard but I prefer to be called by my middle name, Mark.*

Forename is widely used on official forms but is rarely heard in informal speech. It is not, however, the ideal solution, being inappropriate for people whose surname precedes their other names (Hungarians or the Chinese, for example). The same problem may occur with the use of *first name*.

Given name is the preferred expression in American English.

The term *baptismal name* is occasionally used in British English, but like *Christian name*, it is inapplicable to non-Christians.

fish or **fishes**? The plural of *fish* is *fishes*; *fish* is used in a wider range of contexts than the alternative form: • *Fish live in water and breathe through their gills.* • *There are five fish in the pond.* • *Dace, bream, roach, and burbot are all freshwater fishes/fish.*

Considered as a food item, *fish* usually remains in the singular: • *Fish is more expensive than some cuts of meat.*

The plural form *fishes* is most frequently found in technical contexts, often with reference to individual groups or species: • *The major division in this group is between jawless and jawed fishes* (*Longman Illustrated Animal Encyclopedia*). *See also* **phishing**.

fix or **repair**? Both these verbs are used in the sense of 'mend', *repair* being more formal than *fix*: • *Have you fixed the TV yet?* • *He was ordered to repair the damaged boat.* The verb *fix* has a number of other meanings, principally 'make firm' or 'fasten'.

fjord *see* **fiord** or **fjord**?

flagrant *see* **blatant** or **flagrant**?

flagship The noun *flagship*, which denotes the ship that carries the commander of a fleet, is increasingly used in figurative contexts with reference to the most important of a group of products, projects, services, etc.: • *Education policy is the Labour party's flagship.* • *The chain's flagship store is located in a fashionable quarter of San Francisco.*

flair or **flare**? The noun *flair* means 'a natural aptitude or instinct'; *flare* is a noun or verb referring to a sudden burst of flame: • *a flair for cookery* • *the flare of the torch.* The two words are sometimes confused, though not always with the humorous effect of an advertisement from the *Gloucestershire Echo* quoted by 'Peterborough' in the *Daily Telegraph*: • *Chef/Cook. Really talented person with flare required at Burlington Court Hotel, experience essential.*

Both words have additional senses. *flair* is an informal synonym for 'stylishness'; a *flare* is a light signal used especially at sea. *To flare* may also mean 'to become wider': • *a flared skirt.*

flak The use of *flak* in the sense of 'heavy adverse criticism or opposition' is best restricted to informal contexts: • *Civil-service bureaucrats come in for* *a lot of flak from the general public.* The principal meaning of *flak* is 'anti-aircraft fire'; of German origin, the word is an **acronym** of *Flieger* (flyer) *Abwehr* (defence) *Kanonen* (guns).

The spelling *flack*, an anglicised variant, is also occasionally used.

flaming With the advent of electronic communication, the word *flaming* has acquired a new meaning beside 'being on fire'. To users of electronic mail, it now refers also to the sending or receipt of a mass of insulting email: • *Flaming is a phenomenon that can cause its victims considerable distress.*

flammable *see* **inflammable**.

flare *see* **flair** or **flare?**

flaunt or **flout?** *Flaunt* means 'show off' or 'display ostentatiously'; *flout* means 'treat with contempt' or 'disregard': • *to flaunt your wealth* • *to flout the rules.*

The use of *flaunt* in place of *flout* is avoided by careful users in all contexts, but the confusion occurs with some frequency: • *If Christians are to campaign against total deregulation* [of the laws on Sunday trading] ... *they must be seen to obey, and not flaunt, the present law* (Jubilee Centre leaflet). This confusion may be due to the sense of openness that is conveyed by both verbs: the open disregard shown by a person who *flouts* a law may be seen as an open display, or *flaunting*, of contempt.

flee or **fly?** The rather literary verb *flee* means 'run away (from)': • *You must flee the town.* • *They have fled.* • *I fled from the danger.* The verb *fly* is also occasionally used in this sense in literary contexts: • *You must fly the town,*

but is more frequently found in its principal sense of '(cause to) move through the air': • *Most birds can fly.* • *The children were flying a kite.* • *We flew to Paris.* Note the potential ambiguity of the last example, which can mean 'We travelled to Paris by air' or 'We ran away to Paris' – although the second meaning is far less likely.

Both verbs are irregular: *fled* is the past tense and past participle of *flee*; *flew* and *flown* are the past tense and past participle, respectively, of *fly*. A *fly* is also an insect, but the name of the insect that sounds like *flee* is spelt *flea*, with a final *-a*.

fleshly or **fleshy?** *Fleshly* refers to the body as opposed to the spirit; *fleshy* refers to the flesh of a person, animal, fruit, or plant: • *fleshly desires* • *fleshly delights* • *fleshy thighs.* *Fleshly* is occasionally used in place of *fleshy*, but some users prefer to maintain the distinction between the two adjectives.

flier or **flyer?** The spellings *flier* and *flyer* are interchangeable in the sense of 'person or thing that flies', and in such compounds as • *high-flier/high-flyer.*

floor or **storey?** Both these nouns are used to denote a particular level of a building or the rooms on this level. The word *floor* is more frequently used with reference to the interior of the building; *storey*, with reference to the exterior or structure. • *He lives on the fourth floor.* • *The new office block will be ten storeys* [not *stories*] *high.*

In American English the *first floor* of a building is at ground level; in British English this is known as the *ground floor*, the *first floor* being the floor above (called the second floor in

American English). This difference in usage does not apply to the word *storey*. *See also* **storey** or **story?**

flounder or **founder?** To *flounder* is to struggle, move with difficulty, or act clumsily; to *founder* is to fail, break down, collapse, or sink. Both verbs can be used literally or figuratively: • *They floundered in the mud.* • *She floundered on to the end of the speech.* • *The project foundered through lack of support.* • *The ship foundered at the harbour entrance.*

The two verbs are often confused, especially in figurative contexts, *flounder* being used in place of *founder*: • [of the Stoke Mandeville Wheelchair Games] *future Games could flounder unless £2.5 million is raised* (*Bucks Advertiser*). The two words are not unrelated: *flounder* is probably a blend of *founder* and *blunder*. *Founder* itself is ultimately derived from the Latin *fundus*, meaning 'bottom'.

flout *see* **flaunt** or **flout?**

flu The word *flu* – the shortened form of *influenza* – is more frequent in general and some technical contexts than *influenza*: • *She's off work with (the) flu*. *Influenza* tends to be restricted to very formal contexts. *See also* **abbreviations; apostrophe**.

fluorescent This word, which is usually applied to light fittings, colours, paint, etc., may cause spelling problems. Note the order of the vowels in the first syllable (as in *fluoride*), the *-sc-* combination, and the *-ent* ending.

flush *see* **blush** or **flush?**

fly *see* **flee** or **fly?**

flyer *see* **flier** or **flyer?**

fob or **foist?** Both these verbs may refer to the disposal of something unwanted or worthless: • *He fobbed the damaged toys off on Christmas shoppers.* • *She always foists the boring jobs on her assistant.*

Many careful users dislike and avoid the insertion of *off* after *foist*, as in *fob off on*: • *She always foists the boring jobs off on her assistant.*

The verb *fob off* may also be used in the sense of 'appease' or 'put off': • *They fobbed us off with the usual excuses.* *Foist* may not be substituted for *fob* in this sense.

focus The doubling of the final *s* of the verb *focus* before a suffix beginning with a vowel is optional. Most dictionaries give *focused*, *focuses*, *focusing*, etc., as the preferred spellings, with *focussed*, *focusses*, *focussing*, etc. as acceptable variants. The noun *focus* has two plural forms, *focuses* and *foci* [*fōsi*], the latter being largely restricted to technical contexts. The final *s* of the noun *focus* is never doubled before the plural ending.

The noun *focus* is often used in the figurative sense of 'centre of attention or activity': • *The proposed route for the new bypass is the focus of today's meeting.* It is better avoided, however, where emphasis, object, point, etc., would be more appropriate: • *the emphasis* [not *focus*] *on unemployment in the Labour Party's manifesto.* *See also* **spelling**.

foetid *see* **fetid** or **foetid?**

foetus or **fetus?** There are two possible spellings for this word; the first is more frequent in British English, and the second in American English. *Fetus* is the standard spelling in scientific contexts: * *The fetus is no longer viable.* The distinction between *foetus* and *fetus* is in fact spurious, as there is no etymological basis for the *-oe-* spelling, the origin of the word lying in the Latin *fetus. Foetus* has, nonetheless, been in widespread use since the sixteenth century.

 See also -ae- *and* -oe-.

foist *see* **fob** or **foist**?

folk The use of the noun *folk* as a synonym for 'people' is generally considered to have slightly old-fashioned and sentimental associations: * *country folk* * *old folk* * *a name that will be familiar to many folk.* The word is chiefly used adjectivally, in the sense of 'traditional': * *folk music* * *folk dance* * *folklore.*

 Like people, the noun *folk* is used with a plural verb: * *Poor folk often dream of a life of luxury. Folks,* the plural form of the word, is largely restricted to informal contexts, in the sense of 'relatives': * *My folks are coming here tomorrow* or 'people in general': * *That's all, folks!*

following The preposition *following* may be confused with the present participle; it is best avoided where *after* or *because of* would be adequate or less ambiguous: * *They went home after* [not *following*] *the party. Following* may serve a useful prepositional purpose in the dual sense of 'after and as a result of': * *Following the burglary we fitted additional locks to the doors and windows. Following* is also used as an adjective meaning 'next' or 'about to be mentioned': * *I*

left the following morning. * *The following tools will be required...*

follows, as *see* **as follows**.

foment *see* **ferment** or **foment**?

foot or **feet**? The plural of *foot,* as an imperial unit of measurement, may be *foot* or *feet:* * *a six-foot fence* * *five feet tall* * *nine feet eight inches long* * *a pane of glass measuring two foot six by four foot three.* In compound adjectives that precede the noun, the singular form *foot* is always used: * *a three-foot rod.*

 For measurements in feet and inches, *feet* is preferred in more formal and precise contexts: * *seven feet four inches.* In informal usage the word *inches* is omitted and the plural form *foot* is more frequent: * *seven foot four.* In such expressions as *three feet high* or *ten foot wide,* the same distinctions of formality and precision may be applied: * *The wall must be exactly three feet high.* * *The room is about ten foot wide.* For larger measurements, such as the height of a mountain, *feet* is preferred to *foot* in all contexts, but metric equivalents are increasingly being used.

for *see* **because, as, for** or **since**?

for- or **fore-**? The prefix *for-* usually indicates prohibition (*forbid*), abstention (*forbear*), or neglect (*forsake*). The prefix *fore-* means 'before': * *foreboding* * *forecast* * *forefather. See also* **forbear** or **forebear**?; **forgo** or **forego**?

forbade *Forbade,* the past tense of the verb *forbid,* may be pronounced [fŏr*bad*] or [fŏr*bayd*]. The first of these pronunciations, rhyming with *mad* rather than with *made*, is the more frequent.

Forbad, an alternative spelling of *forbade*, is always pronounced [för*bad*].

forbear or **forebear**? *Forbear* is the only accepted spelling of the verb, which means 'to refrain': * *I shall forbear from criticising her appearance.* The noun, meaning 'ancestor', may be written *forebear* or *forbear*, the spelling *forebear* being the more frequent: * *His forebears were wealthy landowners.* The two words are not identical in pronunciation: the verb is stressed on the second syllable [for*bair*]; the noun, whichever spelling is used, is stressed on the first syllable [*for*bair]. *See also* **for-** or **fore-**?

forbid or **prohibit**? Both these verbs are used in the sense of 'refuse to allow', *prohibit* being more authoritative than *forbid*: * *I forbid you to visit her.* * *The rules prohibit us from visiting her.* Note the difference in construction: *forbid* is followed by an infinitive with *to*; *prohibit* is followed by an *-ing* form with *from*. *See also* **forbade**.

forceful or **forcible**? *Forceful* means 'having great force'; *forcible* means 'using force': * *a forceful personality* * *forcible expulsion.* Something that is *forceful* may be contrasted with something that has little force; something that is *forcible* may be contrasted with something that uses no force. In many contexts, in the sense of 'powerful' or 'effective', the two words are virtually interchangeable: * *a forceful/forcible reminder.* (Some people may interpret a *forceful* reminder as one that is powerfully presented, and a

forcible reminder as one that has a powerful effect.) *Forcible* should not be replaced by *forceful* where physical force or violence is involved or implied: * *forcible entry.*

fore- *see* **for-** or **fore-**?

forebear *see* **forbear** or **forebear**?

forefather or **foremother**? *see* **non-sexist terms**.

forego *see* **forgo** or **forego**?

foregone *Foregone*, meaning 'already settled' or 'predetermined', is usually encountered in the phrase *a foregone conclusion*: * *Electoral defeat is a foregone conclusion.* Many people dislike the recent tendency to use *foregone* as a noun: * *It's a foregone that the party will block such action.*

forehead This word is usually pronounced [*forrid*], rhyming with *horrid*. The variant pronunciations [*for*hed] and [*forred*] are widely used and accepted.

FOREIGN WORDS AND PHRASES The following table, on pages 173–9, lists both familiar and less familiar foreign borrowings, with their language of origin in the middle column and their meaning in the right-hand column. Cross-references to main entries in the *Good Word Guide*, e.g. *see* **au fait**, are also included.

foreman or **forewoman**? *see* **non-sexist terms**.

forename *see* **first name, Christian name, forename, given name** or **baptismal name**?

FOREIGN WORDS AND PHRASES

ab initio	Latin	from the beginning
ab ovo	Latin	from the beginning
a cappella	Italian	unaccompanied
addendum	Latin	addition
à deux	French	for two people
ad hoc	Latin	for this purpose (see **AD HOC**)
adieu	French	goodbye
ad infinitum	Latin	endlessly (see **AD INFINITUM**)
adios	Spanish	goodbye
ad lib	Latin	spontaneously
ad nauseam	Latin	interminably (see **AD NAUSEAM**)
ad rem	Latin	to the point
aficionado	Spanish	enthusiast, expert (see **AFICIONADO**)
agent provocateur	French	secret agent
agitprop	Russian	propaganda
aide-de-camp	French	assistant
aide-mémoire	French	reminder
à la carte	French	from a separately priced menu (see **A LA CARTE**)
à la mode	French	chic
al dente	Italian	lightly cooked
alfresco	Italian	out-of-doors
alma mater	Latin	a person's school or college (see **ALMA MATER**)
alter ego	Latin	other self
alumnus/alumna	Latin	former male/female pupil (see **ALUMNUS**)
amanuensis	Latin	secretarial assistant (see **AMANUENSIS**)
amour propre	French	self-esteem
ancien régime	French	the old system
angst	German	anxiety
apparatchik	Russian	underling
a priori	Latin	deductive (see **A PRIORI**)
apropos	French	with regard to, appropriate, incidentally (see **APROPOS**)
au contraire	French	on the contrary
au fait	French	well-informed (see **AU FAIT**)
au naturel	French	with nothing added
au pair	French	live-in domestic helper

au revoir	French	goodbye
badinage	French	humorous banter
beau monde	French	fashionable society
bête noire	French	detested or feared thing or person (*see* **BÊTE NOIRE**)
bijou	French	compact but elegant
bona fides	Latin	good faith (*see* **BONA FIDE**)
bon appétit	French	enjoy your meal
bonhomie	French	geniality
bon mot	French	witticism
bon viveur	French	person who enjoys good living
bon voyage	French	farewell
bouquet garni	French	mixture of herbs
bric-a-brac	French	bits and pieces
carpe diem	Latin	seize the moment
carte blanche	French	freedom of action (*see* **CARTE BLANCHE**)
casus belli	Latin	cause of conflict
cause célèbre	French	notorious affair
caveat emptor	Latin	buyer beware
chargé d'affaires	French	diplomat below ambassador
chef d'oeuvre	French	masterpiece
che sarà sarà	Italian	what will be, will be
chez	French	at the house of
chutzpah	Yiddish	audacity
ciao	Italian	goodbye
compos mentis	Latin	of sound mind
contretemps	French	argument or difficulty
cordon sanitaire	French	protective barrier
coup de grâce	French	decisive blow (*see* **COUP DE GRÂCE**)
coup d'état	French	revolution (*see* **COUP D'ÉTAT**)
crème de la crème	French	the very best (*see* **CRÈME DE LA CRÈME**)
cum laude	Latin	with honours
curriculum vitae	Latin	summary of a person's career (*see* **CURRICULUM VITAE**)
debacle	French	fiasco
de facto	Latin	in actual fact (*see* **DE FACTO**)
déjà vu	French	something already seen or experienced (*see* **DÉJÀ**
de jure	Latin	by legal right (*see* **DE JURE**)

denouement	French	final outcome (*see* **DENOUEMENT**)
de rigueur	French	required by social custom (*see* **DE RIGUEUR**)
diktat	German	order
distingué	French	distinguished
distrait	French	distracted
dolce vita	Italian	the soft life
double entendre	French	phrase with a risqué second meaning (*see* **DOUBLE ENTENDRE**)
du jour	French	of the day, fashionable (*see* **DU JOUR**)
éclat	French	success, ostentation
émigré	French	emigrant
éminence grise	French	influence behind the scenes
en bloc	French	all together (*see* **EN BLOC**)
encore	French	again
en croûte	French	cooked in pastry
en famille	French	with one's family
enfant terrible	French	unorthodox person
en masse	French	in a body (*see* **EN MASSE**)
ennui	French	boredom
en passant	French	incidentally
en route	French	on the way
en suite	French	connected, adjoining bathroom and bedroom (*see* **EN SUITE**)
entente cordiale	French	cordial relationship
entre nous	French	between ourselves
ergo	Latin	therefore
esprit de corps	French	team spirit
et al.	Latin	and other people (*see* **ET AL.**)
ex cathedra	Latin	with authority
ex gratia	Latin	as a favour, by favour (*see* **EX GRATIA**)
ex officio	Latin	by virtue of one's office (*see* **EX OFFICIO**)
ex post facto	Latin	retrospective
extempore	Latin	unpremeditated (*see* **EXTEMPORE** or **IMPROMPTU**?)
factotum	Latin	general employee
fait accompli	French	done deed (*see* **FAIT ACCOMPLI**)
faux	French	artificial
faux pas	French	social blunder (*see* **FAUX PAS**)
femme fatale	French	seductress

fin de siècle	French	end-of-the-century
flambé	French	in flaming liquor
garni	French	served with a garnish
gauche	French	awkward, clumsy
genre	French	style (see **GENRE**)
goujon	French	strip of meat or fish
gravitas	Latin	seriousness (see **GRAVITAS**)
habeas corpus	Latin	writ to summon a person before court
hasta la vista	Spanish	until we meet again
haute couture	French	high fashion
haute cuisine	French	high-quality cuisine
hoi polloi	Greek	common masses (see **HOI POLLOI**)
hors de combat	French	out of action
hors d'oeuvre	French	appetiser (see **HORS D'OEUVRE**)
idem	Latin	something already mentioned
imbroglio	Italian	confusion, muddle
in absentia	Latin	in the absence of a person
in camera	Latin	in private
incognito	Latin	under a false identity
incommunicado	Spanish	out of communication
in extremis	Latin	in extreme difficulty (see **IN EXTREMIS**)
in flagrante delicto	Latin	caught in the act
ingénue	French	naive young woman
in loco	Latin	in place of (see **IN LOCO PARENTIS**)
in memoriam	Latin	in memory of
in situ	Latin	in its existing position
in toto	Latin	completely
in transit	Latin	on the way
in utero	Latin	in the womb
in vitro	Latin	in a test tube
ipso facto	Latin	by the fact itself
je ne sais quoi	French	indefinable quality
jihad	Arabic	holy war
joie de vivre	French	enthusiasm for living
kamikaze	Japanese	suicide, suicidal
kaput	German	dead, defeated, broken
laissez-faire	French	unrestricted (see **LAISSEZ-FAIRE**)

largesse	French	generosity
leitmotiv	German	basic theme
lèse-majesté	French	disrespect
lingua franca	Italian	common language (see **LINGUA FRANCA**)
locum tenens	Latin	temporary substitute
macho	Spanish	ostentatiously masculine (see **MACHO**)
maestro	Italian	master, conductor
magnum opus	Latin	masterpiece (see **MAGNUM OPUS**)
maître d'hôtel	French	headwaiter
malaise	French	unease, debility
mañana	Spanish	tomorrow
manqué	French	unsuccessful
mea culpa	Latin	I am to blame
mélange	French	mixture
ménage	French	household
ménage à trois	French	relationship involving three people
modus operandi	Latin	method or procedure (see **MODUS OPERANDI**)
modus vivendi	Latin	compromise (see **MODUS VIVENDI**)
mot juste	French	appropriate word (see **MOT JUSTE**)
mutatis mutandis	Latin	with necessary changes made
née	French	born (see **NÉE**)
nil desperandum	Latin	never despair
noblesse oblige	French	the obligations of nobility
noli me tangere	Latin	warning against interference
nom de plume	French	pen name
non sequitur	Latin	statement that does not follow logically from what preceded it (see **NON SEQUITUR**)
nouveau riche	French	newly rich person
nouvelle cuisine	French	healthy style of cookery
objet d'art	French	work of art (see **OBJET D'ART**)
oeuvre	French	literary or artistic work
opus	Latin	work (see **OPUS**)
outré	French	unconventional
panache	French	flamboyance
paparazzi	Italian	press photographers (see **PAPARAZZI**)
par excellence	French	beyond compare (see **PAR EXCELLENCE**)
parvenu	French	upstart
pas de deux	French	dance for two

passé	French	outmoded
pastiche	French	imitation
patois	French	non-standard dialect
peccadillo	Spanish	minor vice (*see* **PECCADILLO**)
penchant	French	inclination (*see* **PENCHANT**)
per annum	Latin	annually (*see* **PER ANNUM**)
per capita	Latin	per head (*see* **PER CAPITA**)
per pro	Latin	used when signing a letter on behalf of someone else (*see* **P.P.**)
per se	Latin	in itself, as such (*see* **PER SE**)
persona non grata	Latin	banned or excluded person
petit bourgeois	French	lower middle class
pièce de résis-	French	chief attraction (*see* **PIÈCE DE RÉSISTANCE**)
pied-à-terre	French	temporary lodging
plus ça change	French	the more things change, the more they are the
post hoc	Latin	henceforth
précis	French	summary
prima facie	Latin	at first view (*see* **PRIMA FACIE**)
pro bono publico	Latin	for the public good
pro forma	Latin	invoice sent in advance
pro rata	Latin	proportionately (*see* **PRO RATA**)
protégé(e)	French	pupil (*see* **PRODIGY** or **PROTÉGÉ**?)
quid pro quo	Latin	exchange (*see* **QUID PRO QUO**)
quod erat demonstrandum	Latin	which was to be proved
raison d'être	French	motivation (*see* **RAISON D'ÊTRE**)
re	Latin	concerning (*see* **RE**)
recherché	French	choice, obscure
résumé	French	summary
risqué	French	indelicate, improper
roué	French	rake, debauchee
sangfroid	French	composure, equanimity
savoir faire	French	assurance, capability (*see* **SAVOIR FAIRE**)
sic	Latin	thus (*see* **SIC**)
sic passim	Latin	so throughout
sine qua non	Latin	something essential (*see* **SINE QUA NON**)
smorgasbord	Swedish	buffet
sotto voce	Italian	under the breath

spiel	German	chatter, sales pitch
status quo	Latin	the existing state of affairs
sub judice	Latin	before the court
sub rosa	Latin	in confidence
sui generis	Latin	in a class of its own (*see* **SUI GENERIS**)
table d'hôte	French	fixed price meal (*see* **TABLE D'HÔTE**)
tempus fugit	Latin	time flies
terra firma	Latin	firm ground
tête-à-tête	French	private conversation (*see* **TÊTE-À-TÊTE**)
timbre	French	resonance, tone
tour de force	French	feat of skill or ingenuity (*see* **TOUR DE FORCE**)
trompe l'oeil	French	optical illusion
ultra vires	Latin	outside one's power or scope
verbatim	Latin	word for word
vis-à-vis	French	in relation to (*see* **VIS-À-VIS**)
viva voce	Latin	orally
volte-face	French	about-face
weltanschauung	German	world view
weltschmerz	German	sentimental pessimism
wunderbar	German	wonderful
wunderkind	German	successful young person
zeitgeist	German	spirit of the time

forever or **for ever**? The adverb *forever* may be written as a single word in all contexts, but some people prefer to use the two-word form *for ever* for the principal sense of 'eternally': * *We shall remember her for ever.* * *It will stay there for ever.* * *Liverpool for ever!* In the sense of 'continually' or 'incessantly', the single word *forever* is preferred to the two words *for ever*. * *He is forever changing his mind.* The use of *forever* to mean 'a very long time' is best restricted to informal contexts: * *It will take forever to get this carpet clean.*

foreword or **preface**? Both these nouns are used to denote the statement or remarks that often precede or replace the introduction to a book. *Preface* is the older of the two words and the more frequent; some authorities suggest that a *foreword* is usually written by a person other than the author of the book: * *The foreword will be written by a distinguished historian.* * *Have you read the author's preface?* See also **forward** or **forwards**?; **prefix** or **preface**?

forgo or **forego**? *Forgo* is the usual spelling of the verb that means 'do without' or 'give up', *forego* being an accepted variant spelling of this verb: * *The union will not forgo the right to strike.*

The verb *forego*, meaning 'go before' or 'precede', is most frequently found in the adjectival forms *foregoing* or *foregone*, which have no alternative spellings: * *the foregoing instructions* * *a foregone conclusion. See also* **for-** or **fore**?; **foregone**.

formally or **formerly**? These two adverbs are sometimes confused, being identical in pronunciation. *Formally* means 'in a formal manner'; *formerly* means 'in the past': * *formally dressed* * *Sri Lanka, formerly called Ceylon.*

former and **latter** Of two previously mentioned items or people, *the former* denotes the first and *the latter* the second: * *On Monday evening there will be a lecture on local history and a meeting of the chess club: the former will be held in the main hall, the latter in the lounge.*

Neither the *former* nor the *latter* should be used to refer to a single previously mentioned item; the item may be repeated or a simple pronoun, such as *it* or *this*, may be used: * *The killer left the scene of the crime in a stolen car; the car/this* [not the *latter*] *was later found abandoned in a lay-by.*

Of three or more items or people, the first-mentioned should be referred to as *the first, the first-named,* or *the first-mentioned* (not *the former*) and the last-mentioned should be referred to as *the last, the last-named,* etc. (not *the latter*): * *The secretary, the treasurer, and the chairman had a meeting at the house of the first-named* [not the *former*] *yesterday evening.*

For the sake of simplicity or clarity, *the former, the latter, the first-named, the last-mentioned,* etc., should be avoided if possible by restructuring the sentence or by repeating the names of the items or people concerned.

formerly *see* **formally** or **formerly**?

formidable This word may be stressed on the first syllable [*for*midăbl] or the second syllable [fŏrm*i*dăbl]. The first of these pronunciations is the more widely accepted in British English. *See also* **stress**.

formulae or **formulas**? The noun *formula* has two accepted plural forms, *formulae* and *formulas. Formulae*, pronounced to rhyme with *tree*, is largely restricted to scientific contexts: * *chemical formulae.* For other senses of *formula*, the plural form *formulas* is preferred by most users: * *no easy peace formulas that will resolve the dispute* * *There are many different formulas for success.*

forte The noun *forte*, denoting a person's strong point, may be pronounced as two syllables [*for*tay] or as a single syllable [fort]. The first of these pronunciations is the more frequent of the two, although the second is closer to the French original (*forte* is an English feminine rendering of French *fort*, meaning 'strong; strength'). The two-syllable pronunciation may possibly have been influenced by the musical term *forte*, meaning 'loud' or 'loudly'. Pronounced [*for*ti] or [*for*tay], this word is of Italian origin.

forth or **fourth**? *Forth* means 'forward' or 'out into view' and usually has rather literary overtones: * *She never spoke again from that day forth.* * *He brought forth a knife.* It should not be confused with *fourth*, which refers to the number four: * *This was the fourth time he had taken the test.*

fortuitous or **fortunate**? *Fortuitous* means 'happening by chance' or 'accidental'; *fortunate* means 'having or happening by good fortune' or 'lucky': * *a fortuitous meeting* * *a fortunate child*. A *fortuitous* occurrence is not necessarily good, but the similarity between the two words, and their frequent confusion, has led to the increasing acceptance of 'fortunate' as a secondary meaning of *fortuitous*. Many people object to this usage, which can result in ambiguity: * *a fortuitous discovery* may be accidental, or lucky, or both. Unlike *fortunate*, the adjective *fortuitous* is not applied to people: * *You were fortunate to find another job so quickly*.

forty Note the spelling of *forty*, with the *u* of *four* and *fourteen* omitted. Similarly, *fortieth* has no *u*.

forward or **forwards**? As an adjective, *forward* is never written with a final *s*: * *forward motion* * *a forward remark* * *forward planning*. In some of its adverbial senses, the word may be written *forward* or *forwards*: * *He ran forward/forwards to greet his father*.

Some users restrict the adverb *forwards* to physical movement in the opposite direction to *backwards*; some use *forwards* in the wider adverbial sense of 'ahead in space or time'; others use *forward* for all adverbial senses of the word. In idiomatic phrasal verbs, such as *come forward*, *put forward*, *look forward to*, etc., and in the sense of 'into a prominent position', the adverb *forward* is never written with a final *s*: * *She came forward as a witness*. * *I put forward the proposals at the meeting*.

The word *forward* is also used as a noun (denoting a player or position in various sports) and as a verb: * *to forward a letter*.

Forward, pronounced [for**wă**rd], should not be confused with *foreword*,

pronounced [for**wě**rd] – the introduction to a book.

See also **foreword** or **preface**?; **-ward** or **-wards**?

foul or **fowl**? As a noun, *foul* means 'illegal act': * *The player was sent off for a vicious foul*. It should not be confused with *fowl*, denoting a chicken or similar bird: * *He ate neither fish nor fowl for several weeks*. Both words are pronounced [fowl].

founder *see* **flounder** or **founder**?

fourth *see* **forth** or **fourth**?

fowl *see* **foul** or **fowl**?

foyer In British English this word, meaning 'an entrance hall or lobby in a theatre, hotel, etc.', is usually pronounced [**foi**ay]. The pronunciations [**foi**ĕr] and [fwah**yay**] are also acceptable, the later being an approximation of the French original.

fraction Some people dislike the use of *a fraction* to mean 'a small part' or 'a little': * *We flew there in a fraction of the time it takes to go by sea*. * *Could you turn the volume down a fraction, please?*

A fraction is not necessarily a small part of the whole: nine-tenths is a fraction. To avoid possible ambiguity or misunderstanding, a small fraction should be clearly expressed as such: * *Why dine out when you can eat at home for a small fraction of the cost?* * *Only a small fraction of the work has been completed*. *See also* **hyphen**.

fraught *Fraught with* means 'filled with' or 'charged with': * *fraught with problems* * *The expedition was fraught with danger*. The use of the adjective *fraught* alone, in the sense of 'tense' or 'anxious', is disliked by some people and is best restricted to informal usage: * *a fraught evening* * *He looked fraught.*

-free The adjective *free* is frequently used in combination to indicate the absence of something undesirable or unpleasant: * *lead-free petrol* * *rent-free accommodation* * *additive-free food* * *pollution-free water* * *duty-free spirits* * *a trouble-free life*. Some careful users object to this usage, preferring to replace some compounds by a paraphrase: * *accommodation, for which no rent is paid* * *water that has not been polluted.*

free gift Some users avoid the phrase *free gift*, arguing that it is a tautology, all gifts being necessarily free. Others accept that the phrase has acquired a specific meaning, denoting something given away for promotional purposes.

freeze or **frieze**? The verb *freeze* means 'change from liquid into solid form': * *Water freezes at 0° C*. The noun *frieze* denotes a decorative or ornamental band or strip on a wall: * *a frieze depicting the history of the town*. The two spellings should not be confused. *Freeze* is also used figuratively: * *to freeze prices* * *a pay freeze*.

friable The adjective *friable*, a technical term, means 'crumbly' or 'easily broken up': * *friable soil*. It has no etymological connection with the verb *fry*.

-friendly Some people object to the vogue for attaching the adjective *friendly* to an increasing number of nouns, on the model of **user-friendly**: * *customer-friendly* * *Readers... voted*

M&S Britain's least parent-friendly high street store (*Daily Telegraph*). * *ozone-friendly* * *environment-friendly* * *dolphin-friendly*. In the last three examples, *-friendly* has developed the extended sense of 'not harmful': * *Supermarkets... realised that green products, from ozone-friendly aerosols to bleach-free nappies, can give a marketing edge* (*Daily Telegraph*). *Environment-friendly* has further evolved into the phrase *environmentally friendly*, sometimes hyphenated: * *No one knows the real costs of this new environmentally-friendly policy*. The opposite of *-friendly* is *-hostile* or *-unfriendly*: * *user-hostile* * *ozone-unfriendly*. See also **environment**; **green**.

frieze *see* **freeze** or **frieze**?

frolic The verb *frolic* adds a *k* before suffixes beginning with a vowel: * *frolicked* * *frolicking* * *frolicky*. There is no *k* in the derived adjective *frolicsome*. *See also* **spelling**.

front-line In military contexts, the *front line* is the most advanced or exposed position in a battle. Some people dislike the use of the phrase in figurative or non-military contexts: * *a front-line defender of government policy* * *front-line inner-city areas.*

fuchsia Note the spelling of this plant name, particularly the silent *-ch-*. It is pronounced [*few*shă]. The plant name honours the German botanist Leonhard Fuchs (1501–66).

-ful For nouns ending in *-ful*, such as *cupful, spoonful, sackful, handful, mouthful*, etc., most users prefer the plural form *-fuls*: * *two cupfuls* * *three spoonfuls*. The plural form *-sful*, as in:

* *three cupsful* * *two spoonsful*, is regarded by some authorities as rare or old-fashioned and by others as incorrect; it is best avoided. It is important to recognise the difference between *-ful* and *full*: * *a bucketful of water* denotes the quantity of water held by a bucket, but not the bucket itself; *a bucket full of water* denotes both the bucket and the water it contains.

The tendency to confuse *-ful* with *full* sometimes leads to the misspelling of both nouns and adjectives, such as *spoonful*, *doubtful*, etc., with the ending *-ll* (*see also* **fullness** or **fulness**?).

fulfil Note the spelling of this word: in British English, neither *l* is doubled. The spelling of the derived noun in British English is *fulfilment*. The spellings *fulfill* and *fulfillment* are almost exclusively restricted to American English. However, the final *l* of the verb is doubled in British English before a suffix beginning with a vowel, as in *fulfilled* and *fulfilling* (*see also* **spelling**).

full *see* **-ful**.

fullness or **fulness**? Both spellings are acceptable, *fullness* being the more frequent in British English. In the nouns derived from adjectives ending in *-ful*, the *l* is never doubled: * *faithfulness* * *hopefulness*.

full stop The principal use of the full stop as a punctuation mark is to end a sentence that is neither a direct question nor an exclamation. In creative writing, reference books, etc., the full stop may also mark the end of a group of words that does not conform to the conventional description of a sentence: * *He had drunk six pints of beer and two whiskies. Two very large whiskies.* A full stop is often used in decimal fractions, times, and dates: * *3.6 metres of silk* * *at 9.15 tomorrow morning* * *your letter of 26.6.07.*

Full stops are also used in some abbreviations, although the main problems here concern punctuation. The modern tendency is to omit full stops whenever possible: * *BBC* * *AD* * *D H Lawrence* * *Prof.* Full stops are increasingly being omitted from capital abbreviations: * *USA* * *EU*, and they are always omitted from acronyms: * *NATO* * *UNESCO*. When an abbreviation is a contraction (i.e., the final letter of the abbreviation corresponds with the final letter of the word) there is usually no full stop: * *Mr* * *Dr* * *Rd*. There is more likely to be a full stop when the abbreviation is just the first part of the word: * *Rev.* * *Feb.*, although here too the modern trend is to omit it. Abbreviated names can take a full stop or not: * *C.S. Lewis* * *A S Byatt*. There should be no full stop if a capital letter does not stand for a whole word: one should not write *T.V.* (television) or *D.N.A.* (deoxyribonucleic acid) as *tele-* and *deoxyribo-* are not complete words. There are usually no full stops in the abbreviations of weights and measures: * *km* * *oz* and never in chemical symbols: * *Fe* * *Cu*.

A full stop is sometimes called a *stop*, a *point*, or (in American English) a *period*. When part of email and website addresses it is pronounced as *dot*.

See also **brackets; exclamation mark; question mark; quotation marks; semicolons; sentences.**

fulsome The adjective *fulsome* was derived originally from *full* and the suffix *-some*, and is usually interpreted as meaning 'abundant' or 'generous': * *fulsome praise* * *fulsome compliments.* Note, however, that some people may interpret it as meaning 'offensively excessive, exaggerated, or insincere'. The adjective's derogatory connotations may have developed from a mistaken etymology that associated *fulsome* with *foul.*

fun The use of the word *fun* as an adjective, meaning 'enjoyable' or 'amusing', is disliked by some users and is best restricted to informal contexts: * *a fun game* * *a fun person.* The commercial use of *fun-size* to mean 'small': * *a fun-size packet of sweets* * *fun-size apples,* is also to be avoided.

function The verb *function* is best avoided where *work, perform, operate, serve, act,* etc., would be adequate or more appropriate, particularly in general, non-technical contexts: * *The machine never works* [not *functions*] *properly in very hot weather.* * *The automatic lock serves* [not *functions*] *as a safety device.* Some people also object to the excessive use of the noun *function* as a synonym for 'duty', 'role', 'party', etc.: * *What are the precise functions of bishops and priests in the modern world?*

function word A *function word* is a word that has no real meaning of its own but serves chiefly to create a grammatical relationship between other words. They can be subdivided into conjunctions, such as *and* and *but*; articles, such as *a* and *the*; prepositions, such as *at* and *with*; adverbs, such as *around* and *how*; modal verbs, such as *can* and *will*; primary verbs, such as *be* and *do*; and pronouns, such as *I* and *this.*

functional shift The term *functional shift* describes the process by which a word may shift in grammatical identity from its original function and be used in a new way. Examples include *gift*, which was originally a noun but has subsequently been also used as a verb, and *rubbish*, which began as a noun but came to be used also as an adjective: * *a rubbish salary* and as a verb: * *The teacher rubbished his essay.* Care should be taken in using words that have undergone such shifts in function, as they are often disliked by other users.

fundamental The adjective *fundamental* means 'basic', 'essential', 'primary', or 'principal'; it is best avoided where *important, major, great,* etc., would be more appropriate: * *the fundamental difference between the two systems* * *a major* [not *fundamental*] *improvement in East-West relations.* The noun *fundamental*, which is more frequently used in the plural form, denotes a basic principle, constituent, etc.: * *the fundamentals of the issue.*

funeral or **funereal**? The adjective *funereal* means 'like a funeral; suggestive of death; mournful; gloomy': * *funereal music* * *The atmosphere was funereal.* It should not be confused with the noun *funeral* used adjectivally: * *a funeral service* * *a funeral cortege.*

fungi *Fungi*, one of the plural forms of *fungus*, may be pronounced to rhyme with *try* or *tree*; the *g* may be hard, as in *gum*, or soft, as in *germ*. The pronunciations [*fungg***ī**] and [*funj***ī**], rhyming with *try*, are the most frequent. The first of these is closer to the singular form, which has a hard *g* sound. *Funguses* is an alternative plural of *fungus*. *See also* **spelling**.

furore The final *e* of the noun *furore*, meaning 'uproar' or 'craze', can cause problems of spelling and pronunciation. In British English the *e* is never omitted, while *furor* is the usual American spelling. *Furore* is usually pronounced as a three-syllable word stressed on the second syllable [few*rori*]. It is occasionally pronounced as a two-syllable word stressed on the first syllable [*fewror*]; this is also the pronunciation of the American spelling.

further, furthest *see* **farther, farthest, further or furthest?**

G

Gaelic or **Gallic**? *Gaelic* is a noun or adjective that refers to the Celtic languages of Scotland and Ireland: ▪ *to speak Gaelic* ▪ *a Gaelic word*. *Gallic* is an adjective, meaning 'of France or the French': ▪ *a Gallic custom*. The pronunciation of *Gaelic* is [*gay*lik], with the alternative pronunciation [*ga*lik] used especially in regions where the language is spoken. This second pronunciation is identical to that of *Gallic*, and so may cause confusion or ambiguity in some contexts.

gait or **gate**? *Gait* means 'way of walking or moving': ▪ *He walked along the deck with a rolling gait*. It should not be confused with *gate*, meaning 'movable barrier' or 'point of access': ▪ *There was a queue of people at the gate.*

Gallic *see* **Gaelic** or **Gallic**?

gallop Note the spelling of this verb, particularly the -*ll*- and the final *p*, which is not doubled before -*ed*, -*ing*, etc.: ▪ *The horse galloped across the field.* ▪ *galloping inflation.*

gamble or **gambol**? The verb *gamble* means 'take a risk on a game of chance'; *gambol* means 'skip and jump playfully'. The spelling of these words is sometimes confused, although their meanings are very different: ▪ *He went to the casino to gamble.* ▪ *lambs gambolling in the fields.*

gaol *see* **jail** or **gaol**?

garage This word may be pronounced [*ga*rahzh] or [*ga*rij]. Many users prefer the former pronunciation. The stress falls on the first syllable in British English, although in American English [ga*rahzh*], the second syllable is stressed.

gases or **gasses**? The plural of the noun *gas* is *gases* or, less commonly, *gasses*. *Gasses* is also a form of the verb *gas*, meaning 'affect with a gas' or 'talk idly'. *See also* **spelling**.

-gate The suffix -*gate*, derived from the *Watergate* affair (a scandal involving Richard Nixon, then president of the USA, in 1972), is sometimes attached to other words to denote a political scandal: ▪ *Irangate/Contragate* (an American scandal in 1987 involving the sale of arms to Iran, and use of the profits to supply arms to the anti-Communist Contras in Nicaragua) ▪ *The 'Dianagate' scandal, the disclosure of intimate tapes of conversations believed to be between the princess and James Gilbey, her close friend* (Sunday Times). Many of these coinages are inevitably journalistic and ephemeral in usage and are best avoided in formal contexts.

gate *see* **gait** or **gate**?

gauge This word, which means 'measure or standard', is frequently misspelt. The *u* comes after the *a* and not before it. The correct pronunciation is [gayj]. A mispronunciation [gawj] may arise from the unusual spelling.

gay The adjective *gay* is so widely used as a synonym for 'homosexual' that its use in the original sense of 'cheerful', 'merry', or 'bright' may be open to misinterpretation in some contexts: * *a gay bachelor* * *a gay party.* The noun *gay* is principally applied to a homosexual man, *lesbian* being the preferred term for a homosexual woman: * *a community centre for gays and lesbians.* The noun derived from *gay* in the sense of 'homosexual' is *gayness*; in other senses it is *gaiety.*

In the sense of 'homosexual', *gay* is becoming increasingly acceptable in formal contexts and for many gay people is preferable to *homosexual* itself. Note, however, that its acceptance in this context may be threatened in the long term by a new use of the word to mean 'stupid' or 'rubbish': * *That idea's just so gay.* See also **same-sex**.

gender The word *gender* refers to the grammatical classification of nouns as masculine, feminine, or neuter. When referring to people, the use of *gender*, which can encompass an element of upbringing and choice, as a synonym for 'sex', which is determined at birth, is avoided by many users in formal contexts: * *Applications are invited from suitably qualified candidates of either sex* [not *gender*], although there are occasional formal circumstances in which this is considered appropriate: * *gender studies.* In some compounds in informal use, *gender* is used instead of *sex*, e.g. *gender-bending* – 'the blurring of the difference between the sexes, for example by transvestism'. The frequency of this usage is attributable both to the use of the word *sex* as a synonym for 'sexual intercourse' and to the association in English grammar between gender and sex.

In many languages all nouns are of either masculine or feminine gender: the French word for *flower* is feminine; the Italian word for *carpet* is masculine. In English, however, masculine nouns refer to male people, animals, etc., and feminine nouns to female people, animals, etc.: *king*, *brother*, *drake*, and *bull* are masculine nouns; *heroine*, *queen*, *mother*, *vixen*, and *cow* are feminine nouns. See also **non-sexist terms**; **sexism**.

general or **generic**? The adjective *general* has a wide range of meanings, including 'widespread', 'overall', and 'not specialised or specific': * *general opinion* * *general knowledge.* *Generic* means 'referring to a whole class or group': * *a generic term for products that do not damage the environment.* *Generic* is also used in the sense 'cheaper, because it does not have a trade name': * *a generic drug.*

genetic, **genial** *see* **congenial**, **genial**, **congenital** or **genetic**?

genre The word *genre*, meaning 'category' or 'style', may be pronounced in different ways. The anglicisation of the French pronunciation is [zhonrǎ], but [jonrǎ] is also widely heard. A third pronunciation, [zhahnrǎ], is occasionally used but this is sometimes considered pretentious.

gentleman *Gentleman* is used as a synonym for 'man' in some formal or official contexts and as a term of politeness: * *Show the gentleman to his room.* * *Ladies and gentlemen, may I* *introduce tonight's guest speaker?* The noun *gentleman* has connotations of nobility, chivalry, and good manners: * *a country gentleman* * *If you were a gentleman you'd stand up and give me your seat.* See also **man**; **woman**.

geriatric Many people object to the increasing use of the noun and adjective *geriatric* as derogatory synonyms for 'old person' or 'elderly': * *These geriatric drivers should be banned from the roads.* * *The country is governed by a bunch of geriatrics.* *Geriatrics* is the branch of medical science concerned with the diseases of old age and the care of old people; the use of *geriatric* in such contexts as the *geriatric ward* of the hospital is acceptable to all users.

gerunds *see* **infinitive**; **-ing forms**.

get In formal contexts, *get* can often be replaced with an appropriate synonym, such as *become, buy, obtain, receive,* etc.: * *It is becoming* [not *getting*] *increasingly difficult to obtain* [not *get*] *impartial advice on financial matters.* However, if the synonym sounds clumsy or unnatural in context, or causes ambiguity, *get* should be retained or the sentence restructured. The same principles apply to phrasal verbs, idioms, and other expressions containing *get*, such as *get out* (escape), *get by* (survive), *get dressed* (dress), *get well* (recover): * *I often get up/rise at six.* * *They will get married/marry in the spring.* See also **got**.

geyser The noun *geyser*, meaning 'hot spring' or 'water heater', is usually pronounced [*geezĕr*] in British English and [*gīzĕr*] in American English.

gibe, jibe or **gybe**? The word *gibe*, or variant spelling *jibe*, means 'jeer or taunt': * *gibes/jibes and insults*. *Gybe*, sometimes spelt *gibe* or *jibe*, is a nautical term referring to the movement of a ship's sail.

gild or **guild**? *Gild* is a verb, meaning 'cover with gold' (*see also* **gilt** or **guilt**?) or 'make golden in colour': * *gilded picture frames* * *The setting sun gilded the leaves*. *Guild* is a noun, denoting an organisation of craftsmen, tradespeople, or other people with similar or related interests: * *a guild of wine merchants* * *She belongs to the Townswomen's Guild*. *Gild* is also a rare variant spelling of the noun *guild*.

gilt or **guilt**? *Gilt* is a variant form of the past participle of the verb *gild* (*see* **gild** or **guild**?) used as an attributive adjective in the sense of 'covered with gold': * *a gilt candlestick*. As a noun, *gilt* denotes the gold or other substance used for this covering: * *Some of the gilt had worn away*. It should not be confused with the noun *guilt*, meaning 'responsibility for wrongdoing': * *a feeling of guilt* * *He admitted his guilt*.

gipsy or **gypsy**? This word, meaning 'wanderer', has two spellings: *gipsy* and *gypsy*. Some users prefer the former, but the latter indicates the derivation from Egyptian. At one time this migrant people was thought to have originated from Egypt. Note that either word should be spelled with a capital *G-* when referring to a specific group of such people as opposed to travelling people in general. See also **Roma**; **traveller**.

girl *see* **woman**.

given name *see* **first name, Christian name, forename, given name** or **baptismal name?**

glacier The first syllable of this word, which means 'a vast area of ice', may be pronounced to rhyme with *mass* [*glas*eer] or with *clay* [*glay*seer]. Both pronunciations are acceptable in British English, while [*glay*shĕr] is the usual American English pronunciation.

glamorous Some people object to the frequent use of the adjective *glamorous* as a synonym for 'beautiful', 'romantic', 'exciting', 'interesting', etc.: * *a glamorous setting* * *a glamorous career.* The adjective is best restricted to the combination of showy attractiveness, fashion, romance, excitement, charm, and fascination that is known as *glamour:* * *a glamorous film star* * *a glamorous lifestyle.*

The *u* of *glamour* is usually omitted in the adjective *glamorous*, although some dictionaries acknowledge the rare variant spelling *glamourous*.

glass ceiling A *glass ceiling* is an invisible barrier to promotion, based on sex or race. Increasingly, the expression is being applied to barriers that prevent women from rising to top-level executive positions: * *Does your organisation have a 'glass ceiling'?* * *A motion calling for the removal of the glass ceiling on women becoming bishops is back on the synod's agenda* (*The Guardian*). A glass ceiling was originally conceived of as a hypothetical barrier that allowed people to see a goal while at the same time preventing them from reaching it.

global The adjective *global* is increasingly used with specific reference to geo-political or environmental issues that affect the whole world: * *global consciousness* * *global politics* * *Terrorism is a global issue.* * *Think of the world as a global village.* This usage is probably influenced by the phrase *global warming* (*see* **greenhouse effect**). The use of *global* in such contexts may cause confusion with the more general sense of 'worldwide'.

Globalisation is often used to refer to the process by which local phenomena can assume global relevance: * *the globalisation of terrorism* * *the globalisation of aid programmes.* It is frequently used negatively to describe the process by which large international companies can dominate markets and even economies worldwide: * *protests resulting from the globalisation of modern communications.*

glycerin or **glycerine?** Both spellings are correct. *Glycerin* is the usual spelling in American English, while *glycerine* is the customary spelling in British English.

gobbledygook The noun *gobbledygook* is used in informal contexts to denote the pretentious or incomprehensible jargon of bureaucrats, especially the circumlocutory language of official documents, reports, etc. The alternative spelling, *gobbledegook*, is in regular use. *See also* **officialese.**

gobsmacked The adjective *gobsmacked*, meaning 'astounded; flabbergasted; speechless with amazement', is a slang term that should not be used in formal contexts: * *I was gobsmacked when I found out how much it would cost.* * *There was a long pause (maybe he was gobsmacked at the prospect of me staying at home for another year), then an* *unconvincing 'Never mind' (The Guardian).*

god or **God**? A *god* is any of a number of beings worshipped for their supernatural powers. *God*, written with a capital *G,* is the supreme being worshipped in many religions as the creator and ruler of all: ＊ *the god of war* ＊ *the Greek gods* ＊ *to believe in God* ＊ *for God's sake.* Compounds and derivatives of the noun, whether they refer to a *god* or to *God,* are usually written with a lower-case *g:* ＊ *godly* ＊ *godless* ＊ *godchild* ＊ *godsend.* The adjectives *god-fearing* and *god-forsaken,* however, may be written with a capital or lower-case *g; God-forsaken* may be rendered with or without the hyphen.

gold or **golden**? The word *gold* is used adjectivally to describe things that are made of *gold* or contain *gold:* ＊ *a gold medal* ＊ *a gold mine.* The adjective *golden* usually refers to the colour of *gold:* ＊ *golden hair* ＊ *golden syrup.* In the four preceding examples, *gold* and *golden* are not interchangeable; however, *gold* is sometimes used in the sense of 'gold-coloured' and *golden* in the sense of 'made of gold': *fabric with blue and gold stripes* ＊ *a golden necklace.*

Golden has a number of other meanings, such as 'prosperous': ＊ *golden age,* 'important': ＊ *golden rule,* and 'fiftieth': ＊ *golden anniversary.* The phrase *golden handshake,* denoting a large sum of money paid to a retiring employee, has given rise to *golden hello* (a similar sum paid to a new employee), *golden handcuffs* (a payment made to discourage an employee from leaving), and *golden parachute* (a guarantee of compensa-

tion if the employee is dismissed or demoted following a takeover). A *golden share* is the control held by a national government in a privatised company in order to prevent the company from being taken over by foreign business interests.

good or **well**? *Good* and *well* are sometimes confused. *Good* is used as an adjective after such linking verbs as *be* and *seem* or where a sensory function is involved, while *well* is chiefly used as an adverb after verbs without any sensory function: ＊ *the food smelt good and had been chosen well.* Note the difference between *feel good* and *feel well* (in which well is used as an adjective): ＊ *I don't feel too good* is an informal way of saying ＊ *I don't feel very well* (i.e. *I feel ill*), but in less informal contexts *feel good* has connotations of moral, emotional, or spiritual well-being that *feel well* does not have. *See also* **feel-good factor**.

goodwill or **good will**? The term meaning 'a feeling of kindness and concern', as in: ＊ *a gesture of good will,* can be written either as one word or as two. Some prefer the latter, unless the term is being used in the commercial sense, when it is written *goodwill:* ＊ *They paid £12,000 for the goodwill of the shop and £6,000 for the stock.*

gorilla *see* **guerilla**, **guerrilla** or **gorilla**?

gossip Note the spellings of the derived forms: *gossiped, gossiping, gossiper, gossipy:* ＊ *They gossiped all afternoon* ＊ *a gossipy letter.* The word *gossip* derives from *God* and *sibb* – 'relation' – as in *modern sibling. Gossips* were originally the equivalent of present-day godparents; over the course of time the word became applied to close friends and then to the sense of people who were fond of engaging in idle talk.

got *Got*, the past participle of *get*, is often superfluous in the expressions *have got* (meaning 'possess') and *have got to* (meaning 'must'): * *He has (got) grey hair and a small moustache.* * *They have (got) to win this match to avoid relegation.* In informal contexts, and especially in negative sentences, questions, and contractions, *got* is often retained: * *We haven't got any milk.* * *Have you got enough money?* * *I've got to write to my brother.*

In some contractions, the occasional omission of *got* may cause confusion: * *She's a cat* may mean 'she is a cat' or 'she has a cat'; *She's got a cat* is unambiguous.

Used alone, *got* is the past tense of *get*; it should not be used in place of *have* or *have got*: * *They have/have got* [not *They got*] *three children.* * *I got a new car last week.*

Gotten is an American variant of the past participle *got*; in British English its use is restricted to such expressions as *ill-gotten gains*.

gourmand or **gourmet**? A *gourmand* enjoys the pleasurable indulgence of eating, with or without regard to the quality of the food. *Gourmet*, the more common and also more complimentary of the two terms, refers only to a connoisseur of fine food or drink: * *The size of the meals will satisfy the gourmand; their quality should please the most discriminating gourmet.* To avoid ambiguity, *gourmand* may be replaced by *glutton* in the sense of 'one who eats greedily or to excess'. Many people object to the increasing use of *gourmet* to describe restaurants, meals, etc., in which the food is elab-

orate and expensive but not necessarily of high quality.

Gourmand is usually pronounced [*goor*mănd] or [*goor*mon(g)]; *gourmet* is pronounced [*goor*may]. Both words are occasionally stressed on the second syllable.

government In the sense of 'the group of people who govern a country, state, etc.', *government* may be a singular or a plural noun: * *The government is blamed for the rise in unemployment.* * *The government have rejected the proposal.* See also **collective nouns**; **singular** or **plural**?

graceful or **gracious**? *Graceful* refers to movement, actions, forms, shapes, etc. that have *grace*, in the sense of beauty, charm, or elegance: * *a graceful dance.* *Gracious* means 'kind', 'courteous', 'benevolent', or 'compassionate': * *a gracious gift.* The two words are not interchangeable, although they may occasionally qualify the same noun: * *a graceful gesture* is a beautiful or elegant movement; * *a gracious gesture* is an act of kindness or courtesy.

The adjective *gracious* may also occasionally imply condescension: * *She thanked the waiter with a gracious smile.* In such expressions as *gracious living*, the word conveys an impression of luxury, comfort, elegance, and indulgence.

graffiti Nowadays very few people still object to the widespread use of *graffiti* as a singular noun: * *Graffiti covers the walls of the community centre.* * *Some of this graffiti is quite obscene.* *Graffito*, the singular of this Italian borrowing, meaning 'a little scratch', is used only very occasionally to refer

to a single inscription or drawing: *
*The first graffito appeared the day after
the room was repainted.*

Note the spelling of the word, particularly the -*ff*- and single *t*.

grammar The word *grammar*, which
denotes the rules of a language or a
type of school: * *Latin grammar* * *a
grammar school*, is often misspelt. The
most frequent error is the substitution
of -*er* for the -*ar* ending. Note also the
-*mm*-.

grand- or **great-**? Both these prefixes
are used to denote family relationships that are two or more generations
apart. Either prefix may be used for
the aunts and uncles of a person's parents and the children of his or her
nephews and nieces, *great-* being
more frequent than *grand-*: * *great-
niece* * *grandnephew* * *great-uncle* *
grandaunt. The prefix *grand-* is always
used for the parents of a person's parents and the children of their own
children: * *granddaughter* * *grandfather* * *grandchild* * *grandma*.

The prefix *great-* is also used for the
parents of a person's grandparents and
the children of a person's grandchil-
dren: * *great-grandmother* * *great-
grandson* * *great-grandparent*. (The
father of a person's *great-grandfather* is
a person's *great-great-grandfather*, and
so on.)

grass roots Some people object to the
widespread use of this term both in
political or industrial contexts, and as
a noun meaning 'the fundamental
level' or as an adjective meaning
'fundamental' or 'basic': * *the grass
roots of the problem* * *at the grass-roots
level* * *support for the party at the grass
roots* * *grass-roots opinion*. The noun

grass roots came originally from min-
ing in the USA, referring to the soil
immediately below the surface. It was
subsequently applied to the ordinary
people as opposed to the political
leaders of society. The *grass roots* of a
trade union or other organisation are
its rank-and-file members.

gratuitous The adjective *gratuitous* is
most frequently used in the sense of
'unwarranted' or 'uncalled-for': * *gratuitous violence* * *gratuitous criticism*. The
original meaning of the word is 'free' or
'given without payment'.

gray *see* **grey** or **gray**?

great- *see* **grand-** or **great-**?

Great Britain *see* **Britain**.

Greek or **Grecian**? The adjective *Greek*
means 'of Greece, its people, or its
language'; *Grecian* means 'in the simple but elegant style of classical
Greece': * *Greek history* * *a Grecian
vase*. The adjective *Grecian* was formerly applied to the art, architecture,
literature, culture, etc. of ancient
Greece; in these senses it has been
largely superseded by *Greek*.

The noun *Greek* denotes a native or
inhabitant of Greece; a *Grecian* is a
scholar of classical Greek language or
literature.

green The adjective *green* is now widely
applied to any product, policy, or
ideology that is connected with the
protection of the environment: *
green consumerism * *green issues* * *to
buy green* * *to go green* * *The Whole
Thing is a mail order company dedi-
cated to providing a wide range of over
150 of the greenest products available*

(advertisement, *The Guardian*). As a noun, *green* may be spelt with a lower-case or capital initial letter to denote a person who is generally in support of the protection of the environment, but the lower-case form is probably more frequent in this sense. Spelt with a capital *G*, the word specifically denotes a political party that is chiefly concerned with the protection of the environment: * *to vote Green* * *The Greens have shaken Britain's three big parties by winning 2.25m votes and 15% of the poll in the European elections* (*Sunday Times*).

A *greenfield site* is a rural undeveloped site, often near a town or city, that has not been designated as part of a green belt and so is available for development, e.g. for industrial estates, retail parks, or housing.

The verbal noun *greening* has been coined to denote the process of removing environmentally harmful substances: * *the greening of the city streets* * *the greening of the washing machine* (a reference to 'environment-friendly' detergents). *See also* **brownfield**; **environment**; **-friendly**.

grey or **gray**? This word can be spelt with an *e* or an *a*, although the former is far more frequent in British English. *Gray* is standard in American English.

grieve The verb *grieve* is followed by the preposition *for* or *over*: * *She grieved for* [or *over*] *the death of her horse.*

grill or **grille**? A *grill* is a framework of bars used for cooking food. A *grille* is a grating over a window or door. These words are occasionally confused, especially as *grille* can also sometimes be spelt *grill*.

grisly or **grizzly**? The spellings of these words may sometimes be confused. *Grisly* means 'gruesome'; *grizzly* means 'partly grey': * *a grizzly bear,* or 'whining fretfully': * *a grizzly toddler.*

ground zero The phrase *ground zero* originally described the location immediately above or below the area where a nuclear explosion takes place and, by extension, the starting point or site of activity of some kind, especially of a military nature. Since the terrorist attack on the World Trade Center in New York on 11 September 2001, the phrase has come to be predominantly associated with the site of the former towers and is now normally used chiefly in reference to that event – although it can be used by extension to other similarly devastated sites: * *Prayers at Bali's ground zero* (*The Guardian*).

grow Care should be taken over the metaphorical use of the transitive verb *grow*, as this is considered unacceptable by some people: * *grow a range of products* * *grow their profits* * *grow a successful young team of players.* The literal use of the transitive verb is, however, generally acceptable: * *grow some houseplants.*

growth The word *growth* is used adjectivally, in the sense of 'rapidly developing or increasing', in economic and commercial spheres: * *a growth industry* * *a growth economy.* In other contexts it is often better replaced by a paraphrase: * *Canoeing is a growth sport* could well be changed to: * *The sport of canoeing is increasing in popularity.*

guarantee This word, which is often misspelt, means 'an assurance that a certain agreement will be kept': *The washing-machine was still under guarantee.* It is worth remembering that the vowels of the first syllable are like those in *guard*: *A guarantee guards the rights of the consumer.*

guerilla, guerrilla or **gorilla**? *Guerilla/guerrilla* means 'fighter within an independent army': *a guerrilla war*; a *gorilla* is a large ape. The spellings *guerilla* and *guerrilla* are both acceptable, although many users prefer the latter since it derives from the Spanish *Guerra*, 'a war', with *-rr-*. The usual pronunciation of both words is [gĕrilă]. However, *guerilla/guerrilla* may be pronounced [gerilă] to make it distinct from *gorilla* [gĕrilă].

guesstimate The word *guesstimate*, meaning 'rough estimate', resulted from the combination of *guess* and *estimate*: *He quoted a figure but warned that it was only a guesstimate.* The word is disliked by many people and should be used sparingly and only in informal contexts.

guest The use of the word *guest* as a verb, in the sense of 'be a guest (on a television or radio show)', is disliked by some users and is best restricted to informal contexts: *She guested on his chat show last month.* Unlike *host*, the verb *guest* is not used outside the entertainment industry: *He was a guest at our wedding* [not *He guested at...*].

guidelines Some people object to the increasing use of the plural noun *guidelines* in place of *advice, policy, instructions, rules*, etc.: *New guidelines to establish minimum sentences in rape cases* (*The Guardian*). *The series is within the BBC's guidelines on violence* (*Daily Telegraph*). The noun *guidelines*, which is rarely used in the singular, is now usually written as one word; the hyphenated form *guide-lines* is an accepted but less frequent variant.

guild *see* **gild** or **guild**?

guilt *see* **gilt** or **guilt**?

gut The use of the word *gut* as an adjective, meaning 'instinctive', 'strong', 'basic', or 'essential', is best restricted to informal contexts: *a gut reaction * a gut feeling * gut issues.*

gybe *see* **gibe**, **jibe** or **gybe**?

gynaecology This word, meaning 'the branch of medicine concerned with women's diseases', is frequently misspelt. Note the *y* and, in British English, the *-ae-* (or American English, *-e-*). The word is pronounced [gīnĭkolŏji]. *See also* **-ae-** and **-oe-**.

gypsy *see* **gipsy** or **gypsy**?

H

haemoglobin or **hemoglobin**? This word, describing the red protein in blood, is sometimes misspelt. *Haemoglobin* is the usual spelling in British English, while *hemoglobin* is the accepted spelling in American English.

haemorrhage This noun, meaning 'immense loss of blood', is often misspelt. Note the *-rrh-* and the British English *-ae-*, which is reduced to *-e-* in American English (*see* **-ea-** and **-oe-**).

hail or **hale**? The noun *hail* means 'frozen rain'; the verb *hail* means 'call' or 'be a native of': * *hail a taxi* * *She hails from Scotland. Hail* should not be confused with *hale*, meaning 'vigorous and healthy': * *hale and hearty.*

hair or **hare**? *Hair* describes the fine strands that grow on the skin of human beings and other animals. It should not be confused with *hare*, which describes a species of animal resembling a large rabbit.

half Although *half* is a singular noun, it is followed by a plural verb when it denotes a number rather than an amount: * *Half of the books are missing.* * *Half of the water has evaporated.* In most cases the word *of* is optional: * *Give him half (of) the money.* Such expressions as *a half-hour* and *half an hour, a half-dozen* and *half a dozen, a mile and a half* and *one and a half miles,* etc., are equally acceptable in most contexts. However, the insertion of an extra indefinite article before *half an hour, half a dozen*, etc., is avoided by careful users. *See also* **hyphen**.

half- or **step-**? A person's *step-parent* (*stepmother* or *stepfather*) is the new spouse of a divorced or widowed parent. Any children of this step-parent by previous partners become the person's *stepbrothers* or *stepsisters*. Any children of their father or mother by this step-parent (or any other partner) are their *half-brothers* or *half-sisters*. Confusion arises because half-brothers and half-sisters are usually the offspring of a person's stepmother or stepfather. A person may have both half-brothers (or half-sisters) and stepbrothers (or stepsisters).

Note that *half-* is always attached with a hyphen in this sense, whereas *step-* is attached without a hyphen (except in the case of *step-parent*).

hallo *see* **hello, hallo** or **hullo**?

handful Most users prefer to form the plural *-fuls*: * *handfuls. See also* **-ful**.

handicap The final *p* of the word *handicap* is doubled before a suffix beginning with a vowel: * *handicapped* * *handicapping*. Many people avoid the words *handicap* and *handicapped* in relation to those suffering from various physical or mental disabilities, on the grounds that the terms have negative

195

connotations. Preferred alternatives include *disabled* and *person with disabilities*. See also **disabled**; **spelling**.

hands-on This expression refers to practical or personal involvement in a task: • *This is not a desk job. It is a 'hands-on' sales role* (Daily Telegraph). • *The Prime Minister returned to London last night to resume hands-on control of the Gulf crisis* (The Guardian). The term *hands-on* is often used in the expression *hands-on experience* – practical experience.

hangar or **hanger**? These words are often misspelt. A *hangar* is a building for storing aircraft; a *hanger* is an apparatus on which articles can be hung: • *coat hanger*. To avoid mistakes, remember the *a* in both *aircraft* and *hangar*.

hanged or **hung**? *Hung* is the past tense and past participle for most senses of the verb *hang*; *hanged* is restricted to the meaning 'suspended by the neck until dead', in the context of capital punishment or suicide: • *He hung his coat on the peg.* • *The picture was hung up in the hall.* • *The conspirators were hanged for treason.* • *Her father hanged himself.*

hanger *see* **hangar** or **hanger**?

hang-up The noun *hang-up* is an informal name for a mental or emotional problem or inhibition: • *She's got a hang-up about answering the phone.* The word should not be used in formal contexts. *Hang-up* is usually hyphenated in British English but may be written as one unhyphenated word in American English. The plural of *hang-up* is *hang-ups*.

hanker The verb *hanker* is followed by the preposition *after* or *for*: • *those who hanker after* [or *for*] *power*.

happy The adjective *happy* is followed by the preposition *about* or *with*: • *Are you happy about* [or *with*] *the arrangements?*

hara-kiri *Hara-kiri* is the traditional spelling of this Japanese term, which refers to a ritual act of suicide achieved by cutting open the abdomen: • *to commit hara-kiri.* It is pronounced [*ha*rră *ki*rri]. The variant spelling *hari-kari*, pronounced [*ha*rri *ka*rri] or [*ha*ri *ka*ri], is best avoided.

harangue This word, which means 'a vehement and lengthy speech', as in: • *a long harangue about the state of the economy*, is sometimes misspelt. The *-gue* ending is the same as in *meringue*.

harass This word, meaning 'trouble persistently', is spelt with a single *r* and ends in *-ss*. It is pronounced [*ha*rrăs]. The American pronunciation [hă*ras*] has recently come into British English but is disliked by some people. Note that the same spelling rules apply for *harassment*.

hardly In the sense of 'only just' or 'almost not', the adverb *hardly*, like its synonyms *scarcely* and *barely*, is used with negative force; it is unnecessary to add another negative to the clause or sentence: • *I can* [not *can't*] *hardly see you* (see also **double negative**). Careful users avoid using *than* in place of *when* in the constructions *hardly... when, scarcely... when,* or *barely... when*: • *She had hardly begun to speak when* [not *than*] *he interrupted her.* • *Scarcely had they reached* *the end of the road when* [not *than*] *the rain began.* This confusion may be due to the use of *than* in the construction *no sooner... than*: * *No sooner had I stepped into the bath than* [not *when*] *the doorbell rang.*

Hardly is rarely used as the adverbial form of the word *hard*, which functions both as an adjective and as an adverb: * *a hard surface* * *to work hard* * *hard-earned money.*

hare *see* **hair** or **hare**?

harelip *see* **cleft lip**.

hatred The noun *hatred* is followed by the preposition *for* or *of*: * *Her hatred for* [or *of*] *her father.*

have *see* **of**.

have got (to) *see* **got**.

hazardous The adjective *hazardous* is followed by the preposition *to* or *for*: * *These sharp edges can be hazardous to* [or *for*] *young children.*

he or **she** The use of *he/him/his* as pronouns of common gender, with reference to a person of unspecified sex, is widely considered to be misleading and sexist, as is the use of *she/her/hers* for the same purpose with reference to jobs or activities that are traditionally associated with women: * *The candidate must pay his own travelling expenses.* * *This book will be of great value to the student nurse preparing for her examinations.* The most acceptable substitutes for these pronouns are the cumbersome and pedantic expressions *he or she, he/she, (s)he, his or her*, etc.: * *If a child is slow to learn, he or she will be given extra tuition.* *

The candidate must pay his or her own travelling expenses.

In some cases, the problem may be avoided by restructuring the sentence or making the subject plural, or both: * *Travelling expenses must be paid by the candidate.* * *Candidates must pay their own travelling expenses.* * *Children who are slow to learn will be given extra tuition.* Various attempts to coin new pronouns, such as *tey, hesh*, etc., have met with little success; it has also been suggested that the pronoun *it*, already used of babies, should be extended to human beings of all ages. The solution most often resorted to now is the previously criticised use of *they, them, their*, and *theirs* as singular pronouns (*see* **they**).

head up Many people dislike the use of this phrasal verb in place of the simpler *head*, meaning 'lead' or 'be in charge': * *to head up a team of workers.*

headed for or **heading for**? When the verb *head* is used intransitively, the phrase *headed for* is sometimes wrongly used in place of *heading for*: * *We were heading* [not *headed*] *for Southampton.* * *The government is heading* [not *headed*] *for defeat.*

headmaster or **headmistress**? *see* **non-sexist terms**.

heal or **heel**? *Heal* means 'cure' or 'become sound again'. It should not be confused with *heel*, which refers to the back part of the foot. Note also the spelling of *well-heeled* (meaning 'wealthy'): * *She came from a well-heeled background.*

healthful or **healthy**? *Healthy* can mean 'having good health' or 'promoting good health': * *a healthy child* * *a healthy diet*. *Healthful* is a less frequent synonym of *healthy* in both these senses, but in modern usage it is largely restricted to the sense of 'promoting good health': * *foods that are both healthful and relatively inexpensive.*

hear The verb *hear* is followed by the preposition *of* in the sense 'know about': * *I'd never heard of the disease before*, and by *about* or *of* in the sense 'find out about': * *I only heard about* [or *of*] *his promotion yesterday.*

heard or **herd**? *Heard* is the past participle of the verb *hear*. It should not be confused with *herd*, a noun referring to a large number of cattle or other animals.

hearing-impaired This is the preferred modern alternative to *deaf*, which is considered unacceptable by many people because of its negative connotations.

heaved or **hove**? *Heaved* is the usual form of the past tense or past participle of the verb *heave*: * *He heaved the crate up the steps.* * *She heaved a sigh of relief. Hove* is an archaic variant of *heaved*; it is used facetiously or in nautical contexts, in the past tense or past participle of *heave to* meaning 'stop', and *heave into sight* (or *view*), meaning 'appear': * *We hove to for lunch.* * *A ship hove into sight.* The phrase *heave into sight* (or *view*) is also used in non-nautical (but fairly literary) contexts, usually in the past tense: * *As they rounded the corner, the house hove into view.*

heavy-duty The term *heavy-duty* should be restricted to articles, materials,

etc., that are designed to withstand hard wear or frequent use: * *heavy-duty overalls* * *heavy-duty plastic sheeting*. In other contexts the adjectives *tough* or *strong* may be adequate or more appropriate.

heel *see* **heal** or **heel**?

height This word refers to the distance from the base to the top of an object or person: * *the height of the mountain.* It also means 'most intense point': * *at the height of summer. Height* is sometimes misspelt with the ending *-th*, on the model of *length*, *width*, etc.

heinous This word, meaning 'extremely evil': * *a heinous crime*, is often misspelt and mispronounced. Note the *-ei-* and the stress on the first syllable [*hay*nŭs]. The pronunciation [*hee*nŭs] is also acceptable but [*hī*nŭs] is best avoided.

hello, **hallo** or **hullo**? This word of greeting has various spellings, all of which are acceptable. The first spelling is probably the most frequent in contemporary usage.

help Many people object to the phrases *cannot/can't/could not/couldn't help but*, as in: * *I couldn't help but laugh*, preferring either *I couldn't help laughing* or, less frequently, *I couldn't but laugh*. The idiomatic *cannot/can't/could not/couldn't help* construction, where *help* means 'refrain from', is followed by a present participle.

In the sense of 'assist' or 'contribute', *help* is usually followed by a direct object and/or an infinitive, with or without *to*: * *These pills will help you* (*to*) *sleep.* * *They all helped* (*to*) *tidy the house.* Some users prefer to retain *to* in the absence of a direct object: ● *This money will help to pay for the new car.* ● *This money will help us pay for the new car.* See also **but**.

hemi- *see* **demi-**, **hemi-** or **semi-**?

hence *Hence* means 'from this time' or, more rarely, 'from this place'; it is therefore unnecessary to precede the adverb with *from*: ● *The concert will begin three hours hence.* The use of *hence* in the sense of 'from this place' is largely restricted to very formal or archaic contexts. See also **thence**.

Hence is also used to mean 'for this reason' or 'therefore': ● *My route is more direct, and hence faster, than yours.* ● *Her father drowned at sea, hence her reluctance to go sailing.* In the second of these examples, note that *hence* is often followed by a noun rather than a verb; to replace *hence* with *therefore* would involve rewording the clause: ● *...therefore she is reluctant to go sailing.*

herd *see* **heard** or **herd**?

hereditary or **heredity**? *Hereditary* is an adjective, meaning 'genetically transmitted' or 'inherited'; heredity is the noun from which it is derived: ● *The disease is not hereditary.* ● *Is intelligence determined by heredity or environment?* The two words are sometimes confused, being similar in pronunciation (the *a* of *hereditary* is often elided in speech).

heritage or **inheritance**? The noun *heritage* most frequently refers to cultural items, natural features, or traditions of the past that are handed down from generation to generation and are considered to be of importance to modern society: ● *The pyramids are part of Egypt's heritage.* An *inheritance* is money or property that an heir receives from an ancestor who has died: ● *He squandered his inheritance.* *Inheritance* may also refer to the inheriting of physical or mental characteristics by offspring from their parents. In its broader sense, *heritage* denotes anything that is inherited at birth; it is thus interchangeable to some degree with *inheritance*: ● *the family's rich intellectual heritage/inheritance.*

Some people dislike the indiscriminate application of the word *heritage* to any historical event, building, custom, etc., especially as a means of exploiting its commercial potential in the tourism industry: ● *heritage tours of the docklands.* ● *Tourism and the heritage industry inevitably distort the past by making imitations of historic buildings or changing their use (The Guardian).*

hero or **heroine**? *see* **non-sexist terms**.

hesitance, **hesitancy** or **hesitation**? The nouns *hesitance* and *hesitancy* refer to the state of being *hesitant* (i.e. wavering, irresolute, indecisive, reluctant). *Hesitancy* is the more frequent of these synonyms: ● *There was a note of hesitancy in her voice.* The noun *hesitation* refers to the act or an instance of hesitating: ● *after a slight hesitation* ● *He accepted the offer without hesitation.*

heterogeneous This word is often misspelt. Note the *-eous* ending.

hew or **hue**? *Hew* is a verb meaning 'cut', 'carve', or 'cut down': ● *He hewed down the tree.* ● *They hewed a road through the jungle.* It should not be confused with the noun *hue*, which means 'colour' or 'shade of colour': * *The walls are painted in two hues of pink.*

hiatus The noun *hiatus* is best avoided where *gap*, *break*, or *pause* would be adequate or more appropriate: * *a hiatus in our discussions.*

hiccup or **hiccough**? Both spellings of this word are acceptable but *hiccup* is the more frequent. The word refers to a sudden intake of breath resulting in a characteristic sound. It has the additional informal sense of 'small problem': * *The project is going well apart from a few minor hiccups.*

high or **tall**? Both these adjectives mean 'of greater than average size, measured vertically', but there are differences of sense, usage, and application between them: * *a high mountain* * *a tall woman.* The adjective *tall* is largely restricted to people, animals, and plants and to things that are narrow in proportion to their height; it is the opposite of short: * *a tall tree* * *a tall chimney. High* has the additional meaning of 'situated at a great distance above the base'; it is the opposite of low: * *a high branch* * *a high shelf.*

The two adjectives may be applied to the same noun in different senses: *a high window* is a long way from the floor; *a tall window* is relatively large from top to bottom. The size of the *high window* and the position of the *tall window* are unspecified.

Like other adjectives of magnitude (*long*, *deep*, *wide*, etc.), *high* and *tall* are used in combination with specific measurements regardless of size: * *He is only five feet tall.* * *The wall is less than one metre high.*

high-profile *see* **profile**.

hijack The verb *hijack*, meaning 'seize control of (a vehicle in transit)', is increasingly used in figurative contexts: * *The plane has been hijacked by terrorists.* * *One of their most successful authors has been hijacked by a rival company. Highjack* is a rare variant spelling of the verb.

him or **his**? *see* **-ing forms**.

Hindi or **Hindu**? *Hindi* is a language of India; *Hindu* is a noun or adjective relating to the Indian religion of Hinduism: * *She speaks Hindi.* * *He is (a) Hindu.* The two words should not be confused.

hire or **rent**? Both verbs mean 'have or give temporary use of something in return for payment': * *He hired a suit for the wedding.* * *We rented a flat in the town centre.* * *They hire/rent (out) cars at competitive rates.* The basic difference in sense between the two verbs concerns the length of the period of temporary use and, to some extent, the nature of the item in question: a room or building may be *hired* for a party or conference or *rented* for a longer period of time. Clothes are *hired* (usually for a single occasion), not *rented*; television sets are *rented* (sometimes for a number of years), not *hired*. Cars may be *hired* or *rented*.

The verbs *let* and *lease* are also used in this context, usually with reference to buildings or land: * *She lets the cottage to tourists.* * *Room to let.* * *They leased the land from the council.* * *The council leased them the land.* * *All the company cars are leased.* The subject of *let* is usually the owner of the property rather than the person who pays for temporary use.

his or **her** *see* **he** or **she**.

Hispanic The noun *Hispanic* has become an accepted term for a Spanish-speaking person from Central or South America living in the USA, alongside *Latino* and *Chicano*.

historic or **historical**? The adjective *historic* relates to events, decisions, etc. that are memorable or important enough to earn a place in recorded history; *historical* relates to the study of history and to the past in general: * *a historic election* * *historical records* * *The king's visit to the town was not a historic occasion, it is of historical interest only.* The adjective *historical* is also applied to people, events, etc. that existed or happened in fact, as opposed to fiction or legend: * *a historical character.* The two adjectives are not fully interchangeable, although both may be applied to the same noun. A *historic voyage*, for example, is contrasted with one that is of no lasting significance, whereas a *historical voyage* is contrasted with one that never took place: the voyage of Christopher Columbus to the New World was both *historic* and *historical*. Some people dislike the overuse of *historic* with reference to events that are of ephemeral significance: * *Western Samoa produced the first major upset of the World Cup with a historic victory over Wales...* (*The Guardian*). See also **a** or **an**?

histrionic or **hysterical**? The adjectives *histrionic* and *hysterical* are both used of emotional outbursts but should not be confused: *histrionic* behaviour is a display of insincerity, being deliberately exaggerated for melodramatic effect; *hysterical* behaviour is the result of an involuntary loss of control. The same distinction may be applied to the nouns *histrionics* and *hysterics*, both of which are used with plural verbs, adjectives, etc., in this context (*see* **-ics**).

Histrionics and *histrionic* originally referred to actors and the theatre; *hysterics* and *hysterical* also relate to the mental disorder of *hysteria*.

hi-tech The adjective *hi-tech* specifically refers to high technology, or sophisticated electronics; many careful users object to its indiscriminate application to basic electrical appliances or to anything remotely connected with computing: * *a beautiful hi-tech modern home* * *high-tech benefits* [a reference to the computerisation of the social security benefits system] * *This transition of the cycle from leisure 'toy' to hi-tech pedal machine* (*Daily Telegraph*). The word *hi-tech* has a number of variant spellings: *high-tech, high tech, hi-tec, high-tec*, etc. It is also used as a noun: * *Reflecting the world of high tech* [spelt *hi-tech* in the headline], *the first museum devoted to the chemical industry opens today* (*The Guardian*).

hoard or **horde**? A *hoard* is 'a store reserved for future use'; a *horde* is 'a large crowd': * *hordes of tourists.* These words are often confused, as they have the same pronunciation.

hoarse or **horse**? *Hoarse* describes a voice that is rasping or harsh, typically as the result of an infection or through overuse. It should not be confused with *horse*, which refers to the animal.

hoi polloi This phrase of Greek origin, referring to the common populace, is often misspelt: note the *-oi* ending of both words. Because *hoi* means 'the' in Greek, it is technically redundant, but the phrase is firmly established in English. The phrase is pronounced [hoy pǎ*loy*].

holey *see* **holy, holey** or **wholly?**

holistic The adjective *holistic* is used of any system, method, theory, etc., that deals with the whole rather than with individual parts or members: * *holistic medicine* * *a holistic approach to life.* The term relates to the concept of wholes that are greater than the sum of their parts, of the natural tendency to form such wholes, and of a universe that is composed of such wholes. Many people take care not to overuse or misuse this word.

holocaust The use of the noun *holocaust* to denote any major disaster, especially one that involves great loss of life, is disliked by some users, who prefer to restrict the word to its original meaning of 'total destruction by fire': * *the nuclear holocaust.* The *Holocaust*, usually written with a capital *H*, refers to the massacre of the Jews by the Nazis during World War II.

holy, holey or **wholly?** These three spellings should not be confused. The adjective *holy* means 'sacred'; the adjective *holey*, only used facetiously or informally, means 'having holes'; the adverb *wholly* means 'completely': * *holy relics* * *holey socks* * *wholly convinced. Holy* and *holey* are pronounced [*hō*li]; the pronunciation of *wholly* [*hō*l*li] reflects the *-ll-* spelling.

home or **house?** The word *home* may refer to an actual building where a person has his or her residence, but varies from *house* in conveying an affectionate, even sentimental, sense of 'place of refuge' or 'retreat from the world': * *Home is where the heart is.* * *I'm tired and I want to go home.* * *He has no home to go to. Home* is also useful for describing buildings that are not houses, such as flats. *House* generally refers more dispassionately to a place of residence, usually a single-family dwelling as distinct from a flat or other type of residence: * *All the houses in this street are due for demolition.* Note that many people dislike the use of *home* in the sense of 'care facility', in such uses as *retirement home* or *home for the mentally disabled* – including those who live in or run such places: * *They put the old lady in a home.* * *He should be in a home.*

homely In British English the adjective *homely* is complimentary, meaning 'like home', 'unpretentious', or 'sympathetic'; in American English it has the derogatory sense of 'ugly' or 'unattractive': * *a homely room* * *a homely child.* Misunderstanding is most likely to occur when the adjective is applied to a person, in which case it may be replaced by an appropriate synonym.

homogeneous or **homogenous?** These two adjectives are virtually interchangeable in the sense of 'similar, identical, or uniform in nature, structure, or composition' – *homogeneous* being the more frequent: * *a homogeneous mixture.* In biology, the adjective *homogenous* specifically refers to correspondence or similarity due to common descent.

The two words are closer in spelling and meaning than in pronunciation: *homogeneous* is usually pronounced [homŏ*jee*niŭs] and *homogenous* [hŏ*moj*inŭs].

homograph, homonym or **homophone?** A *homonym* is a word that has the same spelling or pronunciation as another word. There are two kinds of *homonym*: *homograph* and *homophone*. A *homograph* is a word that is spelt like another word, but has a different meaning or origin – for example, *rush*, 'a slender marsh plant', from Old English *risc*, and *rush*, 'to move quickly', from Middle French *ruser*, 'to put to flight'. *Homographs* need not have the same pronunciation, e.g. *lead*, 'to guide', rhyming with *feed*, and the metal *lead*, rhyming with *head*.

A *homophone* is a word that is pronounced in the same way as another but with a different meaning, derivation, or spelling. Examples are *hear–here; rain–reign; right–write; son–sun*.

homophobia The noun *homophobia*, meaning 'fear or dislike of homosexuals', and the derived noun *homophobe* and adjective *homophobic*, are used with increasing frequency: • *The Church has been accused of homophobia.* • *a homophobic police officer.* Some people object to these coinages, on the basis that the *homo-* element can only mean 'same' (as in the word *homosexual* itself) or 'man'.

homophone *see* **homograph, homonym** or **homophone?**

homosexual This word may be pronounced in several ways, two of the most frequent being [homŏseksyool] and [hōmōseksyool]. Some people prefer [hom-] to [hōm-] because, in this case, *homo* is from the Greek *homos* 'same' and not the Latin *homo* 'man'. Note that the shortened form *homo* is usually employed offensively: • *I didn't know he was a homo. See also* **gay**.

honorary or **honourable?** *Honorary* means 'given as an honour, without the usual requirements or obligations' or 'unpaid': • *an honorary degree* • *an honorary member of the society* • *the honorary secretary. Honourable* means 'worthy of honour' or 'showing honour' and is also used as a title of respect: • *an honourable man* • *an honourable deed* • *the Right Honourable Margaret Thatcher.* The two adjectives are not interchangeable in any of their senses, but both may be abbreviated to *Hon.* in titles: • *the Hon. Sec.* • *the Rt. Hon. Margaret Thatcher.*

Note the spellings of the two words: the *u* of *honour* is always absent from *honorary*; it is present in the British spelling of *honourable* but absent from the American spelling of this word.

hoofs or **hooves?** Both *hoofs* and *hooves* are acceptable as the plural of *hoof*, 'the hard bony part of the foot of a horse, cow, etc.'.

hopefully The use of *hopefully* to mean 'it is (to be) hoped (that)' or 'I/we hope (that)' is disliked by some users and is best restricted to informal contexts: • *Hopefully the rain will stop before we leave.* The resistance to this usage is based on a number of arguments, of which the most valid is the possible confusion with the traditional adverbial sense of *hopefully* – 'with hope' or 'in a hopeful manner'. Ambiguity is most likely to occur when the adverb is placed directly before the verb: • *They will hopefully wait for us* may mean 'I hope they will wait for us' or 'they will wait for us with hope'. *Hopefully they will wait for us* and *They will wait for us hopefully* are less ambiguous renderings of the two senses.

Hopefully is favoured by some users as a less cumbersome alternative to 'it is (to be) hoped (that)' and a more impersonal alternative to 'I/we hope (that)'. *See also* **adverbs**; **sentence adverb**.

horde *see* **hoard** or **horde?**

horrible, horrid, horrific or **horrendous?** *Horrible* and *horrid* are virtually interchangeable in the sense of 'very unpleasant'; *horrific* and *horrendous* convey a stronger sense of *horror*. • *a horrid sight* • *a horrible dream* • *a horrific attack* • *the horrendous prospect of nuclear war.* All four adjectives are ultimately derived from the Latin verb *horrere*, meaning 'to tremble or bristle (with fear)'; in formal contexts they are principally used in the sense of 'causing fear or dread'.

The use of *horrible* and *horrid* to mean 'disagreeable' or 'unkind': • *a horrid man* • *a horrible meal,* is best restricted to informal contexts, as is the use of *horrendous* to describe exorbitant prices, very bad weather, etc.

hors d'oeuvre An *hors d'oeuvre* is an item of food served before or as the first course of a meal. Of French origin, the phrase is sometimes misspelt: note particularly the vowel sequence *-oeu-*. The two words are sometimes hyphenated: • *hors-d'oeuvre.* The plural is usually *hors d'oeuvres,* but *hors d'oeuvre,* without the final *-s,* is also acceptable.

The anglicised pronunciation of *hors d'oeuvre* is [or *dervr*] or [or *derv*]: the *h-* and *-s* are silent. If the final *-s* of the plural form *hors d'oeuvres* is sounded, the pronunciation is [or *dervz*]: it can be difficult to say [or *dervrz*].

horse *see* **hoarse** or **horse?**

hospitable This word may be stressed on the first syllable [*ho*spit̆abl] or the second syllable [hos*pit̆*abl]. Some users prefer the former, more traditional pronunciation.

hospitalise Some users dislike the verb *hospitalise,* meaning 'send or admit to hospital', as an example of the increasing tendency to coin new verbs by adding the suffix *-ise* to nouns and adjectives: • *She was hospitalised in the eighth month of her pregnancy.*

host Some people object to the verb *host,* meaning 'act as host at' or 'be the host of': • *He hosted the firm's Christmas party.* • *She is to host the BBC's new quiz show. See also* **guest.**

host or **hostess?** *see* **non-sexist terms.**

-hostile *see* **-friendly.**

hour or **our?** The words *hour* and *our* are both pronounced [*ow̆a*] but have different meanings and should not be confused. *Hour* denotes a period of time, while *our* means 'belonging to us'.

house *see* **home** or **house?**

house style Most newspapers, publishing houses and other organisations that produce written matter of one kind or another have their own *house style,* which provides guidance on stylistic issues for writers and editors and may well be unique to themselves. A good house style guide will cover a wide range of areas of possible contention, with the aim of ensuring stylistic consistency between one piece of writing and another. The best house style guides encompass grammar, punctuation (*eg* or *e.g.*?), spelling, hyphenation (*email* or *e-mail*?), accents, capitalisation (*Internet* or *internet*?), abbreviations and a host of other stylistic issues, and may extend to hundreds of pages. Even relatively brief house style guides should tackle such potentially divisive topics as the use of serial commas in lists of three or more items, spelling preferences for words ending *-ise* or *-ize*, the approach to be taken to various formal names or titles (*US* or *USA*, etc.) and the style for rendering numbers (often spelled out from one to ten and rendered as numerals after that).

If compiling a house style guide, it is a good idea to identify a good dictionary to use as an ultimate authority for spellings, word breaks, etc. not covered in the house guide itself.

hove *see* **heaved** or **hove**?

however The principal adverbial senses of *however* are 'nevertheless', 'in whatever way', and 'no matter how': * *The car doesn't have a large boot; it does, however, have plenty of room inside.* * *However I wash my hair, and however carefully I dry it, it always looks untidy.* For the distinction between *however* and *how ever*, *see* **whatever** or **what ever**? In the sense of 'nevertheless', *however* often serves the same purpose as *but*; careful users avoid using both words in the same sentence or clause unless *however* is being used in one of its other senses: * *The girl screamed; she did not, however, try to escape.* * *The girl screamed, but she did not try to escape.* * *The girl struggled, but however hard she tried, she could not escape.*

Some users always separate *however* (in the sense of 'nevertheless') from the rest of the sentence with commas

or other punctuation marks; others use punctuation marks only where there is a possibility of ambiguity or confusion (*see also* **comma**).

In the sense of 'nevertheless', *however* is usually placed immediately after the word or phrase that it serves to contrast or emphasise: * *my friend, however, does not like the colour* suggests that I like the colour but my friend does not; *my friend does not, however, like the colour* suggests that my friend likes some other feature of the object in question but does not like the colour.

Some users object to the positioning of *however* (in the sense of 'nevertheless') at the beginning or end of a sentence or clause; however, this is generally acceptable in most contexts. *See also* **although** or **however**?

hue *see* **hew** or **hue**?

hullo *see* **hello**, **hallo** or **hullo**?

human Some people dislike the use of *human* as a noun, preferring *human being* (or *man, woman, child, person*, etc.): * *This job can be done more efficiently by a robot than by a human (being)*. Most dictionaries acknowledge the noun *human* as a synonym for *human being*. *See also* **inhuman** or **inhumane**?

humanism or **humanity**? *Humanism* is a philosophy that values human beings and rejects the need for religion. The noun *humanity* refers to human beings collectively; it also means 'kindness': * *for the sake of humanity.* The two nouns should not be confused. *Humanism* also refers to a cultural movement of the Renaissance.

The *humanities* are academic subjects such as history, art, literature, language, and philosophy, as distinct from science.

humanist or **humanitarian**? A *humanist* is a person who supports the philosophy of *humanism* (*see* **humanism** or **humanity**?); a *humanitarian* is a philanthropist, a person who works for the welfare of human beings. The word *humanitarian* is also used as an adjective: * *a humanitarian organisation.*

humanity *see* **humanism** or **humanity**?

humiliation or **humility**? *Humiliation* is a feeling of shame, embarrassment, or loss of pride sometimes caused deliberately by other people; *humility* is the quality of being humble or modest: * *the humiliation of failure* * *the nun's humility.*

humorist The noun *humorist*, meaning 'humorous writer, speaker, etc.', is often misspelt. As in the adjective *humorous*, the *-mour* ending of *humour* is changed to *-mor* before the suffix *-ist*.

humorous This word, meaning 'amusing or funny', is often misspelt. The second *u* of *humour* is dropped before the suffix *-ous*. *Humorous* must not be confused with *humerus*, the long bone in the upper arm.

hung *see* **hanged** or **hung**?

hygiene This word, meaning 'science of ensuring good health', is often misspelt. Note *hy-* and not *hi-* at the beginning of the word, and the *-ie-* in the middle.

hype The word *hype*, used as a noun or verb with reference to extravagant and often deceptive publicity of books, films, etc., is generally regarded as a slang term: * *The launch owed more to hype than to literary merit* (Sunday Times). * *The biggest money-making hype in sports history* (Publishers Weekly) * *Hyping books is big business* (The Bookseller). The word is of uncertain origin: many authorities associate it with the slang use of *hype* as an abbreviation for *hypodermic*; others have suggested a connection with the prefix *hyper-*, meaning 'excessive', as in *hyperbole*.

hyper- or **hypo-**? These two prefixes are often confused. This may result in misunderstanding when each is joined to its relevant suffix. *Hyper-* means 'above or excessively': * *a hyperactive child*; *hypo-* means 'beneath or under': * *a hypodermic syringe*. The prefix *hyper-* is increasingly used as an adjective in its own right, in the sense of 'hyperactive': * *Her son is rather hyper.*

hyperbola or **hyperbole**? These two nouns should not be confused. *Hyperbola* is a technical term used in mathematics to describe a type of symmetrical curve; *hyperbole* means 'exaggeration used for effect in speech or writing': * *I've warned him a million times* is an example of *hyperbole*. Both nouns originate from the same Greek word and they share the derived adjective *hyperbolic(al)*. Note that the final *-e* of *hyperbole* is pronounced, producing the four-syllable word [hī*per*bŏli]. *Hyperbola* is pronounced [hī*per*bŏlă].

hypercritical *see* **hypocritical** or **hypercritical**?

HYPHENS

1 Prefixes	Most standard prefixes are attached without a hyphen: * *unimportant* * *multicoloured* * *prefabricated*. Some users prefer to hyphenate words prefixed with *non-* and words in which the absence of the hyphen would result in a word with a doubled vowel: * *non-flammable* * *pre-eminent* * *co-ordinate*. Such words are widely and increasingly accepted in the single-word forms: * *nonflammable* * *preeminent* * *coordinate*, etc. However, the double *i* of words prefixed by *anti-*, *semi-*, etc., is usually split by a hyphen: * *anti-inflationary* * *semi-independent*. Words prefixed with *ex-* (in the sense of 'former') and *self-* are usually hyphenated: * *ex-wife* * *self-sufficient*. A hyphen is sometimes inserted after the prefix to avoid ambiguity or confusion; for example, to distinguish between the nouns *co-op* (a cooperative) and *coop* (an enclosure), or between the verbs *re-cover* and *recover*, and to clarify the pronunciation and meaning of such words as *de-ice* (*see also* **co-**; **re-**). A hyphen is always used to join a prefix to a word beginning with a capital letter: * *anti-British* * *un-Christian*. *See also* **-like**.
2 Compounds	Many compounds can be written with or without a hyphen, depending on convention, frequency of usage, the writer's personal preference, or the publisher's house style: * *dining room* or *dining-room* * *hard-hearted* or *hardhearted* * *boy-friend* or *boyfriend*. There is a growing tendency towards minimal hyphenation, with the substitution of two words or one word as appropriate. Some fixed compounds of three or more words, such as *son-in-law*, *happy-go-lucky*, etc., are always hyphenated; two-word compound adjectives in which the second element ends in *-ed*, such as *light-hearted*, *blue-eyed*, *short-sighted*, etc., are usually hyphenated (*see also* **4** below). Hyphens can be employed to make new compound verbs out of existing nouns: * *ski-lift*. Some compounds derived from phrasal verbs are always hyphenated: * *broken-down*; some are always solid (not hyphenated): * *breakthrough*; others may be hyphenated or solid: * *takeover* or *take-over* * *rundown* or *run-down*. Note, however, that it is wrong to put a hyphen in the phrasal verb itself: * *You can top up* [not *top-up*] *your mobile here.*
3 Adjectival compounds	Compounds of two or more words used adjectivally before the noun they qualify are usually hyphenated: * *a used-car dealer* sells used cars; * *a plain-chocolate biscuit* is coated with plain chocolate; * *a three-month-old baby* is three months old; * *a once-in-a-lifetime opportunity* occurs only once in a lifetime. These hyphens are often essential to avoid ambiguity: * *a red-wine bottle* is a bottle for red wine; * *a red wine bottle* may be a wine bottle that is red. Similarly, * *a black-cab driver* is a driver of a black cab; * *a black cab driver* [or *cab-driver*] is a cab driver who is black.

4 Adverbial compounds	Adjectives or participles preceded by an adverb are not hyphen-ated if the adverb ends in *-ly:* * *a neatly written letter* * *a letter that is neatly written.* Compounds containing other adverbs, especially those that may be mistaken for adjectives (*well, ill, best, little, half,* etc.) are usually hyphenated when they are used adjectivally before a noun, to avoid ambiguity: * *a half-cooked loaf* * *his best-known novel.* When such compounds occur after the noun, the hyphen is sometimes optional.
5 Repeated compounds	In groups of two or more hyphenated compounds a common element need not be repeated, but the hyphen must not be omitted; the same convention applies to solid compounds, in which the common element may be replaced by a hyphen: * *long- or short-haired dogs* * *salesmen and -women.* Some users dis-like this convention, preferring to retain the full compound in all cases.
6 Numbers	A hyphen is inserted when numbers between 21 and 99 are writ-ten out in full: * *twenty-one* * *thirty-seven* * *eighty-six* ∂ *four hun-dred and fifty-three.* A hyphen is used when fractions are written out, to separate the numerator and denominator: * *three-tenths* * *thirteen-six-teenths* * *two-thirds.*
7 End-of-line hyphens	The other major use of the hyphen is at the end of a line, splitting a word that is to be continued at the beginning of the next line. There are a number of conventions relating to the points at which a word may be divided; these recommended breaks are marked in some dictionaries. There is an increasing tendency for word division to be influenced by phonetic rather than etymo-logical principles * *photog-rapher* [fŏtogrăfĕr], not *photo-grapher.* A word should always be split between syllables, ideally at a natural break: after an existing hyphen; between the elements of a one-word compound, such as *semi-, inter-,* etc.; or before a suffix, such as *-ness, -ment,* etc. Words of one syllable should not be broken. Words should not be broken immediately after the first letter or immediately before the last. It is also important to ensure that the letters on either side of the break will not mislead the reader, especially if they form a word in their own right: * *mace-rate* * *the-rapist* * *mans-laughter* * *not-able* * *rear-range* * *homes-pun* * *leg-end,* and that the hyphen will not be mistaken for a fixed hyphen: * *re-creation* * *un-ionised* * *de-crease* * *ex-tractor.*
8 Hyphens as dashes	In handwritten and typewritten texts a hyphen is often used in place of a **dash**. *See also* **underscore**.

HYPHEN The principal uses of the *hyphen* in English are to join two or more words together, either as a fixed compound or to avoid ambiguity, and to indicate that a word has been broken at the end of a line through lack of space. There are a number of other situations in which the use of the *hyphen* is optional, as described in the panel, on pages 207–8.

hypo- *see* **hyper-** or **hypo-**?

hypocrisy The noun *hypocrisy* is sometimes misspelt, a common error being the substitution of *-cracy* (as in *democracy*) for the *-crisy* ending. Note also the prefix *hypo-*, not *hyper*.

hypocritical or **hypercritical**? These two words are often confused. *Hypocritical* means 'insincere' or 'two-faced'; *hypercritical* means 'excessively critical': ◦ *It would be hypocritical of me to say I enjoyed the concert, when really I thought it was awful.* ◦ *He's so hypercritical about the way I lay the table.* As well as being misspelt, these words are sometimes mispronounced: *hypocritical* is pronounced [hipĕkritikl]; *hypercritical* is pronounced [hīpĕkritikl].

hysterical, hysterics *see* **histrionic** or **hysterical**?

I

I or me? The subject pronoun *I* and the object pronoun *me* are sometimes confused in informal speech, especially in the phrases *It's me* and *Between you and I*. After verbs and prepositions, the object pronoun *me* should be used; before verbs, the subject pronoun *I* should be used: * *They have invited my mother, my father, and me* [not *I*] *to the wedding.* * *He works with Mary and me* [not *I*]. * *My friend and I* [not *me*] *will help*. Confusion and errors occur in the highest places: * *She could give a better answer than that to I and to my honourable friends* (said during Prime Minister's Question Time).

These problems rarely arise when the pronoun stands alone; any confusion may therefore be resolved by mentally removing the other item(s) and assessing the result: * *They have invited me to the wedding.* * *He works with me.* * *I will help.*

The verb *to be*, according to grammatical convention, is an exception: in formal contexts *It is me* is unacceptable to a few careful users, who prefer *It is I*. However, in informal contexts the idiomatic *It's me* is generally considered to be more natural than the pedantic *It's I* and is acceptable to most users.

Many users avoid the phrase *between you and I* in all contexts, although it is often heard in informal speech. *Between you and me*, which conforms to grammatical convention, is the preferred usage. *See also* **as**; **it**; **let**; **myself**; **pronouns**; **than**.

-ible *see* **-able** or **-ible?**

-ic or -ical? Many adjectives are formed by the addition of the suffixes *-ic* or *-ical*: * *cubic* * *symmetrical* * *phonetic* * *geographical*. Sometimes either suffix may be added to the same root. The pairs of words thus created may be virtually interchangeable, such as: * *metric–metrical* * *philosophic–philosophical*, although one is usually more frequent or more specialised than the other. In other pairs the two words may differ in meaning or usage: *see* **classic** or **classical?**; **comic** or **comical?**; **economic** or **economical?**; **electric** or **electrical?**; **historic** or **historical?**; **magic** or **magical?**; **politic** or **political?**

Some adjectives, especially those related to nouns ending in *-ic*, are found only in the *-ical* form: a *critic* may be *critical*; a *sceptic* is *sceptical*. Others, such as *static* or *tragic*, are very rarely, if ever, found in the *-ical* form.

With the exception of *politic* and *public*, all adverbs derived from adjectives ending in *-ic* or *-ical* have the suffix *-ically*: * *tragically* * *critically*.

iconic The adjective *iconic* has acquired cliché status due to its overuse in relatively recent times, when it has been applied to virtually anything considered memorable in some way, from cars and hairstyles to football teams and television advertisements. Careful users avoid using the word except where its appearance is unarguably justified by the context: * *The statue has iconic status.*

-ics A number of words ending in *-ics* may be singular or plural nouns, depending on the sense in which they are used: * *Acoustics is the study of sound.* * *The acoustics of the room have been improved and are now excellent.* Such nouns are usually singular when they denote a science or some other area of study or activity: * *Mathematics was not my favourite subject at school.* * *Gymnastics is just one of her many hobbies.* * *Economics is taught in the sixth form, but politics is not on the curriculum.*

In other contexts, the same nouns may become plural when they refer to a system, set of principles, group of activities, etc.: * *His politics are very left-wing.* * *What are the economics of the coal industry?*

Some nouns, such as *tactics*, *statistics*, and *ethics*, may be singular or plural as described above but also exist in a singular *-ic* form: * *military tactics* * *vital statistics* * *professional ethics* * *her latest tactic* * *an alarming statistic* * *the work ethic.*

Nouns relating to behaviour, such as *heroics* and *hysterics*, are usually plural. *See also* **singular** or **plural**?

identical with or **identical to**? The adjective *identical* may be followed by *with* or *to*: * *This picture is identical with/to the one we saw in the shop.* Some users dislike the phrase *identical to*, considering *with* the more acceptable preposition in this context.

idioms An *idiom* is a more or less fixed expression, such as *out of hand*, *in spite of*, *to come into her own*, or *a storm in a teacup*, the meaning of which is distinct from the individual senses of the words it contains. Many idioms, such as * *have egg on your face* ('be shown to be foolish') and * *be dog tired* ('be very tired after exertion') are best restricted to informal contexts; others, such as * *the salt of the earth* ('people regarded as having praiseworthy qualities'), are acceptable at all levels. *See also* **metaphors**; **similes**.

idiosyncrasy This word is often misspelt, the most frequent error occurring when the ending *-asy* is replaced by *-acy*. The correct ending is like *fantasy* and not like *privacy*. Note also that *i* and *y* each occurs twice.

idle, **idol** or **idyll**? The adjective *idle* means 'not active; lazy': * *an idle machine* * *an idle fellow* * *He is never idle.* An *idol* is an object of worship or admiration: * *a pop idol* * *They bowed before the idol.* An *idyll* is (a piece of writing that depicts) a pleasant or idealised scene or situation: * *an idyll of life on the Pacific island.* Idle and *idol* are sometimes confused, being identical in pronunciation: [īdl]. *Idyll* is pronounced with a short initial *i:* [idil]. *Idyll* is more usually found in the derived adjectival word **idyllic**.

idyllic The first *i* of *idyllic* is usually pronounced as in *ill*, although it may be pronounced as in *item*. The stress occurs on the second syllable in both cases: [idilik] or [īdilik].

i.e. *see* **e.g.** and **i.e.**

if The use of *if* in place of *though* often causes ambiguity: * *The work, if difficult, is rewarding.* * *The service was good, if not excellent.* The first of these examples may mean 'the work is difficult but rewarding' or 'difficult work is rewarding'. It is impossible to ascertain from the second example whether the service was excellent or not.

The use of *if* in place of *whether* may also be confusing in certain contexts: * *Ask him if it is raining* probably means 'ask him whether it is raining (or not)', but it may also mean 'if it is raining, ask him (for a lift, to close the window, etc.)'. *See also* **subjunctive**; **were** or **was**?; **whether**.

if and when Many people object to the frequent use of the phrase *if and when*, which can usually be replaced simply by *if* or *when*: * *We'll move to a larger house if and when we start a family.* The phrase sometimes serves a useful purpose, however: in the example above, the users may not wish to commit themselves on the subject of parenthood; *if* would imply doubt, while *when* would imply certainty.

ill *see* **sick** or **ill**?

illegal *see* **illicit**, **illegal** or **illegitimate**?

illegible or **eligible**? The adjective *eligible*, meaning 'qualified; suitable; worthy': * *to be eligible for a competition* * *an eligible bachelor*, should not be confused with *illegible* (*see* **illegible** or **unreadable**?). Note the differences in spelling between the two words – particularly the *-ll-* and *i-e-* vowel sequence of *illegible*, and the *-l-* and *e-i-* vowel sequence of *eligible*.

Illegible is stressed on the second syllable, [i*lej*ĭbl]; *eligible* on the first, [*el*ijĭbl].

illegible or **unreadable**? The adjective *illegible* describes something that can-

not be deciphered and is therefore impossible to read; *unreadable* means 'uninteresting' or 'badly worded', describing something that cannot be read with enjoyment, ease, or understanding: * *Her handwriting is illegible.* * *He has produced another unreadable novel.* * *The document is unreadable; it must be reworded.* *Unreadable* may be used as a synonym for 'illegible' in certain contexts, but it can cause ambiguity: * *This paragraph is totally unreadable* may be a criticism either of the handwriting (or printing quality), or of the content or wording.

illegitimate *see* **illicit**, **illegal** or **illegitimate**?

illicit or **elicit**? The adjective *illicit* (*see* **illicit**, **illegal** or **illegitimate**?) should not be confused with the verb *elicit*, meaning 'draw out' or 'evoke': * *illicit dealings* * *to elicit the truth.* The two words have the same pronunciation [i*lis*it].

illicit, **illegal** or **illegitimate**? All these adjectives mean 'unlawful', but there are differences of sense, usage, and application between them: * *illicit trade* * *illegal parking* * *an illegitimate attack.* *Illicit* means 'not permitted or approved by law': * *The Government should seek the co-operation of the unions, business and revenue authorities to eradicate illicit and irregular earnings* (*Daily Telegraph*). The word is also used to describe something that is contrary to social custom: * *an illicit relationship.* *Illegal* means 'forbidden by law': * *The possession of such weapons without a licence is illegal in this country.* The word is also used to describe something that contravenes the regulations of a sport, etc.: * *an illegal tackle.* The adjective *illegitimate* is principally applied to children born of unmarried parents: * *the president's illegitimate daughter.* It also describes something that defies reason or logic: * *an illegitimate explanation. See also* illicit or elicit?

illusion *see* **allusion, illusion** or **delusion?**

illusive, illusory *see* **allusive, elusive** or **illusive?**

imaginary or **imaginative?** *Imaginary* means 'unreal' or 'existing only in the imagination'; *imaginative* means 'having or showing a vivid or creative imagination': * *an imaginary house* * *an imaginative designer* * *an imaginative story.* The two adjectives are not interchangeable, although both may occasionally be applied to the same noun: * *an imaginary friend* does not exist; *an imaginative friend* has a lively imagination.

I mean The phrase *I mean* may be used in informal speech to clarify, expand, or correct a previous statement, question, etc.: * *Is your foot very painful, I mean too painful to walk on?* * *She lives in Plymouth, I mean Portsmouth.* In some contexts the phrase serves no useful purpose and may be omitted: * *You could have bought a new umbrella, (I mean) they're not very expensive.*

immanent *see* **eminent, imminent** or **immanent?**

immigrant *see* **emigrant** or **immigrant?**

imminent *see* **eminent, imminent** or **immanent?**

immoral *see* **amoral** or **immoral?**

immovable or **immoveable?** Note that both *immovable* and *immoveable* are considered acceptable spellings of the word: * *The chandelier proved immovable.* * *He inherited the property together with various immoveables.*

immune from or **immune to?** The adjective *immune* is followed by *to* in the literal sense of 'protected against or resistant to disease' and figurative extensions of this sense: * *The plant is immune to fungal disease.* * *She is immune to criticism.* In the figurative sense of 'exempt', *immune* is followed by *from*: * *Nobody is immune from punishment.*

immunity or **impunity?** *Immunity* is exemption or freedom from obligation or duty; *impunity* is exemption or freedom from punishment or harm: * *Diplomatic immunity provides foreign ambassadors with immunity from taxation and enables them to infringe the law with impunity. Impunity* is a restricted form of *immunity*; the word occurs most frequently in the phrase with *impunity. Immunity* also means 'resistance to disease': * *This vaccination may not confer total immunity.*

impact The use of *impact* as a synonym for 'effect', 'impression', or 'influence' is best restricted to contexts in which the effect, impression, etc., is particularly powerful: * *the impact of the government's resignation on the stock market* * *The new packaging has had little effect* [not *impact*] *on sales.* Some people object to all figurative uses of the noun, reserving it for physical collisions and their effects: * *the impact of the bullet on the car door.*

The use of *impact* as a verb meaning 'affect' is best avoided: * *The cutbacks impacted secondary education negatively* could be reworded as: * *The cutbacks had a bad effect on secondary education.* The increasing tendency to follow *impact* with *on* is especially disliked by many people: * *This change will impact severely on small companies.*

impassioned, impassive *see* **dispassionate, impassioned or impassive?**

impel *see* **compel or impel?**

imperial or imperious? The adjective *imperial* means 'of an emperor, empress, or empire'; imperious means 'overbearing' or 'arrogant': * *the imperial palace* * *an imperious gesture.* The two words are sometimes confused in the extended sense of *imperial* – 'majestic', 'regal', or 'commanding': *imperial powers* are those that are as majestic as an emperor's, not those that are domineering and arrogant. Both are derived from the Latin noun *imperium*, meaning 'command'.

The adjective *imperial* also refers to the British system of weights and measures (pounds and ounces, feet and inches, gallons and pints, etc.), which has now been largely replaced by the metric system.

impersonate, personate or personify? To *impersonate* is to imitate or pretend to be somebody else: * *The comedian impersonated Humphrey Bogart.* * *It is a crime to impersonate a police officer.* To *personify* is to represent or embody something abstract or inanimate as a human being: * *He personifies the greed of modern society.* The rare verb *personate* is sometimes used in place of *impersonate* or *personify*.

impinge or infringe? Either verb may be used in the sense of 'encroach': * *They are impinging/infringing on our rights.* Note that in this sense, both verbs are followed by *on* (or *upon*). *Impinge* is used with more abstract nouns: * *everything that impinges on our consciousness.* To *impinge on*, in formal contexts, also means to strike: * *The bullet impinged on the side of the vehicle. Infringe*, used transitively without on, means 'break' or 'violate': * *to infringe the rules.*

implement The verb *implement* is best avoided where *carry out, fulfil, accomplish*, or *put into action* would be adequate or more appropriate: * *His absence will enable us to carry out* [not *implement*] *our plan.* Originally a legal term, the verb *implement* is widely used in official contexts: * *The company has been ordered to implement safety measures as a result of the accident.*

As a noun, *implement* denotes a tool or instrument: * *agricultural implements.* There is a slight difference in pronunciation between the verb and the noun: the final syllable of the verb is sounded [-ment], rhyming with *tent*; the final syllable of the noun is unstressed [-mĕnt], as in *garment*.

implicit *see* **explicit or implicit?**

imply or infer? The verb *imply* means 'suggest' or 'hint at'; *infer* means 'deduce' or 'conclude': * *She implied that there would be some redundancies in the factory.* * *I inferred from what she said that there would be some redundancies in the factory.* To *imply* involves speech, writing, or action; to *infer* involves listening, reading, or observation. The two verbs are frequently confused, *infer* being used in place of *imply*, to the extent that some dictionaries now list 'imply' as an additional sense of *infer*. Many people object to this usage, however; it is therefore advisable to maintain the distinction between the two words. Similarly, the noun *inference* is sometimes used instead of *implication*, but it is preferable to maintain the distinction between these two words: * *the implications* [not *the inferences*] *of the report*.

Infer is stressed on the second syllable; the final *r* is doubled before *-ed*, *-ing*, and *-er*. The noun *inference*, in which the stress shifts to the first syllable, has a single *r*. See also **spelling**.

important or **importantly**? *More important* (short for 'what is more important') is sometimes regarded as an adverbial phrase, the adjective *important* being changed to *importantly*: * *His assistants are very conscientious and, more important(ly), they are utterly trustworthy*. Many users prefer the phrase *more important* in formal contexts, although *more importantly* is becoming increasingly acceptable.

impostor or **imposter**? This word, meaning 'person who fraudulently pretends to be another person', has two spellings, though the spelling *impostor* is more frequently used than *imposter*.

impractical or **impracticable**? *see* **practical** or **practicable**?

impresario An *impresario* is a theatrical producer or sponsor. Note the spelling of the word, particularly the single *s*, unlike *impress*. The usual pronunciation is [imprĕ*sariŏ*]; some people dislike the variant [imprĕ*sairiŏ*]. The plural is formed by adding *-s*, not *-es*: *impresarios*.

impromptu *see* **extempore** or **impromptu**?

improvise This word is sometimes misspelt. Note particularly the *-ise* ending, which does not have *-ize* as a variant (*see* **-ize** or **-ise**?).

impugn or **impute**? These words, both of which are formal, are sometimes confused. To *impugn* is to question the integrity of, implying that someone is not being honourable: * *to dare to impugn his motives*. To *impute* is to attribute, sometimes unjustly: * *it is grossly unfair to impute blame for the crime to them*.

impunity *see* **immunity** or **impunity**?

impute *see* **impugn** or **impute**?

in *see* **at** or **in**?; **into** or **in to**?

inaccessible Note the spelling of this adjective, particularly the single *-in-*, the *-cc-* and *-ss-*, and the *-ible* ending.

inapt or **inept**? The adjective *inapt* means 'inappropriate' or 'unsuitable'; its synonym *inept* is more frequently used in the sense of 'incompetent' or 'clumsy': * *an inapt comparison* * *an inept mechanic*.

inasmuch as This phrase may also be written *in as much as*, although *inasmuch as* is far more frequent: * *The result was significant inasmuch as it demonstrated the power of the individual*. See also **in so far as**.

incentive The noun *incentive* is followed by the preposition *to* or *for*: ● *An incentive to* [or *for*] *their employees to work harder.*

incident The noun *incident* is frequently used in the mass media to denote an action or occurrence that has or is likely to have serious, violent, or political consequences: ● *The incident sparked off a wave of anti-globalism protests.* In other contexts the noun *incident* is principally used with reference to events of minor importance: ● *The unfortunate incident was soon forgotten.*
   Incidents, the plural form, should not be confused with *incidence*, which means 'occurrence', 'rate', or 'frequency': ● *The incidence of crime has fallen in recent months.*

include or **comprise**? *Include* and *comprise* are similar in meaning but not identical. *Include* is less restrictive than *comprise*, suggesting that the things cited are part of a greater number or range of things, while *comprise* implies that the things cited are the entirety of the things under discussion: ● *The list includes a number of conditions.* ● *The document comprises a full confession.*

incomparable This word, meaning 'without comparison', is often mispronounced. The stress falls on the second syllable and not the third. The correct pronunciation is [in*kom*părăbl].

incongruous *see* **congruent** or **congruous**?

incontrovertible The adjective *incontrovertible*, meaning 'undeniable; indisputable', and the derived adverb *incontrovertibly*, are sometimes misspelt. Note the *-ible* (not *-able*) ending. Another frequent error is the substitution of an *a* for the second *o*.

incredible or **incredulous**? *Incredible* means 'unbelievable'; *incredulous* means 'disbelieving': ● *He told her an incredible story.* ● *She looked at him with an incredulous expression.* The use of the adjective *incredible* in the sense of 'wonderful' or 'amazing' should be restricted to informal contexts: ● *We had an incredible holiday.* See also **credible**, **creditable** or **credulous**?

indecent *see* **decent** or **decorous**?

indefinite article *see* **a** or **an**?

indefinitely This word is often misspelt, the most common error being the substitution of an *a* for the final *i*. It is worth remembering that the word *finite* has the same sequence of vowels.

independence and **independent** These words are sometimes misspelt, the most frequent error being the substitution of an *a* for the final *e*. Note, however, that the noun *dependant*, 'person who relies on another for financial support', is spelt with a final *a*.

indexes or **indices**? The noun *index* has two accepted plural forms, *indexes* and *indices*. The use of the plural form *indices*, pronounced [*in*diseez], is largely restricted to mathematics, economics, and technical contexts. For other senses of *index*, especially that of 'alphabetical list', the plural form *indexes* is preferred by most users: ● *This cookery book has two indexes: one lists recipes by name; the other lists principal ingredients.* ● *Book titles and authors' names are entered in separate indexes.*

Indian The adjective and noun *Indian* may refer to India and its inhabitants or to the indigenous peoples of America: * *the Indian Empire* * *an Indian reservation.* This common confusion can be blamed on the explorer Christopher Columbus, who mistook the New World for India.

The term *American Indian* is sometimes used to distinguish these peoples from the Indians of Asia; it is preferred to the older British term *Red Indian*, which refers to the Indians of North America and is now generally considered offensive. It has, however, been largely replaced in its own turn by **Native American.**

An inhabitant of Pakistan, part of the Indian subcontinent, is a *Pakistani*. Asian Indians and Pakistanis living in Britain are usually referred to as *Asians*. Note that the Indian subcontinent itself is today more likely to be referred to as South Asia. *See also* **Asian** or **Asiatic**?

Further confusion may be caused by the term *West Indian*, which refers to inhabitants of the West Indies and their descendants.

indices *see* **indexes** or **indices**?

indict The word *indict*, meaning 'accuse; formally charge', is often mispronounced. The correct pronunciation is [ind*ī*t] – note that the *c* is not pronounced. The *c* is similarly silent in the derived noun *indictment*.

indifferent The adjective *indifferent* should be followed by *to* or *as to*, not *for* or *about*: * *He is indifferent to your criticism.* * *I am indifferent as to the outcome of the trial.* The two principal senses of *indifferent* have undergone a gradual change, from 'impartial' to

'unconcerned' or 'uninterested', and from 'neither good nor bad' to 'below average' or 'poor'. Used in either of its original senses, or even in one of its modern senses, the word is sometimes open to misinterpretation or confusion: * *an indifferent referee* may be impartial, uninterested, neither good nor bad, or poor.

indigenous *see* **native**.

indigenous Australian *see* **Aboriginal** or **Aborigine**?

indignant The adjective *indignant* is followed by the preposition *at* or *about* in the sense of 'indignant at something': * *He was indignant at* [or *about*] *having to do the washing up*. In the sense 'indignant with a person', it is followed by *with*: * *She seemed indignant with me.*

indirect speech *see* **reported speech**.

indiscriminate or **undiscriminating**? Both adjectives refer to a lack of discrimination (in the sense of 'discernment' rather than 'prejudice'); *indiscriminate* has the extended meaning of 'random' or 'unselective': * *indiscriminate killings* * *an undiscriminating palate*. There is a tendency for *undiscriminating* to be preferred to *indiscriminate* with direct reference to people: * *undiscriminating viewers* * *indiscriminate viewing. See also* **discriminating** or **discriminatory**?

indispensable This word, meaning 'absolutely essential': * *In this job, a car and a telephone are indispensable assets*, is sometimes misspelt. The ending is *-able*, and not *-ible* as in *indestructible*.

individual Some users dislike the use of the noun *individual* in place of *person*; they reserve *individual* for contexts in which a single person is contrasted with a group: * *the rights of the individual* * *the person* [not *individual*] *who wrote this article.* The noun *individual* is also used, to derogatory, contemptuous, or humorous effect, to denote a particular kind of person: * *an unpleasant individual* * *an eccentric individual.* This usage is best restricted to informal contexts.

indoor or **indoors**? *Indoor* is an adjective; *indoors* is an adverb: * *an indoor aerial* * *to go indoors* * *Indoor games are played indoors.*

industrial or **industrious**? These two adjectives should not be confused. *Industrial* is derived from the noun *industry* in the sense of 'manufacturing or commercial enterprises'; *industrious* means 'hard-working' (from *industry* in the sense of 'diligence; assiduity'): * *an industrial town* * *an industrious student.*

inedible *see* **eatable** or **edible**?

ineffective, ineffectual, inefficient *see* **effective, effectual, efficacious** or **efficient**?

inept *see* **inapt** or **inept**?

inequality, inequity or **iniquity**? *Inequality* is the state of being unequal or different; *inequity* means 'unfairness'; *iniquity* is wickedness: * *the inequality of their ages* * *the inequity of the law* * *a den of iniquity. Inequity* and *iniquity* are much more formal words than *inequality.* All three nouns may be used in the sense of 'injustice', with different connotations: * *The inequality of the tax system* means that some people pay more tax than others; * *The inequity of the tax system* implies that the system is unfair; * *The iniquity of the tax system* suggests that the system is morally wrong.

in extremis The Latin phrase *in extremis* is used in formal contexts to refer to an emergency or a very serious situation in which extreme methods must be taken: * *The use of these drugs is only permitted in extremis.* In other, especially religious, contexts, the phrase *in extremis* also means 'at the point of death': * *to administer a rite only when the patient is in extremis.* It is sometimes written or printed in italics.

in fact The phrase *in fact* is largely used for emphasis or to expand on a previous statement: * *This legislation will not in fact improve housing conditions in inner-city areas.* * *I'm not familiar with the machine; in fact, I've only used it once.* Since *in fact* means 'actually' or 'in reality', the addition of *actual* is considered by many users to be superfluous: * *He often spends his holidays in France, but in (actual) fact he hates the French.*

Note that it is incorrect to write the phrase as a single word, *infact.*

infamous or **notorious**? Both adjectives mean 'well-known for something bad': *notorious* emphasises the well-known aspect; *infamous* emphasises the bad aspect: * *the execution of this infamous/notorious criminal* * *his notorious lack of punctuality* * *That junction is notorious for accidents.* * *one of Richard III's most infamous deeds.* Note the pronunciation and stress pattern of *infamous* [*in*fămŭs], which is quite different from that of *famous* [*fay*mŭs].

infectious *see* **contagious** or **infectious**?

infer, inference *see* **imply** or **infer**?

inferior The adjective *inferior* is followed by the preposition *to*: * *This novel is inferior to his last one.*

infinite or **infinitesimal**? *Infinite* means 'having no limits' or 'extremely great'; *infinitesimal* means 'negligible' or 'extremely small': * *She has infinite patience.* * *The difference is infinitesimal.* An *infinite amount* is so great that it cannot be measured; an *infinitesimal amount* is so small that it cannot be measured.

infinitive The *infinitive* of a verb, often preceded by *to*, is its basic form, without any of the changes or additions that relate to tense, person, number, etc.: (*to*) *go* is the infinitive of the verb from which the past participle *gone* is derived.

The *infinitive* is used without *to* after a number of auxiliary verbs: * *you can leave* * *they must wait* * *he may object* * *we should succeed*, etc. After a number of other verbs, the infinitive is used with *to*: * *I hope to see it.* * *She refused to come.* * *It never fails to amuse him.* * *Do you wish to go home?* The infinitive (with *to*) is also used after adjectives and nouns: * *easy to mend* * *a book to read.*

In some constructions the infinitive functions as a verbal noun and may be interchangeable with its gerund (*see* **-ing forms**): * *We love walking/to walk.* * *He began writing/to write.* * *To teach/ Teaching young children requires great*

patience. * *To find/Finding another job is not always easy.* In other constructions the infinitive and gerund are not interchangeable: * *able to win–capable of winning* * *a tendency to cheat–a habit of cheating* * *He volunteered to help–he considered helping.*

Replacing an infinitive with a gerund sometimes changes the meaning of a sentence: * *He stopped* [i.e. paused] *to read the notice.* * *He stopped reading the notice* [i.e. He finished reading it]. * *I remembered to lock the door* [i.e. I didn't forget to do it]. * *I remembered locking the door* [i.e. I recalled having locked it]. *See also* **split infinitive.**

For irregular parts of verbs, see table at **verbs**.

inflammable The adjective *inflammable* describes something that will catch fire and burn easily: * *This liquid is highly inflammable. Inflammable* may be wrongly interpreted as the opposite of its synonym *flammable* (by analogy with *sensitive–insensitive; visible–invisible; edible–inedible; capable–incapable;* etc.). The potential danger of such confusion has led to a preference, especially on warning signs and labels, for the less ambiguous terms *flammable* (denoting an inflammable substance) and *non-flammable* (denoting a substance that is not (in)flammable). *Inflammable* also means 'easily angered or excited': * *an inflammable situation.* In this figurative sense it cannot be replaced by *flammable.*

The adjectives *inflammable* and *inflammatory* should not be confused; something *inflammatory* tends to arouse strong or violent feelings: * *an inflammatory speech.*

inflation *Inflation* is a general increase in the level of prices: * *The rate of inflation has risen to 6%*. The word is widely used, especially in informal contexts, to denote the rate of inflation: * *Inflation has risen to 6%*. It is sometimes misinterpreted as being synonymous with the level of prices: * *They say inflation's going down, but my money isn't going any further than it did*. A fall in (the rate of) inflation does not mean a fall in prices; it simply denotes a slower increase.

inflection *Inflection* is the term used for the change in form that words undergo in order to denote distinctions of number, tense, gender, case, etc. It is also used to describe the grammatical relation of a word to its root by inflection. So it is possible to say that the word *tables* is formed by inflection from *table*; *walked* is formed by inflection from *walk*; *heroine* is formed by inflection from *hero*; *them* is formed by inflection from *they*. *See* **derived words**.

The spelling *inflexion* is occasionally seen in British English. This is not incorrect but it is now considered virtually obsolete; *inflection* is the preferred spelling.

inflict *see* **afflict** or **inflict**?

influenza *see* **flu**.

info- Some people dislike the increasing use of *info-*, short for *information*, to form new blends and compounds, especially in informal contexts. * *infotainment* (informative entertainment) * *infomania* (preoccupation with information for its own sake) * *infotech* (information technology). The noun *info* ('information') should be used only in informal contexts.

inform The verb *inform* is best avoided where *tell* would be adequate or more appropriate: * *Please tell* [not *inform*] *your husband that his car is ready for collection*. Unlike *tell*, *inform* should not be followed by an infinitive: * *They told* [not *informed*] *him to leave*. * *They informed me of his departure*.

Inform is also used in the sense of 'inspire', which is closer to the meaning of the Latin verb *informare* 'give shape to', from which it is derived: * *His learning informs his whole discourse*.

informant or **informer**? An *informant* is a person who gives information; an *informer* is a person who gives the police information about criminals and their activities: * *The professor was one of the author's most useful informants*. * *The police were tipped off about the robbery by an informer*. The noun *informer* may also be used in the neutral sense of *informant*, but to avoid misunderstanding it is best restricted to its more specific meaning.

information The noun *information* is followed by the preposition *on* or *about*: * *Do you have any information on* [or *about*] *the company?*

infringe *see* **impinge** or **infringe**?

ingenious or **ingenuous**? *Ingenious* means 'clever' or 'inventive'; *ingenuous* means 'innocent', 'naïve', or 'frank': * *an ingenious idea* * *an ingenuous smile*. The two adjectives are not interchangeable, but are sometimes confused. The noun form *ingenuity*, originally derived from *ingenuous* and formerly used for both adjectives, is now restricted to the sense of 'cleverness' or 'inventiveness'; *ingenuousness* is the noun form of *ingenuous*.

Note the pronunciations of the two adjectives: the *e* of *ingenious* is long, as in *mean*; the *e* of *ingenuous* is short, as in *men*. *See also* **disingenuous** or **ingenuous**?

-ing forms The *-ing* form of a verb may be a present participle or a gerund (verbal noun): * *I am learning Japanese* [present participle]. * *Learning Japanese is not easy* [gerund]. It is sometimes difficult, and often unnecessary, to distinguish between a gerund and a present participle. Problems of usage arise when the gerund has its own subject: * *She disapproves of your using the car.* * *She disapproves of the house where she spent her childhood being demolished.* According to grammatical convention, the possessive form should always be used in such cases. The substitution of *you* for *your* in the first example (or of *me/him/us/them* for *my/his/our/their* in similar cases) would be unacceptable to many users, even in informal contexts. However, the substitution of *childhood's* for *childhood* in the second example would be clumsy, unidiomatic, and also unacceptable to many users.

Between these two extremes – the simple personal pronoun and the complex noun phrase – the possessive form is used with varying degrees of acceptability.

For personal names and nouns relating to people, animals, etc., the possessive form is usually preferred in formal contexts but is sometimes rejected in informal contexts: * *She disapproves of Peter's using the car.* * *She disapproves of the gardener's using the car.* If more than one name or noun is involved, the possessive form is usually rejected in all contexts: * *She disapproves of Michael and Peter using the car.* * *She disapproves of the cook and the gardener using the car.*

For abstract nouns and nouns relating to inanimate objects, which are rarely used with the possessive ending *-'s*, the possessive form is usually rejected: * *She disapproves of the house being demolished.* * *She disapproves of religion being taught in schools.*

In the four preceding examples, the absence of the possessive ending may cause confusion: the reader or listener is momentarily led to believe that *she disapproves of Michael/the cook/the house/religion.* Such confusion can often be avoided by restructuring the sentence or by replacing the gerund with a noun: * *She disapproves of the demolition of the house.*

In some contexts the use of the possessive form with such words as *painting, writing, meeting, cooking,* etc., which may denote either an action or its result, can be ambiguous: * *We were not informed of their meeting* [that they intended to hold a meeting]. * *We were not informed of their meeting* [that they had met].

In other contexts, the use of the possessive form may alter the meaning of a sentence: * *They watched the girl dancing* places the emphasis on the girl; * *They watched the girl's dancing* places the emphasis on the dancing. *See also* **apostrophe**; **dangling participles**; **infinitive**; **participles**; **'s or s'?**; **want**.

inherent This word, meaning 'essential or intrinsic', has two possible pronunciations: [in*heer*ĕnt] or [in*herr*ĕnt]. The first of these is the more traditional, and is preferred by many users.

inheritance *see* **heritage** or **inheritance**?

inhuman or **inhumane**? Careful users maintain the distinction between *inhuman* and *inhumane*. *Inhumane*, the opposite of *humane*, means 'lacking in compassion and kindness; cruel; not merciful': • *inhumane treatment*. *Inhuman*, the opposite of *human*, is stronger and has a wider scope than *inhumane*. To be *inhuman* means to lack all human qualities, not only compassion and kindness: • *inhuman violence* • *inhuman living conditions*. *Inhuman* has the additional meaning of 'not having human form': • *An inhuman shape appeared at the window*.

iniquity *see* **inequality**, **inequity** or **iniquity**?

in-law The use of the plural noun *in-laws*, denoting a person's relatives by marriage, is best restricted to informal contexts: • *My in-laws are coming for dinner on Saturday*. The plural of *mother-in-law*, *father-in-law*, *son-in-law*, *daughter-in-law*, etc. is formed by adding *s* to the first element of the compound: *mothers-in-law*, *fathers-in-law*, etc.

in lieu The phrase *in lieu* (*of*) is best avoided where *instead* (*of*) would be adequate or more appropriate: • *She drove to the airport instead* [not *in lieu*] of taking the train. *In lieu* (*of*) is chiefly used in formal contexts with reference to the replacement of one thing with another or others of equivalent value or importance: • *If they have to work on Christmas Day they should be given time off in lieu*. • *We are sending two bottles of dessert wine in lieu of the champagne you ordered*.

The word *lieu* may be pronounced [lew] or [loo].

in loco parentis The Latin phrase *in loco parentis* is used in formal contexts to mean 'acting for a parent; having the responsibilities of a parent': • *On a school trip, teachers act in loco parentis*. The phrase is pronounced [in lōkō părentis]. It is sometimes written or printed in italics.

innit This is a contraction of *isn't it*, usually employed as a tag question (*see* **questions**) at the end of a statement: • *This is a nice place, innit?* Originally used in working-class speech, *innit* was taken up by black British speakers in the early 1980s as an all-purpose question tag and imitated in turn by young white speakers: • *They're coming to the party, innit? Innit* is a strictly non-standard slang usage and should always be avoided in formal contexts.

innocuous The adjective *innocuous*, meaning 'harmless': • *a few innocuous remarks*, is sometimes misspelt. Note the -*nn*-, the single *c*, and the vowel sequence -*uou*-.

inoculate or **vaccinate**? The verbs *inoculate* and *vaccinate* are virtually synonymous in the sense of 'introduce a vaccine into the body of a person or animal to provide immunity': • *She has been inoculated* [or *vaccinated*] *against whooping cough*. *Inoculate* has a wider range of usage: it may refer to the introduction of a substance other than a vaccine, and is also used in figurative contexts in the sense of 'instil': • *He inoculated his students with egalitarian ideals*.

Note the spelling of *vaccinate*, particularly the *-cc-* and the single *n*.

inoculation This word is often misspelt, the most frequent error being the addition of an extra *n* as in *innocent*. Note the single *c* and the single *l*.

in order that and **in order to** The phrase *in order that* is followed by *may*, *might*, *shall*, or *should* rather than *can*, *could*, *will*, or *would*: * *He moved his suitcase in order that we might* [not *could*] *open the door.* * *She drove him to the station in order that he should* [not *would*] *not miss his train.* These restrictions do not apply to the simpler expression *so that* (*see* **so**), which is often preferable to *in order that* in such contexts.

If the subordinate clause has the same subject as the main clause, *in order that* may be replaced by *in order to* followed by an infinitive: * *He moved his suitcase in order to open the door.* The phrase *in order to* is best avoided where *to* would be adequate: * *He turned the key to* [not *in order to*] *open the door.*

input Many people object to the use of the noun *input* as a synonym for 'contribution': * *We hope to have some input from the teaching staff at tomorrow's meeting.* * *positive input* ('approval or encouragement') * *negative input* ('criticism'). As a noun, *input* may be used to denote the power, energy, data, etc. put into a system or machine, or the resources, labour, raw materials, etc. required for production.

The verb *input* refers to the process of entering data into a computer: * *Travel agents will be able to input data*
direct to a central computer.* In other contexts, use of the verb *input* is generally deprecated, other verbs being preferred: * *contribute* [not *input*] *ideas to a meeting* * *provide with* [not *input*] *equipment.*

inquiry *see* **enquiry** or **inquiry**?

inside of Many people dislike the prepositional phrase *inside of*, meaning 'within' or 'in less than', in which the word *of* is incorrect. The phrase should not be used in formal contexts: * *There was a cheque inside* [not *inside of*] *the envelope.* * *The job was completed inside* [not *inside of*] *two weeks.* The addition of this superfluous *of* to the preposition *inside* may be influenced by the phrase *on the inside*, which is followed by *of* when it is used prepositionally: * *a coupon on the inside of the wrapper.*

in so far as This expression may be written *in so far as* or *insofar as*, the latter being more frequent in American English: * *I'll help you in so far as it is appropriate. See also* **inasmuch as**.

in spite of *see* **despite** or **in spite of**?

install or **instal**? Both spellings of this word are correct, although the first is more frequently used: * *install a central-heating system.* If the spelling *instal* with a single *l* is chosen, then the *l* doubles before the suffixes beginning with a vowel: *installing*, *installed*, *installer*, *installation*.

In British English, *instalment* has a single *l*; in American English it usually has a double *l*.

instantly or **instantaneously**? The adverbs *instantly* and *instantaneously* are virtually interchangeable in the sense of 'immediately' or 'without delay': * *He replied instantly/instantaneously. Instantaneously* has the additional meaning of 'very quickly' or 'almost simultaneously': * *She was hit by the car and died instantaneously.*

instil This word, meaning 'introduce gradually', is often misspelt: it ends in a single *l* in British English. It is worth remembering that the *l* must be doubled before a suffix is added: *instilled. See also* **spelling**.

institute or **institution**? Both nouns are used to denote certain professional bodies and established organisations founded for research, study, charitable work, the promotion of a cause, etc.: * *the Institute of Materials* * *the British Standards Institution* * *the Royal National Institute for the Blind* * *the Royal National Lifeboat Institution.* The nouns also denote the buildings or premises used by these organisations. *Institution* has a range of additional meanings: 'the act of instituting': * *the institution of a new electoral system*; 'an established social custom or practice': * *the institution of marriage*; 'a school or hospital': * *an educational institution.*

The verb *institute* means 'establish', 'initiate', or 'install'.

instructional or **instructive**? *Instructional* is the rarer word and means 'providing instruction(s)'; *instructive* is used in the wider sense of 'informative; enlightening': * *an instructional leaflet* * *an instructive experience.* Both adjectives may sometimes be applied to the same noun: * *an instructional course* is intended to instruct and may succeed or fail in this objective; * *an*

instructive course succeeds in instructing, whether or not this was the intention.

insulate The verb *insulate* is followed by the preposition *from* or *against*: * *The cupboard next to the cooker is insulated from* [or *against*] *the heat of the oven.*

insults Note that the power of an insult depends largely upon the context in which it is uttered and the company to whom it is delivered. Many insults – for example ones that refer to a person's ethnic origins or sexual orientation – may be considered highly offensive when delivered by a person from a different background, but innocuous enough when exchanged between members of the same group; they may even be intended as an inclusive term of affection. Examples include such taboo slang terms as *bugger, nigger* (used by some black people among themselves), and *queer* (used by some gays among themselves).

insurance *see* **assurance** or **insurance**?

insure *see* **assure**, **ensure** or **insure**?

integral Some people object to the frequent use of the phrase *integral part*, in which the adjective *integral* is often superfluous: * *The study of local history is an integral part of the syllabus.* Most parts are *integral*, i.e. 'essential to the completeness of the whole', by definition. In many contexts the word *integral* would be better replaced by *essential, important*, etc.: * *Cash registers have become an integral part of even the most backward industries in these competitive days.* The usual pronunciation of *integral* is [*int*igräl], stressed on the first syllable; many users dislike the variant pronunciation [in*teg*răl], stressed on the second syllable.

integrate The verb *integrate* is widely used in the sense of 'make or become part of a social group': * *One of the aims of our organisation is to integrate ethnic minorities into the community.* * *Newcomers to the village often find it difficult to integrate.* In other contexts *integrate* is often better replaced by *mix, amalgamate, join, combine,* etc.: * *a new television programme that combines* [not *integrates*] *learning with entertainment.*

Note the spelling of *integrate*, which does not begin with the prefix *inter-*.

intense or **intensive**? *Intense* means 'extreme' or 'very strong'; *intensive* means 'concentrated' or 'thorough': * *intense pain* * *intense heat* * *intensive training* * *an intensive search.* The two adjectives are not interchangeable, although both may be applied to the same noun: * *intense/intensive study.* Both adjectives have additional senses: *intense* describes a person who has very strong and deep feelings; *intensive* has specialised meanings in grammar and agriculture and is used in such compounds as *intensive care* and *labour-intensive.*

inter *see* **interment** or **internment**?

inter- or **intra-**? The prefix *inter-* means 'between' or 'reciprocally'; *intra-* means 'within': * *intercontinental* * *interdependent* * *intravenous* * *intramural.* The two prefixes should not be confused: *international* means 'of two or more nations'; *intranational* means 'within one nation'.

The prefix *intra-* is most frequently

found in medical contexts: * *intracranial* * *intramuscular* * *intrauterine.*

intercede This verb, meaning 'mediate', is sometimes misspelt: note the *-cede* ending, as in *concede, precede,* etc. (unlike *proceed, succeed,* etc.).

interface In science, computing, etc., the noun *interface* denotes a surface forming a common boundary or a point of communication. Many people dislike its extended use as a synonym for 'interaction', 'liaison', 'link', '(point of) contact', etc.: * *the interface between professionals and lay people in the caring professions* * *the interface of history and literature* * *at the interface between design and technology.* The verb *interface* is also best restricted to technical contexts: * *The office microcomputers will interface with the main computer.*

interfere The verb *interfere* is followed by the preposition *with* in the sense of 'meddle': * *Don't interfere with my papers.* It is followed by the preposition *in* in the sense of 'intrude': * *The police are reluctant to interfere in a domestic dispute.*

interjections *see* **exclamations**.

interment or **internment**? *Interment* means 'burial'; *internment* means 'imprisonment': * *the interment of the corpse* * *the internment of the terrorists.* The two words should not be confused.

The noun *interment* and the verb *inter* (from which it is derived) are formal words that refer to the depositing of a dead body in the earth or in a tomb. The noun *internment* is derived from the verb *intern*, which refers to the confinement of enemy aliens, prisoners of war, etc. In both nouns and both verbs the stress falls on the second syllable.

The noun *intern*, stressed on the first syllable, is an American name for someone in the final stages of professional training, especially in medicine.

Internet The *Internet*, also written as *internet* and commonly abbreviated to the *net*, is a worldwide network of computer networks which, with its vast amount of information, as well as innumerable forums for discussion and entertainment sites, has been responsible for a communications revolution.

It is significant that the Internet was not set up as a commercial venture and has no central governing authority. This lack of central administration means that users of the new medium have felt free to develop their own styles of communication, unfettered by the rules of conventional grammar and spelling, etc., and making extensive use of shorthand versions of words, symbols, and slang. With time, however, the Internet has adopted its own conventions and etiquette (or *netiquette*) and numerous manuals on using it recommend correct spelling and grammar. *See also* **chat; dot.com; email; netspeak; smiley; Web.**

internment *see* **interment** or **internment?**

interpersonal The adjective *interpersonal*, meaning 'between people', is disliked by some people as a vogue term and can often be replaced by a synonym, such as *social*, or by a simple paraphrase: * *interpersonal skills*

are social skills * *in an interpersonal situation* means 'with people'.

interpretive or **interpretative?** Either adjective may be used, but *interpretative* is the more frequent: * *The appendix contains interpretative/ interpretive notes on the text.*

in that The phrase *in that* means 'because' or 'to the extent that': * *He is unsuitable for the job in that he has no relevant experience.* * *The two machines are different in that one is fully automatic and the other is manually controlled.* In some contexts, however, *in that* may be better replaced by *because* or one of its synonyms: * *We are in financial difficulties because* [not *in that*] *my wife has recently been made redundant.*

in the near future The phrase *in the near future* is disliked by some users as an unnecessarily wordy substitute for *soon*: * *The electronics company is considering relocating to Swindon in the near future.*

in this day and age The cliché *in this day and age* is best avoided where *nowadays, today, now,* etc. would be adequate or more appropriate: * *In this day and age a good education is not a passport to a successful career.*

into or **in to?** *Into* is a preposition with a variety of meanings; *in to* is a combination of the adverb *in* and the preposition or infinitive marker *to*: * *I went into the house.* * *I went in to fetch a book.* * *I went in to tea.* It is important to recognise and maintain the distinction between these uses.

As prepositions, *into* and *in* are occasionally interchangeable: * *He* *put the letter into/in his pocket. Into* usually suggests movement from the outside to the inside, whereas *in* suggests being or remaining inside. In many contexts the two prepositions are not interchangeable: * *They sailed into the harbour at four o'clock.* * *They sailed in the harbour all afternoon.*

intonation *Intonation* is a change in pitch that adds to the meaning of a spoken word, phrase, or sentence. It should not be confused with **stress**, which relates to loudness or emphasis, although the two are often used in combination. In English, *intonation* is most noticeable in questions, where the pitch of the voice tends to rise towards the end: * *When did she arrive?* * *Saturday*? The sentence * *Jane doesn't want a cat,* spoken with rising intonation, means 'Does Jane want a cat?' or 'Is it true that Jane wants a cat?': with falling intonation it is a neutral statement of fact. Other variations in the intonation of the sentence and the stress on individual words may produce a number of alternative interpretations, such as 'I don't believe that Jane wants a cat', 'Jane would like a pet of some sort, but not a cat', and 'Other people want a cat, but not Jane'.

Rising intonation is also heard in lists; falling intonation indicates the end of the list: * *You can have carrots, peas, cabbage, or cauliflower.*

intra- *see* **inter-** or **intra-**?

intransitive *see* **verbs**.

intrinsic or **extrinsic**? The adjective *intrinsic* means 'inherent', 'essential', or 'originating from within': * *The discovery is of great intrinsic interest.*

Extrinsic, the opposite of *intrinsic,* is less frequent in general usage: * *The document is of extrinsic interest only.* The *intrinsic* value of a pound coin, for example, is the value of the metal from which it is made; its **extrinsic** value is one pound.

introvert *see* **extrovert** or **introvert**?

Inuit The term *Inuit* refers to the people of North America and Greenland traditionally known as Eskimos. The term *Inuit* (meaning 'people') is preferred to *Eskimo* (meaning 'eater of raw flesh'), by the Inuit themselves. It may also be used to distinguish this people from the Eskimos of the Aleutian Islands and Siberia. *Inuit,* sometimes spelt *Innuit,* is pronounced [*in*yooit]. The plural is *In(n)uit* or *In(n)uits*.

invalid The adjectival sense of 'not valid' is pronounced with the stress on the second syllable [in*val*id]. The noun sense of 'someone who is ill' is pronounced with the stress on the first syllable, either as [*in*valid] or [*in*valeed]. The verb sense, 'disable' or (usually followed by *out*) 'remove from active service because of illness or injury', may be pronounced [*in*valid], [*in*valeed], or [inva*leed*].

inveigh or **inveigle**? To *inveigh* is to protest strongly; to *inveigle* is to persuade cleverly: * *She inveighed against the inequity of the law.* * *He inveigled us into signing the form. Inveigh,* an intransitive verb, is followed by *against,* whereas *inveigle* is transitive and often used with *into*. The two verbs are both formal and are sometimes confused. Note the *-ei-* spelling of both.

Inveigh is always pronounced [in*vay*]; *inveigle* may be pronounced [in*vay*gl] or [in*vee*gl].

invent, **design** or **discover**? *Invent* and *design* refer to the creation of something new; *discover* refers to the finding of something that is already in existence: * *to invent a machine* * *to design a new computer* * *to discover a cure for cancer.* The three words sometimes overlap in usage. A scientific *discovery* may lead to an *invention*, and *inventions* have to be *designed*. Some people dislike the use of *invent* in place of *design*: a new type of car, for example, that is modelled on existing styles and uses a traditional method of propulsion, is *designed*, not *invented*.

inverse *see* **converse, inverse, obverse** or **reverse**?

inversion *Inversion* is a reversal of the normal order of the elements of a sentence or clause, so that the subject follows the verb: * *There goes the bus.* * *In came Michael.* * *At the bottom of the heap was the missing book.* Inversion is most frequently used in questions: * *Am I late?* It is also used after *so, neither*, and *nor*: * *So are they.* * *Neither do we*, and after some negative words and phrases: * *Never have I heard such nonsense!* * *On no account should he go.* The use of inversion in conditional clauses: * *Had she known about his past, she would not have married him.* * *There's a fire extinguisher here, should you need it*, is rather more formal than the use of an *if* clause: * *If she had known...* * *...if you should need it.*

Inversion is optional after direct speech, but is best avoided if the subject is a pronoun: * *'Go away!' cried the boy.* * *'Go away!' he cried.* In poems

and stories inversion is sometimes used for effect or variety: * *In a hole in the tree lived a wise old owl.* * *Stands the Church clock at ten to three?* (Rupert Brooke).

inverted commas *see* **quotation marks.**

invite Many people dislike the use of the word *invite* as a noun in place of *invitation* – even in informal contexts: * *Have you had an invite to their party?* Note that the stress pattern of the noun *invite* is different from that of the verb: the noun is stressed on the first syllable; the verb is stressed on the second syllable. *See also* **stress.**

in vitro The Latin phrase *in vitro* is used to refer to a method of fertilising a woman's egg by artificial means, outside the woman's body. The literal meaning of *in vitro* is 'in glass'; it is sometimes written or printed in italics, and is pronounced [in *veet*rō]. The abbreviation *IVF* stands for *in vitro fertilisation*.

involve Some people object to the frequent use of the verb *involve* and its derivatives in place of more specific or more appropriate synonyms: * *This proposal will entail* [not *involve*] *further cuts in expenditure.* * *Some changes may be necessary* [not *involved*]. * *I have a number of questions concerning* [not *involving*] *teaching methods and discipline.* * *These fingerprints are evidence of his participation* [not *involvement*] *in the robbery.* Many authorities recommend the restriction of *involve* and its derivatives to the senses of 'entanglement' and 'complication': * *the chairman's involvement in the scandal* * *a long-winded and involved account of the incident.*

inward or **inwards?** In British English, *inward* is principally used as an adjective – *inwards* being the usual form of the adverb meaning 'towards the inside': ⁕ *inward feelings* ⁕ *to push inwards*. The adverb *inward* is more frequently used in American English. *See also* **-ward** or **-wards?**

irascible The formal word *irascible*, meaning 'easily angered', is sometimes misspelt. *Irascible* has a single *r* and ends in *-ible*, unlike its synonym *irritable*. Note also the *-sc-*.

ironic, ironical, ironically *see* **irony**.

iron out The phrasal verb *iron out* is widely used in the metaphorical sense of 'settle', 'resolve', 'solve', or 'remove': ⁕ *We have a few more problems to iron out before work can begin.* It is best avoided, however, in contexts that may be associated with its literal meaning of 'smooth with an iron': ⁕ *The laundry workers have ironed out their difficulties.* ⁕ *The last stumbling block was ironed out at yesterday's meeting.*

irony *Irony* is the use of words to express the opposite of their accepted meaning, often for satirical or humorous effect. Words such as *precious* and *fine* are often used ironically, as in *'This is a fine time to tell me you've no keys!'* Some people object to the frequent use of the noun *irony* and its derivatives to refer to something paradoxical, incongruous, or odd: ⁕ *She resigned when they rejected her proposals; the irony of the situation is that they have now adopted the system she proposed.* ⁕ *It's ironic that he should win a skiing holiday just after breaking his leg.* ⁕ *Ironically, it was the police inspector's car that was stolen.*

The adjectives *ironic* and *ironical* are both in use, *ironic* being the more frequent.

Irony may be used as a form of *sarcasm*, but the two words should not be confused: an *ironic* remark is more witty and less cruel than a *sarcastic* remark.

irrefutable This word, meaning 'impossible to be disproved': ⁕ *irrefutable evidence,* may be stressed on the second or on the third syllable: [irefyootăbl] or [irifyootăbl]. The second pronunciation is becoming more common.

irregardless The word *irregardless* is a non-standard blend of *irrespective* and *regardless*. Most dictionaries do not acknowledge its existence, but it is frequently heard in colloquial usage: ⁕ *'Irregardless of what we say about Robbo, he done a good job,' was a near-miss by Elton Welsby for ITV in Bologna (The Guardian).* The word should be avoided in all contexts; either *irrespective* or *regardless* may be used in its place (*see* **irrespective**).

irregular verbs For irregular parts of verbs, *see* table at **verbs**.

irrelevant This word is frequently misspelt. Note the *-rr-* and the vowels *i-e-e-a*.

irreparable This word, meaning 'unable to be repaired', is often mispronounced. The stress should fall on the second syllable and not the third [irepărăbl]. *See also* **repairable** or **reparable?**

irresistible Note the spelling of this adjective, particularly the *-rr-* and the *-ible* (not *-able*) ending.

irrespective The word *irrespective* is most frequently used in the prepositional phrase *irrespective of*, meaning 'regardless of': * *Applications are invited from all suitably qualified candidates, irrespective of age, sexual orientation, nationality, disability or religion.* The expression *irrespectively of* is generally considered to be unidiomatic.

Unlike *regardless*, *irrespective* should not be used adverbially in other contexts: * *It soon began to rain but they carried on with their game regardless* [not *irrespective*]. See also **irregardless**.

irrevocable In its general sense of 'not able to be changed': * *an irrevocable decision*, the word *irrevocable* is stressed on the second syllable [irĕvŏkăbl]. The pronunciation [irivōkăbl], stressed on the third syllable, is restricted to a few legal or financial contexts, where the sense is literally 'not able to be revoked': * *irrevocable letters of credit*.

is Many people dislike the repetition of *is* in such constructions as *the question is, is there any future in this?* and *the problem is, is it going to work?* Careful speakers and writers use *is* once only, by rewording either part, or avoid such constructions altogether: * *The question is whether or not there is any future in this.* * *We must ask ourselves, is there any future in this?*

-ise *see* **-ize** or **-ise**?

-ism Some people object to the increasing use of the suffix *-ism*, in the sense of 'discrimination', to coin new words modelled on the nouns *racism* and *sexism*: * *legislation against ageism* * *the controversial issue of heterosexism* *

ableism * *heightism*. The use of the suffix to form new nouns in the conventional sense of 'doctrine' or 'system' is acceptable in moderation: * *The 'Third Way' was one of the key ideas of Blairism.*

issue Overuse of *issue* as a euphemistic substitute for words such as *problem* or *difficulty* should be avoided: * *They have relationship issues.* * *He has issues around his appearance.*

-ist or **-ite**? Both these suffixes may be used to denote an adherent, follower, advocate, or supporter of a particular doctrine: * *Stalinist* * *Luddite* * *communist* * *Blairite*. The suffix *-ite* is sometimes used in a derogatory manner: people who call themselves *Trotskyists*, for example, may be described by opponents of Trotskyism as *Trotskyites*. The suffix *-ist*, which is also used to form adjectives, may face the same objection as *-ism*: * *ageist principles* * *heterosexist attitudes* * *classist* * *genderist*.

isthmus The noun *isthmus*, meaning 'narrow strip of land', causes problems of spelling and pronunciation. Note the four adjacent consonants, *-sthm-*. The [th] sound is not heard in the usual pronunciation [ismŭs]; the full pronunciation [isthmŭs] is no more or less correct.

it The pronoun *it* has a wide range of uses: to replace an abstract noun or the name of an inanimate object; as the subject of an impersonal verb, etc.: * *He washed the towel and hung it out to dry.* * *It hasn't rained for a week.* * *I find it difficult to make new friends.* * *It's obvious that she doesn't like him.* For this reason, the use of *it* may sometimes cause ambiguity or confusion: • *She took her purse out of her handbag and put it on the table* [the purse or the handbag?]. • *You can open the window if it gets too hot* [the window or the weather?]. The constructions *it is/was... who* and *it is/was... that* should be used only for emphasis: • *It was she who broke the window, so I don't see why you should pay for the repair.* • *It's the weather that's making me feel tired – I'm not ill.*

In such constructions, the verb agrees with the pronoun or noun that follows *is* or *was*, not with the word *it*: • *It's I who wish* [not *wishes*] *to complain.* • *It was they who were* [not *was*] *at fault.* • *It is the books that make* [not *makes*] *the trunk so heavy.* (Note the use of *I* and *they*, rather than *me* and *them*; see also **I** or **me**?; **pronouns**.)

The construction is not used with *where* or *when*: • *It is in France that the best cheeses are to be found* [not *It is France where...*]. • *It was in 2001 that he won the championship* [not *It was 2001 when...*].

However, the construction should not be confused with such statements as *It was dark when we arrived* and *It's snowing where my parents live* or such expressions as *it is believed that...* and *it is possible that....* See also **its** or **it's**?; **that** or **which**?

italics The word *italic* denotes a sloping typeface that is used for a variety of purposes in English. In handwritten or typewritten texts, underlining is generally used to indicate italics. The principal uses of italics are:

1 For the titles of books, newspapers, magazines, plays, films, works of art, musical works, etc.: • *The Economist*

• *An Ideal Husband,* by Oscar Wilde • Elgar's *Enigma Variations.*

2 For the names of ships, boats, trains, aircraft, etc.: • Sir Francis Chichester sailed around the world in *Gipsy Moth IV.*

3 For the Latin names of plants, animals, etc.: • The tiger, *Panthera tigris,* is found in Asia.

4 For foreign words and phrases that are not fully integrated into the English language: • This was his *pièce de résistance.* • The teacher is *in loco parentis.* It is sometimes difficult to judge whether a foreign word or phrase should be italicised or not. Some dictionaries offer guidance on this matter.

5 To indicate stress or emphasis: • Is it *still* raining? • I don't *like* spiders, but I'm not afraid of them. Careful users avoid excessive italicisation for the purpose of stress or emphasis.

6 To draw attention to a particular word, phrase, or letter: • How do you pronounce *controversy*? • Her surname is spelt with a double *s.*

-ite see **-ist** or **-ite**?

itinerary This word, meaning 'planned route of a journey', is sometimes misspelt. The careful pronunciation [ītinĕrări] should ensure its correct spelling.

its or **it's**? *It's,* a contraction of *it is* or *it has,* should not be confused with *its,* the possessive form of *it*: • *It's easy to tell the difference.* • *It's been raining for several hours.* • *The lion has escaped from its cage.* The insertion of an apostrophe in the possessive form *its* is wrong in all contexts, although it occasionally finds its way into print: • *It's aim is to encourage new ideas and* *developments in the field of learning and teaching English* (advertisement for The English-Speaking Union, *The Guardian*). The omission of the apostrophe in the contraction *it's* is less frequent, but equally unacceptable. *See also* **apostrophe**; **contractions**; **'s or s'**?

IVF *see* **in vitro**.

-ize or **-ise**? In British English, the sound [-īz] at the end of many verbs may be spelt *-ize* or *-ise*: ● *baptize/baptise* ● *realize/realise* ● *recognize/recognise* ● *organize/organise*, etc. Most modern dictionaries, partly because of the American international influence, list *-ize* as the preferred spelling, giving *-ise* as an accepted variant; otherwise, *-ise* is generally as common as *-ize* in British English. There is etymological justification for both spellings, the suffix being derived via French *-iser* from Latin *-izare* and Greek *-izein*.

Whichever spelling is preferred, it is important to be consistent within a single piece of writing, both in the choice of other *-ize/-ise* words and in the spelling of any derivatives ending in *-ization/-isation*, *-izer/-iser*, *-izable/-isable*, etc.

Capsize is the only *-ize* verb of more than one syllable that is never spelt *-ise*.

However, there are a number of *-ise* verbs that cannot be spelt *-ize*; the most common of these are *advertise, advise, chastise, circumcise, comprise, compromise, despise, devise, enfranchise, excise, exercise, franchise, improvise, merchandise, revise, supervise, surmise, surprise,* and *televise. See also* **exercise or exorcise**?

Verbs ending in *-yse*, such as *analyse* and *paralyse*, are never spelt *-yze* in British English.

In American English, *-ize* is always used for verbs that can have either ending in British English, but *-ise* is usually retained for verbs of the *advertise... televise* group. *Analyse, paralyse*, etc. are spelt with a *z* in American English.

Some people object to the modern tendency to create new verbs by the addition of *-ize* or *-ise* to a noun or adjective: ● *pedestrianise* ● *hospitalise* ● *prioritise* ● *finalise* ● *weaponise*. Such verbs are best avoided where a simpler form or synonym exists: *to martyrise* may be replaced with *to martyr*; *to finalise* can often be replaced with *to finish*. However, *-ize/-ise* verbs (and their derivatives) that have neither a one-word equivalent nor a simple paraphrase often serve a useful purpose: ● *to computerise the stock-control system* ● *the decimalisation of British currency*.

J

jail or **gaol**? In British English these two spellings are both acceptable, although many people prefer *jail* – which in American English is the only accepted spelling.

jargon *Jargon* is the technical language used within a particular subject or profession, such as science, computing, medicine, law, accountancy, etc.: * *CVA or cerebral vascular accident is medical jargon for a stroke.* The term is also used to denote the complex, obscure, pretentious or euphemistic language used by estate agents, journalists, sociologists, advertisers, bureaucrats, politicians, etc.: * *In sociological jargon the class system has been replaced with a series of socio-economic groups.*

Jargon of both types is acceptable, and often indispensable, in professional journals and in written or spoken communications between members of the same group. It should be avoided, however, in articles, brochures, insurance policies, etc. that are to be read and understood by lay people, and in conversations with members of the general public. Jargon should not be used to impress, intimidate, confuse, or mislead the outsider.

Jargon sometimes finds its way into everyday language in the form of clichés or vogue words, e.g. *interface*, *traumatic*, *user-friendly*. Many users dislike and avoid such words and expressions.

Jargon should not be confused with **dialect** or **slang**. *See also* **commercialese; journalese; management-speak; officialese**.

jealous The adjective **jealous** is followed by the preposition *of*: * *He was jealous of her success.*

jealousy *see* **envy** or **jealousy**?

jeopardise This word, meaning 'expose to danger', is often misspelt – the most frequent error being the omission of the letter *o*. Note that the vowel pattern is the same as in *leopard*.

jewellery or **jewelry**? This word has two spellings in British English. Both are acceptable although *jewelry*, standard in American English, is less common in British English. The preferred pronunciation is [*jooĕlri*], rather than the dialectal or non-standard [*joolĕri*].

The spelling *jeweller* is more common in British English; *jeweler*, in American English.

jibe *see* **gibe, jibe** or **gybe**?

join or **joint**? The nouns *join* and *joint* are synonymous (but not interchangeable) in the sense of 'place where two parts are joined'. *Join* most frequently refers to the visual effect of the act of joining; the line or seam between two flat or flexible parts (such as paper, fabric, carpet, string, etc.): • *You can hardly see the join.* A *joint* is more practical or functional, joining two rigid three-dimensional parts: • *The pipe was leaking at one of the joints.* • *the joint between the shaft and the head.*

joined-up *Joined-up* is used in expressions such as *joined-up thinking* and *joined-up policy* to describe a logical, coordinated approach to an issue: • *What we need here is some joined-up thinking.* It is presumably derived from *joined-up writing*, regarded as more sophisticated than the individual handwritten lettering of young children. Many people consider it a jargonistic (*see* **jargon**) term that is best restricted to informal contexts.

journalese *Journalese* is a derogatory name for the style of writing or language that is considered to be typical of newspapers. It is characterised by the use of clichés and short sensational synonyms – e.g. *axe, bid, probe* – which occur especially in headlines. The telegraphic style of newspaper headlines sometimes gives rise to ambiguity or confusion: • *Merseyside pioneers abuse teaching pack for schools* (*The Guardian*). (This headline was intended to mean 'A teaching pack about child abuse has been launched on Merseyside', but could be interpreted as 'Pioneers on Merseyside are misusing a teaching pack'.) Careful users avoid such techniques and devices in formal writing. *See also* **jargon**.

judgment or **judgement**? Either spelling of this word is acceptable, although *judgement* was formerly more common in British English and *judgment* in American English. Whichever is adopted, it is advisable to be consistent in the spelling of this word and words such as *abridg(e)ment* and *acknowledg(e)ment*.

judicial or **judicious**? *Judicial* means 'of judgement in a court of law' or 'of the administration of justice'; *judicious* means 'having or showing good judgement' or 'prudent': • *judicial proceedings* • *a judicious choice*. The two adjectives are not interchangeable, although both may be applied to the same noun: • *a judicial decision* is the decision of a court of law; • *a judicious decision* is a wise decision.

Judicial may also mean 'of a judge; impartial; fair'; it is in this sense that it is most likely to be confused with *judicious*.

juncture The phrase *at this juncture* refers to a critical point in time; many people object to its frequent use in place of *now*: • *The leader's resignation at this juncture would have a disastrous effect on the members' morale.* • *I suggest that we take a short break for refreshments now* [not *at this juncture*]. This use of *juncture* has developed from its meaning of 'concurrence or conjunction of events or circumstances'. The noun is rarely used in its original sense, as a synonym of 'junction' or 'joint'.

junta This word refers to a controlling political council and has various pronunciations. The preferred pronunciation is [*juntă*]. Other alternatives such as [*huuntă*] and [*juuntă*] have arisen in imitation of the Spanish pronunciation.

just *Just* has a variety of adverbial senses:

'at this moment', 'exactly', 'only', etc. For this reason it must be carefully positioned in a sentence in order to convey the intended meaning: * *Your son has just eaten two cakes* [i.e. a short time ago]. * *Your son has eaten just two cakes* [i.e. not one or three, etc.]. * *Just your son has eaten two cakes* [i.e. only your son; no one else]. Transposing *just* and *not* may also change the meaning of a sentence: * *I'm just not tired.* * *I'm not just tired; I'm hungry too.* In the sense of 'in the very recent past', *just* should be used with the perfect tense in formal contexts: * *They have just arrived at the station.* Its use with the past tense in this sense (*They just arrived...*) is regarded as an Americanism and is avoided by many careful users, even in informal contexts.

Just may be used in place of, but not in addition to, *exactly*: * *That's just* [not *just exactly*] *what I need.*

K

K The letter *K*, short for *kilo-*, is increasingly used to represent 1000, especially in sums of money: * *a salary of £50K plus company car* * *houses priced from £250K upwards.* The abbreviation is also used in spoken language: * *She was earning a hundred K in the City.* This usage was adopted from the jargon of computing, where *K* may represent 1000 or 1024.

kaleidoscope This word is sometimes misspelt. Note particularly the *-ei* and the first *o* from the Greek *eidos*, meaning 'form'. The correct pronunciation is [kălīdŏskōp].

kerb *see* **curb** or **kerb?**

key Some people object to the increasingly frequent use of the word *key* as an adjective, in the sense of 'fundamental', 'essential', 'crucial', 'most important', 'indispensable', etc.: * *a number of key individuals to manage their top UK stores* * *setting up a policy committee that will take key decisions* (*Sunday Times*). In many contexts it is better replaced by one of its synonyms.

kibbutzim *Kibbutzim* is the plural form of the noun *kibbutz*, denoting a collective community in Israel. *Kibbutz* is pronounced [ki*buuts*], rhyming with *puts*; *kibbutzim* is stressed on the final syllable [kibuut*seem*].

kick-start The figurative use of the verb *kick-start* in the sense of 'take action to get in motion (again)' is becoming rather hackneyed, especially in the phrase *kick-start the economy*: * *Plans to balance income tax cuts with measures to boost business and kickstart the economy will form a key element in the chancellor's strategy* (*Sunday Times*). * *to kick-start the housing market.* The metaphor is derived from the world of motorcycling, where the verb refers to the act of starting an engine by kicking or pressing a pedal.

kid The use of the noun *kid* as a synonym for 'child' or 'young person' is best restricted to informal contexts: * *Things were very different when I was a kid.* * *One of the local kids broke the window.* * *Have you got any kids?*

kidnap The final *p* of the word *kidnap* is doubled before a suffix beginning with a vowel: * *kidnapped* * *kidnapper. See also* **spelling**.

kilo The word *kilo*, pronounced [*kee*lŏ], is most frequently used as an abbreviation for *kilogram*: * *a kilo of sugar* * *50 kilos of coal.* Some dictionaries also list *kilo* as an abbreviation for *kilometre*, but this usage is very rare.

Note that the first syllable of the prefix *kilo-*, in such words as *kilo-*

metre, kilogram, etc., is pronounced like the word *kill*, not *keel*.

kilometre This word may be stressed on the first syllable [*kil*ŏmeetĕ] or on the second syllable [ki*lom*itĕ]. The first of these pronunciations is the more widely accepted in British English. The second, regarded by some as an Americanism, is probably becoming more current in British English. *See also* **meter** or **metre**?; **stress**.

kindly The word *kindly* may be used as an adjective, meaning 'kind' or 'sympathetic', or as an adverb, meaning 'in a kind way': * *a kindly policeman* * *kindly smile* * *They treated us kindly*. The adjective *kindly* has no one-word adverbial form: * *He smiled in a kindly manner*.

The adverb *kindly* is also used in polite or angry requests or commands: * *Patrons are kindly requested to refrain from smoking*. * *Kindly allow me to tell you what happened*. * *Would you kindly take your hand off my knee!* In such contexts it is often better replaced by *please*.

kind of In formal contexts the phrases *kind of*, *sort of*, and *type of* – in which *kind*, *sort*, and *type* are in the singular – should be preceded by *this* or *that* (rather than *these* or *those*) and followed by a singular noun: * *this kind of story* * *that sort of biscuit*. Such expressions as *these kind of stories*, *those sort of biscuits*, etc., are sometimes heard in informal contexts but are disliked and avoided by careful users.

A plural noun may be used if the expression is rephrased: * *Stories of this kind are very popular*. Note that

the verb agrees with *stories*, not *kind*.

Where more than one kind, sort, or type is concerned, the whole expression may be put into the plural: * *She specialises in detective and horror stories: these kinds of stories are very popular*. In such cases, the noun that follows *kinds/sorts/types of* may remain in the singular: *...these kinds of story are very popular*. (Note that the verb here agrees with *kinds*, not story.)

The same principles apply to *kind of*, *sort of*, and *type of* in other contexts: * *a different type of vegetable* * *many different types of vegetable/vegetables*.

The use of *kind of* or *sort of* in place of *rather* or *somewhat* is best restricted to informal contexts: * *I sort of like him.* * *It's kind of warm in here.* The spelling *kinda* is sometimes used in writing to denote 'kind of' in casual speech. *See also* **singular** or **plural**?

kinsman or **kinswoman**? *see* **non-sexist terms**.

knee-jerk In figurative contexts, the term *knee-jerk* is applied to an automatic, predictable, and/or unthinking reaction, as opposed to a more considered response: * *A knee-jerk reaction to the problem could make matters worse.* * *Industrial action is the knee-jerk response of many union leaders.* The term should be confined to informal usage and not be overused. A knee-jerk reaction or response is the metaphorical equivalent of the physical reflex action that results from a light blow just below the kneecap.

kneeled or **knelt**? Either word may be used as the past tense and past participle of the verb *kneel*. *Knelt* is more frequent in British English: *

He knelt on the grass; kneeled is more common in American English. *See also* **-ed** or **t**?

knight or **night**? The word *knight* variously describes an armoured medieval warrior or a romantic hero. It should not be confused with *night*, as in *day and night*, although both words are pronounced the same [nīt].

knit or **knitted**? *Knitted* is the more frequent form of the past tense and past participle of the verb *knit*, especially in the literal sense: ◦ *I (have) knitted a cardigan for the baby.* ◦ *She was wearing a knitted jacket. Knit*, an alternative form of the past tense and past participle, is largely restricted to figurative contexts, especially in combination with an adverb before a noun: ◦ *a closely knit family.*

knot or **not**? *Knot* means 'fastening' or 'tangled mass of hair or thread, etc.': ◦ *She tied a knot in the cord.* It should not be confused with *not*, both words being pronounced [not].

know *see* **you know**.

knowledgeable This word, meaning 'having clear knowledge or understanding', is sometimes misspelt. Note that the final *e* of *knowledge* is retained before the suffix *-able*.

kudos *Kudos*, from Greek, is approximately equivalent to 'prestige' or 'status'. Some people avoid using it on the grounds that it sounds pretentious, although this reservation has become less pronounced over the years as the word has gradually become more widely familiar.

L

laboratory The usual pronunciation of this word in British English is [lǎborrǎtŏri], with the stress on the second syllable; the second *o* is sometimes not sounded. In American English the stress falls on the first and fourth syllables, [lǎbŏrǎtori]; the first *o* is sometimes not sounded.

laborious The word *laborious* is sometimes misspelt, the most frequent error being the insertion of a *u* after the first *o*, as in *labour*.

lack Many people find the use of *lack for* in place of *lack* unacceptable, and the superfluous *for* is best omitted: • *She did not lack* [not *lack for*] *friends*. The use of *lack for* may be influenced by the synonymous phrase *want for*, in which the optional preposition *for* serves the purpose of avoiding ambiguity or confusion with *want* in the sense of 'desire': • *She did not want for friends*.

lacquer This word is sometimes misspelt. Note that it has only one *u*: the word ends in *-er*, and not *-eur* as in *liqueur*.

laden or **loaded**? *Laden*, a past participle of the verb *lade*, is principally used as an adjective, meaning 'weighed down' or 'burdened'; *loaded* is the past tense and past participle of the verb *load*: • *The tree was laden with apples*. • *We overtook a heavily laden lorry*. • *He (has) loaded the car.*

The verb *lade*, meaning 'load with cargo', is rarely used in modern times in any other form, except in the term *bill of lading*. *Loaded* is also used as an adjective in literal and figurative senses: • *a loaded gun* • *a loaded question* ('one that contains hidden implications or is misleading').

The two adjectives should not be confused: • *The van is laden with furniture* implies that the van is weighed down or full to overflowing with furniture; • *The van is loaded with furniture* simply means that the van contains furniture.

lady *see* **woman**.

laid, lain *see* **lay** or **lie**?

laissez-faire The French expression *laissez-faire* is used to refer to the policy of allowing businesses to operate freely without government interference or control. The phrase can also be extended to refer to non-interference with people's freedom of choice: • *parents with a laissez-faire attitude to the bringing up of their children*.

The literal meaning of the expression is 'let people do (as they choose)'. The phrase has the less common variant spelling of *laisser-faire*. Both variants are pronounced [lesay *fair*].

lama or **llama**? The spelling of these words is sometimes confused. A *lama* is a Lamaist monk, the order of Lamaism being a form of Buddhism

239

of Tibet and Mongolia. A *llama* is a South American mammal related to the camel: note the *ll-* at the beginning of this word.

lamentable This word has two pronunciations. The traditional British English pronunciation is [*lam*ĕn*t*ăbl]. The stress may also fall on the second syllable [lă*men*tăbl], although this is disliked and avoided by some users.

languor Note the spelling of this word, particularly the unusual *-uor* ending. *Languor* is a formal word that means 'laziness; weariness'; the derived adjective is spelt *languorous*.

LARGE NUMBERS Confusion sometimes arises over the names and magnitudes of large numbers, which can be significant when discussing economic, financial, scientific matters etc. (*see* following panel on page 241). *See also* **numbers**.

larva or **lava**? These two words are occasionally confused. A *larva* is an insect in its first stage after coming out of the egg. *Lava* is the flowing or hardened molten rock from a volcano. The plural of *larva* is *larvae*, with the second syllable rhyming with *me*.

lasso A *lasso* is a rope with a noose, used for catching horses or cattle. There are two acceptable pronunciations, although [la*soo*] is the more frequent in contemporary British usage. The second pronunciation [la*sō*] was once standard but is now less common.

last To avoid ambiguity, the adjective *last* should be replaced, where necessary, with an appropriate synonym such as *latest*, *final*, or *preceding*: * *His latest*

[not *last*] *novel was published in June.* * *His final* [not *last*] *novel was published in June.* * *The final* [not *last*] *chapter contains a list of useful addresses.* * *The preceding* [not *last*] *chapter contains a list of useful addresses.* The use of *last* may also cause confusion in such phrases as *last Wednesday*, used on a Friday, which may mean 'two days ago' or 'nine days ago'. If the context is clearly in the past, *last* may be replaced by *on* before days of the current week: * *I posted it on* [not *last*] *Wednesday.*

Last may be retained where the context makes its meaning clear: * *His last novel was published posthumously.* * *The identity of the narrator is not revealed until the last chapter. See also* **next** or **this**?

late Used directly before a noun denoting a person, the adjective *late* may mean 'dead' or 'former': * *The widow gave her late husband's clothes to charity.* * *The late president has written his memoirs.* To avoid confusion, *late* (in the sense of 'former') is often better replaced by *ex-* or *former*: * *the ex-chairman* * *my former flatmate*. It is generally unnecessary to add *late* to a person's name in obituaries, death announcements, or in historical contexts.

lath or **lathe**? These two nouns should not be confused. A *lath* is a thin strip of wood; a *lathe* is a machine for shaping wood, metal, etc. Note that it is the noun *lath*, not *lathe*, which is used in the simile *as thin as a lath*. *Lath* is pronounced [lahth]; *lathe* is pronounced [laydh].

lather This word has various pronunciations. The traditional pronunciation rhymes with *gather*, but the

LARGE NUMBERS

The UK and much of the rest of Europe have their own traditional definitions of large numbers, which vary from those accepted in the US and France. Note that the US definitions have largely replaced the traditional definitions in the UK and elsewhere in recent years.

Number	Numerical value (US)	(Europe/traditional)
million (m)	10^6 (1,000,000)	10^6 (1,000,000)
billion (bn)	10^9 (1,000,000,000)	10^{12} (1,000,000,000,000)
trillion (tn/trn)	10^{12} (1,000,000,000,000)	10^{18} (1,000,000,000,000,000,000)
quadrillion	10^{15}	10^{24}
quintillion	10^{18}	10^{30}
sextillion	10^{21}	10^{36}
septillion	10^{24}	10^{42}
octillion	10^{27}	10^{48}
nonillion	10^{30}	10^{54}
decillion	10^{33}	10^{60}
undecillion	10^{36}	10^{66}
duodecillion	10^{39}	10^{72}
tredecillion	10^{42}	10^{78}
quattuordecillion	10^{45}	10^{84}
quindecillion	10^{48}	10^{90}
sexdecillion	10^{51}	10^{96}
septendecillion	10^{54}	10^{102}
octodecillion	10^{57}	10^{108}
novemdecillion	10^{60}	10^{114}
vigintillion	10^{63}	10^{120}
centillion	10^{303}	10^{600}

To these may be added googol (10^{100}) and googolplex (10^{googol})

241

pronunciation rhyming with *father* is becoming more frequent in contemporary usage. The pronunciation [*lay*thĕr] is incorrect.

latter *see* **former** and **latter**.

launch The verb *launch* is widely used in the figurative sense of 'set in motion', 'start', or 'introduce': * *The campaign will be launched next month* * *They have just launched their new perfume*. The word is also used figuratively as a noun: * *He gave a party to celebrate the launch of his latest novel*.

lava *see* **larva** or **lava**?

lavatory *see* **toilet, loo** or **bathroom**?

law and order Careful speakers pronounce this phrase without an intrusive [r] sound between the words *law* and *and*. Similar care should be taken with the pronunciation of other words and phrases containing the sound [aw] followed by a vowel, such as *drawing, awe-inspiring, I saw it*.

lawful, legal or **legitimate**? All these adjectives mean 'authorised by law', but there are differences of sense, usage, and application between them: * *the lawful owner* * *a legal contract* * *a legitimate organisation*. *Lawful* means 'allowed by law' or 'rightful'; it is largely restricted to formal contexts or set phrases, such as *a lawful business*.

Legal is more widely used, having the additional meaning of 'relating to law': * *the legal profession* * *legal advice* * *the legal system* * *legal action*.

The adjective *legitimate* is principally applied to children born in wedlock: * *the king's legitimate son*. It also means 'reasonable', 'logical', 'genuine', or 'valid': * *a legitimate excuse* * *a legitimate reason*.

lay or **lie**? The verb *lay*, which is usually transitive – i.e. has an object – is often confused with *lie*, which is intransitive – i.e. does not have an object: *I'll lay the towel on the sand to dry. She's going to lie down for a while*. Careful users maintain the distinction between the two verbs in all contexts.

Any confusion is probably due to the fact that the word *lay* also serves as the past tense of *lie*: * *The baby lay in his cot and screamed*. * *You'd better lay the baby in his cot*.

The past participle of *lie* is *lain*; the word *laid* (note the spelling) is the past tense and past participle of *lay*: * *They have lain in the sun for too long*. * *We (have) laid our coats on the bed*.

This verb *lie*, meaning 'rest in a horizontal position', should not be confused with the unrelated verb *lie*, meaning 'be untruthful'. The past tense and past participle of the latter are regular: * *He (has) lied about his age*. The present participle of both these verbs is *lying*; the present participle of the verb *lay* is *laying*.

The verb *lay* has a number of specific uses: * *to lay eggs* * *to lay the table* * *to lay a ghost*, etc. The expression *to lay low*, meaning 'to bring down', should not be confused with *to lie low*, meaning 'to stay in hiding'.

The verb *lay* is rarely used without a direct object, a notable exception being in the sense of 'to produce eggs': * *If the hens don't lay, there will be no eggs for breakfast*. The verb *lie* never has a direct object. *See also* **overlay** or **overlie**?; **underlay** or **underlie**?

layman or **laywoman**? *see* **non-sexist terms**.

LDC *see* **development**.

leach or **leech**? These two words are occasionally confused since they are pronounced in the same way. The verb *leach* means 'deprive of something' or 'drain away': • *The colour leached from his face.* It should not be confused with the noun *leech*, which describes a bloodsucking freshwater worm: • *She picked a leech off her leg.*

lead or **led**? These two words are often confused. *Lead* means 'guide by going in front': • *He was leading the walking party*, and is pronounced [leed]. The past tense of this verb is *led*. This is sometimes wrongly spelt as *lead* because the pronunciation is the same as that of the metal: • *as heavy as lead*, pronounced [led].

leadership *Leadership* is the state or rank of a leader; it also denotes qualities associated with a good leader: • *elected to the leadership* • *to lack leadership potential.* Some people dislike the use of the noun in place of *leaders*: • *China's leadership appeared to be stepping up efforts to promote its version of recent history* (*Daily Telegraph*).

leading-edge The adjectival use of *leading-edge* is best avoided where *advanced* or *up-to-date* would be adequate or more appropriate: • *leading-edge technology* • *a leading-edge project.* The noun *leading edge* denotes the forward edge of an aerofoil, wing, etc.; it noun is also used figuratively, in the vogue expression *at the leading edge*: • *This impressive product is at the leading edge of both lexicographical and computer technology* (Harrap catalogue).

A modern derivative of the term is *bleeding-edge*, which refers to the very latest technological advances, as yet largely unproved in real applications and thus carrying a certain degree of risk: • *This company is cautious about adopting bleeding-edge technology that may cause problems in the long run.* See also **cutting edge**.

leading question A *leading question* suggests or prompts the expected or desired answer, such as: • *Did you see the defendant stab his wife with a kitchen knife?* • *Do you approve of the wholesale slaughter of innocent animals for their fur?* Many people object to the frequent use of the term with reference to questions that are challenging, unfair, embarrassing, etc.: • *'Are there going to be any redundancies at the factory?' 'That's a leading question.'*

leak The use of the verb and noun *leak* with reference to the unofficial, surreptitious, or improper disclosure of secret information is acceptable in most contexts: • *Details of the report were leaked to the press.* • *The managing director's secretary denied all responsibility for the leak.* The verb *leak* is used both transitively and intransitively in this sense: • *He leaked the story.* • *The story leaked out.*

leak or **leek**? These two words are occasionally confused since they are pronounced in the same way. *Leak* describes an outpouring of liquid or something else escaping a container: • *oil leaking from the pipe.* It should not be confused with *leek*, which refers to a vegetable with a white bulb and long cylindrical stem: • *a bowl of leek soup.*

leaned or **leant**? Either word may be used as the past tense and past participle of the verb *lean*: ◦ *She leaned/leant forwards to open the window. Leaned* may be pronounced [leend] or [lent]; *leant* is always pronounced [lent]. *See also* **-ed** or **-t**?

leaped or **leapt**? Either word may be used as the past tense and past participle of the verb *leap*: ◦ *They leaped/leapt across the very wide ditch. Leaped* may be pronounced [leept] or [lept]; *leapt* is always pronounced [lept]. *See also* **-ed** or **-t**?

learn or **teach**? The use of the verb *learn* in place of *teach* is wrong: ◦ *He's teaching* [not *learning*] *me to swim*. To *learn* is to gain knowledge; to *teach* is to impart knowledge.

The verb *learn* is followed by the preposition *of* or *about* in the sense 'receive information': ◦ *When did you learn of* [or *about*] *the accident?* It is followed by the preposition *about* in the sense of 'gain knowledge': ◦ *We learnt about the Vikings last week*.

learned or **learnt**? Either word may be used as the past tense and past participle of the verb *learn*: ◦ *Have you learned/learnt the words of the song?* The past tense and past participle *learned* may be pronounced [lernd] or [lernt]; it should not be confused with the two-syllable adjective *learned* [lernid], meaning 'erudite': ◦ *a very learned professor*. *See also* **-ed** or **-t**?; **learn** or **teach**?

learning curve The phrase *learning curve* refers to the process of acquiring new knowledge or experience as if represented by a graph. (The rate of learning is usually not uniform: the curve may rise steeply at the beginning, when a large amount of knowledge is acquired in a relatively short time.) It is a vogue term, often found in business contexts, and should not be overused: ◦ *to help new employees up the learning curve* ◦ *Most schools have only just started their second year of LMS and head teachers admit to being on a steep learning curve* (*The Bookseller*).

learning difficulties In modern usage, this is the approved designation for any condition that hinders a person from absorbing basic information or learning simple skills: ◦ *The local authority is opening a new department to support youngsters with learning difficulties*. ◦ *They employ a number of adults who have learning difficulties*. It has replaced such terms as *retarded* or *mentally handicapped*, which are now considered unacceptable. People with learning difficulties may also be termed *learning-disabled*, although some would consider this jargonistic (*see* **jargon**).

learnt *see* **learned** or **learnt**?

lease *see* **hire** or **rent**?

least-developed countries *see* **development**.

leave or **let**? The use of the verb *leave* in place of *let*, especially in the expressions *let go* and *let be*, is regarded as incorrect and avoided by many users: ◦ *You mustn't let* [not *leave*] *go of the rope*. ◦ *I told the children to let* [not *leave*] *him be*. The expressions *leave alone* and *let alone*, however, are virtually interchangeable in the sense of 'refrain from disturbing, bothering, interfering with, etc.': ◦ *Leave/Let the* *dog alone. Leave alone* also means 'allow or cause to be alone', in which sense it cannot be replaced by *let alone*: * *Please don't leave me alone – I'm afraid of the dark.*

Let alone is also used as a set phrase meaning 'not to mention' or 'still less': * *They can't afford minced beef, let alone fillet steak. See also* **let**.

led *see* **lead** or **led**?

leech *see* **leach** or **leech**?

leek *see* **leak** or **leek**?

leeward This word has two possible pronunciations. The generally accepted pronunciation is [*lee*wărd], but [looărd] is used in nautical contexts.

legacy This word is sometimes misspelt: note the *-acy* ending. With the advent of computers in recent years *legacy* has expanded beyond its original meaning of 'inherited gift' or 'something handed down from an ancestor or predecessor', and may now also refer specifically to essential computer software that has been in use for some time but has become costly and difficult to maintain: * *legacy software * legacy system.*

legal *see* **lawful**, **legal** or **legitimate**?

legalise *see* **decriminalise** or **legalise**?

legendary The use of the adjective *legendary* in the sense of 'very famous or notorious' may be misleading or confusing: * *The legendary Dick Turpin rode a horse called Black Bess. * Listening to recordings of the legendary Andrés Segovia during the 1930s...* (*Reader's Digest*). The context of the

second example makes it clear that Andrés Segovia existed in fact, not in legend, but the first example is ambiguous.

legible or **readable**? The adjective *legible* describes something that can be deciphered and read; *readable* describes something that may be read with interest, enjoyment, or ease: * *legible handwriting * a very readable novel. Readable* is also used as a synonym for 'legible': * *The text is barely readable without a magnifying glass. See also* **illegible** or **unreadable**?

legionary *see* **legionnaire**.

legionnaire Note the spelling of this word, particularly the *-nn-*. A *legionnaire* is a (former) member of a military legion, such as the French Foreign Legion, the British Legion, or the American Legion; the noun also occurs in the name of a serious disease, *legionnaires' disease. Legionnaire* should not be confused with the noun *legionary*, which has a single *n* and specifically refers to a member of an ancient Roman legion.

legitimate *see* **lawful**, **legal** or **legitimate**?

leisure This word, meaning 'time spent free from work', is sometimes misspelt: note the *-ei-* spelling. *Leisure* is commonly pronounced [*lezh*ĕr] in British English and [*leezh*ĕr] in American English.

leisurely The word *leisurely* may be used as an adjective or, more rarely, as an adverb, meaning 'without haste': * *stroll at a leisurely pace * She walked leisurely up the garden.*

lend or **loan**? The word *lend* is used only as a verb; in British English *loan* is used principally as a noun: * *He lent me his pen.* * *Thank you for the loan of your lawn mower.* The use of *loan* as a verb is widely regarded as an Americanism. It is becoming increasingly acceptable, however, with reference to the lending of large sums of money, valuable works of art, etc.: * *The bank will loan us the money we need to finance the setting up of the new venture.* * *This picture has been loaned to the gallery by the Duke and Duchess of Kent.* The use of the verb *lend* in place of *borrow* is wrong: * *Can I borrow* [not *lend*] *your umbrella, please?* To *lend* is to give for temporary use; to *borrow* is to take for temporary use.

length or **duration**?

lengthways or **lengthwise**? Either word may be used as an adverb in British English: * *Fold the sheet lengthways/ lengthwise before ironing it.* As an adjective, and as an adverb in American English, *lengthwise* is preferred to *lengthways. See also* -**wise** or -**ways**?

lengthy The adjective *lengthy* means 'tediously, excessively, or unusually long'; it should not be used in place of *long* as a neutral antonym of *short*: * *The children became very restless during the headmaster's lengthy speech.* * *She has long* [not *lengthy*] *dark hair and brown eyes. Lengthy* may be pronounced [*leng*thi] or [*lenk*thi]. Note the consonant sequence *-ngth-* in the spelling.

leopard This word is sometimes misspelt. The most frequent error is the omission of the *o*, which is not pronounced.

less *see* **fewer** or **less**?

less-developed country *see* **development.**

lest This word, meaning 'in case something bad happens', is a relic of Old English that has become relatively infrequent in everyday conversation. It is followed by *should* or a verb in the **subjunctive**: * *I did not mention it, lest it should give her needless pain.* * *We should go now lest we be late.* Many people consider its use pretentious and avoid it altogether.

let Used in the imperative, *let* should be followed by an object pronoun rather than a subject pronoun: * *Let them try.* * *Let him finish his meal first.* * *Let Paul and me* [not *I*] *see the letter. Let's*, an informal contraction of let us, is used to introduce a suggestion or proposal made to the other member(s) of a group: * *Let's stay here.*

The preferred negative form of *let's* is *let's not*, although *don't let's* is also used in British English: * *Let's not go to the party. See also* **hire** or **rent**?; **leave** or **let**?

LETTER WRITING There are a number of conventions relating to the style and layout of a formal or semiformal letter (*see* following panel on page 247). *See also* **email**.

leukaemia This word is sometimes misspelt. Note the three sets of vowels: *eu, ae,* and *ia* in British English. The American English spelling is *leukemia.*

level The noun *level* serves a useful purpose in a variety of literal and figurative senses but is sometimes superfluous or unnecessarily vague: * *a*

LETTER WRITING

1 Addresses	The sender's address, followed by the date, should appear at the top of the letter, usually in the right-hand corner. The recipient's name and address appear below this, on the left-hand side of the page. Punctuation of the address – a comma at the end of each line (except the final line, which has a full stop) and sometimes after the house number – is optional.
2 Greeting	The salutation (*Dear Sir, Dear Madam, Dear Miss Jones, Dear Mr Brown*, or, increasingly but more controversially, under American influence, *Dear James Chapman*, etc., where the writer wants to avoid the formality of *Dear Mr Chapman* and the informality of *Dear James*) is set on a separate line, beginning with a capital letter and ending with a comma in British English, a colon in American English (*see also* **abbreviations**; **Ms, Mrs** or **Miss**?).
3 Presentation	The letter itself should be divided into paragraphs, with or without indentation. The style and content of the letter depend on the level of formality (*see also* **commercialese**).
4 Closing phrase	The letter is closed with any of a number of fixed phrases, the most frequent being *Yours sincerely* (if the recipient's name is used in the salutation) or *Yours faithfully* (if an impersonal salutation, such as *Dear Sir* or *Dear Madam*, is used). Like the salutation, this phrase is set on a separate line, beginning with a capital letter and ending with a comma.
5 Signature	The signature is usually followed by the sender's name, title, and office (if appropriate).
6 Informal letters	Some of these conventions also apply to informal letters: the position of the sender's address, the punctuation and layout of the salutation and closing phrase, etc. An informal letter may begin with the recipient's first name and end with any of a number of expressions, such as *Best wishes, Yours, Love*, etc. The recipient's name and address are usually omitted and it is rarely necessary to add the sender's name after the signature.

high level of unemployment (high unemployment) • *an increase in the noise level* (more noise) • *decisions made at management level* (decisions made by the management).

liable or **likely**? Both adjectives are used to express probability, followed by an infinitive with *to*. *Liable* refers to habitual probability, often based on past experience; *likely* refers to a specific probability that may be without precedent: • *The dog is liable to bite strangers.* • *The dog is likely to bite you if you pull his tail.* • *The shelf is liable to collapse when it is filled with books.* • *The shelf is likely to collapse if it is filled with books.* Careful users maintain the distinction between the two words. The adjectives *apt* and *prone*, which are similar in sense and usage to *liable*, principally refer to disposition, inclination, or tendency: * *He is apt/prone to lose his temper.*

Liable also means 'responsible (for)' or 'subject (to)': * *She is liable for their debts.* * *He is liable to epileptic attacks.* *Prone* is interchangeable with *liable* in the second of these senses: * *She is prone to indigestion. See also* likely.

liaison The noun *liaison* and its derived verb *liaise* are often misspelt, the most frequent error being the omission of the second *i*. Some people object to the widespread use of *liaison* and *liaise* as synonyms for 'communication', 'communicate', or '(maintain) contact', and the use of *liaison* to refer to an illicit sexual relationship: * *Closer liaison between teachers and social workers might have prevented this tragedy.* * *Overseas travel will be necessary to liaise with subsidiaries and distributors in Europe, North America, and the Far East.* * *His wife found out about his liaison with his secretary.*

libel or **slander**? Both words refer to defamatory statements: *libel* is written, drawn, printed, or otherwise recorded in permanent form; *slander* is spoken or conveyed by gesture. In informal contexts the word *libel* is often used in place of *slander*.

Both words may be used as nouns or as verbs. The final *l* of *libel* is doubled before a suffix beginning with a vowel in British English; the final *r* of *slander* is never doubled. *See also* spelling.

library The pronunciation of this word is [*lī*brări]. Careful users avoid dropping the second syllable [*lī*bri]; never-

theless this pronunciation is frequently heard.

licence or **license**? In British English, the noun is spelt *licence*, the verb *license*: * *a television licence* * *an off-licence* * *poetic licence* * *to license a car* * *(un)licensed premises* * *licensing hours.* In American English, both the noun and verb are spelt *license*.

lichen This word has two pronunciations: [*lī*kĕn] or [*lī*chĕn]. Some people prefer the first of these, which is the same pronunciation as *liken*.

licorice *see* **liquorice**.

lie *see* **lay** or **lie**?

lieu *see* **in lieu**.

lieutenant This word is often misspelt, the most frequent errors occurring in the first syllable: *lieu-*. The pronunciation of this syllable varies: the most frequent in British English is as in *left*; in nautical contexts, the pronunciation is as in *let*; and in American English the pronunciation is as in *loot*.

lifelong or **livelong**? The adjective *lifelong* means 'lasting or continuing for a lifetime': * *my lifelong friend* * *his lifelong admiration for her work.* The adjective *livelong*, meaning 'very long' or 'whole', is chiefly used in the old-fashioned poetic expression *all the livelong day. Lifelong* is usually written as a solid compound, the hyphenated form *life-long* being an accepted but rare variant.

Livelong, which is etymologically unrelated to the word *live*, is pronounced [*liv*long].

248

lifestyle Some people object to the frequent use of the term *lifestyle*, as a synonym for 'way of life', by advertisers, journalists, etc.: * *urban lifestyle* * *consumer lifestyle values* * *lifestyle packaging* * *The spread of Aids is likely to have tremendous effects on the personal lifestyles of many people.* There is an increasing tendency today for *lifestyle* to be written as a one-word compound. It is sometimes hyphenated (*life-style*) but not usually written as two separate words.

lighted or **lit**? Either word may be used as the past tense and past participle of the verb *light*. *Lit* is the more frequent in British English: * *Have you lit the fire?* * *He lit his pipe.* * *The hall was lit by candles.* Used adjectivally before a noun, *lighted* is the preferred form: * *a lighted torch* * *a lighted match* * *a lighted cigarette.* If the adjective is modified by an adverb, however, *lighted* may be replace by *lit*: * *a well-lit room* * *a badly lit stage.*

lightning or **lightening**? These two words are often confused. *Lightning* is a flash of light produced by atmospheric electricity: * *thunder and lightning.* *Lightning* is also used as an adjective to describe things that happen very quickly: * *the lightning strike by postal workers.* *Lightening* is the present participle/gerund of the verb *lighten*: * *lightening someone's load.*

light-year This is a unit of distance, not time; careful users avoid such expressions as: * *It happened light-years ago.* * *The wedding seemed light-years away.* A *light-year* is the distance travelled by light in one year (approximately six million million miles); the term is used in astronomy.

likable see **likeable** or **likable**?

like Many people dislike the use of *like* as a conjunction, introducing a clause that contains a verb; it is best avoided in formal contexts, where *as*, *as if*, or *as though* should be used instead: * *The garden looks as if* [not *like*] *it has been neglected for many years.* * *As* [not *like*] *the headmaster said, corporal punishment is not used in this school.* The use of *like* as a preposition, introducing a noun, pronoun, or noun phrase, is acceptable in all contexts: * *The garden looks like a jungle.* * *Like the headmaster, she disapproves of corporal punishment.* * *His sister writes like him.* * *Like you and me, they are keen amateur photographers.* (Note that the preposition *like* is followed by the object pronouns him, me, etc., not the subject pronouns *he*, *I*, etc.)

The use of *as* in place of the preposition *like* may change the meaning of the sentence: * *As your father, I have a right to know.* * *Like your father, I have a right to know.* * *She plays like a professional.* * *She plays as a professional.* In other contexts, the two prepositions may be virtually interchangeable: * *He was dressed as/like a policeman.* * *They treat me like/as an idiot.*

It is best to avoid the habitual use of *like* in spoken conversation as a meaningless filler: * *He was, like, really angry*; when exaggerating for effect: * *He was like 100 feet tall*; or to introduce speech: * *She was like, 'Where do you think you're going?' and I was like, 'Mind your own business!'*. See also **as**; **such as** or **like**?

-like The suffix *-like* may be attached with or without a hyphen in British English: * *spadelike* or *spade-like* * *autumnlike* or *autumn-like*. When *-like* is added to one- or two-syllable words that do not end in *-l*, the hyphen is often omitted: * *dreamlike* * *birdlike* * *paperlike*, particularly in words that are well-established in the English language, such as *lifelike* and *ladylike*. Words that end in *-l*, especially those that end in *-ll*, and words of three or more syllables usually retain the hyphen when adding *-like*: * *coal-like* * *model-like* * *doll-like* * *potato-like*.

likeable or **likable**? Both spellings of this word are acceptable. *See* **spelling**.

likely In British English the adverb *likely*, meaning 'probably', is not used on its own in formal contexts; it is usually preceded by *very, quite, more,* or *most*: * *They will very likely arrive tomorrow morning.* * *I'll most likely see you at the party.* Some people avoid the problem by using **probably** or by rephrasing the sentence to make *likely* an adjective: * *They will probably arrive tomorrow morning.* * *They are likely to arrive tomorrow morning.*

As an adjective, *likely* may stand alone or be modified by an adverb: * *a likely effect* * *a more likely explanation*. *See also* **liable** or **likely**?

limited Some people object to the use of the adjective *limited* as a synonym for 'small', 'little', 'few', etc.: * *a limited income* * *with limited assistance* * *of limited education*. Limited is best reserved for its original meaning of 'restricted': * *Their powers are limited.* * *We have a limited choice.* * *He finds it difficult to work in a limited space.*

lineage or **linage**? The noun *lineage*, pronounced [*lin*iij], means 'line of descent' or 'ancestry'; the noun *linage*, pronounced [*lin*ij], means 'number of

printed or written lines': * *the emperor's lineage* * *payment based on linage*. Neither word is in frequent use: *lineage* is largely restricted to formal contexts; *linage* to the world of printing and publishing.

Lineage is also used as a variant spelling of *linage*, in which case it is pronounced [*lin*ij].

lineament or **liniment**? The noun *lineament*, meaning 'feature', is largely restricted to formal or literary contexts: * *the noble lineaments of his face*. It should not be confused with the noun *liniment*, denoting a liquid rubbed into the skin to relieve pain or stiffness: * *a bottle of liniment*.

linger The verb *linger* is followed by the preposition *over* in the sense of 'be slow' * *He lingered over his breakfast*. It is followed by *on* in the sense of 'dwell on': * *Don't let your mind linger on the unpleasant details.*

lingua franca A *lingua franca* is a language adopted as a common language by speakers whose native languages are different: * *English is rapidly becoming the lingua franca of the world*. The expression *lingua franca* is pronounced [lingwă *frank*ă]; the plural is *lingua francas* [lingwă *frank*ăs].

The phrase *lingua franca* comes from Italian, meaning 'Frankish language'.

linguist The noun *linguist* may denote a person who knows a number of foreign languages, or a specialist in linguistics – the study of language. * *Mr Evans, an accomplished linguist, was a great help to us on our European tour.* * *At yesterday's lecture the linguist Noam Chomsky expounded his theory of lan-*

guage structure. A *modern linguist* is someone who can speak or is studying modern European languages such as French, German, and Spanish. Although the noun linguist is rarely ambiguous in context, it may be replaced, if necessary, by the synonym *polyglot* (for the first sense) or *linguistician* (for the second sense).

liniment *see* **lineament** or **liniment**?

liquefy or **liquify**? Both spellings of this word are acceptable, although the first is generally preferred.

liqueur or **liquor**? The spellings of these words are sometimes confused. A *liqueur* [li*kyoor*] or, less commonly, [li*ker*] is a sweet alcoholic drink taken after a meal. *Liquor* [*li*kĕr] is any alcoholic beverage.

liquidate or **liquidise**? The verb *liquidate* is used in finance: * *to liquidate a company* * *to liquidate a person's assets*, and as an informal euphemism for 'kill': * *He liquidated his rivals*. To *liquidise* is to make something liquid, usually in a blender or liquidiser: * *Liquidise the fruit and add it to the whipped cream*.

liquify *see* **liquefy** or **liquify**?

liquor *see* **liqueur** or **liquor**?

liquorice There are two possible pronunciations of this word. The traditional pronunciation [*li*kŏris] is preferred by many, but [*li*kŏrish] is also acceptable and widely used. In American English the noun is spelt *licorice*.

lit *see* **lighted** or **lit**?

literal, **literary** or **literate**? *Literal* means 'word for word; exact'; *literary* means 'relating to literature'; *literate* means 'able to read and write: (well-) educated': * *a literal translation* * *the literal meaning of the word* * *literary works* * *a literary critic* * *They are barely literate.* * *a highly literate candidate*. All three adjectives are ultimately derived from Latin *littera* meaning 'letter', but they are not interchangeable in any of their senses.

Some people avoid using *literate* to mean 'well-educated' where there is a risk of ambiguity. In a job advertisement, for example, *literate* may refer to anything from a basic ability to read and write to degree-level qualifications.

In such combinations as * *computer literate*, the word *literate* is reduced to the sense of 'competent; able; experienced'.

literally The use of the adverb *literally* as an intensifier, especially in figurative contexts, is disliked by many users: * *It literally rained all night.* * *I was literally tearing my hair out by the time they arrived.* The effect of this usage may be misleading or ambiguous: * *We were literally starving*, or quite absurd: * *She literally laughed her head off.*

As the opposite of *figuratively*, *literally* may be used to indicate that a metaphorical expression is to be interpreted at its face value: * *The dog had literally bitten off more than it could chew.*

literary, **literate** *see* **literal**, **literary** or **literate**?

literature Some people object to the use of the noun *literature*, with its connotations of greatness, to denote brochures, leaflets, and other written or printed matter: * *They're sending us some literature about holidays in the Far East.* The principal objection is not that *literature* is an unnecessary synonym for some other noun – it has no one-word equivalent in general use for this sense – but 'that so reputable a word should be put to so menial a duty' (H.W. Fowler, *A Dictionary of Modern English Usage*).

little *see* **few; fewer** or **less?**

live The adjective *live*, meaning 'not pre-recorded': * *a live broadcast* * *live music*, is increasingly used in the extended sense of 'actually present': * *They have never performed in front of a live audience.* This usage inevitably leads to humorous associations with the principal meaning of *live*, i.e. 'living' or 'alive', in contrast to 'dead'.

livelong *see* **lifelong** or **livelong?**

livid The adjective *livid* may be used to describe a range of colours, from the dark purple colour of a bruise, through the greyish-blue colour of a *livid* sky, to the pale complexion of somebody who is *livid* with fear. *Livid* is perhaps most frequently used in the sense of 'very angry': * *His mother will be livid when she finds out.* This usage is best restricted to informal contexts.

living room *see* **lounge.**

llama *see* **lama** or **llama?**

loaded *see* **laden** or **loaded?**

loan *see* **lend** or **loan?**

loath, loth or **loathe?** *Loath* and *loth* are different spellings of the same adjective, meaning 'unwilling' or 'reluctant'; *loathe* is a verb, meaning 'detest': * *He was loath/loth to move to London.* * *He loathes working in London.* *Loath* and *loathe* are frequently confused: * *The team would be loathe to see the manager go.* For this reason some users prefer *loth*, the more distinctive spelling of the adjective. The adjectives *loath* and *loth* are pronounced [lōth], with the final *th* sound of *bath*; the verb *loathe* is pronounced [lōdh], with the final *th* sound of bathe.

Note the spelling of the adjective *loathsome*, which may be pronounced [*lōdh*sŏm] or [*lōth*sŏm].

locale, locality or **location?** All three nouns mean 'place', but they are not altogether synonymous. *Locale*, the most formal of the three, refers to a place that is connected with a particular event or series of events: * *an unlikely locale for a human rights convention* (example adapted from COBUILD corpus). *Locality* often refers to a neighbourhood or geographical area: * *There are a number of bookshops in the locality.* *Location* means 'site' or 'situation' and is often used as a formal or pretentious substitute for the nouns *place, position,* etc. (*see also* **locate**): * *to move to a different location* * *the location of the town hall.*

locate The verb *locate* and its derived noun *location* are best avoided where *find, situate, place, position,* etc. would be adequate or more appropriate: * *I can't find* [not *locate*] *my front-door key.* * *The shrub should be planted in a sheltered position* [not *location*]. *

Offices in a prestigious part of the City [not *a prestigious City location*].

location *see* **locale, locality** or **location**?

lone *see* **alone** or **lone**?

longevity This word, meaning 'long length of life', is usually pronounced [lon*jev*īti] although [long*jev*īti] is also frequently used. The pronunciation [long*gev*īti] is non-standard.

longitude This word, referring to the distance west or east of the Greenwich meridian, may be pronounced with a *j*-sound [*lon*jityood] or a *g*-sound [*long*gityood]. Note that there is no *t* before the *i* in *longitude*, either in spelling or pronunciation, unlike in *latitude*.

loo *see* **toilet, lavatory, loo** or **bathroom**?

looked-after *see* **care**.

loose or **loosen**? The verb *loose* means 'release', 'set free', or 'undo'; the verb *loosen* means 'make or become less tight': • *She loosed the lion from its cage.* • *He loosened his belt.* The two verbs are not interchangeable. The adjective *loose*, which means 'free' or 'not tight', may be applied to something that has been *loosened*: • *The lion was loose.* • *His belt was loose.*

The verb *loose* is rarely used in modern times. It is occasionally confused with the verb *lose*, which is similar in spelling and pronunciation (*loose* is pronounced [loos]; *lose* is pronounced [looz]).

lorry *Lorry* and *lorry driver*, the traditional British English terms, are increasingly being overtaken by their American equivalents *truck* and *truck driver* or *trucker*.

lose *see* **loose** or **loosen**?

lot The expressions *a lot (of)* and *lots (of)* are best avoided in formal contexts, where they may be replaced by *many, much, a great deal (of), a good deal (of)*, etc.: • *We have many* [not *lots of*] *books.* • *They received a great deal of* [not *a lot of*] *help.* Note that *a lot* should never be written *alot*. *See also* **many; much; singular** or **plural**?

loth *see* **loath, loth** or **loathe**?

lots *see* **lot**.

loud or **loudly**? *Loud* may be used as an adjective or adverb: • *a loud noise* • *He shouted as loud as he could.* The adverb *loudly* may be substituted for *loud* in all its adverbial uses except the phrase *out loud*, meaning 'audibly': • *She read the poem out loud* [not *out loudly*]. It is not always acceptable, however, to use the adverb *loud* in place of *loudly*: • *They protested loudly* [not *loud*] *and angrily.* • *loudly* [not *loud*] *dressed in a blue-and-yellow striped jacket.*

lounge The *lounge* of a private house or flat is the room used for relaxation, recreation, and the reception of guests, as opposed to the *dining room*: • *She showed the vicar into the lounge.* Some people consider the synonyms *sitting room* and *living room* to be less pretentious than *lounge*. The word *lounge* also denotes a room in a hotel, pub, club, or airport: • *Coffee will be served in the lounge.* • *The passengers waited in the departure lounge.*

The noun *parlour*, an old-fashioned synonym for *lounge*, is derived from the French verb *parler*, meaning 'to speak': * *The maid has tidied the parlour*. The word *parlour* also has a number of specific uses: * *beauty parlour* * *ice-cream parlour*.

The term *drawing room* (short for *withdrawing room*), another synonym, has connotations of grandeur and formality: * *The ladies retired to the drawing room*.

Sitting room, *living room*, *drawing room*, and *dining room* are sometimes hyphenated in British English.

lour or **lower**? *Lower* in the sense of 'look sullen; look gloomy or threatening' may also be spelt *lour* and is pronounced to rhyme with *tower*: * *clouds lowering/louring over the sea*. The word is etymologically unrelated to *lower*, used as an adjective to mean 'relatively low', and as a verb to mean 'move down'. *Lower* in these senses is pronounced to rhyme with *mower*.

low or **lowly**? The adjective *low*, the opposite of *high*, has a number of senses: * *a low wall* * *a low temperature* * *a low voice* * *low morale* * *to feel low*. The adjective *lowly*, meaning 'humble' or 'inferior', is much more restricted in usage and is formal: * *their lowly abode* * *a lowly job*. Both adjectives may be applied to the same noun with different connotations: * *the low status of women in 18th-century society* * *the lowly status of the gardener*.

As an adverb, *lowly* can mean 'in a low manner' or 'in a lowly manner', but it is very rarely used in either sense. The word *low* may be used adverbially: * *to lie low* * *to bow low* * *low-heeled shoes* * *a low-cut neckline*.

lower *see* **lour** or **lower**?

lower-case *see* **capital letters**.

low-key Some people object to the frequent use of the adjective *low-key*, meaning 'of low intensity', in place of *modest*, *restrained*, *subdued*, unassertive, etc.: * *The reception was a very low-key affair*. The variant *low-keyed* is also used from time to time.

lowly *see* **low** or **lowly**?

low-profile *see* **profile**.

Ltd *see* **plc**.

lumbar or **lumber**? These two words are identical in pronunciation and are sometimes confused. *Lumbar* is an adjective used in medical contexts, referring to the lower part of the back and sides: * *a lumbar puncture* * *the lumbar vertebrae*. *Lumber* is used as a noun or verb. In the sense of 'unwanted articles', the noun *lumber* is chiefly found in British English: * *the lumber room*; in the sense of 'timber' it is chiefly found in American English: * *heaps of lumber*. The verb *lumber* means 'move heavily, awkwardly, etc.': * *An elephant lumbered past*; in the sense of 'burden' it should be restricted to informal contexts: * *I got lumbered with the job of delivering the leaflets*.

lunch or **luncheon**? Both nouns denote a midday meal: a *luncheon* is usually a formal social occasion; *lunch* is often a light informal meal or a fuller meal at which business is conducted: * *The Prince of Wales was the guest of honour at the luncheon*. * *We stopped at a pub for lunch*. * *They discussed the terms of* *the contract at their business lunch.* The use of *luncheon* as a synonym for 'lunch' is generally considered to be old-fashioned, surviving only in such terms as *luncheon meat* and *luncheon* voucher. *See also* **dinner, lunch, tea** or **supper?**

lure *see* **allure** or **lure?**

luxuriant or **luxurious?** *Luxuriant* means 'profuse', 'lush', or 'fertile'; *luxurious* means 'sumptuous' or 'characterised by luxury': * *luxuriant vegetation* * *a luxurious hotel.* The two adjectives are not interchangeable: *luxuriant* is principally applied to things that produce abundantly; *luxurious* to things that are very comfortable, expensive, opulent, self-indulgent, etc. The noun *luxury* is also used as an adjective, meaning 'desirable but not essential': * *luxury goods.* Some people dislike its use as a synonym for 'luxurious', especially in advertisements: * *a luxury car* * *a luxury hotel* * *luxury flats*, etc.

lying *see* **lay** or **lie?**

M

macabre Note the spelling of this word, which ends in *-re* in both British and American English. It means 'relating to death; gruesome': * *a macabre tale.* The *r* is not always sounded in speech, the pronunciations [măkahbĕ] and [măkahbrĕ] being equally acceptable to most people.

machinations This word, meaning 'devious plots or conspiracies', is traditionally pronounced [makinayshŏnz], although the alternative pronunciation [mashinayshŏnz] is becoming increasingly common.

machismo The noun *machismo*, denoting aggressive masculinity: * *the machismo of the leader*, may be pronounced [makizmō] or [machizmō]. Note that the *ch* does not have the *sh* sound of *machine*. Derived from a Spanish word meaning 'male' (*see* **macho**), it is a derogatory word that is disliked by some users of British English and is best restricted to informal contexts.

macho The adjective *macho*, the Spanish word for 'male', has derogatory connotations in English, describing a man who displays his masculinity in an aggressive or ostentatious way: * *a macho image* * *the macho hero.* Like **machismo**, *macho* should not be used in formal contexts or overused in informal contexts: it is sometimes better replaced by *masculine*, *virile*, *male*, etc. The *ch* in *macho*, unlike

machismo, is always pronounced [ch], not [k]: [*machō*].

macro- and **micro-** *Macro-* means 'large'; *micro-* means 'small'. Both prefixes are used in scientific and technical terms, such as: * *macroeconomics* * *microorganism* * *macrobiotic* * *microwave* * *macrocosm* * *microcosm* * *macroscopic* * *microscopic* * *microprocessor* * *microchip*. The use of *macro-* and *micro-* in other contexts, e.g. * *macrocontract* * *microskirt*, in place of the adjectives *large*, *great*, *small*, *tiny*, etc., is best avoided. The insertion of a hyphen between the prefix *macro-* or *micro-* and a word beginning with a vowel is optional: for example, *macroeconomics* and *microorganism* may be replaced with *macro-economics* and *micro-organism*. *See also* **hyphen**.

Madam or **Madame**? *Madam* is a polite term of address for woman; the word may be written with a capital or lowercase *m*: * *Would madam like a cup of coffee?* * *Can I help you, Madam? Madame*, written with a capital *M*, is the French equivalent of *Mrs*: * *Wax models of famous people are displayed at Madame Tussaud's.* The usual English pronunciation of both words is [*mad*ăm]; *Madame* is also pronounced [*mă*dam] or [*mă*dahm] – anglicised forms of the French pronunciation.

Madam is also used as an impersonal salutation in letter writing and as a formal title of respect: * *Dear Madam* * *Madam President.* In both these uses the word is always written with a capital *M*.

Mesdames, the plural of the French word *Madame*, also serves as the plural form of *Madam*. It is usually pronounced [*may*dam] in English.

The noun *madam* denotes a woman who runs a brothel or a girl who is impudent, conceited, precocious, badly behaved, etc.

mad cow disease This is the popular name for the cattle prion disease, bovine spongiform encephalopathy (BSE); note that it is not the approved term for the condition among scientists or farmers. Note also that *mad cow disease* only affects cattle. The human version is *variant CJD*, a new form of *Creuzfeldt-Jakob Disease*, thought to be caused by exposure to BSE.

magic or **magical**? The adjective *magic* is more closely related to the art or practice of magic than magical, which is used in the wider sense of 'enchanting': * *a magic wand* * *a magic potion* * *a magic spell* * *a magical experience* * *the magical world of make-believe*. The two adjectives are virtually interchangeable in many contexts, although *magic* is retained in certain fixed expressions, such as: * *magic carpet* * *magic lantern*, etc., and *magical* is sometimes preferred for things that happen as if by magic: * *a magical transformation*. *Magic*, but not *magical*, is also used in informal contexts to mean 'wonderful': * *The holiday was magic!*

magnate or **magnet**? These two words are occasionally confused. A *magnate* is a person with great wealth or influence. A *magnet* is a piece of iron or other substance that attracts iron.

Figuratively, *magnet* is used to describe a person or place that attracts many people: * *The region became a magnet for computer businesses*. The endings of the words are pronounced *magnate*: [-ayt] and *magnet*: [-it].

magnitude The noun *magnitude* is best avoided where *size, extent, importance, greatness*, etc. would be adequate or more appropriate: * *the magnitude of the problem*. The expression *of the first magnitude* is used in astronomy to describe the brightness of a star; its figurative use, in the sense of 'greatest' or 'most important', is disliked by some people: * *a disaster of the first magnitude*.

magnum opus The Latin expression *magnum opus* is used to refer to the greatest work produced by a writer, artist, musician, etc. The phrase *magnum opus* is pronounced [magnŭm ōpŭs]. Its plural forms are *magnum opuses* and *magna opera* [magnă ōpĕră].

Mahomet *see* **Muslim** or **Moslem**?

mail Since the development of worldwide electronic networks, the word *mail* – which originally referred solely to traditional postal services – has come to represent a much wider range of communications: * *He spent the morning opening the mail*. * *The message on the screen told her she had mail*. Thus, while *let me mail you the results* may still be understood to mean that the material in question will be sent by post, it could also mean that some electronic means is intended. To avoid confusion, careful users should specify the method they intend to use, whether it be *snail mail* (conventional post), *email* (a typed message sent via the Internet), *voicemail* (a telephone message recorded electronically), etc.

maintenance The noun *maintenance*, which is related to the verb *maintain*, is often misspelt, a common error being the substitution of *-tain-* for *-ten-* in the middle of the word. Note also the *-ance* ending.

major Some people dislike the frequent use of the adjective *major* in place of *great*, *important*, *chief*, *principal*, *serious*, etc.: * *There was certainly major news interest in the details of the background of a man convicted of murdering five members of his family* (*Daily Mail*). Although *major* is an accepted synonym of these words, it should not be used to excess.

majority and **minority** *Majority* means 'more than half of the total number'; *minority* means 'less than half of the total number': * *the majority of the books* * *a minority of his friends.* *Majority* and *minority* should not be used to denote the greater or lesser part of a single item: * *the greater part* [not the *majority*] *of the house* * *less than half* [not the *minority*] *of the meal.*

A *majority* may be as small as 51%; a *minority* may be as large as 49%. For this reason, *majority* and *minority* are best avoided where *most*, *a few*, etc. would be more appropriate.

Majority and *minority* may be singular or plural nouns. If the people or items in question are considered as a group, a singular verb is used; if they are considered as individuals, a plural verb is used: * *Only a minority was in favour of the proposal.* * *The majority have refused to pay.*

The two nouns also denote the difference between the greater and lesser numbers; in this sense they are always singular: * *The Labour candidate's majority has increased. See also* **collective nouns**; **singular** or **plural**?

male or **masculine**? The adjective *male* refers to the sex of a person, animal, or plant; it is the opposite of **female**: * *a male kangaroo* * *male genital organs.* *Masculine* is applied only to people (or their attributes) or to words (*see* **gender**); it is the opposite of **feminine**: * *masculine strength.*

With reference to people, *male* is used only of the sex that does not bear children; it is used to distinguish men or boys from women or girls but has no further connotations: * *We have a male French teacher and a female German teacher.*

Masculine, on the other hand, may be used of both sexes; it refers to characteristics, qualities, etc. that are considered typical of, or traditionally associated with, men: * *a masculine walk* * *masculine clothes.*

The noun *male* is best reserved for animals and plants, *man* and *boy* being the preferred terms for male human beings, unless the question of age makes these nouns inappropriate: * *Haemophilia is almost exclusively restricted to males.*

For male, female, and neutral (gender-inclusive) terms for people, *see* table at **non-sexist terms**. *See also* **boy**; **chauvinism**; **man**.

malevolent, **malicious** or **malignant**? All these adjectives mean 'wishing harm to others', but there are differences of sense, usage, and application between them: * *a malevolent look* * *malicious gossip* * *cruel, malignant intentions. Malignant* is the strongest of the three, describing an intense desire for evil. It is common in medical contexts, in the sense of 'cancerous', 'resistant to treatment', or 'uncontrollable': * *a malignant tumour.*

The adjectives *malevolent* and *malicious* are interchangeable in many contexts. *Malicious*, the more frequent, is also used in law with reference to premeditated crime: * *malicious intent.*

man Many people consider the use of the noun *man* as a synonym for 'person' to be ambiguous and/or sexist: * *the best man for the job* * *All men are equal.* With reference to individual human beings of unspecified sex, it is usually possible to use *person, people, human being, individual, everyone, worker(s), citizen(s)*, etc., in place of *man* or *men*: * *the best person for the job* * *All people are equal.* Idiomatic expressions, such as *the man in the street, to a man, as one man*, or *be one's own man*, and compounds, such as *manhole, manpower, man-made*, or *man-hour*, should not be changed but may be replaced with a synonym or paraphrase if necessary: * *without exception* (for *to a man*) * *be independent* (for *be one's own man*) * *workforce* (for *manpower*) * *synthetic* (for *man-made*).

Some users also object to the verb *man*, preferring *operate, staff, work, run*, etc.

The use of *man* in the sense of 'male adult' dates from around the 11th century. In Old English, the noun *man* denoted a human being of either sex, and the nouns *wer* and *wīf* were used to distinguish between male and female (respectively). *Wīf* was subsequently combined with *man* to form *wīfman*, from which the noun *woman* is derived. The word *wīf* also survives in the noun *wife* and

in compounds such as *fishwife* and *midwife*, where the *-wife* element simply means 'woman' and does not necessarily refer to a married woman. *See also* **boy; chair; gentleman; male** or **masculine?; mankind; non-sexist terms; sexism; woman.**

manageable This word, meaning 'able to be controlled': * *manageable in small numbers*, retains the *-e-* to indicate the softness of the *g*.

management-speak The informal term *management-speak*, alternatively known as *bizspeak* or *corporate-speak*, refers to the jargon of the modern corporate workplace. The language of business executives and middle-ranking functionaries in a wide range of commercial enterprises on both sides of the Atlantic, it is frequently lampooned both inside and outside the corporate world, especially when encountered outside the context of the office, and many people consequently avoid its use. Often of US origin and reflecting the influence of buzz words and political correctness, it is constantly evolving, and users of such euphemistic jargon may easily find that terms they thought current are considered outdated by others.

Notorious examples of contemporary *management-speak* that could easily be replaced by plainer terms include: *action* (do), *baseline* (starting point), *blue sky thinking* (thinking up ideas), *dialogue* (discuss), *facilitate* (help), *fast-track* (speed up), *get one's ducks in a row* (get organised), *going forward* (in the future), *idea shower* (brain storm), *incentivise* (reward), *interface* (communicate), *joined-up* (working together), *loop back* (return to), *mission statement* (aim), *outcomes* (results), *pre-prepare* (prepare), *push the envelope* (innovate), *rationalise* (cut), *run it up the flagpole and see if anyone salutes it* (try something and see what happens), *slippage* (delay), *stakeholder* (client or other interested party), *think outside the box* (look at things differently), *touch base* (talk), *value-added* (extra). *See also* **commercialese**.

manager or **manageress**? *see* **non-sexist terms**.

mandatory The adjective *mandatory* is usually pronounced [*man*dătŏri]. The alternative pronunciation [man*day*tŏri] is disliked by many users and is best avoided.

Some people object to the frequent use of *mandatory* as a synonym for 'compulsory', 'obligatory', or 'essential': ● *A degree in archaeology is desirable, but not mandatory, for this post.*

man-hours *see* **non-sexist terms**.

mankind The use of the noun *mankind* to denote human beings collectively may be confused with its second sense of 'men in general' (as opposed to *womankind*, meaning 'women in general'): ● *the future of mankind*. Many users dislike the word *humankind*, coined as a replacement for the first sense of *mankind*. *Humanity* may be ambiguous, having the additional meaning of 'kindness', but *the human race* is acceptable to most: ● *the future of the human race. See also* **man**; **non-sexist terms**.

man-made *see* **non-sexist terms**.

manoeuvre This word is sometimes misspelt. Note the vowel sequence

-oeu- and the -re ending in British English; the American spelling is *maneuver*. The derived adjective is *manoeuvrable* in British English, *maneuverable* in American English. *See also* **-ae-** and **-oe-**.

manpower *see* **non-sexist terms**.

mantel or **mantle**? A *mantel*, or more commonly a *mantelpiece*, is a shelf forming part of an ornamental structure round a fireplace. A *mantle* is a cloak or something that covers: ● *shrouded in a mantle of secrecy*. The spellings *mantle* and *mantlepiece* are also possible for the fireplace shelf, but are rarer.

many In formal contexts, the adjective *many* may be used in place of the informal expressions *a lot (of)* and *lots (of)* (*see* **lot**). *Many* is also used in informal contexts, especially in negative and interrogative sentences: ● *She doesn't buy many clothes.* ● *Have you got many pets?* In some positive sentences, however, *a lot of* and *lots of* are more idiomatic than many in informal contexts: ● *We have a lot of* [not *many*] *books. Many* denotes a large number (as opposed to *much*, which denotes a large amount); it is therefore used with a plural verb: ● *Many have disappeared.* ● *Many houses were destroyed.* However, in the idiomatic expressions *many a...* and *many's the...* a singular verb is used: ● *Many a child has dreamt of becoming a film star.* ● *Many's the time I've walked down this road.*

margarine The usual pronunciation of this word has a soft *g*: [marjăreen]. The original pronunciation, with a hard *g*, as in *Margaret*, is now rarely used, even though it is more in keeping with the spelling and the etymology of the word.

marginal Some people object to the use of the adjective *marginal* as a synonym for 'small' or 'slight': * *marginal changes* * *a marginal improvement* * *a marginal effect* * *a student of marginal ability*. *Marginal* means 'close to a margin or limit', sometimes with reference to a lower limit: * *marginal profits* * *a ceremony of marginal, not primary, importance*.

The adjective also has a number of specific uses, notably in politics: * *a marginal seat* (or *constituency*) is one in which the Member of Parliament has only a small majority. *Marginal* is also used to describe land on the edge of cultivated areas that is too poor to produce many crops.

marginalise The verb *marginalise* means 'treat as unimportant' or 'relegate to the fringes (of society, an organisation, etc.)'. Sometimes spelt *marginalize* (*see* **-ize** or **-ise**?), it is chiefly used in the passive: * *Britain fears being marginalised in the EU.* * *Opponents of a stern military response risk being marginalised on the back benches.* * *The arts are no longer marginalised* (*The Guardian*). A vogue term, *marginalise* is disliked by some people as an example of the increasing tendency to coin new verbs by adding the suffix *-ise* to nouns and adjectives. It should not be overused in formal contexts.

marital *see* **martial** or **marital**?

market forces The phrase *market forces* refers to anything that affects or influences the free operation of trade in goods or services, such as competition or demand, as opposed to (artificially imposed) government controls. It is in danger of becoming overused as a vogue term: * *The printing of this holy work* [the Bible] *should be subjected to market forces* (*The Bookseller*). * *Green market forces are working in the appliance manufacturers' favour* (*Daily Telegraph*).

marquess or **marquis**? A *marquess* is a British nobleman who ranks below a duke and above an earl; a *marquis* is a nobleman of corresponding rank in other countries. The word *marquis* is sometimes used in place of *marquess*. Note that *marquess* is a masculine title, despite the apparently feminine ending *-ess*. The female counterpart of a marquess or marquis is called a *marchioness*, although the term *marquise* is sometimes used for the non-British feminine title.

Marquess and *marquis* have the same pronunciation, [*mar*kwis], in British English, but the non-British title is sometimes pronounced [mar*kee*].

marshal *see* **martial** or **marshal**?

martial or **marital**? These two adjectives are sometimes confused, being similar in spelling. *Martial* means 'of or relating to war or military matters': * *martial music* * *martial arts* * *martial law*. *Marital* means 'of or relating to marriage': * *marital problems* * *marital status* * *marital vows*. The word *marital* is also found in the adjectives *extramarital*, *premarital*, etc., and *martial* in the compound noun and verb *court-martial*.

martial or **marshal**? The pronunciation of these two words is identical and they are sometimes confused. The adjective *martial* means 'of or relating to war or military matters' (*see* **martial** or **marital**?). *Marshal* may be used as a noun, meaning 'officer' or 'official', or as a verb, meaning 'arrange', 'assemble', or 'guide': * *Field Marshal Montgomery* * *One of the marshals pushed the damaged car off the racetrack.* * *to marshal the facts* * *We were marshalled into the courtroom.* Note that the second element of the compound noun and verb *court-martial* is *-martial* not *-marshal*.

The word *marshal* is sometimes misspelt with *-ll* at the end. The *-l* should be doubled only before *-ed*, *-ing*, and *-er* (in British English), and in the surname *Marshall*.

masculine *see* **male** or **masculine**?

massage The verb *massage* is increasingly used in the figurative sense of 'manipulate (figures, data, etc.) to make them more acceptable': * *to massage the accounts* * *to massage the results of the survey.* This usage is best restricted to informal contexts. Note also the noun phrase *massage parlour*, which is sometimes employed as a euphemism for brothel.

masterful or **masterly**? *Masterful* means 'domineering'; *masterly* means 'very skilful': * *His masterful approach made him unpopular with the staff.* * *The team reached their fifth World Cup final with a display of masterly efficiency* (*The Guardian*). The two adjectives relate to different senses of the noun *master*, from which they are both derived: 'person in authority' (*masterful*) and 'expert' (*masterly*).

Masterful is sometimes used in place of *masterly*: * *a masterful performance by the soloist*, but many users

prefer to maintain the distinction between the two words.

mat, **matt** or **matte**? The adjective *matt*, meaning 'not shiny', has the variant spellings *mat* and *matte*. *Matt* is the most frequent spelling in British English: * *a matt finish* * *matt black paint.* The spelling *mat* is preferred in American English.

materialise Some people dislike the use of the verb *materialise* in place of *happen* or *turn up*: * *The threatened strike is unlikely to materialise.* * *Her friends didn't materialise so we left without them.* In formal contexts the word is best restricted to its original meaning of 'make or become real': * *They watched in horror as the spirit materialised before their very eyes.*

mathematics *see* **-ics**.

matrimony This word, describing the state of *marriage*, is sometimes mispronounced. The correct pronunciation is [*mat*rimŏni], with the stress on the first syllable.

matrix The noun *matrix* denotes the substance or environment within which something originates, develops, or is contained. It is also a technical term in fields such as mathematics, computing, printing, anatomy, and linguistics. In general contexts matrix is disliked by many as a vogue word; it is often better replaced by *setting*, *background*, *framework*, *environment*, etc.: * *the matrix in which primitive societies evolved.* *Matrix* has two plural forms, *matrices* or *matrixes*, either of which is acceptable to most users.

matt, **matte** *see* **mat**, **matt** or **matte**?

mattress Note the -tt- and the -ss in this word, which is often misspelt.

maximal, maximise see **maximum**.

maximum The noun and adjective *maximum* refer to the greatest possible quantity, amount, degree, etc.: * *a maximum of twenty guests* * *the maximum dose.* The noun *maximum* has two plural forms, commonly used in technical contexts: *maximums* and *maxima.*

The adjective *maximum* is more frequent than its synonym *maximal.*

The verb *maximise* means 'increase to a maximum'; it is best avoided where *increase* would be adequate or more appropriate: * *The initial brief is to maximise sales of existing products.* Some people also dislike the use of *maximise* to mean 'make maximum use of': * *to maximise resources.*

may or **might**? *Might* is the past tense of *may* (see **can** or **may**?): * *She may win.* * *May we sit down?* * *I thought she might win.* * *He said we might sit down.* In the last two examples, *might* cannot be replaced with *may.* In the first two examples, however, *might* can be substituted for *may* with a slight change of meaning: * *She might win* expresses a greater degree of doubt or uncertainty than *She may win.* * *Might we sit down?* is a more tentative request than *May we sit down?* *May* and *might* are both used in the perfect tense. *May have* expresses a possibility that still exists; *might have* expresses a possibility that no longer exists: * *She may have won: I didn't hear the result.* * *She might have won if she hadn't fallen on the last lap.*

maybe or **may be**? *Maybe*, meaning 'perhaps': * *Maybe the letter will come*

tomorrow, is often confused with the phrase *may be,* the verb *may,* and the verb *be*: * *It may be that she has missed the train.*

mayoress A *mayoress* is the wife of a male mayor, or a woman who assists or partners a mayor of either sex at social functions and on ceremonial occasions. The use of the term *mayoress* to denote or address a female mayor is incorrect.

me see **I** or **me**?

me or **my**? see **-ing forms**.

mean see **I mean**.

meaningful The adjective *meaningful* should be avoided where *important, significant, serious, worthwhile,* etc. would be adequate or more appropriate: * *a caring, loving, and meaningful relationship* * *a meaningful experience. Meaningful* is best reserved for its literal sense of 'having meaning': * *meaningful utterances* * a meaningful smile * *a highly meaningful pause.*

means In the sense of 'method', *means* may be a singular or plural noun; in the sense of 'resources' or 'wealth' it is always plural: * *A means of reducing engine noise was developed.* * *Several different means of transport were used.* * *His means are insufficient to support a large family.* See also **singular** or **plural**?

meantime or **meanwhile**? *Meantime* is chiefly used as a noun, in the phrases *in the meantime* and *for the meantime; meanwhile* is chiefly used as an adverb: * *He wrote a letter in the* meantime. ⁕ *We have enough for the meantime.* ⁕ *Meanwhile, I had phoned the police.* Meantime may also be used as an adverb, in place of *meanwhile*, and *meanwhile* as a noun, in place of *meantime*, but these uses are less frequent.

medal or **meddle**? These two words should not be confused. *Medal* is a noun, denoting a metal disc, cross, etc. given as an award; *meddle* is a verb, meaning 'interfere': ⁕ *a gold/silver/bronze medal* ⁕ *Don't meddle in other people's affairs.*

media The word *media*, frequently used to refer to television, radio, newspapers, etc. as means of mass communication, is one of the plural forms of the noun *medium*: ⁕ *The media act as publicity agents for writers.* ⁕ *Television is an influential medium.* The plural of *medium* in the sense of 'spiritual intermediary' is *mediums*. Either plural form may be used for other senses of the noun: 'agency through which something is transmitted': ⁕ *the mediums* [or *media*] *of air and water for transmitting sound*; 'means of communication': ⁕ *English and French are the media* [or *mediums*] *of instruction.*

The increasing use of *media* as a singular collective noun is unacceptable to some people and is best avoided: ⁕ *There has been a failure to educate the young to the benefits of trade unions, leaving the field open for a hostile media* (*The Guardian*). *Media* is also used adjectivally in front of other nouns: ⁕ *a media event* is an event that is deliberately created for extensive coverage by the mass media.

mediaeval *see* **medieval** or **mediaeval**?

mediate In the sense of 'mediate in a situation', the verb *mediate* is followed by the preposition *in*: ⁕ *An independent adviser was called in to mediate in the dispute.* In the sense of 'mediate between people', it is followed by *between*: ⁕ *Who will mediate between the union and the management?*

medicine The word *medicine* is sometimes misspelt, the most frequent error being the substitution of *e* for the first *i*. This letter is sometimes not sounded in speech, resulting in the two-syllable pronunciation [*med*sin]. Some users prefer the full pronunciation, [*med*isin].

medieval or **mediaeval**? Both spellings of this word are acceptable. The spelling *medieval* is far more frequent in British English and is standard in American English. *See also* **-ae-** and **-oe-**.

mediocre This word, meaning 'of indifferent quality', is sometimes misspelt: note the ending, *-cre*. Some users object to such expressions as *quite mediocre* and *very mediocre*, considering that something either is or is not mediocre.

Mediterranean Note the spelling of this word, particularly the single *t*, the *-rr-*, and the *-ean* ending. It may help to associate the central syllables with the Latin word *terra*, meaning 'earth; land', from which they are derived.

medium, mediums *see* **media.**

meet with In British English the phrasal verb *meet with* should be restricted to the sense of 'experience' or 'receive': ⁕ *I hope he hasn't met with an accident.* ⁕

Does it meet with your approval? The American use of *meet with* in the sense of 'have a meeting with' is disliked by many British users: * *We met with the managing director this morning.*

The phrasal verbs *meet up with* and *meet up* are widely regarded as unnecessary synonyms for 'meet' and are best avoided, especially in formal contexts: * *I met (up with) her at the theatre.* * *They met (up) in the park.*

mega- Some people object to the use of the prefix *mega-*, meaning 'great' or 'large', in non-technical contexts, as in: * *mega-motorway* * *mega-trend* * *mega-merger* * *mega-bid* * *megabucks* * *megathon*. The prefix is often used as an adjective in its own right, meaning 'very large and impressive': * *The new leisure complex is really mega.* This usage is best restricted to very informal contexts.

In science, the prefix *mega-* means 'one million': a *megaton* is one million tons. In computing, the prefix *mega-* means 2^{20}; a *megabyte* is 1,048,576 bytes.

meltdown In nuclear physics, the noun *meltdown* refers to the melting of the core of a nuclear reactor, caused by a defect in the cooling system. It is also used figuratively with reference to any disastrous event, especially a stock-market crash: * *Meltdown Monday*. Given the very serious nature of a meltdown (in the literal sense of the word), some people object to the figurative application of the term to comparatively trivial issues, such as a fall in company profits.

melted or **molten?** *Melted* is the past tense and past participle of the verb *melt*; it is also used as an adjective: * *The chocolate (has) melted.* * *Serve the asparagus with melted butter. Molten* is used only as an adjective, meaning 'melted' or 'liquefied': * *molten iron* * *molten rock*. The use of the adjective *molten* is restricted to substances that become liquid at very high temperatures.

membership *Membership* is the state of being a member: * *to apply for membership*. The noun is also used to denote the number of members of an organisation: * *Membership has increased this year.* Some people dislike its frequent use in place of *members*, however: * *We must consult the membership.*

memento The word *memento* is sometimes misspelt, the most frequent error being the substitution of *o* for the first *e*, through confusion with such words as *moment* and *momentum*. It may help to associate the *mem-* with *memory* and *remember*. *Memento* has two acceptable plural forms, *mementos* and *mementoes*.

mental The use of the adjective *mental* as a synonym for 'stupid', 'foolish', 'mentally ill', 'mentally deficient', etc. should be avoided as it is very likely to cause offence: * *They must be mental to set off in such terrible weather.* * *Her youngest son's a bit mental, and the other children tease him.* The principal meaning of *mental* is 'of or involving the mind': * *mental illness* * *mental arithmetic*. The adjective is also used in the sense of 'relating to disorders of the mind': * *a mental hospital* * *a mental patient*, although recent usage prefers * *psychiatric hospital* and * *a psychiatric patient*, and a mentally ill person would more correctly be described as being *in poor mental health*.

The term *mentally handicapped* was formerly the accepted term for a person suffering from intellectual impairment of some kind. Note that many people now avoid the term, preferring such alternatives as *learning-disabled* (*see* **learning difficulties**).

mentholated or **methylated**? These two words should not be confused. *Mentholated* refers to the addition of *menthol*, a medicinal substance found in peppermint oil; *methylated* refers to the addition of the poisonous substance *methanol*: * *a mentholated lozenge* * *methylated spirits*.

meretricious or **meritorious**? *Meretricious* means 'superficially attractive' or 'insincere'; *meritorious* means 'having merit' or 'praiseworthy': * *meretricious glamour* * *a meritorious deed*. Both adjectives are fairly formal in usage. The adjective *meretricious* originally meant 'of a prostitute'; like *meritorious*, it is ultimately derived from the Latin verb *merere*, meaning 'to earn' or 'to deserve'.

Note the spellings of the two words, particularly the second vowel: *meretricious* has the *e* of its Latin root; *meritorious* has the *i* of *merit*.

merge The verb *merge* is followed by the preposition *with* or *into* in the sense of 'merge with [or into] something else': * *On the horizon, the sea appeared to merge with* [or *into*] *the sky*. In the sense of 'merge with another business, company, etc.', it is followed by *with*: * *Cadbury merged with Schweppes*; in the sense of 'form a combined group' it is followed by *into*: * *The three companies merged into one*.

meta- Some people object to the increasing use of the prefix *meta-* in the sense of 'transcending' or 'of a higher order': * *A suggestion of metafiction, of uncertainties found to be themselves fictionally productive* (*London Review of Books*). * *Could this be a symptom of a developing metaculture?* * *Large parts of the town centre are now dominated by cinemas and other manifestations of meta-entertainment*. The prefix has a number of other accepted meanings: 'change': * *metamorphosis*; 'after', 'behind', or 'beyond': * *metatarsus*.

metal or **mettle**? These two words, which have the same pronunciation, are sometimes confused. A *metal* is one of a group of mineral substances that are good conductors of heat and electricity. *Mettle* means 'strength of character': * *He was given no chance to prove his mettle*. The confusion may arise from the fact that *mettle* was originally derived from *metal*.

metaphors A *metaphor* is a figure of speech in which a word or phrase is used, not with its literal meaning, but to suggest an analogy with something else. The comparison is implicit, not introduced by *like* or *as* (compare **synonym**) * *the winds of change* * *an icy voice* * *stone deaf*. Many expressions used in everyday speech are metaphorical, but are so frequently used that they are hardly thought of as metaphors: * *the arm of a chair* * *a branch of a bank*, and many occur in well-known idioms: * *not up my street* * *feel under the weather* * *if you play your cards right*.

Metaphors have been used very successfully and with striking effect in literature. There are biblical examples: * *Thy word is a lamp unto my feet*

(Psalm 119:105) and countless poetic ones: * *I see a lily on thy brow... and on thy cheek a fading rose* (Keats, *La Belle Dame Sans Merci*). However, as used by modern politicians and journalists, metaphors can often be tired and overworked: * *the cure for unemployment* * *fighting against inflation* * *light at the end of the tunnel.*

Mixed metaphors, where two or more different metaphors are used in one sentence, should be avoided: * *In resurrecting these allegations they are just fuelling the flames of racism.* * *The committee's task was to iron out all the bottlenecks in the system.*

meter or **metre**? The spelling of these words is often confused, probably partly because the American spelling of the measurement *metre* is *meter*. In British English, a *meter* is a measuring instrument: * *gas meter* * *speedometer*. A *metre* is the basic metric measurement of length and is used in derived measurements: * *kilometre* * *millimetre*. *Metre* is also the technical term for the regular rhythmic arrangement of syllables in poetry. Note however that in compounds describing such measures, the spelling -*meter* is followed: * *pentameter* ('a line having five stresses').

methodology The noun *methodology* denotes a body or system of methods, rules, principles, etc. used in a particular area of activity: * *the methodology of teaching.* Many people dislike the use of the noun in other contexts, especially as a synonym for 'method': * *experimental design methodology* * *unstructured pragmatic methodologies*, and this is best avoided.

methylated *see* **mentholated** or **methylated**?

meticulous The adjective *meticulous* is widely used and accepted as a synonym for 'painstaking' or 'scrupulous': * *meticulous attention to detail* * *a meticulous secretary*. Some people, however, object to the use of the adjective in a complimentary manner, restricting it to the pejorative sense of 'fussy' or 'excessively careful': * *If you weren't so meticulous you'd have finished the cleaning hours ago.*

Meticulous originally meant 'timid', being ultimately derived from *metus*, the Latin word for 'fear'.

metonym A *metonym* is a word or phrase that is used as a substitute for something else to which it is related or of which it is a part. Thus, *Rome* may serve as a metonym for the hierarchy of the Roman Catholic Church, *Hollywood* for the US film industry, and *the crown* for the monarchy. Care should be taken to use only metonyms whose relevance will be correctly interpreted.

metre *see* **meter** or **metre**?

mettle *see* **metal** or **mettle**?

micro- *see* **macro-** and **micro-**.

mid *see* **amid**, **amidst**, **mid** or **midst**?

middle *see* **centre** or **middle**?

midget *see* **dwarf**.

midwifery This word is sometimes mispronounced. In British English the correct pronunciation is [*mid*wifěri]. In American English, -*wif*- may be pronounced like *wife*. See also **man**.

might *see* **can** or **may**?; **may** or **might**?

migraine The usual pronunciation of this word, meaning 'a severe and recurrent headache', is [*mee*grayn]. The alternative pronunciation [*mī*grayn] is also acceptable and is standard in American English.

mileage or **milage**? *Mileage* is the more frequent spelling of this word, *milage* being an accepted but rare variant: * *The exceptionally low mileage makes this car a good buy.* In its figurative sense of 'benefit' or 'usefulness', the noun is avoided by some users in formal contexts: * *It was an interesting subject, though, and the chairman... got the maximum intellectual mileage out of it* (*The Guardian*). *See also* **spelling**.

militate or **mitigate**? The verb *militate*, which is usually followed by the preposition *against*, and occasionally by *for*, means 'have a powerful influence or effect': * *His left-wing opinions militated against his appointment as headmaster.* The verb *mitigate* means 'moderate' or 'make less severe': * *The judge's decision did little to mitigate the suffering of the bereaved parents.* * *mitigating circumstances.* The two verbs are occasionally confused, *mitigate* being wrongly used in place of *militate*.

milkman or **milkwoman**? *see* **non-sexist terms**.

millennium This word and its plural form *millennia* are often misspelt, the most frequent error being the omission of the second *n*: * *Over the millenia, as earth movements cause new formations* (*Reader's Digest* advertisement for *Marvels and Mysteries of the World Around Us*). Spelling mistakes may be avoided by associating the word, which means 'a thousand years', with the *-ll-* of *millipede* and *millimetre* (from Latin mille 'thousand') and the *-nn-* of *annual* and *perennial* (from Latin *annus* 'year').

The phrase *the millennium* was much used around the year 2000 to refer to the start of the new (third) millennium: * *celebrations to mark the millennium.*

There is some confusion about when millennia start and end. As there was no year 0 AD, we calculate in thousand-year segments from the year 1 AD. This means that the second millennium began on 1 January 1001 and ended on 31 December 2000. Despite this reckoning, in modern usage 1 January 2000 (rather than the strictly correct 1 January 2001) is often considered to have been the beginning of the third millennium. *See also* **centuries**.

millionaire The word *millionaire* is sometimes misspelt. Note the *-ll-*, but only one *n*.

mimic This word, meaning 'imitate': * *He likes mimicking the teachers*, is sometimes misspelt. Note that a *k* is added before the suffixes *-ed*, *-ing*, and *-er*. *Mimicry* does not, however, have a *k*. *See also* **spelling**.

mincemeat The noun *mincemeat* principally denotes the sweet mixture of dried fruit, suet, sugar, and spices that is used to fill mince pies, traditionally baked and eaten at Christmas. To avoid confusion, meat that has been minced (minced meat) is usually called *mince* in British English and *ground meat* in American English.

miner or **minor**? These two words are occasionally confused. A *miner* is a person who works underground in a mine; *minor* is an adjective that is the opposite of major, meaning 'less important; relatively unimportant': * *have a minor part in a play*; it is also used to refer to a musical scale. As a noun, *minor* means a person who is still legally a child – a person who has not yet reached the age of majority. *Miner* and *minor* have the same pronunciation: [*mī*něr].

miniature *Miniature*, meaning 'small in size', is sometimes misspelt. Note the *-iat-*.

minimal, minimise *see* **minimum**.

minimum The noun and adjective *minimum* refer to the smallest possible quantity, amount, degree, etc.: * *a minimum of four employees* * *the minimum requirements*. The noun *minimum* has two plural forms, commonly used in technical contexts: *minimums* or *minima*.

Some users dislike the frequent use of *minimal* in the sense of 'very small': * *The response to our advertisement was minimal – we received only two applications.* * *minimal effort* * *minimal risk.* Note also that *minimal* should never be used with a modifier: * *rather minimal.*

The verb *minimise* means 'reduce to a minimum'; it is best avoided where *reduce* would be adequate or more appropriate: * *The new safety regulations should minimise the danger.* Some people also object to the widely accepted use of *minimise* to mean 'play down' or 'belittle': * *to minimise your achievements.*

minor *see* **miner** or **minor**?

minority *see* **majority** and **minority**.

minus The use of the preposition *minus* in the sense of 'without' or 'lacking' is best restricted to informal contexts: * *She came home minus her umbrella.* Some people also avoid using the noun *minus* as a synonym for 'disadvantage' in formal contexts: * *Having to move to the South is one of the minuses of my new job: we'll never be able to afford to buy a house there. See also* **plus**.

minuscule This word is often misspelt, the most frequent error being the substitution of an *i* for the first *u*. The word is pronounced [*min*ŭskyool].

minutiae The plural noun *minutiae*, meaning 'small, minor, or trivial details', may be pronounced [mi*new*shiee] or [mī*new*shiee]: * *The minutiae of the problem are of no interest to me. Minutia*, the singular form of the noun, is rarely used.

The noun *minutiae* is best avoided where *details* would be more appropriate: * *discuss the details* [not *minutiae*] *of a contract.* Note the spelling of *minutiae*, particularly the three final vowels, *-iae*.

miscellaneous This word, meaning 'of a variety of items', is sometimes misspelt. Note particularly the *-sc-*, the *-a-*, and the *-eous* ending.

mischievous The correct pronunciation of this word is [mis*chiv*ŭs]. The mispronunciations [mis*chee*vŭs] and [mis*chee*viŭs] are heard from time to time but are avoided by careful speakers. The word is often misspelt: particular attention should be paid to the order and position of the vowels.

misogynist Note the spelling of *misogynist*, which refers to a person who hates women. The word derives from Greek *misos* ('hatred') and *gyne-* ('woman') – as in *gynaecology*, the branch of medicine concerned with women's diseases. *Misogynist* is usually pronounced [miso*j*inist], although the first syllable is very occasionally pronounced with a long *i*, as in *my*.

Miss *see* **Ms, Mrs or Miss?**

miss The verb *miss*, meaning 'regret the loss or lack of', is sometimes wrongly used with *not*: * *I miss not having a car* means 'I was happier before I had a car', not 'I wish I had a car'. This error is not confined to informal spoken contexts: * *Passengers... ask me* [a ship's doctor] *if I miss not being a 'proper' doctor* (Reader's Digest). *See also* **air miss** or **near miss?**

misspelled or **misspelt?** Either word may be used as the past tense and past participle of the verb *misspell*: * *You have misspelt/misspelled my name.*

    Misspelled may be pronounced [mis*spelt*] or [mis*speld*]; *misspelt* is always pronounced [mis*spelt*]. Note the spellings of the two words, particularly the single *l* of *misspelt* and the *-ss-* of both words. *See also* **-ed** or **-t?**

MISSPELLINGS Some words present a particular hazard as regards their correct spelling. *See* the panel on page 271 for the correct spellings of some frequently misspelled words in English. *See also* **-able** or **-ible?; -ae-** and **-oe-; Americanisms; -ant** or **-ent?; -ize** or **-ise?; plurals;** and **individual entries.**

mistrust *see* **distrust or mistrust?**

misunderestimate *see* **estimation.**

misuse *see* **abuse or misuse?**

mitigate *see* **militate or mitigate?**

mix Some people object to the increasing use of the noun *mix* in place of *range*: * *A wide mix of subjects will be taught at the college.* In the sense of 'combination' or 'mixture', *mix* is found in compounds such as *marketing mix*, 'the various elements that need to be coordinated in a marketing plan'. Some users, however, object to its use in formal contexts.

mnemonic The word *mnemonic*, referring to something that aids the memory (e.g. the spelling rule '*i* before *e* except after *c*'), causes spelling and pronunciation problems. The initial *m* is silent; the word is pronounced [ni*monik*].

mobile As a noun, *mobile* has enjoyed a massive revival in use in recent years through the widespread introduction of *mobile phones* (portable telephones commonly referred to simply as *mobiles*): * *I tried to reach you on your mobile. Mobile telephone* or *mobile phone* is usually preferred to *mobile* in formal contexts. *Mobile phone* has largely replaced the former terms *cellphone* and *cellular phone* in British English.

moccasin This word, used to describe a soft leather shoe without a heel, is sometimes misspelt. Note the *-cc-* but single *s*.

modal *see* **verbs.**

modern or **modernistic?** The adjective *modern* means 'of the present time' or 'contemporary'; *modernistic* means

MISSPELLINGS

aberration	descendant	integrated	preparation
abbreviation	desiccated	intercede	privilege
accelerate	desperate	instalment	proceed
accessory	detach	instil	procession
accommodate	**diarrhoea**	itinerary	professional
accommodation	disappoint	jeopardise	pronunciation
achieve	discrepancy	laborious	psychiatry
achievement	ecstasy	legacy	questionnaire
acquaint	eighth	liaise	queue
acquiesce	embarrass	liaison	receipt
address	enthral	lieutenant	receive
admissible	exaggerate	liquefy	relevant
advantageous	exceed	loose	relieve
ancillary	excite	lose	reminiscent
anonymous	exhilarate	maintenance	resistant
appalling	exorbitant	manoeuvre	responsible
asphalt	foreign	marshal	resuscitate
assassinate	foreigner	Mediterranean	rhythm
assimilate	forfeit	millennium	rigorous
authoritative	friend	millionaire	sacrilege
beautiful	fulfil	miniature	sacrilegious
besiege	gauge	minuscule	scissors
billionaire	grammar	miscellaneous	secretary
broccoli	grandad	mischievous	seize
buoyant	granddaughter	misspell	separate
Caribbean	guarantee	mnemonic	sergeant
categories	haemorrhage	modelled	sheriff
ceiling	harass	necessarily	siege
cemetery	harassed	necessary	skilful
census	harassment	niece	suddenness
chief	height	noticeable	supersede
commemorate	hindrance	occasionally	tariff
commissionaire	honorary	occurrence	threshold
commitment	humorist	omission	tranquillity
committed	humorous	omitted	traveller
compulsory	humour	oscillate	unnecessary
concede	hygiene	parallel	unwieldy
conceit	hypocrisy	paralleled	vaccination
conceive	idiosyncrasy	perceive	vacillate
conscience	illegible	perennial	variegated
conscientious	inconceivable	perseverance	vigorous
consensus	indefinitely	personnel	weight
curriculum	indispensable	playwright	weird
deceive	innocuous	possess	whether
definitely	inoculation	precede	wholly
dependant (noun)	inseparable	preceding	withhold
dependent	install	predecessor	
(adjective)			

'characteristic of modern trends, ideas, etc.' and is sometimes used in a derogatory way: * *modern society* * *modernistic architecture.* *Modern* has a wider range of sense and usage than *modernistic*, which is largely restricted to objects, designs, thoughts, etc. that are conspicuously modern or unconventional.

modus operandi The Latin phrase *modus operandi* is used in formal English to refer to a particular method of working: * *The committee discussed the modus operandi of the new working party.* The phrase *modus operandi* is pronounced [mōdŭs opĕrandee, opĕrandī]; its plural is *modi operandi* [mōdi].

modus vivendi The Latin phrase *modus vivendi* is principally used in formal English to denote an arrangement or compromise between conflicting parties: * *This modus vivendi enabled them to complete the job without further disruption.* The literal meaning of the phrase is 'way of living', but some people object to its use in place of the English expression way of life.

The word *modus* is pronounced [mōdŭs]; *vivendi* may be pronounced [vivendee] or [vivendī].

Mohammed *see* **Muslim** or **Moslem**?

molten *see* **melted** or **molten**?

momentary or **momentous**? *Momentary* means 'lasting for a very short time'; *momentous* means 'of great significance': * *a momentary lapse* * *The Commons... took the momentous step of opening its doors to the television cameras for the first time* (*The Guardian*). The two adjectives relate to different

senses of the noun *moment*, from which they are both derived: 'a very short time' (*momentary*) and 'significance' (*momentous*).

Note the difference in stress between the two adjectives: *momentary* is stressed on the first syllable, *momentous* on the second. The adverb *momentarily* should also be stressed on the first syllable [mōmĕntărĭli]; the pronunciation [mōmĕnterrili] is unacceptable to many people.

mongolism *see* **Down's syndrome**.

mongoose The plural of the noun *mongoose* is *mongooses*; the word should not be treated as a compound of the noun *goose* (the plural of which is *geese*). *Mongoose* is derived from the word *mangūs*, of Indian origin, and is etymologically unrelated to *goose*.

monogram or **monograph**? A *monogram* is a design made up of a person's initials: * *There was a monogram on the corner of the handkerchief.* A *monograph* is a learned book, treatise, etc. about a single subject: * *He wrote a monograph on Oliver Cromwell.* The two nouns should not be confused.

moot The adjective *moot*, meaning 'debatable' or 'open to question', rarely occurs outside the fixed phrase *a moot point*: * *Whether she will accept this offer is a moot point.* The verb *moot*, meaning 'put forward for debate', is most frequently used in the passive in formal contexts: * *The subject was mooted at our last meeting.*

moral or **morale**? These two spellings are sometimes confused. *Moral* means 'concerned with the principles of right and wrong': * *the gradual erosion* *of moral standards. Morale* is the extent of confidence and *optimism in a person or group:* * *After the election defeat, the party's morale sank to an alltime low. Moral* is stressed on the first syllable [morrăl]; *morale* is stressed on the second syllable [mo*rahl*].

more The adverb *more* is used to form the comparative of a number of adjectives and adverbs: * *She is more intelligent than her sister.* * *The trains run more frequently in the summer months. More* should not be used with adjectives that already have the comparative ending -*er*, such as *happier, older*, etc. Other uses of the word *more* – as the comparative of *much* or *many*, or in the sense of 'further' or 'additional' – may lead to confusion: * *She has more beautiful dresses* may mean 'her dresses are more beautiful (than mine/ yours/etc.)', 'she has other dresses that are more beautiful (than this one)', 'she has a greater number of beautiful dresses (than you/me/etc.)', or 'she has other beautiful dresses (in addition to this one)'.

The phrase *more than one*, although it implies a plural subject, is used with a singular verb: * *More than one accident has happened at this junction.* If the sentence is reworded, however, a plural verb is used: * *More accidents than one have happened at this junction. See also* **comparative** and **superlative**; **singular** or **plural**?

mortgage This word is sometimes misspelt, the most frequent error being the omission of the silent *t*.

mortgagee or **mortgagor**? A *mortgagor* is a person who borrows money by means of a mortgage; a *mortgagee* is the person or organisation, e.g. a building society or bank, that lends the money. The two nouns should not be confused: the *mortgagors* are the people who are mortgaging their property, i.e. using it as security for a loan; the *mortgagees* are those who receive this security, not the recipients of the loan itself.

Moslem *see* **Muslim** or **Moslem**?

most The adverb *most* is used to form the superlative of a number of adjectives and adverbs: * *This is the most expensive picture in the shop.* * *The prize will be awarded to the child who writes the most neatly. Most* should not be used with adjectives that already have the superlative ending -*est*, such as *saddest, youngest*, etc. Other uses of the word *most* – as the superlative of *much* or *many*, or in the sense of 'very' – may cause ambiguity: * *This teacher has the most intelligent pupils* may mean 'this teacher has the greatest number of intelligent pupils' or 'this teacher's pupils are the most intelligent in the school'; * *She danced most gracefully* may mean 'she danced very gracefully' or 'she danced more gracefully than the other dancers'. *See also* **comparative** and **superlative**.

The use of *most* in place of *very* is generally best avoided, although it is acceptable in certain contexts: * *I am most grateful for your assistance.* * *He spoke most rudely of his former employers.*

The adverb *mostly*, meaning 'mainly' or 'usually', should not be confused with *most*: * *He writes mostly* [not *most*] *for children.* * *Old people are most* [not *mostly*] *at risk.* In some contexts the substitution of *most* for *mostly*, or vice versa, changes the meaning of the sentence: * *Our friends are mostly helpful. – Our friends* *are most helpful.* • *The shop sells most books.* – *The shop sells mostly books.*

motif or **motive**? These words are sometimes confused. A *motif* is a recurrent feature that establishes a pattern throughout a work of art, etc.: • *a design with a feather motif.* A *motive* is a reason for a course of action: • *no apparent motive for the crime.*

motivation Many people dislike and avoid the use of the noun *motivation*, which means 'incentive' or 'drive', in place of *reason* or *motive*: • *his reason* [not *motivation*] *for deserting his wife and family.* Some people also object to the frequent use of the noun in its accepted sense of 'providing with an incentive' in the context of industrial psychology: • *the motivation of the workforce.* As Roland Gribben remarked in the *Daily Telegraph*: 'Motivation is a grossly overworked and abused term for getting the best or more out of people.'

Similar objections may be applied to the use of the verb *motivate* in place of *cause*, and of *motivated* as a synonym for 'keen': • *an action that may cause* [not *motivate*] *her to change her mind* • *a highly motivated sales manager* • *a self-motivating entrepreneur.*

motive *see* **motif** or **motive**?

mot juste The French expression *mot juste* is used in English to refer to the exactly appropriate word or phrase: • *This dictionary of synonyms will help you find the mot juste.* The literal meaning of *mot juste* is 'right word'. It is sometimes written or printed in italics. Its anglicised pronunciation is [mōzhoost]. The plural is *mots justes*,

with the same pronunciation as the singular.

mouse The plural of the noun *mouse*, in the sense of 'small animal', is *mice*. In computing contexts, where a *mouse* is an electronic device used to move the cursor on the screen, the preferred plural form is *mice*, though the plural form *mouses* is sometimes used.

mousse The noun *mousse* denotes a creamy or foamy preparation. Some types of mousse are for eating: • *chocolate mousse* • *salmon mousse*; some are for cosmetic purposes: • *styling mousse* • *body mousse.* Note the spelling of this word, which should not be confused with the animals *moose* and *mouse.* The pronunciation of this word is [moos].

moustache This word is sometimes misspelt: the most frequent error is the substitution of *u* for the *-ou-* in British English. The British English spelling is *moustache*; the American English spelling *mustache*. Note also the *-che* ending.

movable or **moveable**? This word has two different spellings. Both are acceptable, although the first spelling, *movable* – which omits the *e* before the suffix *-able* – seems to be more frequent in contemporary usage. *See also* **spelling**.

move the goalposts To *move the goalposts* is to change the rules, requirements, etc., usually to the advantage of the person or organisation that sets and changes the rules: • *The Government is moving the goalposts again from April 6, with the cut-off point* [for eligibility for income support] *reduced* to 16 hours a week (*The Guardian*). The verb *move* is sometimes replaced by *shift* or *change*. The expression is best restricted to informal contexts.

mowed or **mown**? Either word may be used as the past participle of the verb *mow*: * Have you mowed/mown the grass yet? When the participle is used as an adjective, *mown* is preferred to *mowed*: * a neatly mown lawn * new-mown hay.

The past tense of the verb *mow* is always *mowed*: * I mowed the grass yesterday.

Mr *see* **Ms, Mrs** or **Miss**?

Ms, Mrs or **Miss**? *Ms*, *Mrs*, and *Miss*, shortened forms of the archaic title *Mistress*, are used before the names of girls and women, according to age and marital status, in letter writing and as polite terms of address. *Miss* is traditionally used for girls, unmarried women, and married women who have retained their maiden name: * Miss Mary Baker * Miss Davies * Miss Elizabeth Taylor. In formal contexts, two or more girls or unmarried women with the same surname should be referred to as the *Misses Brown/Smith/*etc. rather than the *Miss Browns/Smiths/*etc.

Mrs, pronounced [*mi*siz], is used before a woman's married name: * Mrs Anne Johnson * Mrs Johnson.

Ms, pronounced [miz] or [mĭz], is used before the name of a woman of unknown or unspecified marital status. It was introduced as a feminine equivalent of the masculine title *Mr*, which makes no distinction between married and unmarried men. Because of its feminist associations, however, the title *Ms* is disliked by some people.

Ms is most frequently used in place of *Miss*, but is best avoided when referring to elderly unmarried women or young girls (*see also* **sexism**).

The titles *Ms, Mrs*, and *Mr* are usually written without a full stop. *See also* **abbreviations**.

much The use of the adjective *much* in positive sentences is best restricted to formal contexts: * They own much land. * There is much work to be done. Even in formal contexts, some users prefer to replace *much* with *a large amount of, a great deal of*, etc.: * They own a large amount of land. * There is a great deal of work to be done.

In informal contexts, *much* may be replaced with *a lot of* or *lots of*: * There is a lot of work to be done.

In negative and interrogative sentences, *much* is acceptable in all contexts: * They don't own much land. * Is there much work to do? *See also* **lot; many; very**.

mucous or **mucus**? These two words are sometimes confused. *Mucous* is the adjective from the noun *mucus*; *mucus* is the secretion produced by *mucous membranes*.

muesli The noun *muesli*, denoting a type of breakfast food, causes problems of spelling and pronunciation. Note the -*ue*- in the first syllable, and the -*li* ending. The usual pronunciation is [*mew*zli], with the first syllable pronounced as in *music*, but the pronunciation [*moo*zli] is also acceptable.

Muhammad *see* **Muslim** or **Moslem**?

multi- Some people object to the increasing use of the prefix *multi-*, meaning 'many', to coin new words that are often better expressed by a paraphrase: * *a multirole device* * *a multistage process* * *her outstanding multi-tasking abilities* ('her abilities to perform many tasks at the same time'). * *Specialist skills are now ignored or swamped in the drive for multi-skilling* (*The Guardian*). In neologisms of this kind a hyphen is sometimes inserted between the prefix and the word to which it is attached.

muscle or **mussel**? *Muscle* means 'fibrous tissue' or 'strength': * *His muscles bulged as he took the strain.* * *The new squad has plenty of muscle.* It should not be confused with *mussel*, which refers to a bivalve mollusc: * *The stone was covered by mussels.*

Muslim or **Moslem**? Nowadays the preferred spelling for a follower of the Islamic faith is *Muslim*, rather than the older spelling *Moslem*. *Muslim* is pronounced with the vowel sound as in *put* [*muuz*lim] or as in *cup* [*muz*lim].

The most accepted spelling of the name of the prophet of Islam is *Muhammad*, rather than *Mohammed* or *Mahomet*.

mussel *see* **muscle** or **mussel**?

must The auxiliary verb *must* expresses obligation, compulsion, necessity, resolution, certainty, etc.: * *We must obey the rules.* * *They must go.* * *I must finish writing this letter.* * *You must be very thirsty.* In other tenses, and in the negative, *must* is usually replaced by *have to*: * *We had to obey the rules.* * *They don't have to go.* The negative form *must not* (or *mustn't*) expresses prohibition: * *They must not go.*

The past tense *must have* is used only to express certainty: * *You must have been very thirsty.*

The use of *must* as a noun, meaning 'something necessary or essential', is best restricted to informal contexts: * *Waterproof clothing is an absolute must for a sailing holiday.*

mute *see* **deaf-mute**; **dumb** or **mute**?

mutual, **common** or **reciprocal**? A *mutual* action or emotion is done or felt by each of two or more people to or for the other(s): * *mutual help/ destruction/admiration/hatred*/etc. * *The feeling is mutual.* The adjective *mutual* is superfluous in such phrases as: * *a mutual agreement* * *a mutual exchange* * *their mutual love for each other.*

The frequent use of *mutual* in place of *common*, meaning 'shared' or 'joint', is disliked by many users: * *a mutual friend* * *mutual interests* * *a mutual problem.* However, the other senses of *common* can cause ambiguity: * *a common friend* may mean 'an unsophisticated, rude friend' as well as 'a friend shared by two people'. Thus expressions such as * *our joint friend* * *the friend we have in common* * *the friend we share* could be used instead.

Reciprocal and *mutual* are synonymous in the principal sense of the latter: * *reciprocal help* * *reciprocal hatred.* *Reciprocal* can also be used to describe an action or emotion that is done or felt in return: * *He praised her new novel, and she expressed reciprocal admiration for his latest film.*

my or **me**? *see* **-ing forms.**

myself The use of the pronoun *myself* for emphasis is acceptable to most

users but disliked by some: * *I disap-*
prove of such behaviour myself. * *I*
myself have never met her. Myself
should not be used in place of *I* or *me*
in the following sentences and similar
constructions: * *My sister and I* [not
myself] *will do the gardening.* * *The*
bill was paid by Richard and me [not
myself]. *See also* **I** or **me**?; **self**.

mythical or **mythological**? *Mythical*
means 'imaginary'; *mythological*
means 'of mythology': * *a mythical*
danger * *a mythological kingdom.* Both
adjectives also mean 'of a myth or
myths', in which sense they are virtually interchangeable: * *a mythical/*
mythological character.

N

naive, naïve or **naïf?** This word, meaning 'innocent' or 'credulous', is most commonly spelt *naive* or *naïve*. The French masculine adjective *naïf* is no longer used, *naive* (or *naïve*) being used to describe people of both sexes.

The derived noun is most commonly spelt *naivety* or *naïvety*, although the variants *naiveté* and *naïveté* are also found.

Naive is pronounced [nīeev] or [naheev]. *Naivety* is pronounced [nīeevĕti] or [naheevĕti].

naked or **nude?** A person wearing no clothes at all may be described as *naked* or *nude:* ⁕ *pictures of naked/nude men.* The adjective *naked*, however, has a wider range of usage and application than *nude*, which is largely restricted to artistic or pornographic human nakedness, or to nudism: ⁕ *nude photography* ⁕ *nude bathing* ⁕ *a naked* [not *nude*] *body buried in a shallow grave* ⁕ *naked* [not *nude*] *children playing in the sand.*

Naked is also used as a synonym for 'bare' or 'uncovered' in other contexts: ⁕ *a naked room* ⁕ *naked flame.*

name In British English the verb *name*, in the sense of 'name a person or a thing', is followed by the preposition *after:* ⁕ *He was named after his grandfather.* In American English it is followed by *for:* ⁕ *The airport is named for John F. Kennedy.*

naphtha This word, meaning 'petroleum', is sometimes misspelt. Note the consonant sequence *-phth-;* note also the spellings of the compounds *naphthalene* and *naphthene.*

nation *see* **country** or **nation?**

native The word *native*, used in the sense of 'non-white person' (originally applied to the indigenous inhabitants of lands colonised by the West), is derogatory and offensive: ⁕ *The settlers intermarried with the natives.* The noun and adjective *native* may be applied to people or animals born in a specified place: ⁕ *native Spaniards.* As a noun, *native* is followed by the preposition *of:* ⁕ *She's a native of Sweden.* As an adjective, it is followed by *to:* ⁕ *The bird is native to Australia.* This usage is generally acceptable, but some people prefer to avoid the word *native* where there is a danger of confusion with the derogatory sense: ⁕ *the indigenous inhabitants* [not *natives*] *of Tasmania.*

Native American *Native American* is the preferred modern term for a person descended from one of the indigenous peoples of the Americas: ⁕ *The rights of Native Americans must be defended.* It replaces such former terms as *Red Indian* and *American Indian*, which are no longer considered acceptable. Some Native Americans prefer such terms as *First Nations* or *Original Americans*, but these are uncommonly heard outside the Native American community itself. Note that the term is often also rendered as *native American.*

naturalist or **naturist**? A *naturalist* is a person who studies animals and plants, or an advocate of *naturalism* (in art, literature, philosophy, etc.); a *naturist* is a *nudist*: * *Naturalists will appreciate the flora and fauna of the island; naturists can take advantage of its secluded beaches.*

nature Such phrases as *of this/that nature* and *in the nature of* are often better replaced by more concise or less vague expressions: * *Crimes like that* [for *of that nature*] *should be severely punished.* * *This new method of assessment is like* [for *in the nature of*] *an examination.* The word *nature* is used in other unnecessary circumlocutions: * *a problem of a difficult nature* is *a difficult problem* * *a remark of a flippant nature* is *a flippant remark.*

naturist *see* **naturalist** or **naturist**?

naught or **nought**? These two words are sometimes confused. *Naught* means 'nothing' and is used in idiomatic expressions such as *set at naught* ('consider unimportant') and *come to naught* ('produce no successful results'): * *All our plans came to naught.* In British English *nought* is used to represent the figure *0* (*see also* **zero**): * *The number 100 has two noughts.* * *play the game of noughts and crosses.* In American English, however, *naught* is used for the mathematical sense.

nauseous The use of the adjective *nauseous* in the sense of 'nauseated' or 'suffering from nausea' is acceptable in American English but best avoided in British English: * *I feel sick* [not *nauseous*]. The principal meaning of *nauseous* in British English is 'nauseating' or 'causing nausea': * *a nauseous smell.*

naval or **navel**? These two words are sometimes confused. *Naval* is used to describe something connected with the navy: * *a naval officer* * *naval warfare*. The *navel* is the small depression in the middle of the abdomen where the umbilical cord was formerly attached, and the word is also used in the phrase *navel orange*.

near or **nearly**? In the sense of 'almost', the adverb *near* is sometimes interchangeable with *nearly*: * *I nearly* [or *near*] *forgot.* * *It's near* [or *nearly*] *impossible.* This use of *near* may be considered informal or archaic, and *nearly* is a safer choice in most contexts. Used in combination with an adjective, and especially one that is placed before the noun, *near* may be preferred to *nearly* and is usually attached with a hyphen: * *a near-perfect copy* * *a near-successful attempt.*

nearby or **near by**? There is often confusion as to whether this term should be one word or two. *Nearby* is the preferred form for both adjectival and adverbial senses: * *Wolverhampton, Dudley, and other nearby towns. Near by* may still be used in the adverbial sense: * *a town near by* * *He lives near by.*

nearly *see* **near** or **nearly**?

near miss *see* **air miss** or **near miss**?

necessarily There are two possible pronunciations for this word. In the traditional pronunciation, the first syllable is stressed [*nesĕsĕrĭli*], but this is very difficult to say unless the speaker is speaking slowly and carefully. Many users dislike the alternative pronunciation, which has the main stress on the third syllable [nesĕserrĭli].

necessary This word, meaning 'essential', is often misspelt. Note the single *c* and the *-ss-*.

née *Née*, the feminine form of the French word for 'born', is used to indicate the maiden name of a married woman: * *Mrs Susan Davies, née Eliot.* The pronunciation of *née*, which is sometimes written without an accent, is [nay].

Née should not be used to indicate a man's original name or pseudonym, nor a remarried woman's previous married name: * *Ringo Starr, born* [not *née*] *Richard Starkey* * *Jacqueline Onassis, formerly* [not *née*] *Jacqueline Kennedy.*

need *Need* may be used as a full verb, in the sense of 'require' or 'be obliged', or as an auxiliary or modal verb, indicating necessity or obligation: * *We need help.* * *Your daughter needs to wear glasses.* * *He need not leave.* * *Need she reply?* The use of *need* as an auxiliary verb is indicated by the absence of *-s* in the third person singular and the omission of *to* in the following infinitive.

The auxiliary verb *need* is used only in questions and negative sentences (*see* the last two examples above), and in certain constructions that have negative force, such as: * *All she need buy is food.* * *He need do no more than wait.* * *You need only ask.* * *Nobody need suffer.*

The full verb *need* may also be used in questions and negative sentences: * *He doesn't need to leave.* * *Does she need to reply?*

In the sense of 'require', *need* is followed by the *-ing* form of the verb, or by a past participle preceded by *to be*, not by the past participle alone: * *This shirt needs washing* [not *washed*]. * *This shirt needs to be washed.*

needless to say The idiomatic expression *needless to say* is frequently used for emphasis, especially in informal contexts: * *Needless to say, the unions intend to campaign against the proposed legislation.* The expression is disliked by those who choose to interpret it literally, but is acceptable to most people.

negative A negative word is one that is used to deny or contradict something. Words such as *no, not, nobody, never,* and *nothing* make the clause in which they appear a negative one. Care must be taken as to where a negative word is placed in a sentence; usually the negative word is placed with the clause whose truth is being denied: * *He said he had never been there.* * *He never said he had been there.* The exception is with verbs such as *believe, think, except, imagine,* etc., where the negative word is generally placed before the verb: * *I don't think you know what you're talking about* [rather than *I think you don't know...*]. * *She didn't expect them to return before dark* [rather than *She expected them not to return...*].

The adjective *negative* is often used in a very general way to mean not only 'lacking in positive features', but also 'pessimistic; unenthusiastic': * *You're taking a rather negative view.* * *I felt very negative about all his suggestions. See also* **double negative**.

neglectful, negligent or **negligible**? Both *neglectful* and *negligent* mean 'careless' or 'heedless'; *negligible* means 'very small', 'trivial', or 'insignificant': * *a neglectful mother* * *a negligent driver* * *negligible effect.* The adjectives *neglectful* and *negligent* are not completely synonymous: *negligent* often implies habitual or more serious neglect or negligence, which may be punishable by law.

Note the spelling of *negligible*, especially the two *i*'s.

negligible *see* **neglectful, negligent** or **negligible?**

negotiate The usual pronunciation of this verb is [nigōshiayt]. Some people dislike the variant pronunciation [nigōsiayt], in which the *sh* sound is replaced by *s*.

Negress, Negro *see* **black.**

neither As an adjective or pronoun, *neither* is used with a singular verb: * *Neither towel is clean.* * *Neither of the towels is* [not *are*] *clean.* In the *neither... nor* construction, a singular verb is used if both subjects are singular; a plural verb is used if both subjects are plural: * *Neither his brother nor his sister has* [not *have*] *been invited.* * *Neither his parents nor his friends have been invited.*

Careful users avoid the use of a plural verb with the pronoun *neither*, or with singular subjects in a *neither... nor* construction – especially in formal contexts. Nevertheless it occurs with some frequency: * *Neither the ship nor its cargo were able to be salvaged.*

When a combination of singular and plural subjects occurs in a *neither... nor* construction, the verb traditionally agrees with the subject that is nearest to it: * *Neither his brother nor his parents have been invited.* * *Neither his friends nor his sister has been invited.* The same principle is applied to singular subjects that are used with different forms of the verb: * *Neither you nor he has* [not *have*]

been invited. * *Neither my husband nor I have* [not *has*] *been invited.* If the resulting sentence sounds awkward or unidiomatic, it may be reordered or rephrased.

The alternatives presented in a *neither... nor* construction should be grammatically balanced: * *She travelled neither by boat nor train* may be changed to: * *She travelled neither by boat nor by train* or: * *She travelled by neither boat nor train.*

As a pronoun, *neither* should be used only of two alternatives: * *There are two cars outside, but neither is mine.* * *None* [not *Neither*] *of the three candidates arrived on time.* However, the use of the *neither... nor* construction with three or more subjects is acceptable to some people: * *They eat neither meat nor fish nor eggs.*

The first syllable of *neither* may be pronounced to rhyme with *try* or *tree*. The pronunciation [nīdhĕr] is more frequent in British English. *See also* **double negative; either; none; nor.**

nephew There are two acceptable pronunciations for this word: [nevew] and [nefew]. Some people prefer the first. In American English [nefew] is standard.

nerve-racking *see* **rack** or **wrack?**

net *see* **Internet; netspeak.**

net or **nett?** The word *net*, referring to what remains after the deduction of tax, expenses, loss, packaging, etc., is sometimes spelt *nett*: * *net* [or *nett*] *income* * *net* [or *nett*] *profit* * *net* [or *nett*] *weight* * *500 kg net* [or *nett*] * *to net* [or *nett*] *£2000 a month.* Both spellings are acceptable in British English, but *net* is the more common.

netspeak The advent of the computer age, and the development of the worldwide network of computers known as the **World Wide Web** (or Web) or the **Internet** (or *net*), has inspired a substantial body of new coinages and linguistic conventions. This is sometimes treated as a separate language in its own right and identified as *netspeak*. Usages include *netizens*, *netiquette* (the conventions of *netspeak*), *Netlish* or *Weblish* (*netspeak* as a version of English), *netwallah* (a net administrator), and such technical terms as *byte*, *cookie*, *crash*, *domain name*, *firewall*, *hit*, *offline*, *search engine*, *server*, and *URL*. The temptation to relax the rules of grammar – for instance by running sentences together without a full stop and ignoring upper-case/lower-case distinctions (even rendering the personal pronoun *I* as *i*) – may offend many users. Some *netspeak* terms and acronyms have already been absorbed into mainstream English: examples include *404* (meaning 'clueless', from an error message numbered 404) and *FAQ* (abbreviation for 'frequently asked question'). *See also* **acronyms; chat; email; Internet; smiley; text messaging.**

network The word *network* is used as a verb in telecommunications, computing, and the media; it is also increasingly used in general contexts to mean 'communicate or make contact with other people in a similar situation': ● *to network with clients* ● *Women also often mentioned the help, advice and support they had received from networking with other women* (*The Bookseller*). ● *Those four people... network extensively and draw on specialist help as appropriate* (*Alpha*). ●

Networking... is one of the current buzz-words of the enterprise industry (*The Guardian*). In computing, *networking* is the connecting of computers located in different places as a means of transferring and sharing information. *Social networking* refers to social interaction through web-based online communities aimed at people who share similar interests or activities.

neuron or **neurone**? The conventional spelling of this word, referring to a nerve cell, in scientific contexts is *neuron*. In more general non-technical contexts, however, *neurone* is the usual spelling.

neutral For male, female, and neutral (gender-inclusive) terms for people, *see* table at **non-sexist terms.**

never Careful users avoid the use of *never saw/took/went/*etc. in place of *did not see/take/go/*etc. – usually for emphasis – in all but a few informal spoken contexts: ● *I never said a word! Never* means 'at no time' and should not be used when referring to a single occasion: ● *I never met his wife.* ● *I did not meet his wife in town yesterday.* The word is sometimes used informally as a substitute for a simple negative when expressing surprise: ● *He never expected that to happen.* ● *We never thought it would work.* ● *I never knew you could play the guitar.*

nevertheless *see* **none the less** or **nevertheless**?

next or **this**? The adjective *this* is often used in place of *next* with reference to days of the current week, months of the current year, etc.: ● *I'm not going* to the club this Friday. ● She's getting married this September. As a result, the use of *next* in similar contexts may lead to ambiguity or confusion: the phrase *next Friday*, used on a Tuesday, for example, may mean 'three days hence' or 'ten days hence'. *See also* **last**.

nice The adjective *nice*, in the sense of 'pleasant', 'agreeable', 'kind', 'attractive', etc., is often better replaced by an appropriate synonym, especially in formal contexts: ● *an attractive* [not *nice*] *garden* ● *a pleasant* [not *nice*] *afternoon*. In the sense of 'subtle' or 'precise', *nice* is acceptable in all contexts: ● *a nice distinction*.

Nice is ultimately derived from the Latin adjective *nescius*, meaning 'ignorant'; it was originally used in the now obsolete sense of 'foolish'.

niceness or **nicety**? Both these nouns are derived from *nice*. *Niceness* is used in the general senses of 'pleasantness', 'kindness', etc.; *nicety* is restricted to the sense of 'subtlety; precision' and specifically refers to refined details: ● *the niceness of the weather/his sister* ● *a nicety of grammar* ● *the niceties of etiquette*.

niche This word may be pronounced to rhyme with *pitch* or *leash*. The second of these pronunciations is closer to the French origin, and is more frequent than the anglicised [*nich*]. The word *niche* is increasingly used with reference to a gap in the market, especially a gap that can be profitably filled: ● *niche marketing* ● *Niche retailers like Sock Shop, Tie Rack and Knobs & Knockers have shown that they struggle when times get hard* (*The Guardian*).

night *see* **knight** or **night**?

nil *see* **zero**.

nimby *Nimby*, an acronym of 'not in my back yard', is used with reference to a person or people who object to proposed new developments, such as roads or power stations, in the vicinity of their houses: ● *the Nimby syndrome* ● *If he has changed his mind, and is now a true non-Nimby, he should withdraw his objection to having homes at the bottom of his garden* (*The Guardian*). The noun *nimbyism* has been coined to denote this selfish opposition (the protesters usually have no objection to the development being sited elsewhere): ● *Their deep dislike of the kind of gung-ho development and growth-at-all-costs going on in their communities... is not crude Nimbyism, as Nicholas Ridley would have us believe* (*Daily Telegraph*).

no *see* **no on**e or **no-one**?; **yes** and **no**.

nobody *see* **no one** or **no-one**?

no-brainer This is a slang term for a question or problem whose solution requires little or no intelligence: ● *The first question was a real no-brainer*. As a relatively recent vogue term, it is best restricted to very informal contexts.

noisome The adjective *noisome* means 'offensive' or 'noxious' and is used in formal contexts; it has no connection, etymological or otherwise, with the noun *noise*: ● *a noisome smell*.

non- The prefix *non-* is used to form a simple or neutral antonym of the word to which it is attached: ● *a non-professional golfer* ● *non-Christian religions*.

The prefix *un-*, attached to the same words, may have stronger negative force: *an unprofessional* or *un-Christian act*, for example, violates professional ethics or Christian principles.

Many people object to the frequent use of the prefix *non-* to coin unnecessary antonyms: * *non-presence* (for *absence*) * *non-permanent* (for *temporary*) * *non-success* (for *failure*) * *non-obligatory* (for *optional*). Note that, though in fairly wide use, the term *non-white* to describe a person who does not belong to the white racial grouping may be considered offensive by some people because of its assumption that white is the standard skin colour. A more politically correct alternative is *person of colour*. *See also* **hyphen; inflammable**.

none The use of a singular or plural verb with the pronoun *none* depends on the sense and context in which it is used: * *None of the milk was spilt.* * *None of my friends has/have seen the film.* In the first of these examples, *none*, like milk, must be used with a singular verb. In examples of the second type, some people prefer a singular verb in formal contexts, especially if *none* is used in the sense of 'not one'. In informal contexts, or in the sense of 'not any', a plural verb is more common. *See also* **singular** or **plural?**

none the less or **nevertheless?** These two synonyms are sometimes confused. Traditionally, *none the less* has been written as three separate words, although *nonetheless* is gradually being accepted. *Nevertheless* is always written as one word. In American English both words are written as single words.

non-flammable *see* **inflammable**.

non sequitur The Latin expression *non sequitur* is used in formal contexts to refer to a statement that does not follow logically from what has just been said. An example of a *non sequitur* is: * *If all males are mortals then all mortals are males.* The literal meaning of *non sequitur* is 'it does not follow'.

NON-SEXIST TERMS – *see* table on pages 285–6.

no one or **no-one?** Many users prefer the two-word compound *no one* to the hyphenated form *no-one*. Unlike *anyone*, *everyone*, and *someone*, *no one* should not be written as a one-word compound. The pronoun *no one* and its synonym *nobody* are interchangeable in all contexts; both are used with a singular verb but are sometimes followed by a plural personal pronoun or possessive adjective (*see* **they**): * *No one/Nobody likes to see their children suffer.*

nor *Nor* is used in place of *or* in the *neither... nor* construction (*see* **neither**); it is also used to introduce a negative alternative that stands as a separate clause: * *I speak neither German nor Spanish.* * *She hasn't been to America, nor has her sister.* * *He never watches television, nor does he listen to the radio.* In many other contexts *nor* and *or* are interchangeable: * *The library is not open on Thursday mornings, nor/or at the weekend.* * *We have no food to eat nor/or clothes to wear.*

Many users prefer *or* to *nor* where the negative force of an auxiliary verb covers both alternatives: * *They cannot sing or dance.* * *She has not eaten her biscuits or drunk her tea.*

NON-SEXIST TERMS

The following table lists words showing male, female, and neutral (gender-inclusive) terms. Cross-references – e.g. *see* **mankind** – are also included to main entries in the *Good Word Guide* where there is a fuller discussion.

Male	Female	Neutral (gender-inclusive)
actor	actress	actor
airman	airwoman	pilot
author	authoress	author or writer (*see also* -**ess**)
barman	barmaid	bartender
businessman	businesswoman	(business) executive
cameraman	camerawoman	camera operator or photographer
chairman	chairwoman	chairperson or chair (*see* **chair**)
clergyman	clergywoman	member of the clergy
comedian	comedienne	comedian or comic or comic actor or comic entertainer
congressman	congresswoman	member of congress
countryman	countrywoman	native/inhabitant of ... or compatriot
craftsman	craftswoman	craftsperson or craftworker
draughtsman	draughtswoman	draughter or draughtsperson
dustman	dustwoman	refuse collector or refuse operative or cleansing operative
fireman	firewoman	firefighter
forefather	foremother	ancestor or forebear or forerunner
foreman	forewoman	supervisor
headmaster	headmistress	headteacher or head
hero	heroine	hero
host	hostess	host or (tour) guide
kinsman	kinswoman	relative or relation
layman	laywoman	lay person or member of the laity
man (noun)	woman	person or individual or human being (*see* **man**)
man (verb)		operate or staff or run or work or equipment
manager	manageress	manager
man-hours		working hours or work hours
mankind	womankind	the human race or human beings (*see* **mankind**)

Male	Female	Neutral (gender-inclusive)
man-made		synthetic or artificial or manufactured
manpower		workforce or personnel or staff
milkman	milkwoman	milk roundsperson or dairy salesperson
poet	poetess	poet (see also -ess)
policeman	policewoman	police officer
postman	postwoman	delivery officer
salesman	saleswoman or sales girl	salesperson or sales executive or (sales) representative or sales assistant or shop assistant or sales clerk (American)
sculptor	sculptress	sculptor
serviceman	servicewoman	member of the armed forces
spokesman	spokeswoman	spokesperson or representative or official
sportsman	sportswoman	sportsperson
statesman	stateswoman	statesperson or leader or public figure
steward	stewardess (air hostess)	flight/cabin attendant
usher	usherette	usher
waiter	waitress	waiter or server
weatherman	weathergirl	meteorologist or weather forecaster
workman	workwoman	worker or artisan

The use of *nor* at the beginning of a sentence is generally acceptable: * *Nature is slow to compensate for deforestation. Nor has man been able to make good the damage* (*Daily Telegraph*).

normalcy or **normality**? These two nouns are synonymous derivatives of the adjective *normal*. *Normality* is the preferred form in British English; *normalcy* is chiefly used in American English.

north, North or **northern**? As an adjective, *north* is always written with a capital *N* when it forms part of a proper name: * *North America* * *the*

North Sea. The noun *north* is usually written with a capital *N* when it denotes a specific region, such as the northern part of England: * *House prices are lower in the North.* In other contexts, and as an adverb, *north* is usually written with a lower-case *n*: * *We travelled north for ten days.* * *They live in north London.* * *The wind is blowing from the north.* The adjective *northern* is more frequent and usually less specific than the adjective *north*: * *the northern part of the country* * *in northern France.*

Like *north*, *northern* is written with a capital *N* when it forms part of a proper name, such as *Northern Ireland*. With or without a capital *N*, it also means 'of the North': • *a northern/ Northern accent.*

northward or **northwards**? *Northward* is the correct choice when an adjective is needed: • *a northward direction.* Either *northward* or *northwards* may be used when an adverb is required: • *They travelled northward from the city.* • *The skies were full of birds flying northwards.* See also **-ward** or **-wards**?

no sooner *see* **hardly**.

nostalgia The noun *nostalgia* and its derivatives are most frequently used with reference to a wistful or sentimental yearning for the past: • *She remembered the seaside holidays of her childhood with a deep nostalgia.* • *Listening to old records always makes me nostalgic.* The original meaning of 'homesickness' is now rather dated. The use of the adjective *nostalgic* in the sense of 'causing nostalgia', rather than 'feeling nostalgia', is disliked and avoided by some users: • *the nostalgic sound of the church bells.*

not The position of the word *not* in a negative sentence may affect its meaning and can sometimes lead to ambiguity: • *All children are not afraid of the dark.* • *We did not go because it was raining.* • *He is not trying to win.* • *He is trying not to win.* The first of these examples, which literally means 'No children are afraid of the dark', is easily reworded: • *Not all children are afraid of the dark.* The second example may be reordered or expanded for clarity: • *Because it was raining we did not go.* • *We did not go because it was raining, we went because we were bored.* The frequent use over

recent years of *not* as a one-word contradiction of what has just been said is disliked by many people and should be restricted to very informal contexts: • *That's a really cool hat you're wearing – not!* See also **knot** or **not**?; **not only... but also**.

notable, noted or **noteworthy**? *Noted* means 'famous': • *a noted scientist* • *The area is noted for its spectacular scenery.* *Notable* and *noteworthy* both mean 'worthy of notice or of being noted': • *a notable* [or *noteworthy*] *achievement,* but *noteworthy* is usually used to describe facts or events rather than people: • *It was noteworthy that the average price remained the same despite the effects of inflation.* A person or thing that is *notable* or *noteworthy* deserves notice, admiration or renown; a person or thing that is *noted* has already received notice, admiration, or renown.

notable or **noticeable**? The adjective *notable* means 'remarkable' or 'worthy of note'; *noticeable* means 'perceptible' or 'obvious': • *a notable achievement* • *a noticeable change in temperature.* The two words should not be confused. The final *e* of the verb *notice* is retained in *noticeable*, whereas the final *e* of *note* is omitted in *notable*.

noted, noteworthy *see* **notable, noted** or **noteworthy**?

nothing but The phrase *nothing but...* is used with a singular verb, even if the noun that follows *but* is plural: • *Nothing but crumbs was* [not *were*] *left on the plate.* When *nothing but* is followed by an infinitive, the word *to* is omitted: • *They have done nothing but cry since you left.*

The same rules apply to the synonymous phrase *nothing except*: * *Nothing except his shoes was found.*

noticeable *see* **notable** or **noticeable**?

not only... but also The words or clauses that follow *not only* and *but also* must be grammatically balanced: * *I have lost not only my purse but also my car keys* [not *I have not only lost...*]. * *They not only broke the world record for long-distance swimming but also raised several thousand pounds for charity* [not *They broke not only...*]. In many contexts the word *also* can be omitted: * *He not only wrote to the headmaster but (also) consulted his solicitor.*

notorious *see* **infamous** or **notorious**?

nought *see* **naught** or **nought**?

nouns *Nouns* are the names of things, places, or people. The main division of nouns is into 'countable' and 'uncountable': countable nouns are those which can be preceded by *a* or *the*, or by a number or word denoting number: * *a goat* * *three lemons* * *the priest* * *several books.* Uncountable nouns are nouns of mass: * *flour* * *water.* Some words can be countable or uncountable, according to how they are used: * *Have a beer.* * *Beer is fattening.* Proper nouns refer to a single particular person or thing and begin with a capital letter: * *Trevor Jones.* Exceptionally, proper nouns can be made plural: * *the Americas* * *There are two Susans on the staff.*

Nouns can often be used as adjectives, when they sometimes form one word with another noun, or are hyphenated, or remain as two words: * *postbox* * *tea-tray* * *Christmas cake.* They are more likely to be hyphenated when the two nouns are used together adjectivally before a third noun: * *Christmas-cake decorations* * *a bathroom-fittings shop.*

The use of nouns as verbs has a long history. We use the verb to question without thinking that it was originally a noun. Such phrases as: * *to paper a room* * *to tin fruit* * *to pencil it in* are also so frequently used as to be wholly acceptable. However, many people dislike more modern innovations, such as: * *Let me example that for you.* * *They text each other every month.* * *He rubbished their policies.* * *to modern.* See also **hyphen**; **verbs**.

noxious or **obnoxious**? Both these adjectives can mean 'extremely unpleasant', but *obnoxious* usually refers to a person and *noxious* to something that is physically or morally harmful: * *their obnoxious children* * *noxious fumes.* Both words are ultimately derived from the Latin *noxa*, meaning 'injury'.

nubile The adjective *nubile*, derived from the Latin word for 'marriageable', is frequently applied to any sexually attractive young woman, especially in jocular or informal contexts: * *His friend's nubile sister was sunbathing in the garden.* Some people object to this usage, restricting the term to its original meaning. The use of the adjective *nubile* to describe attractive married women or unattractive unmarried women is therefore best avoided.

nuclear Most people dislike and avoid the occasional use of *nuclear* as a noun, meaning 'nuclear power': * *a* *national debate about nuclear.* This usage is also potentially confusing, as the word *nuclear* may also refer to *nuclear warfare, nuclear missiles, nuclear fission, nuclear energy,* etc. The term *nuclear winter* refers to a period with very little light, heat, or growth that would follow a nuclear war.

In the phrase *nuclear family* the adjective *nuclear* simply means 'forming a nucleus'.

The phrase *go nuclear,* in the sense 'be very annoyed', should not be used in formal contexts.

Nuclear is pronounced [*ny*ookleeă] in British English and [*nook*leeă] in American English. It is sometimes mispronounced as if the word ended in *-cular,* especially in American English.

nude *see* **naked** or **nude**?

number The phrase *a number of...* is used with a plural verb; the phrase *the number of...* is used with a singular verb: * *A number of pupils were late.* * *The number of pupils has increased. See also* **amount** or **number?**; **singular** or **plural**?

numbers *Numbers* that occur in printed or written texts may be expressed in figures or written out in full, according to the nature of the work, the context, the writer's personal preference, or the publisher's house style. In mathematical, scientific, technical, commercial, or statistical texts, numbers are usually expressed in figures throughout. In the case of decimal numbers, these are usually expressed in figures with a full stop representing the decimal point: * *3.6* * *11.25.*

In other works, specific measurements or sums of money, page numbers, dates, and numbers higher than one hundred (except two hundred, three hundred, four thousand, five million, etc.) are usually expressed in figures.

Some writers and publishers spell out numbers from one to ten only; some spell out numbers from one to twenty; others spell out all numbers up to one hundred. It is important to be reasonably consistent within a single piece of writing, but some users prefer not to mix figures and words in the same sentence: * *There are nine boys and fifteen* [not *15*] *girls in his class.* * *We invited 130 guests but only 80* [not *eighty*] *turned up.*

The time may be expressed in words or figures: * *twenty past three* * *3.20* * *eight o'clock* * *8 o'clock.* Times using the 24-hour clock are written as figures: * *16.25* * *0700 hours.*

Numbers of five or more digits are separated by commas or spaces into groups of three: * *45,069/45069* * *3,728,960/3728960.* Four-digit numbers are usually printed or written without commas or spaces: * *5069* * *8960.*

Some numbers have acquired their own particular semantic value: * *We need to review the 999* [emergency] *services.* * *The shop is open 24/7* [24 hours per day, 7 days per week]. * *new security measures introduced in the wake of 9/11* [the terrorist attacks on the USA on 11 September 2001]. *See also* **a.m.** and **p.m.**; **dates**; **hyphen**; **large numbers**.

nutritional or **nutritious**? *Nutritional* means 'relating to nutrition (the process of taking food into the body and absorbing it)'; *nutritious* means 'nourishing': * *the nutritional requirements of a baby* * *a very nutritious meal.* The adjective *nutritional* is increasingly used with reference to the content of processed and other foods: ● *Nutritional labelling must be made compulsory* (Sunday Times). ● *People should have enough nutritional information to make dietary changes* (Daily Telegraph).

The more formal adjective *nutritive* may be used in place of *nutritional* or *nutritious*, but it more frequently replaces the former: ● *New recommendations have been made by the Ministry of Agriculture, Fisheries and Food for the way in which nutritive values are displayed* (Kellogg's Rice Krispies packet).

nutritive *see* **nutritional** or **nutritious**?

O

O or **oh**? *O*, always written with a capital, is a rarer, more poetic variant of the exclamation *oh*: ● *O come all ye faithful.* ● *O* [or *Oh*] *for the school holidays!* ● *'I can't come and see you later, I'm afraid.' 'Oh well, never mind.'* ● *She burst into tears, crying, 'Oh dear! Oh dear! Oh dear!'* ● *I just thought... oh, never mind.*

OAP *see* **senior citizen**.

oar, or or **ore**? These three words are occasionally confused, as they are pronounced in the same way: [or]. *Oar* refers to a paddle used to propel a rowing boat: ● *The oars dipped in the water.* *Or* is a conjunction linking two or more alternatives: ● *right or wrong.* *Ore* refers to mineral from which metals may be extracted: ● *iron ore.*

obeisance *Obeisance* is a very formal word meaning an attitude or gesture of deference or respect: ● *to pay obeisance* ● *to make an obeisance.* It is not synonymous with *obedience*, although both nouns are derived from Old French *obeir*, 'to obey'. Note the spelling of *obeisance*, particularly the *-ei-* and the *-ance* ending.

object The *object* of a clause or sentence is the noun, pronoun, or phrase that is affected by the verb. The object usually follows the verb. An object may be *direct* or *indirect*. In the sentence: ● *The dog buried the bone*, *the bone* is the direct object and there is no indirect object. In the sentences: ● *I gave the child a book* and ● *She bought the child a book*, a *book* is the direct object and the *child* is the indirect object. Many sentences that contain both a direct and an indirect object can be rephrased using the prepositions *to* or *for*: ● *I gave a book to the child.* ● *She bought a book for the child.* Compare **subject**.

objective or **subjective**? The adjective *objective* means 'not influenced by personal feelings, beliefs, or prejudices'; its antonym *subjective* means 'influenced by personal feelings, etc.': ● *This is a subjective opinion: I find it hard to be objective when we're discussing my own daughter's career.* Some users consider the adjectives to be unnecessary synonyms for *fair*, *impartial*, *personal*, *biased*, etc.

The noun *objective* is best avoided where *goal*, *aim*, *purpose*, *object*, etc. would be adequate or more appropriate: ● *the purpose* [not *objective*] *of this meeting.* ● *Our aim* [not *objective*] *is to provide equal opportunities for all.*

objet d'art The plural of the phrase *objet d'art*, meaning 'small object of artistic worth', is formed by adding *-s* to the first word – *objets d'art*. Of French origin, the phrase is sometimes written or printed in italics in English texts. Note the spelling of *objet*, which lacks the *c* of the English word *object*.

obliged or **obligated**? Both these adjectives may be used in the sense of

291

'morally or legally bound': * *He felt obliged/obligated to report the accident.* The use of *obligated* is largely restricted to formal contexts.

Obliged has the additional meaning of 'physically constrained' or 'compelled': * *They were obliged to remain in their seats.*

oblivious The adjective *oblivious* is often used in the sense of 'unaware' or 'heedless': * *He remained in the shelter of the tree, oblivious of the fact that the rain had stopped.* Some people object to this usage, restricting the adjective to its original sense of 'no longer aware' or 'forgetful': * *Oblivious of the need for caution, she stepped out of the car to photograph the lions.*

The frequent use of the phrase *oblivious to*, rather than *oblivious of*, is unacceptable to some users and is best avoided in formal contexts: * *oblivious of* [not *to]* *the dangers* * *oblivious of* [not *to]* *my presence.*

obnoxious *see* **noxious** or **obnoxious**?

obscene Some people object to the increasing use of *obscene* as a general term of strong disapproval: * *Recent large pay awards to some company directors are obscene, the Bishop of Manchester... has told the General Synod in York* (*Daily Telegraph*). The primary meaning of *obscene* is 'offensive to accepted standards of decency': * *obscene language* * *an obscene picture.*

The word *obscene* is sometimes misspelt: note that the second syllable is identical with the word *scene*.

observance or **observation**? The noun *observance* denotes either the act of

complying or a ritual custom or practice; *observation* denotes either the act of watching or noticing or a remark or comment: * *observance of the rules* * *religious observances* * *their observation of human behaviour* * *an observation made by his client.*

obverse *see* **converse, inverse, obverse** or **reverse**?

obviate To *obviate* something is to make it unnecessary or to dispose of it: * *The management's new proposals obviated our complaints.* The word is largely restricted to formal contexts and should not be used as a pretentious synonym for 'remove' or 'get rid of'. The verb *obviate* is unconnected in meaning to the adjective *obvious*, although the two words are etymologically related.

Some users avoid the construction *obviate the need for*, arguing that *the need for* is redundant: * *A reduction in inflation would obviate* [*the need for]* *higher pay rises.*

occasion The verb *occasion* is best avoided where *cause, bring about*, etc. would be adequate: * *The accident was caused* [not *occasioned]* *by a fault in the braking system.* Note the spelling of the word *occasion*, particularly the *-cc-* and single *s*.

occupied or **preoccupied**? Applied to a person, *occupied* means 'busy'; *preoccupied* means 'absorbed in a particular train of thought (often to the exclusion of all else)': * *I was occupied with the preparations for the carnival.* * *Try to keep everybody occupied.* * *He was preoccupied with his marital problems.* * *She seemed preoccupied.* Being *occupied* may involve the mind and/or the body, whereas being *preoccupied* usually involves the mind alone.

occurrence This word is often misspelt. A frequent error is the substitution of *-ance* for the *-ence* ending. Note also the *-cc-* and *-rr-*, as in *occurred* and *occurring*.

octopus The plural of the noun *octopus*, denoting a sea animal with eight tentacles, is *octopuses*. As the word is ultimately of Greek origin, the plural form *octopi* is incorrect; *octopodes* is permissible but pedantic.

oculist *see* **optician, ophthalmologist, optometrist** or **oculist?**

odious or **odorous?** *Odious* means 'extremely unpleasant'; *odorous*, a very formal word, means 'having a particular smell': * *an odious man* * *an odorous room.* The two adjectives should not be confused. Like the noun *odour*, *odorous* may refer to a pleasant or an unpleasant smell. Note that the *u* of *odour* is dropped before the *-ous* ending of *odorous*.

The word *odious*, not *odorous*, is used in the saying 'Comparisons are odious'.

-oe- *see* **-ae-** and **-oe-.**

oesophagus or **esophagus?** This word, describing the part of the alimentary canal linking the pharynx and the stomach, is spelt differently in British and American English. *Oesophagus* is the usual spelling in British English, while *esophagus* is the accepted spelling in American English.

of The preposition *of* is sometimes wrongly substituted for the verb *have*, or, more frequently, for its contraction *'ve*: * *They should have* [not *of*] *refused.* * *She must've* [not *must of*] *forgotten.* * *He could have* [not *of*] *tried.* This substitution, caused by the similarity in pronunciation between the two words when unstressed, is wrong. The use of such phrases as *of a Friday, of an evening*, etc. in place of *on Fridays, in the evening*, etc. should be restricted to informal contexts: * *I go shopping of a Tuesday afternoon.* See also **off**.

of course The phrase *of course* serves a number of useful purposes, but should not be used to excess. It has a variety of connotations, some of which may cause offence.

Used for emphasis, either alone or to introduce a reply, the phrase may convey impatience or politeness: * *'Did you remember to post my letter?' 'Of course (I did).'* * *'May I use your telephone?' 'Of course (you may).'*

Used in the sense of 'naturally' or 'admittedly', it may be patronising, superior, sympathetic, or apologetic: * *It is of course impossible to communicate with the dead.* * *I knew his uncle, of course. I don't believe you ever met him, did you?* * *Of course you're tired, you've had a long journey.* * *I may be wrong, of course.*

off The use of the preposition *off* in place of *from*, to indicate the source of an acquisition, is considered wrong by many people, even in informal contexts: * *I bought it from* [not *off*] *my sister.* The phrase *off of* is also wrong and should be avoided in all contexts: * *He jumped off* [not *off of*] *the wall.* * *Take your feet off* [not *off of*] *the table.*

The word *off* is usually pronounced

to rhyme with *scoff*; the variant pronunciation [awf] is generally considered to be old-fashioned or affected. *See also* **off-limits**.

offence This word, meaning 'action causing displeasure; illegal act', is sometimes misspelt. Note the *-c-* not *-s-* in British English (American English, *offense*). The derived adjective is spelt *offensive* in both British and American English.

offer or **proffer**? Both verbs mean 'present for acceptance': * *He proffered* [or *offered*] *his passport.* * *She offered* [or *proffered*] *her sympathy. Offer* has a much wider range of usage; *proffer* is largely restricted to formal contexts and should not be used as a pretentious substitute for *offer. Proffer* cannot be used in place of *offer* in more complex constructions: * *He offered* [not *proffered*] *her a glass of champagne.* * *They offered* [not *proffered*] *us £2000 for the car.*

official or **officious**? The adjective *official* means 'authorised', 'formal', or 'of an office'; *officious*, which is generally used in a derogatory manner, means 'interfering', 'bossy', 'self-important', or 'offering unwanted advice or assistance': * *an official strike* * *an official visit* * *an officious clerk.* The two words should not be confused. In the field of diplomacy, the adjective *officious* means 'informal' or 'unofficial': * *an officious agreement.* This sense is not in general usage.

officialese *Officialese* is a derogatory name for the style of writing or language that is considered to be typical of official forms, reports, memoranda, letters, leaflets, and other bureau-cratic documents. Known informally as *gobbledegook, officialese* is characterised by the use of pompous and wordy language, obscure jargon, and long unintelligible sentences. An example quoted by Tom Vernon in *Gobbledegook* is from a Department of Employment form: * *In certain circumstances that condition may be modified to enable those persons who claim benefit early in their insurance life to treat as paid in one tax year all class 1 (standard rate) contributions paid in the period starting with the year in which they first became liable for such contributions, and ending with the day from which benefit is claimed.*

Widely satirised in the media, government departments have tried in recent years – and with some success – to eliminate officialese by simplifying vocabulary and circumlocutory phrases, shortening sentences, and personalising instructions. *See also* **commercialese**; **jargon**; **management-speak**.

officious *see* **official** or **officious**?

often The words *oftener* and *oftenest* are accepted comparative and superlative forms of the adverb *often*, but many users prefer *more often* and *most often*, especially in formal contexts: * *It rains most often in the autumn.* * *Which car do you use oftener?* The *t* of *often* is rarely sounded, the most frequent pronunciation of the word being [ofĕn]. The pronunciation [oftĕn] is heard from time to time, but the variant [awfĕn], which sounds like *orphan*, is generally considered to be old-fashioned or affected.

oh *see* **O** or **oh**?

OK or **okay**? The term *OK* or *okay*, denoting agreement or approval, may be used as an adjective, adverb, noun, or verb: ❋ *That's OK.* ❋ *The meeting went OK.* ❋ *Has she given us the OK/okay?* ❋ *They are unlikely to okay/ OK the suggestion.* As the term is most frequently used in informal speech, the variations in its written form are not of great importance.

In informal writing, the extended form *okay* is generally preferred for the verb, especially if inflectional endings are to be added: ❋ *The project has been okayed by the committee.*

The two-letter form *OK* is now rarely written with full stops in British English: ❋ *It looks O.K. to me.*

old age pensioner *see* **senior citizen** or **old age pensioner**?

older, **oldest** *see* **elder**, **eldest**, **older** or **oldest**?

omelette This word is sometimes misspelt. In British English the spelling is *omelette*; in American English, *omelet*. Note the first *e*. The word is pronounced [*om*lit].

omission This noun, meaning 'the act of omitting' or 'something omitted', is often misspelt. The most frequent error is the substitution of *-mm-* for the single *-m-*. Note also the *-ission* ending (not *-ision* or *-ition*).

on The relatively recent tendency to construct phrases around *on* – such as *one-on-one* (meaning 'individual-to-individual' or 'person-to-person') and *white-on-white* (meaning 'white against white') – is disliked by some users and best restricted to informal contexts: ❋ *The increasing incidence of white-on-white violence is worrying. One-on-one* is an American variant of the phrase *one-to-one*, which is more acceptable in British English: ❋ *It's time we had a proper one-to-one discussion about this. See also* **onto** or **on to**?; **upon** or **on**?

one The pronoun *one*, representing an indefinite person, is usually followed in British English by *one's, oneself,* etc., rather than by *his, himself,* etc.: ❋ *One should be kind to one's friends.* If the resulting sentence sounds clumsy or unidiomatic, it may be paraphrased: ❋ *When one lives on one's own one often talks to oneself,* for example, may be changed to: *People who live on their own often talk to themselves.*

In American English, however, *one* is usually followed in such contexts by *his, himself,* etc.: ❋ *One often talks to himself.* ❋ *One should be kind to his friends.*

When the pronoun *one* represents a specific person, it is always followed by *his, her,* etc.: ❋ *The twins' tastes are not identical: one drinks her* [not *one's*] *coffee black, the other drinks it white.*

In formal contexts the impersonal pronoun *one* is sometimes preferred to *you,* although *you* is becoming increasingly common, even in such formal contexts as reference books. The use of *one* in place of *I* or *we,* however, is widely considered affected and is best avoided, especially in informal contexts: ❋ *I have* [not *One has*] *never been very good at sport.* ❋ *We hope* [not *One hopes*] *that the situation will improve.*

The constructions *one in three/five/ ten/*etc. and *one of the...,* followed by a plural noun, should be used with a singular verb: ❋ *One in four teachers is in favour of corporal punishment.* ❋

One of the eggs is broken. However, a plural verb is often seen or heard after the construction *one in...*: • *One in ten men are thought to have a drink problem* (BBC radio news). The constructions *one of those... who* and *one of the... that* are followed by a plural verb: • *He is one of those people who are never satisfied.* • *It is one of the shortest books that have ever been published.*

In some contexts the word *one* is superfluous: • *His smile was not a friendly one,* for example, may be more concisely expressed as: *His smile was not friendly. See also* **each other** or **one another**?; **singular** or **plural**?; **you**.

ongoing Many people object to the use of the adjective *ongoing* in place of *continuing, developing, in progress,* etc.: • *ongoing research* • *an ongoing investment programme in manufacturing technology.* The cliché *ongoing situation* is also widely disliked. The word *ongoing* sometimes appears in hyphenated form: • *We put you through the world's most advanced management training courses, followed by on-going personal development* (*Executive Post*).

on-line The term *on-line,* which relates to equipment that is directly connected to and/or controlled by a central computer, is sometimes used in the extended sense of 'in direct communication with': • *on-line to the president.* It should not be confused with *on-stream*: • *Rent A Film... will be getting in the party spirit to celebrate a very special service which has just come on line at their plush, newly-refurbished premises* (*Littlehampton Guardian*). The phrase *on-line* often refers specifically to being connected to the internet: • *Is your computer on-line yet?* • *I haven't gone on-line yet today.* When used as an attributive adjective, the phrase is usually spelt as one word: • *Let me tell you about our online services.*

only In some written sentences the adverb *only* must be carefully positioned as near as possible to the word it refers to in order to convey the intended meaning: • *She eats fish only on Fridays* [i.e. not other days]. • *She eats only fish* [i.e. nothing else] *on Fridays.* • *Only she* [i.e. She is the only one who] *eats fish on Fridays.* In speech, where the stress and intonation of the sentence should eliminate any ambiguity, and in written sentences that are not open to misinterpretation, *only* may be placed in its most idiomatic position, i.e. between the subject and the verb or between an auxiliary verb and a main verb: • *He only needs one more to complete the collection.* • *They have only sold three books.*

The use of *only* as a conjunction, in place of *but* or *however,* is best restricted to informal contexts: • *I'd like to go to Canada, only I can't afford the air fare.*

Some people object to the use of the phrase *only too* as an intensifier, reserving it for the sense of 'regrettably': • *I am very* [not *only too*] *pleased to help.* • *The new container, which is supposed to be childproof, is only too easy to open. See also* **not only... but also**.

onomatopoeia *Onomatopoeia* is the formation of words that imitate the sound associated with an object or action: • *cuckoo* • *moo* • *clang* • *croak* • *hiss* • *twitter.* It also refers to the use of words, usually in poetry, in such a way as to suggest the sound described. An example is:

Keeping time, time, time,
In a sort of Runic rhyme,
To the tintinnabulation that so
   musically wells
From the bells, bells, bells, bells.
                (Edgar Allan Poe, *The Bells*)

on-stream The term *on-stream* relates to an industrial process or plant that is in production or about to go into production or operation, or to the launching of a new advertising campaign, etc.: * *The rest of the country should be on-stream by the end of 2015.* It is sometimes possible to replace the phrase *come on-stream* with *open*, *begin*, etc.

The hyphen is often omitted when *on-stream* is employed as an attributive adjective: * *An onstream date of 2020 is proposed.*

onto or **on to**? The preposition *onto* may be written as one or two words: * *She drove onto/on to the pavement. On to* may also be a combination of the adverb *on* and the preposition or infinitive marker *to*, in which case it should not be written as one word: * *She drove on to London.* * *She drove on to find a hotel.*

onward or **onwards**? In British English, *onward* is principally used as an adjective, *onwards* being the usual form of the adverb meaning 'ahead': * *Onward motion* * *to march onwards.* The adverb *onward* is more frequently used in American English. *See also* **-ward** or **-wards**?

operative Many users dislike the frequent use of the noun *operative* in place of worker, especially in non-industrial contexts: * *a strike by cleaning operatives at the hospital.*

ophthalmologist *see* **optician, ophthalmologist, optometrist** or **oculist**?

opposite The noun *opposite* is followed by *of*, not *to*: * *Hot is the opposite of* [not *to*] *cold.* As a preposition, opposite may be followed by *to* (not *of*) but usually stands alone: * *the car park opposite (to) the station.* The adjective *opposite* may be used with *to* or *from*: * *He sat on the opposite side to/from her.*

oppress, repress or **suppress**? These verbs are similar in meaning: all three refer to subjugation or restraint. *Oppress* means 'subjugate by force, cruel treatment, etc.'; the direct object of the verb is usually a group of people: * *a regime that oppresses women* * *the oppressed workers.* The verb *repress* is also used in this sense, but more frequently refers to the act of concealing or controlling feelings: * *I repressed the urge to hit him.* * *a repressed desire.* In psychology, *repress* means 'banish or exclude (thoughts, feelings, etc.) from the conscious mind or awareness' – an act that may lead to psychological problems: * *repressed sexuality.* The verb *suppress* has the more general meaning of 'restrain' or 'control': * *She couldn't suppress her laughter. Suppress* also means 'withhold' or 'crush': * *to suppress information* * *to suppress a rebellion.* Note the differences in spelling, particularly the *-pp-* of *oppress* and *suppress* and the *-p-* of *repress*.

optician, ophthalmologist, optometrist or **oculist**? All four nouns denote people who are concerned with defects or diseases of the eyes. The word *optician*, probably the most familiar, may denote an *ophthalmic optician* or a *dispensing optician*.

An *ophthalmic optician* is qualified to test eyesight and prescribe corrective lenses. A *dispensing optician* makes and sells glasses (and other optical equipment).

An *ophthalmologist* is a doctor who specialises in eye diseases. *Optometrist* is a less common name for an *ophthalmic optician*; *oculist* is synonymous with *ophthalmologist*.

The word *ophthalmologist* is sometimes misspelt, the most frequent error being the omission of the first *h*. It is usually pronounced [ofthal-mólójist]; many users dislike the pronunciation of the first syllable to rhyme with *hop*, rather than *scoff*.

optimal *see* **optimum**.

optimistic Many people object to the frequent use of the adjective *optimistic* as a synonym for 'hopeful', 'confident', 'cheerful', 'favourable', 'encouraging', etc.: ● *She is optimistic that the car will be found.* ● *They have produced an optimistic report on the company's prospects.* In general usage, *optimistic* principally relates to a tendency to see or expect the best, or to take a favourable view of things: ● *Throughout his illness he remained optimistic.*

optimise *see* **optimum**.

optimum The adjective and noun *optimum* refer to the most favourable or advantageous condition, amount, degree, etc.: ● *the optimum speed* ● *A temperature of 158°C is the optimum.* The noun *optimum* has two plural forms, usually encountered in technical contexts: *optimums* and *optima*.

Many people dislike the frequent use of the adjective *optimum* and its synonym *optimal* in the sense of 'best': ● *a manufacturing programme designed to make optimum use of all available resources* (*Executive Post*). ● *A combination of olive oil and butter will produce the optimal result.*

The verb optimise means 'make the most of' or 'make as efficient as possible': ● *to optimise the potential of the business* ● *to optimise the production process.*

opt in *see* **opt out**.

optometrist *see* **optician, ophthalmologist, optometrist** or **oculist**?

opt out *Opt out* means 'choose not to participate or be involved', with the implication that a person or organisation that does not opt out is automatically included: ● *to opt out of society* ● *schools that have opted out* (*of local government control*). In the opposite situation, where people or organisations are automatically excluded unless they choose to participate, the verb *opt in* may be used: ● *A survey into public attitudes to kidney donation found that most people are willing to donate their kidneys but they are against a scheme to 'opt out' of donorship rather than the present scheme of 'opting in'* (*New Scientist*).

opus The formal noun *opus*, denoting a musical work or other artistic composition, may be pronounced [ópŭs], with the long *o* of *open*, or [opŭs], with the short *o* of *operate*. Both pronunciations are acceptable, but the first is more common. *Opus* also has two plural forms, *opuses* and *opera*. As the word *opera* exists as a singular noun in its own right, some users prefer *opuses*: the phrase *Mozart's opera*, for example, may refer to a single operatic composition or to all of Mozart's musical works.

or When *or* connects two or more singular subjects, a singular verb is used: * *Perhaps Peter or Jane knows* [not *know*] the answer. A plural verb is used if both subjects are plural: * *Carrots or parsnips are served with this dish.* In a combination of singular and plural alternatives, the verb traditionally agrees with the subject that is nearest to it: * *One large pot or two small ones are needed.* * *Two small pots or one large one is needed.* The same principle is applied to singular subjects that are used with different forms of the verb: * *Are you or your wife going to the concert?* If the resulting sentence sounds inelegant or unidiomatic, a second verb may be added: * *Am I the winner or is he?*

The use of *or* at the beginning of a sentence is generally acceptable: * *We may go to London tomorrow. Or we may stay at home.*

For the use of a comma before *or* in a series of three or more items, *see* **comma**. *Or* may also be preceded by a comma in other contexts, especially if it introduces a synonym rather than an alternative: * *the policy of glasnost, or openness. See also* **and/or**; **either**; **nor**; **oar, or** or **ore?**

oral *see* **aural** or **oral?**; **verbal** or **oral?**

ordinance or **ordnance?** An *ordinance* is a decree or regulation; the noun *ordnance* denotes military supplies or artillery. Neither word is in frequent use: *ordinance* is largely restricted to local government contexts; *ordnance*

is chiefly associated with Ordnance Survey maps.

The similarity in spelling often leads to confusion between the two words.

ore *see* **oar** or **ore?**

organic The adjective *organic* is applied to methods of food production that do not make use of chemical fertilisers, pesticides, etc.: * *organic farming* * *organically produced fruit.* Some people dislike the increasing tendency to apply the adjective directly to the produce itself: * *organic food* * *organic vegetables.* This objection is based on the fact that all meat, fruit, and vegetables may be described as *organic* in the principal sense of 'relating to or derived from living plants or animals'.

orient or **orientate?** Both forms of the verb are acceptable: *orient*, the standard form in American English, is preferred by some users as the shorter and simpler alternative, but *orientate* is the more frequent in British English. To *orient* originally meant 'to face east'; the variant *orientate* was probably a back formation from the noun *orientation.* The verb is often used reflexively, meaning 'get your bearings' or 'adjust to new surroundings': * *They found it difficult to orient/orientate themselves in the unfamiliar town.*

The past participle is increasingly used in the sense of 'inclined towards': * *a commercially orientated service* * *a science-oriented course.* Many people dislike this usage, which is generally avoidable and often quite superfluous: examples include *the local government service designed to meet locality-oriented needs* rather than *to meet the needs of the locality* and job advertisements that call for *experience in product-orientated development* (product development) or *engineering-orientated environments* (engineering). *See also* **disorient** or **disorientate**?

Oriental The use of *Oriental* as a noun describing a person from one of the countries of East Asia is no longer considered acceptable. The preferred modern alternative is *South-East Asian*.

orthopaedic or **paediatric**? Both these adjectives are used in medical contexts and they are often confused. *Orthopaedic* refers to the treatment of bones, joints, muscles, etc.; *paediatric* refers to the treatment of children. The *-paed-* element in both words is derived from the Greek word for 'child': an *orthopaedic specialist* was originally concerned with the bones, joints, etc. of children but now treats people of all ages. Note that there is no connection with the *ped-* element of *pedestrian* and *pedal*, which is derived from the Latin word for 'foot'.

In American English the *-ae-* of *orthopaedic* and *paediatric* is reduced to *-e-* (*see also* **-ae-** and **-oe-**).

oscillate or **osculate**? To *oscillate* means 'move from one position, mood, or value to another; fluctuate or swing': * *The value of the pound oscillated between 1.50 and 1.70 US dollars.* * *His moods oscillated between anger and indifference.* *Osculate* is a much rarer word mainly used in humorous contexts to mean 'to kiss'.

ostensible or **ostentatious**? *Ostensible* means 'apparent'; *ostentatious* means 'showy': * *the ostensible reason for her absence* * *an ostentatious display of grief.* Both adjectives are ultimately derived

from the Latin verb *ostendere*, meaning 'show', and neither is complimentary: *ostensible* has connotations of falseness or deception; *ostentatious* suggests pretentiousness or vulgarity.

other than The use of *other than* as an adverbial phrase is disliked by some users: * *They were unable to escape other than by squeezing through the narrow window.* Its adjectival use, however, is acceptable to all: * *There was no means of escape other than the narrow window.*

Other than is best avoided where *apart from* would be more appropriate: * *There was a narrow window; apart from* [not *other than*] *that, there was no means of escape.*

The construction *other... than* should not be replaced by *other... but* or *other... except*: * *He had no other friend than* [not *but*] *me.* * *Every other card than* [not *except*] *yours arrived on time.* If the word *other* is omitted, however, *but* or *except* may be substituted for *than*.

otherwise Some people object to the frequent use of *otherwise* as an adjective or pronoun: * *All essays, finished or otherwise, must be handed in tomorrow morning.* * *The entire workforce, union members and otherwise, went on strike. Otherwise* may be replaced by *not* in the first of these examples and by *others* in the second. The use of *otherwise* in combination with an adverb is acceptable to all: * *The window was broken, accidentally or otherwise, by one of your children.*

In the sense of 'or else', *otherwise* should not be preceded by *or*: * *Turn the volume down, otherwise you'll wake the baby.*

OTT *see* **over the top.**

ought The auxiliary verb *ought*, expressing duty, obligation, advisability, expectation, etc., is always followed by an infinitive with *to*: • *They ought to visit her more often.* • *Ought we to have invited your sister?* • *You oughtn't to leave your car unlocked.* • *The meat ought to be cooked by now.* The negative and interrogative forms *didn't ought to, hadn't ought to, did we ought to, had I ought to*, etc. are regarded as wrong by careful users.

Ought to can occasionally be replaced by *should*: • *The meat should be cooked by now.* In most contexts, however, *ought* expresses a stronger sense of duty, obligation, advisability, etc. than *should*. *See also* **should** or **would?**

our *see* **hour** or **our?**

our or **us?** *see* **-ing forms.**

ourself or **ourselves?** When referring to people in general or to an individual person, the singular pronoun *ourself* is occasionally used in preference to the plural form *ourselves*: • *We can decide that for ourself.* • *'Oh dear, have we hurt ourself?' she said to the child.* This is likely to be considered an outdated or even incorrect usage, however, and *ourselves* is the safer option in most contexts.

out The verb *out*, meaning 'expose the homosexuality of', is a relatively recent coinage derived from the phrase *come out (of the closet)*, which refers to a person revealing their own homosexuality': • *The militant gay group which threatened to 'out' MPs and other leading figures for not disclos-ing their homosexuality... said it was all a hoax* (*The Guardian*). The verb *out* and its associated noun *outing* are increasingly used in other contexts: • *Indiscriminate 'outings' [of people alleged to have collaborated with the former communist secret police] prompted Mr Havel to announce that he himself had been listed as a 'candidate for collaboration' in 1965* (*The Guardian*).

out or **out of?** In recent years the prepositional phrase *out of* has been reduced with increasing frequency to out: • *He stormed out the door.* • *She looked out the window.* This tendency is disliked by many people and is best restricted to very informal contexts.

outdoor or **outdoors?** *Outdoor* is an adjective; *outdoors* is an adverb: • *outdoor sports* • *outdoor pursuits* • *to play outdoors* • *Outdoor clothes are worn outdoors.* The word *outdoors* is also used as a noun: • *the great outdoors.*

outing *see* **out.**

outlet Some people object to the frequent use of the noun *outlet* in place of shop: • *The product is available at a number of retail outlets in London.* In commercial contexts, *outlet* also means 'market': • *The company has yet to find outlets for its solar-powered torches.*

out of *see* **out** or **out of?**

outplacement The noun *outplacement* refers to advice and assistance given to people who have been made redundant (or who are about to be made redundant): • *outplacement counselling* • *outplacement consulting*. The use of the noun *outplacement* as a euphemism for 'making redundant' is best avoided.

outrageous This word, meaning 'shocking or unconventional': • *outrageous manners*, is sometimes misspelt. The *e* of *outrage* is retained before the suffix *-ous* to indicate the softness of the *g*.

outside of Many people dislike the prepositional phrase *outside of*, in which the word *of* is incorrect. The phrase is best avoided in formal contexts: • *There was a taxi outside* [not *outside of*] *the house*. The addition of this superfluous *of* to the preposition *outside* may be influenced by the prepositional phrase *out of* or by the phrase *on the outside*, which is followed by *of* when it is used prepositionally: • *a label on the outside of the box*.

outward or **outwards**? In British English *outward* is principally used as an adjective, *outwards* being the usual form of the adverb meaning 'towards the outside': • *the outward journey* • *to pull outwards*. The adverb *outward* is more frequently used in American English. *See also* -**ward** or -**wards**?; **above** or **over**?

overall The word *overall* is best avoided where *total, whole, comprehensive, general, average, inclusive, altogether,* etc. would be adequate or more appropriate: • *his general* [not *overall*] *appearance* • *the total* [not *overall*] *cost of the project* • *The journey will take five days altogether* [not *overall*]. In some contexts *overall* is superfluous: • *an overall increase in production.*

The use of the word *overall* in its original sense of 'from end to end' is acceptable to all users: • *the overall length of the room.*

overexaggerate Careful users avoid this emphatic form of *exaggerate* on the grounds that the prefix *over-* is redundant: • *The importance of this development cannot be overexaggerated.*

overkill The frequent use of the noun *overkill* in the sense of 'excess' is disliked by some users: • *In the coverage of the election the media have been accused of overkill.* The noun is particularly undesirable in contexts that may be associated with the literal meaning of the verb *kill*: • *We must avoid overkill in the presentation of our anti-abortion campaign.*

The term *overkill* originally denoted a greater capacity than necessary for destruction, with specific reference to nuclear weapons: • *The de-escalation of the arms race has reduced the problem of overkill.*

overlay or **overlie**? Both verbs are used transitively: *overlay* has the past tense and past participle *overlaid*; *overlie* has the past tense *overlay* and the past participle *overlain*. *Overlay* means 'cover or superimpose', and is often used in the passive: • *floorboards overlaid with old rugs*; • *the atmosphere was overlaid with a sense of nostalgia*. Either *overlay* or *overlie* is used in the sense of 'cause the death of, by lying on': • *The sow overlay the piglet.*

Overlie is used less frequently and means 'lie over or upon': • *rocks overlain by alluvial deposits.*

overly Many people object to the use of the adverb *overly* in place of *too, excessively,* etc.: • *She was not overly enthusiastic about my idea.* • *He is overly sensitive to the slightest criticism.* In some contexts the need for *overly* can be obviated by attaching the prefix *over-*, with or without a hyphen, to the relevant adjective: * *over-enthusiastic* * *oversensitive*.

overtone or **undertone**? In the figurative sense of 'implicit shade of meaning or feeling', these two nouns are virtually synonymous, although *overtone* may convey an additional effect and *undertone* an underlying effect. Both are more frequently used in the plural: * *overtones of malice* * *undertones of discontent* * *political overtones* * *religious undertones*. The words are not interchangeable in their other meanings; *overtone* is a technical term in music and *undertone* denotes a hushed voice: * *to speak in an undertone*.

overview The noun *overview* is best avoided where *survey*, *summary*, etc. would be adequate or more appropriate: * *a general overview of the situation*.

owing *see* **due to**, **owing to** or **because of**?

oxymoron An *oxymoron* is a phrase in which two apparently contradictory words are combined: * *a cowardly hero* * *cruelly kind*.

P

pace The Latin word *pace*, usually printed in italics, means 'with due respect to' and is used when stating an opinion contrary to that of the specified person: ◦ *The teaching profession, pace George Bernard Shaw, is not a refuge for those who cannot do anything else.* *Pace* is a two-syllable word with at least two accepted pronunciations, [*pay*si] and [*pah*chay]. Since the word is largely restricted to formal written contexts, the problem of pronunciation does not frequently arise.

package The word *package* and the expression *package deal* are widely used to denote a set of proposals or offers that must be accepted or rejected as a whole: ◦ *a new package of measures dealing with pay and working conditions.* In other contexts, *package* is often better omitted or replaced by a more appropriate noun: ◦ *Japan's recent announcement of a substantial package of extra spending* (Sunday Times). ◦ *Hammicks has spent over £100,000 on a retail design package* (The Bookseller).

Some people also object to the frequent use of the verb *package* in place of present: ◦ *the different ways in which the major political parties were packaged during the election campaign.*

paediatric *see* **orthopaedic** *or* **paediatric**?

pain *or* **pane**? These two words are occasionally confused since they are pronounced the same. *Pain* means 'acute physical or mental discomfort': ◦ *The morphine should stop the pain.* ◦ *Her remarks caused him great pain.* The word *pane* refers to a sheet of glass or other material: ◦ *The explosion broke three panes of glass.*

pajamas *see* **pyjamas** *or* **pajamas**?

palate This word, meaning 'the top part of the inside of the mouth' or 'sense of taste': ◦ *a cleft palate* ◦ *He has a sensitive palate*, is sometimes misspelt. It should not be confused with *palette*, the board on which an artist mixes colours; nor with *pallet*, a flat platform used in stacking and moving stored goods, and also a hard bed or straw mattress.

palindrome A *palindrome* is a word, phrase, or sentence that reads the same whether read forwards or backwards. Examples include such words as *noon* and *madam*, such names as *Anna* and *Hannah*, and, more ambitiously, such phrases as 'Able was I ere I saw Elba' (supposedly said by the exiled Napoleon).

pallor The noun *pallor*, meaning 'paleness', is sometimes misspelt. Note the final *-or*, as in *stupor*, rather than *-our*.

palpable The use of the adjective *palpable* in the extended sense of 'easily perceived', in place of obvious, manifest, plain, etc., is disliked by some people: * *a palpable lie.* Derived from the Latin verb *palpare*, meaning 'touch', palpable was originally restricted to what could be touched or felt: * *palpable warmth.*

panacea The noun *panacea* denotes a universal remedy for all ills; it should not be used with reference to individual problems or troubles: * *Efficient use of energy saves money but is not a panacea for solving carbon dioxide pollution* (*Daily Telegraph*). Often used disparagingly, the word is more frequently found in figurative contexts than in its literal sense of 'cure-all'.

Note the spelling of *panacea*, which is derived from the prefix *pan-*, meaning 'all', and the Greek word for 'cure'. It is pronounced [panăseeă].

pane *see* **pain** or **pane**?

panic The word *panic* adds a *k* before the suffix *-y*, and before suffixes beginning with an *e* or *i* such as *-ed*, *-er*, and *-ing*: * *panicky* * *They panicked.* * *Stop panicking! See also* **spelling**.

paradigm The noun *paradigm* is best avoided where *example*, *model*, *pattern*, etc. would be adequate or more appropriate: * *a paradigm of enterprise and initiative* * *a paradigm of the problems faced by the unemployed.* *Paradigm* specifically denotes a clear or typical example; it should not be confused with the noun *paragon*, meaning 'model of excellence'. The word is often encountered in the phrase *paradigm shift*, which describes a fundamental change of direction or in underlying attitudes, etc.

Paradigm is pronounced [parră-dīm]; the *g* is silent. In the adjective *paradigmatic*, pronounced [parrădig*ma*tik], the *g* is sounded.

paraffin This word is sometimes misspelt: note the single *r* and *-ff-*, as in *raffle*.

paragon *see* **paradigm**.

paragraphs A *paragraph* is a subdivision of a written passage, which usually deals with one particular point or theme. It expresses an idea that, though it relates to the sense of the whole passage, can to some extent stand alone. There is no specified length for a paragraph; it can be one sentence or over a page long. However, very short successive paragraphs, as are found in advertisements and popular journalism, can have a rather disjointed effect, while very long paragraphs can give the impression of heavy material that can be read through only in a slow, laborious manner. The most effective writing usually mixes longer and shorter paragraphs.

A paragraph starts on a new line and is usually indented. In a passage of dialogue, each act of speech normally starts a new paragraph.

parallel This word is sometimes misspelt. Note the single *r*, the *-ll-*, and then the single *l*. The spelling of some derived forms and compounds varies: * *paralleling or parallelling* * *paralleled or parallelled* * *parallelism* * *parallelogram* * *unparalleled.*

paralyse This word is sometimes misspelt. The spelling in British English is *paralyse* [not *-yze*]; in American English, *paralyze. See also* **-ize** or **-ise**?

parameter Many people object to the frequent use of the noun *parameter*, a mathematical term, as a synonym for 'limit', 'boundary', 'framework', 'characteristic', or 'point to be considered': * *A business must operate within the parameters of time, money, and efficiency.* * *We keep on refining our mailing selection parameters* (*The Bookseller*). * *What are the parameters of the problem?* Note the pronunciation of *parameter*, which is stressed on the second syllable [păr*am*itĕr].

Care should be taken not to confuse *parameter* with *perimeter*, which means 'boundary' or 'outer edge': * *Guards were posted along the perimeter.*

paranoid The adjective *paranoid* principally relates to a mental disorder (*paranoia*) characterised by delusions of persecution or grandeur: * *Often, he* [a schizophrenic] *feels himself to be persecuted – a paranoid delusion that occasionally leads to violence* (*Reader's Digest*). Some people object to the frequent use of *paranoid* and *paranoia* with reference to any intense suspicion, distrust, anxiety, fear, obsession, etc.: * *It gives me an interest-free overdraft of £250 so I don't have to get paranoid at the end of the month* (advertisement, *Sunday Times*).

The word *paranoid* is also used as a noun, although this may cause offence. Its synonym *paranoiac*, pronounced [parră*no*ïk] or [parră*no*iak], is less common.

Note the spelling of *paranoia*, particularly the vowel sequence -*oia*.

paraphernalia The noun *paraphernalia*, sometimes used with derogatory connotations, denotes all the miscellaneous items associated with a particular activity: * *the paraphernalia of photography.* It is also used in more abstract contexts: * *the paraphernalia of buying a new house. Paraphernalia* is a plural noun, but it is frequently used with a singular verb: * *His camping paraphernalia is stored in the attic.* This usage is generally acceptable. Note the spelling of the word, particularly the unstressed syllable -*phern*-.

parentheses *see* **brackets**.

parenting The word *parenting*, which means 'being a parent' or 'parental care', is increasingly used to emphasise the joint responsibility of both parents in all aspects of a child's upbringing, and to avoid the sexual stereotypes and traditional roles associated with the words mother and father and their derivatives: * *the advantages of shared parenting* * *a guide to parenting the gifted child.* This expression is disliked by those who object to the use of nouns as verbs.

par excellence The French expression *par excellence* is used to refer to a person or thing that is better than all others of its kind: * *He is a news reporter par excellence.* Note that the expression *par excellence* comes after the noun to which it refers, and is sometimes written or printed in italics. Its anglicised pronunciation is [par *eks*ĕlahns].

parliament The noun *parliament*, meaning 'legislative authority, assembly, or body', is usually written with a capital *P* when it denotes a specific parliament, especially that of the United Kingdom: * *The issue will be debated in Parliament this afternoon.* The usual pronunciation of parliament is [*par*lămĕnt]; the pronunciations [*par*limĕnt] and [*par*lyămĕnt] are accepted variants. Note the spelling of the word, particularly the central vowels.

parlour *see* **lounge**.

part and **parcel** The phrase *part and parcel*, meaning 'included as an essential aspect of something else', is sometimes rendered incorrectly as *part and partial*: ◦ *Physical exhaustion is all part and parcel of being a top athlete.*

partially or **partly**? Both adverbs mean 'not completely' or 'to some extent', but there are differences of sense, usage, and application between them: ◦ *facilities for the blind and partially sighted* ◦ *The course consists partly of oral work and partly of written work.* In some contexts the two adverbs are virtually interchangeable: ◦ *a partly/ partially successful attempt.* It can be helpful to think of *partly* as meaning 'concerning one part; not wholly': ◦ *The woman's face was partly hidden* [i.e. only part of her face was hidden] by *her veil.* ◦ *The art treasures were partly on permanent loan to the museum and partly in the possession of the Adams family.* *Partially* may then be used to mean 'to a limited extent; not completely': ◦ *The woman's face was partially hidden* [i.e. her whole face may have been hidden but to a limited degree] *by her veil.* ◦ *His hopes were partially frustrated by the lack of full commitment by his fellow workers.*

However, in actual usage such guidelines tend to be ignored, and the words are used interchangeably, with *partly* being the more frequent. The H.M. Customs and Excise VAT notice on Partial Exemption (1984),

for example, describes those registered for VAT as *partly exempt*, even though the notice is titled Partial Exemption.

participles All verbs have *present participles*, which are formed with *-ing*: ◦ *seeing* ◦ *walking*, and *past participles*, formed with *-d* or *-ed* for regular verbs and in other ways for irregular verbs: ◦ *loved* ◦ *finished* ◦ *given* ◦ *gone* ◦ *thought. Participles* are often used as adjectives: ◦ *broken promises* ◦ *a leaking tap.* They are also used, with an inversion of the usual sentence construction, to introduce a sentence such as: ◦ *Sitting in the corner was an old man.* ◦ *Attached to his wrist was a luggage label.* Care should be taken with such introductory participles, as they are sometimes used to link items that are quite unrelated: *see* **dangling participles**.

The pronunciation most frequently used is [par*ti*sipl]; [*par*tisipl] is an older variant. *See also* **-ed** or **-t**?; **-ing forms**; **stress**. For irregular parts of verbs, *see* table at **verbs**.

particular Used for emphasis, the adjective *particular* is often superfluous: ◦ *Do you have any particular preference?* ◦ *This particular dress was worn by Vivien Leigh in Gone with the Wind.* Many people dislike this usage, reserving the adjective for that which is exceptional, special, specific, or worthy of note: ◦ *This discovery is of particular importance.*

partly *see* **partially** or **partly**?

PARTS OF SPEECH Words can be grouped into classes, commonly called *parts of speech*, which share the same grammatical function within sentences. They include nouns, verbs, adjectives, pronouns, adverbs, prepositions, conjunctions, and interjections, as described in the following panel and in more detail under their own entries elsewhere in the text.

passed or **past**? These spellings are sometimes confused. *Passed* is the past tense and past participle of *pass*: ∘ *We passed the station.* ∘ *The years have passed by so quickly. Past* is used for all other forms: noun, adjective, preposition, and adverb: ∘ *Your past is catching up with you.* ∘ *the past weeks* ∘ *She ran past the sign.* ∘ *It's five past three.* ∘ *The plane flew past.*

passive A *passive verb* is one in which the subject receives the action of the verb (*compare* **active**). The sentence ∘ *The play was written by Oscar Wilde* contains the passive verb *was written.* The subject of a passive verb is the direct object of the verb in a corresponding active sentence. The subject of the above example, *the play*, is the direct object of the active equivalent, *Oscar Wilde wrote the play.*

A passive verb is usually formed from part of the verb *be* followed by a past participle: ∘ *The woman was struck on the head.* ∘ *The house had been demolished.*

Many users prefer to replace a passive clause or sentence with its simpler active equivalent, but this is not always possible. For example, it is impossible to convert the two examples in the previous paragraph into the active unless it is known who or what struck the woman and demolished the house.

PARTS OF SPEECH

1 Nouns	Nouns are the names of things, places, or people: ∘ *a goat* ∘ *school* ∘ *Trevor Jones.*
2 Pronouns	Pronouns are words that are used to replace nouns or noun phrases to refer to something or someone: ∘ *I* ∘ *it* ∘ *you* ∘ *they.*
3 Adjectives	Adjectives are words that provide information about a noun: ∘ *fat* ∘ *happy* ∘ *dirty.*
4 Adverbs	Adverbs modify other parts of speech and answer questions such as how?, when?, where?: ∘ *quietly* ∘ *tomorrow* ∘ *there.*
5 Verbs	Verbs are 'doing' words that refer to actions, occurrences, or existence: ∘ *enjoy* ∘ *fall* ∘ *stop.*
6 Prepositions	Prepositions are words that show the relation of a noun or other word acting as a noun to the rest of the sentence: ∘ *at* ∘ *with* ∘ *before.*
7 Conjunctions	Conjunctions are words that link two or more words, clauses, or sentences: ∘ *and* ∘ *but* ∘ *when.*
8 Interjections	Interjections are words, phrases, or sentences that stand outside the usual structure of sentences. They usually express a strong feeling, such as surprise, anger, shock, excitement (*see also* **exclamations**): ∘ *Gosh!* ∘ *Oh dear!*

past *see* **passed** or **past**?

patent This word may be pronounced [*pay*tĕnt] in all senses in British English: • *to patent/apply for a patent for a new invention* • *patent leather shoes*, and as the adverb *patently* [*pay*tĕntli]: • *It is patently obvious she's lying*. In legal and official contexts, in the noun and verb senses of the word – '(obtaining) the official rights to a product' – *patent* is usually pronounced [*pat*ĕnt].

In American English [*pat*ĕnt] is used for all senses.

pathetic The use of the adjective *pathetic* in the derogatory sense of 'contemptible' or 'worthless' is best restricted to informal contexts: • *The comedian made a pathetic attempt to mimic the president.* • *Don't be so pathetic!* The principal sense of *pathetic* is 'arousing pity or sorrow': • *The sick child made several pathetic attempts to stand up.*

pathos *see* **bathos** or **pathos**?

patriot This word, meaning 'one who loves his or her country', has two acceptable pronunciations: [*pay*triŏt] or [*pat*riŏt].

patron *see* **client** or **customer**?

pay- In recent years the prefix *pay-* has been adopted in a wide range of contexts, with reference to payment for services at the time they are received: • *pay-as-you-go* • *pay-per-view* • *pay-per-listen*. Care should be taken not to overuse the prefix, especially in contexts where it is unnecessary or inappropriate.

PC *see* **political correctness**.

PE *see* **AD** and **BC**.

peaceable or **peaceful**? The adjective *peaceable*, meaning 'disposed to peace', 'peace-loving', or 'not aggressive', is principally applied to people: • *the peaceable inhabitants of the town* • *a peaceable temperament*. *Peaceful*, the more frequent of the two adjectives, means 'characterised by peace', 'calm', or 'not violent': • *a peaceful scene* • *a peaceful demonstration* • *peaceful coexistence*. Note the spelling of **peaceable**, particularly the second *e* (*see also* **spelling**).

peak, **peek**, or **pique**? These three words are occasionally confused, since they are all pronounced in the same way [peek]. *Peak* refers variously to a mountain, summit, or cap brim or, as a verb, to the action of reaching a high point: • *The climbers reached the peak around noon.* • *The storm peaked around midnight.* • *He tapped the peak of his cap with his forefinger.* It should not be confused with *peek*, which denotes a brief glimpse: • *He could not resist a quick peek at the menu*, or with *pique*, which means 'resentment' or 'hurt pride': • *He changed his mind in a fit of pique.*

peal or **peel**? These two words are pronounced in the same way but have different meanings. *Peal* refers to the sound of bells ringing: • *the peal of church bells* or to a long loud sound • *a peal of distant thunder* • *peals of laughter*. *Peel* as a noun refers to the skin of a fruit: • *orange peel*; and as a verb means 'remove the skin of a vegetable or piece of fruit': • *to peel the potatoes.*

pedal or **peddle**? The word *pedal* relates to a foot-operated lever: * *the soft pedal on a piano* * *a pedal bin* * *to pedal a bicycle*. To *peddle* is to sell small articles or illegal goods, such as drugs, or to put forward ideas or information: * *to peddle brushes/heroin /gossip*. The two verbs should not be confused. The verb *peddle* is a back formation from the noun *pedlar*, denoting a person who goes from place to place selling goods. In other senses of the verb *peddle*, the spelling *peddler* is often used in place of *pedlar*: * *a drug peddler* * *a peddler of ideas*. In American English *peddler* is preferred for all senses; in British English *pedlar* is usually retained in its original sense. Note the single *d* and the *-ar* ending of *pedlar*.

In British English the final *l* of the verb pedal is doubled before a suffix beginning with a vowel: * *pedalled* * *pedalling*. The American spellings are *pedaled, pedaling*, etc. *See also* **spelling**.

pedigree The noun *pedigree* denotes an ancestral line or line of descent, specifically that of a purebred animal; some people dislike its use as a synonym for 'record' or 'background': * *a pedigree of success spanning over 50 years in the radio and television rental and retail field* (*Executive Post*).

pedlar *see* **pedal** or **peddle**?

peek *see* **peak, peek** or **pique**?

peel *see* **peal** or **peel**?

peer or **pier**? *Peer* variously means 'equal', 'member of the nobility', or, as a verb, 'take a close look at someone or something': * *He was much admired by*

his peers. * a *peer of the realm* * *He peered at the signature*. It should not be confused with *pier*, which refers to a jetty or platform on stilts: * *There were two boats tied up at the pier*.

pence As *pence* is one of the plural forms of the noun *penny*, many people object to the use of the term *one-pence piece* to denote a penny coin: * *Does the machine still take one-pence pieces?* The plural noun *pennies* is used with reference to a number of coins, whereas *pence* usually refers to a sum of money: * *My purse is full of pennies.* * *The envelopes cost fifteen pence each.* * *Can you give me ten pennies in exchange for a ten-pence piece?* After the decimalisation of British currency in 1971, the abbreviation *p*, pronounced [pee], was often used in speech to distinguish between old and new pennies or pence. This usage has continued, but is best restricted to informal contexts: * *Can you lend me twenty p?*

The pronunciation of the word *pence* was also affected by decimalisation: the sum of *6d* was pronounced [*siks*pĕns], with the stress on the first syllable, whereas *6p* is usually pronounced [*siks*pens], with equal stress on both syllables.

pendant or **pendent**? The noun *pendant*, denoting a type of necklace, has the rare variant spelling *pendent*. The word *pendent* is also used as an adjective, in the sense of 'hanging', with the (less frequent) variant spelling *pendant*.

peninsula or **peninsular**? These two spellings are sometimes confused. A *peninsula* is a long narrow section of land that is almost surrounded by water but which in fact is joined to the

mainland. The adjective is *peninsular*:
* *the Peninsular War of 1808 to 1814.*

pennies, penny *see* **pence**.

pensioner *see* **senior citizen** or **old age pensioner**?

people *People* is usually a plural noun, but in the sense of 'nation', 'race', or 'tribe' it may be singular or plural: * *a nomadic people of Africa* * *all the peoples of the world* * *The French people are renowned for their culinary expertise.* The use of the alternative plural form *persons* to denote a number of human beings is best restricted to formal contexts: * *No more than eight persons may use the lift.* * *There are four people* [not *persons*] *in the waiting room.* With reference to a group or body of human beings, the word *people* is preferred in all contexts: * *a meeting place for young people* * *representatives of the people.*

Note that when referring to a single group or to people in general, the possessive of people is formed by adding *'s*: * *He is the people's favourite.* When referring to several groups or nations the possessive is formed by adding *s'*: * *an oppressed peoples' organisation.*

people with disabilities This is the preferred modern term for people with physical or mental disabilities, replacing such former terms as *handicapped* and *retarded*: * *The building has been specifically designed to meet the needs of people with disabilities. See also* **disabled**.

per The preposition *per*, meaning 'for each' or 'in each', is often better replaced by *a* or *an*: * *four times a* [not *per*] *month* * *60p a* [not *per*] *metre.* In

some contexts, however, *per* must be retained: * *Use two ounces of cheese per person.* * *The left-luggage attendant charges one pound per item per day.* Many people consider the use of *per* in place of *by* to be excessively formal or affected: * *The parcel will be sent per Securicor. See also* **as per**; **per annum**; **per capita**; **per cent**; **per se**.

per-, pre- or **pro-**? These three prefixes sometimes cause confusion in the spelling and usage of certain pairs of words. *See* **persecute** or **prosecute**?; **perspective** or **prospective**?; **precede** or **proceed**?; **prerequisite** or **perquisite**?; **prescribe** or **proscribe**?

per annum The Latin phrase *per annum*, meaning 'for each year', is best restricted to formal contexts: * *You will be paid a salary of £12,000 per annum.* In other contexts the more informal phrase *a year* is preferred: * *It costs several hundred pounds a year, excluding petrol, to keep this car on the road. See also* **per**.

per capita The adverbial or adjectival phrase *per capita* is widely used in English in the sense of 'for each person': * *the minimum cost per capita* * *a per capita allowance of ten pounds.* Some people object to this usage as an inaccurate translation of the Latin phrase, which literally means 'by heads': * *The estate will be divided per capita.*

per cent The phrase *per cent* is used adverbially, in combination with a number, in the sense of 'in or for each hundred': * *an increase of 25 per cent* * *75 per cent of the students.* Some people dislike the use of *per cent* as a noun meaning 'one-hundredth' or 'a percentage': the phrase *half a per cent*, for example, is better replaced by *half of one per cent*.

In American English *per cent* is usually written as one word: ● *100 percent*; in British English the two-word form is preferred. *See also* **percentage; singular** or **plural?**

percentage Many people object to the use of a *percentage* to mean 'a small part', 'a little', or 'a few': ● *Only a percentage of the workforce will be present.* A *percentage* may be as small as 1 per cent or as large as 99 per cent; in the sense of 'proportion' the noun often needs a qualifying adjective for clarity: ● *A small percentage of the money is used for administration costs.* ● *A large percentage of the stock was damaged in the fire.* When discussing a particular percentage, prefaced by the, a singular verb should be used: ● *The percentage of passes is lower this year.* When *percentage* is prefaced by *a,* the verb usually agrees with the following noun: ● *A small percentage of new vehicles are defective.* ● *A large percentage of the work has already been done.*

Percentage is sometimes better replaced by *number, amount, part,* or *proportion; a high percentage* by *many* or *much; a lower percentage* by *fewer* or *less,* etc.

The use of the noun *percentage* as a synonym for 'advantage' or 'profit' is best restricted to informal contexts: ● *There's no real percentage in sending your children to a private school.*

perceptible, perceptive or **percipient?** The adjective *perceptible* means 'perceivable', 'noticeable', or 'recognisable'; *perceptive* means 'observant', 'discerning', or 'sensitive': ● *a perceptible change* ● *a perceptive remark.*

Percipient, which is virtually synonymous with, but less common than, *perceptive*, is largely restricted to formal contexts: ● *a percipient writer.*

The adverbs *perceptibly* and *perceptively* are often confused, being similar in spelling and pronunciation: ● *The children were perceptibly quieter when their teacher was present.* ● *She spoke perceptively of the composer's orchestral works.*

peremptory or **perfunctory?** *Peremptory* means 'commanding; dogmatic; positive; decisive': ● *a peremptory order* ● *a peremptory man* ● *in a peremptory tone of voice* ● *a peremptory knock at the door. Perfunctory* means 'quick; careless; cursory; superficial': ● *a perfunctory glance at the letter.* Both adjectives are largely restricted to formal contexts; they should not be confused. *Peremptory* is usually pronounced [pĕremptŏri], with the stress on the second syllable, but [perrĕmptŏri], stressed on the first syllable, is an acceptable alternative.

perennial *see* **annual, biennial** or **perennial?**

perfect Many people avoid using such adverbs as *very, rather, more, most, less, least,* etc. to qualify the adjective *perfect,* meaning 'faultless', 'unblemished', 'complete', or 'utter': ● *This book is in less perfect condition than that one.* ● *It was the most perfect diamond that he had ever seen.* The expressions *nearly perfect* and *almost perfect,* however, are generally acceptable. The pronunciation of the adjective *perfect* is different from that of the verb. The adjective is stressed on the first syllable [perfikt], whereas the verb is stressed on the second syllable [pĕrfekt].

perfunctory *see* **peremptory** or **perfunctory**?

perimeter *see* **parameter**.

perk *see* **prerequisite** or **perquisite**?

permissible or **permissive**? These two adjectives are derived from the verb *permit*, meaning 'allow' or 'authorise'. *Permissible* means 'permitted'; *permissive* means 'tolerant': ● *the smallest permissible investment* ● *a permissive attitude*. *Permissive* sometimes implies disapproval of such tolerance (or of the thing tolerated), especially when it is used with reference to sexual indulgence: ● *the permissive society*. Note the spelling of *permissible*, particularly the *-ible* ending.

perpetrate or **perpetuate**? *Perpetrate* means 'commit' or 'perform'; *perpetuate* means 'cause to continue' or 'make perpetual': ● *to perpetrate a crime* ● *to perpetuate a tradition*. The two verbs should not be confused.

per pro. *see* **p.p.**

perquisite *see* **prerequisite** or **perquisite**?

per se The Latin phrase *per se*, meaning 'by itself' or 'in itself', is best restricted to formal contexts: ● *The discovery is of little importance per se*. Note the spelling and pronunciation of the word *se* [say].

persecute or **prosecute**? *Persecute* means 'harass' or 'oppress'; *prosecute* means 'take legal action against': ● *They were persecuted for their beliefs*. ● *Trespassers will be prosecuted*. The two verbs should not be confused.

perseverance The noun *perseverance* is sometimes misspelt. A common error is the addition of an extra *r* before the *v*. Note also the *-ance* ending.

persevere The verb *persevere* is followed by the preposition *in* or *with*: ● *They persevered in* [or *with*] *their efforts to dam the stream*.

person Many people prefer to use the noun *person*, rather than *man*, to denote a human being whose sex is unspecified: ● *We need to take on another person to deal with the backlog*. The substitution of *person* for *man* in such words as *chairman, salesman, statesman, spokesman, layman, craftsman*, etc. is a more controversial issue: ● *Mr Smith has resigned as chairperson of the committee.* ● *Mrs Liz Forsdick... will act as 'linesperson' in the third qualifying round game* (*The Guardian*).

Some users apply the terms *chairman, salesman*, etc. to both men and women: ● *The chairman of the CBI's Smaller Firms Council, Mrs Jean Parker* (*The Guardian*). Others use the more or less acceptable feminine forms *chairwoman, saleswoman*, etc. for women: ● *The appointment was announced yesterday by ChildLine's chairwoman, Miss Esther Rantzen* (*The Guardian*).

As a general rule the substitution of *person* for *man*, in any context, is best avoided if a simpler or more idiomatic solution can be found: the use of *someone else* instead of *another person*, *nobody* instead of *no person*, *crew of four* instead of *four-person crew*, and so on.

Person has two plurals, *persons* and *people*. See also **agreement**; **chair**; **man**; **non-sexist terms**; **people**; **person**; and **sexism**.

personage or **personality**? Both nouns are applied to famous people, but they are not synonymous. *Personage* is used in formal contexts to refer to an important or distinguished person; a *personality* is a famous person from the world of show business, sport, etc.: * *members of the royal family and other personages* * *The shop will be opened by a TV personality.* The principal meaning of the noun *personality* is 'character': * *She has a delightful personality.* * *Personality is more important than looks.*

personal *see* **personally; personnel**.

personality *see* **personage** or **personality**?

personally Some people dislike the use of the adverb *personally* for emphasis: * *I personally prefer to spend my holidays at home.* Similar objections may be raised to the unnecessary use of the adjective *personal* in such expressions as: * *a personal friend* * *her personal opinion* * *a personal visit*, etc.

In some contexts, however, *personally* and *personal* may serve the useful purpose of distinguishing between the unofficial and the official, the private and the professional, etc.: * *I personally think you should accept their offer, but as your solicitor I must advise you to make further enquiries.* * *He is a business acquaintance but not a personal friend.*

personal pronouns *see* **pronouns**.

persona non grata The Latin expression *persona non grata* is used to refer to someone who is unwelcome or unacceptable: * *After his book was published, he became persona non grata with*

certain foreign powers. The phrase, which is sometimes written or printed in italics, literally means 'person not acceptable' and is pronounced [per*so*na non *grah*ta]. Its plural is *personae non gratae* [per*so*nee non *grah*tee].

personate, personify *see* **impersonate, personate** or **personify**?

personification *Personification* refers to the practice of attributing human characteristics to animals, inanimate objects, or abstract ideas: * *The orangutan winked at me, for all the world like a knowing old man.* * *Gravity is the sworn enemy of the paraglider.* Such personifications are acceptable in poetic and informal contexts, but should generally be avoided in formal contexts. One aspect of *personification* is the tradition of allotting specific genders to various inanimate objects, such as cars and ships, which are frequently described as feminine (despite recent official decisions to end this practice): * *She's a beautiful little craft.*

personnel Many people object to the frequent use of the noun *personnel* in place of *staff, workforce, workers, employees, people*, etc.: * *They do not have enough personnel to cope with the increased workload.* The word *personnel* is principally used to denote the employees of a large company or organisation, considered collectively, or the department that is concerned with their recruitment and welfare: * *hospital personnel* * *the personnel officer.* Note, however, that the job description *personnel officer* is now often restyled as *human resources officer* (or *manager*). *Personnel* may be a singular or plural noun, but it should not be used with a specific number: * We are moving four people [not *personnel*] from the sales office to the production department.

Note the spelling of *personnel*, particularly the *-nn-* and the second *e*, and the pronunciation of the word, with the primary stress on the last syllable [persŏ*nel*]. The noun *personnel* is sometimes confused with the adjective *personal*: * There will be strong prospects of long-term personnel development for... the truly commercial engineer (Sunday Times).

person of colour *Person of colour* is a preferred modern alternative to such terms as *coloured* and *nonwhite*, which many people find unacceptable: * *This council welcomes applications from persons of colour.* Many users find the term ponderous, however, and it has yet to enjoy wide acceptance.

persons *see* **people**.

perspective or **prospective**? *Perspective* is a noun, meaning 'view', 'aspect', or 'objectivity'; it should not be confused with the adjective *prospective*, meaning 'expected', 'likely', or 'future': * *a different perspective* * *a prospective employer*. In painting, drawing, etc., the noun *perspective* principally refers to the representation of three-dimensional objects and their relative sizes and positions on a flat surface. Its figurative use in the phrase *in perspective* is derived from this sense: * *You must try to put things in perspective: the loss of one customer is relatively unimportant when the future of the company is at stake.*

perturb *see* **disturb** or **perturb**?

perverse or **perverted**? *Perverse* means 'obstinate' or 'contrary'; *perverted* means 'corrupt' or 'characterised by abnormal sexual behaviour': * *a perverse refusal* * *a perverted attack*. The two adjectives should not be confused: to call a man *perverted* is a far more serious and offensive accusation than to call him *perverse*. Both adjectives may be applied to the same noun in different contexts: * *He took a perverse delight in making her wait.* * *He took a perverted delight in torturing his victims.*

phase *see* **faze** or **phase**?

phenomena *see* **phenomenon** or **phenomena**?

phenomenal The use of the adjective *phenomenal* as a synonym for 'extraordinary', 'remarkable', 'prodigious', or 'outstanding' is disliked by some: * *a phenomenal achievement.*

phenomenon or **phenomena**? *Phenomena* is the plural form of the noun *phenomenon*: * *This phenomenon is of great interest.* * *Such phenomena are not easy to explain.* The use of *phenomena* as a singular noun – a frequent error – is wrong: * *'The development of the Muslim community in Britain is only a recent phenomena and needs proper research,' Mr Ayman Ahwal, London spokesman of the World Muslim League, said (The Times).*

Careful users avoid overuse of the word *phenomenon*, resisting the tendency in recent years to apply the word to anything mildly unusual: * *The increasing number of police on the streets is a recent phenomenon.*

-phile, **-phobe** or **-phone**? These suffixes are sometimes confused. The suffix *-phile* is applied to a person who likes something very much: * *Her husband is a real anglophile*, whereas *-phobe* indicates that a person has a strong aversion to something: * *Her boss was a technophobe who hated computers.* The suffix *-phone* refers to a person who speaks a particular language: * *His wife is a Francophone.*

philosophy The noun *philosophy* is best avoided where *idea, view, policy*, etc. would be adequate or more appropriate: * *My philosophy is that children should be seen and not heard.* * *The company has a philosophy of sound management practices at the local level.*

phishing Note the spelling of this word, which refers to the modern phenomenon of attempting to gain passwords or other confidential information through the sending of fraudulent emails purporting to be from a person's bank or other trustworthy source: * *Home computers are the latest target of large-scale phishing campaigns.* The initial *ph*, not to be confused with the *f* of conventional *fishing*, was probably arrived at through the influence of *phreaking*, a slang term describing the activities of those who experiment with and exploit modern telecommunications systems (itself a result of the combining of *phone* and *freak*).

phlegm This word causes problems with spelling and pronunciation. Note the initial *ph-* spelling, pronounced [f], and the silent *g*. The word is pronounced [flem].

-phobe, -phile or **-phone?** *see* **-phile, -phobe** or **-phone?**

phobia A *phobia* is an abnormal or irrational fear or aversion: * *He has a phobia about flying.* * *She has a phobia of spiders.* The noun should not be used as a synonym for 'dislike', 'dread', 'obsession', 'inhibition', etc.: * *She has a phobia of losing her car keys.* * *He has a phobia about undressing in front of other people.* See also **suffixes**, page 391–402.

phone Use of the noun and verb *phone* in place of *telephone* is becoming increasingly acceptable: the telephone directory is now officially entitled 'The Phone Book' – the term long used to describe it in informal contexts. The shortened form *phone* is best avoided, however, in formal contexts: * *The phone's ringing.* * *You'd better phone the doctor.* * *The cost of your telephone call will be refunded.* * *Please write or telephone for an application form.* See also **abbreviations**; **apostrophe**.

-phone, -phile or **-phobe?** *see* **-phile, -phobe** or **-phone?**

phoney or **phony?** The more usual spelling of this word, meaning 'fake', is *phoney* in British English, and *phony* in American English.

phosphorous or **phosphorus?** *Phosphorous* is the correct spelling for the adjective meaning 'containing phosphorus' or 'of or relating to phosphorus': * *The craft will probe the phosphorous clouds. Phosphorus* is the correct spelling for the noun referring to the chemical element: * *The industrial uses of phosphorus.*

photo The use of the noun *photo* in place of *photograph* is best restricted to informal contexts: * *Did you take a photo of the baby?* * *This pass is not valid without a photograph of the holder.* The plural of *photo* is *photos*. The word *photo* is not generally used as a shortened form of the verb *photograph*. *See also* **abbreviations**; **apostrophe**.

phrasal verbs *see* **verbs.**

phrase A *phrase* is a group of words that function together as a noun, verb, adjective, adverb, preposition, etc.: * *the red car* * *give up* * *highly polished* * *at the back of the room* * *with reference to*. *See also* **clause**; **sentences.**

physician or **physicist**? A *physician* is a doctor of medicine; a *physicist* is a scientist who has specialised in physics: * *the number of physicians in the National Health Service* * *physicists involved in nuclear research*. The two nouns should not be confused. The term *physician* is chiefly used to distinguish qualified medical practitioners in non-surgical fields from surgeons. In everyday usage the term *doctor* is preferred; *physician* sounds formal or old-fashioned in British English.

physiognomy Note the spelling of this word, which means 'the outward appearance of a person considered to show the person's character'. The most frequent error is to omit the silent *g*.

picaresque or **picturesque**? A *picaresque* story is one that deals with the adventures of a rogue. Examples of picaresque novels in English include Daniel Defoe's *Moll Flanders* and Henry Fielding's *Jonathan Wild*. *Picturesque* is used much more fre-

quently and means 'attractive and charming; quaint' and 'evocative; vivid': * *picturesque villages* * *picturesque language*. *Picaresque* derives ultimately from Spanish *picaro*, meaning 'a rogue; wily trickster'.

picnic This word adds a *k* before the suffixes *-er*, *-ed*, and *-ing*: * *picnickers* * *They picnicked in the woods*. *See also* **spelling.**

picturesque *see* **picaresque** or **picturesque**?

pidgin or **pigeon**? These two words may sometimes be confused. *Pidgin* is a language that is a mixture of two other languages: * *pidgin English*. A *pigeon* is a grey bird with short legs and compact feathers: * *the pigeons of Trafalgar Square*. *Pigeon* also has the informal, rather old-fashioned sense of 'concern': * *that's his pigeon*.

pièce de résistance The phrase *pièce de résistance*, meaning 'main dish of a meal; most outstanding or impressive item', is of French origin and is sometimes written or printed in italics in English texts: * *The designer's pièce de résistance was the exquisite dress worn by the princess at her wedding*. Note the accents, which serve to distinguish *pièce*, pronounced [pyes], from the English word *piece* [pees], and *résistance* [rezis*tahns*] from the English word *resistance* [rizis*tăns*]; these accents should never be omitted. The plural is formed by adding *-s* to the first word: *pièces de résistance*.

pier *see* **peer** or **pier**?

pigmy *see* **pygmy** or **pigmy**?

pique *see* **peak, peek** or **pique**?

piteous, pitiable or **pitiful**? All these adjectives mean 'arousing or deserving pity', in which sense they are virtually interchangeable in many contexts. There are, however, slight differences of usage and application between them: * *a piteous cry* * *a pitiable figure* * *a pitiful sight*. Note the spelling of *piteous*, the least frequent of the three adjectives, in which the *t* is followed by *e* rather than *i* (as in *pitiable* and *pitiful*).

Pitiable and *pitiful* have the additional meaning of 'arousing or deserving contempt': * *Their pitiful offer of a two per cent pay rise was immediately rejected by the union.*

pivotal Some users dislike the frequent use of the adjective *pivotal* in the sense of 'crucial or very important': *

to come to a pivotal decision. Note the pronunciation of *pivotal*, which is stressed on the first syllable [*piv*ŏtăl].

place or **plaice**? These two words are occasionally confused, since they are pronounced in the same way [plays]. *Place* means 'location' or 'position': *Everything is back in its place.* * *What a delightful place.* It should not be confused with *plaice*, which refers to a large flat-bodied sea fish: * *They had a fine catch of plaice.*

PLACE NAMES Difficulty can sometimes arise concerning the Anglicisation of the names of countries, towns and geographical features elsewhere in the world. This is especially true where naming conventions change as a result of political, cultural or other influences (*see* following panel).

PLACE NAMES

Accepted modern name	Former name
Beijing (China)	Peking
Belarus	Byelorussia
Belize	British Honduras
Bengaluru (India)	Bangalore
Benin	Dahomey
Bishkek (Kyrgystan)	Frunze
Cambodia	Kampuchea
Chemnitz (Germany)	Karl-Marx-Stadt
Chennai (India)	Madras
Dhaka (India)	Dacca
Guangzhou (China)	Canton
Harare (Zimbabwe)	Salisbury

Ho Chi Minh City (Vietnam)	Saigon
Kanpur (India)	Cawnpore
Kiribati	Gilbert Islands
Kochi (India)	Cochin
Kolkata (India)	Calcutta
Mafikeng (South Africa)	Mafeking
Mallorca (Spain)	Majorca
Menorca (Spain)	Minorca
Moldova	Moldavia
Mumbai (India)	Bombay
Myanmar	Burma
Nizhny Novgorod (Russia)	Gorky
Polokwane (South Africa)	Pietersburg
Puducherry (India)	Pondicherry
St Petersburg (Russia)	Leningrad
Samoa	Western Samoa
Tuvalu	Ellice Islands
Sri Lanka	Ceylon
Thiruvananthapuram (India)	Trivandrum
Vanuatu	New Hebrides
Varanasi (India)	Benares
Yangon (Myanmar)	Rangoon
Xi'an (China)	Sian

plain or **plane**? These words are sometimes confused. The main noun sense of *plain* is 'level, treeless expanse of land': * *the vast plains of the prairies.* *Plane* as a noun is a shortened form of *aeroplane*; a carpenter's tool; or a surface in geometry. *Plain* has several adjectival senses including 'straightforward', 'simple', and 'clear'; the adjectival use of *plane* means 'flat': * *a plane surface.*

The idiomatic expression *plain sailing* is used to describe easy progress: * *Once I've mended this switch, the rest will be plain sailing. See also* **plane**.

PLAIN ENGLISH The most effective writing is both clear and concise. By observing some basic rules about writing and speech, anyone may be confident of conveying their meaning both neatly and efficiently. *See* the following panel.

plaintiff or **plaintive**? These words are sometimes confused. A *plaintiff* is the person who commences legal action in a court; *plaintive* means 'mournful and melancholy': * *a plaintive song*.

plane The use of the noun *plane* as a shortened form of *aeroplane* is acceptable in most contexts: * *What time does your plane leave?* * *More than 250 people were killed in the plane crash.* *See also* **abbreviations**; **apostrophe**; **plain** or **plane**?

plastic The first syllable of the word *plastic* may be pronounced with the short *a* of *plan*, or with the long *a* of

PLAIN ENGLISH	
1 Vocabulary	It is good practice to prefer simple, shorter, and generally more straightforward words to longer, more complicated ones that may be unfamiliar to others. The inappropriate use of longer words or jargon can easily lead to an impression of pretentiousness. Longer words are preferable, however, where there is no simpler equivalent or where the use of an alternative word might lead to confusion or ambiguity (as is often the case in scientific or other technical contexts). Conversely, the use of slang should be restricted to only the most informal of communications.
2 Grammar	Care should always be taken to observe grammatical convention at a level appropriate to the context. The rules may be relaxed somewhat for such communications as emails or brief notes or memos, but should be strictly observed in more formal contexts, such as treatises, official reports, or articles for publication. Use of incorrect grammar can readily lead to misunderstandings on the part of a reader and may also create an unfavourable impression on the recipient. Many tips on using effective grammar will be found in specific articles throughout this book. These include the preference for using verbs in place of nouns and the use of active verbs instead of passive ones.
3 Explanation	It is sensible to assume that some readers or listeners may not be familiar with the meaning of specialised vocabulary or with the background to what is being communicated. If the use of such language cannot be avoided, it is good practice to explain anything that may not be known by the reader or listener. Such explanations should not, however, be inserted where this might create the impression that the writer or speaker is 'talking down' to their audience.
4 Conciseness	Language should be used with accuracy and precision. Careful readers and writers avoid long, rambling sentences and make their point in as clear, simple, and brief a manner as possible. The use of abbreviations and acronyms can contribute to conciseness, though care should be taken not to employ them where they may not be understood.

plant. The first of these pronunciations, [*pla*stik], is more frequent than the second, [*plah*stik]. Many people object to the informal use of the noun *plastic* to mean '(payment by) credit cards': * *I very rarely pay by cash these days – I usually use plastic.*

platform Some people dislike as an Americanism the use of the noun *platform* to denote the declared policies and principles of a political party or candidate, but it is generally acceptable: * *Their unilateralist platform will win them few votes in the forthcoming election.*

playwright *see* **dramatist** or **playwright**?

plc This abbreviation for *public limited company* is often written or printed in lower-case letters, without full stops. A *public limited company* is a company whose shares can be bought and sold on the stock exchange, as opposed to a private limited company, which has the abbreviation *Ltd* (spelt with a capital *L* and usually without a full stop) after its name.

pleaded or **pled**? In British English *pleaded* is the usual form of the past tense and past participle of the verb *plead*: * *'Save my child,' she pleaded.* * *They had pleaded with him to stay.* *Pled* is an American, Scottish, or dialectal variant of pleaded.

Plead has particular significance as a legal term in the context of a defendant admitting or denying guilt: * *She pleaded guilty when the case came to court.*

pleasantness or **pleasantry**? *Pleasantness* is an uncountable noun, meaning 'the state of being pleasant': * *the*

pleasantness of the weather. Pleasantry is chiefly used in more formal English in the plural form *pleasantries*, meaning 'polite, casual, friendly, agreeable, or amusing remarks': * *to exchange pleasantries.*

plenty The use of *plenty* as an adverb, in place of *quite* or *very*, is regarded by some as non-standard: * *The house is plenty big enough for us.* * *She was plenty upset when she heard the news.* The second of these uses is generally considered to be an Americanism.

The adjectival use of *plenty* without *of* is also unacceptable to many users: * *They have plenty toys to play with.*

plethora The phrase *a plethora of* implies excess or superfluity; it should not be used as a pretentious synonym for 'a large number of' or 'plenty of': * *a plethora of houses for sale*, for example, describes a situation in which there are too many houses on the market – far more than the number of prospective buyers – with the result that many will remain unsold.

plum or **plumb**? These two words are occasionally confused, since they are pronounced in the same way. *Plum* variously refers to the fruit of the plum tree or to something of choice quality: * *She served up a dish of plums and custard.* * *He's landed a plum job with the government.* It should not be confused with *plumb*, which means 'install piping for water' or 'probe': * *He has plumbed in the new sink.* * *She plumbed the depths of despair.* Note also the spelling of *plumb line*, denoting a line with a weight attached that is used to check or determine verticality. Both words are pronounced [plum].

plurals The regular way of forming *plurals* for English words is to add an -*s*, except for words ending in -*s*, -*x*, -*ch*, -*sh*, and -*z*, where -*es* is added: * *ships* * *houses* * *buses* * *foxes* * *churches* * *sashes* * *buzzes*. Of course, there are many irregularly formed plurals. Words ending in a consonant and then -*y* have -*ies* in the plural: * *fairies* * *ponies*, with the exception of proper nouns, which have -*s* or -*ies*: * *I've invited the Joneses and the Hartys*. * *the Two Sicilies*. Some words ending in -*f* or -*fe* have -*ves* in the plural: * *halves* * *wives*, while others simply add -*s*, and others allow a choice: * *beliefs* * *hoofs–hooves*. Some words ending in -*o* add -*es*, others just an -*s*. It is impossible to formulate a general rule here, although note the frequently used *potatoes* and *tomatoes*, which both end -*es*. Note also that shortened forms ending in -*o* just add -*s*: * *photos* * *pianos* * *radios* * *stereos* * *videos*. Some nouns ending in -*s* are already plural and cannot be pluralised: * *trousers* * *spectacles* * *scissors*. With various animal names, the plural form is the same as the singular: * *deer* * *sheep* * *bison*; the same applies to a number of other words that can be treated as either singular or plural: * *crossroads* * *the accused*. Several English words have plurals not formed in any of the ways described above: * *man–men* * *child–children* * *mouse–mice* * *goose–geese* * *foot–feet*. There is no rule about these words and it is impossible to generalise from them; the plural of *mongoose* is *mongooses* [not *mongeese*].

Foreign words sometimes take a regular English plural and sometimes the plural of the appropriate language: often, either is regarded as correct: * *châteaus/châteaux*. Latin or Greek words frequently take the plural of their original language. The -*is* ending of such nouns as *analysis* and *thesis* changes to -*es* in the plural: * *analyses* * *theses*. The endings -*ix* and -*ex* may change to -*ices* (*see* **appendixes** or **appendices?**; **indexes** or **indices?**); the ending -*a* may add an -*e* (*see* **formulae** or **formulas?**); the endings -*on* and -*um* may change to -*a* (*see* **media**; **phenomenon** or **phenomena?**); and the ending -*us* may change to -*i* (*see* **fungi**).

Difficulties often arise with the plurals of compound nouns. The general rule is that when the qualifying word is an adjective, the noun is made plural: * *courts martial* * *poets laureate*, although in less formal usage the second word is made plural: * *poet laureates*. If both words are nouns, the second is made plural: * *town clerks*, although *woman teacher* becomes *women teachers*. In compounds of a noun and a prepositional phrase or adverb, the noun is made plural: * *mothers-in-law* * *hangers-on* * *men of war*. If no words in the compound are nouns, then -*s* is added at the end: * *forget-me-nots* * *go-betweens* * *grown-ups*.

On using singular or plural verbs, *see* **singular** or **plural?**

plus The prepositional use of *plus* in the sense of 'with the addition of' is acceptable in all contexts: * *My savings, plus the money my grandmother left me, are almost enough to buy a car.* Note that the verb agrees with savings; if the sentence is reordered to make *money* the principal subject, a singular verb must be used: * *The money my grandmother left me, plus my savings, is almost enough to buy a car.*

Some people avoid using the noun *plus* as a synonym for 'advantage' in formal contexts: * *Being within walking distance of the station is one of the pluses of living on this estate.*

The expression *an added plus* is tautological and should be avoided.

The construction *plus which* is avoided by many speakers, particularly when beginning a new sentence or clause: * *I'm fed up and I've had enough. Plus which, I'm tired.*

The use of *plus* in the sense of 'and' or 'with' is best restricted to informal contexts: * *He's afraid to go sailing because he can't swim, plus he suffers from seasickness.* * *She was met at the airport by her son plus his new girlfriend.* See also **minus**.

p.m. *see* **a.m.** and **p.m.**

pneumatic and **pneumonia** Note the spelling of these words, particularly the silent initial *p* and the *-eu-* of the first syllable. The prefix *pneum-* is derived from a Greek word meaning 'air', as in *pneumatic* ('using compressed air'), or 'breath', as in **pneumonia** ('inflammation of the lungs').

poet or **poetess**? *see* **-ess**; **non-sexist terms**.

poignant This word, meaning 'distressing', is usually pronounced [*poyny*ănt] although [*poyn*ănt] is also acceptable. The *g* is silent.

policeman or **policewoman**? *see* **non-sexist terms**.

politic or **political**? *Politic* means 'prudent', 'shrewd', or 'cunning': *political* means 'of politics, government, policy-making, etc.': * *a politic decision* * *a political party*. The two adjectives should not be confused. *Politic*

was originally synonymous with *political*: this sense of the word survives only in the expression *the body politic*, meaning 'the state'.

Note the different stress patterns of the two words: *politic* is stressed on the first syllable, *political* on the second.

political correctness *Political correctness*, or *PC*, is the avoidance of words, phrases, or actions that may be deemed offensive by a particular section of society, such as ethnic minorities, homosexuals, women, and **blind**, **deaf**, **disabled** or old people: * *Speakers have been asked not to use descriptions deemed politically incorrect on grounds of race, disability and gender* (*Daily Telegraph*). It extends beyond vocabulary, to the way in which people are portrayed in television advertisements, children's books, etc. and the way in which they interact in their working or social lives. The term is most frequently used in situations where this anxiety to avoid offence seems excessive, and is often the subject of humorous exaggeration: * *The legions of the politically correct continue to direct their accusations of racism, sexism, stoutism and inappropriate body language at every area of our public and private life, sniffing out imaginary insults and creating antagonism in their wake* (*Daily Telegraph*). *Political correctness* also strives to project a more positive image of negative or undesirable qualities, with the substitution of such euphemisms as *deficiency achievement* for failure. Other examples of terms proposed as politically correct alternatives include *person of size* for *fat*, *aurally inconvenienced* for *deaf*, and *companion animal* for *pet*.

Of American origin, *political correctness* is often regarded in Britain as unacceptable interference with English usage and the natural development of the English language. Nevertheless, it has served a useful purpose in drawing people's attention to the need for sensitivity in their use of words and images, and not all its suggested changes are necessarily for the worse. *See also* **abled**; **ableism**; **ageism**; **challenged**; **non-sexist terms**; **sexism**.

politics *see* **-ics**.

poltergeist The word *poltergeist*, denoting a mischievous spirit, is sometimes misspelt: note the *-er-* in the middle and the *-ei-* in the final syllable. The word is pronounced [*pol*tĕrgīst].

populace or **populous**? These two words are occasionally confused, since they are pronounced in the same way: [*pop*yoolăs]. *Populace* is a noun meaning 'inhabitants' or 'the ordinary people': * *The cries roused the populace.* *This news will not go down well with the general populace.* *Populous* is an adjective meaning 'densely populated' or 'crowded': * *California is the nation's most populous state.*

pore or **pour**? These spellings are sometimes confused. *Pore* as a verb means 'look intently': * *They pored over the map*; *pour* means 'cause to flow': * *She poured the tea.* The noun *pore* refers to a minute opening in the skin.

portmanteau word *see* **blends**.

Portuguese This word is sometimes misspelt; note the second *u* and the *-e-* that follows it.

position To *position* is to put carefully and deliberately in a specific place; the verb is best avoided where *place*, *put*, *post*, *situate*, *locate*, etc. would be adequate or more appropriate. * *She positioned the mat on the carpet to hide the stain.* * *He put* [not *positioned*] *his dirty plate on top of the others.* * *The offices are situated* [not *positioned*] *in the town centre.* Some people also dislike the unnecessary use of the noun *position* in many contexts: for example, it is usually possible to replace the verbal phrase *be in a position to* with *be able to* or *can*: * *I am not in a position to answer your questions.*

possessed The adjective *possessed* is followed by the preposition *of* in the sense 'having': * *He is possessed of an ability to communicate with animals.* In the sense 'dominated', it is followed by the preposition *by*: * *She was possessed by a desire for revenge.* * *possessed by a demon.*

possessives The two ways of showing that a noun is one of possession are the apostrophe and the use of the word *of*: * *Anne's car* * *the company's profits* * *the rabbits' burrow* * *soldiers of the Queen.* The apostrophe is used more frequently than *of* and there is no firm rule as to where it is appropriate to use *of*. It is possible to say either: * *the table's leg* or *the leg of the table*, but where there is a recognised phrase containing *of*: * *the Valley of the Rocks*, an apostrophe cannot be substituted. *Of* is usually used of inanimate things; when it is used of people an apostrophe is generally used as well: * *a friend of Peter's*. It is also often used for geographical regions: * *the wines of France* * *the cities of Europe.*

In cases of joint possession the

apostrophe belongs to the last owner mentioned: * *Tom and Lucy's house* * *Beaumont and Fletcher's plays*. With a compound noun the last word takes the apostrophe: * *the lady-in-waiting's dress* * *the county court's judge*.

Care should be taken with such phrases as *one of the residents' dogs*, which might mean 'the dogs belonging to one of the residents' or 'one of the dogs jointly owned by the residents'. It is better to rephrase such an expression to avoid ambiguity. *See also* **apostrophe**; **'s or s'?**

post- Some people object to the frequent use of the prefix *post-*, meaning 'after', to coin new adjectives, often of a futuristic nature: * *post-nuclear Britain* * *post-feminist literature* * *Russia has shivered in the cold wind of economic reality throughout the post-Communist period*, or to produce cumbersome phrases that could be reworded more elegantly: * *post-September 11 anxiety* * *post-retirement financial planning*.

posthumous This word causes problems with spelling and pronunciation. In speech the *h* is silent [*post*ewmŭs]; the first syllable is not as in *post*, but as in *possible*.

postman or **postwoman**? *see* **non-sexist terms**.

pour *see* **pore or pour?**

power The word *power* is sometimes used adjectivally to refer to an important business occasion. For example * *a power breakfast* [or *lunch*] is a meeting of influential people from e.g. politics, business, or the media that is held over breakfast (or lunch). This vogue usage is best restricted to informal contexts.

p.p. The abbreviation *p.p.* (or *per pro.*), short for the Latin phrase *per procurationem*, is used when signing a letter on behalf of somebody else. The Latin phrase means 'by proxy' or 'through the agency of', and the abbreviation should precede the name of the person signing the letter. In modern usage the abbreviation is frequently interpreted as 'for and on behalf of' and placed before the name of the person on whose behalf the letter is signed. This 'incorrect' sequence is so well established that the correct usage could lead to misunderstanding.

practical or **practicable**? The adjective *practical* has a wide range of senses; the principal meaning of *practicable* is 'capable of being done or put into practice'. A *practicable* suggestion is simply possible or feasible; a *practical* suggestion is also useful, sensible, realistic, economical, profitable, and likely to be effective or successful: * *It may be practicable to create jobs for everyone but this would not be a practical solution to the problems of unemployment*. Careful users maintain the distinction between the two words, which is also applicable to their antonyms, *impractical* and *impracticable*: * *It's impractical to use the washing machine when you only have a couple of shirts to wash*. * *It's impracticable to use the washing machine when there is a power cut*. *Unpractical*, a less frequent antonym of *practical*, may refer to a person who lacks practical abilities.

Additional senses of *practical* include 'not theoretical', 'suitable for use', 'skilled at doing or making things', and 'virtual': * *a practical* *course in first aid * a more practical layout for the kitchen * My brother is not a very practical man. * She has practical control of the company. See also* **practically**.

practically The adverb *practically* is widely used as a synonym for 'almost', 'nearly', 'virtually', etc.: * *I practically broke my ankle.* Some people dislike this usage, which can lead to confusion with one of the more literal senses of the word: * *It is practically impossible,* for example, may mean 'it is impossible in practice' or 'it is almost impossible'. *See also* **practical** or **practicable**?

practice or **practise**? The noun is *practice*, the verb is *practise*: * *the doctor's practice * the doctor who practises in our town.* In American English both the noun and verb are spelt *practice*.

practitioner This word is sometimes misspelt, the most frequent error being the substitution of *c* or *s* for the final *t*.

pray or **prey**? These spellings are sometimes confused. The verb *pray* means 'speak to God': * *pray for forgiveness.* The verb *prey*, which is usually followed by *on* or *upon*, means 'hunt' or 'obsess': * *The lion preys on other animals. * The problem is preying on my mind.* The noun *prey* means 'animals hunted for food': * *birds of prey.* Spelling mistakes may be avoided if *pray* is associated with *prayer*.

pre- *see* **hyphen; per-, pre-** or **pro-**?; **pre-war**.

precautionary measure The phrase *precautionary measure* can usually be replaced by the noun *precaution,*

which denotes a measure taken to avoid something harmful or undesirable: * *The police closed the road as a precaution(ary measure) against flooding.*

precede or **proceed**? *Precede* means 'come before', 'go before', or 'be before'; *proceed* means 'continue', 'go on', or 'advance': * *September precedes October. * The text is preceded by an introduction. * I am unable to proceed with this work. * They proceeded to dismantle the car.* The two verbs should not be confused or misspelt: note the different spelling but identical pronunciation of the second syllables, *-cede* and *-ceed* [*-seed*].

precedence or **precedent**? The noun *precedence* means 'priority' or 'superiority'; the noun *precedent* denotes a previous example that may serve as a model (in a court of law or elsewhere): * *Should this work take precedence over our other commitments? The guests were seated in order of precedence. * The committee's decision has set a precedent for future claims. * This result is without precedent.* Both nouns are derived from the verb *precede* (*see* **precede** or **proceed**?); to interchange them is wrong.

The pronunciation of *precedence* is [*presidĕns*]. The noun *precedent* is pronounced [*presidĕnt*], but the rarer adjective is pronounced [*priseedĕnt*].

precipitate or **precipitous**? The adjective *precipitate* means 'rushing', 'hasty', 'rash', or 'sudden'; *precipitous* means 'like a precipice' or 'very steep': * *a precipitate decision * their precipitate departure * a precipitous slope.* The substitution of *precipitous* for *precipitate* is disliked by some users but acknowledged by most dictionaries. *Precipitate*, however, should not be used in the sense of 'precipitous'.

The word *precipitate* is also used as a verb and as a noun. In the pronunciation of the adjective and noun, the final syllable is unstressed: [pri*si*pităt]. The verb has the same primary stress pattern but the final syllable is pronounced to rhyme with *gate*.

preclude *see* **exclude** or **preclude**?

precondition *see* **condition** or **precondition**?

predecessor The noun *predecessor* denotes the previous holder of an office, post, etc.: * *Her predecessor had left the accounts in a mess.* Although the words *predecessor* and *decease* (meaning 'death') are both derived from the Latin verb *decedere*, a predecessor is not necessarily dead: the Latin verb means 'go away', not 'die'. Note the spelling of *predecessor*, particularly the *c* and *-ss-* and the *-or* ending.

predicate The *predicate* is that part of a sentence or clause that includes information about the **subject**, but excludes the subject itself. Thus, in *the President conceded defeat*, the predicate is *conceded defeat*. See also **predict** or **predicate**?

predicative *see* **adjectives**.

predict or **predicate**? To *predict* is to foretell; the verb *predicate* means 'affirm', 'declare', or 'imply': * *It is impossible to predict the result of tomorrow's match.* * *They predicated that the accident had been caused by negligence.* In British English the verb

predicate is rare and largely restricted to formal contexts. In American English, however, it is widely used as a synonym for 'base' or 'found': * *Her decision was predicated on past experience.*

In grammar and logic the word *predicate* is also used as a noun (*see* **predicate**).

The verb *predicate* is pronounced [*predi*kayt]; the noun is pronounced [*predi*kăt].

predominantly or **predominately**? Although the adverb *predominantly* is the more common form, *predominately* is also correct and shares the same meaning of 'to a prevailing or dominant degree': * *a predominantly white colour* * *a predominately Roman culture.*

preface *see* **foreword** or **preface**?; **prefix** or **preface**?

prefer The elements that follow the verb *prefer* should be separated by *to*, not *than*: * *I prefer cricket to football.* * *She prefers watching television to reading a book.* If these elements are infinitives, the preposition *to* (and the second infinitive marker) may be replaced by *rather than* in informal contexts: * *He prefers to walk rather than (to) drive.* In formal contexts the sentence should be rephrased: * *He would rather walk than drive.* * *He prefers walking to driving.*

Careful users avoid qualifying the verb *prefer* and its derived adjective *preferable* with such adverbs as *more*, *most*, etc.: * *Which dress do you prefer* [not *prefer most*]? * *Quiet background music is acceptable but complete silence is preferable* [not *more preferable*].

The verb *prefer* is stressed on the

second syllable; the final *r* is doubled before *-ed*, *-ing*, and *-er*. In the adjective *preferable*, the adverb *preferably*, and the noun *preference*, the stress shifts to the first syllable and the second *r* is not doubled. The pronunciation of *preferable* with the stress on the second syllable [prifĕrăbl] is widely disliked. *See also* **spelling**.

prefix or **preface**? The words *prefix* and *preface* are most frequently used as nouns (*see* **foreword** or **preface**?; **prefixes** and **suffixes**). As verbs, both can mean 'add at the beginning' or 'put before', although *preface* is more common: ● *She prefaced/prefixed her speech with a few words of welcome.* Some users dislike this use of the verb *prefix*, reserving it for the literal sense of 'add as a prefix': ● *The word 'organised' may be prefixed by 'dis-' or 'un-'.*

prefixes and **suffixes** *Prefixes* and *suffixes* are elements attached to a word in order to form a new word. *Prefixes* are attached to the beginnings of words and include: ● *un-* ● *dis-* ● *anti-* ● *non-* ● *ex-*. *Suffixes* are attached to the ends of words and include: ● *-ism* ● *-ful* ● *-dom* ● *-logy* ● *-ship*. *Prefixes* are sometimes used with hyphens, sometimes not: ● *disenchanted* ● *ex-husband*: *see* **hyphen**.

There are some cases where a word cannot stand alone without its prefix: ● *uncouth* ● *disgruntled* ● *dishevelled* ● *unkempt*, although *gruntled*, *kempt*, etc., are occasionally used jocularly.

Most affixes are in productive use: they can be attached to any appropriate noun. However, new coinages involving affixes are often disliked: *see*, for example, **macro-** and **micro-**.

PREFIXES	
Cross-references – e.g. *see* **aero** or **air**? – to main entries in the *Good Word Guide* where there is a fuller discussion are also included.	
a-	**1** without; not: ● *asymmetrical* **2** in; on; at: ● *ashore*
aero-, air-	aircraft: ● *aeronautics see* **aero** or **air**?
ambi-	both; two: ● *ambidextrous*
ante-	before: ● *antenatal see* **ante-** or **anti-**?
anthropo-	human: ● *anthropology*
anti-	against: ● *anti-aircraft see* **ante-** or **anti-**?
arch-, archi-	chief: ● *archenemy see* **arch-** and **archi-**
astro-	stars: ● *astronomy*
audio-	hearing or sound: ● *audiovisual*
auto-	self: ● *autobiography*
be-	(used to make verbs): ● *becalm*
bi-	two; twice: ● *bicycle see* **bi-**
biblio-	book: ● *bibliography*
bio-	life: ● *biography* ● *biology see* **bio-**
by-	less important: ● *by-election*
centi-	one hundredth: ● *centimetre*
chron-	time: ● *chronological*
co-, col-, com-, con-, cor-	together; with: ● *collect* ● *combine see* **co-**
contra-	against; opposite: ● *contradict*
counter-	**1** opposite: ● *counteract* **2** corresponding; matching: ● *counterpart*
cyber-	computers: ● *cybercafé see* **cyber-**
de-	**1** take away something: ● *dethrone* **2** go back: ● *decode see* **de-**

deca-	ten times: * decagon see **deca-** or **deci-**?	**hect-, hecto-**	one hundred: * hectare
deci-	one tenth: * decibel see **deca-** or **deci-**?	**hemi-**	half: * hemisphere see **demi-**, **hemi-**, or **semi-**?
demi-	half: * demigod see **demi-**, **hemi-** or **semi-**?	**epta-**	seven: * heptagon
di-	two: * diphthong * dioxide	**hexa-**	six: * hexagon
dia-	through; across: * diameter	**homo-**	same: * homogeneous
digi-	digital: * digibox	**hydro-**	water: * hydroelectricity
dis-	1 not: * disagree * dissimilar 2 opposite: * disconnect see **dis-** or **dys-**?	**hyper-**	much more than normal: * hypermarket see **hyper-** or **hypo-**?
dys-	abnormal: * dysfunction see **dis-** or **dys-**?	**hypo-**	under: * hypodermic see **hyper-** or **hypo-**?
e-	1 electronic: * email 2 European: * e-number see **e-**	**ig-, il-, im-, in-, ir-**	not: * ignoble * illogical * impossible
eco-	environment; ecology: * eco-friendly * eco-aware see **eco-**	**il-, im-, in-, ir-**	in; into: * income * irrigate
electro-	electricity: * electrolysis	**infra-**	below: * infra-red
em-, en-	1 used to make verbs): * enthrone * enrich * enable 2 in; into: * enlist	**inter-**	1 between: * intermediary 2 from one to another: * interchange see **inter-** or **intra-**?
equi-	equal: * equidistant	**intra-**	inside: * intravenous see **inter-** or **intra-**?
Euro-	Europe; European Union: * Eurocrat see **euro-**	**kilo-**	one thousand: * kilometre
ex-	1 former: * ex-president 2 out of: expel see **ex**	**macro-**	large: * macrocosm see **macro-** and **micro-**
extra-	outside: * extraterrestrial	**mal-**	bad: * malfunction
for-	prohibition: * forbid see **for-** or **fore-**?	**mega-**	1 million: * megawatt 2 big: * megaphone see **mega-**
fore-	1 front: * foreword 2 before: * foretell see **for-** or **fore-**?	**meta-**	1 change; after: * metamorphosis 2 transcending: * meta-fiction see **meta-**
geo-	earth: * geology	**micro-**	small: * microscope see **macro-** and **micro-**
grand-	parents of your parents; children of your children: * grandfather * granddaughter see **grand-** or **great-**?	**mid-**	middle: * midday
		milli-	one thousandth: * millimetre
		mini-	small: * minibus
great-	parents of your grand-parents; children of your grandchildren: * great-grandmother * great-grand-son see **grand-** or **great-**?	**mis-**	bad; badly: * mislead
		mono-	one: * monotony
		multi-	many: * multicoloured see **multi-**
haemo-	blood: * haemorrhage	**neo-**	new: * neoclassical

neuro-	mind or nerves: • *neurosis*
non-	not: • *nonstop see* **non-**
ob-	against: • *obstruct*
octa-, octo-	eight: • *octagon* • *octopus*
omni-	all: • *omnipotent*
ortho-	correct: • *orthodox*
out-	1 greater than: • *outlast* 2 outside: • *outbuilding*
over-	1 above: • *overhang* 2 too much: • *overdo see* **overly**
penta-	five: • *pentagon*
peri-	around: • *perimeter*
photo-	1 light: • *photosynthesis* 2 photography: • *photocopy*
physio-	nature: • *physiology*
poly-	many • *polygon*
post-	after: • *postscript* • *post-war see* **post-**
pre-	before: • *prelude*
pro-	1 in favour of: • *pro-African* 2 substitute: • *pronoun*
proto-	first; original: • *prototype*
pseudo-	not real; pretended: • *pseudonym*
psycho-	mind; behaviour: • *psychology*
quad-	four: • *quadrangle*
quin-	five: • *quintet*
re-	again: • *reappear see* **re-**
retro-	back: • *retrograde see* **retro**
self-	oneself: • *self-confident see* **self**

semi-	half: • *semicircle see* **demi-, hemi-** or **semi-**?
sept-	seven: • *septet*
sex-	six: • *sextet*
socio-	social; society: • *sociology*
sub-	1 under: • *subsoil* 2 less than • *subnormal*
super-	1 over: • *superimpose* 2 greater: • *supersonic see* **super-**
sym-, syn-	together with: • *sympathy* • *synthesis*
techno-	practical skill and science: • *technology see* **techno-**
tele-	distant: • *telephone* • *television see* **tele-**
theo-	God: • *theology*
thermo-	heat: • *thermometer*
trans-	across: • *transcontinental*
tri-	three: • *triangle*
turbo-	1 driven by a turbine: • *turbojet* 2 powerful: • *turbo computer see* **turbo-**
ultra-	beyond: • *ultraviolet see* **ultra**
un-	1 not: • *unhappy* 2 opposite: • *undo* • *untie see* **non-**
under-	1 below: • *undergrowth* 2 too little: • *underdeveloped*
uni-	one: • *unity*
vice-	assistant: • *vice-president*
video-	video: • *videolink*

prelude Some people dislike the frequent use of the noun *prelude* in the sense of 'introduction': • *The leaders had an informal meeting this morning as a prelude to next week's summit in Geneva.* The noun *prelude* is principally used to denote a piece of music: • *one of Chopin's preludes.*

premier The adjective *premier* is best avoided where *foremost, principal, first*, etc. would be adequate or more appropriate: • *We consulted one of the country's premier authorities on the subject. Premier* is pronounced [*premyĕr*] or [*premiĕr*], the first syllable having the short *e* of *them*, not the long *e* of *theme*. It should not be confused with **premiere**, which is sometimes pronounced in the same way.

premiere Some people dislike the use of the word *premiere* as a verb, meaning 'give the first performance of': * *The film will be premiered in New York.* The verb is also used intransitively: * *The play premiered in the West End.*

The noun *premiere*, meaning 'first performance', is acceptable to all users: * *the world premiere of Andrew Lloyd Webber's latest musical.*

Premiere may be pronounced [*prem*iair] or [*prem*iĕr]. It is sometimes spelt with a grave accent on the second *e*, as in the French word from which it is derived: *première. See also* **accents.**

premises The noun *premises*, denoting a building (or buildings) and any accompanying land or grounds, is always plural: * *Their new premises are on the other side of the railway line.* The singular noun *premise*, which is not used in this context, means 'assumption' or 'proposition'; it has the variant spelling *premiss*.

premiss *see* **premises.**

preoccupied *see* **occupied** or **preoccupied**?

preparation The noun *preparation* is sometimes misspelt, a frequent error being the substitution of *-per-* for *-par-*, as in *desperation*.

prepositions *Prepositions* are such words as: * *at* * *with* * *of* * *up* * *before* that show the relation of a noun or noun equivalent to the rest of the sentence. It is frequently claimed that

there exists a grammatical rule that sentences should never end with a preposition. It is true that prepositions, as their name implies, usually precede the noun or pronoun to which they are attached: * *It was under the chair.* * *They drove to Birmingham*, but it certainly does not have to be in this position. * *Which village did you stay in?* and * *In which village did you stay?* are both possible, although the latter sounds more formal. In some cases it is hardly possible to put the preposition anywhere but at the end of the sentence: * *What is he up to?* * *It isn't worth worrying about.* A reliable rule is that the preposition should be placed where it sounds most natural.

The 'rule' about not ending a sentence with a preposition originated in the fact that a Latin sentence cannot end with a preposition, but there is no reason for this to have any implication for English usage.

A preposition does not need to be repeated when it applies to two elements of a sentence: * *They went to France and Italy.* * *He behaved with tact and discretion*, although the preposition must be repeated if ambiguity might otherwise arise. * *They were arguing about physical fitness and about drinking spirits* could have a different meaning if the second *about* were omitted.

On the use of a preposition with a particular verb, adjective, or noun, *see* **individual entries.**

prerequisite or **perquisite**? A *prerequisite* is a precondition; a *perquisite* is a benefit, privilege, or exclusive right: * *A degree is not a prerequisite for a career in journalism.* * *A company car is often regarded as a perquisite.* In the sense of 'incidental benefit', the noun *perquisite* is largely restricted to formal contexts – the abbreviation *perk* being the usual form elsewhere: * *one of the perks of the job*. See also **prerequisite** or **requisite?**

prerequisite or **requisite?** Both these words may be used as nouns or adjectives. *Requisite* relates to anything that is required, necessary, essential, or indispensable; *prerequisite* relates to something that is required in advance: * *Does the building have the requisite number of fire exits?* * *The shop sells pens, paper, and other writing requisites.* * *Physical fitness is prerequisite to/a prerequisite of success at sport.* See also **prerequisite** or **perquisite?**

prescribe or **proscribe?** To *prescribe* is to lay down as a rule or to advise or order as a remedy; to *proscribe* is to condemn, prohibit, outlaw, or exile: * *The union has prescribed a new procedure for dealing with complaints.* * *Surrogate motherhood has been proscribed in Britain.* * *Proscribing the doctor's habit of prescribing* (*Daily Telegraph* headline). The two verbs are similar in pronunciation but almost opposite in meaning: a *prescribed book* is recommended, a *proscribed book* should not be read; a *prescribed drug* should be taken, a *proscribed drug* is banned.

presently Some people object to the increasingly frequent use of the adverb *presently* in place of *currently*, *at present*, or *now*: * *Mr Iain Duncan-Smith, presently leader of the opposition* * *The company presently manufactures components for the electronics industry.* The word has long been used in this sense in Scotland and America.

The principal meaning of *presently*

in British English is 'soon': * *We walked on a little further and presently we reached the inn.* * *I'll phone him presently.*

preside The verb *preside* is followed by the preposition *at* or *over*: * *The chairman presided at* [or *over*] *the meeting.*

pressure or **pressurise?** The verb *pressure*, which literally means 'apply pressure to', is frequently used in the figurative sense of 'coerce': * *They were pressured into accepting the pay rise.* The literal meaning of the verb *pressurise* is 'increase the pressure in', but it is also used figuratively in British English: * *Aircraft cabins are pressurised to maintain normal atmospheric pressure at high altitudes.* * *They were pressurised into accepting the pay rise.*

Some dislike and avoid the figurative use of *pressurise* and *pressurised*, especially in potentially ambiguous contexts: * *The ability to work effectively in a pressurised stimulating environment is essential* (*Daily Telegraph*).

prestige The noun *prestige*, denoting the high status, esteem, or renown derived from wealth, success, or influence, is usually pronounced [pres*teezh*]. *Prestige* is also used adjectivally: * *a prestige company* * *a prestige car*. See also **prestigious**.

prestigious The adjective *prestigious* is frequently used in the sense of 'having or conferring prestige': * *new ways of raising money for the country's most prestigious opera house* * *The company will shortly be relocating to prestigious new offices in the City.* The original meaning of *prestigious* was less complimentary: derived from the Latin word for 'conjuring tricks', it was used as a synonym for 'fraudulent' or 'deceitful'.

Unlike *prestige*, *prestigious* has the anglicised pronunciation [pres*tij*ŭs].

presume *see* **assume** or **presume?**

presumptuous or **presumptive?** *Presumptuous* means 'bold', 'forward', or 'impudent'; *presumptive* means 'based on presumption or probability' or 'giving reasonable grounds for belief': * *It's rather presumptuous of him to make such a request.* * *This is only presumptive evidence.* The adjective *presumptive* is also used in the term *heir presumptive*, which denotes a person whose right to succeed or inherit may be superseded by the birth of another.

Note the spelling of *presumptuous*, particularly the second *u*.

pretence, pretension or **pretentiousness?** The noun *pretence* denotes the act of pretending; a *pretension* is a claim; *pretentiousness* means 'ostentation' or 'affectation': * *She made a pretence of closing the door.* * *He has no pretensions to fame.* * *Their pretentiousness does not impress me.*

In some contexts *pretence* may be used in place of *pretension*, especially to denote a false or unsupported claim; both nouns may be used in the sense of 'pretentiousness'.

Compare the spellings of *pretension* and *pretentiousness*, particularly the *s* of the former and the second *t* of the latter. In American English the *c* of *pretence* is replaced by *s*.

prevaricate or **procrastinate?** To *prevaricate* is to be evasive, misleading, or untruthful; to *procrastinate* is to delay, defer, or put off: * *She prevaricated in*

order to avoid revealing her husband's whereabouts. * *He procrastinated in the hope of avoiding the work altogether.* The two verbs should not be confused: *prevaricate* is partially derived from the Latin word *varus*, meaning 'crooked'; *procrastinate* contains the Latin word *cras*, meaning 'tomorrow'.

prevent When the verb *prevent* is followed by an *-ing* form in formal contexts, the *-ing* form should be preceded either by *from* or by a possessive adjective or noun: * *They prevented me from winning.* * *They prevented Andrew from winning.* * *They prevented my winning.* * *They prevented Andrew's winning.* In informal contexts the last example may be considered unnatural or unidiomatic, and the word **from** may be omitted from the first two examples: * *They prevented me/Andrew winning.* See also **-ing forms**.

preventive or **preventative?** Either word may be used as an adjective or noun, but *preventive* is the more frequent: * *preventive measures* * *preventative surgery* * *This drug is used as a preventive/preventative.* Some users consider *preventative* to be a needlessly long variant.

In medical and technical contexts the adjective is used with reference to procedures that forestall disease, damage, breakdown, etc., rather than curing or repairing it: * *preventive medicine* * *preventive maintenance.*

pre-war This word is usually hyphenated, although some dictionaries list it as a one-word compound (*see also* **hyphen**). *Pre-war* is generally used as an adjective: * *pre-war conditions* * *reverting to pre-war practices.* Its adverbial use is less frequent, the phrase *before the war* being preferred by some users: • *These houses were built pre-war/before the war.*

In general usage, *pre-war* usually refers to the period preceding World War II, but in some contexts the reference may be to World War I or, more rarely, to a different war. This can occasionally lead to ambiguity or confusion: • *pre-war house prices in the Falkland Islands.*

prey *see* **pray** or **prey?**

price *see* **cost** or **price?**

prima facie This Latin phrase is used adverbially or adjectivally in the sense of 'at first sight', '(based) on first impressions', or 'apparently true': • *Her argument seems reasonable prima facie.* • *There is prima facie evidence to support his case.* Largely restricted to formal contexts, the phrase is pronounced [*prī*mă *fay*shee].

primarily Many users prefer to stress this word on the first syllable, [*prī*mărĕli], but this is very difficult to say unless the speaker is speaking slowly and carefully. The pronunciation with the stress on the second syllable [prī*merr*ĕli] is becoming increasingly common in British English, although disliked by many. It is the standard pronunciation in American English. *See also* **stress**.

prime Some people dislike the frequent use of the adjective *prime* in the sense of 'best', 'most important', 'principal', etc., especially when it is applied to something that is not of the highest quality, significance, or rank: • *in prime condition* • *the prime position* • *a prime example.*

primeval This word, meaning 'of the first ages', is usually spelt *primeval* but in British English may also be spelt *primaeval*. *See also* **-ae** and **-oe**.

primitive *see* **savage**.

principal or **principle?** These two spellings are often confused. The adjective *principal* means 'of the most importance': • *the principal cause*; the noun *principal* refers to the head of an organisation: • *the principal of a college*. *Principle* is always a noun and refers to a fundamental truth or standard: • *moral principles*. The adjectival form is *principled*. *In principle* means 'in theory'; *on principle* means 'because of the principle'.

principal parts The *principal parts* of a verb are the main inflected forms from which all the other verb forms can be derived. In English they usually include the infinitive, the present participle, the past tense, and past participle. The principal parts of *give*, for example, would be: • *give, giving, gave, given*. Often the past tense and past participle are the same, and do not both have to be listed: • *walk, walking, walked*. The present participle is not always included when it is derived regularly, as in: • *know, knew, known*. For irregular principal parts, *see* table at **verbs**.

principle *see* **principal** or **principle?**

prioritise The verb *prioritise*, meaning 'put in order of priority' or 'give priority to', is disliked by some users as an example of the increasing tendency to coin new verbs by adding the suffix *-ise* (or *-ize*) to nouns and adjectives: • *The methods of increasing industrial* *output have been prioritised.* • *Where women are, in fact, seen to prioritise their career, they are considered in some way 'unnatural', 'unfeminine' or 'on the shelf'* (*The Bookseller*).

prior to Many people object to the unnecessary use of the phrase *prior to* in place of the simpler and more natural preposition *before*: • *Players and singers rehearsed the works during the afternoon prior to performing them in the evening* (*Chichester Observer*). The use of *prior* as an adjective is acceptable to all: • *I would like to come but unfortunately have a prior engagement.*

prise or **prize**? For the meaning 'to force open', either spelling can be used in British English, but *prise* is more common: • *In the end we managed to prise the lid off. Prize* is the only possible spelling for the noun meaning 'a reward' and the verb 'value greatly': • *Gloria won first prize in the competition.* • *The thieves made off with most of their prized possessions.* In American English, the spelling *prize* is more common than *prise* for the sense 'force open'.

pristine The use of *pristine* to mean 'spotlessly clean', 'pure', or 'as good as new' is acceptable to most users: • *a pristine tablecloth* • *He made the packet look untouched and in pristine condition* (*Daily Telegraph*). A few people object to this usage, restricting the adjective to its earlier sense of 'original' or 'primitive': • *The mists of a pristine swamp* • *The pristine severity of the Benedictine rule was moderated in the course of time.*

The second syllable of *pristine* may be pronounced to rhyme with *mean* or *mine*.

privacy This word has two pronunciations in British English: [*prĭvăsi*] and [*prīvăsi*]. The standard American English pronunciation is [*prīvăsi*].

privilege This word, meaning 'special right or advantage', is often misspelt. Note particularly the second *i* and the first *e*. Remember also that there is no *d* as in *ledge*.

prize *see* **prise** or **prize**?

pro- *see* **per, pre-** or **pro-**?

probe In the headline language of popular newspapers, the noun *probe* is often used in place of the longer *enquiry* or *investigation*: • *Crucial questions the BBC poll probe must answer* (*Sunday Times*). In medicine a *probe* is a slender instrument for examining a wound or cavity; *space probes* examine and investigate the expanse beyond the earth's atmosphere.

In non-technical contexts *probe* is more frequently used as a verb: • *After further gentle probing, Mark revealed some new details of the incident. See also* **journalese**.

procedure or **proceeding**? The noun *procedure* denotes a way of doing something; the noun *proceeding* (or, more frequently, *proceedings*) means 'something that is done': • *to follow the established procedure* • *to take part in the proceedings.* The two words should not be confused. Note the difference in spelling, particularly the *-ced-* of *procedure* and the *-ceed-* of *proceeding*.

proceed *see* **precede** or **proceed**?

proceeding *see* **procedure** or **proceeding**?

process The noun *process* is always pronounced with the stress on the first syllable, [*prō*ses]. (The pronunciation [*pros*es], with a short *o*, is largely restricted to American English.) The verb *process* is also stressed on the first syllable in most contexts; however, in the rare sense of 'move (as if) in a procession': • *They processed down the avenue*, the second syllable is stressed, [prŏ*ses*]. This rare sense, a back formation from *procession*, is etymologically distinct from the noun and other meanings of the verb.

pro-choice *see* **pro-life**.

procrastinate *see* **prevaricate** or **procrastinate?**

prodigal *Prodigal* means 'recklessly wasteful', 'extravagant', or 'lavish': • *Her brother has always been prodigal with his money.* • *They were prodigal of praise.* The use of the adjective *prodigal* to mean 'returning home after a long absence' (based on a misunderstanding of the word in the New Testament parable of the prodigal son, Luke 15:11–32) is disliked and avoided by some careful users: • *Prodigal performers from the Bosham Players are to return home 40 years on* (*Chichester Observer*).

The use of the noun *prodigal*, however, in the extended sense of 'returned wanderer' or 'repentant sinner', rather than the traditional sense of 'spendthrift', is acceptable to most: • *The prodigal has returned.*

prodigy or **protégé?** The noun *prodigy*, meaning 'marvel', is used to denote an exceptionally talented person, especially a child: • *Tracy Austin, then 14, was starting to be acknowledged as one of the first child prodigies in professional tennis* (*Daily Telegraph*). A *protégé* is someone who receives help, guidance, protection, patronage, etc. from a more influential or experienced person: • *one of Lord Olivier's protégés.* The two nouns should not be confused. Derived from the French word *protéger*, meaning 'protect', the noun *protégé* has the (optional) feminine form *protégée*.

produce or **product?** Both these nouns denote something that is produced. *Produce* refers to things that have been produced by growing or farming, whereas *product* usually refers to industrially produced goods: • *farm produce* • *the company's latest product.* The noun *product* is also used in more abstract senses: • *He is a product of the public-school system.* • *the product of a vivid imagination* • *Such attitudes are the product of ignorance and suspicion.*

Note that some people object to the word *product* being applied to ideas or other things that are not actually physically produced: • *The latest product from the building societies is a high-interest account for children.*

Both nouns are pronounced with the stress on the first syllable. The verb *produce*, however, is stressed on the second syllable: [prŏ*dews*].

productivity The noun *productivity*, frequently used in industrial contexts, relates to efficiency or rate of production; it is not synonymous with output, which denotes the amount produced: • *a productivity bonus* • *The installation of new machinery will increase the company's productivity*; *employing more workers will only increase its output.*

professional The adjective *professional* is applied to people who are engaged in a profession or who take part in a sport or other activity for gain: * *doctors, lawyers, and other professional people* * *a professional golfer/actor/writer/musician.* The noun *professional* is used to denote such people. In general usage the word *professional*, in the sense of '(person) engaged in a profession', may refer to any career that requires advanced learning and/or special training, such as law, medicine, theology, accountancy, engineering, teaching, nursing, and the armed forces. Many users object to the wider application of the term to include other middle-class occupations: * *a marketing professional* * *sales professionals* * *recruitment professionals.*

Note the spelling of the word *professional*, which has one *f*, and *-ss-*.

professor This word is sometimes misspelt. Note the single *f*, the *-ss-*, and the *-or* ending.

proffer *see* **offer** or **proffer**?

proficient The adjective *proficient* is followed by the preposition *in* or *at*: * *Applicants must be proficient in* [or *at*] *French and German.*

profile The noun *profile* is widely used in the expression *keep a low profile*, meaning 'be inconspicuous or unobtrusive' or 'avoid attention or publicity': * *The group has kept a low profile since the arrest of its leader.* Two adjectival compounds, *low-profile* and *high-profile*, have developed from this use: * *a low-profile investigation* * *The star has lived a low-profile existence since the scandal appeared in the press.*

The noun *profile* is also used alone in a further extension of this sense: * *She* [Joan Bakewell] *is credited with raising the profile of arts coverage on television* (*Sunday Times*). * *You can't risk loss of profile, market share, and media appeal* (*The Bookseller*).

The word *profile* is also occasionally used as a verb, meaning 'construct a profile of': * *The new leader has been profiled in most of the leading newspapers.* See also **visible**.

profoundly deaf *Profoundly deaf* is the preferred modern term to describe a person who is both deaf and unable to speak: * *A special school for the profoundly deaf.* It replaces such former terms as *deaf-mute* and *deaf-and-dumb*, which are now avoided because of their negative connotations.

prognosis *see* **diagnosis** or **prognosis**?

program or **programme**? Both these words may be used as nouns or verbs. In British English the spelling *program* is restricted to the computing sense of '(provide with) a series of coded instructions': * *a computer program* * *to program a computer.* *Program* is also the American spelling of the word *programme*. The noun *programme* has a variety of senses and uses, such as 'broadcast', 'list', 'plan', and 'schedule': * *a television programme* * *a theatre programme* * *the programme for tonight's concert* * *a research programme* * *a housing programme* * *the programme of events.*

The verb *programme* means 'plan', 'schedule', or 'cause to conform to particular instructions', although some object to this usage: * *The new road is programmed for completion next spring.* * *He has been programmed to respond in this way.*

In British English the final *m* of *program* is doubled before *-ed, -ing, -er,* and *-able.* In American English *programmed, programming,* etc. are sometimes spelt with a single *m.*

The spelling *programme* was adopted from the French in the 19th century; *program,* which is now regarded as an Americanism, was the original spelling of the word in British English.

progressive tense The *progressive* (or *continuous*) *tense* describes those forms of verbs that describe an ongoing or unfinished action: * *We were driving towards London.* * *They are deceiving themselves.* Note that some verbs cannot be used in the progressive tense: * *I am having black hair.*

prohibit *see* **forbid** or **prohibit?**

project As a noun, the word *project,* meaning 'scheme or plan', is usually pronounced [*pro*jekt]. The alternative [*prŏ*jekt] is sometimes heard but is avoided by careful users. The verb *project,* meaning 'protrude' or 'estimate for the future', is pronounced [prŏ*jekt*].

prolific The adjective *prolific* means 'very productive'; it is applied to the person or thing that produces, rather than to what is produced: * *A prolific author, she writes two or three new novels every year.* Many people object to the use of *prolific* as a synonym for 'abundant' or 'numerous': * *Her prolific novels deal with a wide range of subjects.*

prone *see* **liable** or **likely?**; **prostrate, prone** or **supine?**

pronouns *Pronouns* are words that are used to replace nouns or noun phras-

es to refer to something or someone: * *I* * *she* * *him* * *it* * *you* * *they,* etc. The main difficulty that arises with pronouns is in the use of the personal pronoun, where many people are confused between the subject and object forms. Such phrases as: * *Everything comes to he who waits.* * *It was up to Julia and I,* though incorrect, are frequently used. Remember that after verbs and prepositions, the object pronoun (*me, him, her, us, them*) should be used: * *Everything comes to him who waits.* * *It was up to Julia and me.* The confusion can be resolved by mentally changing the sentence slightly: * *Things come to him* [not *he*]. * *It was up to me* [not *I*]. Before verbs, the subject pronouns (*I, he, she, we, they*) should be used: * *I* [not *me*] *and my friend will come.* * *She* [not *her*] *and her colleague are arguing.* Perhaps because of this uncertainty about the personal pronoun, another frequent mistake is the use of a reflexive pronoun instead of a personal pronoun: * *It was written by another author and me* [not *myself*].

A further difficulty with pronouns is that of uncertainty of reference. This can occur in sentences containing *it*: * *We took the bus although it was late.* It is unclear whether the bus was late or the time was late. *See also* **I** or **me; it; them.**

pronunciation The recommended *pronunciation* of English words found in dictionaries and grammar books is usually what is known as *RP* or *received pronunciation,* which more or less represents the speech of educated middle-class people from the South-East of England. Until comparatively recently, *RP* was regarded as 'correct' and other pronunciations were sometimes thought of as, if not actually incorrect, at least inferior. Most people now accept that there is no one standard form of English pronunciation that is correct. There is great regional variety within the United Kingdom and further variations in the speech of other English-speaking countries, and there is nothing incorrect about a pronunciation that is standard to a particular community or region. It is perfectly valid, then, to say [bath] instead of [bahth] if a person comes from northern England, or for an American to say [misl] instead of [misīl]. There is, however, still the possibility of mispronunciations, where a certain pronunciation is not an accepted regional variation and would generally be regarded as a mistake – for example, pronouncing *gist* as [gist] instead of [jist]. It should also be noted, though, that pronunciation is not static; it changes over the years and new pronunciations, which were originally resisted by careful speakers, sometimes eventually become the standard form.

A frequent mistake is to misspell *pronunciation* as *pronounciation*. The recommended pronunciation is [prănunsi*ay*shăn], not [prănownsiayshăn]. *See also* **law and order** and other individual entries.

propeller This word for a rotating device with blades is usually spelt with the ending *-er*, though *-or* is occasionally found.

proper nouns *see* **capital letters; nouns.**

prophecy or **prophesy**? These spellings and pronunciations are sometimes confused. The noun meaning 'prediction' is spelt *prophecy* and pronounced [*prof*isi]. The verb meaning 'utter predictions' is spelt *prophesy* and pronounced [*prof*isī]. *Advice* and *advise* are a similar noun-verb combination, spelt with a *c* for the noun and an *s* for the verb.

proportion The noun *proportion* denotes a ratio; it is best avoided where *part, number, some,* etc. would be adequate or more appropriate: ● *The proportion of female students to male students has increased.* ● *Some* [not *A proportion*] *of his friends are unemployed.* Such phrases as *a small(er) proportion* and *a large(r) proportion* may be replaced by *few, less, many, more,* etc.: ● *many* [not *a large proportion*] *of our employees* ● *less* [not *a smaller proportion*] *of their money.*

Some people also dislike the use of the plural noun *proportions* in place of *size* or *dimensions*: ● *Men of his proportions have difficulty finding clothes that fit.* ● *They set sail in a ship of enormous proportions.*

proportional or **proportionate**? The adjectives *proportional* and *proportionate* are virtually synonymous in the sense of 'in proportion': ● *a proportionate* [or *proportional*] *increase in spending* ● *the cooking time is proportional* [or *proportionate*] *to the size of the joint of meat.* In the phrase *proportional representation,* denoting a type of electoral system, the adjective *proportional* cannot be replaced by *proportionate.*

proposal or **proposition**? Both these nouns can mean 'something that is proposed, suggested, or put forward for consideration', but they are not always interchangeable: ● *the government's latest proposal/proposition* ●

That's an interesting proposition/ proposal. * *an insurance proposal* * *a business proposition.* The two words have other specific senses that should not be confused: a *proposal* is an offer of marriage; a *proposition* is an invitation to extramarital sex. The verb *proposition* usually relates to this meaning of the noun (and is much more common than the noun in this sense): * *He propositioned his secretary;* it should not be used in place of *propose.*

Some people dislike the informal use of the noun *proposition* in the sense of 'person', 'thing', etc.: * *The new manager is a formidable proposition.* * *Recycling may not be an economic proposition.* In both these examples the adjective phrase could be replaced by the adjective alone.

proprietary Note the spelling of this word, which is used to refer to goods sold under a particular trade name – and especially the second *r*, the *-ie-*, and the *-ary* ending. The *a* is not always sounded in speech.

pro rata The Latin expression *pro rata* is used in formal contexts to mean 'in proportion to an amount': * *a part-time job at a salary of £20,000 per year paid pro rata.* The expression *pro rata* is pronounced [prō *rah*tă].

proscribe *see* **prescribe** or **proscribe?**

prosecute *see* **persecute** or **prosecute?**

prospective *see* **perspective** or **prospective?**

prostate or **prostrate?** The word *prostate* refers to a gland around the neck of the bladder in men and other

male mammals: * *He's going into hospital to have his prostate (gland) removed.* It should not be confused with the adjective *prostrate*, which means 'lying face downwards', 'exhausted', or 'overcome': * *He stepped over the prostrate body of the prisoner.* * *They were prostrate with anguish.*

The word *prostrate* is also used as a verb. The adjective is stressed on the first syllable; the verb is stressed on the second syllable.

prostrate, prone or **supine?** *Prostrate* and *prone* mean 'lying face downwards'; *supine* means 'lying face upwards'. In these senses the adjectives *prone* and *supine* are largely restricted to formal or literary usage, or to contexts where the distinction between 'face downwards' and 'face upwards' is particularly important or relevant. Elsewhere, the adjective *prostrate* (with its additional meanings of 'exhausted' or 'overcome': *see* **prostate** or **prostrate?**) is more common than *prone* and may also be used in place of *supine* or in the general sense of 'lying flat': * *She lay prostrate with exhaustion.*

protagonist Some people object to the frequent use of the noun *protagonist* to denote a supporter – especially a leading or notable supporter – of a cause, movement, idea, political party, etc.: * *The Bush regime has been the chief protagonist in calls for action against maverick states.* * *I would find myself a protagonist of a movement to introduce sanctions on those who do not use these established trade tools* (*The Bookseller*). In such contexts *protagonist* may be better replaced by an appropriate synonym, such as *cham-*

pion, *advocate*, or *proponent*. The traditional meaning of *protagonist* is 'the leading or principal character in a play, story, etc.': * *Wheeler and Webb then added a third series, starting with 'Murder Gone to Earth' (1937), ...in which the protagonist was a country doctor* (*Daily Telegraph*). In this sense it should not be necessary to qualify the noun with such adjectives as *chief*, *main*, *leading*, *principal*, etc.

protect The verb *protect* is followed by the preposition *from* or *against*: * *This vaccination will protect you from* [or *against*] *a number of tropical diseases.*

protégé *see* **prodigy** or **protégé**?

protein Note the spelling of this word, especially the *-ein* ending. It is an exception to the 'i before e' rule (*see* **spelling**).

pro tem The expression *pro tem* is a shortened form of the Latin phrase *pro tempore*, meaning 'for the time being' or 'temporarily': * *Mr Jones will take charge of the sales department pro tem.*

proved or **proven**? *Proved* is the past tense of the verb *prove* and the usual form of its past participle in British English: * *They (have) proved their innocence.* As a variant form of the past participle, *proven* is largely restricted to the Scottish legal phrase *not proven*. In British English it is more frequently used as an adjective: * *a proven remedy* * *proven skills* * *a proven liar.*

The accepted pronunciation of the word *proven* is [*proov̆en*], although the pronunciation [*prōv̆en*] is also heard from time to time, particularly

in the Scottish legal phrase mentioned above.

proverbial The cliché *the proverbial...* is often used when (part of) a proverb or other idiomatic expression is quoted: * *It's like taking the proverbial horse to water.* * *We found ourselves up the proverbial creek.* Some dislike the use of the adjective *proverbial* as a synonym for 'famous' or 'notorious': * *the proverbial British weather.*

provided or **providing** The expressions *provided* (*that*) and *providing* (*that*) mean 'on the condition (that)': * *You may have a dog provided/providing that you look after it yourself.* Some consider *provided* (*that*) more acceptable than *providing* (*that*). The inclusion or omission of *that* is optional in most contexts.

The use of *provided* or *providing* in place of *if* is usually unnecessary and sometimes wrong: * *I'll clean the windows this afternoon if/provided/providing it doesn't rain.* * *We'll miss our train if* [not *provided/providing*] *we don't leave soon.*

provident or **providential**? These two adjectives, both used in formal contexts, should not be confused. *Provident* means 'showing or exercising foresight' or 'thrifty'; *providential* means 'fortunate' or 'relating to divine providence': * *They should have been more provident with their resources.* * *A providential shower of rain brought the game to an end.*

providing *see* **provided** or **providing**?

psychedelic The adjective *psychedelic*, describing hallucinogenic drugs or their effects, is sometimes spelt *psychodelic.* This spelling is acknowledged by some dictionaries but is unacceptable to many users, on the grounds that the adjective is derived from the word *psyche* rather than the prefix *psycho-*. The use of the adjective *psychedelic* in the sense of 'vividly coloured or patterned' should be restricted to informal contexts.

psychiatrist, psychoanalyst *see* **psychologist, psychiatrist, psychoanalyst** or **psychotherapist**?

psychological moment Of German origin, the phrase *psychological moment* is generally used with reference to the most appropriate time to produce the desired effect: ◦ *He waited until she had digested the news of his promotion and then, at the psychological moment, he proposed to her.* This usage derives from a misinterpretation of the German original, which would have been more accurately translated as *psychological momentum.*

The expression should not be used in place of *turning point, nick of time,* etc., or in contexts where the noun *moment* would be better qualified by a different adjective, such as *crucial, critical, exact,* or *precise*: ◦ *She lost her concentration at the critical* [not *psychological*] *moment.*

psychologist, psychiatrist, psychoanalyst or **psychotherapist**? These words are sometimes confused. A *psychologist* is a person who studies psychology, the study of the human mind and reasons for human behaviour. A *psychiatrist* is a doctor who is concerned with psychiatry, the branch of medicine concerned with the treatment of mental illness. A *psychoanalyst* is someone who treats

people with mental disorders by means of psychoanalysis, i.e. by bringing patients' mental processes into consciousness by allowing them to talk freely about themselves, especially their early childhood experiences. A *psychotherapist* is someone who treats people with mental, emotional, or psychosomatic disorders using psychological methods.

publicly This word is frequently misspelt; there is no *k* before the suffix *-ly*. This word does not conform to the normal rule that adjectives ending in *-ic* have an adverb ending in *-cally*, as in *tragic–tragically.*

pudding *see* **dessert, sweet, pudding** or **afters**?

punctilious or **punctual**? These two adjectives should not be confused. *Punctilious* is the more formal of the two and means 'scrupulously correct' or 'attentive to detail'; *punctual* means 'prompt; exactly on time': ◦ *He is very punctilious about etiquette.* ◦ *If you're called for an interview, be punctual.*

PUNCTUATION The primary purpose of *punctuation* is to clarify the writer's meaning. In speech the meaning is conveyed by the use of emphasis and pauses; punctuation has to serve the same purpose with written language. Lack of punctuation or incorrect punctuation can lead to misunderstanding and ambiguity. The importance of punctuation in conveying meaning can be illustrated by the various levels of punctuation in the following sentences: ◦ *My son who is a psychiatrist said Geoff is insane.* The sense here is that one of my sons was commenting on Geoff's mental state. • *My son, who is a psychiatrist, said Geoff is insane.* The suggestion here is that I have only one son and he was commenting on Geoff's mental state. • *'My son, who is a psychiatrist,' said Geoff, 'is insane.'* Here Geoff is commenting on his son's mental state.

Punctuation is sometimes a matter of rules and sometimes a matter of style or personal preference. A heavily punctuated passage of writing is unpleasant to read and, in general, it is preferable to use the minimum amount of punctuation consistent with conveying the meaning clearly. *See* the following panel for a brief description of different types of punctuation, which are discussed at greater length under their own headword.

PUNCTUATION	
1 Apostrophe	An apostrophe (represented by ') is used mainly to denote possession: • *This is my mother's car.* • *That is her parents' house.* It may also be used to indicate that a letter is (or that letters are) missing: • *It's starting to rain.* • *He didn't come.* • *They could've gone the other way.* Care should be taken not to insert apostrophes where they are not needed: • *apples* [not *apple's*] *for sale.* • *The dog wagged its* [not *it's*] *tail.*
2 Asterisk	An asterisk (represented by *) is used to draw the reader's attention to a footnote, or to indicate that certain letters have been omitted, typically to avoid rendering a swearword in full: • *Some bas***d cut me up on the way to work this morning!*
3 Brackets	Brackets (otherwise called parentheses and represented by ( )) are used in pairs around clauses or other parts of a sentence that can be left out without altering the sentence's grammatical structure: • *She picked up her hat (a present from her daughter last Christmas) and placed it on her head.* • *The tall man (the boy's uncle) frowned and shook his head.*
4 Bullet point	A bullet point (represented by • or ▪ or various other shapes) may be used to separate items in a list. Where a bullet point introduces a full sentence the convention is to begin with a capital letter and end with a full stop or semi-colon.
5 Colon	A colon (represented by :) is used to separate two main clauses where the second clause expands on or explains the first: • *The skies were heavy and grey: a storm was gathering.* • *She would say only this: she had never meant to hurt anyone.* It may also be used to introduce a list: • *It takes three things to succeed in business: imagination, money, and determination.* • *These three boys will be sent home: Tom, Dick, and Harry.*
6 Comma	The comma (represented by ,) has several different uses. It may be used to separate items in a list: • *Blood, sweat, and tears* • *Red, white, and blue.* Note that in such lists the final comma before *and* or *or* is optional. A comma can also be inserted between clauses: • *If you can't stand the heat, get out of the kitchen.* • *As far as I know, nothing's happened yet.* It may also appear, in pairs, around phrases or clauses that could be

343

	omitted without altering the grammatical structure of the surrounding sentence: • *The ship, which had been built before the war, was not sea-worthy.* • *Her father, a policeman in London, died years ago.* Note that a comma should not be placed where it separates a subject from its verb. There should be no comma in the following two sentences: • *The bird with the biggest wingspan, is the condor.* • *The player criticised by the referee after the game, was sent off in his next match.*
7 Dash	A dash (represented by –) is usually employed as an alternative to a colon: • *That is how he does everything – recklessly and without thinking first.* Dashes may also be used in pairs to separate a clause or phrase within a sentence, in much the same way as a pair of brackets: • *The team – which hasn't won all season – is now languishing at the bottom of the league.* Care should be taken not to confuse dashes with hyphens.
8 Ellipsis	An ellipsis (represented by …) may be used to indicate that something is missing: • *The table was heaped with tomatoes, onions, peppers … everything he needed to make the dish.* • *But the story, as he was soon to discover, was far from over …*
9 Exclamation mark	An exclamation mark (represented by !) is used at the end of an exclamation or interjection: • *Good heavens!* • *What a pity!* • *Ow!*
10 Full stop	Full stops (represented by .) are used to close sentences and in abbreviations: • *a.m.* • *e.g.* • *Nov.* Note, however, that full stops are not generally used where the abbreviation includes the last letter of the word: • *Dr* • *Dept* • *Ltd* • or in metric measurements: • *cm* • *kg* • *ml.*
11 Hyphen	The hyphen (represented by -) is used in various compound nouns, adjectives, etc.: • *well-developed* • *long-established* • *great-grandfather.* Note that while hyphens may be used in certain two-part nouns, as in *Let's get a top-up at the bar,* they are never used when these are turned into verbs, as in *Let's top up the drinks.* It may also be employed to break a word at the end of a line in printed texts. Caution should be exercised, however, where the addition of a hyphen may lead to confusion as to meaning: • *a red-wine bottle* • *a red wine bottle.*
12 Question mark	A question mark (represented by ?) is used at the end of a question: • *Are you coming?* • *You didn't get it?*
13 Quotation marks	Quotation marks (otherwise called inverted commas and represented by "or"") are used in pairs around direct speech or quotations: • *'Give me some money,' he demanded.* • *He shrugged and told her, 'Do as you would be done by.'* Note that any punctuation closing the quotation should be placed before the final quotation mark: • *'Now we'll have a short break,' the manager announced.*

14 Semicolon	A semi-colon (represented by ;) is used between two main clauses that are linked, but could otherwise be separated into simple sentences: • *The time dragged by very slowly; it seemed midnight would never come.* It may also be used to separate items in a list, especially one of the items already contains a comma: • *Her father insisted that she study reading, writing, and arithmetic; classical philosophy; and the scriptures.*
15 Solidus	A solidus (otherwise called a stroke, slant, slash mark, forward slash, oblique, or virgule and represented by /) is used to separate alternatives: • *This is not a yes/no question.* • *Each applicant should sign his/her name below.* It may also be used in writing dates, as a replacement for *per* or to indicate a break in verse, among other roles: • *9/11* • *100 km/hr* • *A little learning is a dangerous thing/Drink deep, or taste not the Pierian spring.*

pupil or **student**? In British English the noun *pupil* denotes a child at school or a person receiving instruction from an expert; a *student* is a person who studies at an institute of further or higher education, such as a college or university: • *a pupil at the local infant school* • *a painting by one of Michelangelo's pupils* • *while she was a student at Oxford.* Influenced by American usage, the application of the noun *student* to *schoolchildren*, especially the older pupils at a secondary school, is becoming increasingly frequent in British English.

purposely or **purposefully**? *Purposely* means 'on purpose; intentionally' and usually refers to the reason for doing something; *purposefully* means 'in a determined way; with a definite purpose in mind' and usually indicates the manner in which something is done: • *He purposely left his umbrella behind.* • *She strode purposefully into the room.* The two adverbs are sometimes confused.

pusillanimous. The adjective *pusillanimous*, used in formal contexts to mean 'timid' or 'cowardly', is sometimes misspelt. Note the -*ll*-, the single *n*, and the -*ous* ending.

putrefy This word, used in formal English to mean 'decompose' or 'rot', is sometimes misspelt. Note the ending -*efy* (like *stupefy*), in spite of the spelling of the related word *putrid*.

pygmy or **pigmy**? Both of these spellings are acceptable, although some users prefer the *y* spelling, as it shows the word's Greek origins: *pygmaios* ('dwarfish'). *Pygmy* should be written with an initial capital letter when it is used to refer to a member of one of the tribes of equatorial Africa.

pyjamas or **pajamas**? The spelling *pyjamas* is used in British English; *pajamas* is the usual form in American English. The word comes originally from the Urdu and Persian *pay* (meaning 'leg') and *jama* (meaning 'clothing').

Q

quality The word *quality* is often used adjectivally as a synonym for 'excellent' or 'of superior quality': * *quality goods* * *quality fiction* * *a quality newspaper*. Some people object to this usage on the grounds that the noun *quality* does not always denote excellence: the quality of a product, service, etc., may be good, mediocre, or bad.

quantum leap Many people object to the frequent use of the term *quantum leap* (or *quantum jump*) to denote a great change or advance: * *The administration must make the 'quantum leap' to negotiations with the new rebel government.* The term is borrowed from the field of physics, where it refers to a sudden transition that is discernible but far from great.

quarrelled or **quarreled**? In British English the correct spelling of the word is *quarrelled*: * *They quarrelled over a woman.* In American English, however, the accepted spelling is *quarreled*: * *We should not have quarreled over something so minor.*

quasi The Latin word *quasi*, meaning 'as if', may be combined with adjectives, in the sense of 'virtual', 'seemingly', 'partly', or 'almost', or with nouns, in the sense of 'resembling', 'so-called', or 'apparent': * *quasi-religious* * *quasi-official* * *quasi-republics*. The hyphen is sometimes omitted but the words are never written as a one-word compound.

Quasi may be pronounced [*kwayzi*], [*kwaysi*] or [*kwahzi*].

quay This word for 'landing place' is sometimes misspelt. Although pronounced like *key*, note its totally different spelling.

queer The use of *queer* as an informal, often derogatory, synonym for 'homosexual' dates back to the early 20th century. In recent years it has been replaced by the word **gay**, which is not derogatory. Although the term *queer* sounds dated in modern usage when used by a heterosexual, it is increasingly used in a non–derogatory manner among homosexuals.

query The verb *query* is best avoided where *ask* or *question* would be more appropriate: * *'Where do you live?' she asked* [not *queried*]. The word *query* has connotations of doubt: a *query* is a question prompted by doubt; to *query* is to cast doubt on: * *They accepted his statement without query.* * *We queried the bill.*

quest The noun *quest* is followed by the preposition *for* or *of*: * *The never-ending quest for the truth.* * *She travelled the world in quest of her missing brother.*

question *see* **beg the question**; **leading question**; **question mark**; **questions**; **rhetorical question**.

question mark The primary use of the *question mark* is as a substitute for a full stop at the end of a sentence that is a direct question: * *Where are you going?*, and at the end of a quoted question, within the quotation marks: * *'Where are you going?' he asked.* It is not used for an indirect question: * *He asked me where I was going.* A question mark may appear after a question that is not a complete sentence: * *Beer? Wine? Red or white?* It may also appear after a sentence which is not actually in question form but where the rising intonation of speech would indicate a question: * *You can't mean that?* * *She's really going to do it?*

A question mark usually follows a request: * *Could I possibly have a cup of tea?* If the request is more of an instruction, especially if it is lengthy, it normally ends with a full stop rather than a question mark: * *Would all ladies who wish to travel to the gardens by coach kindly remain here for a short time.*

If a verb of thinking follows a direct question it takes a question mark unless the question is in the past, where it has the force of reported speech: * *Where are they now, I wonder?* * *Where were they now, I wondered.* It would be incorrect to write: * *Where are they now? I wonder*, although it is occasionally possible for a question mark to appear in the middle of a sentence: * *The question Why me? is one that cannot be answered.* This is disliked by some people who insist that, as a question mark has the force of a full stop, it cannot appear except at the end of a sentence, or in quotation marks or parentheses.

A question mark can be used to show that a fact is dubiously true: * *Ambrose Bierce (1842–?1914).* It is sometimes also used, humorously or ironically, to express doubt: * *my devoted (?) little brother,* but only in very informal contexts. Similarly, doubled question marks and the combination of question marks and exclamation marks should be avoided in formal writing.

questionnaire This word is sometimes misspelt. Note the *-nn-*, unlike the single *n* in *millionaire*. The traditional pronunciation of the first syllable was [kest-], but in contemporary usage the first syllable is generally pronounced as in *question*: [kweschŏn*air*].

questions A *question* is a word, phrase, or sentence that asks for information and requires an answer (*see also* **rhetorical question**). Questions often begin with *how, what, when, where, which, who,* or *why*: * *How did you find out?* * *Where is it?* * *Which one?* * *Why?* They may begin with an inverted verb: * *Is he old enough?* * *Are you hungry?* * *Must she?* * *Will the car be ready tomorrow?* Direct questions are always followed by a question mark; indirect questions, which occur in **reported speech**, do not have a question mark at the end: * *She asked me what I was doing.*

Other words, phrases, and sentences may become questions by the addition of a question mark in written or printed texts, or by intonation in speech: * *You've sold it?* * *Coffee?*

A *tag question* is an inverted form of the verb *be, have, do, can, must,* etc. that is added to a statement. Usually, a positive statement is followed by a negative tag question, and vice versa: * *He's tall, isn't he?* * *You work in a bank, don't you?* * *She can't swim, can* *she?* ∘ *The clock hasn't stopped, has it?* Tag questions usually require a 'yes' or 'no' answer but they are sometimes rhetorical. A positive statement followed by a positive tag question may be more of an exclamation than a question: ∘ *They want higher wages, do they!* Negative tag questions usually contain the contraction *-n't*; the full form *not* is heard only in very formal contexts or in dialectal English: ∘ *You left the car unlocked, did you not?*

queue *see* **cue** or **queue**?

quick The use of the word *quick* as an adverb should generally be avoided in formal contexts: ∘ *Please reply quickly* [not *quick*] *to avoid disappointment.* ∘ *Come quick!* The comparative and superlative forms *quicker* and *quickest* are more informal than *more quickly* and *most quickly*: ∘ *Some plants grow more quickly/quicker than others.* ∘ *The German athlete ran the quickest/most quickly. Quicker* may be preferred to *more quickly* when the adverb is preceded by *any*: ∘ *Can you drive any quicker?*

The use of the adverb *quick* in fixed combinations, such as *quick-drying paint*, *quick-frozen food*, etc., is acceptable in all contexts.

quid pro quo A *quid pro quo* is something given to someone in return for something else: ∘ *They felt obliged to write research papers as a kind of quid pro quo for their fees.* ∘ *to exchange information on a quid pro quo basis.* The phrase *quid pro quo* is Latin in origin, meaning 'something for something'. Its English plural is *quid pro quos*.

quiet or **quieten**? Both these verbs may be used to mean 'soothe, calm, or allay' or 'make or become quiet'; in the second of these senses the verb is often followed by *down*. In British English the verb *quiet* is largely restricted to the first sense and to formal usage, and *quieten* to the second: ∘ *We must try to quiet his doubts.* ∘ *The children quietened down when their mother appeared.* In American English the verb *quiet* is preferred in both senses.

quit or **quitted**? Either word may be used as the past tense and past participle of the verb *quit*. In British English *quitted* is preferred by some users in formal contexts, but the American variant *quit* is becoming increasingly frequent, particularly in informal contexts: ∘ *They quitted/quit the building without delay.* ∘ *He has quit/quitted his job.*

quite In the sense of 'completely', 'totally', or 'entirely', the adverb *quite* is generally used with adjectives that cannot be qualified by *very*: ∘ *a quite excellent result* ∘ *a quite unnecessary remark* ∘ *It is quite impossible!* ∘ *The ring is quite worthless.* Used with other adjectives, quite usually has the meaning 'somewhat', 'fairly', or 'rather': ∘ *They are quite useful.* ∘ *The film is quite frightening.* In some contexts, however, the adverb may be ambiguous: ∘ *The room is quite clean.* ∘ *The bucket is quite full.*

In the sense of 'fairly', the adverb *quite* usually precedes the indefinite article: ∘ *quite an easy question* ∘ *quite a long time.* The adjectival use of the expression *quite a/an*, meaning 'remarkable' or 'exceptional', is best restricted to informal contexts: ∘ *She has quite a collection.* ∘ *That was quite a meal.*

quitted *see* **quit** or **quitted**?

quiz Some people dislike the use of the verb *quiz* in the sense of 'interrogate': • *The police quizzed him about his involvement in the affair.* This usage is widely regarded as journalese. A further objection to the verb is raised by those who feel that the lighthearted connotations of the noun *quiz* (in the sense of 'general knowledge game or competition') are inappropriate to the seriousness of a police interrogation.

quotation marks *Quotation marks* are used at the beginning and end of direct quotations: • *He said, 'I'm going out now.'* • *'All right,' she replied, 'but don't be late.'* Only the words actually spoken are placed within the quotation marks; they are not used in reported speech: • *'I am tired,' she said.* • *She said that she was tired.* However, in reported speech, a person might use quotation marks in order to draw attention to the fact that the speaker has used certain words, particularly if wishing to dissociate themselves from the expression used: • *He said he was in an 'ongoing situation'.* The convention in British English has been for punctuation to come inside the quotation marks only when it is part of the actual quotation. However, the comma usually also comes within the quotation marks when it is followed by *he said*, *Martha replied*, etc.: • *'I wish,' she said, 'you would go away.'* In sentences where the quoted matter is not followed by *he said* or similar, then the comma takes its logical position: • *He said, 'I'm happy', but I knew he was lying.* • *He loves Kipling's 'If', and is constantly quoting it.* In

American English the comma would appear within the quotation marks in the last example; full stops also always appear within the quotation marks in American English: • *See Fowler's section on 'hackneyed phrases.'* whereas in British English, when the quoted material is not a complete sentence or utterance, the full stop falls outside the quotation marks: • *He said I should work at 'improving my image'.*

Either single or double quotation marks can be used, but when there is a quotation within a quotation, double marks must be used inside single ones – or vice versa: • *She commented, 'I wish he wouldn't call me "sweetie".'*

Quotation marks are used instead of italics for various short literary and musical works (*see* **titles**). They are also sometimes used by writers to indicate slang or as an apology for using a particular word or expression: • *I gather my writing is thought to lack 'pizzazz'.* And they are used in various specialised writings to indicate meanings or interpretations: • *The word hence means 'from this time'.*

quote The noun *quote* (short for *quotation*) and the plural form *quotes* (short for *quotation marks*) are best restricted to informal contexts: • *It's a quote from Shakespeare.* • *We'd better get a quote for having the fence repaired.* • *Should the last sentence be in quotes?* The word *quote* is also used in speech to introduce a direct quotation: • *The chairman said, quote, there will be no further redundancies this year, unquote.* (The addition of *unquote* at the end is optional.)

R

race Many users avoid the term *race*, denoting a particular people or racial group, because of its controversial associations. Preferred terms include *ethnic group*.

racism or **racialism**? Both these nouns are used in the sense of 'racial prejudice or discrimination', *racism* being more frequent than *racialism* in modern usage: • *The company was accused of racism in its recruitment policy.*

rack or **wrack**? These two words are sometimes confused. A *rack* is a framework for storing or displaying things: • *a luggage rack* • *a shoe rack*; it is also an instrument of torture: • *on the rack*. As a verb, *rack* means 'cause to suffer pain': • *racked with uncertainty*; a person also *racks their brains*. The expression *rack and ruin*, 'a state of collapse', may also be spelt *wrack and ruin*; *nerve-racking*, 'causing great anxiety and tension', has the variant spelling *nerve-wracking*. *Wrack* is seaweed.

racket or **racquet**? Either spelling is acceptable for describing the implement used in sport for striking the ball: • *tennis racket/racquet* • *the game of rackets/racquets*. The spelling *racket* has the additional noun senses of 'loud noise': • *That music is a terrible racket,* and 'illegal business': • *involved in a drugs racket*.

rail The verb *rail* is followed by the preposition *at* or *against*: • *Protesters railed at* [or *against*] *the reform of the abortion law.*

rain, **reign**, or **rein**? These spellings are sometimes confused. *Rain* refers to water falling from clouds: • *The rain eased at noon*. *Reign* refers to the rule of a monarch or other leader, while *rein* describes one of the leather straps used to control a horse: • *the reign of the present queen* • *pull on the reins*. The noun *rein* is also used in such expressions as *give free rein to* ('allow freedom to') and *keep a tight rein on* ('control strictly'). The verb *reign* means 'exercise royal authority': • *King Henry VIII reigned from 1509 to 1547*. *Reign* is also used to describe a powerful prevalent power or influence: • *the reign of terror in Uganda under Idi Amin* • *Peace has reigned in Europe since 1945.*

raise or **raze**? The verb *raise* means 'move to a higher position': • *He raised the trophy high*; *raze* means 'destroy completely': • *The city was razed to the ground*. The two spellings should not be confused. The verb *raze* has the variant spelling *rase*, though *raze* is more frequent in modern usage.

raise or **rise**? Both these verbs mean 'move to a higher or upright position' or 'increase'. *Raise* is transitive, *rise* is intransitive: • *She raised her arm.* *They may raise the price.* • *I watched the smoke rise.* • *The temperature was rising*. The verb *raise* is also used in the sense of 'bring up', 'rear', or 'breed': * *He was raised in Cornwall.* * *We raise Highland cattle.* (Some people regard this usage as an Americanism.) *Rise*, an irregular verb, has a number of specialised uses: * *She rose at dawn.* * *The dough has risen.*

The noun *rise* means 'increase': * *a pay rise* * *a rise in unemployment.* In American English *raise* is used in place of *rise* to denote an increase in salary, wages, etc.: * *He asked for a raise*; this usage is sometimes found in British English, but is disliked by many. *See also* **arise** or **rise?**; **raise** or **raze?**

raison d'être The phrase *raison d'être*, of French origin, is used in English to denote a reason or justification for existence; it is best avoided where *reason*, *explanation*, etc. would be adequate or more appropriate: * *Helping the bereaved is the organisation's raison d'être.* * *The Prime Minister explained the reason* [not *raison d'être*] *for the government's change of policy.* Note the spelling of the phrase, particularly the circumflex accent on the first *e*. The anglicised pronunciation is [*rayz*on *de*trĕ].

rang *see* **ringed, rang** or **rung?**

rapt or **wrapped?** These spellings are sometimes confused. The adjective *rapt* means 'engrossed or absorbed': * *rapt with wonder* * *They listened with rapt attention.* *Wrapped* is the past tense of the verb *wrap*, meaning 'enfold': * *She wrapped the shawl round the baby.* Note that *wrapped* can also be used figuratively: * *He is completely wrapped up in his work.*

rarefy This word, meaning 'make rare or less dense', is sometimes misspelt. Note the *-efy* ending, unlike *purify*,

intensify, etc. The variant spelling *rarify* is acknowledged by some dictionaries but is best avoided. The past participle *rarefied*, used as an adjective meaning 'exalted', 'exclusive', or 'thin', is the most common form: * *rarefied atmosphere.*

rat The word *rat* has been in common use for many years as an insult for someone who has behaved despicably or deceitfully, but in recent times it has enjoyed renewed currency in a number of combined forms. Some, such as * *mall rat* (for a person who spends many hours shopping) or * *love rat* (for a man who cheats on his partner), are broadly contemptuous in tone, while others, such as * *rug rat* (for a small child), are grudgingly affectionate.

rateable or **ratable?** Both spellings of this word are acceptable, but *rateable* is preferred by some users: * *rateable value.* *See* **spelling.**

rather The adverb *rather* may be used with *would* or *had*, but *would* is more frequent in modern usage – *had* being rather formal: * *They would/had rather watch television than listen to the radio.* * *She would/had rather you stayed at home.* The contraction *'d*, which may represent either *would* or *had*, is often used in informal contexts: * *I'd rather write than telephone.*

The substitution of *rather than* for *than* after a comparative is wrong: * *He is more interested in the customs and traditions of Elizabethan times than* [not *rather than*] *in the political events of the period.*

Some people object to the use of *rather* before *a* or *an* when the following noun is qualified by an adjective, preferring *it's a rather expensive car* to *it's rather an expensive car.* If the noun is not qualified by an adjective, *rather* must precede the indefinite article: • *He's rather a coward.* See also **should** or **would**?

ravage or **ravish**? These two verbs should not be confused. *Ravage* means 'cause great damage to' and 'devastate'; *ravish* means 'delight or enrapture': • *The country was ravaged by war.* • *They were ravished by the beauty of the sunset. Ravish* has the additional meaning of 'rape' or 'carry off by force': • *She was ravished by her captors.*

Both verbs are largely restricted to formal contexts. The word *ravage* is also used as a noun, in such phrases as *the ravages of time*, and the word *ravish* in the adjectival form *ravishing*: • *You look ravishing in that dress.*

raze *see* **raise** or **raze**?

re The use of the preposition *re*, meaning 'with reference to' or 'in the matter of', should be restricted to the heading or opening of a business letter: • *Re: Interest rates for personal loans.* • *Re your advertisement in Country Life.* In other contexts *re* can usually be replaced by *about, concerning*, etc.: • *I am producing a documentary about* [not *re*] *the problems faced by single parents.* • *We have received many complaints concerning* [not *re*] *the proposed route for the new bypass.*

Re is usually pronounced to rhyme with *bee.* The pronunciation [ray] is also heard from time to time, but is incorrect. *See also* **commercialese**.

re- The prefix *re-*, meaning 'again', should be followed by a hyphen in compounds that might be confused with existing or more familiar words.

Such verbs as *re-sound, re-lease*, and *re-sign* (meaning 'sound again', 'lease again', and 'sign again'), for example, are thus distinguished from the verbs *resound, release*, and *resign.*

The use of a hyphen in the words *re-educate, re-election, re-entry, re-erect, re-examine*, etc. is optional (*see also* **hyphen**). Some people prefer to retain the hyphen in such words as *re-invent, re-arrest*, etc., to avoid confusion with *rein, rear*, etc.

Careful users avoid the tautological addition of the adverbs *back* and *again* to verbs that begin with the prefix *re-*: • *She returned* [not *returned back*] *to England in 1945.* • *I refer you to the opening paragraph* [not *I refer you back*].• *We are redecorating the lounge* [not *redecorating again*]. • *He made me rewrite the article* [not *rewrite again*]. The use of *again* in the last example would imply that the article had been written more than twice: • *He was not satisfied with my second draft and made me rewrite the article again.* See also **rebound** or **re-bound**?; **recount** or **re-count**?; **recover** or **re-cover**?; **recreation** or **re-creation**?; **reform** or **reform**?; **relay** or **re-lay**?; **represent** or **re-present**?; **resort** or **re-sort**?

reaction The noun *reaction*, which denotes a spontaneous or automatic response, is best avoided where *reply, response, answer, opinion*, etc. would be more appropriate: • *On hearing the alarm, his reaction was one of panic.* • *We had hoped for a more favourable response* [not *reaction*] *from the committee.* • *Please study these proposals and give me your opinion* [not *reaction*]. A *reaction* can only occur in response to something else; the word should not be used in place of *effect, influence*, etc.: • *What was the effect* [not *reaction*] *of the news on her family?*, but: * *What was the reaction of her family to the news?*

readable see **legible** or **readable**?

real Many people object to the frequent use of the adjective *real* in place of *important*, *serious*, etc., or simply for emphasis: * *a real achievement* * *a real problem* * *the real facts* * *in real life*. The adverbial use of *real* in the sense of 'really' or 'very' is an American or dialectal usage: * *He's real clever.*

real or **reel**? *Real* means 'existent', 'actual', or 'verifiable': * *The country in which the story is set is not real.* * *The real reason for her resignation came out later.* It should not be confused with *reel*, which describes a revolving device of some kind or, as a verb, means 'stagger' or 'whirl': * *A fisherman's reel.* * *He reeled with shock.*

realism or **reality**? *Reality* is the state of being real, or the state of things as they really are: * *Daydreams are an escape from reality.* * *We must face reality.* *Realism* is the acceptance of reality, a practical rather than idealistic attitude of mind: * *Problems like this must be approached with realism and common sense.* In art, literature, etc., the term *realism* denotes a style in which things are depicted as they really are, as opposed to abstract art, romantic literature, etc.

realistic Many users dislike the frequent use of the adjective *realistic* as a synonym for 'sensible', 'practical', 'reasonable': * *a realistic proposal* * *a realistic alternative* * *a realistic offer*.

reality see **realism** or **reality**?

really Excessive use of the adverb *really* is best avoided, even in informal contexts. *Really* can often be replaced by a different intensifier, such as *very*, *extremely*, *thoroughly*, *truly*, etc., or omitted altogether: * *It was really late when they arrived and we were really worried.* * *Wait until the paint is really dry.* * *I really enjoyed that holiday.* * *She really hates her job.*

reason Careful users regard the tautological construction *the reason is/was because* as wrong, preferring the *reason is/was that* or a simpler paraphrase using *because* alone: * *The reason for the delay is that* [not *because*] *there are road works in the town centre.* * *The reason I opened the window was that* [not *because*] *there was a wasp in the room.* * *I opened the window because there was a wasp in the room.* Similar objections are raised to the use of such constructions as *the reason is due to*, *the reason was on account of*, etc.

The phrase *the reason why* is acceptable to some users but disliked by others: * *the reason why he resigned.* In such contexts, *why* may be replaced by *that* or omitted altogether; if a noun can be substituted for the verb, the phrase *the reason for* may be used instead: * *the reason (that) he resigned* * *the reason for his resignation.*

rebound or **re-bound**? These two spellings are sometimes confused. The verb *rebound* means 'spring back': * *The ball rebounded.* *Re-bound*, spelt with a hyphen, is the past tense and past participle of the verb *re-bind* (or *rebind*), meaning 'bind again': * *The book has been re-bound.*

rebound or **redound**? *Rebound* means 'spring back': * *The ball rebounded.* *

The success of the project threatens to rebound upon the government. In the figurative sense *redound* is sometimes used in place of *rebound*; however, most careful users prefer to restrict *redound* to the sense 'contribute or lead to': • *Your skilful performance redounds to your benefit.* Only *rebound* is used as a noun • *The rebound bounced off Smith's arm.* • *marry someone on the rebound.*

receipt This word, meaning 'written confirmation that something has been paid or received', is sometimes misspelt. Note the *-ei-* spelling, and the silent *p*. *See also* **spelling**.

receive This word is often misspelt. Note the *-ei-* spelling, which conforms to the rule 'i before e except after c'. *See also* **spelling**.

recess The noun *recess* may be pronounced [*rises*] or [*reeses*]. Some users of British English prefer the first pronunciation, with the stress on the second syllable, but the second – stressed on the first syllable – is becoming increasingly common.

recession *see* **depression** or **recession**?

reciprocal *see* **mutual**, **common** or **reciprocal**?

reckon The use of the verb *reckon* in place of think, expressing a personal opinion, is best restricted to informal contexts: • *He reckons the other team will win.* In the sense of 'consider' or 'regard', however, *reckon* is acceptable in all contexts: • *She is reckoned to be one of the most talented musicians of her generation.*

recoil The verb *recoil* is followed by the preposition *from* or *at*: • *She recoiled from* [or *at*] *the prospect of meeting him again.*

recommend This word, meaning 'praise or suggest as suitable', is often misspelt. Note the single *c* and the *-mm-*.

reconnaissance This word, meaning 'exploration or survey of an area for military intelligence purposes', is often misspelt. Note the *-nn-* and *-ss-*. Note also the spelling of the verb *reconnoiter*, meaning 'make a reconnaissance'.

recount or **re-count**? These two spellings are sometimes confused. The verb *recount* means 'narrate': • *He recounted his experiences during the war.* The verb *re-count*, with a hyphen, means 'count again', and the noun *re-count*, which is used more frequently than the verb, means 'second count': • *to demand a re-count of the votes.*

recourse, **resort** or **resource**? Similarities in the sense, usage, form, and pronunciation of these words may lead to confusion. All three can refer to a source of help or an expedient: • *Violence was our only recourse/resort/ resource.* In the expressions *have recourse/resort to* and *without recourse/ resort to*, *recourse* and *resort* are virtually interchangeable but cannot be replaced by *resource*. *Recourse* is the more frequent noun in such contexts, *resort* being used as a verb in similar constructions: • *I hope he will not have recourse to violence.* – *I hope he will not resort to violence.* • *They settled the dispute without recourse to violence.* – *They settled the dispute without resorting to violence.*

In the expression *as a last resort/*

resource, the nouns *resort* and *resource* are interchangeable but cannot be replaced by *recourse*. *Resort* is generally considered to be the more idiomatic choice in such contexts: • *She turned to violence as a last resort.*

recover or **re-cover**? These two spellings are sometimes confused. *Recover* means 'regain': • *She recovered her health.* *Re-cover*, with a hyphen, means 'give a new cover to': • *The upholsterer re-covered the chair.*

recreation or **re-creation**? The spellings of these words are sometimes confused. *Recreation* means 'relaxation; leisure (pursuit)': • *a recreation ground.* *Re-creation*, with a hyphen, is less frequently used and means 'a new creation': • *the re-creation of the Wild West for the film set.*

recuperate The verb *recuperate*, meaning 'recover', is sometimes misspelt, a common error being the substitution of *-coup-* for *-cup-*, as in the verb *recoup*. Note that the verb is always used intransitively: • *It will take him weeks to recuperate.*

recur The word *recur*, meaning 'happen again', should never be followed by *again*: • *Make sure this situation does not recur.*

Red Indian *see* **Native American**.

redouble or **reduplicate**? The verb *redouble* means 'increase' or 'intensify': • *We redoubled our efforts.* The rarer and more formal verb *reduplicate* means 'repeat' or 'double'; it also has the specialised sense of 'repeat (a syllable)', as in the words *bye-bye*, *papa*, etc. Note that in general usage

redouble does not refer to the act of doubling something.

redound *see* **rebound** or **redound**?

redundant Some people object to the frequent use of the adjective *redundant* in place of *unnecessary*, *superfluous*, *irrelevant*, *unimportant*, etc.: • *Our second car will become redundant when my husband starts commuting by train.* • *The cancellation of the dinner-dance made the baby-sitting problem redundant.*

reduplicate *see* **redouble** or **reduplicate**?

reek or **wreak**? *Reek* means 'stink' or 'smell strongly': • *The flat reeked.* • *The affair reeked of state interference.* It should not be confused with *wreak*, which means 'cause havoc' or 'inflict violence': • *The storm wreaked havoc in the harbour.* See also **wrought**.

reel *see* **real** or **reel**?

refer The verb *refer* is stressed on the second syllable; the final *r* is doubled before *-ed*, *-ing*, and *-er*. In the noun *reference* the stress shifts to the first syllable, and the second *r* is not doubled. For the use of the adverb *back* with the verb *refer*, see **re-**. See also **spelling**.

referee or **umpire**? Both nouns denote a person who ensures that a game is played according to the rules and settles any disputes that may arise during the course of the game. A *referee* supervises such sports as football, boxing, etc.; an *umpire* supervises such sports as tennis, cricket, baseball, hockey, etc. A *referee* is also a person who supplies a professional or character reference for a job applicant, prospective tenant, etc. The noun *umpire* is not used in this sense.

referendum The noun *referendum* has two plural forms, *referendums* and *referenda*. *Referendums* is the more frequent in general usage: * *Their proposed referendums on nuclear disarmament and the return of capital punishment will be welcomed by many.*

reflective or **reflexive**? These two adjectives should not be confused. *Reflective* is used in the literal sense of 'reflecting light' or the figurative sense of 'thoughtful; contemplative': * *a reflective stripe across the back of the jacket* * *in a reflective mood. Reflexive* is a grammatical term: * *reflexive verb* * *reflexive pronoun.*

reflexive A *reflexive* verb is a transitive verb in which the subject and object are the same: * *I washed myself.* * *She hid herself behind a tree.* * *He perjured himself.* * *The directors awarded themselves large pay increases.* The pronouns *myself, yourself, himself, herself, itself, oneself, ourselves, yourselves,* and *themselves* are called *reflexive pronouns. See also* **self**; **verbs**.

reform or **re-form**? These spellings are sometimes confused. The verb *reform* means 'change by improvement': * *plans to reform the tax system. Re-form*, with a hyphen, means 'form again': * *After a lapse of ten years, the club decided to re-form.*

refrigerator Note the spelling of this word, particularly the *-er-* in the middle and the *-or* at the end. There is no *d* in *refrigerator*, unlike in the informal short form *fridge*.

refute or **deny**? The verb *refute* means 'prove to be false'; *deny* means 'declare to be false': * *He refuted their accusations by producing a receipt for the camera.* * *He denied their accusations but was unable to prove his innocence.* The use of *refute* in place of *deny* is avoided by many careful users but nevertheless occurs with some frequency.

regard In the sense of 'consider' the verb *regard* should be used with the preposition *as*: * *She regards her mother as her friend.* * *This novel is regarded as the author's masterpiece.* The verb *regard* has a number of other senses and is also used in the prepositional phrase *as regards*, meaning 'with respect to', 'about', or 'concerning': * *As regards your suggestion, the committee will discuss it at tomorrow's meeting. As regards* should not be confused with the phrases *with regard to* and the less frequent *in regard to,* used in similar contexts, in which the word *regard* is a noun and does not end in *s*. In mid-sentence these compound prepositions are often better replaced by *about, concerning,* or *regarding.*

The noun *regard* is used in a variety of other expressions. *Have regard for* means 'show consideration for': * *They have no regard for her safety.* The plural noun *regards,* meaning 'greetings', occurs in such expressions as *with kind regards* (used to close a letter) and *give regards to*: * *Please give my regards to your daughter when you next see her. Compare* **consider**.

regardless *see* **irrespective**.

registry office or **register office**? Both these terms are used to denote the place where civil marriages are conducted and where births, marriages, and deaths are recorded. *Registry office* is the more frequent term in general usage, *register office* being largely restricted to formal contexts.

regrettably or **regretfully**? These two adverbs are sometimes confused. *Regrettably* relates to something that causes regret; *regretfully* relates to somebody who feels regret: * *This year's profits are regrettably low.* * *She regretfully turned down their offer.* *Regrettably*, not *regretfully*, may be used to mean 'it is regrettable that': * *Regrettably, the house does not have a garage.* The increasing use of *regretfully* in place of *regrettably* in this sense may be due to confusion with **hopefully**, **thankfully**, etc.

reign, rein *see* **rain, reign** or **rein**?

reiterate The verb *reiterate* means 'repeat' or 'say or do repeatedly'; it should not be used with the adverb *again* (*see also* **re-**): * *The Prime Minister was simply reiterating the promises made in the party manifesto.*

relation or **relationship**? Both these nouns may be used in the sense of 'connection', but they are not interchangeable in all contexts: * *Is there any relation/relationship between unemployment and crime?* * *This evidence bears no relation* [not *relationship*] *to the case.* * *What is his relationship* [not *relation*] *to the deceased?* The noun *relationship* is preferred for human connections; *relation*, for more abstract connections. A similar distinction may be applied to the use of *relationship* and the plural noun *relations* in the sense of 'mutual feelings or dealings': * *business relations* * *an intimate relationship* * *the government's relations with the*

unions * *his relationship with his wife.* *See also* **relation** or **relative**?

relation or **relative**? Either noun may be used to denote a person connected to another by blood, marriage, or adoption: * *Most of her relations/relatives are going to the wedding.* * *I have a distant relation/relative in Canada.* *See also* **relation** or **relationship**?

relative clause *see* **clause**; **comma**; **that** or **which**?

relatively The adverb *relatively* implies comparison; many people object to its use as a synonym for 'fairly', 'somewhat', 'rather', etc., where there is no comparison: * *After the heat of the kitchen the lounge felt relatively cool.* * *Our records are fairly* [not *relatively*] *up to date.*

relay or **re-lay**? These two spellings are sometimes confused. The verb *relay* means 'pass on': * *to relay a message.* The verb *re-lay*, spelt with a hyphen, means 'lay again': * *to re-lay a carpet.* The past tense and past participle of *relay* is *relayed*; the past tense and past participle of *re-lay* is *re-laid*.

The word *relay* is also used as a noun: * *The switch is operated by a relay.* * *They worked in relays.* In this usage, and in such phrases as *relay race*, *relay* is stressed on the first syllable. The verbs *relay* and *re-lay* may be stressed on either syllable; *re-lay* is sometimes stressed on both.

relevant This word is sometimes misspelt. Note particularly the second *e*.

reliable or **reliant**? The adjective *reliable* means 'dependable' or 'able to be trusted': * *a reliable car* * *Some of the* *author's sources are not very reliable.* The adjective *reliant*, meaning 'dependent', is chiefly used in the phrase *be reliant on*: * *We were reliant on their assistance.*

relocate The verb *relocate*, frequently used in business and industrial contexts, is widely regarded as a pretentious synonym for 'move': * *the latest major firm to relocate to Basingstoke* * *Unemployment in the North is forcing many families to relocate.*

remedial or **remediable**? *Remedial* means 'intended as a remedy'; *remediable* means 'able to be remedied': * *remedial treatment* * *a remediable problem.* The two adjectives should not be confused. *Remedial* is specifically applied to the teaching of slow learners: * *remedial education* * *a remedial course.*

Remediable is less frequent than its antonym *irremediable*: * *The damage is irremediable.*

Both adjectives are stressed on the second syllable, unlike the word *remedy* from which they are derived. *Remedial* is pronounced [rimeediăl], *remediable* is pronounced [rimeediăbl].

remembrance The noun *remembrance*, meaning 'the act of remembering', 'memory', or 'memento', is often misspelt, the most frequent error being the substitution of *-ber-* for *-br-*, as in the verb *remember*. Note also the *-ance* ending.

remind The verb *remind* is followed by the preposition *of* in the sense 'cause to think of': * *The smell of pine forests reminds me of my childhood in Scotland.* It is followed by *about* or *of* in the sense of 'cause to remember': * *She reminded me about* [or *of*] *the promise I had made.*

reminiscent This word is sometimes misspelt. Note particularly the *-sc-*, as in *scent*.

remission or **remittance**? Both these nouns are derived from the verb *remit*. *Remittance* is largely restricted to official contexts, in the sense of 'payment': * *Please enclose this counterfoil with your remittance.* *Remission* has a wider range of uses and meanings, such as 'reduction in the length of a prison sentence', 'abatement of the symptoms of a disease', 'discharge; release': * *the remission of sins.* Careful users maintain the distinction between the two words.

remit The noun *remit* is best avoided where 'task', 'responsibility', 'brief', etc. would be adequate or more appropriate: * *The quality control function will also be part of your remit* (*Executive Post*). As a synonym for the wordy expression *terms of reference*, denoting the scope of an investigation, *remit* is welcomed by many users: * *Financial matters are not part of the inquiry's remit.*

The verb *remit* is pronounced [rimit]. The noun may also be stressed on the second syllable, but its usual pronunciation is [reemit]. *See also* **stress**.

remittance *see* **remission** or **remittance**?

renege The traditional pronunciation of this word, which means 'not keep (a promise, agreement, etc.)' is [rineeg], but [rinayg] is also frequently used and is acceptable.

Note the spelling of *renege*, particularly the *-ege* ending. The spelling *renegue* is a less frequent variant.

The verb *renege* is followed by the preposition *on*: * *They reneged on the deal.*

rent *see* **hire** or **rent**?

repair *see* **fix** or **repair**?

repairable or **reparable**? Both these adjectives mean 'able to be repaired'; careful users apply *repairable* to material objects and *reparable* to abstract nouns: • *The car is badly damaged but repairable.* • *His loss is scarcely reparable.* The two adjectives relate to different senses of the verb *repair*: 'mend' or 'restore' (*repairable*) and 'remedy' or 'make good' (*reparable*).

Reparable, which is stressed on the first syllable, [*rep*ărăbl], is less common than its opposite, *irreparable*: • *These allegations have done irreparable harm to his political career.*

Repairable is stressed on the second syllable, [rip*air*ăbl]; its opposite is *unrepairable*: • *These shoes are unrepairable.*

repel *see* **repellent** or **repulsive**?

repellent or **repulsive**? *Repellent* and *repulsive* mean 'causing disgust or aversion'. *Repulsive* is the stronger of the two adjectives, both of which are ultimately derived from the Latin verb *repellere*, meaning 'repel': • *His deformed body was a repellent sight.* • *The partially decomposed corpse was a repulsive sight.* • *The principles of Communism are repellent to some; the doctrines of Nazism were repulsive to many.* The adjective *repellent* is also used in combination to mean 'driving away' or 'resistant': • *insect-repellent cream* • *water-repellent fabric.* *Repellant* is a less frequent spelling of the noun and adjective *repellent*.

The verb *repel* is a weaker synonym of *repulse*. The use of the verb *repulse* in the sense of 'disgust' or 'cause aver-

sion' is disliked by some users, who restrict it to the sense of 'drive back' or 'rebuff': • *The inhabitants repulsed the invading army.* • *He repulsed her offer of friendship.* *Repel* may be used in any of these senses.

repent The verb *repent* may be followed by the preposition *of*: • *He repented (of) his dissolute youth.*

repercussions The word *repercussions* is best avoided where *result, consequence, effect*, etc. would be adequate or more appropriate: • *the repercussions of a ban on smoking in restaurants.* The noun *repercussion* literally means 'reverberation' or 'rebound'; in figurative contexts it should be restricted to indirect or far-reaching effects: • *the repercussions of a serious accident at one of Britain's nuclear power stations.*

repertoire or **repertory**? The noun *repertoire* principally denotes the musical or dramatic works, poems, jokes, etc. that a person or group is able or prepared to perform: • *That song is not in her repertoire.* The word *repertory* is also used in this sense, but is more frequently applied to a company of actors that presents a repertoire of plays at the same theatre: • *a repertory company* • *a repertory theatre* • *to act/be performed in repertory.*

repetitious or **repetitive**? The adjective *repetitive* means 'characterised by repetition'; *repetitious* means 'characterised by unnecessary or tedious repetition': • *a repetitive rhythm* • *repetitious arguments.* *Repetitive*, the more frequent of the two adjectives, is also sometimes used in the derogatory sense of *repetitious*, but careful users avoid this: • *a lengthy repetitious* [not *repetitive] description of the ceremony.*

Note the spellings of *repetitious*, *repetitive*, and the related noun *repetition*, particularly the second *e*, which is sometimes wrongly replaced by *i*.

replace or **substitute**? The verb *replace* means 'take the place of'; the verb *substitute* means 'put in the place of': • *I substituted his painting for her photograph.* • *Her photograph was replaced with his painting.* • *His painting was substituted for her photograph.* • *His painting replaced her photograph.* *Substitute* is always used with the preposition *for*; *replace* may be used with the preposition *with* or *by* (especially in passive sentences): • *Her photograph was replaced by his painting.*

All the examples above refer to the act of removing her photograph and putting his painting in its place. The two verbs are often confused in such contexts, *substitute* being used instead of *replace*, but careful users maintain the distinction between them.

replica Some people object to the frequent use of *replica* in place of *copy*, *duplicate*, *reproduction*, *model*, etc.: • *He bought a plastic replica of the Eiffel Tower.* • *This article is a replica of yesterday's editorial.* • *legislation to ban replica guns.* The noun *replica* principally denotes an exact copy of a work of art, especially one made by the original artist. The phrase *exact replica* is therefore tautologous.

reported speech Reported speech, also called indirect speech, differs from direct speech in a number of ways. In direct speech the actual words of the speaker are given, enclosed in **quotation marks** in written or printed texts: • *Mary said, 'I've lost my ring.'* In

reported speech quotation marks are not used for this purpose: • *Mary said that she had lost her ring.* Note the differences between the two examples above. The subject pronoun *I* usually changes to *he* or *she* in reported speech; *we* often changes to *they*. The subject pronoun *you* may change to *I* in reported speech if it refers to the person who is reporting the speech: • *Peter said, 'You need a new battery.'* • *Peter said that I needed a new battery.*

The use of the word *that* to introduce reported speech is optional. In formal contexts *that* is usually included.

Note also the change of tense in reported speech: *I've lost* becomes *she had lost*; *you need* becomes *I needed*. Thus the present tense usually changes to the simple past; *has* and *have* change to *had*; *will* changes to *would*: • *He said, 'Anne will be late.'* • *He said that Anne would be late*; *am* and *is* change to *was*; *are* changes to *were*, etc.

represent or **re-present**? These spellings are sometimes confused. *Represent* means 'act in place of': • *The team will represent the whole school. Re-present*, with a hyphen, means 'present again': • *He re-presented the series of lectures the following autumn.*

repress *see* **oppress, repress** or **suppress**?

reproach The verb *reproach* is followed by the preposition *with* or *for*: • *She reproached me with [or for] my carelessness.*

repulse, repulsive *see* **repellent** or **repulsive**?

reputable The adjective *reputable* should be stressed on the first syllable, [*repy*uutăbl]. The pronunciation [ri*pew*tăbl], with the stress on the second syllable, is incorrect.

requisite *see* **prerequisite** or **requisite?**

research The word *research* is traditionally pronounced with the stress on the second syllable [ri*serch*]. In recent years, however, many people have taken to placing the stress on the first syllable [*ree*serch] and this is now widely considered a valid alternative for the noun, though rarely for the verb.

resin or **rosin?** *Resin* is a natural substance exuded by plants, insects, etc., or a synthetic substance that resembles natural *resin*. *Rosin* is a type of natural resin used on the bow of a stringed instrument to increase friction, on the hands of a gymnast to increase grip, etc. *Resin* is pronounced [*rez*in]; *rosin* is pronounced [*roz*in].

resort or **re-sort?** The noun *resort* means 'place of rest or recreation': ● *seaside resorts*. The verb *resort* means 'turn to': ● *I hope he will not resort to violence*. The verb *re-sort*, with a hyphen, means 'sort again'; ● *re-sort all the index cards*. *Resort*, both as a noun and as a verb, is pronounced with a *z* [ri*zort*]; *re-sort* is pronounced with an *s* [ree*sort*].

resort, resource *see* **recourse, resort** or **resource?**

respectable, respectful or **respective?** These three adjectives should not be confused. *Respectable* means 'worthy of respect'; *respectful* means 'showing respect'; *respective* means 'separate; several' (*see* **respective** or **respectively?**): ● *In those days acting was not considered a respectable profession*. ● *a*

respectful silence ● *Jane and Michael collected their respective children and went home.*

respective and **respectively** The words *respective* and *respectively* should be used only where there would be a risk of ambiguity or confusion in their absence: ● *The workers explained their respective problems to the shop steward.* ● *Toys and furniture are sold on the second and third floors respectively.* Without *respective*, the first example could imply that all the workers had the same problems; without *respectively*, the second example might suggest that toys and furniture are sold on both floors. In other contexts the words are often unnecessary or inappropriate: ● *Paul and Sarah got into their (respective) cars and drove away.* ● *Each book must be returned to its (respective) shelf.* ● *She worked (respectively) in Paris, Vienna, and Rome.*

respite This word, meaning 'relief, delay': ● *no respite from the toil,* is often mispronounced. The stress falls on the first syllable, unlike *despite*, which has the stress on the second syllable. The second syllable may be pronounced [*res*pit] or [*res*pīt], although some users prefer the former pronunciation.

restaurateur Note the spelling of this formal word for a person who runs a restaurant; there is no *n* as in restaurant. *Restaurateur* is pronounced [restără*ter*].

restive or **restless?** The adjective *restive* means 'resisting control'; *restless* means 'fidgety' or 'agitated': ● *The teacher tried to discipline his restive pupils.* ● *Some of the congregation* *became restless during the long sermon.* Careful users avoid the use of *restive* in place of *restless*. The two adjectives are etymologically unrelated: *restive*, which originally meant 'refusing to move', is derived from the same Latin source as the noun *rest* (meaning 'remainder'); *restless*, the opposite of *restful*, is derived from the noun *rest* (meaning 'repose'), which is of Germanic origin.

restrain *see* **constrain** or **restrain?**

restrictive clause A *restrictive clause* limits the meaning of another part of a sentence: * *The pistols which are on the wall were carried by my great-grandfather at Waterloo.* Here the restrictive clause *which are on the wall* makes it clear which particular pistols are being referred to, and also implies that there are some other pistols elsewhere in the room. Note the contrast with *The pistols, which are on the wall, were carried by my great-grandfather at Waterloo,* in which the non-restrictive clause *which are on the wall*, preceded and followed by commas, implies that these are the only pistols under consideration and conveys the incidental information that they are on the wall. *See also* **comma; that** or **which?**

resuscitate This word, meaning 'revive': * *All attempts to resuscitate him with the kiss of life failed*, is often misspelt. Note particularly the *-sc-* in the middle of the word.

retch or **wretch?** *Retch* means 'heave prior to vomiting': * *The gore made him retch*. It should not be confused with *wretch*, which denotes a pitiable or wretched person: * *The wretch had no shoes, and rags for clothes.*

retread The noun *retread* denotes an old tyre with a new outer surface; it is synonymous with *remould*. Many people object to the metaphorical application of the word *retread* to people, such as politicians returning to parliament after a spell out of office or retired people returning to paid employment: * *There will be a number of retreads in the new government.*

retro The prefix *retro-*, meaning 'backwards', is increasingly used as an adjective in its own right, describing fashions, styles, ideas, etc., that have been revived from the past: * *the retro look/sound* * *His latest film is unashamedly retro.* * *Retro British nursery food is just so now* (*The Guardian*).

return *see* **re-**.

returner A *returner* is a person who returns to work after an extended period of absence from paid employment, such as a woman who resumes her career after spending a number of years bringing up her children: * *Few employers are actually offering women returners a new deal... but a wealth of information on the subject is available* (*The Guardian*). * *Current trends are centring on more widely appealing 'returner schemes' which offer career breaks of between two and five years* (*The Guardian*).

reveille This word may be pronounced [rivali] or [riveli], the former being the more usual pronunciation. Note also the spelling; the word is derived from the French *réveiller* 'awaken'.

revenge or **avenge?** Both these verbs refer to the act of repaying a wrong. The person who *revenges* is usually the offended or injured party; a person who *avenges* is usually a third party acting on behalf of another: * *I will revenge myself on those who cruelly humiliated me.* * *He planned to avenge his brother's death by drowning the murderer's daughter.* * *He avenged his murdered brother.* This distinction is not observed by all users in all contexts, however, and *revenge* is often interchangeable with *avenge*. *See also* **revenge** or **vengeange**?

revenge or **vengeance**? Both these nouns may be used in the sense of 'retaliation' or 'retribution': * *The destruction of her parents' home was an act of revenge/vengeance.* Some users associate *revenge* with the subjective or personal act of revenging and *vengeance* with the objective or impersonal act of avenging (*see* **revenge** or **avenge**?): * *They humiliated me, but I will take my revenge.* * *He sought vengeance for the murder of his brother.*

reverend or **reverent**? *Reverend* is a title used by members of the clergy: * *Reverend Jones took the service.* It is abbreviated to *Rev.* It should not be confused with *reverent*, an adjective meaning 'respectful': * *He handled the relic with reverent awe.*

reversal or **reversion**? *Reversal* is the act of reversing; *reversion* is the act of reverting: * *the reversal of this trend* * *reversion to his former way of life.* The two nouns should not be confused.

reverse *see* **converse**, **inverse**, **obverse** or **reverse**?

reversion *see* **reversal** or **reversion**?

review or **revue**? These two spellings are sometimes confused. *Review*, as a noun, is a 'critical appraisal': * *a review of her latest novel*, or a 'reassessment': * *The minister ordered an urgent review of prison security.* A *revue* is a light theatrical show consisting of sketches, songs, etc.: * *the annual Christmas revue.* *Revue* may also be spelt *review*, but this is best avoided in order to maintain the distinction between the two words.

rhetorical question A *rhetorical question* is one which is asked for effect, and to which no answer is expected: * *What is the world coming to?* * *How can people behave like that?* The question is sometimes asked so that it can be answered immediately by the speaker: * *Why are we on strike? I will tell you why...* A rhetorical question is sometimes just a rephrased statement, put in question form for greater emphasis: * *Was there ever a more unfortunate person?*

rheumatism This word for an illness that causes pain in the muscles or joints is sometimes misspelt. Note particularly the first syllable, *rheum-*.

rhinoceros The name of this animal is often misspelt. Note particularly the *rh-*, and the *c* in the middle of the word.

rhododendron This word is sometimes misspelt. Note particularly the *rh-* at the beginning and the *-do-* in the middle. The word *rhododendron* comes originally from the Greek *rhodon* (meaning 'rose') and *dendron* (meaning 'tree').

rhythm This word is frequently misspelt. Note particularly the first *h* and the *y*.

ribald This adjective, meaning 'coarse or crude': * *ribald language*, is often mispronounced. The pronunciation is [rĭbăld]; careful users regard the alternative [rĭbawld] as unacceptable.

ricochet This word, used to describe bullets, etc. that rebound, is usually pronounced [rĭkŏshay] although [rĭkŏshet] is also acceptable. There are alternative present and past participles: *ricocheting* [rĭkŏshaying] or *ricochetting* [rĭkŏsheting], and *ricocheted* [rikŏshayd] or ricochetted [rĭkŏshetid].

right or **rightly**? Both these adverbs may be used in the sense of 'correctly' or 'properly'. *Right* is generally placed after the verb, *rightly* before the verb: * *Have I spelt your name right?* * *He rightly stopped at the zebra crossing.* * *You're not holding your fork right.* * *She rightly held her fork in her left hand.* The phrase *if I remember right/rightly* is a notable exception to this rule.

Right has a number of other adverbial uses: * *Turn right at the next junction.* * *They went right home.* * *We live right at the top of the hill.* *Rightly* also means 'justly' or 'suitably': * *She was rightly annoyed by their behaviour.* * *Am I rightly dressed for the trip?* The two adverbs are not interchangeable in any of these senses.

In informal contexts, *right* is sometimes used to mean 'very' and *rightly* to mean 'with certainty': * *We're right pleased to see you.* * *He doesn't rightly know.*

right or **write**? *Right* variously means 'correct', 'good', or 'of or relating to the side opposite left': * *Everything is now right and proper.* * *He was in the right.* * *The car turned to the right.* It

should not be confused with the verb *write*: * *She writes a thousand words a day.* The word *wright* generally appears combined with other words to describe someone who pursues a particular trade: * *wheelwright* * *shipwright* * *millwright* * *playwright.* See *also* **dramatist** or **playwright**?

rigor *see* **rigour** or **rigor**?

rigorous This word is sometimes misspelt. The *u* of *rigour* is dropped in front of the suffix -*ous*.

rigour or **rigor**? *Rigour*, meaning 'harsh conditions; severity': * *the rigours of winter*, should not be confused in British English with the medical *rigor*: * *rigor mortis*. Note, however, that in American English *rigour* is spelt *rigor*.

ring or **wring**? These two verbs are sometimes confused, being identical in pronunciation. *Ring* means 'make a resonant sound' or 'surround or mark with a ring'; *wring* means 'twist' or 'squeeze': * *to ring a bell* * *I asked her to ring any errors in red ink.* * *wringing their hands* * *Shall I wring out the wet clothes?* The past tense and past participle of *wring* is *wrung*, which should not be confused with *rung* (*see* **ringed, rang** or **rung**?).

ringed, rang or **rung**? *Ringed* is the past tense and past participle of the verb *ring* in the sense of 'surround or mark with a ring': * *He ringed all the words that had been misspelt.* * *The birds have been ringed for identification.* *Rang* is the past tense and *rung* the past participle of the verb *ring* in the sense of 'sound (a bell)': * *She rang the bell.* * *The telephone has not rung.* The substitution of *rung* for *rang* is now restricted to dialectal usage; it is considered incorrect in formal British English.

rip-off Derived from the slang verb *rip off*, meaning 'steal' or 'cheat', the noun *rip-off* is principally applied to overpriced goods or the practice of charging exorbitant prices: * *This handbag is an absolute rip-off – it's not even made of real leather.* * *I had to pay £10 to get in – it's a rip-off!* Extending this sense of 'exploitation', *rip-off* is also used to denote an inferior film, book, etc. that seeks to exploit the success of another by imitation.

The noun *rip-off* should not be used in formal contexts.

rise *see* **arise** or **rise**?; **raise** or **rise**?

risky or **risqué**? These two words are sometimes confused. *Risky* refers to an action that may lead to danger, failure, injury or loss: * *It's too risky to try and pursue a career in acting.* *Risqué* means slightly improper or indecent: * *tell risqué jokes.*

risqué *see* **risky** or **risqué**?

road or **street**? Generally the noun *road* is used to denote a thoroughfare between towns or cities or in the suburbs of a town or city; a *street* is a thoroughfare in the town or city centre: * *a country road* * *a one-way street* * *the road to Brighton* * *the streets of London* * *a new housing estate on Park Road* * *their Oxford Street store.* There are, however, numerous exceptions to this rule, especially in the naming of roads and streets. Through its association with inner-city areas the word *street* has acquired certain negative connotations, and it is rarely used in the names of thoroughfares on new

estates. It is used in a number of words and expressions related to prostitution: * *on the streets* * *streetwalker*, and also in neutral idioms such as *streets ahead*, meaning 'much better': * *She's streets ahead of her sister at maths*, and *(right) up my street*, meaning 'suited to my interests or experience': * *This project is right up my street. See also* **street-**.

rob The verb *rob*, meaning 'steal money or property from' or 'take away an important quality from' is followed by the preposition *of*: * *He robbed his employers of thousands of pounds.* * *The incident robbed him of his dignity. See also* **burgle**, **rob** or **steal**?

role Some people object to the frequent use of the noun *role* as a synonym for 'place', 'function', 'position', 'part', etc.: * *the role of religion in modern society* * *a proven track record in a technical sales role* * *A new manager is now sought to play a key role in determining the company's future strategy.* The noun *role* is principally used to denote the part played by an actor. In psychology and sociology it refers to the part played by an individual in a social situation: * *role reversal* * *role-playing.* The word is sometimes spelt with a circumflex accent over the *o*, as in the French word from which it is derived: * *rôle.* It should not be confused with the English noun *roll*, to which it is etymologically related.

Roma *Roma*, or Romany, is the approved modern replacement for the former term *gipsy*, which is felt by many people to have acquired negative connotations over the centuries. *Roma* is used in both singular and plural contexts, though the correct singular form is *Rom*. Note, however, that *Roma* has yet to become widely accepted and that *gipsy* remains the more common term. *See also* **traveller**.

roofs or **rooves**? The plural of the word *roof*, 'covering of a building', is usually *roofs*, pronounced [roofs] or [roovz]. The spelling of the plural *rooves* is less common.

root *see* **rout** or **route**?

rosin *see* **resin** or **rosin**?

roughage This word, meaning 'coarse food; dietary fibre', is sometimes misspelt. Note the *-gh-* in the middle of the word.

round *see* **around** or **round**?

rouse *see* **arouse** or **rouse**?

rout or **route**? The noun *rout* means 'overwhelming defeat' or 'disorderly retreat'; the noun *route* means 'road' or 'course': * *They put the enemy to rout.* * *The procession took a different route this summer.* The risk of confusion is greater when the words are used as verbs, especially in the past tense: * *They routed the enemy.* * *The procession was routed along a different road.* The *e* of *route* is sometimes retained in the spelling of the present participle.

The phrasal verb *rout out*, meaning 'find by searching' or 'force out', is a variant of the verb *root*, meaning 'rummage', and is etymologically unrelated to the verb *rout* discussed above.

Rout is pronounced [rowt], rhyming with *out*, in all its senses and uses. The pronunciation of *route* is identical with that of *root* in British English; in American English *route* may be pronounced [root] or [rowt].

rowlock This word, for the device in a boat that holds an oar in place, is usually pronounced [*rol*ŏk]. In nontechnical contexts, *rowlock* is sometimes pronounced [rōlok].

rubbish The use of the word *rubbish* as a verb, meaning 'criticise severely' or 'condemn as worthless', is disliked by many users and should be avoided in formal contexts: * *The report rubbishes the new GCSE examinations.*

rung *see* **ringed**, **rang** or **rung**?

run-up Some people dislike the frequent use of the noun *run-up*, adopted from the field of athletics, to denote the period preceding an important event: * *the last few days in the run-up to the general election* * *The run-up to the anniversary of soldiers being deployed on the streets of Northern Ireland* (BBC TV).

rural or **rustic**? Both these adjectives relate to the countryside, country life, country people, farming, etc. *Rural* is used as a neutral opposite of urban; *rustic* has the connotations of simplicity, crudeness, quaintness, or lack of sophistication: * *rural schools* * *a rural setting* * *rural areas* * *rustic food* * *a rustic cottage* * *rustic manners*. Careful users maintain the distinction between the two words.

Russian or **Soviet**? The word *Russian* relates to the country of *Russia*, which formed the major part of the Soviet Union from 1922 to 1991, and its people: * *the Russian composer Rimsky-Korsakov* * *a Russian manufacturing* *company*. The word *Soviet* is used with reference to people and events of the years when the Soviet Union was in existence: * *Soviet space missions* * *a Soviet politician*. The noun and adjective *Russian*, formerly loosely applied to all the constituent republics of the Soviet Union and their people, should not be used with reference to (the people of) Ukraine, Lithuania, etc. since their independence in 1991.

S

's or s'? Possessive nouns are usually formed by adding *'s* to singular nouns, an apostrophe to plural nouns that end in *s*, and *'s* to irregular plural nouns that do not end in *s*: * *Jane's pen* * *the boy's father* * *the directors' cars* * *women's clothes*. In the possessive form of a name or singular noun that ends in *s*, *x*, or *z*, the apostrophe may or may not be followed by *s*. The final *s* is most frequently omitted in names, especially names of three or more syllables that end in the sound [z]: * *Euripides' tragedies* * *Berlioz' operas*. For words of one syllable, *'s* is generally used: * *St James's Palace* * *the fox's tail* * *Liz's house* * *the boss's secretary*. The presence or absence of the final *s* in other possessives of this group depends on usage, convention, pronunciation, etc.: * *the princess's tiara* * *Jesus' apostles* * *the rhinoceros'(s) horn* * *Nostradamus'(s) prophecies*. *See also* **apostrophe; contractions; -ing forms; possessives; sake.**

sac or sack? These two spellings are sometimes confused. The noun *sac* is largely restricted to scientific contexts, where it denotes a baglike part of an animal or plant: * *a fluid-filled sac*. A *sack* is a large bag used to hold coal, potatoes, etc. In informal contexts, *sack* is also a noun or verb referring to dismissal from employment: * *They got the sack.* * *We sacked them.*

 The word *sac*, of French origin, occurs in the compound *cul-de-sac*, meaning 'dead end'.

saccharin or saccharine? The sweet powder that is used as a sugar substitute is spelt *saccharin*, without a final *-e*; *saccharine* is an adjective meaning 'excessively sweet': * *The drink is sweetened with saccharin.* * *a saccharine smile*. The use of *saccharine* in place of *saccharin* is acknowledged by some dictionaries but is widely regarded as incorrect. Note also the *-cc-* and *-ar-* of both words.

sack *see* **sac or sack?**

sacrilegious This word, which means 'showing disrespect towards something holy', sometimes causes problems with spelling. Note the position of the first *i* and *e*, which are in the opposite order in the word *religious*.

sail or sale? *Sail* means 'expanse of canvas or cloth used to propel a vessel using windpower': * *The crew lowered the sail as the gale gathered strength*. It should not be confused with *sale*, which denotes the selling of something: * *a house sale*.

sake The noun *sake* is usually preceded by a possessive adjective or noun: * *for their sake* * *for Edward's sake* * *for pity's sake* * *for old times' sake*. If the preceding noun ends in the sound [s], the possessive form is not used, although an apostrophe may be added: * *for goodness sake* * *for conscience' sake*.

Such expressions as *for all our sakes* and *for both their sakes*, using the plural form of *sake*, are disliked by some users but acceptable to most. They may be replaced by *for the sake of us all, for the sake of both of them*, etc.

salable *see* **saleable** or **salable**?

salary or **wage**? Both these nouns denote the money paid to employees at regular intervals in return for their services. A *salary* is usually paid monthly to professional people or non-manual workers; a *wage* is usually paid weekly to manual workers or servants: * *My salary barely covers our mortgage repayments and living expenses.* * *the minimum wage for factory workers.* The noun *wage* is often used in the plural form *wages*: * *a bricklayer's wage(s)* * *He seems to spend most of his wages on cigarettes and alcohol.* The noun *wages* is not used with a singular verb, except in the well-known biblical quotation *the wages of sin is death* (Romans 6:23).

sale *see* **sail** or **sale**?

saleable or **salable**? Both spellings of this word are acceptable, but *saleable* is the more usual in British English. *See* **spelling**.

salesman or **saleswoman**? *see* **non-sexist terms**.

salivary This word has two possible pronunciations. The more traditional has the stress on the first syllable [*sali*vări]; the pronunciation [să*lī*vări], with the stress on the second syllable, is perfectly acceptable and is more frequently used.

salon or **saloon**? *Saloon* is the anglicised form of the French word *salon*. Both words entered the English language in the 18th century and have developed a number of individual meanings. *Salon* is most frequently found in the names of certain places of business, such as: * *beauty salon* * *hairdressing salon.* A *saloon* is a large room in a public house or on a ship: * *We went into the saloon (bar)*; it also denotes a type of car: * *the most popular saloon (car).* A *salon* is also a room for receiving visitors in a large house, or an assembly of important political or artistic guests: * *the literary salons of 17th-century Paris.*

salubrious or **salutary**? *Salubrious* means 'wholesome' or 'conducive to health'; *salutary* means 'beneficial', 'causing improvement', or 'remedial': * *a salubrious climate* * *a salutary warning* * *We decided to look for a more salubrious hotel.* * *Spending a few days in prison can be a salutary experience for young offenders.* The adjective *salutary* was formerly synonymous with *salubrious* but is rarely used in this sense today. Both adjectives are ultimately derived from the Latin word *salus*, meaning 'health'.

Note the spelling of *salutary*, which ends in *-ary*, not *-ory*.

same The use of *same* as a pronoun is best restricted to business or official contexts: * *I enclose my passport, as requested; please return same by registered post.* This usage is widely regarded as commercialese, and another pronoun, such as *it* or *them*, can usually be substituted for *same*: * *He found an old blanket and used it* [not *same*] *to line the dog's basket.* Nouns qualified by the adjective *same* are usually followed by *as*: • *He works for the same company as his brother-in-law.* • *She sent me the same book as you gave her last Christmas.* In the second example, and in similar sentences, *as* is often omitted or replaced by *that*: • *the same suit that he wore for his wedding.*

same-sex The adjective *same-sex* has appeared with increasing frequency in reference to homosexual relationships: • *Same-sex marriages are on the increase.* Many users prefer it to the more slangy and less neutral *gay*, though others consider it both unnecessarily jargonistic and euphemistic compared with *homosexual*.

sanatorium A *sanatorium* is a medical establishment for the treatment and care of people, especially those suffering from long-term illnesses. Note the spelling of this word in British English, particularly the second *a* and the *o*. The spelling *sanitarium* is an American English variant. The plural forms of both spellings may end in *-riums* or *-ria*.

sanction The noun *sanction* has two senses that appear to contradict each other. It may mean 'official authorisation or permission': • *The project has been given the sanction of the board of directors.* This use is largely restricted to formal contexts, and the noun is perhaps more frequently found in the plural form *sanctions*, referring to coercive measures taken against a state or institution: • *economic sanctions against Iraq* • *to impose political sanctions.* The verb *sanction* means 'permit' or 'authorise': • *The law does not sanction the use of violence in such cases.* It should not be used in the sense of 'impose sanctions'.

sank, sunk or **sunken**? The past tense of the verb *sink* is *sank* or *sunk* – *sank* being the more frequent. The usual form of its past participle is *sunk*; *sunken* is largely restricted to adjectival use: • *The dog sank its teeth into the man's leg.* • *One of the boats has sunk.* • *We are diving for sunken treasure.*

sarcasm, sarcastic *see* **irony**.

sat *see* **sitting** or **sat**?

sate, satiate or **satisfy**? The verb *satisfy* means 'supply' or 'fulfil': • *Her needs had been satisfied.* • *This should satisfy their demands.* The verbs *sate* and *satiate* may mean 'satisfy fully', but are more frequently used in the sense of 'supply or fulfil to excess': • *to satiate a person's appetite* • *Television viewers are sated with imported comedy shows.* A person who is *satisfied* has had enough; a person who is *sated* or *satiated* has usually had too much. *Sate* and *satiate* are used in formal contexts and are largely synonymous, but *sate* is very rarely used as an active verb. The nouns *satiety* and *satiation* are derived from *satiate*. *Satiation* means 'the act of satiating' or 'the state of being satiated'; *satiety* is used only in the second of these senses. Both nouns are used only in formal contexts.

Note the change in pronunciation of the first *t* in *satiate* [*say*shiayt] and *satiety* [să*tī*ĕti].

satire or **satyr**? *Satire* is the use of irony or parody to mock folly and evil in human behaviour, politics, religion, etc.; a *satyr* is a mythological creature in the form of a goatlike man, associated with lechery. The two nouns should not be confused in usage or pronunciation: *satyr* rhymes with *matter*, whereas the second syllable of *satire* rhymes with *fire*.

satisfy *see* **sate, satiate** or **satisfy?**

saturate The verb *saturate* is followed by the preposition *with* or *in*: * *The rug was saturated with* [or *in*] *dirty water.*

satyr *see* **satire** or **satyr?**

savage The use of the word *savage* to describe a person from a technologically undeveloped culture is no longer considered acceptable and should be avoided: * *The sailors found themselves surrounded by savages brandishing spears.* Note that for similar reasons the term *primitive* may also cause offence.

savoir faire The French expression *savoir faire* is used in formal contexts to refer to an ability to act appropriately in different situations, and especially to behave with self-confidence in social situations: * *to display/lack savoir faire.* The phrase is sometimes hyphenated in English and is pronounced [savwah *fair*]. Its literal French meaning is 'knowing how to do'.

saw, soar, or **sore?** The spellings of these three words are sometimes confused. *Saw* is the past tense of the verb *see*: * *I saw her yesterday* and also denotes a serrated blade used for cutting wood, etc.: * *The saw bit into the bark of the tree. Soar* means 'fly' or 'rise rapidly': * *The bird soared on the breeze.* * *Inflation is soaring. Sore* means 'painful' or 'hurting': * *The child has a sore elbow.* * *My heart is sore.*

says This word is sometimes mispronounced. The form of the verb *say* used in the present tense with *he, she,* or *it* is *says,* pronounced [sez].

scallop The standard pronunciation of this word, which means 'a shellfish with two flat fan-shaped shells', is [*skol*ŏp]. An alternative, which rhymes with *gallop,* is often heard but is avoided by careful users.

scant or **scanty?** Both these adjectives mean 'limited', 'barely enough', or 'meagre'. *Scant* is more formal and less frequent than *scanty,* being chiefly used in front of certain abstract nouns: * *He paid scant attention to my words.* * *She has scant regard for the law. Scanty* is used before or after a wider range of nouns: * *Their knowledge is rather scanty.* * *a scanty bikini* * *a scanty collection of books. Scant* is also used with units of measurement to mean 'barely' or 'slightly less than': * *a scant two ounces.*

scarcely *see* **hardly.**

scared As an adjective, *scared* is followed by the preposition *of*: * *He's scared of spiders.* As a past participle, *scared* is followed by the preposition *by*: * *We were scared by their threats.*

scarfs or **scarves?** Either *scarfs* or *scarves* is acceptable as the plural of the noun *scarf,* denoting a piece of cloth worn around the neck or on the head.

scarify The verb *scarify* should not be used in place of *scare,* to which it is unrelated in meaning and origin. *Scarify* tends to be used in formal contexts and means 'scratch or break up the surface of': * *to scarify the skin* *before administering a vaccine* ● *to scarify the topsoil of a field.* In figurative contexts it is used in the sense of 'wound with harsh criticism': ● *a scarifying review.* The traditional pronunciation of *scarify* is [*ska*rrifī], with [*skai*rifī] being an accepted and frequently encountered variant.

scarves *see* **scarfs** or **scarves**?

scenario The noun *scenario* is frequently used to denote a projected or imagined future state of affairs or sequence of events: ● *a scenario in which the superpowers would have recourse to nuclear weapons.* Many people object to the frequency of this usage, especially in contexts where *plan*, *programme*, *scene*, *situation*, etc. would be adequate or more appropriate. The clichés *nightmare scenario* and *worst-case scenario*, both of which mean 'the worst thing that could happen', are also best avoided wherever possible. The principal meaning of *scenario* is 'outline or synopsis of a play, film, opera, etc.'. The word is usually pronounced [*sin*ariō]; some users dislike the variant pronunciation [*sinairi*ō].

sceptic or **septic**? The pronunciation of these two words is sometimes confused. A *sceptic* (American English, *skeptic*) is a person who has doubts about accepted beliefs or principles, and is pronounced [*skep*tik]. *Septic* is an adjective meaning 'infected with harmful bacteria': ● *a septic wound*, and is pronounced [*sep*tik].

sceptical The adjective *sceptical* is followed by the preposition about or of: ● *I remain sceptical about* [or of] *her motives. See also* **cynical** or **sceptical**?

schedule This word, meaning 'plan or timetable': ● *The train was behind schedule again*, is usually pronounced [*shed*yool] in British English. The word may also be pronounced [*sked*yool], particularly in American English. The verb *schedule*, 'to plan', should not be overused.

schism The traditional pronunciation of this word, meaning 'separation into opposed groups', is [sizm], with a silent *ch*. The alternative pronunciation [skizm] is perfectly acceptable.

schizophrenic The adjective *schizophrenic* relates to the mental disorder *schizophrenia*, which is characterised by hallucinations, delusions, social withdrawal, emotional instability, and loss of contact with reality: ● *Another sufferer believes during a schizophrenic attack that he is in command of a spaceship, 2,000 years in the future* (*Reader's Digest*). The use of the adjective *schizophrenic* in the extended sense of 'inconsistent', 'contradictory', 'unpredictable', 'capricious', etc. is disliked and avoided by most users.

Note the spelling of *schizophrenic* and *schizophrenia*, and the difference in pronunciation between the two words: *schizophrenic* is pronounced [skitsŏ*fren*ik], with a short *e*; *schizophrenia* [skitsŏ*free*niǎ] has a long *e*.

scone The pronunciation of this word is a favourite topic for debate; both [skon] and [skōn] are equally acceptable. The parish of *Scone* in East Scotland, the original site of the stone on which Scottish kings were crowned, is pronounced [skoon].

Scotch, **Scots** or **Scottish**? All these adjectives mean 'of Scotland', but there are differences of usage and application between them. *Scottish*, the most common, is used in a wide range of contexts: * *Scottish history* * *a Scottish town* * *Scottish Gaelic* * *a Scottish name* * *Scottish dancing* * *a Scottish poet.*

The adjective *Scotch* was formerly used for such purposes but is now restricted to a number of fixed phrases, in the sense of 'produced in Scotland' or 'associated with Scotland': * *Scotch whisky* * *Scotch broth* * *Scotch mist.*

Scots is usually applied to people: * *the Scots Guards* * *a Scotsman* * *a Scotswoman.* The last two examples may be replaced by the noun *Scot*, which means 'a native or inhabitant of Scotland': * *She married a Scot.* The collective name for the people of Scotland is the *Scots* or the *Scottish*. The noun *Scots* also denotes a variety of English spoken in Scotland.

In some contexts two of the adjectives are interchangeable: * *a Scots/Scotch pine* *a Scottish/Scotch terrier* * *a Scottish/Scots accent.*

sculpt or **sculpture?** The verbs *sculpt* and *sculpture* are synonymous and virtually interchangeable in all contexts: * *He sculpted/sculptured a copy of the Venus de Milo in marble.* * *She paints and sculpts/sculptures in her attic studio.*

sculptor or **sculptress?** *see* **non-sexist terms**.

sea or **see?** *Sea* means 'ocean' or 'wide expanse of something': * *They set sail upon the sea.* * *A sea of eager faces.* It should not be confused with the verb *see*, meaning 'catch sight of': * *Did you see that? See* is also occasionally used as a noun to refer to the office or jurisdiction of a bishop: * *the see of Rome.*

seamless This word, meaning 'having no seam' or 'uninterrupted', is sometimes misspelt. Note particularly the *-ea-* in the middle of the word: * *a seamless blouse* * *a seamless transition from one story to another.* The word *seemless* is an archaic word meaning 'unseemly; shameful; unfitting' (*Oxford English Dictionary*).

seasonal or **seasonable?** *Seasonal* means 'of or occurring in a particular season'; *seasonable* means 'suitable for the season' or 'opportune': * *seasonal vegetables* * *seasonal work* * *seasonable weather* * *seasonable advice.* The two adjectives should not be confused.

secateurs This word, meaning 'pruning shears', is sometimes misspelt. Note the single *c* and the *-eurs* ending.

second or **secondly?** *see* **first** or **firstly?**

second-guess The verb *second-guess*, of American origin, means 'predict', 'anticipate', or 'evaluate with hindsight': * *On a scale of difficulty of one to 10, second-guessing the travel market this year is 12* (*The Guardian*). Some people object to the use of this Americanism in British English.

secretary The word *secretary* is sometimes misspelt: note the *-ary* ending, which is attached to the letters of the word *secret*. The *a* of secretary is rarely sounded in the British English pronunciation [*sek*rĕtri]. Careful users always sound the first *r*, however, and object to the pronunciation [*sek*ĕtri]. The usual American English pronunciation is [*sek*rĕterri].

see *see* **sea** or **see?**

seed *see* **cede** or **seed**?

seeing as or **seeing that?** The construction *seeing as*, meaning 'since', is disliked by some people and should be used only in very informal contexts: *We will help you out, seeing as you helped us. Seeing that* is the more correct form of the conjunction: *We should go at once, seeing that it is already late.*

seem When the verb *seem* is used in the negative, the word *not* (or other negative element) may be placed before or after the verb: * *She didn't seem to understand.* * *She seemed not to understand.* * *The weather doesn't seem likely to improve.* * *The weather seems unlikely to improve.* The use of *didn't seem, doesn't seem*, etc. is best avoided in formal contexts; similarly, the phrases *cannot seem, can't seem, couldn't seem*, etc. should be restricted to informal speech: * *He couldn't seem to hear us.* * *I cannot seem to find the key.* In formal writing, such phrases may be replaced by *seem unable* or simply *cannot*: * *He seemed unable to hear us.* * *I cannot find the key.*

seemless *see* **seamless**.

seize This word, meaning 'take eagerly or by force': * *He seized the money and ran*, is sometimes misspelt. Note the order of the vowels *-ei-*, which does not correspond to the usual 'i before e' rule. *See also* **spelling**.

self Many people dislike and avoid the use of the word *self* as a pronoun, even in informal contexts: * *tickets for husband and self*. The noun *self* and its plural form *selves* are acceptable to all users: * *his usual self* * *their true selves*.

The suffixes *-self* and *-selves* are used to form the reflexive pronouns *myself, yourself, ourselves, themselves*, etc.: * *She killed herself while under the influence of drugs.* Some people object to the use of these pronouns for emphasis: * *The house itself will be demolished next week.* * *He has not driven the car himself.*

The prefix *self-* is always attached with a hyphen: * *self-catering* * *self-confident* * *self-propelled* * *self-sufficient*.

Some people object to the increasing use of the prefix *self-* to coin new verbs: * *self-pick strawberries* * *We teach them to be aware, to self-market, to look at the future, perhaps in a slightly different way* (The Guardian). * *Farmers may one day be able to graze 'self-dipping' sheep, which do not need to be dunked in chemicals to deter attacks by pests and parasites* (Daily Telegraph). Such verbs can often be replaced by a more acceptable phrase using a reflexive pronoun, such as *market yourself* in place of *self-market. See also* **hyphen; myself**.

sell-by date This phrase literally means 'the date by which perishable goods should be sold', but it is increasingly used in figurative contexts, meaning 'no longer useful or effective; out-of-date': * *The government is past its sell-by date.* * *ideas that have passed their sell-by date.* It should not be overused in this sense. Other phrases adopted from commercial usage include *best-before date* and *shelf-life*: * *the best-before date for new entrants to the profession* * *She was forced to admit that she was approaching the end of her shelf-life as a marriage prospect.*

semantics, semiotics or **semiology?** *Semiotics* (or *semiology*) is the study of the properties of sign systems, especially as used in human communication. *Semantics*, one part of *semiotics*, is the study of the meaning of linguistic signs. For example, discussion of the meaning of the words *book, moon*, or *yellow* belongs to *semantics*, whereas the wider cultural aspects of raising eyebrows when people greet each other at a distance belongs to *semiotics*.

semi- *see* **demi-, hemi-** or **semi-**?

semicolons Unlike many of the other punctuation marks, there is no occasion on which the *semicolon* cannot be replaced by another form of punctuation or sentence construction, and its use appears to be gradually declining. It is mainly used between clauses that are linked by sense but are not joined by a conjunction, and that could each stand as a separate sentence: * *I am very tired; I am also hungry.* * *The night was dark; the rain fell in torrents.* It is frequently used before such phrases as *however, none the less*, and *nevertheless*: * *This precaution is recommended; however, it is not compulsory.*

The semicolon can sometimes be replaced by a comma, but in sentences where clauses already contain commas, the semicolon is often used to separate the clauses: * *Eliot, though born in America, was a British subject; he lived, worked, and died in England.* The semicolon can also be used in order to establish subsets in a long list or series separated by commas: * *Applicants must have a good honours degree, preferably in English; a lively writing style, a knowledge of magazine publishing, and proven editorial experience; an ability to work under pressure, to cooperate with colleagues, and to work flexible hours.*

semiotics, semiology *see* **semantics, semiotics** or **semiology**?

senior citizen or **old age pensioner**? Both these expressions are used with reference to people who are over the age of retirement. The expression *senior citizen* (or the shortened form senior) is considered a euphemism by most: * *There are courses for senior citizens at the university.* * *Senior citizens are entitled to reduced bus and train fares.* The term *old age pensioner* specifically denotes a person who receives a state retirement pension. *Old age pensioner*, often shortened to pensioner or abbreviated to *OAP*, may have connotations of dependence: * *helping old age pensioners in the community* * *pensioners who are unable to pay their fuel bills.*

sensible or **sensitive**? The most frequent meaning of *sensible* is 'having or showing common sense; not foolish; practical': * *a sensible child* * *sensible advice* * *the sensible thing to do* * *sensible shoes. Sensitive* means 'easily hurt or irritated', 'having awareness', 'delicate', or 'reacting to very small differences': * *sensitive skin* * *He's very sensitive about his large nose.* * *We are sensitive to your problems.* * *a sensitive issue* * *a sensitive instrument.* Note that, by extension, *sensibility* denotes a person's emotional or aesthetic awareness, while *sensitivity* refers more generally to a person's emotional or physical responses: * *Her association with famous painters of the day is a testament to her artistic sensibility.* * *The school must show sensitivity to the parents' wishes.*

sensitive The adjective *sensitive* is followed by the preposition *to* in the sense 'affected by': • *He is too sensitive to criticism*, and by *about* in the sense 'self-conscious': • *She is very sensitive about her large nose.*

sensual or **sensuous**? Both these adjectives relate to the gratification of the senses. Something that is *sensual* appeals to the body, arousing or satisfying physical appetites or sexual desire; something that is *sensuous* appeals to the senses, sometimes especially the mind, being aesthetically pleasing or spiritually uplifting: • *to indulge in the sensual pleasures of eating and drinking* • *the sensual movements of the striptease artist* • *the sensuous movements of the ballerina* • *to appreciate the sensuous music of Elgar's cello concerto.* The use of the adjective *sensual* sometimes implies disapproval, whereas *sensuous* is generally used in a favourable manner.

Sensuous was coined originally by the English poet John Milton in the mid-17th century.

sentence adverb A sentence adverb is a word that qualifies an entire sentence: • *Militarily the campaign was a great success.* It should be noted that sentence adverbs that relate more to the speaker's attitude than to the content of the sentence itself may incur criticism: • *Personally I think it's a mistake.* • *Thankfully no one was hurt.* • *Hopefully everything will go well.*

sentences A *sentence* can be defined as 'a grammatically complete unit consisting of one or more words, which starts with a capital letter and ends with a full stop, question mark, or exclamation mark'. The old rule that 'all sentences must contain a verb' holds good for most kinds of writing,

but it is a rule that is often legitimately broken, for example: • *Whatever for?* • *For heaven's sake!* • *Yes, of course.* Verbless sentences are often used for stylistic effect, particularly in order to emphasise or qualify a previous statement: • *It was an illusion, he told himself. A trick of the light.* • *He's as rich as Croesus. Possibly richer.*

Sentence structure and word order in English are partly a matter of rules and partly a matter of style. The normal word order is subject-verb-object; for example: • *The dog bit the postman* cannot be changed to *The postman bit the dog* without changing the sense of the sentence. However, a speaker or writer can choose their word order in sentences like: • *After lunch we could go for a walk. – We could go for a walk after lunch.* • *Even more delicious is her chocolate mousse. – Her chocolate mousse is even more delicious.* See also **inversion**.

sentiment or **sentimentality**? A *sentiment* is a feeling, emotion, attitude, or opinion: • *anti-communist sentiment.* • *These are my sentiments on the matter.* *Sentimentality* is the state of being sentimental, with particular reference to excessive indulgence of the emotions: • *the sentimentality of the film* • *She kept his handkerchief under her pillow for reasons of sentimentality.* *Sentiment* may also refer to indulgence of the emotions, but it is more neutral than *sentimentality*: • *He seems to be totally lacking in sentiment.*

separate This word is often misspelt. Note the vowels; the most frequent error is to replace the first *a* with an *e*. It may help to associate the central syllable -*par*- with the central letters of the word *apart*. The verb *separate* is followed by the preposition *from*: * *Keep raw meat separate from cooked meat.*

septic *see* **sceptic or septic?**

sequence of tenses When you change a verb from the present tense to the past tense, other verbs in the sentence may change too, according to a fixed pattern. This is known as the sequence of tenses: * *He said, 'I know it is too late.' – He said that he knew it was too late.* * *She said, 'I am glad I sold my house.' – She said that she was glad she had sold her house.* See also **tense**.

serf or surf? These two words are occasionally confused, as they are pronounced in the same way. *Serfs* were agricultural labourers in feudal times, who had to work on their master's land. *Surf* is the breaking swell of the sea. As a verb, *surf* means 'ride the surf' or, in the informal expression *surf the net*, to look generally on the Internet for information of interest.

sergeant The spelling of *sergeant* is often a source of error. A *sergeant* is a middle-ranking non-commissioned officer in an army, etc., or an officer in a police force. A *sergeant-major* is a non-commissioned officer of the highest rank. A *serjeant-at-arms* is an officer in a parliament; a *serjeant-at-law* a former rank of barrister.

serial *see* **cereal or serial?**

series The word *series* can be treated as either a singular or a plural noun, depending upon whether one or more series is being discussed: * *A series of programmes has been agreed.* * *Several series of programmes have been agreed.*

seriously The adverb *seriously* is best avoided where *very* or *extremely* would be adequate or more appropriate: * *They seemed to be having a very* [not *seriously*] *good time.* * *Her parents are extremely* [not *seriously*] *rich.* The adjective *serious* is also overused in the sense of 'great', especially in the phrase *serious money*, meaning 'a large amount of money'.

serve The verb *serve* is followed by the preposition *as* or *for*: * *The sofa serves as* [or *for*] *a spare bed.*

service The verb *service* is best avoided where *serve* would be adequate or more appropriate: * *Labour MPs have accused Thames Water officials of spending too much time on privatisation issues rather than servicing customers* (*Daily Telegraph*). * *A national organisation has been formed to service the local groups.* The principal meanings of the verb *service* are 'overhaul': * *The mechanic serviced the car*, and 'pay interest on a debt'.

serviceable This word, meaning 'ready to be used; durable': * *The television had been repaired and was now serviceable*, is sometimes misspelt. The *e* is retained before the suffix *-able* in order to retain the soft *c* sound. *See also* **spelling**.

serviceman or servicewoman? *see* **nonsexist terms**.

session *see* **cession or session?**

sewed or sewn? Either word may be used as the past participle of the verb *sew*: * *I have sewn/sewed a patch over the hole.* *Sewn* is often preferred to *sewed*, especially when the participle is used as an adjective: * *a neatly sewn hem*. The past tense of *sew* is always *sewed*: * *She sewed the lace along the edge*.

The verb *sew* and its derivatives should not be confused with *sow* (*see* **sowed** or **sown?**).

sexism The use of sexist language can often be avoided by the substitution of neutral synonyms or simple paraphrases, without recourse to clumsy or controversial neologisms. Those opponents of sexism who coin such expressions as *the artist's mistress-piece* and *to person the telephones* do little to further their cause. The most frequent examples of sexism include the use of the noun *man* in place of *person*; *lady* or *girl* in place of *woman*; *he*, *him*, and *his* as pronouns of common gender; and the titles *Mrs* and *Miss* (*see* **he** or **she**; **man**; **Ms, Mrs or Miss?**; **woman**).

The problems of sexism arising from occupational titles fall into three categories. The words *engineer* and *nurse*, for example, are of neutral gender but are traditionally associated with men and women respectively. For this reason the terms *female engineer*, *male nurse*, etc. are sometimes used to avoid confusion. This is often quite unnecessary: * *Dr Tony Butterworth, 40, a former male nurse, has been appointed Britain's first Professor of Community Nursing at Manchester University* (*Daily Telegraph*).

The ban on sexual discrimination in job advertisements has encouraged the substitution of neutral synonyms for occupational titles that specify sex: *foreman* and *charwoman*, for example, may be replaced by *supervisor* and *cleaner*; *fireman* and *cameraman* by *firefighter* and *camera-operator*; *policeman* and *policewoman* by *police officer*;

salesman and *saleswoman* by *sales representative* or *shop assistant*.

Some people also dislike use of feminine suffixes: *The fête was opened by the comedienne Victoria Wood*. * *Her sister is an usherette at the local cinema*. * *He married a successful authoress*. See also -**ess**; **non-sexist terms**; **person**; **political correctness**.

sexy *Sexy*, an informal adjective meaning 'arousing sexual interest' or 'sexually aroused', has increasingly become used as a synonym for 'attractive', 'enjoyable', 'exciting', or 'fashionable' in contexts that are completely devoid of sexual connotations: * *'Crime,' according to an independent television producer recently, 'is very sexy this year.'* (*The Guardian*). * *Boots wanted a presence in some of the sexier parts of the retailing business* (*The Guardian*).

Shakespearean or **Shakespearian?** This word, meaning 'of or having the characteristics of Shakespeare': * *a Shakespearean sonnet*, may end with *-ean* or with *-ian*.

shall or **will?** The traditional distinction between *shall* and *will* is that *shall* is used in the first person and *will* in the second and third persons as the future tense of the verb *to be*. Furthermore, *will* is used in the first person and *shall* in the second and third persons to express determination, compulsion, intention, willingness, commands, promises, etc.: * *I shall wash the dishes later*. * *He will come back tomorrow*. * *We will not obey you*. * *They shall apologise immediately*. In informal contexts the problem rarely arises, the contraction *'ll* being used to represent both *shall* and *will* in all persons.

Outside England, especially in American, Scottish, and Irish English, the distinction between *shall* and *will* is more simply defined, *shall* being used in all persons to express determination, compulsion, etc., and *will* as the future tense of the verb *to be*, with an increasing tendency to use *will* in all senses. Modern usage in England is following this trend, although *shall* is retained in official contexts: * *Passengers shall remain seated until the vehicle is stationary.*

The use of *shall* and *will* in questions is a more complex issue. * *Shall I stay?* means 'Do you want me to stay?' * *Shall we go?* is a suggestion or proposition. * *Will I/we win?* means 'Am I/Are we going to win?' * *Shall you pay the bill?* means 'Are you going to pay the bill?' * *Will you pay the bill?* is a request.

shaved or **shaven**? *Shaved* is the past tense of the verb *shave* and the usual form of the past participle: * *He (has) shaved off his beard.* *Shaven*, a variant form of the past participle, is largely restricted to adjectival use: * *the shaven heads of the monks* * *a clean-shaven young man.*

she *see* **he** or **she**; **female** or **feminine**?

shear or **sheer**? *Shear* means 'cut or break off' or 'remove or deprive': * *The mast had sheared off halfway up.* * *Millions have been sheared off the budget.* It should not be confused with *sheer*, which means 'utter' or 'vertical': * *sheer cheek* * *a sheer drop.*

sheared or **shorn**? *Sheared* is the past tense of the verb *shear*; *shorn* is the usual form of its past participle: * *They sheared the sheep.* * *They have*

shorn the sheep. * *You will be shorn of your power.* The past participle *sheared* is used in the technical sense of 'deformed', 'distorted', 'fractured', or 'broken': * *The head of the screw has sheared off.*

Shorn is also used as an adjective: * *a shorn lamb* * *his shorn hair.*

sheer *see* **shear** or **sheer**?

sheikh The preferred pronunciation of this word, which means 'an Arab chief or ruler', is [shayk]. The alternative pronunciation [sheek] is not generally accepted. Note the spelling of this word; the spelling *sheik* is an accepted variant.

shelf-life *see* **sell-by date**.

sheriff This word is often misspelt. Note the single *r* in the middle of the word and the *-ff* ending.

shined or **shone**? *Shone* is the past tense and past participle for most senses of the verb *shine*; *shined* is restricted to the meaning 'polished': * *The sun (has) shone all day.* * *He shone his torch on the statue.* * *They (have) shined our shoes.*

ship *see* **boat** or **ship**?

shone *see* **shined** or **shone**?

shoot *see* **chute** or **shoot**?

shorn *see* **sheared** or **shorn**?

should or **would**? In reported speech, conditional sentences, and other indirect constructions, the use of *should* and *would* follows the pattern of *shall* and *will* (as the future tense of the verb *to be*); *would* is always used in the second and third persons and often replaces *should* in the first person: ◦ *We said we should/would stay until Saturday.* ◦ *She thought you would fail.* ◦ *If you were in trouble I should/would help you.* ◦ *He would open the door if he had the key. Would* is also the correct choice when asking a question: ◦ *Would you like to see the rest of the house?* A similar convention applies to the use of *should* and *would* in polite or formal constructions: ◦ *We should/would be delighted to see you.* ◦ *I should/would like to buy a pair of sandals.* ◦ *She would be pleased to oblige.* ◦ *They would prefer to play outside.*

In informal contexts, the distinction between *should* and *would* does not arise, the contraction *'d* being used to represent both *should* and *would* in all persons.

In the sense of 'ought to' *should* is used in all persons: ◦ *We should visit her more often.* ◦ *You should be able to see it from here.* There is sometimes a risk of ambiguity in the first person: ◦ *I thought I should accept their offer* may be a paraphrase of 'I thought I ought to...' or the past tense of 'I think I shall...'

In the sense of 'used to' *would* is used in all persons: ◦ *When we were on holiday we would sometimes spend all day on the beach.* ◦ *Before his retirement he would always get up at seven o'clock.*

On the use of *should* (or *would*) *of* for *should* (or *would*) *have, see* **of**. *See also* **rather**; **shall** or **will?**; **subjunctive**.

shrank, shrunk or **shrunken?** *Shrank* is the past tense of the verb *shrink*, and *shrunk* the usual form of its past participle – the variant *shrunken* being

more frequently used as an adjective: ◦ *He shrank from telling her the truth.* ◦ *My pullover has shrunk.* ◦ *A shrunken old woman stood in the doorway.* The use of *shrunk* in place of *shrank* is also acknowledged by some authorities.

Siamese twins *see* **conjoined**.

sibling The noun *sibling*, which denotes a brother or sister, is a useful word that is unfortunately disliked by many users and largely restricted to formal contexts and sociological jargon: ◦ *the twins' relationship with their siblings* ◦ *sibling rivalry.* The use of *sibling* and *siblings* to simplify such sentences as: ◦ *He would like to have a sibling* [rather than a brother or sister] *to play with* and: ◦ *All her siblings* [rather than brothers and sisters] *have left home* has yet to gain general acceptance.

sic The Latin word *sic*, meaning 'so' or 'thus', is used in printed or written text (often in a quotation) to indicate that an unlikely, unexpected, questionable, or misspelt word or phrase has in fact been accurately transcribed: ◦ *He spoke of a need for 'more thorough analysation [sic]' of the results. Sic* is enclosed in square brackets and inserted immediately after the word or phrase it refers to. The use of italics is optional.

sick or **ill?** In British English, to feel *sick* is to feel nauseated or queasy, to feel *ill* is to feel unwell: ◦ *She was sick yesterday* usually means 'she vomited yesterday': ◦ *She was ill yesterday* means 'she was not well yesterday'. The adjective *ill* is not usually used in this sense before a noun, *sick* being preferred: ◦ *a sick* [not *ill*] *man.* (*Ill* may, however, precede a noun in the sense of 'bad': * *ill fortune* * *ill treatment* * *ill health*.) *Sick* is also used with reference to absence from work because of illness: * *to go sick* * *off sick* * *sick pay* * *sick leave*.

In American English, *sick* and *ill* are interchangeable in most contexts, *ill* being the more formal of the two adjectives.

sideline Some people dislike the increasing use of the verb *sideline*, meaning 'prevent from taking part' or 'put out of action': * *This country must not be sidelined at the United Nations*. * *The old guard has been sidelined by the new administration*. Of sporting origin, the verb *sideline* has been used in American English since the 1940s, usually with reference to illness or injury that puts a player out of action.

siege This word, meaning 'the surrounding of a fortified place to force a surrender', is sometimes misspelt. Note the order of the vowels *-ie-*, which conforms to the normal 'i before e' rule. *See also* **spelling**.

sight or **site**? *see* **cite**, **sight** or **site**?

significant The adjective *significant* means 'having meaning': * *a significant detail* * *a significant gesture*. Its frequent use as a synonym for 'important', 'large', 'serious', etc., is disliked by some: * *a significant writer* * *a significant increase* * *a significant problem*.

silhouette This word, meaning 'outline; shadow', is sometimes misspelt, the most frequent error being the omission of the silent *h*. Note also the *-ette* ending. The word derives from the name

of the French politician Étienne de *Silhouette* (1709–67), perhaps because of his small-minded economies.

silicon or **silicone**? *Silicon* is an element that occurs in sand and is used in alloys, glass manufacture, and the electronics industry: * *silicon chip*. *Silicone* is a compound that contains *silicon* and is used in lubricants, polishes, and cosmetic surgery: * *silicone rubber*. The two words should not be confused. The final syllable of *silicon* is unstressed; the final syllable of *silicone* rhymes with *bone*.

similar Note the spelling of this adjective, particularly the single *m* and *l* and the *-ar* ending. The adjective *similar* is followed by the preposition *to*: * *Their car is similar to ours*. The alternative *similar as* is incorrect.

similes A *simile* is a figure of speech which, like a metaphor, suggests a comparison or analogy. However, a simile expresses the comparison explicitly and is usually introduced by *like* or *as*: * *teeth like pearls* * *as wide as the ocean*. (In the second example, the first *as*, before wide, is optional.) *Similes* are used in many well-known idioms: * *good as gold* * *dry as dust* * *bold as brass*, and many similes are so overworked as to have become clichés: * *to run like the wind* * *a voice like thunder* * *eyes like stars*.

Similes can be used to good effect, particularly in humorous or ironical prose: * *Jeeves coughed one soft, low, gentle cough like a sheep with a blade of grass stuck in its throat* (P.G. Wodehouse, *The Inimitable Jeeves*). * *A laugh swept through the conference hall as a drip of water might sweep through the Kalahari* (*The Times*).

They are more often used seriously in poetry:

> Life, like a dome of many-coloured glass,
> Stains the white radiance of Eternity.
> (Shelley, *Adonais*)

simplistic The adjective *simplistic* means 'oversimplified' or 'naive'; it should not be used in place of *simple*: * *a simplistic explanation of the theory of relativity* * *a simple* [not *simplistic*] *explanation for her behaviour. Simplistic* is generally used in a derogatory manner: * *His simplistic solution to the problem was rejected without further discussion.*

simulate or **stimulate**? These two verbs are sometimes confused. *Simulate* means 'feign', 'imitate', or 'reproduce for the purpose of study, training, experiment, etc.': * *to simulate indifference* * *simulated leather* * *The process is simulated in the laboratory. Stimulate* means 'arouse' or 'excite': * *He stimulated his pupils' interest.* * *a stimulating experience.* See also **dissemble, dissimulate** or **simulate**?

simultaneity The traditional pronunciation of this noun, derived from *simultaneous*, is [sĭmŭltăneeiti], although [sĭmŭltănayiti] is also heard. The American English pronunciation is [sīm-].

simultaneous This word, meaning 'happening at the same time', may cause problems with pronunciation. The usual pronunciation is [sĭmŭltaynius]; in American English, [sīm-].

since *see* **ago** or **since**?; **because, as, for** or **since**?

sincerely The adverb *sincerely* is sometimes misspelt. Note the *-cere-* in the middle, and the *-ly* (not *-ley*) ending.

sinecure The noun *sinecure*, meaning 'a job or position in which payment is received for little or no work', is often mispronounced. The correct pronunciation of this three-syllable word is [sīnikewr]: the *i* is long, as in *wine*, and the first *e* is not silent.

sine qua non The expression *sine qua non*, which is largely restricted to formal contexts, denotes an essential or indispensable condition or requirement: * *Mutual trust is a sine qua non of a successful marriage.* Of Latin origin, the phrase literally means 'without which not'.

The word *sine* may be pronounced [sīni], [sini], or [sinay]; *qua* may be pronounced [kway] or [kwah]; *non* may rhyme with *gone* or *bone*.

singeing or **singing**? *Singeing* is the present participle of the verb *singe*, meaning 'burn slightly': * *It is difficult to iron this blouse without singeing the lace.* The *e* of *singe* is retained in *singeing* to keep the *g* soft and to distinguish it from *singing*, the present participle of the verb *sing*: * *The birds were singing in the trees. Singeing* is pronounced [sinjing]; *singing* is pronounced [singing]. Careful speakers do not insert the hard *g* sound, as in *single*, into *singing*, *singer*, etc.

singular or **plural**? As a general rule, a singular verb is used with a singular subject and a plural verb is used with a plural subject. Problems arise when the subject is a noun or phrase that can be singular or plural, and when a singular subject is separated from the verb by a number of plural nouns (or vice versa): * *A list of the names and addresses of new members is* [not *are*] *available on request.* Such nouns as *audience, government, jury, committee, family, crowd, herd*, etc., and other collective nouns followed by *of* (*a bunch of flowers, a flock of geese, a gang of thieves*, etc.), are used with a singular verb if the people or items in question are considered as a group, and with a plural verb if they are considered as individuals.

Any corresponding pronouns or possessive adjectives should agree with the chosen verb: * *The audience were asked to remain in their* [not *its*] *seats.* * *The jury has to consider all the evidence before it* [not *they*] *can reach a verdict.* American English treats groups as singular more than British English does: * *Harvard plays Yale,* but: *Oxford play Cambridge.*

Measurements, sums of money, percentages, etc. are used with a singular verb if they are considered as a single entity: * *Four metres is all we need.* * *Ten pounds is not enough.* * *Fifteen per cent is a generous increase.*

Two or more nouns joined with *and* are used with a plural verb unless they represent a single concept: * *His sister and her friend were killed in the accident.* * *Gin and tonic is a popular drink.* However, nouns and phrases joined to the principal subject with *as well as, together, with, plus*, etc. are regarded as parenthetical; the verb agrees with the principal subject alone: * *A valuable painting, as well as her engravings, was destroyed in the fire.* * *Her engravings, together with a valuable painting, were destroyed in the fire.* See also **any; collective nouns; committee; either; foot** or **feet?; government; -ics; kind of; majority** and **minority; more; neither; none; number; one; or; plus; there is** or **there are?; together with.**

sink or **sync?** *Sink* is a verb meaning 'go down' or 'reduce', or a noun meaning 'basin for washing': * *as the sun sinks in the west* * *Hopes were sinking fast.* * *the kitchen sink.* It should not be confused with *sync*, which is an abbreviated form of *synchronisation*: * *The two systems run in sync.*

siphon or **syphon?** This word, meaning '(draw off liquid by means of a) tube using atmospheric pressure', can be spelt with an *i* or a *y.* Some users prefer the *i* spelling, since this reflects the original Greek, *siphōn.*

Sir *Sir* is a polite term of address for a man: * *Thank you very much, sir.* The word is usually written with a lowercase *s* in such contexts, but as an impersonal salutation in letter writing it is always written with a capital: * *Dear Sir. Sir*, with a capital *S,* is also the title of knights and baronets: * *Sir Lancelot* * *Sir Humphrey Appleby.* Note that it is correct to use *Sir* with a person's first name alone but not with his surname alone: * *Sir Humphrey* [not *Sir Appleby*].

sitting or **sat?** The substitution of *sat*, the past participle of the verb *sit*, for the present participle *sitting* is found in some dialects of English: * *They were sitting* [in some dialects *sat*] *in the garden.* *Sat* is correctly used in the passive form of the transitive verb *sit*: * *We were sat at this table by the head waiter.*

site or **cite?** *see* **cite, site** or **sight?**

sitting room *see* **lounge.**

situation In the sense of 'state of affairs' the noun *situation* often serves a useful purpose, but it should not be used to excess: * *We discussed our financial situation with the bank manager.* * *They are trying to improve the unemployment situation.* In some contexts *situation* is quite superfluous: * *a crisis situation* is *a crisis* * *an interview situation* is *an interview. See also* **ongoing**.

sixth This word may be pronounced [siksth] or [sikth], although some people dislike the omission of the second [s] sound.

sizeable or **sizable**? Both spellings of this word are acceptable. *See* **spelling**.

skilful The adjective *skilful*, meaning 'possessing skill', is sometimes misspelt. The final *l* of *skill* is dropped in British English before the suffix *-ful*, but in American English the *-ll* is retained: *skillful*.

skill The noun *skill* is followed by the preposition *at* or *in*: * *The job requires considerable skill at* [or *in*] *dealing with difficult people.*

slander *see* **libel** or **slander**?

slang *Slang* is unauthorised language, often but not necessarily coarse, which stands in the linguistic hierarchy between general informal speech and the specific vocabularies of professional and occupational jargon. Innovative and dramatic, slang is the most ephemeral of languages, continually coining new terms and discarding old ones, which are either abandoned to obscurity or transferred into the respectability of the standard language. Slang includes the shortening of words: * *biz* (business) * *vibes* (vibrations); onomatopoeic words: * *zap*; rhyming slang or abbreviations of it: * *skin and blister* (sister) * *plates* (feet, from *plates of meat*); terms from the criminal and drug subcultures: * *grass* (a police informer, or alternatively marijuana) * *porridge* (time spent in prison) * *speed* (an amphetamine drug).

Many slang terms are existing words given new meanings. Examples include: * *cool* (impressive) * *wicked* (great).

A sparing use of slang can be effective, except when the context is too formal for it to be appropriate. However, slang becomes obsolete or old-fashioned very quickly and the use of out-of-date or overworked slang can make speech or writing seem dated and tedious. *See also* **drugs slang**.

slash The symbol /, called a *slash*, is widely used in computing, both in command lines for computer software and in Internet addresses. Note that a forward slash (/) is the form used in Internet addresses, while a backward slash (\) is used to identify computer files, etc. *See also* **solidus**.

sled, sledge or **sleigh**? All these nouns denote vehicles that are used on snow for transport or for recreation. *Sledge*, the most common in British English, is replaced by *sled* in American English. *Sleigh* usually refers to a large sledge that is pulled by animals; the smaller sledge that is used for sliding downhill is also known as a *toboggan*: * *a picture of Father Christmas on his sleigh* * *children playing on their sledges/sleds.*

sleight The word *sleight*, most frequently used in the phrase *sleight of hand* ('dexterity in using the hands to perform conjuring tricks, etc.') is sometimes misspelt and mispronounced. Note the -*ei*- spelling and the pronunciation [slīt], not [slayt].

slough *Slough* is pronounced [slow], rhyming with *how*, in the sense 'swamp; state of hopeless dejection': • *in the slough of despond*, and [sluf] when referring to the cast-off skin of a snake or the verb 'shed or abandon'.

slow The use of the word *slow* as an adverb should generally be avoided in formal contexts: • *Time passes slowly* [not *slow*] *in prison.* • *You'd better drive slow in this fog.* The comparative and superlative forms *slower* and *slowest* are more informal than *more slowly* and *most slowly*: • *She eats more slowly/slower than you.* • *Michael works the slowest/most slowly. Slower* may be preferred to *more slowly* when the adverb is preceded by any: • *I can't walk any slower.*

The use of the adverb *slow* in fixed combinations, such as *slow-moving traffic, a go-slow*, etc., is acceptable in all contexts.

smart In modern usage the adjective *smart*, meaning 'intelligent', is often applied to devices that use sophisticated electronic technology: • *smart card* (a plastic bank card with an integral microprocessor) • *smart house* (a house with computer-controlled heating, lighting, etc.) • *smart weapon* (a bomb or other missile that can be automatically guided to its target). The word can also mean 'efficient', in which case it does not necessarily imply the use of the latest technology alone: • *Work smart by getting a good night's sleep* • *Time-smart travellers check into airports during off-peak hours.*

smear The increasing use of the noun *smear* to denote a defamatory attack, often involving slander or libel, is disliked by many users: • *Their allegations of professional misconduct are the latest in a series of smears.* • *the victim of a smear campaign.* The noun is particularly frequent in the headline language of popular newspapers.

smelled or **smelt**? Either word may be used as the past tense and past participle of the verb *smell*: • *The cake smelled /smelt delicious. See also* -**ed** or -**t**?

Smelled may be pronounced [smelt] or [smeld]; *smelt* is always pronounced [smelt].

smiley A *smiley* is the popular name for an emoticon, a symbol used in electronic communications to indicate the writer's response. The restrictions imposed by keyboards mean that most smileys are rendered sideways.

:-)	smiling
(-:	smiling back
:-))	very happy
:-D	laughing
:-(	sad
:-<	very sad
>:(	angry
:-o	shock
:-*	kiss
[ ]	hug
;-)	winking
@)-'-,-	a rose

SMS *see* **text messaging.**

snail mail *see* **mail.**

sneaked or **snuck**? *Sneaked* is the standard past form of *sneak*: * *They sneaked into the house.* The alternative form *snuck* is disliked by many people, although its history in American English goes back to the 19th century. Today it remains confined largely to the USA.

so The phrase *so that*, expressing purpose, is sometimes reduced to *so* in informal contexts. In formal speech and writing the word *that* should be retained: * *The gate had been left open so (that) we could drive in.* To introduce a result or consequence, *so* may be used alone in all contexts: * *The gate had been left open, so we drove in.*

The phrase *so as*, which also expresses purpose, is followed by an infinitive with *to* and should not be confused with *so that*: * *She wore gloves so as not to leave fingerprints.* * *She wore gloves so that* [not *as*] *she would not leave fingerprints.* *So as to* is best avoided where *to* would be adequate: * *He closed the window (so as) to keep out the rain.* See also **as**; **in order that** and **in order to**; **so-called**.

soar *see* **saw, soar** or **sore**?

so-called The adjective *so-called* is generally used in an ironic sense, implying that the following word is inaccurate or inappropriate; * *a so-called friend* * *their so-called supporters* * *This year's so-called disastrous summer was actually quite good, the London Weather Centre said yesterday* (*Daily Telegraph*). Some people dislike the increasing use of the adjective in neutral contexts: * *The so-called black economy regularly comes under fire.*

Note that it is unnecessary to put quotation marks around an expression immediately following *so-called*: * *the so-called special services* [not *the so-called 'special services'*].

Used without a hyphen after the noun it qualifies, *so called* may be interpreted more literally: * *the peewit, so called because of its characteristic cry.*

sociable or **social**? *Sociable* means 'friendly', 'companionable', or 'convivial'; *social* means 'of society' or 'promoting companionship': * *a sociable guest* * *a sociable dinner party* * *a social worker* * *a social club.* The two adjectives are not interchangeable in these senses, although both may be applied to the same noun: * *a sociable evening with friends at the pub* * *a social evening for new members.*

Both words also mean 'gregarious', *sociable* being used in the sense of 'liking the company of others' and *social* in the sense of 'living with others': * *She is more sociable than her sister, who hardly ever goes out.* * *Ants are social insects.* See also **antisocial**, **asocial**, **unsocial** or **unsociable**?

social networking *see* **network**.

sole or **soul**? *Sole* means 'single': * *A sole walker paced the beach.* It should not be confused with *soul*, meaning 'spirit'.

solidus The *solidus* is also known as the *stroke, slant, slash mark, forward slash, oblique,* or *virgule.* Its main use is in separating alternatives: * *A doctor must use his/her diagnostic skill in such cases.* * *You need butter and/or margarine to make pastry.* It is also used, as in this book, to indicate that both of two alternatives are correct or appropriate: * *a terrible/terrific amount of work.*

The solidus is used in the percentage sign %, and is sometimes used for writing fractions: * *2/3*. It is used instead of the word *per* in expressions like: * *35 km/hr*. It is used in certain abbreviations: * *a/c* * *c/o*, and to separate successive time units: * *the financial year 2012/13* * *July/August and in dates:* * *1/11/13*.

A further use of the *solidus* is to indicate the breaks in lines of verse, when a poem is not set out in its separate lines: * *We are the hollow men/ We are the stuffed men/Leaning together* (T.S. Eliot). *See also* **slash**.

soluble or **solvable**? Either adjective may be used to describe something that can be solved: * *a soluble/solvable problem*. *Soluble* is more frequently used to describe something that can be dissolved, especially something that dissolves easily in water: * *soluble aspirin*.

somebody or **someone**? The pronoun *somebody* and its synonym *someone* are interchangeable in all contexts. Both are used with a singular verb but are sometimes followed by a plural personal pronoun or possessive adjective (*see* **they**): * *Somebody/Someone has parked their car in our drive*.

someday, **someplace**, and **sometime** *Someday* and *sometime*, which both mean 'at some undefined time', are accepted as standard English: * *I shall get round to it someday*. * *We must go there sometime. Someplace*, however, is considered an Americanism that should be restricted to informal contexts: * *I know I left that file here someplace*. Note that *someday* is sometimes rendered as two words: * *We met some day soon after the Liberation*, whereas *sometime* is always rendered as one

word when used as an adjective or adverb. *See also* **sometime** or **some time**?

somersault Note the spelling and prnunciation of this word, which means 'acrobatic roll'. The first two syllables are pronounced like *summer*, but are spelt *somer-*; the last syllable is pronounced like *salt*, but spelt *-sault*.

-something Many people dislike the frequent use of the words *twentysomething, thirtysomething, fortysomething*, etc., with reference to people in their *twenties/thirties/forties/*etc. These words may be used as adjectives or nouns: * *The studio panel was formed... of five well-heeled thirtysomething artsy liberals* (*Sunday Times*). * *He was reluctant to admit to being fortysomething*. * *Are the thirtysomethings leaving childbearing too late for safety?* (*The Guardian*). The expression derives originally from the popular 1980s American television series *Thirtysomething*, which described the lives and lifestyles of a group of people born in the late 1940s or early 1950s and who had therefore reached their thirties during the 1980s.

sometime or **some time**? These spellings are occasionally confused. *Sometime* is used as an adverb to mean 'at some point in time': * *I'll come and see you sometime*, and as an adjective to mean 'former': * *Sir Percy Cooper, the sometime President of the Yachting Association. Some time* means 'a period of time': * *I need some time to think*. * *I've been worried about her for some time now*.

sooner *see* **hardly**.

sophisticated The adjective *sophisticated* is frequently applied to machines or devices, in the sense of 'complex' or 'advanced': * *Our client... develops and manufactures sophisticated electrical and electronic products and systems* (*Sunday Times*). This usage may be extended to the methods or techniques involved in producing such equipment: * *sophisticated technology.* When it is extended to people, however, there is a risk of confusion with the principal sense of the adjective, 'refined' or 'cultured': * *the best-documented UFO case in history – one which has managed to perplex and astonish some of the most sophisticated scientists in the world* (*The Bookseller*). Some people also dislike the increasing tendency to describe children and adolescents as *sophisticated* simply because they are at ease with modern technology and have expensive tastes (largely due to their susceptibility to marketing and peer pressure), as such attributes have little to do with refinement or culture.

sore *see* **saw, soar** or **sore**?

sorry The adjective *sorry* is followed by the preposition *for* or *about*: * *I'm sorry for* [or *about*] *what I said yesterday.*

sort of *see* **kind of.**

soul *see* **sole** or **soul**?

source The use of the word *source* as a verb, meaning 'find a source of', is disliked by many users: * *He had difficulty sourcing the material for his thesis.* In commercial contexts the term *sourcing* is used with reference to the discovery of suppliers: * *Responsible for a team of buyers and* *accountable for the effective sourcing and procurement of all the company's supplies* (*Executive Post*).

south, South or **southern**? As an adjective, *south* is always written with a capital *S* when it forms part of a proper name: * *South Africa* * *the South Pole.* The noun *south* is usually written with a capital *S* when it denotes a specific region, such as the southern states of the USA: * *The secession of the South precipitated the American Civil War.* In other contexts, and as an adverb, south is usually written with a lower-case *s*: * *Many birds fly south for the winter.* * *Only the south wall of the city remains intact.* * *The island of Tasmania lies to the south of Australia.*

The adjective *southern* is more frequent and usually less specific than the adjective *south*: * *the southern slopes* * *in southern Italy.*

Like *south*, *southern* is written with a capital *S* when it forms part of a proper name, such as the *Southern Cross.* With or without a capital *S*, it also means 'of the South': * *speaking with a southern/Southern drawl.*

southward or **southwards**? *Southward* is the correct choice when an adjective is needed: * *a southward direction.* Either *southward* or *southwards* may be used when an adverb is required: * *They travelled southward from the city.* * *The skies were full of birds flying southwards. See also* **-ward** or **-wards**?

Soviet *see* **Russian** or **Soviet**?

sowed or **sown**? Either word may be used as the past participle of the verb *sow*, but *sown* is the more frequent: * *I have sown/sowed some more parsley in the herb garden.* The past tense of the verb *sow* is always *sowed*: * *They sowed the field with wheat.*

The verb *sow* and its derivatives should not be confused with *sew* (*see* **sewed** or **sewn**?).

spam *Spam* is a trade name for a type of tinned chopped meat. With the development of electronic communications, however, it has acquired a new use as a noun referring to unsolicited, usually commercial, messages sent via email to a large number of recipients: * *How to block spam on your PC.* See also **flaming**.

span *see* **spun** or **span**?

spastic The term *spastic* is no longer considered acceptable as a description for a person who has cerebral palsy; it is now also dated as an insult for a person who lacks physical coordination or is in some way incompetent.

spatula The noun *spatula*, meaning 'flat-bladed utensil', is sometimes misspelt. Note that the word ends in *-a*, not *-ar* or *-er*.

-speak Some people object to the overuse of the suffix *-speak*, meaning 'jargon' or 'characteristic language', which is attached to nouns, proper names, or prefixes and is derived from the term *newspeak* coined by George Orwell in his novel *Nineteen Eighty-Four*: * *computerspeak* * *techspeak* * *econospeak* * *Joy-rides bill themselves as 'the travel sickness tablet for children', which is, to say the least, a cheeky bit of marketing-speak* (*Sunday Times*). In view of its etymology, it is appropriate that the suffix should have established itself in the English language during the 1980s. *See also* **-babble**.

spearhead The verb *spearhead* is best avoided where *lead* would be adequate: * *an opportunity exists for a profit-oriented manager who can spearhead the company's continued expansion.*

speciality or **specialty**? *Speciality* is used in British English and *specialty* in American English to denote a special skill or interest or a product, service, etc. that is specialised in: * *Wildlife photography is his speciality.* * *Steak tartare is a speciality of the house.* In British English the noun *specialty* is sometimes used in place of *speciality*. It is chiefly used to denote an area of medicine that is specialised in.

specially *see* **especially** or **specially**?

specialty *see* **speciality** or **specialty**?

species This word is normally pronounced [*spee*sheez]; careful users avoid the alternative pronunciation, [*spee*seez]. Like *series*, the word has the same form in the singular and plural: * *a species/several different species.*

spectrum The noun *spectrum* is best avoided where *range* would be adequate or more appropriate: * *a wide spectrum of experience* * *across the whole spectrum* * *at the other end of the political spectrum.* The noun *spectrum* principally denotes the series of colours produced when white light is dispersed. It has two plural forms, *spectra* and *spectrums*.

speculate The verb *speculate* is followed by the preposition *on* or *about*: * *There's no point in speculating on* [or *about*] *what might happen.*

speech-impaired *see* **dumb** or **mute**?

speeded or **sped**? *Sped* is the past tense and past participle of the verb *speed* in the sense of 'move or go quickly'; *speeded* relates to the sense of 'drive at excessive speed' and to the phrasal verb *speed up*, meaning 'accelerate': * *We sped through the water.* * *The days have sped by.* * *He has never speeded on a motorway.* * *The workers speeded up when the supervisor arrived.*

spelled or **spelt**? Either word may be used as the past tense and past participle of the verb *spell*: * *Have I spelt/spelled your name right? Spelled* may be pronounced [spelt] or [speld]; *spelt* is always pronounced [spelt]. *See also* **-ed** or **-t**?

spellcheckers A *spellchecker* is a facility in computer software that draws the user's attention to misspelt words, i.e. words that do not match any word in the computer's dictionary. It is important to remember that spellcheckers do not highlight words that are correctly spelt but used in the wrong context, e.g. *to* for *too*, *lead* for *led*, *their* for *there*, *that* for *than*, or *form* for *from*. Over-reliance on spellcheckers can result in such mistakes being made with increasing frequency. *See also* **homograph**, **homonym** or **homophone**? and **individual entries**.

SPELLING English spelling is notoriously difficult to learn, for native English speakers as well as for foreign students. However, it is to some extent governed by rules, some of which are described in the panel below. *See also* **-able** or **-ible**?; **-ae-** and **-oe-**; **Americanisms**; **-ant** or **-ent**?; **-ize** or **-ise**?; **misspellings**; **plurals**; and individual entries for particular words that cause difficulty.

spelt *see* **spelled** or **spelt**?

spend Many people dislike the use of the word *spend* as a noun, meaning 'amount spent' or 'amount to be spent': * *an advertising spend of £20,000.* It is best replaced by an appropriate synonym or paraphrase.

spilled or **spilt**? Either word may be used as the past tense and past participle of the verb *spill*: * *He has spilt/spilled his coffee.* * *The children spilled/spilt out of the school.*

  Spilt is the usual form of the adjective in British English: * *It's no use crying over spilt milk.*

  Spilled may be pronounced [spild] or [spilt]; *spilt* is always pronounced [spilt]. *See also* **-ed** or **-t**?

spin In recent years the word *spin* has acquired a new meaning, referring to the practice of presenting or interpreting facts or events in a favourable light: * *This story is a prime example of Labour government spin.* A *spin doctor* is a person employed by a political party, government department, etc. to manipulate that organisation's public face in the light of current events: * *Almost everyone who took part in the travelling circus of the election became so bewitched by the spin doctors, photo opportunities and in-jokes of each campaign that we lost sight of one fundamental reality* (*The Observer*).

  The expression derives from the spin given to a ball in certain sports in order to control its direction through the air or the way in which it bounces.

split infinitive A *split infinitive* occurs when an adverb is inserted between *to* and the infinitive form of a verb: * *to*

SPELLING

1 Doubling of consonants	Final consonants are sometimes doubled when a suffix starting with a vowel is added. With single-syllable words this applies when the final consonant is preceded by a single vowel: * *hit–hitting* * *drop–dropped*. If the word has more than one syllable, the consonant is doubled if the last syllable is stressed and the final consonant is preceded by a single vowel: * *refer–referred* * *commit–committed*. Exceptions are words with a final -*l*, which is doubled even if the syllable is unstressed: * *traveller* (but *traveler* in American English); and * *worshipped* * *handicapped* * *kidnapped* (not always doubled in American English) * *leapfrogged* * *jetlagged* * *outfitter*. A final -*c* is not doubled, but is changed to -*ck*- before a suffix beginning with a vowel: * *panic–panicked*.
2 y and i	When a suffix is added to a word that ends in -*y*, the y becomes an *i* only if the preceding letter is a consonant: * *silly–sillier* * *hurry–hurried*. Exceptions are: * *said* * *laid* * *paid* and in words where a suffix beginning with an *i* is added, such as -*ing*: * *try–trying*.
3 Final -e	When a suffix beginning with a vowel is added to a word with a silent final -*e*, the e is dropped: * *rate–rating*. A growing trend is to drop the -*e*- before the suffixes -*able* and -*age*: * *likeable–likable* * *sizeable–sizable* * *mileage–milage*. If the word ends in -*ge* or -*ce* the e is not dropped before *a* and *o*: * *outrageous* * *peaceable*. The e is not dropped if the suffix begins with a consonant: * *excitement*, except -*ly* (see **4 below**).
4 -ly suffix	When -*ly* is added to a word it remains unchanged except for the endings -*ll* and -*le* which change to -*lly* and -*ly*: * *nice–nicely* * *full–fully* * *noble–nobly*. Exceptions are: * *truly* * *duly* * *wholly*.
5 ie and ei	The rule 'i before e except after c' applies to most words where the sound those letters represent is [ee]. Examples of words that have 'i before e' include: * *achieve* * *belief* * *believe* * *brief* * *chief* * *diesel* * *field* * *frieze* * *grief* * *hygiene* * *niece* * *piece* * *priest* * *relief* * *relieve* * *reprieve* * *shield* * *shriek* * *siege* * *thief* * *yield*. Examples of words 'except after c' include: * *ceiling* * *conceit* * *conceive* * *deceit* * *deceive* * *perceive* * *receipt* * *receive*. Exceptions include: * *caffeine* * *Keith* * *Neil* * *protein* * *seize* * *Sheila* * *species* * *weir* * *weird*. When the sound represented is [ay] then *ei* is used: * *beige* * *deign* * *eight* * *feign* * *feint* * *freight* * *heinous* * *neighbour* * *reign* * *rein* * *reindeer* * *sleigh* * *veil* * *vein* * *weigh* * *weight*.

boldly go. The practice is disliked by some but very widely used: * *Microsoft, the world's largest software corporation, would be forced to radically alter the way it does business with rivals and suppliers* (*The Guardian*). Split infinitives have a long history and the objection to them is comparatively recent. As with the opposition to ending sentences with prepositions,

grammarians based their objections on the rules of Latin grammar.

Since so many people dislike split infinitives it is probably best to try to avoid them, at least in formal speech and writing. They can sound awkward or unpleasant, particularly when more than one word comes between *to* and the verb: * *He tries to on the one hand explain...* However, there are some sentences in which it is preferable to split an infinitive, especially in order to avoid ambiguity: * *He failed to entirely comprehend me.* The revised ordering *He entirely failed to...* or *He failed to comprehend me entirely* would suggest complete, not partial, failure. * *We expect to further modernise our services.* The revised ordering *We expect further to modernise...* suggests moreover. * *They were plotting secretly to destroy the files.* Was the plotting or the intended destruction secret? * *I would not expect anyone who has not read Joyce fully to understand the play.* Read Joyce fully or understand fully?

Another argument for disregarding the rule is that sometimes the rhythm of spoken English makes the split infinitive sound natural and its avoidance awkward. Compare: * *I hope to really enjoy myself* with *I hope really to enjoy myself.*

spoiled or **spoilt**? Either word may be used as the past tense and past participle of the verb *spoil*: * *The bad weather spoiled/spoilt our holiday.*

Spoilt is the usual form of the adjective in British English: * *a spoilt child.*

Spoiled may be pronounced [spoild] or [spoilt]; *spoilt* is always pronounced [spoilt]. *See also* **-ed** or **-t**?

spokesman or **spokeswoman**? *see* **non-sexist terms.**

sponge The verb *sponge* is followed by the preposition *off* or *on*: * *You can't sponge off* [or *on*] *your family for the rest of your life.*

spontaneity The traditional pronunciation of this noun, meaning 'the quality of behaving in a natural, impulsive way', is [spontǎneeiti] but the pronunciation [spontǎnayiti] is probably more frequently heard.

spoonful Most users prefer to form the plural *-fuls*: * *spoonfuls. See* **-ful.**

sportsman or **sportswoman**? *see* **non-sexist terms.**

spouse The use of the noun *spouse* in place of *husband* or *wife* is best avoided where the sex of the person is known: * *The broadcaster Sue Baker and her husband* [not *spouse*] *were the guests of honour.* The words *spouse* and *spouses* may, however, serve as useful replacements for the phrases 'husband or wife', 'husbands and wives', etc., especially in formal contexts: * *Please give details of any other properties owned by you or your spouse.* * *Use of the car park is restricted to members and their spouses.*

The noun *spouse* is usually pronounced [spows], the pronunciation [spowz] being an accepted variant.

sprang or **sprung**? *Sprang* and *sprung* are both used as the past tense of the verb *spring*. *Sprang* is the standard form in British English: * *The man sprang from the bushes.* Both *sprang* and *sprung* are commonly used in American English: * *She sprung out of the door.* * *The lizard sprang out of his hand.* Note that *sprung* is the only acceptable form of the past participle in both British and American English: * *The lizard had sprung out of his hand.*

spun or **span**? *Spun* is the past tense and part participle of the verb *spin* in modern usage; *span* is an archaic form of the past tense: * *He spun the wheel.* * *This yarn has been spun by hand.*

squalor This word, meaning 'dirtiness; wretchedness': * *the squalor of the slums*, is sometimes misspelt. In both British and American English the ending is *-or*, as in *tremor*.

squaw *Squaw* is a Narragansett word meaning 'woman' and became a generic term for any woman of Native American origin. In recent years, however, the word has acquired negative connotations through its more general use and it is now considered unacceptable in virtually every context.

squeaky-clean The adjective *squeaky-clean*, which originated in advertising, is often used in the figurative sense of 'beyond reproach' or 'above suspicion': * *the squeaky-clean image of this generation of pop-stars* * *The president must be squeaky-clean*. Users of this expression should be aware of its possible derogatory connotations: there may be an implication that the person or thing so described is too good to be true.

stadiums or **stadia**? *Stadiums* is the more usual plural of the noun *stadium*, but either word may be used: * *New football stadiums have been built throughout Britain in recent years.* * *The city has two football stadia.*

stair or **stare**? *Stair* means 'one of a series of steps': * *The stair creaked beneath his foot.* It should not be confused with *stare*, which means 'look hard': * *She stared in horror.* * *a sad, faraway stare.*

stalactite or **stalagmite**? *Stalactites* and *stalagmites* are tapering masses of calcium carbonate that form in limestone caves. A *stalactite* hangs from the roof; a *stalagmite* rises from the floor. The classic method of distinguishing between the two words is to associate the *c* of *stalactite* with that of ceiling and the *g* of *stalagmite* with that of ground.

stanch or **staunch**? Either word may be used as a verb, meaning 'stop (the flow of)', *staunch* being more frequent than *stanch* in modern usage: * *I staunched/stanched the flow of blood with a handkerchief.* * *She staunched /stanched the wound.* * *This offer is no remedy to recruitment and retention problems within our universities: It won't staunch the brain drain* (*The Guardian*). *Stanch* is also a rare variant of the adjective *staunch*, meaning 'loyal' or 'firm': * *a staunch supporter.*

The word *stanch* is pronounced [stahnch]. *Staunch* is occasionally pronounced in the same way, but its usual pronunciation is [stawnch], rhyming with *launch*.

standing or **stood**? The substitution of *stood*, the past participle of the verb *stand*, for the present participle *standing* is found in some dialects of English: * *She was standing* [in some dialects *stood*] *in front of the mirror.* *Stood* is correctly used in the passive form of the transitive verb *stand*: * *The bottle should be stood in a cool place for two hours.*

stank or **stunk**? Either word may be used as the past tense of the verb *stink*, but *stunk* is the only form of its past participle: * *The room stank/ stunk of cigarette smoke.* * *These boots have stunk* [not *stank*] *of manure since my visit to the farm last week.*

stare *see* **stair** or **stare**?

state-of-the-art Some users dislike the adjective *state-of-the-art*, which relates to the current level of technical achievement, development, knowledge, etc.: • *Heart of the system is a state-of-the-art desktop copier with a host of time-saving features* (*Sunday Times*). • *state-of-the-art computer technology*. It is best avoided where *modern* or *up-to-date* would be adequate or more appropriate: • *They [Venture Scouts] use state-of-the-art camp stoves for cooking* (*Daily Telegraph*).

statesman or **stateswoman**? *see* **non-sexist terms.**

stationary or **stationery**? These two words are often confused. *Stationary* means 'not moving': • *a stationary car*; *stationery* means 'writing materials': • *office stationery*. To avoid confusion, remember that *stationery* is sold by a *stationer* – a trader whose name, like *baker* and *grocer*, ends in *-er*.

statistics *see* **-ics.**

status In British English the word *status* should be pronounced [*stay*tŭs], with the first syllable like *state*. The pronunciation [*stat*ŭs], with the first syllable as in *static*, is an American English variant.

staunch *see* **stanch** or **staunch**?

stay or **stop**? The substitution of the verb *stop* for *stay* in the sense of 'reside temporarily' or 'remain' is found in some dialects of English: • *We stayed [in some dialects stopped] with my sister for a few days*. The use of the verb *stop* with reference to a break in a journey is generally acceptable: • *We stopped at my sister's house for a cup of tea on the way home.*

steal *see* **burgle, rob** or **steal**?

steal or **steel**? *Steal* means 'take something illegally': • *He stole three cars in two days*. It should not be confused with *steel*, which refers to a hard alloy of iron: • *The building is mostly steel and glass*. In informal contexts, *steal* is a noun meaning 'bargain': • *At £10 it's a steal.*

step or **steppe** *Step* variously means 'footstep', 'footprint', 'raised surface', 'stage in progress', etc.: • *He paused a few steps away from the body*. • *She heard steps on the floor above*. • *She mounted the step*. • *The next step will be to contact the vendors*. It should not be confused with *steppe*, which denotes a broad, treeless plain: • *the harsh climate of the Siberian steppes.*

step- *see* **half-** or **step-**?

stereo- This word has the alternative pronunciations [*ste*rriō] and [*stee*riō], both of which are acceptable, although the former is more frequent in contemporary usage.

steward or **stewardess**? *see* **non-sexist terms.**

sticky The word *sticky* has acquired at least two new meanings in recent years. Many people use it to refer to small self-adhesive squares of paper widely used as memos in everyday life: • *She pressed a sticky on the front door to remind her husband to feed the pets*. It is also used in computing to describe the electronic equivalent of a paper reminder: • *A sticky popped up* on the screen reminding him to check his email. The term may also be encountered in electronic communications as an adjective describing an Internet site that attracts and retains large numbers of visitors.

stiletto Note the spelling of this word, which refers to a woman's shoe with a high narrow heel, particularly the single *l* and the *-tt-*. The plural is either *stilettos* or *stilettoes*, the former being accepted by more authorities.

stimulant or **stimulus**? Both these nouns are used to denote something that stimulates activity. *Stimulant* is specifically applied to drugs, alcohol, etc., whereas *stimulus* is a more general synonym for 'incentive': ● *Caffeine is a stimulant.* ● *They responded to the stimulus of competition.* A *stimulant* increases activity; a *stimulus* initiates activity. The plural of *stimulus* is *stimuli*, which may be pronounced [*stim*ewlī] or [*stim*ewlee].

stimulate *see* **simulate** or **stimulate**?

stimulus *see* **stimulant** or **stimulus**?

stoical The adjective *stoical*, meaning 'resigned to or unaffected by suffering': ● *a stoical attitude to death*, is pronounced [*stō*ikl]. The *o* and *i* are pronounced separately, not as the *oi* sound of *soil*. The word *stoic* may be used as a variant of *stoical* or as a noun: ● *She's a real stoic.*

    Spelt with a capital *S*, the noun and adjective *Stoic* refer to a school of ancient Greek philosophy.

stood *see* **standing** or **stood**?

stop *see* **stay** or **stop**?

storey or **story**? These two spellings are sometimes confused. The word *storey*, meaning 'level of a building': ● *He lives on the second storey.* ● *a multi-storey car park*, is spelt with an *e*; the plural is *storeys*. *Story* means 'tale': ● *Tell me a story*; its plural is *stories*. In American English the sense 'level of a building' may also be spelt *story*, with the plural *stories*.

straight or **strait**? The word *straight* is most frequently used as an adjective or adverb: ● *a straight line* ● *I went straight there.* It is sometimes used as a noun, meaning 'straight line or part': ● *the home straight* (of a racecourse). The word *strait* is an archaic adjective meaning 'narrow; restricted'; in modern usage it is most frequently found in the form of the plural noun *straits*, meaning 'difficult circumstances': ● *in dire straits.* In the sense of 'narrow channel', the noun *strait* (or *straits*) also occurs in proper names: ● *the Straits of Dover.* The two words have different origins: *straight* comes from the Old English *streccan* ('to stretch'), whereas *strait* is ultimately derived from the Latin *stringere* ('to bind tightly').

    The two spellings are interchangeable only in certain compound words (*see* **straitjacket** and **straitlaced**). *See also* **straightened** or **straitened**?

straightaway or **straight away**? This expression, meaning 'without delay': ● *I'll be going to the shops straightaway*, may be written as one word or two.

straightened or **straitened**? These words are sometimes confused. *Straightened* means 'made straight': ● *The road has been straightened.* *Straitened*, which is derived from the archaic adjective *strait* (*see* **straight** or strait?), means 'restricted': * *in strait-ened circumstances.*

strait *see* **straight** or **strait**?

straitened *see* **straightened** or **strait-ened**?

straitjacket and **straitlaced** A *strait-jacket* – a constricting jacket used to restrain a violent person, and also, in extended senses, 'something that restricts' – may also be spelt *straight-jacket*: * *The government finds itself in a straitjacket/straightjacket.* In the same way, *straitlaced*, meaning 'puritanical', may also be spelt *straightlaced*: * *a very straitlaced/straightlaced maiden aunt.* See also **straight** or **strait**?

strata *see* **stratum** or **strata**?

stratagem or **strategy**? A *stratagem* is a scheme, trick, or ruse; *strategy* is the art of planning a campaign: * *to devise a new stratagem* * *the strategy involved in a game of chess.* The use of *strategy* in the extended sense of 'plan' or 'method' overlaps with that of *stratagem.*

Both nouns are ultimately derived from the Greek word for 'a general', and are principally applied to warfare – a *stratagem* being an artifice for deceiving the enemy, and *strategy* being the science or art of conducting a war.

stratum or **strata**? *Strata* is the plural form of the noun *stratum*: * *from a different social stratum* * *in one of the upper strata of the rock.* The use of *strata* as a singular noun is wrong, but nevertheless is occurring with increasing frequency, especially in figurative contexts: * *in that strata of society.*

street *see* **road** or **street**?

street- In such words and phrases as *streetwise* and *street-cred(ibility)*, *street-* refers to the culture of young people, especially young working-class inhab-itants of the inner cities: * *a streetwise kid.* * *This year's batch of school-leavers are optimistic and streetwise, according to a study commissioned by the TSB bank* (*The Guardian*). The meaning has recently widened to include the culture of those familiar with the lat-est trends, fashions, topical issues, etc.: * *To be successful in the public relations industry, you need more than just street credibility.* * *Ladas and Skodas snubbed as car thieves opt for 'street cred'* (headline, *The Guardian*). *Street* is occasionally used as an adjec-tive in slang usage in its own right, meaning 'accepted by young people or those familiar with the latest trends, etc.': * *He isn't street enough.* See also **-cred**.

strength This word is sometimes mis-pronounced [strenth]. The correct pronunciation is [strength], but the variant pronunciation [strenkth] is acceptable to most users.

stress Some languages have a fairly reg-ular stress pattern, but English stress patterns are varied and subject to change over time. As foreign words become absorbed into the English language they often change their stress to a more English-sounding one: * *bureau* * *chauffeur.* Two-syl-lable words are more likely to be stressed on the first syllable, but when a word serves as both a noun (or adjective) and a verb, it is normally stressed on the first syllable as a noun (or adjective), and the second as a verb: * *permit* * *rebel* * *present* * *con-flict* * *insult* * *absent.*

Most three-syllable words have their stress on the first syllable, and several of those words which have their stress on the second are widely coming to be pronounced with the stress on the first: * *contribute* * *subsidence*. Words with four or more syllables usually have their stress on the second or third syllable. Some people find difficulty in pronouncing those multisyllabic words that traditionally have been stressed on the first syllable, and such words are coming to be pronounced with the stress on a later syllable: * *applicable* * *demonstrable* * *formidable*.

Individual words may be stressed in speech for emphasis: in written and printed texts such words are indicated by italics: * I *like* walking in the rain. See also **intonation**.

stringed or **strung**? *Stringed* is an adjective derived from the noun *string*; *strung* is the past tense and past participle of the verb *string*: * *a stringed instrument* * *a twelve-stringed guitar* * *His squash racket was strung by an expert.* * *The children (have) strung decorations around the room.* Strung is also used adjectivally before a noun, often in combination with an adverb: * *a newly strung violin*.

strive The verb *strive* is followed by the preposition *for* or *after*. * *Some minority groups are still striving for* [or *after*] *equality of opportunity.*

student *see* **pupil** or **student**?

stumble The verb *stumble* is followed by the preposition *across* or *on*: * I *stumbled across* [or *on*] *the solution to the problem.*

stunk *see* **stank** or **stunk**?

stupefy This word, meaning 'bewilder or amaze', is sometimes misspelt. Note the ending -*efy* (like *putrefy*), in spite of the spelling of the related word *stupid*.

stupor This word, meaning 'a drowsy dazed state': * *in a drunken stupor*, is sometimes misspelt. Note the final -*or*, as in *torpor*, rather than -*our*.

subconscious or **unconscious**? Both these adjectives mean 'without (full) awareness', but *subconscious* implies a greater degree of consciousness than *unconscious*: * *a subconscious desire* * *unconscious resentment.* In psychology both words relate to parts of the mind that can influence behaviour.

Unconscious has the additional senses of 'not conscious', 'unaware', and 'unintentional': * *He lay unconscious for two hours.* * *They were unconscious of the danger.* * *It was an unconscious insult.*

subject The *subject* of a clause or sentence is the noun, pronoun, or phrase that controls the verb (*See also* **active**; **passive**). The subject usually precedes the verb, unless the clause or sentence is a question. In the sentence: * *The dog buried the bone*, the *dog* is the subject. In the sentence: * *Does he like them?*, the pronoun *he* is the subject. In more complex sentences, the subject may be a clause, such as *Why she resigned* in the sentence: * *Why she resigned remains a mystery.*

The subject determines the form of the verb: a singular subject is used with a singular verb and a plural subject is used with a plural verb: * *She often goes to the cinema* [singular subject *she*, singular verb *goes*]. * *The children go to school by bus* [plural subject *children,* plural verb *go*]. * *The legs of the table are loose.* In the last example, note that the verb agrees with *the legs,* not with *the table. See also* **object**; **predicate**; **singular or plural?**

subjective *see* **objective or subjective?**

sub judice The legal term *sub judice* is Latin in origin; it is used to refer to a case that is still being considered by a court of law and therefore cannot be discussed in public: * *He declined to comment further, as the matter was still sub judice.* The expression is pronounced [sub *jood*ĭsi]. Its literal meaning is 'under a judge'.

subjunctive The *subjunctive* is the grammatical set ('mood') of forms of a verb used to express possibilities or wishes rather than facts. With most verbs the subjunctive form is its basic form minus the *-s* ending of the third person singular, but *to be* has the past tense subjunctive *were.* The subjunctive is largely falling into disuse but survives in such idioms as: * *be that as it may* * *as it were* * *far be it from me* * *come what may.* The main use of subjunctives is in clauses introduced by *that* and expressing a proposal, desire, or necessity: * *It is vital that she leave immediately.* * *I suggested to Mark that he drop in for a coffee sometime.* * *They demanded that he answer their questions.* This usage is more popular in American English than in British English, where *should* is often inserted before the verb: * *It is vital that she should leave immediately.*

The other use of subjunctives is in clauses introduced by *if, though,* or *supposing*: * *If you were to go, you might regret it.* * *It's not as though he were a bachelor.* It is now very unusu-

al to use such a construction with any subjunctive form other than *were. See also* **if**; **were or was?**

subordinate clause *see* **clause.**

subpoena This word, referring to a writ requiring a person to appear in court, is sometimes misspelt: note particularly the *-oe-.* The pronunciations [sŭb-*pee*nă] or [sŭ*pee*nă] are both acceptable. The word comes from the Latin *sub poena,* meaning 'under penalty'.

The present participle of the verb *subpoena* ('issue with a subpoena') is *subpoenaing;* the past tense and past participle are *subpoenaed,* pronounced [-*pee*nĕd].

subsequent *see* **consequent or subsequent?**

subsidence The traditional pronunciation of this word, which means 'falling or sinking': * *cracks due to subsidence,* is [sŭb*sī*dĕns]. The alternative pronunciation [*sub*sidĕns] is also widely used and is generally acceptable.

subsidiarity The noun *subsidiarity* is often used in the context of the European Union, where it refers to the principle that political decisions should be made at the lowest level. Thus some issues may be dealt with by countries that belong to the EU rather than by the EU itself.

subsidiary The noun and adjective *subsidiary,* which means 'auxiliary; subordinate', is sometimes misspelt. Note that the word ends in *-iary,* not *-uary* or *-ary.*

substance abuse or substance misuse? These terms are often treated as synonymous, both relating euphemistically to the incorrect use of drugs. The phrase *substance abuse* always implies deliberate misuse of drugs, chemicals, etc., while *substance misuse* can encompass both deliberate and accidental misuse.

substantial or **substantive**? Both these adjectives refer to the basic substance or essence of something, but neither is in frequent use in this sense. *Substantial* usually means 'of considerable size, importance, etc.': * *a substantial improvement* * *a substantial meal. Substantive*, a rarer word, is used to mean 'real; firm': * *substantive measures to curb inflation*. In grammar, the word *substantive* is a noun or adjective relating to words that have the function of a noun.

Note that *substantial* is stressed on the second syllable [sŭbstanshăl]. As a noun, *substantive* is stressed on the first syllable [substăntiv], but as an adjective it is more frequently stressed on the second syllable [sŭbstantiv].

Some people object to the use of *substantial* as a pretentious synonym for 'large', 'big', etc.: * *a substantial pay rise*. The increasing tendency to use *substantive* in this sense is widely regarded as incorrect: * *Substantive numbers of students are opting for more vocational courses*.

substitute *see* **replace** or **substitute**?

subsume The verb *subsume* means 'incorporate within a larger category or group' or 'classify under a general rule or heading'; it should not be used as a pretentious synonym for 'include' or 'contain': * *The concept of a classless society is subsumed within the doctrine of Marxism*.

subtle This word, meaning 'slight', 'understated', or 'ingenious': * *subtle differences in meaning* * *subtle innuendoes*, is sometimes misspelt. Note particularly the *-b-* in the middle of the word, which is pronounced [sutăl].

succeed *see* **accede** or **exceed**?

successfully or **successively**? These two adverbs are sometimes confused. *Successfully* means 'with success'; *successively* means 'in succession': * *The surgeons operated successfully*. * *The sales figures fell for several months successively*.

such The use of the construction *such... that* (or *such... who*) in place of *such... as* is avoided by careful users: * *such tools as* [not *that*] *are needed for the job* * *such people as* [not *who*] *are eligible for supplementary benefit*. The construction *such... that* may, however, be used to indicate a result: * *He earns such a pittance that he can't afford to buy food for his family*.

The use of *such* or *such a/an* before an adjective preceding a noun, in the sense of 'so' or 'very', is disliked by a few users but acceptable to most: * *Such careless driving should not go unpunished*. * *I have never seen such a small house*. * *You have such beautiful clothes.* * *It was such a difficult question*.

The phrase *such that* is reserved for constructions describing the consequences of something: * *The gravity of the situation was such that the whole project was threatened. See also* **such as** or **like**?

such as or **like**? *Such as* introduces an example; *like* introduces a comparison: * *Dairy products, such as milk and cheese, should be kept in a cool place*. *

Dairy products, like fresh meat, should be kept in a cool place. * *He directed several horror films, such as Dracula.* * *He directed several horror films like Dracula.* The potentially ambiguous use of *like* in place of *such as* is disliked by some people but frequently occurs in general usage: * *He gave Danielle gifts like a £1,500 ruby and diamond necklace, a matching ring and earrings* (*Daily Telegraph*). The use of *such as* in place of *like* is largely restricted to formal contexts: * *Shoes such as these are ideal for indoor sports.*

Careful users avoid substituting *such as* for *as*: * *When the Post Office is closed, as* [not *such as*] *on Sundays, stamps may be obtained from the machine outside.* * *The pizza can be cooked in a number of ways, as by* [not *such as by*] *baking it in a hot oven for twenty minutes.* In the second example, *as by* may be replaced by *such as.*

suffer from or **suffer with**? *Suffer from* means 'have (an illness or disability)'; *suffer with* means 'experience pain or discomfort because of (an illness or disability)': * *I suffer from hay fever.* * *I have been suffering with my hay fever today.*

Suffer with is often followed by a possessive. It should not be used in place of *suffer from*.

SUFFIXES *Suffixes* are elements attached to the ends of words and include: * *-ism* * *-ful* * *-dom* * *-logy* * *-ship*. See following panel for a list. Cross-references – e.g. *see* **-able** or **-ible**? – to main entries in the *Good Word Guide* are also included where there is a fuller discussion. *See also* **prefixes** and **suffixes**.

SUFFIXES

-able, -ible	1 able to be ...: * *enjoyable* 2 that may cause: * *objectionable* 3 that belongs to: * **fashionable** *see* **-able** or **-ible**?
-age	an action, condition, or charge: * *breakage* * *postage*
-aholic	obsessed by ...; addicted to: * *shopaholic see* **-aholic**
-al	1 an action: * *removal* 2 relating to: * *postal* * *central* * *dental*
-an, -ian	1 (a person) coming from a country: * *Canadian* 2 a person who is an expert at something: * *mathematician*
-ance, -ence, -ancy, -ency	a quality, state, or action: * *assistance* * *ascendancy*
-ant, -ent	(a person or thing) that does something: * *pleasant* * *student* * *dependent see* **-ant** or **-ent**?
-ar	like; belonging to: * *solar* * *molecular*
-ary	1 connected with: * *monetary* 2 a person doing something: * *missionary* 3 a place for: * *aviary*
-ate	1 having a quality: * *fortunate* 2 a chemical compound: * *carbonate* 3 cause to have or become: * *hyphenate see* **-ate**
-atic	(used to make adjectives): * *problematic*
-ation	an action, state, or condition: * *pronunciation* * *moderation*
-babble	jargon: * *technobabble see* **-babble**

-cide	killing: * *insecticide*
-cy	a state or quality: * *secrecy*
-dom	**1** a state or condition: * *freedom* **2** an area ruled: * *kingdom* **3** a group of people: * *officialdom*
-ed	**1** (used to make the past tense and past participles of verbs): * *extended* * *gained* **2** showing or having a quality or state: * *surprised* * *long-sighted see* **-ed** *or* **-t?**
-ee	**1** a person to whom something is done or given: * *addressee* **2** a person in a particular state or condition: * *refugee see* **-ee** *or* **-er?**
-eer	a person who does something or is concerned with something: * *mountaineer*
-en	**1** (cause to) become: * *harden* **2** made of: * *wooden*
-enabled	capable of working with: * *WAP-enabled see* **enable**
-ence, -ency	*see* **-ance**
-ent	*see* **-ant**
-er	**1** (also **-r**) (used to make the comparative of adjectives): * *faster* * *nicer* * *tidier* **2** (also **-or**) a person or thing that does something: * *cooker* * *sailor* * *transmitter* **3** a person working in a job: * *writer* * *painter* **4** a person who lives in a place: * *Londoner* **5** a person or thing that has or is something: * *teenager see* **-ee** *or* **-er?;** **-er** *or* **-or?**
-ery, -ry	**1** a place where an activity or business is done: * *bakery* **2** a group of things: * *cutlery* **3** a condition: * *bravery* **4** the practice of: * *cookery*

-es	*see* **-s**
-ese	a place of origin or language: * *Chinese* * *journalese*
-ess	(used to make the feminine of nouns): * *lioness* * *countess see* **-ess**
-est	(used to make the super-lative of adjectives): * *fastest* * *tidiest*
-ette	**1** small: * *cigarette* **2** (used to make feminine nouns): * *usherette*
-fold	having a number of parts or multiplied by a number: * *fivefold*
-ful	**1** having a quality: * *painful* **2** the amount that a ... can hold: * *spoonful see* **-ful**
-fy, -ify	make or become: * *simplify* * *liquefy*
-gate	a political scandal: *Irangate see* **-gate**
-gon	an angle: * *polygon*
-hood	a state or condition; time of being something: * *man-hood* * *childhood*
-i	(a person) belonging to a region or people: * *Iraqi* * *Bangladeshi*
-ian	*see* **-an**
-ible	*see* **-able**
-ic, -ical	related to: * *poetic* * *fanatical see* **-ic** *or* **-ical?**
-ice	(used to make abstract nouns): * *cowardice*
-ics	a science, subject, or group of activities: * *physics* * *politics* * *acrobatics see* **-ics**
-ide	a chemical compound: * *cyanide*
-ie	*see* **-y**
-ify	*see* **-fy**

-ine	made of; like; connected with: * *crystalline*
-ing	1 (used to make the present participle of verbs): * *eating* 2 an action, process, or result; thing: * *meeting* * *wedding* * **welding** see **-ing forms**
-ion	an action, process, or state: * *creation* * *tension*
-ious	having a quality: * *suspicious*
-ise, -ize	make or become: * *equalise* see **-ize** or **-ise**?
-ish	1 (belonging to) a country or language: * *Swedish* 2 about: * *seventyish* 3 like, having the bad qualities of: * *childish* * *foolish* 4 to some extent: * *brownish* * *tallish*
-ism	1 a system of beliefs, etc.: * *socialism* 2 a quality, practice, or action: * *heroism* * *criticism* see **-ism**
-ist	1 (a person) following a system of beliefs, etc.: * *communist* 2 a person who does something: * *motorist* see **-ist** or **-ite**?
-ite	(used in the name of a chemical substance): * *bauxite*
-itis	a disease: * *tonsillitis*
-ity, -ty	a quality, state, or condition: * *stupidity* * *flexibility*
-ive	that will cause something; having a quality: * *productive* * *digestive*
-ize, -ise	make or become: * *equalize* see **-ize** or **-ise**?
-less	not having: * *harmless*
-let	something small: * *droplet*
-like	like: * *dreamlike* see **-like**

-logy	a science or subject: * *biology* * *geology*
-ly	1 (used to make adverbs): * *nicely* 2 having qualities of: * *brotherly* 3 happening at regular times: * *yearly*
-man	a person who lives in a place or does something: * *chairman*
-ment	a state, condition, quality, result, or process: * *enjoyment* * *management* * *arrangement*
-most	the furthest: * *eastmost*
-ness	a state, quality, or condition; example of this: * **kindness** * *brittleness*
-nik	person connected with ...: * *refusenik* see **-nik**
-oid	like: * *humanoid*
-or	see **-er**
-ory	1 a place for: * *observatory* 2 having a quality: * *contributory*
-ous	having a quality: * *poisonous*
-phile	(a person) liking something very much: * *francophile* see **-phile**, **-phobe** or **-phone**?
-phobia	fear: * *claustrophobia*
-proof	resisting something: * *waterproof*
-r	see **-er**
-rage	outburst of anger: * *road rage*
-ry	see **-ery**
-s, -es	1 (used to make plurals): * *books* * *pencils* * *horses* 2 (used to make the third person singular of present tense of verbs): * *eats* * *rides*
-'s	of ...: * *John's* * *house's* * *children's* * *houses'* see **'s** or **s'**?

-ling	someone or something small: * *duckling*
-ship	1 a state: * *friendship* 2 a skill: * *craftsmanship*
-some	causing: * *troublesome*
-speak	jargon, characteristic language: * *computerspeak* see -**speak**
-th	1 (used to make adjectives from numbers): * *fifth* 2 a state: * *width*
-tion	an action, process, state, or result; thing: * *completion* * *imagination*
-ty	see -**ity**
-ward, -wards	in a direction: * *homewards* see -**ward** or -**wards**?
-ways	showing direction: * *sideways* see -**wise** or -**ways**?
-wise	1 in such a way: * *crosswise* 2 as far as ... is concerned: * *weatherwise* see -**wise** or -**ways**?
-woman	a woman who lives in a place or does something: * *saleswoman*
-y	1 having a quality: * *dusty* * *sandy* * *sunny* 2 (also -**ie**) (used as an affectionate name) small: * *bunny* * *daddy* * *auntie* 3 the act of doing something; condition or state: * *enquiry* * *envy*

sui generis The Latin expression *sui generis* is used in formal contexts to refer to a unique person or thing, one that is in a class of its own: * *The taxation rules were sui generis, and could not be applied generally.* The expression literally means 'of its own kind' and is pronounced [sooi *jenĕris*].

suit or **suite**? These two nouns should not be confused. A *suit* is a set of clothes, one of the four sets of playing cards, or an action in a court of law: * *a trouser suit* * *to follow suit* * *a lawsuit.* A *suite* is a set of furniture, a set of rooms, a group of followers, or a musical composition with several movements: * *to re-upholster a suite* * *the honeymoon suite* * *a ballet suite.* *Suit* and *suite* are most frequently confused in the expressions *three-piece suit* (a pair of trousers, a jacket, and a waistcoat) and *three-piece suite* (a sofa and two armchairs).

Note the difference in pronunciation between the two words: *suite* is pronounced [sweet]; *suit* is pronounced [soot] or [syoot], although the last of these pronunciations is becoming less usual and may be considered old-fashioned.

suite or **sweet**? These two words are occasionally confused since they are both pronounced [sweet]. *Suite* variously means 'set of matching furniture', etc. (*see* **suit** or **suite**?): * *a new suite of software applications* * *This suite is the composer's masterpiece.* * *He arrived with a suite of advisers.* It should not be confused with *sweet*, which as a noun refers to a chocolate, toffee, etc.: * *What is your favourite sweet?* and as an adjective means 'sugary', 'pleasing', 'kind', etc.: * *a sweet taste* * *a sweet gesture* * *How sweet of them!*

summon or **summons**? To *summon* is to send for, call upon, or muster; to *summons* is to serve with a legal summons (an order to appear in court): * *I was summoned to the managing director's office.* * *He was summonsed for speeding.* The verb *summon* may be used in place of the verb *summons*: * *He was summoned for speeding.*

Of the two words, only *summons* is used as a noun: * *I received a summons from the managing director.* * *He received a summons for speeding.*

sunk, sunken *see* **sank, sunk** or **sunken**?

super- Some people object to the frequent use of the prefix *super-*, in the sense of 'surpassing all others' or 'to an excessive degree', to coin new nouns and adjectives: * *a superbug that is resistant to most antibiotics* * *those superfit people who put the rest of us to shame.* See also **macro-** and **micro-**; **mega-**.

supercilious This word, meaning 'haughty in a condescending disdainful manner', is sometimes misspelt. Note the single *c* and single *l*.

superior The adjective superior is followed by the preposition *to*: * *This wine is superior to the wine we had in the restaurant.*

superlative *see* **comparative** and **superlative**.

supersede This word, meaning 'replace', is sometimes misspelt. The most common mistake is to confuse the *-sede* ending with the *-cede* ending of *precede*. *Supersede* comes from the Latin *supersedere*, 'to sit above'.

supervise *Supervise*, meaning 'oversee': * *She supervised the plans for the party*, is sometimes misspelt; the *-ise* ending cannot be spelt *-ize*: *see* **-ize** or **-ise**? Note also the *-or* ending of *supervisor*, not *-er*.

supine *see* **prostrate, prone** or **supine**?

supper *see* **dinner, lunch, tea** or **supper**?

supplement *see* **complement** or **supplement**?

suppose or **supposing**? Either word may be used to introduce a suggestion or hypothesis, *suppose* being preferred by some users in formal contexts: * *Suppose/Supposing we sell the car?* * *Suppose/Supposing the train is late.* Only *supposing* can be used in the sense of 'if' or 'assuming': * *I'll buy her some chocolates on the way home, supposing the corner shop is still open.*

suppress *see* **oppress, repress** or **suppress**?

sure This word, pronounced [shor], is sometimes misspelt: note particularly the *su-* at the beginning of the word. The use of *sure* as an intensifying adverb is disliked by many people and is best restricted to very informal contexts: * *I was sure relieved to see your car.*

surf *see* **serf** or **surf**?

surprised *Surprised* is followed by the preposition *by* in the sense of 'taken unawares' and by *at* in the sense of 'amazed': * *The thief was surprised by the owner of the car.* * *I was surprised at her ignorance.* In the second sense *surprised* may also be followed by an infinitive with *to* or a clause introduced by *that*: * *He was surprised to see you.* * *They were surprised that we won.*

The idiomatic use of a double negative in such sentences as *I shouldn't be surprised if it doesn't rain* is acceptable to most users in informal contexts, provided that the meaning is clear. The construction is best avoided if there is a risk of ambiguity.

surveillance This word, meaning 'careful observation', is usually pronounced [ser*vay*lĕns]. The pronunciation [ser*vay*ĕns], imitating the French original, sounds rather affected.

susceptible The adjective *susceptible* is followed by the preposition *to* in the sense of 'easily influenced or affected' and by *of* in the formal sense of 'capable' or 'admitting': ▪ *susceptible to flattery* ▪ *susceptible to hay fever* ▪ *susceptible of a different interpretation*. Note that *susceptible* ends in *-ible*, not *-able*. The *-sc-* combination can also cause spelling mistakes.

suspect or **suspicious**? The word *suspect* may be used as a verb, noun, or adjective; *suspicious* functions only as an adjective. In its adjectival sense of 'causing suspicion' or 'open to suspicion', *suspect* is sometimes virtually synonymous with *suspicious*: ▪ *a suspect/suspicious package* ▪ *The scheme sounds rather suspect/suspicious*. However, only *suspicious* can be used in the sense of 'feeling or showing suspicion': ▪ *The police were suspicious* [not *suspect*] *of her behaviour*. Similarly, only *suspect* can be used in the sense of 'possibly false or unreliable': ▪ *a suspect banknote* ▪ *The braking system is suspect*. As a noun, *suspect* describes a person who is under suspicion of being responsible for a crime or other misdeed. Note the difference in pronunciation between the verb *suspect*, which is stressed on the second syllable [sŭs*pekt*], and the noun and adjective, stressed on the first syllable [*sŭs*pekt].

suspense or **suspension**? Both these nouns are derived from the verb *suspend*, meaning 'hang'. *Suspense* is largely restricted to the figurative sense of 'a state of uncertainty, anxiety, insecurity, or excitement': ▪ *Don't keep me in suspense any longer! Suspension* means 'the act of suspending' or 'the state of being suspended'; it is also used in the figurative senses of 'interruption; deferment; postponement' and 'temporary debarment or expulsion': ▪ *the suspension of an insurance policy* ▪ *The offending players face suspension from the team*. The two nouns are not interchangeable in any context.

suspicious *see* **suspect** or **suspicious**?

sustainable In modern usage the adjective *sustainable* has developed a specialised application to natural resources that can be renewed: ▪ *sustainable forests*, and to activities that do not damage the environment: ▪ *sustainable development*.

swam or **swum**? *Swam* is the past tense of the verb *swim*; *swum* is the past participle: ▪ *The dog swam to the shore.* ▪ *the lake where they had swum.*

swap or **swop**? Both spellings are acceptable for this informal word meaning 'exchange': ▪ *to swap stamps* ▪ *swop homes for a holiday*. *Swap* is the more traditional spelling, but *swop* is a frequently used variation. The word originates from the Middle English *swappen*, which meant 'to strike' – from the custom of striking or shaking hands on a bargain.

swat or **swot**? These spellings are sometimes confused. *Swat* means 'strike with a blow': ▪ *to swat flies*; it may also be spelt *swot*, although many careful users avoid this spelling. *Swot* is an informal word meaning 'study hard': ▪ *swotting for exams.*

sweet *see* **dessert, sweet, pudding** or **afters**?; **suite** or **sweet**?

swelled or **swollen**? Either word may be used as the past participle of the verb *swell. Swelled* is the more neutral form; *swollen* often indicates an undesirable or harmful increase or expansion: * *The population has swelled in recent years.* * *The disaster fund was swelled by a generous contribution from the mayor.* * *His wrist has swollen to twice its normal size.* * *The stream was swollen by the melted snow.* The past tense of *swell* is always *swelled*: * *The population swelled.* * *His wrist swelled.*

  Swollen is the usual form of the adjective: * *She crammed a few more sweets into her swollen pockets.* * *My ankle is badly swollen.* The adjective *swelled* is largely restricted to the informal American English phrase *swelled head*, denoting conceit, which is usually replaced by *swollen head* in British English.

swingeing Note the pronunciation and spelling of this word, which means 'severe': * *swingeing cuts in public expenditure* * *swingeing tax increases.* The word is pronounced [*swin*jing]; the *-e-* distinguishes it from *swinging* and indicates the softness of the *g*. The word derives from Old English *swengan*, 'to beat or flog'. *See also* **spelling**.

swipe The verb **swipe** has acquired a new meaning with the advent of electronic credit and debit cards, etc., describing the action of passing such a card through an electronic reading device: * *Let me swipe your card for you.* Careful users restrict the word to informal contexts.

swollen *see* **swelled** or **swollen**?

swop *see* **swap** or **swop**?

swot *see* **swat** or **swot**?

syllable A *syllable* is a unit of a word that contains a vowel sound or something that resembles a vowel sound. The words *by*, *tune*, and *through* have one syllable; the words *doctor*, *table*, and open have two syllables; the word *secretary* has three syllables if the *a* is not sounded and four syllables if the *a* is sounded.

syllabus The plural of this word, which means 'the subjects studied in a particular course', is usually *syllabuses*. *Syllabi*, pronounced [-bī], is the less frequent plural form.

symbol The noun *symbol* is followed by the preposition *of* in the sense 'an emblem': * *An olive branch is a symbol of peace*, and by *for* in the sense 'a sign': * *A diagonal cross is the symbol for multiplication. See also* **cymbal** or **symbol**?

sync *see* **sink** or **sync**?

syndrome Some people object to the frequent use of the noun *syndrome* in non-medical contexts to denote any set of characteristics, actions, emotions, etc.: * *She is suffering from the only-child syndrome.* In medicine the noun *syndrome* denotes a group of signs and symptoms that indicate a physical or mental disorder: * *Down's syndrome.*

synecdoche This term, describing a word that is used to refer to something of which it is just a part, is sometimes misspelt. Note particularly the *y* and the *-doche* ending, and do not be tempted to put an *h* after the first *c* as well. An example of *synec-doche* is: * *I've got some wheels so we can drive over there tonight.* The word is pronounced [si*nek*dŏkee].

synergy In technical contexts the noun *synergy*, pronounced with a soft *g* sound [*sinĕ*ji], denotes the combined action and increased effect of two or more drugs, muscles, etc., working together. Some people dislike the introduction of the noun *synergy* into general usage: * *Synergy, as business people know, is bringing several elements together to make a product greater than the parts* (Islwyn Borough Council advertisement). * [of the Cadbury-Schweppes merger] *The growth of vending machines has provided the magic synergy which such mergers are always supposed to produce* (*The Guardian*). The concept of *synergy* is sometimes explained in mathematical terms as 2+2=5.

synonymous Note the spelling of this word, particularly the vowel sequence *-y-o-y-o*. The phrase *synonymous with* means 'being a synonym of', but in general contexts it is frequently used in the sense of 'closely associated with': * *The verb 'jump' is synonymous with 'leap'.* * *Our name is synonymous with excellence. See also* **antonym**.

syphon *see* **siphon** or **syphon?**

systematic or **systemic?** The adjective *systematic* means 'methodical; well-ordered; well-planned': * *a systematic approach to the problem* * *You must try to be more systematic.* A rare synonym of *systematic*, the adjective *systemic* is most frequently found in biological contexts, in the sense of 'affecting or spreading through the whole system, body, plant etc.': * *a systemic disease* * *a systemic fungicide.*

T

-t *see* -ed or -t?

table d'hôte On a menu in a restaurant, *table d'hôte* refers to a meal that consists of set prearranged courses with a limited selection of dishes and served to all guests at a fixed price. The expression comes from French and means literally 'host's table'. Its anglicised pronunciation is [tahbĕl dōt]. *See also* à la carte.

tactics *see* -ics.

tag question *see* questions.

tail or **tale**? *Tail* variously refers to the flexible rear part of an animal or to the end of something: * *The horse's tail brushed his face.* * *The tail of the aircraft was riddled with bullet holes.* It should not be confused with *tale*, meaning 'story': * *a sad tale about doomed love.*

take *see* bring or take?

tall *see* high or tall?

tantamount The adjective *tantamount* is followed by the preposition *to*: * *Her offer was tantamount to bribery.*

target The noun *target* is now most frequently used in its metaphorical meaning of 'an aim or goal'. The verb form is more recent, and is often followed by *on* or *at*: * *The advertising campaign is to be carefully targeted at the 18–25 age group.* * *a benefit which*

is easy to understand, popular, fair, ...and actually targets those who genuinely need it* (The Guardian). Although many people object to the use of target as a verb, it has a long history: the *Oxford English Dictionary* cites an example from 1837.

Note that the final *t* is not doubled in front of suffixes: * *targeted* * *targeting.*

Target is often used in expressions such as *target date*, meaning 'the date set for the completion of work, etc.': * *target markets* * *consumer-targeted material.*

tariff This word is sometimes misspelt. Note the single *r* and the -*ff* ending.

task This verb is used in business jargon to mean 'assign a job to someone': * *Susan was tasked with investigating potential suppliers.*

task force A *task force* is a group of people formed in order to undertake a particular objective, usually of a military nature: * *The captain led a task force to blow up the bridge.* * *A task force was sent to the Falklands.* The most frequent use refers to subsections of the armed forces dispatched to deal with particular crises. However, it is sometimes used in a civilian context: * *A Home Office task force is to investigate the rise in crime.*

tasteful or **tasty**? These two adjectives relate to different senses of the word *taste*. *Tasteful* is applied to things that indicate good taste, in the sense of 'aesthetic discrimination'; *tasty* is applied to things that have good taste, in the sense of 'flavour': * *tasteful furnishings* * *a tasty meal*. Careful users maintain the distinction between the two words. *Tasty* also has the slang meaning of 'sexually attractive': * *His sister's rather tasty*, and is sometimes used to mean 'excellent; notable': * *a tasty song* * *a tasty little villain*. Some people object to these extended usages.

tautology *Tautology* is the avoidable repetition of an idea already expressed in different words: * *a new innovation* * *a brief moment*. Many well-established English phrases contain tautologies: * *circle round* * *free gift* * *join together* * *all-time record*, etc. It is not difficult to avoid the cruder tautologies: * *a dead corpse* * *an empty bottle with nothing in it*, but many tautologies arise unintentionally from carelessness about the meanings of words. To speak of *unlawful murder* is tautologous because *murder* means 'unlawful killing'. In * *She repeated it again*, *again* is redundant as *repeat* means 'to say again'. People also speak of * *SALT talks* * *OPEC countries* * *a PIN number*, presumably not realising that the word following the abbreviation is a repetition of the final word of the abbreviation.

Tautologies are in general to be avoided but can sometimes be used deliberately for emphasis: * *a tiny wee mite*.

tea *see* **dinner, lunch, tea** or **supper**?

tea or **tee**? *Tea* refers to a hot drink or to a light afternoon meal: * *Would you like a cup of tea?* * *Time for tea*. It should not be confused with *tee*, which refers to the small peg on which a golfer places the ball before playing the first shot of a hole: * *The ball kept rolling off the tee*.

teach *see* **learn** or **teach**?

team or **teem**? These two words are sometimes confused, being identical in pronunciation. *Team* is most frequently used as a noun, meaning 'group of people (or animals) who work or play together': * *a valuable member of the sales team* * *the captain of the hockey team* * *a team of oxen*. *Teem* is a verb, meaning 'pour' or 'bound': * *It was teeming with rain*. * *The village was teeming with tourists*. The word *team* is also used as a verb, often followed by up, meaning 'join to make a team': * *Michael teamed up with Peter*.

technical or **technological**? *Technical* means 'having or concerned with special practical knowledge of a scientific or mechanical subject'; *technological* means 'using science for practical purposes' and is used particularly of modern advances in technical processes: * *technical skills* * *a technical college* * *a technological breakthrough*. A second meaning of the word *technical* is 'marked by a strict interpretation of law or a set of rules': * *a technical offence* * *a technical advantage*.

techno- The prefix *techno-* relates to art, craft, technology, or technical matters. Some people object to its frequent use in the coining of new words in the sense of 'relating to high technology, especially computers'. *Techno-* may be used with or without a hyphen: * *technophobia* * *technofreak* * *techno-politics*. *See also* **hi-tech**.

technological *see* **technical** or **technological?**

tee *see* **tea** or **tee?**

teem *see* **team** or **teem?**

tele- The prefix *tele-*, from a Greek word meaning 'far', is found in such words as *television, telephone, telescope*, etc. It is increasingly used in the senses of 'relating to television' or 'by telephone': * *telebook* * *telecast* * *televangelism* * *teleshopping* * *telemarketing* * *teleworking* * *Telecommuting is the name given to working from home by linking up to your office computer over the telephone line (The Guardian).* Some people dislike such neologisms, despite the fact that most of them retain the original sense of 'far', since a thing transmitted by television or telephone must originate at a distance.

telephone *see* **phone**.

televise This word is often spelt incorrectly with a *z* instead of an *s*. To avoid mistakes, remember that the *s* in television remains unchanged. *Televise* is one of the verbs ending in *-ise* that cannot be spelt *-ize*: *see* **-ize** or **-ise?**

temerity or **timidity?** The word *temerity* is sometimes mistakenly used where *timidity* is intended, though their meanings are completely different. *Temerity* means 'audacity or recklessness'; *timidity* means 'lacking courage or self-confidence; easily frightened or alarmed'. The two words are not exact opposites. The opposite of *timidity* is *courage* or *confidence*, which have positive connotations, whereas *temerity* has negative ones. It suggests a rash contempt of

danger or disapproval, with a lack of reserve that may be interpreted as ill mannered: * *He had the temerity to interrupt the meeting.*

temperature *Temperature* means 'the degree of heat or cold as measured on, for example, a thermometer'. To take someone's temperature is to use a thermometer to determine the person's body heat. The word is often used to denote abnormally high body heat or fever: * *running a temperature* * *She's got a temperature*, but this is best avoided in writing and formal contexts. A metaphorical use of *temperature* describes the emotional state of a group of people: the *temperature* is raised or low according to whether they are agitated or calm.

temporal or **temporary?** These two words are sometimes confused. *Temporal* means 'relating to secular, ordinary, or worldly things; not spiritual': * *temporal matters/authority*; 'relating to time': * *spatial and temporal connections*; and 'relating to the parts of the brain near the temples': * *temporal arteritis*. *Temporary* means 'lasting for only a limited period of time; not permanent': * *temporary accommodation* * *a temporary loss of memory*. The adjective *temporary* may be pronounced as a three- or four-syllable word, with the stress on the first syllable: [*temp*rări] or [*temp*ŏrări]. Some careful users prefer the four-syllable pronunciation. The pronunciation [*temp*ări], omitting the [-(ŏ)r-] sound, is widely regarded as careless or incorrect.

The adverb *temporarily* should be stressed on the first syllable in British English; the pronunciation [tempŏrairili] is restricted to American English.

temporise *see* **extemporise** or **temporise**?

tense The tense of a verb is a set of forms expressing distinctions of time. Some modern grammarians say that fundamentally there are only two real tenses in English: the present: *It is hot today*, and the past: *It was cloudy yesterday*. The future is simply formed by the addition of *will* or *shall*, etc.: *It will be fine tomorrow*, and all other changes of tense are marked by using *be*, *have*, or both combined, with the past or present participle of the verb: *She is dancing*. *He was talking*. *I'll be thinking of you*. *They had ridden for three days*. *I shall have finished it by then*. *They had slept until noon*. *He had been praying*. *She has been working*. *They will have been travelling all day*.

The tense system becomes more complicated when there is more than one verb in a sentence. In such sentences there is a main clause, containing the most important verb, and a subordinate clause or clauses containing the other verb(s): *I thought that I knew him*. Here the main clause *I thought* is in the past tense, and the subordinate clause *that I knew him* follows the lead of the main clause and is in the same tense. This is by no means always the case, for it is quite possible for the clauses to refer to different times: *I believe I met him last week*. When the main clause is in the future, the verb of the subordinate clause is usually in the present: *I will look him up when I go to London*. When the main clause is in the past but the subordinate clause expresses some permanent fact, then that clause can be in the present: *She had learnt that Paris is a capital city*. In sentences referring to the future as viewed from the past, the subordinate verb usually changes to the past tense: *I hope they will succeed* becomes *I hoped they would succeed*.

The present tense is not used solely in expressions of events in the present. It is frequently used to express the future: *I leave on Thursday*. *The President speaks to the nation tonight*. The present is also habitually used in newspaper headlines to describe past events: *Van makes U-turn into path of coach* (*The Times*).

The verb form that is generally used for expressing recent events or actions is the *present perfect*, which is formed by adding *have* to the past participle of a verb: *You've already told me*. *He's just seen his mother*. *Has she turned up yet?* In informal American English the simple past tense is used in such sentences: *You already told me*. *He just saw his mother*. *Did she turn up yet?* and this form is also beginning to be used in British English. *See also* **participles**; **sequence of tenses**; **subjunctive**; **verbs**.

terminal or **terminus**? Used as a noun meaning 'end or finishing point', these words are often synonymous. Both can mean the finishing point of a transport line, but in Britain *terminal* is used for airlines, *terminus* for railways, while either can be used for bus routes. *Terminal* as an adjective can mean 'of, at, the end' or 'leading to death': *a terminal illness*. Other meanings of *terminal* as a noun include: 'a device on a wire or battery for an electrical connection', and 'an instrument through which a user can communicate with a computer'.

terminate *Terminate*, meaning 'bring to an end, form the ending of, close', is increasingly used in the context of ending employment. From speaking of *terminating someone's contract*, etc., some people have gone on to use *terminated* as a synonym for *dismissed*: * *The workers were terminated when profits fell.* Terminate is also used of buses and trains to mean 'stop at a particular place and go no further': * *This train terminates here.* An extension of its sense 'bring to an end' has resulted in its adoption as a euphemism for killing someone: * *Orders have gone out for the general to be terminated.*

Another popular use relates to ending pregnancies. A *termination* is synonymous with an abortion, although largely confined to medical contexts and not the preferred term in popular use.

Terminated, with the addition of *with* or *in*, is a fashionable alternative to resulted in in sports commentaries: * *The match terminated in a draw.*

terminus *see* **terminal** or **terminus**?

terrible or **terrific**? *Terrible* can be used as a general term of disapproval or can mean 'very bad' or 'causing distress': * *a terrible singer* * *a terrible accident* * *a terrible sight.* Terrific, on the other hand, expresses approval: * *Chartres has a terrific cathedral.* Both can mean 'unusually great': * *There's a terrible/ terrific amount of paperwork here.* The adverbs *terribly* and *terrifically* may be used as intensifiers to express either approval or disapproval: * *a terribly/ terrifically dull lecture* * *a terribly/ter- rifically good book.*

While both words derive from *ter- ror*, they are now far removed from any suggestion of fear. Both should be restricted to informal contexts.

tête-à-tête This compound, meaning 'intimate conversation between two

people', is of French origin. Note the accents, which should not be omitted when the term is used in English texts. The anglicised pronunciation is [taytah*tayt*].

text Since the advent of **text messaging**, the word *text* has been increasingly used as a verb to describe the process of sending keyed text from one mobile telephone or pager to another: * *Please text the details to me* * *She texted me with the results.* Some people dislike this appropriation of the noun as a verb, but it is now generally accepted as a standard form.

text messaging The introduction of the Short Message Service (SMS) in the 1990s, enabling the transmission of keyed messages by mobile telephone or pager (*text messaging*), has led to the development of an abbreviated form of **netspeak**. The small screen size on which messages appear means that extensive use is made of acronyms and other abbreviations, often based on the sound of individual letters and numbers, which are not always immediately comprehensible. For a selection of these, *see* the table below. *See also* **smiley**.

@TEOTD	at the end of the day
10Q	thank you
1OTD	one of these days
2Day	today
4eva	for ever
B4	before
BBL	be back later
BRB	be right back
Bsy	busy
BTDT	been there, done that
CUl8r	see you later

c%l	cool
CUO	see you online
EZ	easy
F2T	free to talk?
G2G	got to go
HHOJ	ha ha, only joking
LO	hello
M8	mate
MMYT	mail me your thoughts
Msg	message
NE1	anyone
NOYB	none of your business
PCM	please call me
ROTFL	rolling on the floor laughing
RUOK	are you ok?
SWDYT	so what do you think?
TXT	text
XLNT	excellent
Xxx	kisses
YYSW	yeah, yeah, sure, whatever
Zzzz	I'm tired

than *Than* is used to link two halves of comparisons or contrasts: * *Jack is taller than Jill.* * *I am wiser now than I was at that time.* Care must be taken with pronouns following than; the general rule is to remember the missing verb: * *You are older than I (am).* If there is no obvious implied verb, the object form follows: * *Rather you than me!* However, the form that is considered correct by careful users sometimes sounds stilted: * *She runs faster than he* is correct, but *She runs faster than him* is more frequently used. * *She runs faster than he does* is both correct and natural-sounding.

Note that it is incorrect to follow *than* with *what*: * *He is cleverer than* [not *than what*] *I am.*

thankfully As an adverb from *thank*, *thankfully* means 'in a thankful, relieved, or grateful way': * *They received the good news thankfully.* It is also used to mean 'it is a matter of relief that': * *Thankfully, he has survived the operation.* Many people dislike the second use of *thankfully*, although it is not as widely objected to as the similar use of *hopefully*. It can also occasionally lead to such ambiguous statements as: * *Thankfully, she went to church on Sunday.*

thank you *Thank you, thanks, many thanks*, etc., are expressions of gratitude: * *Thank you for a lovely evening.* They are also used in acceptance: * *'Have a sweet.' 'Thanks, I will.';* as a polite refusal in conjunction with no: * *'Have a sweet.' 'No, thanks.';* in a firm and less polite refusal: * *I can manage without your advice, thank you very much*; and to show pleasure: * *Now David's got a new job, we're doing very nicely, thank you very much.* Thanks can indicate responsibility or blame: * *Thanks to your coaching, I passed my exam.* * *Thanks to their incompetence, we lost the contract.* Thank heavens, thank goodness, and thank God are general expressions of relief: * *Thank heavens you're all right.* *'Peace has been declared.' 'Thank goodness!'*

Thank you is sometimes spelt as one word or hyphenated, when it is used as a noun or attributively: * *We said our thankyous and left.* * *a thank-you letter.*

that *That* is used as a conjunction or relative pronoun to introduce various types of clause; in some cases it can be omitted from both written and spoken English. As a conjunction it can usually be omitted: * *I'm sure (that) you're lying.* It cannot be left out when used with a noun: * *the fact that grass is green*, or with certain verbs, usually of a formal nature – for example *assert, contend*. It must not be left out when its omission could lead to ambiguity: * *I said last week you were wrong* might mean either 'I said that last week you were wrong' or 'I said last week that you were wrong'. Used as a relative pronoun *that* can be omitted when it is the object: * *the man (that) I love*, but not when it is the subject: * *the thing that upsets me*.

The use of *that* as an adverb: * *He's not that fat* is best avoided in formal contexts.

that or **this**? The difference between the pronouns *that* and *this*, referring to objects or people, is one of distance. *That* is further away from the speaker than *this*: * *Give me that.* * *Take this.* When the pronouns represent abstract concepts, *that* traditionally refers to something in the past (or something previously mentioned), whereas *this* refers to something in the future (or something about to be mentioned): * *This is what I want you to do.* * *That is what I expected you to do.* The use of *this* in place of *that* in such contexts may be ambiguous and is best avoided.

that or **which**? Whether to use *that* or *which* depends on whether it appears in a restrictive clause (a clause that limits the meaning of another part of a sentence) or a non-restrictive clause (a clause that conveys parenthetical or incidental information). *That* and *which* are both used in restrictive (or defining) clauses: * *the school that/which they go to*. Furthermore, a restrictive clause is not followed by a comma: * *The school that I go to burnt*

down. In non-restrictive (or non-defining) clauses, only *which* can be used: * *The programme, which was broadcast by the BBC, caused much controversy.* Non-restrictive clauses are always preceded by a comma and, unless at the end of a sentence, followed by one. Some people dislike the use of *which* in restrictive clauses, maintaining that only *that* can be used. However, the usage described above is widespread and generally accepted. *Which* is also useful to relieve a sentence that already has several thats: * *His Ford Capri. He remembered that that was the car which* [not *that*] *had run out of petrol on the M1.* On the use of *that* or *who/whom, see* **who**. *See also* **comma**; **restrictive clause**.

the *The* is the most frequently used word in the English language. Its pronunciation is usually a straightforward matter: before consonants it is pronounced [dhĕ]; before vowels or an unaspirated *h* it is pronounced [dhee]. The use of [dhee] before consonants has become common in recent years, particularly by broadcasters, but it is disliked by many people. One use of *the* is to single out one of a class as the best or most significant of a class: * *Is that* the *Michael Jackson?* * *It's* the *place to go for curry.* In these cases the is emphasised and pronounced [dhee].

theft *see* **burgle, rob** or **steal**?

their, there or **they're**? These three words are sometimes confused. *Their* means 'of them or belonging to them': * *their house. There* means 'in or to that place': * *over there. They're* is a contraction of *they are*: * *They're/They* *are always late*. Another frequent mistake is the wrong spelling of *theirs* as *their's*. The correct usage is as in: * *The car was theirs. See also* **they**.

them or **their**? *see* **-ing forms**.

theme park A *theme park* is an amusement park in which the displays and entertainments are organised round one particular idea or group of ideas, e.g. space travel or the Wild West.

themself The reflexive pronoun *themself* is unacceptable to careful users, being associated with the controversial singular usage of *they, them, their*, etc. (see **they**): * *Somebody has been helping themself to my whisky.* * *Walking through Pilsen, the casual observer might easily think themself back in 1945 (The Times*, cited in *English Today).*

thence *Thence* is a formal and almost archaic word with three meanings: 'from there, from that place': * *We drove to York and thence to Scotland*; 'from that premise, or for that reason': * *She proved that x was an even number and thence that it must be 42*; and 'from that time': * *His wife died ten years ago and thence he has become a recluse.* As *from* is contained in the meaning of *thence*, it is incorrect to say from thence (*see* **hence**; **whence**).

Thence is sometimes mistakenly used to mean 'to there', instead of the even more archaic *thither*.

there *see* **their**, **there** or **they're**?

there are *see* **there is** or **there are**?

therefore *Therefore* means 'for that reason, consequently, as this proves': * *I dislike worms; therefore I avoid digging*

the garden. * *Scotland is part of Great Britain; therefore the Scots are British. Therefore* normally appears at the beginning of a clause and is not followed by a comma. If it appears parenthetically within a clause it has a comma before and after: * *It appears, therefore, that he must be guilty.*

Note that *therefore* and *thus* are not always synonymous: * *She spoke thus* [i.e. in such a way].

there is or **there are**? Normally, *there is* should precede a singular noun, and *there are* a plural: * *There is a black car outside.* * *There are three bottles on the table.* However, *there is* is widely used in various expressions where *there are* is formally correct. These include situations where the plural noun is regarded as a single unit: * *There is three tons of coal here*; where the first of a list of nouns is singular: * *There is a rabbit, two gerbils, and some white mice*; where two nouns are regarded as a single entity: * *There is fish and chips for supper*, and when considering a situation in its entirety: * *There is my job and career prospects at stake.*

The use of the contraction *there's* followed by a plural is almost universal in informal speech: * *There's two good films showing*, although unacceptable in formal speech and writing.

they *They, them, their*, etc. are being used increasingly to refer to singular entities: * *Anyone can apply if they have the qualifications.* Such use, in conjunction with *anyone, someone, no one, everyone*, is well established, and in formations such as: * *No one's seen John, have they?* is becoming generally acceptable. However, many careful users object to such phrases as *a person on their own*. The use of *he* and *his* has a male bias unacceptable to many, while *he or she* or *his or her* often sounds clumsy or stilted. Probably the best solution is to make the noun plural to agree with *they* or *their*: * *people on their own.* See also **he** or **she**; **themself**.

they're *see* **their**, **there** or **they're**?

third or **thirdly**? *see* **first** or **firstly**?

third-generation This adjectival phrase, denoting something that belongs to a third developmental stage, is particularly associated with computer technology, but has also come to be applied to mobile telephones: * *These third-generation phones offer vast new commercial possibilities.* On the same model, people also talk of *fourth-generation, fifth-generation,* etc.: * *a fourth-generation i-Pod* * *the sixth-generation Golf GTI models.*

third world *see* **development**.

thirst The verb *thirst* is followed by the preposition *for* or *after*: * *They thirsted for* [or *after*] *revenge.*

this Careful users avoid using *this* as an intensifier before a noun in the place of such definite articles *as a, an, the,* etc.: * *Then this bloke came along and this policeman told him to keep his distance.* See also **next** or **this**?; **that** or **this**?

thoroughfare The noun *thoroughfare,* meaning 'way through', is sometimes misspelt and/or mispronounced, the most frequent error being the substitution of *through-* for *thorough-*.

though *see* **although** or **though**?

thrash or **thresh**? The verb *thrash* means 'flog or beat with repeated blows' or 'defeat': * *As a child, he was frequently thrashed by his father.* * *We thrashed the opposition.* *Thresh* means 'separate seeds of cereal from husks by beating'. *Thrash,* usually with *about,* can also mean 'move violently': * *He thrashed his arms about like a windmill,* and is used in the idiomatic phrasal verb *thrash out* meaning 'discuss in detail until a solution is found': * *Let's thrash out this problem together.*

The two words are occasionally confused, partly because *thresh,* with the meaning given above, is sometimes spelt *thrash.*

threshold Note that there is only one *h* in the middle of this word, unlike in the word *withhold.* *Threshold* may be pronounced either [*thresh*hōld] or [*thresh*ōld].

threw or **through**? *Threw* is the past participle of the verb *throw*: * *She threw the ball up in the air.* It should not be confused with *through,* which means 'across', 'among', or 'past': * *He ran through the grass.* * *They fought their way through the mob.*

thus The slightly formal adverb *thus* means 'in such a manner, in the way indicated, consequently': * *His father died in a hunting accident and he thus became a baron.* *Thus far* means 'to this extent, up to now': * *Thus far we have succeeded.* * *Go thus far but no further.*

The word *thusly,* sometimes used in American English, is unacceptable in written or spoken British English. See also **therefore**.

tide or **tied**? *Tide* refers to the ebb and flow of the sea or a movement of

something in a particular direction: *
*The tide rolled in until the rock was
covered.* * *The tide of opinion appears
to be flowing against the prime minister.* It should not be confused with
tied, the past tense and past participle
of the verb *tie:* * *He tied his bootlace.*

till or **until**? Both words mean 'up to the
time that; up to as far as': * *I will
work until I drop.* * *Carry on till you
reach the traffic lights.* They are interchangeable although *until* is slightly
more formal and *till* is more likely to
be used in speech. *Until* is usually
more appropriate as the first word of
a sentence: * *Until they go, we shall
have no peace.*

    Till is not an abbreviation of *until,*
so *'til* and *'till* are incorrect.

timidity *see* **temerity** or **timidity**?

tire or **tyre**? The rubber outer part of a
wheel is known as a *tire* in American
English and as a *tyre* in British
English. *Tire* can also mean 'grow
weary' or 'lose interest': * *He never
tires of being with me.* * *They seem to
tire of cricket very quickly.*

titillate or **titivate**? Literally, *titillate*
means the same as *tickle,* but it is
almost always used figuratively in the
sense of 'stimulate or arouse pleas-
antly': * *Her interest titillated his van-
ity.* *Titivate* is occasionally confused
with *titillate,* but its meaning is 'tidy
or smarten up': * *I must titivate myself
for the party.* *Titillate* is sometimes
used to mean 'excite mild sexual
pleasure' and in modern usage it often
has negative connotations of super-
ficiality or self-indulgence: * *Readers
of sensationalist tabloids are titillated
by reports of sexual offences.*

    Note the spelling of *titillate,* espe-
cially the *-t-* and *-ll-* (unlike the single
-v- of *titivate*).

titles Generally the titles of literary
works, musical works, works of art,
films, etc. are set in italics or, in handwriting and in typescript, underlined:
* *I saw *King Lear* last night.* * *She
sang the title role in *Carmen*.* *
Constable's *Flatford Mill*.* The Bible
and the names of its individual books
are not set in italics, and neither are
the Talmud, the Torah, or the Koran.

    Titles of newspapers and periodi-
cals are set in italics. Normally the
definite article before the name is not
italicised: * the *Daily Mail. The Times*
and *The Economist* are exceptions.

    The titles of long poems are usually
set in italics, but short ones in inverted commas: * Keats's *Endymion* *
Keats's 'To Autumn'. *See also* **Ms, Mrs**
or **Miss**?

to or **too**? These two spellings are sometimes confused. *To* is used with the
infinitive and as a preposition; *too* is
an adverb, meaning 'also' or 'excessively': * *to go home* * *Give it to me.* *
too much noise * *Mary came too.*

tobacconist This word, for a person or
shop that sells tobacco, cigarettes,
cigars, etc., is sometimes misspelt.
Like *tobacco,* there is a single *b* and
-cc-; note also the single *n.*

together with *Together with* means 'in
addition to': * *The chairman of the
company, together with three of the
directors, has resigned.* Note that the
verb *has* agrees with the singular noun
chairman: the phrase introduced by
together with does not form part of
the subject of the sentence. If *together*

with is replaced by *and*, the verb becomes plural: • *The chairman of the company and three of the directors have resigned.*

toilet, lavatory, loo or **bathroom**? *Toilet*, *lavatory*, and *loo* are virtually interchangeable in British English: • *I need to go to the toilet.* • *We're out of lavatory paper.* • *Where's the loo? Bathroom* is used in American English as a synonym for *toilet*, but in Britain its main meaning is a room containing a bath but not necessarily a toilet. *Toilet* is probably the most widely used term in British English, although *loo* is very commonly used in all but the most formal situations.

Toilets is usually used on signs in public places.

The use of *toilet* or *lavatory* is often considered a class marker in Britain. Upper- and middle-class people tend to use *lavatory*, while lower-middle and working-class people use *toilet* and regard *lavatory* as affected or impolite. *Loo* is classless.

tolerance or **toleration**? Both these words are nouns from *tolerate*, but *tolerance* is 'the capacity to tolerate', while *toleration* is 'the act of tolerating': • *His tolerance is unlimited.* • *Her toleration of his habits demonstrates her good nature. Tolerance* is generally used with reference to respect for the beliefs of others, although in the context of official government policy, *toleration* is used: • *religious toleration.*

Tolerance has several technical meanings in mathematics, statistics, physics, and medicine: an accepted deviation from a standard measurement; the ability of substances to endure heat, stress, etc., without being damaged; the capacity

of a person's body to withstand harmful substances, etc.

too *see* **to** or **too**?

torpor This word, meaning 'inactive condition', is sometimes misspelt. Note the final *-or*, as in *stupor*, rather than *-our*.

tortuous or **torturous**? *Tortuous* means 'twisting; winding' and, figuratively, 'complex, devious, or over-elaborate': • *a tortuous road* • *a tortuous policy. Torturous* comes from *torture* and means 'inflicting torture; agonising or painful': • *a torturous illness. Torturous* is sometimes used to mean 'complicated' or 'twisted', but careful users restrict it to the use suggesting physical or mental pain. The context often leads to confusion: • *a tortuous decision* might mean a complex one or might be a mistake for a *torturous decision* – one that is painful to make.

total *Total* is used as a noun: • *The total was 115*, a verb: • *Profits this year total one million pounds*, and an intensifying adjective suggesting completeness: • *a total failure* • *a total stranger.* As a verb, it is also used (chiefly in American English) as a slang term meaning 'wreck' or 'destroy utterly': • *He has totalled the car.* Some people dislike the use of *total* as an intensifying adjective synonymous with utter or complete, maintaining that the word should be used only when there is a sense of parts being added to produce a whole, as in: • *the total cost.*

Another disputed use is where the noun already suggests totality; some people think *total* is redundant in phrases like *total annihilation* or the *sum total.*

tour de force The French expression *tour de force* is used to refer to a performance or achievement that shows great skill, strength, etc.: * *a theatrical tour de force*. The expression is sometimes spelt with hyphens, *tour-de-force*. Its plural is *tours de force*. The singular and plural are both pronounced [toor dĕ fors].

tourniquet This word, meaning 'a bandage tied tightly round an arm or leg to stop bleeding', may be pronounced [*toor*nikay] or [*tor*nikay] in British English. In American English the final syllable is pronounced [-kĕt].

toward or **towards**? In British English *toward* is a rare adjective meaning 'afoot', 'imminent', or 'favourable', or a variant of *towards*, the usual form of the preposition meaning 'in the direction of' or 'with regard to': * *They walked towards the hotel.* * *What are his feelings towards her?* The preposition *toward* is more frequently used in American English.

The adjective *toward* is pronounced [*tō*ărd]; the preposition *toward(s)* is pronounced [tŏ*word(z)*]. *See also* **-ward** or **-wards**?

town *see* **city** or **town**?

town house A *town house* suggests an urban terraced house, usually with three or more storeys. However, when speaking of someone's *town house*, this can also mean a house in town belonging to a rich person whose main residence is in the country: * *They used their town house for Veronica's ball.*

toxic The meaning of the adjective *toxic* as 'poisonous' or 'deadly' has been extended in the wake of the world-wide financial collapse of 2008–9, chiefly in the phrase 'toxic debt', which describes an asset (such as a sub-prime mortgage) that was once worth something but is now considered valueless or at least of uncertain, probably negligible, value: * *Home loans have become toxic debts that none of the banks want to have anything to do with.* As some people find this and other similar recent coinages jargonistic, their use is best restricted. *See also* **credit crunch**.

track record The phrase *track record*, meaning 'record of past performance', is frequently used as an unnecessary extension of the word *record*, or as a synonym for 'experience', especially in job advertisements: * a *sound track record in R&D* * a *successful track record in sales and marketing*. Care should be taken to avoid overusing this expression.

trade names *Trade names* are names given to articles by their manufacturers. Some have unofficially become treated as quasi-generic names for articles of their kind, although manufacturers guard their protected legal status jealously * *Hoover* * *Biro*. All nouns that are actually *trade names* should be spelt with an initial capital letter, although this is frequently overlooked, as in: * *Please use a black fountain pen or biro.* * *She wore a crimplene dress.* When the noun has given rise to a verb, it is frequently found spelt with a lower-case initial letter, though this is technically incorrect: * *He hoovered the carpet.*

trade union or **trades union**? The generally accepted singular noun is *trade* union, with the plural *trade unions*. There is no good grammatical reason for the use of *trades union* or *trades unions*, although both are frequently used. However, the official title of the TUC, the central association of British trade unions, is the *Trades Union Congress*, and this title should be used when referring to that organisation.

trafficker This word is sometimes misspelt. The word *traffic* adds a *k* before the suffixes *-er*, *-ed*, and *-ing*: * *drug traffickers* * *illegal arms trafficking*. See also **spelling**.

trait This word may be pronounced [tray] or [trayt], although careful users prefer the first pronunciation. In American English [trayt] is standard.

tranche The noun *tranche* is best avoided where *section*, *group*, *portion*, or *instalment* would be adequate or more appropriate: * *a tranche of the population* * *payable in three tranches*. Of French origin, the word *tranche* entered the English language via the terminology of the Stock Market, where it means 'a block of bonds or government stock'.

tranquillity This word, meaning 'peaceful state': * *the perfect tranquillity of the lake*, is often misspelt. Note the *-ll-* and the final single *t*.

transformation, transfiguration, transmigration or **transmutation**? *Transformation* describes a fundamental change in someone or something: * *She has undergone a transformation in recent months*. * *The country is in the midst of a dramatic economic transfor-*

mation. * *Transfiguration* is virtually synonymous with *transformation* but is used in more literary contexts: * '*It was less a reform than a transfiguration. The former curves of sensuousness were now modulated to lines of devotional passion*' (Thomas Hardy, *Tess of the d'Urbervilles*). In the New Testament, the *transfiguration* of Jesus Christ is 'the revelation of the glory of Jesus Christ, shortly before his death, at which his disciples caught sight of him in his full majesty' (*NIV Thematic Study Bible*). *Transmigration* is quite distinct in meaning, variously denoting the movement of people from one place to another or to the journey of the soul from one body to another at death: * *The transmigration of rebel Kurds*. * *She did not believe in the transmigration of souls*. *Transmutation* signifies a change in something from one state to another: * *the transmutation of liquid to gas*.

transient or **transitory**? Both words mean 'short-lived; lasting only a brief time': * *It is just a transient/transitory phase*. The words are virtually interchangeable but have a slightly different feel about them. *Transient* often suggests passing by quickly, perhaps because of rapid movement from place to place: * *transient summer visitors*. *Transitory* often carries a suggestion of regret about the way desirable things change or disappear: * *the transitory nature of human love*.

Transient is sometimes used as a noun to denote a person who stays for only a short time in any one place.

transitive *see* **verbs**.

translate or **transliterate**? To *translate* is to express in a different language; to *transliterate* is to write or print using a different alphabet. The Greek word *petra*, for example, may be transliterated as *petra* and translated into English as 'rock'. The two verbs should not be confused.

transmigration, transmutation *see* **transformation, transfiguration, transmigration** or **transmutation?**

transparent This word has various pronunciations, all of which are acceptable. The most frequent in contemporary usage is [trans*pa*rrĕnt], but the pronunciations [trahns*pa*rrĕnt] and [trans*pai*rĕnt] are also heard. The *s* is sometimes pronounced with a *z* sound.

transpire *Transpire* means 'become known; come to light': * *It later transpired that the President had known of the plan all along.* It is also widely used to mean 'happen or occur': * *I will let you know what transpires*; many people dislike this second use, although it has a well-established history. *Transpire* is also sometimes used to mean 'turn out or prove to be': * *He transpired to be her cousin*, and even 'arrive or turn up': * *Subsequently dozens of letters transpired.* Both such uses are incorrect.

transport or **transportation?** *Transport* is used in British English both for the system and for means of conveying: * *public transport* * *I have my own transport.* In American English *transportation* is often used: * *the fastest form of transportation* * *The goods were packed ready for transportation*, and this usage is now sometimes found in British English. *Transportation* is used in both British and American English

to mean 'the banishment of convicts': * *The sentence was transportation to Australia.*

Transport is also used in formal English to mean 'the state of being carried away by emotion': * *a transport of joy.*

transverse or **traverse?** *Transverse* is an adjective meaning 'lying or set across; at right angles': * *a transverse section.* *Traverse* is a verb meaning 'cross; go across' or a noun meaning 'way or path across': * *The river traverses two counties.* * *The traverse of this mountain is dangerous to inexperienced climbers.*

traumatic *Traumatic* is the adjective from *trauma*, which means 'a wound or injury' and it is still used in this sense in medical contexts: * *traumatic fever.* However its main use is with the figurative meaning of 'causing great and deeply disturbing emotional shock': * *a traumatic bereavement* * *the traumatic effects of divorce* * *the traumatic experience of a concentration camp.* Both *traumatic* and *trauma* have become very much overworked and are often used for cases of mild distress or annoyance: * *I spent a traumatic evening filling in my tax return.* * *the trauma of moving house.*

The usual pronunciation of *trauma* is [*traw*mă]; the pronunciation [*trow*mă] is used less frequently.

travel This word is sometimes misspelt. In British English the final *l* is doubled before the suffixes *-ed*, *-ing*, and *-er*: * *well-travelled* * *travelling fast along the motorway* * *commercial travellers.* American English retains the single *l*: * *traveled* * *traveler* * *travelling.* See also **spelling.**

traveller The noun *traveller* simply means 'someone who travels', but in certain circumstances it can convey something more specific. In former times, *fellow traveller* was a euphemism for someone who was a member of the Communist Party, or who had Communist sympathies: * *We never suspected he was a fellow traveller*, and it has since been applied in other political contexts. The term *traveller* is also employed as an alternative to the more prescriptive, and more contentious, *gipsy* to describe a person who lives an itinerant life on the road, in which case it is sometimes rendered with an initial capital letter. A *new age traveller* is an itinerant who pursues a freewheeling, hippy lifestyle: * *The whole neighbourhood was up in arms when some new age travellers set up camp on the village green. See also* **gipsy; Roma.**

traverse *see* **transverse** or **traverse?**

treble or **triple?** Both words can be used as a noun, verb, and adjective and are virtually interchangeable in meaning. However, *treble* is preferred by many careful users when the meaning is 'three times as great': * *treble the sum*, and *triple* when the meaning is 'consisting of three parts': * *a triple jump.* The words have distinctly different meanings in the context of music. *Treble* refers to a high-pitched voice or instrument, or a singer who performs at this pitch, whereas *triple* is used of rhythm: * *a treble recorder* * *triple time.*

tremble The verb *tremble* is followed by the preposition *at* in the sense of 'respond to something frightening': * *I trembled at the thought,* and by *with*

in the sense of 'show fear, excitement, etc.': * *The children were trembling with fear.*

tremor This word, meaning 'shaking or quivering action': * *earth tremors,* is sometimes misspelt. Note the ending *-or*, not *-our.*

triage This word, describing the practice of treating sick or injured people in order, according to the seriousness of their condition, is often misspelt. Note particularly the *-age* ending. The word is pronounced [*tree*ahj] or [*tree*ahzh].

tribe *Tribe*, in its sense of 'people' or 'social group', is often avoided by careful users because of its negative connotations, which imply that the group in question is primitive and uncivilised: * *The local tribe were quickly subdued by the colonists.* Use of *tribe* in a figurative sense, to describe a family gathering or group of other people, is best restricted to informal contexts: * *Here comes my sister with all her tribe.*

trillion *see* **billion.**

triple *see* **treble** or **triple?**

triumphal or **triumphant?** These adjectives are often confused. *Triumphal* is connected with the celebration of a victory, usually of a military nature: * *triumphal arch* * *A triumphal march was played as the victorious army paraded through the streets. Triumphant* means 'victorious; exulting or rejoicing in success': * *The team were triumphant.* * *Having succeeded in her task, she returned with a triumphant smile. Triumphant* is the more frequently used word, *triumphal* being restricted to narrower, more formal contexts.

trivia *Trivia* means 'matters of very minor importance': * *the trivia of village gossip* * *Why waste hours fussing over the trivia of everyday life?* The word is actually a plural, so careful users would not say, for example: * *Such trivia is beneath my notice.* However, *Such trivia are beneath my notice* has a stilted and unnatural sound, so most users would substitute such phrases as: * *trivial matters* * *trivial issues* * *trivial things* for *trivia* in the preceding example.

troop or **troupe**? These words are sometimes confused. A *troop* is a military unit or group of people or things: * *troops of soldiers* * *a Scout troop.* *Troop* is also used as a verb in informal English to mean 'move as a large group': * *Then they all trooped off home.* A *troupe* is a group of actors or performers: * *a troupe of travelling acrobats.* The words *trooper* and *trouper* are also sometimes confused. A *trooper* is a cavalry soldier, especially a private, and in American and Australian English a mounted policeman: * *swear like a trooper* means 'swear a lot'. A *trouper* is a member of a troupe of dancers, singers, etc.

trooping the colour To *troop the colour* is to parade the flag of a regiment ceremonially along the ranks of soldiers of that regiment: * *trooping the colour* * *the trooping of the colour.* Written with capital initials, the phrase *Trooping the Colour* refers to the annual parade in London, usually attended by the Queen, the Prime Minister, and other dignitaries: * *We*

went to watch the ceremony of *Trooping the Colour.* Since the ceremony is officially called *Trooping the Colour*, some people object to the phrase the *Trooping of the Colour:* * *We went to watch the Trooping of the Colour.* However, this example reads awkwardly without the *of* (or the first *the*): * *We went to watch (the) Trooping the Colour.* A possible solution is to use *Trooping the Colour* adjectivally: * *We went to watch the Trooping the Colour ceremony.*

troupe *see* **troop** or **troupe**?

truculent This adjective, which means 'sullenly or defiantly aggressive', is sometimes misspelt; note the *-ucu-* and the *-ent* ending. The correct pronunciation is [*truk*yuulĕnt].

truism The narrower meaning of *truism* is 'a statement of self-evident truth, one containing superfluous repetition of an idea': * *It is a truism to speak of single bachelors.* The word is more widely used to mean 'a statement of a fact that is too obvious to be thought worth stating': * *the truism that stars are only visible at night.* *Truism* is sometimes used as though it were a synonym for *fact* or *truth* in such phrases as: * *the truism that heterosexuals can contract AIDS*, but such use is widely regarded as unacceptable.

truly The adverb *truly* is sometimes misspelt. Note that the final *-e* of *true* is dropped when the adverbial suffix *-ly* is added.

try and or **try to**? The two expressions are virtually interchangeable: * *Try and catch me!* * *Try to tell the truth. Try* *and* is colloquial and very frequently used; it is unacceptable only in formal written English. Note that *try to* sounds better in a negative context: • *She didn't even try to be polite*, and only *try to* can be used in the past tense: • *They tried to break into the house.*

tsar or **czar**? This word – the title of any of the former Russian emperors – is spelt **tsar**, **czar**, or, rarely, **tzar**. It is pronounced [zah]. Many users prefer the spelling *tsar*, because it more accurately reflects the Russian word as written in the Cyrillic script. The spelling *czar* shows the origin of the word from the Gothic *kaisar*, and ultimately the Latin *Caesar*.

The word has been revived in recent years as an informal title for a person who has been appointed head of an official committee or other body, but in this sense it is usually spelt *czar*: • *He is the government's new drugs czar.*

tun *see* **ton, tonne** or **tun**?

tunnel This word is sometimes misspelt. In British English the final *l* is doubled before the suffixes *-ed*, *-ing*, and *-er*: • *They tunnelled under the hill.* American English retains the single *l*: • *tunneled. See also* **spelling**.

turbid, turbulent or **turgid**? The adjective *turbid*, used in formal contexts, is sometimes confused with *turbulent* or *turgid*. *Turbid* means 'opaque; cloudy; muddy; dense': • *a turbid pool*, whereas *turbulent* means 'in a state of agitated

movement or confusion': • *turbulent seas* • *a politically turbulent period of history.* The adjective *turgid* means 'swollen' or 'distended': • *The turgid river had overflowed its banks.* Both *turbid* and *turgid* may be applied in formal and figurative contexts to linguistic or literary style, *turbid* meaning 'confused' and turgid 'bombastic': • *turbid/ turgid prose.*

turbo- The prefix *turbo-* is applied to a machine that is driven by a turbine: • *turbofan* • *turbojet.* Its association with turbo-charged cars, in which performance is improved by the use of a turbine, sometimes leads to a mistaken interpretation and application of the prefix in the sense of 'fast' or 'powerful': • *a turbo model of a computer.* This extension of usage is best avoided.

turbulent, turgid *see* **turbid, turbulent** or **turgid**?

turquoise The name of this greenish-blue mineral has various pronunciations. The most frequent in contemporary usage is [*ter*kwoiz], but [*ter*-wahz], [*ter*kwois], and [*ter*koiz] are also heard.

twelfth Careful users avoid dropping the *f* in the pronunciation of this word [twelfth]. The word is, however, frequently pronounced without the *f*.

type of *see* **kind of.**

tyre *see* **tire** or **tyre**?

U

uber- This German prefix, meaning 'over', has been absorbed into English in recent years to describe a person who ranks above their peers in a particular field: * *an uberchef* * *an uber-model*. As a vogue term, it is best restricted to informal contexts. The word is sometimes rendered in its original German form, with an umlaut, as *über*. * *There's a certain irony in this story: a sceptic and über-rationalist finding a cure for his illness in a mysterious hotchpotch of Chinese herbs* (*The Guardian*).

ultimate *Ultimate* is used mainly as an adjective meaning 'last, final, eventual': * *the ultimate goal*, or 'fundamental': * *ultimate truths*. As a noun it has traditionally simply meant 'something ultimate' or 'the extreme': * *the ultimate in wickedness*. This last use is increasingly being extended, particularly in advertising and journalism, to mean 'the best possible; the most modern or advanced thing': * *the ultimate in swimming pools* * *the ultimate in high technology*. This vogue use, disliked by some, has some similarity with the phrase *the last word*.

ultra *Ultra* is an adjective meaning 'going beyond' or 'extreme' and is also used as a prefix with other words, either with or without a hyphen. In the sense of 'extremely' it is used in such words as: * *ultra-modern* * *ultra-radical*. In the sense of 'beyond the range of' it is used in: * *ultrasonic* *

ultramicroscopic. *UHT* stands for ultraheat-treated and *UHF* for ultra-high frequency.

umbilical This word may be stressed on the second syllable, [um*bil*ikl], or on the third: [umbi*līk*l].

umpire *see* **referee** or **umpire?**

un- *see* **non-**.

unanimous *Unanimous* means 'of one mind; in complete agreement': * *The committee reached a unanimous decision*. It can only be used when several people all agree about something, and cannot be used as a synonym for 'wholehearted' or 'enthusiastic', as in: * *Many of the group were prepared to give the project their unanimous backing*. When a vote is taken, someone can only be said to have been *elected unanimously*, or *a motion passed unanimously*, if every person present voted in favour. If there are any abstentions the motion is said to be passed *nem con*, which is an abbreviation of the Latin *nemine contradicente* – 'no one contradicting'.

unaware or **unawares?** *Unaware* is an adjective meaning 'not aware; not knowing about; not having noticed': * *I was unaware that you were coming.* * *He seemed unaware of the reaction he was causing*. It is occasionally used as an adverb, but the usual adverb is *unawares*, meaning 'unexpectedly, without warning', often in *caught unawares* or *taken unawares*: * *The landslide caught the villagers unawares. Unaware* is often followed by *of* or *that*, but *unawares* cannot precede another word in that way.

uncertain The adjective *uncertain* is followed by the preposition *of* or *about*: * *She was uncertain of* [or *about*] *the terms of the contract.*

unconscious *see* **subconscious** or **unconscious?**

under *see* **below, beneath, under** or **underneath?**

under foot or **underfoot?** This term should be spelt as one word, not as two separate words: * *It was rather wet underfoot.*

underhand or **underhanded?** Both *underhand* and *underhanded* are used as adjectives to mean 'sly; marked by dishonesty, trickery, and deception': * *They used the most underhand/underhanded methods in their campaign.* Both words can be used in the context of some sports, meaning 'with the hand below the shoulder or elbow': * *underhand shooting* * *aiming underhanded. Underhanded* is also occasionally used to mean 'short of the required number of workers'.

underlay or **underlie?** Both verbs are used transitively; *underlay* has the past tense and past participle *underlaid; underlie* has the past tense *underlay* and the past participle *underlain. Underlay* means 'cover the bottommost part of': * *to underlay the carpet with felt. Underlie* is used more frequently and means 'form the cause or basis of': * *This trend has underlain many of the changes in present-day society;* it is most often used in the adjectival form *underlying*: * *the underlying reasons for the conflict.*

underline *see* **underscore.**

underneath *see* **below, beneath, under** or **underneath?**

underprivileged *Underprivileged* has become a fashionable adjective to use in connection with those lacking the standard of income and opportunities enjoyed by other members of the society in which they live: * *She started a clinic for underprivileged children.* * *Many young criminals come from underprivileged backgrounds.* It is used as a noun as well as an adjective: * *His concern for the underprivileged drew him towards social work as a career.* Its real meaning is not 'lacking in privileges' but rather, 'lacking in rights; disadvantaged' or at least lacking in those social and economic rights considered to be fundamental in Western developed society.

underscore *Underscoring* (or *underlining*) a letter, word, phrase or sentence by inserting a line beneath it serves to draw the reader's attention to it: * *This door <u>must</u> be kept locked.* * *Do not block this entrance <u>at any time</u>.* * *<u>These cliffs are dangerous</u>.* Although useful for emphasising important words or passages, underscoring should not be employed too frequently, as this dilutes its impact and may render the text difficult to read and absorb properly. Attention should also be paid to context: it is appropriate to use underscoring for headings in a technical or official document, for instance, but not (generally speaking) in narrative writing. Note also that many people take particular objection to passages that are underlined not once but twice or even three times. In email addresses, care should be taken not to confuse an underscore (_) with a hyphen (-). In proofreading, underscored text indicates that it is to be typeset in italics.

undertone *see* **overtone** or **undertone**?

underway or **under way**? Careful users prefer to write this expression, meaning 'moving; in progress', as two words: • *Preparations for the new project are now well under way.* The one exception to this is when it appears as an adjective preceding a noun: • *The aircraft rendezvoused for underway fuelling.* • *the then underway project.* The expression is, however, increasingly being spelt as one word in all contexts. The spelling *under weigh* is wrong; it probably arises from confusion with the nautical expression *weigh anchor*, meaning 'raise anchor'.

undiscriminating *see* **indiscriminate** or **undiscriminating**?

undoubtedly *Undoubtedly, no doubt, doubtless, without (a) doubt* are all adverbs expressing that something is not disputed. However, *undoubtedly* and *without a doubt* express that idea much more positively and strongly than the other expressions: • *She is undoubtedly the best student in her year.* *No doubt* and *doubtless* are much weaker expressions, often suggesting that the user is in fact not completely certain, or is even harbouring doubts: • *No doubt he is very clever but I still can't understand what he is saying.* As

doubtless is an adverb, *doubtlessly* is incorrect.

Some people mistakenly spell *undoubtedly* as *undoubtably*, perhaps confusing it with *indubitably*, which is a more formal and even stronger expression suggesting that something cannot possibly be doubted: • *It was indubitably evident that he had acted in a manner which was utterly unacceptable.*

uneatable *see* **eatable** or **edible**?

unequivocally Note that the adverb *unequivocally* has the ending -*ally*, not -*ably*. It is derived from the adjective *unequivocal*, meaning 'clear; plain'.

unexceptionable or **unexceptional**? *Unexceptionable* means 'inoffensive; not liable to be criticised or objected to': • *His behaviour had been unexceptionable, so he could not understand how he could have offended his hosts.* *Unexceptional* means 'usual, normal, or ordinary': • *The weather was unexceptional for the time of year.* It is, however, more frequently used to suggest that something is dull or disappointingly commonplace: • *I had heard enthusiastic reports of his playing, but I found this an unexceptional performance.* The words are often confused, partly because it is quite possible for something to be both inoffensive and rather dull.

unfair The adjective *unfair* is followed by the preposition *to* or *on*: • *The present system is unfair to* [or *on*] *the self-employed.*

-unfriendly *see* **-friendly**.

uninterested *see* **disinterested** or **uninterested**?

unique *Unique* means 'being the only one of its kind': • *Every snowflake has a unique pattern*. A thing is either unique or it is not, so careful users dislike such expressions as *so unique, rather unique, very unique*, etc., and something cannot be *more unique* or *less unique* than something else. *Almost* and *nearly* are the only modifiers generally acceptable with *unique*. The word is widely used with a weaker meaning of 'unrivalled; outstanding', but many people object to such use. Intensifiers are often used with *unique*: • *It was absolutely unique*, but such expressions should be restricted to informal use.

United Kingdom *see* **Britain**.

United States, United States of America *see* **America**.

unlike Careful users avoid employing *unlike* as a conjunction: • *The man worked unlike he'd ever worked in his life*.

unmistakable or **unmistakeable**? Both spellings of this word are acceptable, but *unmistakable* is the more usual in British English. *See* **spelling**.

unnecessary The adjective *unnecessary* is sometimes misspelt. Note the -*nn*- (from the addition of the prefix **un**- to the adjective *necessary*), the single *c*, and the -*ss*-.

unorganised *see* **disorganised** or **unorganised**?

unpractical *see* **practical** or **practicable**?

unprecedented A *precedent* is 'an earlier example or occurrence of a similar thing', so *unprecedented* means 'never having happened before; completely new or original': • *His score was unprecedented in the history of cricket*. It has recently become a popular word, particularly in the media, where its meaning has weakened to 'extremely great': • *The film is enjoying an unprecedented success*.

unreadable *see* **illegible** or **unreadable**?

unrepairable *see* **repairable** or **reparable**?

unsociable, unsocial *see* **antisocial, asocial, unsocial** or **unsociable**?

until *see* **till** or **until**?

unused Like *used*, the word *unused* may be pronounced with the [s] sound of the noun use or the [z] sound of the verb use. In the phrase *unused to*, meaning 'unaccustomed to', *unused* is pronounced [un*yoost*]: • *I am unused to driving on the right-hand side of the road*. The adjective *unused*, meaning 'not being used' or 'never having been used', is pronounced [un*yoozd*]: • *Many of the rooms are unused.* • *Unused pills and tablets should be returned to the pharmacy for safe disposal*.

unwaged The adjective and noun *unwaged* refers to anybody who does not receive a wage or salary. Such people include the unemployed, full-time mothers or housewives, students, and old age pensioners: • *The membership fee is £5 (or £3 for the unwaged)*. The euphemistic use of the term *unwaged* in place of *unemployed*, with reference to those who are out of work and seeking employment, is on the increase, though some might argue that it could be misleading.

unwanted or **unwonted**? *Unwanted* means simply 'not wanted': * *She gave her unwanted clothes to the Oxfam shop. Unwonted means 'out of the ordinary; unusual': * The drug gave him an unwonted feeling of euphoria.* The two words are confused because people sometimes mistakenly spell *unwanted* as *unwonted*, and frequently pronounce *unwonted* as *unwanted*. *Unwanted* should be pronounced [un*won*tid] and unwonted [un*wōn*tid], with the stressed syllable pronounced the same as for the word *won't*.

unwieldy This word is often misspelt: note particularly the *-ie-* in the middle.

up-front Some people dislike the increasing use of the term *up-front*, meaning 'paid in advance, at the beginning, or as a deposit': * *an up-front payment* * *They want £500 up-front and the remainder in monthly instalments.* The term should not be overused, and is best restricted to informal contexts.

upload *see* **download** and **upload**.

upon or **on**? These two words are synonyms and virtually indistinguishable in use: * *She threw herself upon the sofa.* * *He walked on the beach. On* is more frequently used; *upon* has a more formal sound and is rarely heard in spoken English. In some cases usage is dictated by the fact that one or the other word is normal in a particular idiom: * *once upon a time* * *on the contrary.*

Upon is used between two repeated nouns to suggest large numbers: * *We walked mile upon mile.*

uptalk This term refers to the increasing modern tendency to deliver statements as though they are questions, with the voice rising at the end of the sentence. Sometimes called *upspeak* or *HRT* (high-rise terminals), *uptalk* is variously thought to have originated in the USA, Canada, Australia, or New Zealand. It has become a target of criticism in recent years, especially in Britain. Popularly associated with teenagers in particular, it has also been detected among older and younger speakers: * *Then we went round to Jack's house? Which was, like, really great? And then we out for a meal? And we all had the same things?*

Careful speakers avoid using *uptalk*, not only because it can be irritating to the listener, but also because it can project an image of weakness or insecurity, as if the user lacks confidence in the opinions he or she is advancing with such tentative intonation.

upward or **upwards**? In British English *upward* is principally used as an adjective, *upwards* being the usual form of the adverb meaning 'to a higher level': * *an upward trend* * *to float upwards.* The adverb *upward* is more frequently used in American English.

The phrase *upwards of*, meaning 'more than', is disliked by some people: * *The newly privatised company is in contention with America's Pratt & Whitney to supply the engines for upwards of 100 Boeing 757s that Texas Air is planning to order* (*Sunday Times*). See also **-ward** or **-wards**?

urban or **urbane**? *Urban* means 'of a town or city': • *Unemployment is higher in urban areas.* *Urbane* is used of someone who is sophisticated and polite, with a smooth and easy manner in any social situation: • *He turned out to be an elegant and urbane man who charmed them all.* *Urbane* actually derives from *urban*, for it describes a manner thought to be characteristic of a person who came from a city.

urinal This word may be stressed on either the second syllable, [yuur*ī*nl], or the first syllable [*yoo*rinl] in British English. The American English pronunciation is stressed on the first syllable.

us *see* **we**.

us or **our**? *see* **-ing forms**.

US, USA *see* **America**.

usable or **useable**? Both spellings of this word are acceptable, but *usable* is the more frequent in British English. *See* **spelling**.

usage or **use**? *Usage* is the way in which something, especially language, is used; the noun *use* denotes the act of using: • *This book deals with problems of usage.* • *in contemporary usage* • *the use of wood as an insulator* • *The photocopier is in use.* Careful users maintain this distinction between the two words, avoiding such phrases as: • *a ban on the usage of hosepipes.* Either *usage* or *use* may be used in the sense of 'amount or degree to which something is used': • *increased usage/use of electricity,* although some people dislike the use of usage in this context.

Usage also means 'treatment': • *rough/gentle usage.* The noun *use* has a variety of other meanings, such as 'usefulness': • *What's the use of trying?*; 'wear': • *to deteriorate through use*; 'need': • *Do you have a use for this box?*; and 'the right to use': • *to have the use of a company car.*

Note the difference in pronunciation between the noun *use* [yoos] and the verb *use* [yooz]. *Usage* may be pronounced [yoosij] or [yoozij].

useable *see* **usable** or **useable**?

used In the phrase *used to*, *used* is pronounced [yoost]. *Used* as an adjective, for example in: • *used cars*, and as the past tense and past participle of the verb *use*, is pronounced [yoozd].

used to *Used to* either means 'accustomed to': • *I have got used to the noise*, or refers to a habitual action or situation in the past: • *She used to play squash regularly.* Difficulties arise over negative and question forms of the phrase in its second meaning. In negative forms the more formal *used not to* or the more informal *did not/didn't use to* are both acceptable: • *He used not to be so aggressive.* • *She did not use to like fish.* Both *usen't to* and *didn't used to* are heard, but are avoided by careful users.

In the question form, the formal and rather old-fashioned *used X to?* and the less formal *did X use to?* are both correct: • *Used there to be a lake in that wood?* • *Did Henry use to visit you? Did X used to?* or *didn't X used to?* are frequently heard, though disliked by many careful users. As no form sounds completely natural and correct many people would reconstruct the sentence and say, for example: •

Was there once a lake in that wood? See also **used**.

user-friendly *User-friendly* is a term used in computing to describe software that is simple to use, being designed to assist the user and forestall any potential problems: ● *a user-friendly program.* The term is increasingly found in other fields, meaning 'easy to operate or understand', and describing electrical appliances, cars, books, etc.: ● *A drive to make the National Health Service 'user-friendly' was launched yesterday* (*Daily Telegraph*). This implied association with advanced technology may impress some people but will alienate others; it is therefore advisable to reserve the term for its original purpose.

User-hostile and *user-unfriendly*, opposites of *user-friendly*, are also found in certain contexts: ● *complex, user-hostile systems which require complicated languages to programme and are hard to understand* (*The Guardian*). See also **-friendly**.

usher or **usherette**? *see* **non-sexist terms**.

utilise *Utilise* means 'use in a practical and effective, profitable or productive way': ● *They utilised every machine that was available.* It can also mean 'make good use of something not intended for the purpose': ● *She utilised her tights when the fan belt broke*; or 'make use of something that might be thought useless': ● *She utilised all the scraps for stuffing cushions. Utilise* is often used, particularly in business jargon, as though it were merely a synonym for *use*: ● *Successful applicants will be able to utilise their experience and skills in this field.* However, careful users restrict the word to the narrower senses described above.

V

vacant or **vacuous**? Both these adjectives mean 'empty', but they are not generally interchangeable in usage. The adjective *vacant* is most frequently applied to a flat, room, seat, post, etc. that is not occupied by a person or people: *a hotel with vacant rooms* *The post remained vacant for several months after her resignation.* The adjective *vacuous* is used in formal contexts, often in the derogatory sense of 'apparently devoid of intelligence; inane; mindless': *a vacuous remark* *Modern pop music is vacuous, repetitive, and uninspiring.* Both *vacant* and *vacuous* may also be applied to a person's expression, or to a gaze or stare: *a vacant expression* suggests a temporary lack of concentration, attention, or awareness; *a vacuous expression* suggests a lack of intelligence.

vacation In British English the primary meaning of the noun *vacation* is 'the period when universities and law courts are not officially working': *She went home for the Christmas vacation.* Students often shorten the word informally to *vac.*

In American English the main meaning of vacation is 'a holiday': *They took a vacation in Miami.* It is also used as a verb: *We vacationed in Europe last year.*

A further meaning of the word is 'vacating; making vacant or empty': *The landlord insisted on immediate vacation of the house.*

vaccinate *see* **inoculate** or **vaccinate**?

vacuous *see* **vacant** or **vacuous**?

vagary The noun *vagary*, meaning 'whim', 'caprice', or 'unpredictable change': *the vagaries of the weather*, causes problems of pronunciation. In British English the noun is usually pronounced [*vay*gări]; the pronunciation [vă*gairi*] is less frequent and may be regarded as an Americanism. Note also that there is no *i* after the *g*, either in pronunciation or spelling.

vain, vane or **vein**? These three words are sometimes confused, being identical in pronunciation. *Vain* is an adjective, meaning 'conceited; excessively proud' or 'worthless; futile': *the vain parents of talented children* *a vain attempt to increase productivity.* It is also used in the phrase *in vain*, meaning 'to no avail': *She tried in vain to dissuade him.* *Vane* and *vein* are nouns: a *vane* is a flat blade moved by wind or water: *a weather vane*; a *vein* is a blood vessel, a thin layer of ore in rock, etc. *Vein* is also used in figurative contexts, referring to a style, mood, quality, or trait: *another remark in the same vein* *a vein of irony in the novel.*

vale or **veil**? *Vale* means 'valley' or 'dale': *The hill commands fine views of the vale.* It should not be confused with *veil*, which describes a fine layer of lace or other material masking a view:

432

• *The bride lifted her veil.* • *The mountains were hidden by a veil of mist.*

value-added The adjective *value-added*, meaning 'having extra value' or 'having extra features', has appeared with increasing frequency in recent years: • *value-added food products*, • *value-added services*. Care should be taken not to overuse the phrase in these figurative applications, as many people find it jargonistic.

vantage *see* **advantage** or **vantage**?

vaporise Note the spelling of the verb *vaporise*, meaning 'change into vapour'. The *-u-* of *vapour* is dropped before the suffix *-ize*. The variant spelling **vaporize** is equally correct (*see* **-ize** or **-ise**?).

variant CJD *see* **mad cow disease**

variegated This word, meaning 'having different colours; diverse': • *variegated leaves*, is sometimes misspelt. Note the *e* between the *i* and the *g*.

various Many people dislike the use of *various* as a pronoun, usually followed by *of*, and seek alternative wordings: • *He was betrayed by various of his colleagues.*

've *see* **of**.

veil *see* **vale** or **veil**?

vein *see* **vain, vane** or **vein**?

venal or **venial**? *Venal* means literally 'for sale' and is used either of individuals who are capable of being 'bought' or corrupted, or of systems which operate by bribery and corruption: • *Their legal system is so venal that criminals openly offer bribes in court*. *Venial* means 'pardonable; excusable' and is applied to minor faults and offences: • *He was inclined to be thoughtless but that was a venial fault in one so young.* In Roman Catholic theology a *venial sin* is one that does not deprive the soul of divine grace, as opposed to a mortal sin.

vengeance *see* **revenge** or **vengeance**?

venial *see* **venal** or **venial**?

venue The usual meaning of *venue* is 'the place where a meeting, event, or gathering happens': • *We have not yet decided on the venue for the annual conference.* There is a sense of people coming together to a particular place for a purpose. However, recent usage, to the dislike of some, makes *venue* virtually synonymous with *place*, *scene*, or *setting*, as the site of any activity: • *A valley in South Wales is the venue for this experiment in self-sufficient communal living.*

verbal or **oral**? *Verbal* means 'expressed in words', while oral means 'relating to the mouth' or 'expressed in speech'. Something *verbal* can be expressed in either speech or writing. However, a *verbal agreement* is generally understood to mean one that is spoken and not written. Some careful users feel that, despite the established use of *verbal* in this way, it is always better to use an *oral agreement*, as there is no risk of misunderstanding or ambiguity with the word *oral*.

verbal nouns *see* **infinitive**; **-ing forms**.

verbs *Verbs* refer to actions, occurrences, or existence. They vary in form according to the tense or mood used, usually in a predictable way but, with irregular verbs, in various different ways which need to be learned. Verbs differ in their functions. One distinction is between *transitive* and *intransitive verbs*. A transitive verb is one that needs a direct object – for example, *like*. A person cannot just 'like'; he or she has to like someone or something. Either it must take a direct object: * *He likes chocolate*, or it can be used in the passive: * *She is liked by everyone*. Intransitive verbs do not take a direct object. *Fall*, for example, is an intransitive verb: * *The leaves are falling from the trees*. Some verbs can be used both transitively and intransitively in different constructions: * *The boat sailed out of the harbour. – She sailed the boat out of the harbour.*

Some transitive verbs are *reflexive verbs*, where the subject and object are the same: * *perjure yourself*. In this example the verb is always reflexive; you cannot perjure anyone or anything other than yourself. But some verbs are not always used reflexively: * *I introduced myself to our hostess. – I introduced Chris to our hostess.*

Auxiliary verbs are those used with other verbs, enabling them to express variations in tense, mood, voice, etc. The most frequently used auxiliaries are *be, have*, and *do*: * *He is tired.* * *I have finished.* * *We did not agree.* Be is used to form the passive: * *It was discussed.* Other auxiliaries include: *shall, should, can, could, will, would, may, might*, and *must*: * *I shall accept the offer.* * *You must stop immediately.* This second group of auxiliary verbs, which cannot be used as full verbs

(unlike *be, have*, and *do*), are also called *modal verbs*.

Phrasal verbs are verbs that include an adverb, preposition, or both: * *give in* * *throw away* * *take to*. Many such verbs have meanings that go beyond the sum of their parts; for example, *came by*: * *I came by* [i.e. obtained or received] *that engraving in Venice*. Some mean no more than the words suggest: * *keep down* * *stay away*. Many users dislike the modern trend to extend ordinary verbs so that they become phrasal verbs, while adding nothing to their meaning: * *I consulted (with) my accountant*. New verbs are formed in various ways. One way is by converting nouns: * *He serviced her car* (*see* **nouns**). A variation of this is the formation of *compound verbs*: * *to rubber-stamp* * *blue-pencil* * *inflation-proof* * *top-score* * *fundraise* * *downgrade*. These verbs are often disliked when first introduced but they have the advantage of economy, if not of elegance. * *I shall word-process the letters* is briefer than *I shall produce the letters on a word processor*. For other ways of forming new verbs *see* **back formation**; **-ize** or **-ise**? *See also* **active**; **compound**; **dare**; **finite verb**; **infinitive**; **-ing forms**; **need**; **participles**; **passive**; **principal parts**; **subjunctive**; **tense**.

verbs – *see* **IRREGULAR VERBS** table, on pages 434–7.

vermilion The noun and adjective *vermilion*, meaning 'bright red', is sometimes misspelt. Note that *vermilion* has a single *l*, unlike the word *million*.

vertex or **vortex**? A *vertex* is the highest point or a point at which two or more lines intersect; a *vortex* is the spiralling

IRREGULAR VERBS

Cross-references – e.g. *see* **hanged** or **hung**? – to main entries in the *Good Word Guide* are also included where there is a fuller discussion.

Infinitive	Past tense	Past participle
abide	abode, abided	abode, abided
arise	arose	arisen
awake (*see* **awake**, **awaken**, **wake** or **waken**?)	awoke	awaked, awoken
be	was; were	been
bear	bore	borne
beat	beat (*see* **beat** or **beaten**?)	beaten
become	became	become
befall	befell	befallen
beget	begot	begotten
begin	began	begun
behold	beheld	beheld
bend	bent	bent
beseech	besought	besought
beset	beset	beset
bespeak	bespoke	bespoken
bet	bet, betted (*see* **bet** or **betted**?)	bet, betted
bid	bade, bid	bidden, bid
bide	bode, bided	bided
bind	bound	bound
bite	bit	bitten, bit
bleed	bled	bled
bless	blessed, blest (*see* **blessed**)	blessed, blest
blow	blew	blown
break	broke	broken

Infinitive	Past tense	Past participle
breed	bred	bred
bring	brought	brought
broadcast	broadcast, broadcasted	broadcast, broadcasted
build	built	built
burn	burnt, burned (*see* **burned** or **burnt**?)	burnt, burned
burst	burst	burst
buy	bought	bought
cast	cast	cast
catch	caught	caught
choose	chose	chosen
cleave	clove, cleft	cloven, cleft
cling	clung	clung
come	came	come
cost	cost	cost
creep	crept	crept
cut	cut	cut
deal	dealt	dealt
dig	dug	dug
do	did	done
draw	drew	drawn
dream	dreamt, dreamed (*see* **dreamed** or **dreamt**?)	dreamt, dreamed
drink	drank	drunk
drive	drove	driven
dwell	dwelt, dwelled (*see* **dwelled** or **dwelt**?)	dwelt, dwelled
eat	ate	eaten
fall	fell	fallen
feed	fed	fed
feel	felt	felt
fight	fought	fought
find	found	found

Infinitive	Past tense	Past participle
flee	fled	fled
fling	flung	flung
fly	flew	flown
forbear	forbore	forborne
forbid	forbade, forbad (see **forbade**)	forbidden
forecast	forecast, forecasted	forecast, forecasted
forget	forgot	forgotten
forgive	forgave	forgiven
forsake	forsook	forsaken
freeze	froze	frozen
get	got (see **got**)	got; gotten (American)
gild	gilded	gilded, gilt
gird	girded, girt	girded, girt
give	gave	given
go	went	gone
grind	ground	ground
grow	grew	grown
hang	hung, hanged (see **hanged** or **hung**?)	hung, hanged
have	had	had
hear	heard	heard
heave	heaved, hove (see **heaved** or **hove**?)	heaved, hove
hew	hewed	hewed, hewn
hide	hid	hidden
hit	hit	hit
hold	held	held
hurt	hurt	hurt
inlay	inlaid	inlaid
keep	kept	kept

Infinitive	Past tense	Past participle
kneel	knelt, kneeled (see **kneeled** or **knelt**?)	knelt, kneeled
knit	knitted, knit (see **knit** or **knitted**?)	knitted, knit
know	knew	known
lay (see **lay** or **lie**?)	laid	laid
lead	led	led
lean	leant, leaned (see **leaned** or **leant**?)	leant, leaned
leap	leapt, leaped (see **leaped** or **leapt**?)	leapt, leaped
learn	learnt, learned (see **learned** or **learnt**?)	learnt, learned
leave	left	left
lend	lent	lent
let	let	let
lie (see **lay** or **lie**?)	lay	lain
light	lighted, lit	lighted, lit
lose	lost	lost
make	made	made
mean	meant	meant
meet	met	met
mislay	mislaid	mislaid
mislead	misled	misled
mistake	mistook	mistaken
misunderstand	misunderstood	misunderstood
mow	mowed	mown, mowed (see **mowed** or **mown**?)
overtake	overtook	overtaken

Infinitive	Past tense	Past participle
partake	partook	partaken
pay	paid	paid
plead	pleaded, pled (see **pleaded** or **pled**?)	pleaded, pled
prove	proved	proved, proven (see **proved** or **proven**?)
put	put	put
quit	quitted, quit (see **quit** or **quitted**?)	quitted, quit
read	read [red]	read [red]
rend	rent	rent
ride	rode	ridden
ring	rang (see **ringed**, **rang** or **rung**?)	rung
rise	rose	risen
run	ran	run
saw	sawed	sawn
say	said	said
see	saw	seen
seek	sought	sought
sell	sold	sold
send	sent	sent
set	set	set
sew	sewed	sewn, sewed
shake	shook	shaken
shear	sheared	shorn, sheared
shed	shed	shed
shine	shone, shined	shone, shined
shoe	shod	shod
shoot	shot	shot
show	showed	shown, showed

Infinitive	Past tense	Past participle
shrink	shrank, shrunk (see **shrunk**, **shrank**, **shrunk** or **shrunken**?)	shrunk
shut	shut	shut
sing	sang	sung
sink	sank, sunk (see **sank**, **sunk** or **sunken**?)	sunk
sit	sat	sat
slay	slew	slain
sleep	slept	slept
slide	slid	slid
sling	slung	slung
slink	slunk	slunk
slit	slit	slit
smell	smelt, smelled (see **smelled** or **smelt**?)	smelt, smelled
smite	smote	smitten
sow	sowed (see **sowed** or **sown**?)	sown, sowed
speak	spoke	spoken
speed	sped, speeded (see **speeded** or **sped**?)	sped, speeded
spell	spelt, spelled (see **spelled** or **spelt**?)	spelt, spelled
spend	spent	spent
spill	spilt, spilled (see **spilled** or **spilt**?)	spilt, spilled
spin	spun, span (see **spun** or **span**?)	spun

Infinitive	Past tense	Past participle
spit	spat	spat
split	split	split
spoil	spoilt, spoiled (see **spoiled** or **spoilt**?)	spoilt, spoiled
spread	spread	spread
spring	sprang	sprung
stand	stood	stood
stave	staved, stove	staved, stove
steal	stole	stolen
stick	stuck	stuck
sting	stung	stung
stink	stank, stunk (see **stank** or **stunk**?)	stunk
strew	strewed	strewn, strewed
stride	strode	stridden
strike	struck	struck
string	strung	strung
strive	strove	striven
swear	swore	sworn
sweep	swept	swept
swell	swelled (see **swelled** or **swollen**?)	swollen, swelled
swim	swam (see **swam** or **swum**?)	swum
swing	swung	swung
take	took	taken
teach	taught	taught
tear	tore	torn
tell	told	told
think	thought	thought
thrive	throve, thrived	thriven, thrived

Infinitive	Past tense	Past participle
throw	threw	thrown
thrust	thrust	thrust
tread	trod	trodden, trod
unbend	unbent	unbent
undergo	underwent	undergone
understand	understood	understood
undertake	undertook	undertaken
underwrite	underwrote	under-written
undo	undid	undone
upset	upset	upset
wake (see **awake**, **awaken**, **wake** or **waken**?)	woke, waked	waked, woken
wear	wore	worn
weave	wove, weaved	woven
wed	wedded, wed (see **wed** or **wedded**?)	wedded, wed
weep	wept	wept
win	won	won
wind	wound	wound
withdraw	withdrew	withdrawn
withhold	withheld	withheld
withstand	withstood	withstood
wring	wrung	wrung
write	wrote	written

motion of a whirlpool or whirlwind or, metaphorically, an activity that draws people or things into it like a whirlpool or whirlwind: * the vertex of a triangle * the vortex of rebellion. The plural of *vertex* is *vertexes* or *vertices*; the plural of *vortex* is *vortexes* or *vortices*.

very *Very* can be used as an intensifier before most adjectives and adverbs: * *very unpleasant* * *very efficiently.* However, before past participles, *much* is used instead of *very*: * *It was much improved.* The exception is when the past participle is used adjectivally: * *She was very excited.* Some words come into a grey area where either *very* or *much* can be used: * *She was very/much distressed.* *Much* usually has a more formal sound. There are other participles which cannot take either *very* or *much* as an intensifier, although they can take *very* if an adverb is interposed: a person cannot be *very wounded* but can be *very badly wounded*; it is impossible to say *very mended* but possible to say *very neatly mended.*

veterinary This word causes problems with spelling and pronunciation. Note the *-erin-* and the *-ary* ending. The word is frequently pronounced [vetĕnri], [vetĕnĕri], or [vetrinri], although careful users insist on the pronunciation with five syllables: [vetĕrinĕri]. The expression *veterinary surgeon* is usually shortened to *vet.*

via *Via* means 'by way of' and is used when talking of the route for a journey: * *They went to Australia via Hong Kong.* * *Your best route would be via the M6.* It is also used to mean 'by means of': * *I'll return it via Fred*, or to speak of a means of transport: * *We crossed the Channel via the ferry*, but many people dislike these usages, particularly the latter.

The pronunciation normally regarded as correct is [vīă], although [veeă] is sometimes heard.

viable *Viable* means 'capable of living or surviving independently': * *a viable*

foetus. In this sense it can be used figuratively of new communities: * *When the colony shows itself to be viable, it will be granted independence.* The meaning has been extended to 'capable of carrying on without extra (financial) support': * *The business is expected to be commercially viable within two years.*

Sometimes the meaning is even further extended to become synonymous with *workable, practicable, feasible*: * *a viable partnership* * *a viable plan*, but many people object to this loose usage.

vice versa This expression, meaning 'with the order reversed', is usually pronounced [vīsĕ versă]. Alternative pronunciations for the first word are [vīsi] and [vīs].

vicious or **viscous**? *Vicious* means 'wicked' or 'ferocious'; *viscous* describes a liquid that is thick and sticky: * *a vicious dog* * *viscous paint.* The two adjectives are sometimes confused, being similar in form and pronunciation. The *c* of *vicious* is soft [vishŭs]; the *c* of *viscous* is hard [viskŭs]. The word *viscous* is largely restricted to formal or technical contexts.

The word *vicious* also occurs in the expression *vicious circle*, denoting a problematic situation that creates new problems leading back to the original situation: * *the vicious circle of debt.* This is often incorrectly rendered as *vicious cycle.*

victuals This word, meaning 'supplies of food', is pronounced [vitlz]. A *victualler*, 'a licensed purveyor of spirits', is pronounced [vitlĕr].

video- The prefix *video-*, from the Latin *videre* meaning 'to see', is found in such words as *video-recorder, video-phone*, and *video-camera*. It is increasingly used in the senses of 'relating to video' or 'by video', sometimes hyphenated and sometimes unhyphenated: * *videolink* * *Video-conferencing is the latest factor in revolutionising boardroom practice around the world.*

vigorous This word, meaning 'healthy and strong', is often misspelt. Note that the *u* of *vigour* is dropped before the suffix *-ous*.

vilify Note the spelling of this verb, used in formal contexts to mean 'malign; defame', particularly the single *l*.

virtual The word *virtual* has acquired new relevance with the development of computer technology, being used to describe the hypothetical environments created by computer games, the Internet, etc.: * *virtual community* * *virtual classroom* * *virtual advertising*. Care must be taken with the use of *virtual* and *virtually* in this and other senses, to avoid ambiguity. *Virtual reality* originally referred chiefly to interactive computer games, where the player's movements may be mirrored by a character in a hypothetical computer-generated world. The phrase has since come to be used more widely, in particular to television shows that invite some degree of viewer participation: * *Television ratings on both sides of the Atlantic are now dominated by the virtual-reality game show.*

virus A virus is the causative agent of a disease, but the word is frequently used of the disease itself: * *He's recovering from a very nasty virus.* The word is also often used in a metaphorical sense for an influence or ideology that is thought to be corrupting people's minds: * *the virus of anti-Semitism that spread throughout Germany in the 1930s.* In computing, it denotes a code or program that can spread through a computer system, corrupting or destroying data.

vis-à-vis *Vis-à-vis* literally means 'face to face' and is most frequently used as a preposition to mean 'in relation to': * *We shall have to change our policy vis-à-vis the law.* It also means 'opposite' or 'face to face with' and is sometimes used as a noun to mean 'someone or something opposite another; a counterpart'. It is also occasionally used as a synonym for *tête-à-tête*, meaning 'a private conversation between two people'. It is pronounced [veezahvee].

viscous *see* **vicious** or **viscous?**

visible There is a recent fashionable use of *visible* to mean 'in the public eye; well known': * *He's one of the more visible cabinet ministers.* It can also be more or less synonymous with having a high profile, with the meaning of 'being in a position where a person's actions are liable to become subject to public comment or notice': * *The role of Director of Social Services is an increasingly visible one.* As some object to these uses of *visible*, care should be taken to avoid overworking this word.

vision statement *see* **mission statement.**

visit or **visitation?** In its most frequent use, *visit* is a verb meaning 'pay a call on, stay with as a guest, stay somewhere temporarily' and a noun meaning 'an act of visiting': * *I will visit Venice when I am in Italy.* * *He was on a visit to his daughter.* A *visitation* is an official or formal act of visiting: * *The vicar's work includes the visitation of parishioners in hospital,* and is often found in humorous use, referring to an unwelcome visit: * *I'm awaiting a visitation from the VAT man. Visitation* can also refer to the visit of a supernatural being: * *a visitation of angels,* and is also used in referring to an act of affliction, either natural or divine: * *the visitation of the Black Death* * *the visitation of God's wrath.*

visually impaired *Visually impaired* is the preferred modern alternative to *blind,* which is considered unacceptable by many people because of its negative connotations.

vital The adjective *vital* is followed by the preposition *to* or *for:* * *Their co-operation is vital to* [or *for*] *the success of the mission.*

vitamin The traditional British pronunciation of this word is [*vĭt*ămin]. The American English pronunciation [*vī*tămin], the first syllable of which rhymes with *bite,* is now acceptable in British English, although disliked by some people.

voluntarily Careful users of British English stress this word on the first syllable [*vol*ĕntĕrili]. Such users object to the alternative pronunciation, with stress on the third syllable [volĕn*te*rili], though this is acceptable in American English.

vortex *see* **vertex** or **vortex**?

vote The idiomatic expression *to vote with your feet* means to show disapproval of something by staying away, not participating in it, not buying it and so on. The underlying image is of a dissatisfied crowd of people walking out of an auditorium or a hall. Recently it has been used in an opposite sense meaning to show approval by attending or taking something up in large numbers, but this is strictly incorrect.

vowel A *vowel* is the sound represented by any of the letters *a, e, i, o,* and *u* in the English language. The presence of a vowel at the beginning of a word may affect the form or pronunciation of the preceding word (*see* **a** or **an**?; **the**).

Note that in such words as * *unit* and * *uranium,* the letter *u-* produces the combined consonant and vowel sound [yoō]. *Compare* **consonant.**

W

w- or wh-? The spellings of words beginning with *w-* and *wh-* are easily confused, since the majority of English speakers pronounce them the same (exceptions include Scottish speakers of English). Examples of such confusable words include *which* and *witch*, *watt* and *what*, and *while* and *wile*, all of which have different meanings. Note that a small number of words can be spelt either way with the same meaning, e.g. *wacky/whacky*, *weal/wheal*.

wage, wages *see* **salary** or **wage**?

waist or **waste**? These two words are occasionally confused since they are pronounced the same [wayst]. *Waist* refers to that part of the body between the ribs and the hips and thus to any similar narrow part of something: * *The dancer had a tiny waist.* It should not be confused with *waste*, which as a noun means 'rubbish' or 'unwanted material': * *The process creates little waste*, and as a verb, 'squander': * *to waste well-earned money.*

wait or **weight**? These two words are occasionally confused since they are pronounced the same [wayt]. *Wait* means 'stay' or 'delay action': * *They waited until the parade had passed.* It should not be confused with *weight*, which is chiefly used as a noun meaning 'heaviness' or 'relative mass': * *He took the weight of the sack on his shoulders*, and is also used as a verb (*see*

weigh or **weight**?). *See also* **await** or **wait**?

waiter or **waitress**? *see* **non-sexist terms**.

waive or **wave**? These two words are sometimes confused. The verb *waive* means 'relinquish': * *The judge waived the penalty*; *wave* means 'move to and fro': * *wave goodbye* * *The corn waved in the wind.* The noun *wave* means 'ridge of water'. The noun *waiver* comes from the verb *waive*: * *a waiver clause in a contract.* It must not be confused with the verb *waver*, which means 'fluctuate or hesitate; become unsteady': * *Throughout his suffering his faith never wavered.* * *a wavering voice.*

wake, waken *see* **awake, awaken, wake** or **waken**?

wander or **wonder**? These spellings are sometimes confused. *Wander* means 'roam aimlessly': * *He wandered through the streets*; *wonder* means 'be astonished at' or 'think about': * *I wonder where she is.* The pronunciation of wander is [*wond*ĕr]; the pronunciation of *wonder* [*wund*ĕr] rhymes with *thunder*.

wannabee A *wannabee* is a person who strives to emulate another, especially a young fan who mimics a famous person in appearance, behaviour, etc.: * *a horde of Madonna wannabees.* The

442

word *wannabee*, from the phrase *(I) want to be (like...)*, is sometimes spelt *wannabe*. It is best restricted to informal contexts.

want As a verb the main meanings of *want* are 'to desire': * *I want a bigger car*, 'to need': * *That door wants mending*, and 'to lack': * *The door wants a handle*. As a noun it means 'something desired; a desire for something; a lack' or is used as a synonym for poverty: * *the want experienced by the unemployed*. *Want to* is often used in informal contexts to mean 'ought to': * *You want to be more careful*. There is controversy over whether *want* can be used with a present participle, as in: * *I want my hair cutting*; this usage is a standard regional variation in British English, although more people would say *I want my hair cut*. This latter form can lead to ambiguity: * *I want the picture fixing on the wall* is clearer than * *I want the picture fixed on the wall*, which could indicate a desire for a particular picture. * *I want the picture to be fixed on the wall* is unambiguous and avoids the use of the present participle, which is generally considered unsuitable for any but informal use.

-ward or **-wards**? The adverbial suffixes **-ward** and **-wards** are used to indicate direction. Both forms are equally correct, although *-wards* is usually preferred in British English and *-ward* in American English. Most of these adverbs have a related adjective ending in *-ward*. The adjectival suffix cannot be replaced by *-wards*.

For further discussion and additional information, *see* **afterward** or **afterwards**?; **backward** or **backwards**?; and other individual entries.

ware or **where**? *Ware* is usually used in the plural, meaning 'goods' or 'products': * *Customers flocked to see the company's wares*. It should not be confused with *where*, meaning 'to or at what place': * *Let me show you where to go*.

-ware or **-wear**? The ending *-ware* denotes goods of the specified type or material; the ending *-wear* denotes clothing: * *glassware* * *computer software* * *knitwear* * *leather footwear*. The two endings are sometimes confused: * *Dawn French, who is planning to open a knitware shop* (*The Bookseller*). In computing, the ending *-ware* has been used to coin a number of nouns on the model of *hardware* and *software*. These include: * *groupware* (a set of related software) * *courseware* (educational software) * *vapourware* (software that has yet to be produced) * *liveware* (human beings).

warn or **worn**? These two words are occasionally confused since they are pronounced the same [worn]. *Warn* means 'caution' or 'advise of danger': * *They were warned about their behaviour*. It should not be confused with *worn*, the past participle of *wear*, which is also used as an adjective: * *That tyre is badly worn*.

was *see* **were** or **was**?

wastage or **waste**? *Waste* is used as a verb, noun, and adjective. As a noun its main meanings are 'squandering, using carelessly or ungainfully': * *It was a complete waste of time and money*; or 'rubbish; unwanted material': * *Get rid of all this waste*. *Wastage* is a noun meaning 'loss due to leakage, decay, erosion, evaporation, etc.' * *the wastage of water from a reservoir* * *Petrol stored*

in garages is subject to wastage.
Another meaning, usually occurring
in the phrase *natural wastage*, refers to
the loss of employees through resignation, retirement, or death. *Wastage*
is sometimes used as a synonym for
waste but it should be confined to the
meanings outlined above.

waste *see* **waist** or **waste**?

watercooler TV The term *watercooler
TV* refers to popular television programmes that are the subject of informal conversation among friends or
work colleagues (i.e. the sort of programmes that people talk about
around the office watercooler). These
may be soap operas, reality TV shows,
situation comedies, etc.; the term is
generally not applied to documen-
taries or current-affairs programmes
that would provoke more serious
discussion.

wave, **waver** *see* **waive** or **wave**?

way The use of *way* as an adverb, meaning 'considerably', is best restricted to
informal contexts: ● *The film is way
too long.* ● *Her hair is way too short.* It
should also be restricted to very informal contexts when used as an adverb
meaning 'extremely': ● *That's a way
cool jacket.*

-ways *see* **-wise** or **-ways**?

we *We* is used to mean 'I and one or
more other people': ● *We should get a
divorce.* ● *Shall we all go for a walk?* It
was formerly used by monarchs to
mean 'I': ● *We grant by royal decree...*,
and is sometimes used by writers to
give an impression of impersonality: ●
We shall discuss this in a later chapter.

We may be used to mean 'you', usually
in addressing children or invalids in a
somewhat patronising manner: ● *We
are in a nasty temper today, aren't we?* ●
Are we feeling better this morning?

Mistakes are sometimes made in
the use of *we* and *us*. *We* is correct
with a plural noun as the subject: ●
We children used to play there. Us is
correct when the noun is the object: ●
It won't help us workers.

weal, **wheal** or **wheel**? The noun *wheel*,
denoting a circular object, is by far
the most common of these three
words: ● *the wheels of a bicycle* ● *a
steering wheel* ● *a spinning wheel.* The
nouns *weal* and *wheal* are interchangeable in the sense of 'raised
mark on the skin (usually caused by a
blow from a whip, cane, etc.)', *weal*
being the more common: ● *The weals
[or wheals] on his back suggested that
he had been beaten. Weal* is also an
archaic or literary word meaning 'welfare' or 'prosperity': ● *the public weal* ●
the common weal.

-wear *see* **ware** or **wear**?

weather, **wether** or **whether**? These
three spellings are sometimes confused. The noun *weather* (*see* **weather
conditions**) and the conjunction
whether are far more common than
the noun *wether*, which denotes a
(castrated) male sheep.

weather conditions *Weather* means 'the
condition of the atmosphere, especially in respect of sunshine, rainfall,
wind, etc.'. As the word contains condition in its meaning, careful users
maintain that it is tautological to talk
of *weather conditions*, as in: ● *The bad
weather conditions stopped play.* ● *The*

freezing weather conditions in the north will not improve.

weatherman or **weathergirl**? *see* **non-sexist terms**.

weaved, **wove** or **woven**? The usual past tense of the verb weave is *wove*: * *She wove the cloth herself.* * *The spider wove its web. Woven* is the usual past participle: * *It was woven by hand.* * *They were wearing woven garments.* In some senses of *weave*, *weaved* is used for the past tense or past participle, as when *weave* means 'contrive or produce a complicated story': * *She weaved a sinister plot*; 'lurch or stagger': * *He weaved drunkenly down the street*; and 'move around vehicles to avoid hitting them': * *The car weaved in and out of all the traffic.*

web *see* **World Wide Web**.

weblish *see* **netspeak**.

wed or **wedded**? The use of the verb wed in the sense of 'marry' is rather old-fashioned, formal, or literary; in modern usage it is chiefly found in newspaper headlines: * *Doctor weds former patient.* Either *wed* or *wedded* may be used as the past tense or past participle of the verb in this sense: * *They wed [or wedded] the following spring.* * *They were wed [or wedded] by her uncle.* When the past participle is used adjectivally (often in combination with an adverb), *wed* is preferred to *wedded*: * *the newlywed couple* * *her twice-wed father.* In the formal and figurative sense of 'committed' or 'closely connected', the past participle *wedded* is preferred to *wed*: * *He seems wedded to the idea.* * *Malnutrition is wedded to poverty.*

Wednesday The name of this day of the week is usually pronounced [*wen*zdi], although careful users prefer to sound the *d* [*wed*nzdi] or [*wed*nzday].

weigh or **weight**? To *weigh* is to measure the weight of something; to *weight* is to add weight to something: * *The box weighs 3 kg.* * *We weighted the tarpaulin with stones so that it would not blow away.* Both words may be used in the figurative sense of 'oppress': * *They were weighed/ weighted down with problems.*

Weigh is the more frequent of the two verbs, being used in a variety of other senses: * *to weigh* ['raise'] *anchor* * *to weigh up* ['assess'] *the pros and cons* * *to weigh* ['consider carefully'] *one's words.* The verb *weight* is also used in the sense of 'bias': * *The legislation must not be weighted towards the rich.* A London *weighting* allowance is an extra sum of money paid to some people who work in London, where the cost of living is high.

Note the *-eigh-* spelling of the two words. *Weight* is sometimes misspelt with the ending *-th*, on the model of length, width, etc. *See also* **wait** or **weight**?

weird This word, meaning 'uncanny or extraordinary', is sometimes misspelt. Note the *-ei-* spelling.

well *see* **as well as**; **good** or **well**?

well or **well-**? When used as part of an adjectival compound, such as *well-aimed*, whether *well* is hyphenated or not depends on its position in relation to the noun or verb in the sentence. If placed before the noun, a hyphen is usual: * *a well-aimed remark.* If placed after the verb, it is usual to omit the hyphen: • *Her remarks were well aimed.*

were or **was**? Difficulty is sometimes experienced in the use of the subjunctive form *were* in phrases expressing supposition. The basic rule is to use *were* when the suggestion is of something hypothetical, unlikely, or not actually the case: • *If I were you, I'd leave him.* • *She talks to me as if I were three years old.* If the supposition is factual or realistic, *was* is used: • *I'm sorry if I was rude.* When a supposition might be possible or factual then either *was* or *were* may be used: • *They behaved as if it was/were their own house.* The more doubt there is, the more appropriate it is to use *were.*

west, West or **western**? As an adjective, *west* is always written with a capital *W* when it forms part of a proper name: • *the West End* • *the West Country.* The noun *west* is usually written with a capital *W* when it denotes a specific region, such as the non-communist countries of Europe and America: • *She defected to the West in 1986.* In other contexts, and as an adverb, *west* is usually written with a lower-case *w*: • *Drive west until you reach the border.* • *We camped on the west bank of the river.* • *The sun sets in the west.*
   The adjective *western* is more frequent and usually less specific than the adjective *west*: • *the western side of the island* • *in western Scotland.* Like *west, western* is written with a capital *W* when it forms part of a proper name, such as *Western Australia.* With or without a capital W, it also means 'of the West': • *western/Western technology.* A *western* is a film, novel, etc. about life in the western USA in the 19th century.

westward or **westwards**? *Westward* is the correct choice when an adjective is needed: • *a westward direction.* Either *westward* or *westwards* may be used when an adverb is required: • *They travelled westward from the city.* *The skies were full of birds flying westwards. See also* **-ward** or **-wards**?

wet or **wetted**? The verb *to wet* means 'make wet': • *Don't keep wetting your lips,* and 'urinate in or on something': • *Children often wet their beds when they are anxious.* The usual past tense or participle is *wet*: • *The baby has wet its nappy again.* However, in the passive, *wetted* is used. *The sheets have been wetted* is less ambiguous than *the sheets have been wet.*

wet or **whet**? These two spellings are sometimes confused. *Wet* means 'cover with moisture': • *to wet one's lips*; *whet* means 'stimulate or sharpen': • *whet someone's appetite.* A *whetstone* is a stone used for sharpening knives, etc.; a *wet stone* is simply a stone that is damp.

wether *see* **weather, wether** or **whether**?

wetted *see* **wet** or **wetted**?

wh- *see* **w-** or **wh-**?

whammy *see* **double whammy**.

wharfs or **wharves**? Either *wharfs* or *wharves* is acceptable as the plural of the noun *wharf,* denoting a place where ships dock for loading and unloading. *Wharves* is the more usual form.

what A difficulty in the use of the pronoun *what* is whether it should be followed by a singular or plural verb. In general, the rule is that when *what* means 'that which' it takes a singular verb, even if the complement is plural, and when it means 'those which' it takes a plural verb: * *What we need is a ladder.* * *What he likes best is expensive restaurants.* * *I mentioned what I thought were the most important points.* *What* cannot follow a noun or pronoun. Constructions such as: * *the man what I was talking to* are wrong.

what or **which**? In a question, the use of *what* or *which* affects the interpretation of the meaning. *Which* chooses from a limited range of alternatives; *what* is used in more general enquiries. Thus * *Which film are you going to see?* suggests that the speaker has several possible films in mind; whereas * *What film are you going to see?* shows that the speaker is probably unaware of the choice of the various films.

whatever or **what ever**? If *ever* is used to intensify *what*, the expression is written as two words in formal writing: * *What ever* ['What on earth'] *did he say next?* In less formal writing, one word is sometimes used, but careful writers object to this. If *whatever* means 'no matter what', it is written as one word: * *I'll write whatever I like.* * *Whatever the weather he always wears a vest.* * *There is no chance whatever of him winning.* A similar rule applies to the use of *how ever* and *however*, *when ever* and *whenever*, *where ever* and *wherever*, *which ever* and *whichever*, and *who ever* and *whoever*. * *How ever did you find out?* – *However carefully I wash my hair, it always looks untidy.* * *Where ever did*

you buy such a hat? – *Wherever you travel, you'll find businesses that accept our credit card.* * *Who ever told you that?* – *Whoever wrote this had a strange sense of humour.*

wheal, wheel *see* **weal, wheal** or **wheel**?

whence *Whence* is a formal, rarely used word meaning 'from where; from what place': * *The monster returned to the swamp whence it had appeared. From whence* is more frequently used; as in: * *The country from whence they came*, although the *from* is redundant, being contained in the meaning of *whence*, and many people consider *from whence* to be incorrect. However, as *whence* is now a word whose use tends to sound old-fashioned, affected, or jocular, it is probably better to avoid both *whence* and *from whence* altogether. *See also* **hence; thence.**

whenever or **when ever**? *see* **whatever** or **what ever**?

where *see* **ware** or **where**?

whereabouts The noun *whereabouts*, meaning 'place where somebody or something is', may be used with a singular or plural verb: * *The whereabouts of the original manuscript remains* [or *remain*] *a secret.* * *Her whereabouts are* [or *is*] *unknown.*

wherever or **where ever**? *see* **whatever** or **what ever**?

whet *see* **wet** or **whet**?

whether *Whether* can be used to introduce an indirect question: * *He asked whether we were going.* Here it is synonymous with *if* but sounds rather more formal. *Whether* is also used to introduce alternatives or consider possibilities and is virtually interchangeable with *if*: • *I wonder whether/if she'll come.* • *I don't know whether/if it is correct.* In these cases there is some confusion concerning the use of *whether or not*, as in: • *He has not decided whether* (or *not*) *to stay.* Here, where the sense is 'if he is staying', the *or not* can be considered redundant; it is only necessary when the sense is 'regardless of whether or not', as in: • *He has decided to stay, whether or not he can afford it. See also* **weather**, **wether** or **whether**?

which *see* **that** or **which**?; **what** or **which**?

while or **whilst**? As a conjunction *while* means 'during the time that; as long as'; it is also used to mean 'although; whereas': • *I shall be doing his work while he's away on holiday.* • *Elizabeth votes Labour while her husband votes Conservative. Whilst* has the same meanings but is rarely used; it tends to sound formal and old-fashioned. Many people dislike the use of *while* or *whilst* in the sense of 'although; whereas', as it can give rise to ambiguity. • *While she was studying literature she disliked poetry* could mean 'during the time she was studying literature' or 'although she was studying literature'.

whisky or **whiskey**? The alcoholic drink distilled in Scotland is spelt *whisky*, which is the more frequent spelling in British English. The alcoholic drink distilled in the USA or Ireland is spelt *whiskey*, the usual spelling in American English.

white As a term describing skin colour, *white* is less contentious than *non-white* (*see* **non-**), but is still avoided by some users. An alternative is to refer to a person's geographical origin, rather than his or her skin colour: • *Europeans are a minority in this part of the world.*

who The pronoun *who* is normally used in reference to human beings (*which* being used for non-humans): • *the man who runs the shop.* However, it is acceptable to use *who* in referring to animals, to countries in certain contexts, and to a group of people, especially when taking a plural verb: • *cats who refuse to eat leftovers* • *Greece, who joined the European Community in 1981* • *the band who plays the loudest. That* can be used to refer to human beings and things in defining clauses (*see* **that** or **which**?): • *the man that* [or *who*] *runs the shop* • *the band that* [or *who* or *which*] *plays the loudest* • *the woman that* [or *who*, or the formally correct *whom*] *you just saw.*

Care must be taken with the punctuation of phrases containing *who*. • *The boys, who attend public schools, regularly drink in pubs* changes its meaning if the commas are omitted. Without the commas, *who* introduces a restrictive (or defining) clause, suggesting *specific boys*: those that attend public school. With commas, the additional clause merely adds extra information about the boys.

who or **whom**? *Who* is used when it is the subject of a verb and *whom* when it is the object of a verb or preposition: • *the boy who delivers the papers* • *the woman whom you just saw* • *the people to whom I was talking. Whom* is falling into disuse, especially in questions. * *Whom did you give it to?* is formally correct but most people would now use *who*. As a relative pronoun, *whom* should still be used, when correct, in formal writing. While many careful users feel that it is important to use *whom* when it is correct to do so, most would consider that the use of *who* for *whom* is far less of a mistake than the use of *whom* when *who* is correct, as in: * *The children, whom she thought were dead, had been saved*. The temptation is to use *whom* because it is felt that this is the object of *she thought*, but it is not. *She thought* is a more or less independent part of the sentence; it could even be moved to another part of the sentence. It is not an object of *she thought* that is needed, but a subject (*who*) of the phrase *were dead*.

whodunit This word, used in informal contexts to describe a detective story, may be spelt *whodunit* or, less frequently, *whodunnit*. It is, of course, an abbreviation of the ungrammatical *who done it?*

whoever or **who ever**? *see* **whatever** or **what ever**?

whoever or **whomever**? Many users are unclear about the difference between these two words. Both mean 'whatever person'; *whoever*, like *who* (see **who** or **whom**?), is used as the subject of a verb: * *Whoever broke it must pay for the repair*, and *whomever*, like *whom*, is used as the object of a verb or preposition: * *Bring whomever you want to the party*. Since it sounds very formal, *whomever* has become relatively rare and is now commonly replaced by *whoever*.

wholly *see* **holy**, **holey** or **wholly**?; **spelling**.

whom *see* **who** or **whom**?

whomever *see* **whoever** or **whomever**?

whoop This word, meaning 'express delight', as in: * *Sally whooped excitedly*, is sometimes mispronounced. The correct pronunciation is [woop]; note, however, that whooping as in whooping cough is pronounced [hooping].

whose or **who's**? These spellings are sometimes confused. *Whose* means 'of whom' or 'of which': * *the children, whose father had left them* * *political parties whose ideas are old-fashioned* * *Whose book is that? Who's* is a contraction of *who is* or *who has*: * *Who's coming to dinner tonight?* Some people object to the use of *whose* in the sense of 'of which', referring to things rather than people: * *an old teapot, the handle of which* [not *whose handle*] *had been broken for many years*. Others, however, find the construction *the... of which* an unnecessarily wordy substitute for *whose*....

wicked Like **bad**, the adjective *wicked* is used as a slang term of approval, especially by young people: * *His new bike is well wicked*. Jonathon Green in *Neologisms: new words since 1960* comments on its origin: 'The term has arrived via two borrowings: the first from standard English via black Americans, and subsequently by the white young from their black counterparts.'

wilful Note the spelling of this word, which has a single *l* in the middle and at the end in British English. In American English the -ll ending of *will* is retained in the spelling *willful*.

will *see* **shall** or **will**?

window *Window* has various well-established metaphorical uses. It can mean 'something that allows people to see something they might otherwise not see': * *The programme is a window on the closed world of the monastery*; or 'an opportunity to display something': * *The exhibition is the annual window of domestic design*. A more recent use is 'a gap; an interval of time': * *a window of opportunity*, though care should be taken to avoid overworking this expression: * *Is there a window in my diary next week for that meeting with Dempster?* (Vodafone advertisement, *Daily Telegraph*). * *There should be a clear window between the arrival of the interim report and the publication of the final conclusions*.

-wise or **-ways**? The suffix *-ways* combines with certain abstract nouns to form an adverb meaning 'in (such) a way, direction, or manner': * *sideways* * *lengthways*. It has a more limited use than *-wise*, which can combine with various nouns to mean either 'in the position or direction of': * *clockwise* * *lengthwise* or 'in the manner of': * *to walk crabwise*. The use of *-wise* to mean 'in respect of' in such expressions as: * *moneywise* * *weatherwise* * *careerwise* * *taxwise* * *performancewise* is becoming increasingly popular, but is disliked by many people.

with When a singular subject is linked to something else by *with* it should take a singular verb: * *The Prime Minister with senior members of the*

Cabinet has been considering the problem. The same rule applies even when a singular subject comprises several individuals or entities: * *The band with members of the road crew has been given rooms at a local hotel*. The usual pronunciation in British English is [widh]; [with] is a regional variation.

withhold This word, meaning 'keep back', is sometimes misspelt. Note the *-hh-* in the middle of this word, unlike in the word *threshold*. The correct pronunciation [widh*hōld*] should ensure that the word is spelt correctly.

woman As a general term for an adult female human being, *woman* is more acceptable than *female*, *girl*, or *lady*. * *The prize was won by a woman from Brighton*. The noun *female* (*see* **female** or **feminine**?) is best reserved for animals and plants. It may be applied to human beings when the question of age makes *woman* or *women* inappropriate: * *He shares the house with five females: his wife and their four young daughters*. In most other cases it is considered inelegant, contemptuous, or offensive. As an adjective, however, *female* is only marginally less acceptable than *woman* and is preferable to *lady*: * *There are two female doctors and one male doctor at the local surgery*. * *Female drivers do not have more road accidents than male drivers*.

A *girl* is a female child or adolescent. The term is often used as a synonym for 'woman' but is considered patronising or disrespectful by some people in some contexts, especially when used by men.

The word *lady* has connotations of nobility, dignity, and good manners: * *the Lady of the manor*. * *She may be* wealthy but she's no lady! It is used in polite address, as in formal or official contexts: * This lady would like to speak to the manager. * Ladies and gentlemen... * Give that lady your seat. However, it is sometimes regarded as a term of condescension, especially in such phrases as the cleaning lady, which may be replaced by the cleaning woman or, more simply, the cleaner.

As a general rule, female, girl, and lady are best restricted to contexts where male, boy, or gentleman would be used of the opposite sex. See also man; non-sexist terms; sexism.

wonder The verb wonder is followed by the preposition at in the sense of 'marvel': * I wondered at his strength, and by about in the sense of 'speculate': * I wondered about the reason for his departure. See also **wander** or **wonder**?

wont This old-fashioned word is used to mean 'inclined or accustomed': * They were wont to have tea at 4 o'clock every day, and in the expression as is one's wont. Its pronunciation is the same as that of the word won't: [wōnt].

wood or **would**? Wood refers to trees or timber: * They entered the wood. * The frame is made of wood. It should not be confused with the modal verb would: * She would not do as she was told.

woolly Note the spelling of this word: -oo- and -ll- in British English; -oo- and a single l in American English. Similarly, the adjective woollen has -ll- in British English and a single l in American English.

workman or **workwoman**? see **non-sexist terms**.

World Wide Web The term World Wide Web (commonly referred to simply as the web) describes the global network of computers linked by the **Internet**. In practice, the term is generally treated as synonymous with Internet or net, although some people make a distinction between the World Wide Web (the mass of documents and other material available by such electronic means) and the Internet (the actual connections between these sites). In electronic addresses World Wide Web is abbreviated to www; in other contexts it is usually abbreviated to WWW.

worn see **warn** or **worn**?

worship The single final p doubles in front of most suffixes beginning with a vowel in British English: * worshipped * worshipper * worshipping. American English retains the single p. Worshipful always retains the single p. See also **spelling**.

worthwhile or **worth while**? The traditional rule is that this expression is written as two words after a verb and as one word in front of a noun: * It is worth while spending a little more money. * a project that is worth while — a worthwhile project. Increasingly, however, the tendency is to write this expression as one word in all contexts.

would see **of**; **should** or **would**?; **wood** or **would**?

wove, woven see **weaved, wove** or **woven**?

wrack see **rack** or **wrack**?

wrapped *see* **rapt** or **wrapped?**

wreak *see* **reek** or **wreak?**

wreath or **wreathe?** *Wreath* is a noun describing a circular garland of flowers and foliage of the type commonly displayed at funerals: ● *There was a single wreath on the coffin. Wreathe* is a verb meaning 'encircle' or 'twist': ● *The mist wreathed around the trees. Wreath* is pronounced [reeth], while *wreathe* is pronounced [reedh].

wretch *see* **retch** or **wretch?**

wring The verb *wring* is followed by the preposition *from* or *out of*: ● *They tried in vain to wring the truth from* [or *out of*] *her. See also* **ring** or **wring?**

wright *see* **right** or **write?**

write *see* **right** or **write?**

WRITING TIPS It can be helpful when approaching a writing task of any kind to consider it as having four distinct stages. For example, in a letter, consider the following:

WRITING TIPS	
1 Thinking	It is always good policy to devote time to thinking about the task in hand and about the aims to be fulfilled before putting pen to paper or touching the computer keyboard. This is arguably the most important stage in the whole process, as the success of the finished piece of writing will depend largely upon the quality of the thinking and researching done at the outset. Experienced writers know the value of good preparation and recognise that time spent at this initial stage is never wasted. In the case of an email or a letter, this would include thinking about who the message is being sent to, the content of the message, and the response that is desired from the recipient.
2 Organising	It is essential to give some thought to planning how best to organise and present your writing, making decisions about the proposed structure, layout, etc. There may be more than one way to present an argument or other material, and choosing between these alternatives at this early stage may save a lot of time later. Being properly organised will reduce the overall time needed to complete the task and will help ensure that all the intended aims are met at the desired standard. If there is a deadline to be met, it is vital to decide how much time to dedicate to the task, making sure there will still be an opportunity at the end to go back over what has been written and make any necessary corrections and improvements.
3 Writing	The best writers pay careful attention to grammar and vocabulary as they set about committing their ideas in written form. The richness of the English vocabulary often provides writers with a range of alternatives, and it is important to select from these with care, guided not only by personal preference but also by the context in which the words will appear and the familiarity of the intended readership with more complicated terms, among other considerations. Consulting dictionaries and thesauruses can be helpful here. It is essential to observe grammatical conventions at all times: many readers will fail to understand what is being

	said if a piece of writing is badly assembled, or may not bother to try deciphering it at all. When unsure about how to say something, the writer may consult a guide such as this one for a solution. All writers will experience moments when they cannot think what to write next; in such circumstances it may be helpful to read through what has already been written to see if this suggests a way in which to continue. Note that many writers make revisions to what has been previously written as they go along, instead of waiting until they reach the end and going back.
4 Checking	Careful writers always read through what they have written to make corrections and improvements to vocabulary, grammar, and content, as well as refining the presentation and layout and ensuring that all the initial aims have been met. The importance of revision cannot be overstated, though all too many writers tend to neglect this exercise. It is immediately obvious to the practised eye when a piece has not been properly checked, as even the most experienced writers can easily make spelling mistakes or accidentally repeat material, omit words, or fall prey to grammatical howlers. The spellchecking facilities on modern computers go some way towards simplifying the revision process, although there are limitations to their effectiveness and they are no substitute for a careful read-through when the task is completed. It can be useful, however, to get someone else to look over the finished piece as well, as they might spot mistakes that the writer has missed or suggest improvements that may not have occurred to the author.

wrought *Wrought* is an archaic form of the past tense and past participle of the verb *work*. It is still used adjectivally in such expressions as *wrought iron*. *Wrought* is sometimes wrongly used as the past tense of *wreak*, meaning 'inflict; cause': • *The hurricane wreaked* [not *wrought*] *havoc throughout the countryside*. • *She wreaked* [not *wrought*] *vengeance on the bullies*.

www, WWW *see* **World Wide Web**.

wysiwyg The term *wysiwyg*, used in computing and pronounced [*wizi*-wig], is an acronym for *what you see is what you get*: the display on the computer screen is an exact representation of what will appear on the printout. The term is sometimes spelt *WYSIWYG* or *Wysiwyg*: • *Offering full Wysiwyg (what you see is what you get), including the enhancements such as bold, italics, inverse, tone and outlines* (*Daily Telegraph*).

X

Xerox This word should be spelt *Xerox* if it is referring to the trademarked noun for a type of photographic copier or process. The verb, meaning 'copy on a Xerox machine', is spelt with a lower-case *x*. *Xerox* is pronounced [*zee*roks].

Xmas *Xmas*, an abbreviation for *Christmas*, is used particularly in commercial contexts and newspaper headlines. The *X* derives from the Greek *chi*, the initial letter of *Christos*, Greek for *Christ*. Some people, particularly Christians, find the word offensive and it is generally considered suitable only for informal writing. When reading the word aloud it is preferable to pronounce it as Christmas, and only actually to say [*ek*smăs] when this spelling is emphasised.

X-ray or **x-ray**? The noun is nearly always written with a capital *X*; the verb is written with a capital or lower-case letter: • *He had an X-ray/He was X-rayed* [or *x-rayed*] *after the accident.*

Y

ye *Ye* is the archaic plural of *thou*, which subsequently became an equivalent of *you*. The use of *ye* (meaning 'the') to suggest antique, rustic charm, as in: *Ye Olde Teashoppe*, was formerly fashionable, but in contemporary usage is best avoided except in ironic contexts. This second sense of *ye* actually came about through medieval mistranscription of the runic letter *thorn*.

yes and **no** In discussing affirmative or negative expressions there is the option of writing, for example, either: * *She said yes to the offer* or: *She said, 'Yes' to the offer*. The latter carries more of an implication that the person actually used the word *yes* or *no*. In phrases where there is no suggestion of someone actually using the word, it is better not to have yes or no in inverted commas: * *He says yes to life.* * *She won't take no for an answer.*

  Phrases such as: * *He said (that) yes, he agreed* are acceptable. The *yes* is dispensable but adds emphasis.

yet *Yet* has various meanings: 'up till now; so far': * *It has not yet been decided*; 'even': * *a yet greater problem*; 'in addition': * *yet more presents*; 'at some future time': * *We'll do it yet*; and 'nevertheless': * *slow, yet sure*. In several of its meanings *yet* is more or less interchangeable with *still*, but in the sense of 'as before': * *It is yet raining*, *yet* is now archaic, and *still* is required.

  When the meaning is 'up till now; so far' *yet* cannot be used with the simple past tense, except in informal American English: * *Did she go yet?*

yoghurt The most frequent spelling of this word is *yoghurt*. Acceptable alternatives are *yogurt* and *yoghourt*. The usual pronunciation is [*yogĕrt*] in British English and [*yōgĕrt*] in American English.

yoke or **yolk**? These words are sometimes confused. *Yoke* means 'connecting bar or bond': * *yoked oxen* * *under the yoke of slavery*. A *yolk* is the yellow part of an egg: * *Would you like your yolk hard?*

you *You* is often used to mean 'people in general' in place of the slightly more formal *one*: * *You certainly get a good meal at that restaurant.* * *You hold a hammer like this.* * *They* [i.e. 'The authorities'] *fine you on the spot if you've not got a ticket.* * *It's really embarrassing when you forget someone's name.* * *Dentists say you should clean your teeth at least twice a day*. Although *one* is less frequently used than *you*, it is sometimes better to use *one* to avoid possible confusion as to whether the speaker is talking personally or generally. It is also important to be consistent in the use of either *you* or *one* throughout a single piece of writing. The personal pronoun *you* is either singular or plural. All attempts to indicate that more than one person is being addressed (*you all, you lot, you guys*, etc.) are informal. *See also* **-ing forms**.

you know The expression *you know* is used by speakers who are not sure about what they have just said or who are not sure what to say next: * *I just wondered... you know... if you might like to come with me to the theatre.* The expression is frequently used with this function but is very widely disliked.

your or **you're**? These two words may be confused. *Your* means 'belonging to you': * *your house* * *your rights.* *You're* is a contraction of *you are*: * *Hurry up, you're going to be late!* Note also the spelling of *yours*: * *That's mine, not yours*; spelling it with an apostrophe (*your's*) is wrong.

yourself Careful speakers avoid using *yourself* as a replacement for *you*: * *Would yourself care to sit here, next to me?* * *That's a question for yourself.*

yuppie *Yuppie*, often spelt *yuppy*, is a North American coinage which came into frequent use in Britain in the mid-1980s. It stands for 'young urban (or upwardly mobile) professional' and is used to designate well-educated young adults, living in cities, working in well-paid occupations, and enjoying a fashionable way of life.

Z

zero The digit *0* has a variety of names. *Nought* (*see also* **naught** or **nought?**) and (less frequently) *zero* are the general terms: ⁎ *The number 1000 has three noughts* [or *zeros*]. ⁎ *You've missed a nought off the end – it should be two hundred thousand, not twenty thousand.* In scientific contexts, and for expressing temperatures, etc., *zero* is preferred: ⁎ *Water freezes at zero degrees Celsius.* *Zero* is also used in countdowns: ⁎ *five, four, three, two, one, zero.* When 'spelling out' a number, such as a telephone number or account number, the name of the letter *O* (pronounced like the word *oh*) is used in British English: ⁎ *The dialling code for Liverpool is oh-one-five-one.*

In sport, the terms *love* and *nil* are used for a score of *0*: ⁎ *four love in the final set.* ⁎ *At half-time the score was two nil.*

The plural of *zero* is *zeros* or *zeroes*. Either form is acceptable, but *zeros* is the more frequent, being preferred by many users.

zeugma This term denotes a figure of speech in which a word (usually a verb or adjective) applies to more than one other word in the sentence, often in different senses: ⁎ *She drove the car too fast and her instructor to despair.* *Zeugma* is pronounced [*zyoog*mă] in British English and [*zoog*mă] in American English.

zoology This word, referring to the biological study of animals, has two pronunciations; the more frequent is [zoo*olō*ji], though careful users prefer [zō*olō*ji].

Your Turn

Questions to test your knowledge of words. Answers on page 460.

Grammar

Which of these alternatives is correct?

1 He is one of the few who *know/knows* how to work the machine.
2 The woman *who/whom* he married was a blonde.
3 *She didn't do nothing/She didn't do anything.*
4 We spent the evening at *Colin and Gerry's/Colin's and Gerry's* house.
5 They would *had/have had* no other choice.
6 We plan to *marry/marrying* next year.
7 Each of you *has/have* done your share.
8 This is the *best/better* of the two options.
9 If she comes, I *go/will go.*
10 The boy *laid/lay* the gun on the floor.

Plain English

Find a simpler alternative to these jargonistic words and phrases.

1 terminological inexactitude
2 pre-owned
3 get one's ducks in a row
4 incentivise
5 push the peanut forward
6 pre-prepare
7 think outside the box
8 low-hanging fruit
9 paradigm shift
10 push the envelope

Punctuation

Identify the correctly punctuated sentence.

1 (a) Potatoe's for sale.
  (b) Potatoes for sale.
  (c) Potatoes' for sale.
2 (a) The bag contained hammers, and nails.
  (b) The bag, contained hammers and nails.
  (c) The bag contained hammers and nails.
3 (a) The children learn reading and writing; mathematics; and history.
  (b) The children learn reading; and writing mathematics; and history.
  (c) The children learn reading; and writing; mathematics; and history.
4 (a) Three main colours – red, white and blue – appear on the flag.
  (b) Three main colours/red, white and blue/appear on the flag.
  (c) Three main colours: red, white and blue, appear on the flag.
5 (a) The trip starts on Tuesday however we can't go.
  (b) The trip starts on Tuesday, however we can't go.
  (c) The trip starts on Tuesday; however, we can't go.
6 (a) Name the actor who (starred in the film).
  (b) Name the actor who starred in the film.
  (c) Name the actor who starred in the film?

458

7 (a) 'Hello' said the man clutching his wounded arm.

  (b) Hello! said the man, clutching his wounded arm.

  (c) 'Hello,' said the man, clutching his wounded arm.

8 (a) 'Give me a break!!!' I told him.

  (b) 'Give me a break!' I told him.

  (c) 'Give me a break' I told him!

9 (a) The teacher asked, 'What is he doing now?'

  (b) The teacher asked, 'What is he doing now'?

  (c) The teacher asked, 'What is he doing now!'

10 (a) He asked his daughter what she wanted for her birthday.

  (b) He asked his daughter what she wanted for her birthday?

  (c) He asked his daughter, what she wanted for her birthday?

Spelling

Which spelling is correct?

1 They *complemented/complimented* him on his performance.

2 She dug her spoon into the *yolk/yoke* of the egg.

3 The book will have a brief *forword/forward/foreword*.

4 The press is *censored/censured/censered* by the government.

5 The company agreed to *wave/waive* the usual charges.

6 He says he must adhere to the highest *principles/principals*.

7 She went out with her *friends/friends/frends*.

8 She *siezed/seized* the gun before he could reach it.

9 We are *truly/truely* sorry for the mistake.

10 I was in *ecstacy/ecstasy/exstacy*.

Usage

Which alternative seems best to you?

1 (a) There aren't no sweets left.

  (b) There isn't any sweets left.

  (c) There aren't any sweets left.

2 (a) You should of said something.

  (b) You should have said something.

  (c) You should a said something.

3 (a) They're putting there things over their.

  (b) They're putting their things over there.

  (c) Their putting they're things over there.

4 (a) There are fewer shoes on this shelf.

  (b) There are less shoes on this shelf.

  (c) There is less shoes on this shelf.

5 (a) It's hard to see its nest.

  (b) Its hard to see it's nest.

  (c) It's hard to see it's nest.

6 (a) Who's shoes are these?

  (b) Whose shoes are these?

  (c) Whom's shoes are these?

7 (a) They blamed Henry and myself.

  (b) They blamed Henry and I.

  (c) They blamed Henry and me.

8 (a) I borrowed the money off a friend.

  (b) I borrowed the money from a friend.

  (c) I borrowed the money off of a friend.

9 (a) I prefer these kind of boots.

  (b) I prefer this kind of boots.

  (c) I prefer this kind of boot.

10 (a) It's they who are wrong.

  (b) It's them who are wrong.

  (c) It's they who is wrong.

Answers

Grammar
1 know
2 whom
3 didn't do anything
4 Colin and Gerry's
5 have had
6 to marry
7 has
8 better
9 will go
10 laid

Spelling
1 complimented
2 yolk
3 foreword
4 censored
5 waive
6 principles
7 friends
8 seized
9 truly
10 ecstasy

Plain English
1 lie
2 secondhand
3 get organised
4 offer rewards
5 make progress
6 prepare
7 look at things differently
8 easy pickings
9 new way of thinking
10 innovate

Usage
1 (c)
2 (b)
3 (b)
4 (a)
5 (a)
6 (b)
7 (c)
8 (b)
9 (c)
10 (a)

Punctuation
1 (b)
2 (c)
3 (a)
4 (a)
5 (c)
6 (b)
7 (c)
8 (b)
9 (a)
10 (a)